MODEL &
MINIATURE
RAILWAYS

MODEL & MINIATURE RAILWAYS

CHARTWELL BOOKS INC.

Volume Editor: **J. T. Shackleton**
General Editors: **J. H. L. Adams and P. B. Whitehouse**
Picture Editors: **Janice Every, Rosemary Lister and Michele Monk**

This edition is published by Chartwell Books
Inc., a division of Book Sales Inc., 110 Enterprise
Avenue, Secaucus, New Jersey 07094 by arrangement
with The Hamlyn Publishing Group Ltd., U. K.
© Text and illustrations copyright New English
Library Ltd., 1976. New English Library,
Barnard's Inn, Holborn, London, England.
Printed by Fratelli Spada, Ciampino, Rome.
Library of Congress Catalog Card Number 76-11707
ISBN 0 89009 066 1

Contents

Introduction

Almost as soon as the smoke had dispersed from the first primitive railway engines that rattled, creaked and belched their way across the nineteenth century landscape, people began to make models of trains. As early as 1813, when the makers of active steam locomotives could be counted on one's fingers, von Gerstner of Prague made display models for demonstration purposes. In 1826, the German firm Hess, of Nuremberg, was advertising a tinplate toy train. During the next two decades in France and Germany it was possible to buy "at a cheap price" (to quote Hess's advertising) bulky model locomotives resembling the *Rocket* and coaches based, like their prototype, on the principles of the stage coach. These models usually had neither track nor power; they were simply pushed across the nursery floor. But by the 1850s, in the United States as well as in Europe, clockwork power had been introduced. Usually the mechanism was inside the locomotive, although one crude tinplate model of the period had a more unusual means of propulsion. The gaudy locomotive and its four-wheeled coaches were attached to a metal bar, to which was fixed a clockwork mechanism which rotated the bar slowly through 360 degrees, thus giving the illusion of motion to the train.

It was not long before people began to realise one of the crowning glories of the steam locomotive: that its basic principle of steam produced in a boiler driving the wheels through cylinders and cranks was infinitely reducible. A methylated spirit lamp heating a boiler filled with water could produce the steam power for small simple model engines that soon earned themselves the nickname "dribblers". These sturdy little engines were not at first controllable; without regulators or track they simply careered across the floor and were quite capable of inflicting considerable damage on the household gods before they were brought to a stop.

Whilst such toys as these were by no means exorbitantly priced, it is important to stress that they were quite beyond the means of the average family until the advent of mass production techniques around the turn of the century. The poor had to be content with cast-offs or crude wooden models, often home-made but possessing great charm, as the many examples which survive in toy museums and private collections throughout the world will testify. It is true that the vast majority of model trains in the nineteenth century were crude replicas, bearing little resemblance to any known prototype. But scale models were being produced throughout the period, though usually on a one-off basis for decoration or showcase exhibition. A young man who, as a child, had been fired with the unique and indescribable enthusiasm for trains by his early tinplate toys, might choose to enter one of the great Victorian railway workshops as an apprentice. Here, before coming to grips with the real thing, he might well have been required to work first on building an exact scale replica of one of the companies' locomotives. Many of these models survive today, magnificent testimonials to the engineering skill and craftsmanship of the nineteenth century; the chapter on the collection of such models in the Science Museum, London, illustrates some of the finest examples. Indeed, the Norris locomotive here must rank as one of the earliest running models, being built to 3in scale in 1836 as a promotional device for potential buyers of Norris engines in Europe. Engineers and instrument makers also made accurate scale models of high quality and finish, either for amusement or for private customers. H J Wood, father of Sir Henry Wood, the conductor and founder of London's famous Promenade Concerts, was one of these, who enlarged his part-time modelling activities into a full-time model-making business, with premises in the prestigious West End of London. Henry Greenly and W J Bassett-Lowke were other pioneers in the production of high quality models, available (at a price) to the general market.

As the work of these and later modellers shown in this book will testify, the scope of model railways extends far beyond the playroom and the toyshop. A good piece of model engineering, be it a replica of a locomotive, a signal box or a goods vehicle, forms a valuable historical record, especially since many of the prototypes have long since fallen under the wrecker's hammer. And even though many of the items covered in this book are technically toys, nonetheless the survival of amusements of our childhood is one of the principle ways in which we can recreate bygone years. In recent times collectors have come to realise the interest and picturesque qualities of toy trains, and have made treasures out of what were once worn-out amusements; few people can resist the charming gurglings of an old "dribbler" in steam once again, or look dispassionately on brightly-painted clockwork locomotive with its hopelessly and delightfully inaccurate coaches hurtling around a circle of tinplate track. These models brought limitless pleasure to their original owners, and are now bringing the same delight to new generations. This book tells, in words and pictures, their story.

EARLY TINPLATE

Overleaf: Bing 1900 gauge 1 clockwork engine
in Midland Railway livery. *Simon Goodyear*

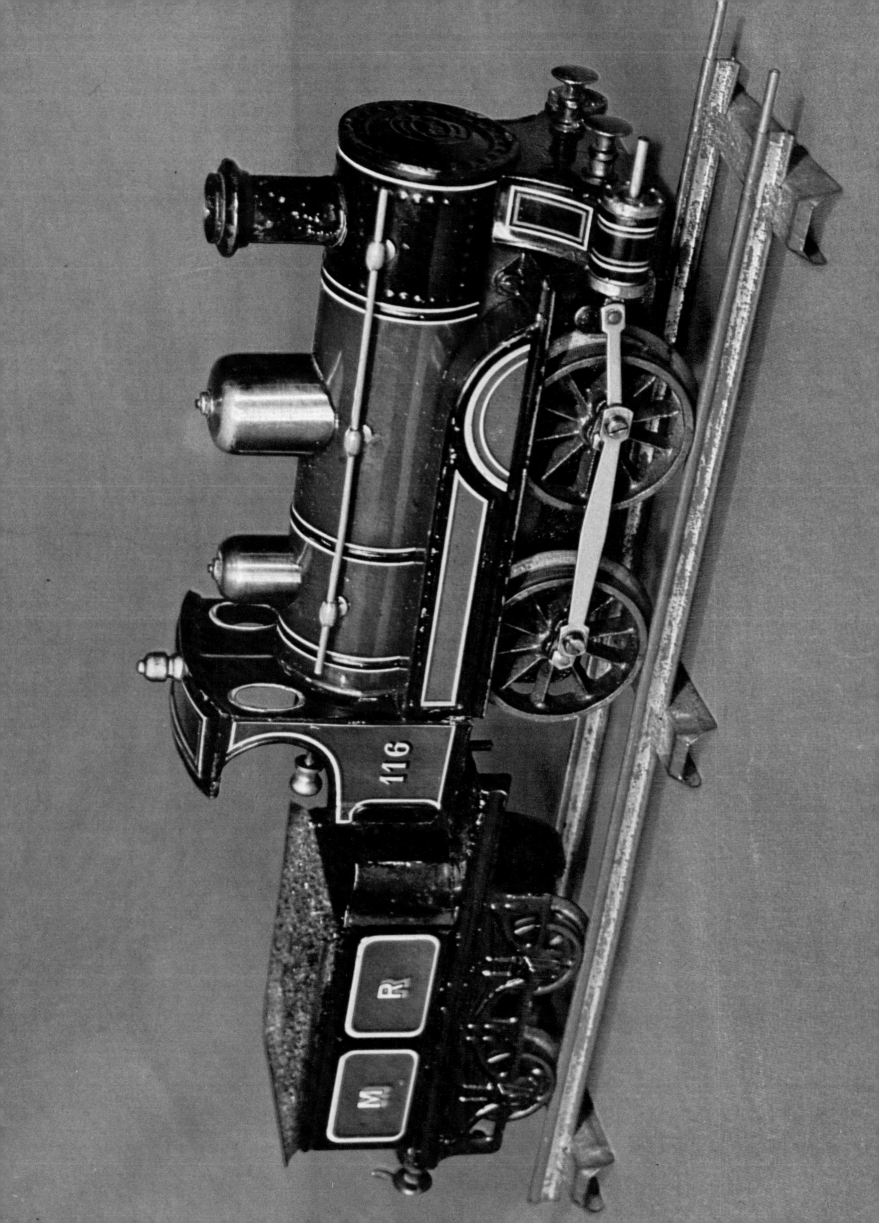

THOSE GLAMOROUS TINPLATE TRAINS

"The description 'tinplate trains' was first applied in the early 1900s to toy trains using a sectional metal track made of this same material," quotes Louis H Hertz, on page 25 of his classic book "Collecting Model Trains". Such tinplate trains were the forerunners of the highly sophisticated model railways of today. Before them, perhaps as early as the forties of the last century, these were simple floor trains, pulled by a string, and a very few steam models. Old advertisements found by the author in his researches at Nuremberg suggest that the first clockwork toy trains were made there in 1855 by the firm of S Güntermann. Louis Hertz writes that in 1856, George W Brown and Co of Forestville also began to put clockwork into small tinplate locomotives with only three wheels, arranged like a tricycle. Forestville was part of Bristol, Connecticut (USA) which at that time was a clockmaking centre.

Now, the real trains ran on rails, but this was not so easy to copy on a small scale. It needed wheels with a depth of flange and a width of tread proportionately far bigger than on the real vehicles, to prevent derailments on uneven track, with rails also out of scale for reasons of strength. Also the question of curves came up, because large radii could not be accommodated on the floor of a room, let alone a table top. From continued researches at Nuremberg it seems that the firm of Johann Andreas Issmayer

founded there in 1866 was the first to succeed in manufacturing clockwork trains running on circular track and thus providing the second stage in the story of tinplate trains. These trains were widely copied in one form or another by several Nuremberg toy makers, and by the eighties live steam locomotives, running on track, known as "dribblers" were also on offer. Sometimes the axles of engines and cars were set radially, so these trains could only run (always in the same direction) on a circle of exactly matching radius. The gauges differed widely between 2 and 4 inches and were not always consistent even for trains made by one manufacturer. The track circle was now made in sections (therefore called sectional track) the rails being rolled from tinplate and each section joined to the next by spikes.

It was Märklin of Göppingen in Württemberg who brought order into the track chaos when he first showed his new train lines at the Leipzig Fair in 1891. His sectional track was made in lengths which allowed the laying out of regular geometric figures. He added further points and crossings to match. The diameter of a full circle varied of course, with the track gauge.

The gauges were also standardised, measured from centre to centre of the rails. At first there were three gauges.

Above: A primitive: A gauge O Märklin train set circa 1900. *Egmont Fisher*

The then smallest (48mm) received the number 1, 54mm was numbered 2 and the largest (75mm) became gauge 3. When, before long, Märklin introduced smaller trains for a gauge of 35mm, there was nothing for it but gauge O.

Märklin adopted the same hollow tinplate rails for all his gauges, using a rounded rail head of 3mm diameter. Thus, the actual gauge measured between the rails was always 3mm less than the nominal dimensions. This gave the British equivalents as follows: O: 32mm = $1\frac{1}{4}$in, 1: 45mm = $1\frac{3}{4}$in, 2: 51mm = 2in, 3: 72mm = $3\frac{13}{16}$in.

The standards set by Märklin for his rails and even their radii were immediately accepted by Bing and soon by the other Nuremberg firms, but the 75mm gauge 3 remained a typical Märklin gauge, that of 67mm (or 64mm inside the rails) being preferred by other manufacturers, perhaps because it was already well established in Great Britain by steam locomotive modellers as $2\frac{1}{2}$in gauge. Bassett-Lowke's consulting engineer, Henry Greenly, based his standards on Märklin's track measurements. Ives of Bridgeport, the leading American toy-maker, introduced gauge O to that country and thus settled the way for mass produced track trains in the United States. Gauge 1 came later. Both gauges were also adopted in France. This first step to universal standardisation was carried out so that trains of various makers could be used together.

But cheap toy trains were often made in smaller gauges than O, sometimes OO or OOO, ranged from 24mm to the 30mm which Issmayer continued to the firm's demise.

Märklin also took the lead in the production of line accessories, such as station buildings, goods depots, post offices, loco sheds, signals, cranes, lamp posts, tunnels and even customs posts—an assortment never surpassed by any other manufacturer. So it might be said that before Märklin there were only toy trains, with Märklin the age of Miniature Railways began.

The turn of the century brought two important events in the tinplate story. At the Paris World Exhibition of 1900 Bing, then already the biggest toy manufacturer, exhibited their wide range including trains, doubtless influenced by Märklin. Young W J Bassett-Lowke visited the stand. Let us quote from this firm's book "Fifty Years of Model Making" as to what followed: "So impressed was Bassett-Lowke by the workmanship in these Paris exhibits that he arranged for locomotives of his own designs to be constructed by Continental manufacturers while the development of small fittings and parts made in Northampton continued. The late Mr Stefan Bing (who was Governing Director of the Nuremberg firm) was keenly interested in producing model railways to English designs . . ." This contract with Bing led to the birth of the first commercial scale model.

The second important event at the turn of the century was the introduction of electrically driven trains. Indeed, the use of electric motors to drive copies of the contemporary tramcars was already known. Apart from some early attempts by skilful electricians, the first mention which the author has found of electric trains made commercially by the toy industry, comes from the Bavarian Provincial, Industrial, Arts and Crafts Exhibition held in 1882 at Nuremberg. There the firm of Ernst Plank "again showed various very pretty novelties, of which we would only mention the electric railway and electric motors . . . numerous spectators came along as soon as the notice announced that the electric railway and the motor were put to work". Soon after this Carette and Schoenner, both in Nuremberg and, in the States, Carlisle & Finch of Cincinnati followed with simple electrically driven model tramcars. Mains electricity was not yet available in the home, so this sort of train needed wet batteries, and later dry ones. Complete sets of electric trains with engines of steam or electric outline and sectional track, matching the existing clockwork and steam train sets were offered by Märklin in the 1900 catalogue. By then, electric current had begun to be used for domestic lighting and this allowed trains to be run from the mains, which increased their attraction. The current, in most cases 110 volts, was reduced to 40 or 60 volts by lamp resistances, but the full voltage was possible between track and earth, so it was a method not without its dangers. Transformers which eliminated this disadvantage could only be employed when direct current began to be replaced by alternating. The Knapp Electric Novelty Company of New York offered transformers in their 1911/1912 catalogue. With direct current house supply, in-

Above: A "Dribbler" of English manufacture circa 1900. *Egmont Fisher*

Left: A "Dribbler" made by Ernst Planck of Nuremburg between 1890 and 1900. A 2½in gauge steam driven engine fired by methylated spirits, which was not intended for use on track. These engines were called "Dribblers" because of the trail of water and oil from the cylinders. *K A C Melvin*

stead of transformers rotary converters were developed. In Great Britain the use of accumulators remained the rule, still recommended in Bassett-Lowke's Model Railway Handbook in his 12th edition, but this method was finally rendered obsolete by the introduction of transformer and rectifier units.

Development of miniature trains before the outbreak of the First World War led to a wide range of price and quality. On the one hand there were cheap toy trains with clockwork engines, often sold as complete sets with accessories in a box. You could buy such an outfit for less than a shilling, consisting of a locomotive, a tender and a coach, and a circle of track made up of four pieces. Yet these little toy trains, primitive as they were, introduced the model train hobby to many people. The mass production of such trains made it possible to build more ambitious models at prices within the reach of a large public. The trend towards ever more realistic models culminated in the famous Bassett-Lowke range.

The First World War wrought radical changes in the tinplate train industry. The blockade of Germany by the Allies stopped the export of tinplate trains of which Germany had a near monopoly. The consequences were dramatic in the USA. Firms there began fierce competition, with more and better models, which culminated during the post war years in luxurious train "consists" to which were given high-sounding names, even if they were only simple freight trains. The 1930s saw the most glamorous and glorious age of American tinplate, but the grand old firm of Ives, pioneer of it all, fell a victim of the Wall Street crash of 1929.

The prevailing atmosphere in Great Britain during the war is best demonstrated by the words, "It is our intention to spare no effort to wrest this business from the Germans," quoted from the catalogue of the short-lived firm of Jubb. However, even Hornby, a leader of the toy world thanks to his "Meccano", had to suspend manufacture in 1915; he returned with increased vigour to fight successfully against the renewed competition of the German firms after 1918.

The products of his factories, the old one at Binns Road in Liverpool, the new one at Bobigny near Paris, spread rapidly across the world.

He was not the only one in France. The old established firm "Le Jouet de Paris", better known by its later trade mark JEP, which before the war could hardly survive the German toy invasion, completely updated its range of trains and won a good place in the tinplate train market. The short-lived firm of Marescot produced a scale tinplate Etat 4-6-2 in O gauge, with accurately modelled Walschaerts valve gear for the first time. With this went four different types of coach, and the complete set achieved near-photographic realism. The range was taken over by Fourneneau.

An inevitable victim of the war in Germany was the distinguished French-owned Nuremberg firm of Georges Carette. Bing, the first to make a hopeful start, brought out some very fine, often British-inspired models, but was in the long run doomed by the Jewish blood of its proprietors. Hitler's arrival swept away many of the old Nuremberg toy

manufacturers. Karl Bub could have taken Bings' inheritance and did produce some coaches and goods wagons, using tools purchased from Bing, but failed finally, his products being far from real scale models. Märklin, who had at first lagged considerably behind their competitors in their cheap ranges, with antiquated models, though still of their traditional quality, introduced their first "scale" models of German locomotives in 1930 and quickly ascended to the highest quality of tinplate.

In the winter season of 1923 Bing launched the first trains in 16mm gauge, named OO gauge, manufactured to designs and samples made by Henry Greenly and sold in the United Kingdom by Bassett-Lowke as "the table railway". This was the first portent of a new tinplate age. The Leeds Model Company began marketing gauge O goods wagons with moulded plastic bodies in 1937—the

first deviation from the traditional tinplate. Dorfan, at Newark New Jersey (USA) founded by Nuremberg emigrants, started (in the early 1920s) the idea of using die-cast zinc alloy for locomotive bodies, and this new material was widely adopted by the other American train manufacturers. From 1935, when the Nuremberg firm Trix came out with its gauge OO "Trix Express" trains, these alloys began to be employed on this side of the Atlantic as well. These events heralded the radical change which, after World War 2 dealt the final death-blow of the tinplate train. Fortunately, the gay colours, and the multifarious (and sometimes monstrous) versions of long vanished or non-existent prototypes still appeal to an increasing number of train lovers who make a hobby of collecting these old trains and thus saving them for posterity from an untimely end in the scrap heap.

Top left: A clockwork gauge 1 train set made by Bing—circa 1900.
Collection John Bevan, B Monaghan

Top right: The early 1900's. This type of 2-2-0 locomotive, referred to as a "Stork Legs" type, was made by Johann Falk of Nuremburg. Gauge O steam. Two oscillating cylinders and fitted with safety valve and whistle, but non-reversing. *K A C Melvin*

Centre: Gauge 2 Bassett-Lowke Great Central Railway 4-4-2/T of about 1915 with a rare Märklin hospital van complete with interior fittings of 1905 and two scarce Bing express carriages—a blue dining car and a brown sleeping car. *Gustavo Reder*

Bottom left: A Märklin gauge O train set of the early 1900s with clockwork engine (cylinders missing), a mail van, an open ended passenger carriage and a hospital van. *Gustavo Reder*

Facing page top: A Märklin gauge O clockwork LNER 0-4-0T of the 1920s/30s. *K A C Melvin*

Facing page centre: Hornby 1929. The smallest and cheapest of the Hornby range, gauge O non-reversing clockwork, supplied singly or in a boxed set complete with coach and rails. *K A C Melvin*

Above right: A gauge O two speed clockwork model of an electric locomotive made about 1945 by a Swiss firm called Buko (A Bucherer et Cie, Diepoldsau.) *K A C Melvin*

Centre right: Examples of gauge O and 1 rolling stock made by Märklin in the 1930s. *Egmont Fisher*

Below: French gauge O. An electric 2-4-0 made by JEP at the end of the 1920s, complete with train. *Gustavo Reder*

Overleaf: A gauge O clockwork model made by Bing for export sales in America. *K A C Melvin*

AMIDST CLOUDS OF STEAM

Live steam in O gauge could be called a captivating anomaly—it was messy, inefficient and uncontrollable, yet completely fascinating. In the larger gauges, of course, steam was an accepted and practical thing, so the increasing popularity of O gauge naturally stimulated demand for the same "real" motive power in this smaller scale. The demand was met by numerous types of "pot boiler" whose performance was often spectacular, if rather intractable in view of the limitations of size and cost.

Many of the O gauge steamers running on British tracks were of foreign origin, but the home-produced articles of the 1920s and 1930s included several which have a justifiable claim to fame. Even if they were not scale models in the strictest sense, these modestly priced live steamers brought the thrill of steam to the model railway operator of slender means.

One such example was produced by a then familiar name, Clyde Model Dockyard, of Glasgow. During the 1920s their range included a small four-wheel tank locomotive offered at a price of 12s 6d. Proudly advertised as "British Made" it was in appearance little more than the

Above: A very early model steam locomotive of about 1890 by Glasgow Model Dockyard.
K A C Melvin

bare minimum of loco, with an open-rear cab, a modicum of bunker and "paddle-box" splashers. The boiler was a brass tube with safety valve and filler, and there were two brass oscillating cylinders. Further details included "correct section cast metal loco wheels with flanges and tread turned and polished". Each locomotive had been "tested under steam". It was available "painted and lined in correct railway colours, LMS or LNER", and would steam about 15 minutes on one filling. A larger model, priced at 21s, would run for about half a mile on one filling.

Bassett-Lowke at the same period offered a range of steamers, including an 0-4-0 of decidedly LNWR flavour, price £2 7s 6d. "Those who know the pre-war quality of German locomotives will know that it is not easy to surpass some of their best work, but our model makers at Northampton have done this".

Further up their price range was a 4-4-0 designed by Henry Greenly and "conceived on massive lines"; at £4 10s this was a popular model, though it was later "somewhat outclassed", as Bassett-Lowke said, by their new Mogul of 1925. The Mogul was based on an actual prototype which it well resembled, but it was by no means cheap at £5 5s.

There was still a market to be tapped by an impressive low-priced steamer that really looked like a "big" express engine that would appeal especially to the younger enthusiast. This was where the Bowman 234 came in with a flourish.

"Be a real engine driver! Think of owning a real locomotive that goes by steam and yet is as safe as clockwork! A real replica of the great expresses you see thundering through the countryside!"

That was the dazzling prospect offered by the Bowman 234 when it burst upon the scene in 1928, advertised as "The most wonderful model steam loco ever made!"

"Think of the joy such an engine can add to your railway system! It runs on your O gauge track and pulls your rolling stock 1½ miles amidst clouds of steam from the chimney and the true exhaust sound of a real locomotive."

As to its performance, "the Wonder Bowman Loco" pulled six large coaches for a distance of 183 miles during the British Industries Fair of 1928. During this marathon "it was refuelled every 40 minutes . . . A £5 foreign steam engine refused to pull half the load and ran for 12 minutes only, on one filling".

The "Bowman Express Locomotive Model 234" was produced by Bowman Models, of Dereham, Norfolk, makers also of miniature stationary steam engines. It was priced at £1 7s 6d, plus 7s 6d for the tender. "It's the biggest you've ever seen", they said of their new loco, and certainly it could lay claim to be one of the largest ever O gauge models. "Note the massive proportions" —and indeed you could hardly fail to notice, for the first impression of the 234 was its size, which would not have disgraced 1 gauge tracks. With its tender it was 1ft 8in in length, while its height from rail to top of chimney was 4½ inches. The loco alone weighed 5lb. Size of course was the secret of its success, for it had the ability to go on producing steam to keep it pounding away on its long run.

It was equally massive in construction, which was of "solid brass and steel throughout". Frames were of heavy steel plate and wheels of turned steel, while the boiler was of heavy seamless

brass tested to three times the working pressure. Cylinders were of drawn brass ⅜ by ⅞ inch, with pistons of solid brass with grooved oil rings and felt oiling pads. Even the packing was substantial; the 234 came in no flimsy carton but in a stout wooden box.

In theory the Bowman 234 was a 4-4-0 but in fact the driving wheels were not coupled. The oscillating cylinders drove on to the rear pair of wheels, the front pair simply being journalled in a slot. The lamp with its array of wicks was fixed beneath the cab floor. Safety had been given proper consideration: "Absolute safety is secured by the new Bowman safety valve which, having no rubber, cannot possibly stick, and the lamp automatically cuts off the supply of spirit if the locomotive is overturned". Steam was taken from the "firebox" end of the boiler and led to the cylinders by pipes running along the footplate. Controls there were none; there was no regulator and no reverse.

Launching the 234, Bowman organised a sort of Train Week: "from October 8 to 13 you can see this loco running under steam—at your shop". But hurry though: "2s Deposit secures your loco for Christmas. The demand for this loco is so great that we may be sold out by Christmas. Make sure of yours now . . ."

To complete the train, Bowman produced coaches of the same ample proportions, with cut-out windows and opening doors. And it was also appro-

priate that suitably tough track should be provided. "Extra strong rails for this loco, 6s dozen . . . Strong enough to stand on . . ."

Bowman offered other steam locos of more modest dimensions if of hardly less solid construction: "every part of heavy gauge brass or steel". For example there was the Model 300; priced at 18s 6d this was a stocky four-wheel tank loco, though again the wheels were not coupled. It was fitted with oscillating cylinders of ⅜ inch by ¾ inch stroke, had an overall length of 8¾ inches and a weight of 1¾lb. With side tanks and open-rear cab and finished in either LMS or LNER colours, it was advertised in no uncertain terms:

"Here is a marvel of model engineering. A wonder of massed production methods which has brought a real substantial British steam engine of the type usually obtainable for 30s to 40s within the reach of everybody. Its power is guaranteed equal to any 30s steam loco on the market. Indoors it will haul from six to nine trucks at a steady speed for ¾ mile non-stop and yet will rush round with a very light load without leaving the rails".

The generally similar but slightly larger Model 265 weighed in at 2½lb and had a length of 10½ inches, with a correspondingly enhanced performance. This "sturdy tank loco will draw heavy rolling stock 1½ miles on one filling". Its price was 22s 6d.

Clearly not to be outdistanced by any

Left: The Bowman Express Locomotive Model 234. Note the oscillating cylinder and lack of coupling rod, also the external steam pipe. *J Joyce*

Below: The Bowman Model 234 in LMS black livery and numbered 13000! *C M Whitehouse*

rival, Bassett-Lowke in 1931 introduced their new "Enterprise" steam loco in hardly less emphatic terms and equally with an obvious eye on the younger enthusiast:

"A Record Breaker. At a Record Breaking Price. Boys! You are looking at the most wonderful model steam locomotive for the price that ever hummed along the rails! Never before have the shillings bought such supreme quality, power and realism. The Enterprise is the result of exhaustive experiments. Under test she ran for 55 minutes non-stop, covering 1¾ miles and hauling five long bogie coaches. Open her throttle and she will do the same for you! Just like the real thing!"

Like the Bowman 234, Enterprise was a 4-4-0 but this time the driving wheels were coupled. Outlines were still simple and proportions generous, while the specification was little less impressive.

The frames of Enterprise were of tinned steel plate while the driving wheels were of cast iron and the bogie and tender wheels of anti-friction metal. The boiler was of rolled sheet brass, tested to 45lb per square inch, and the double-action cylinders were fitted with stainless steel pistons, piston rods and valves, while an added virtue was reversing by means of slip eccentrics. Coupling rods and connecting rods were nickel plated. Fittings included a combined safety valve and filler, whistle, water level plug, and an automatic lubricator in the smokebox with level indicator and filling plug.

Enterprise was available in a choice of styles: black with red lining, red with yellow lining, and green with white lining. Price including tender was £2 10s;

that is, noticeably more than the Bowman 234 but less than half the price of Bassett-Lowke's well-known Mogul.

Bassett-Lowke described Enterprise as "the most powerful gauge O steam locomotive ever produced commercially" and quoted one "satisfied customer" in testimony of its prowess:

"Even hardened model railway men have raised their eyebrows at this performance of the Enterprise. Under test she ran 1 hour 10 minutes light, hauled 26 Bassett-Lowke wagons for 52 minutes, and started no less than 35 vehicles without apparent effort".

Enterprise was joined in 1937 by its big brother "Super Enterprise", Bassett-Lowke's new "smasher" as they called it. They explained its raison d'etre as follows:

"The model realist who is not satisfied with the limitations of clockwork or even electricity in the working of his O gauge line, and who wishes to see signs of steam about his system, has long desired a 4-6-0 model at a moderate price, and at length we are able to meet his wishes . . . Based on our successful Enterprise design, the new 4-6-0 is a massive and handsome engine, with all the internal arrangements which made the 4-4-0 so reliable a machine".

The specification for Super Enterprise was basically similar to Enterprise, though with some refinements apart from the extra pair of coupled wheels. It was fired by a vaporising spirit lamp and was superheated, as well as being fitted with a regulator operated from the cab. The inclined cylinders drove on to the centre pair of coupled wheels.

Super Enterprise was a sturdy looking engine with a Belpaire firebox, unlike the

round-topped firebox of the Enterprise. Although, as its makers admitted, it was of freelance design, it did bear a general resemblance to a Patriot or Baby Scot of the LMS or a Southern Lord Nelson, while they pointed out that the LNER version was "similar to the Sandringham class". Super Enterprise was available finished in the colours of three of the Big Four; as well as LNER 2871, it came as LMS 5524 and SR 851, these two versions being fitted with "true to prototype" smoke deflectors. It was additionally obtainable in a goods livery of black with red lines and numbered 2495. The original price was £3 17s 6d.

The Super Enterprise 4-6-0 represented the final phase in this long heritage of low-priced O gauge pot boilers. With its stable companions Enterprise and Mogul it was reintroduced after the war, but by then this unsophisticated age of excitement in "real" motive power had ended. All these small steamers had brought joy to many enthusiasts, even if they were not without their spice of hazards.

An extract from one of the instruction leaflets well sums up the unpredictability that was part of their attraction: "If the engine through excessive speed turns over, do not try to blow the lamp out, but stand the model upright immediately by catching hold of the front buffers and the cab". Maybe O gauge steam was not the most suitable motive power for serious model railway operation—but it was lots of fun!

Above: The Bowman Tank Locomotive Model 300 in LNER Livery. *G Brown*

Below: The Bassett-Lowke "Enterprise" in green livery. *P B Whitehouse Collection*

SCALE GAUGE & SPACE

The development of railway modelling can be summed up quickly by saying that there has been a steady progression from the large to the small, with at the same time, a slow improvement in scale standards. Like most summaries of a complex history, this is a gross over-simplification. In fact, although there has been a gradual drift down in size, it has occured in quite definite steps, while the improvements in scale proportions have also taken the same erratic course. There are solid reasons why this has happened, bound up with social and economic changes which are far from complete.

There are three main divisions in this story, punctuated by the two world wars. In each a subtly different pattern has been evident, and there is distinct evidence that a further change is in the offing. Throughout the entire period there has been one abiding problem. The standard gauge of 4ft 8½in—a nominal figure since it does vary slightly in practice—is very awkward indeed. It is very difficult to express a model gauge in inches and arrive at a respectable scale. Some of the guesses have turned out to be substantially inaccurate, causing a great deal of heartburning and acrimony. Indeed, it is as well at this point to mention that the opinions expressed in this are the author's.

In the beginning each manufacturer was a law unto himself, so when the first attempt to standardise took place, a modicum of compromise was needed.

There is little doubt that the leading characters in this important matter were Henry Greenly and W J Bassett-Lowke. Four gauges were standardised and in general use, in descending order Gauge 3 (2½in gauge, ½in scale), Gauge 2 (2in gauge 7/16in scale), Gauge 1 (1¾in gauge, ⅜in scale), and Gauge O (1¼in gauge, ¼in scale).

Initially Gauge 2 was the most popular. It was big enough to be robust and reliable, but small enough to go indoors. To modern minds, this seems incredible, but it is important to realise that in Edwardian days hobbies were the privil-

Above: Two pictures of a London & South Western railway bogie express locomotive No 593 gauge 3 (2½in gauge) built by Bing for Bassett-Lowke 1903-04. Certainly not a child's toy. *A Moreland*

Bottom Left: NER 4-4-0 built by Carette for Bassett Lowke (1909) gauge 3 (2½in). *Collection McCrindell. Photo Sharpe*

ege of the wealthy. Gauge 2 permitted a choice of steam or electricity—clockwork was practicable, but only for strong adults, the heavy springs needed a deal of winding! These were not toys. Nor were Gauge 1 models. This slightly smaller scale gradually overtook Gauge 2 in popularity, it was ideally suited for a modest villa in the better part of town. Again one had the choice of steam, electricity and clockwork, though the latter was frowned upon by the serious enthusiast as being toylike.

Gauge O was basically a toy system, useful where space was limited. Live steam was a trifle unreliable in such a small locomotive—even though it was normal to put on a grossly over-large pot boiler. Electric traction had limited appeal—few homes had a mains supply and charging accumulators was a messy and inconvenient business. More im-

portant, in those days permanent magnets were usually made from carbon steel and were not only massive, but very unreliable. Motors had wound fields, and since in many cases silk covered wire was used—varnished wire was a trifle unreliable—they tended to be large, and required either an erratic sequence reverser, a fearsome device, or the rather temperamental polarised switch. When reduced to O gauge dimensions, such motors were decidedly troublesome. However, clockwork was cheap and simple.

Then for the first time, enthusiasts made an interesting discovery. One or two blessed with room for a Gauge 1 line realised that by using the smaller scale they could lay down a large system, with lots of stations, and with a little ingenuity and imagination produce a model of an actual main line.

It is important to realise that in this initial stage the number of serious railway modellers in the country was relatively small, and therefore the luxury of four different dead scale rail sections, together with a complete selection of chairs, fishplates and other parts was commercially impracticable. A compromise was made. The selection was somewhere between 7/16in and $\frac{1}{8}$in scale, about right for the two main gauges, a little light for 3 gauge—which was not very popular anyway—but very much too large for O gauge. This was not so serious as it might have seemed, because it did provide ample clearance for the deep flanges used by the toymakers, whose wheels were made from two pieces of dished tinplate, beaded together along the top of the flange. Some moves might have been taken towards a more accurate rail section but for the unfortunate upheaval of World War 1.

Many early models have survived. The reason is simple: those in Gauge 1 and larger represented a considerable capital outlay; even where treated as toys, they were special toys, reserved for high days and holidays, and usually only brought out under papa's supervision. Only the more toylike O gauge were, to any real extent, destroyed. The Gauge 1 Association has been assiduous in preserving some really choice specimens, whilst strangely enough, Gauge 3 models have survived to enable at least one contemporary enthusiast to build a garden layout in this almost forgotten lavish

Top: Gauge 1 0-4-4T of 1909 by Märklin.
A Morland

Left: Gauge 1 (1¾in gauge) layout in the attic: a section of J Francis Parker's vintage railway.

scale.

It is perhaps worth mentioning here that the USA manufacturers worked on individual lines. Only two gauges were in use, the Standard Gauge, 2⅛in, and Gauge O. Separated by an ocean, they did not enjoy the close co-operation that existed among Europe's model manufacturers, before the war put paid to this happy state of affairs.

In the early 1920s the hobby began to pick up the threads again, with one important difference. The use of ¼in scale for O gauge is clearly wrong; the models are undersize, or the track is over gauge. In Britain a scale of 7mm to the foot, recommended before the war by Henry Greenly, came into vogue with a gauge of either 1¼in, 32 or 33mm. With the rather wide wheels still in use it didn't make much difference either way! In due course it became standardised at 32mm.

Gauge 1, with ⅜in scale has a nominal track gauge of 1¾in, and here 10mm scale, which works out at 4ft 6in on a gauge of 45mm was preferred. However, this size was a little too big, and slowly it dropped in popularity. Gauge 2 sank, after a premature attempt to form an association failed to get under way.

Various individuals had already experimented with a smaller scale. Retrospectively, one regrets that the decision was taken to halve O gauge, had they decided to reduce Gauge 1 by half it is probable that the entire course of railway modelling might have been changed for the better. However, Bing, the big Nuremberg toymakers, produced the first commercial half-O models in the mid twenties, first as a non-reversing clockwork model and then as an electric set. These models were all 2-4-0 tanks. The electric models had a vertical armature with a wound field. Reversal was by a lineside trip. A little later Bonds produced a permanent magnet replacement for DC working.

These early half-O models were so puny that the locomotives could just about manage four of the small four wheeled tinplate coaches. But the sets were relatively cheap, and two persuasive writers, Edward Beal in Scotland and Allan Lake Rice (using the pen-name Eric LaNal) in the USA were fascinated by this size. Both independently came to the same conclusion, the true scope of half-O lay in a fairly large room where, at last it was possible to create a real miniature railway.

At this point trouble enters. The Bing wheels were equally happy on either 16.5mm or ⅝in gauge and the scale was known as OO or HO according to the whim of the builder. There was also a certain amount of difference in pronounciation. It must be remembered that gauges were *numbered* and the original sizes stopped, logically, at 1. Nought gauge was an afterthought. When something smaller was needed, the confusion between the Roman O and the Hindu Zero took over, and imperceptibly gauge nomenclature changed to letters. For a time, ⅝in gauge was known as "double nought".

Now the Bing models were nondescript, but built to roughly Continental loading gauge. When adapted for British usage, the coaches and wagons could be made to about 3½mm scale, but the sheer size of the motor made it difficult to make a locomotive to this scale unless one built one's own motor. However, there was another possibility. If the bodies were made to 4mm scale, everything was lovely. Maybe the track was undergauge, but since the rather heavy wheels were about 4mm scale across their faces, it all helped.

At about the same time one or two Gauge O workers were asking themselves why a serious railway modeller need be forced to use rails designed for obsolescent gauges. Agreed, the nice new Hornby trains, cheap and quite reliable, would run over these rails, but surely, they were building scale models.

Before anything could happen, Wall Street collapsed, the Great Depression hit Europe and no manufacturer felt in the least inclined to invest in new tools and equipment, let alone rock the boat.

When, in the mid thirties, the economic situation began to stabilise, two developments occurred. The half-O business had polarized. There was HO, 3½mm scale on 16.5mm gauge and OO, 4mm scale, also on 16.5mm gauge. For a time components were available for both scales, but for a number of reasons the great majority of British railway modellers settled on OO while the rest of the world went HO.

The most significant development around this time was the formation of the NMRA, the American association of railway modellers which, from the start established wheel and track standards. Here they did much good, but unfortunately, their influence has been greatly overestimated in Britain. It is often said that had we such a body, the OO mix up would never have happened. It is therefore

worth pointing out that the NMRA standardised Gauge O at $\frac{1}{4}$in scale, and since manufacturers also had to cater for the popular Lionel system, with deep flanges, the net result is that in O and its associated sizes in the USA there have been just as many variations as exist in 4mm scale in Britain! Their success in HO is an historic accident; the first American manufacturer to go in for ready-to-run HO train sets began by producing kits for the scale market and as a result used his existing wheels.

However, to return to the 1930's, the move towards finer track standards for O was given a great impetus by the work of W S Norris, a wealthy enthusiast who decided that the old standards were not good enough, and instead had rail and wheels made to his own specification. The result was what is now known as fine scale O, or lately, OF. While not exactly to scale (the wheels were still slightly too broad, the flanges too deep) the resulting models were beautifully proportioned and looked right. They also worked well. There were one or two unfortunate concomitants of Norris' work. First, because he was rich many people claimed that one needed a deep pocket to work in OF, which is not so. Second, it has long been believed that Norris worked more exactly to scale, whereas all he did was to use a scale section rail and, accordingly a finer section wheel. Apart from this nothing was altered, the improvement in appearance occured because the track looked right! He built two superb layouts; the second remained technically unfinished at his death, though most modellers would have been satisfied with something half as good.

The 1930s were undoubtedly the high peak of Gauge O development. At the cheap end there was the Hornby range, including the realistic No 2 special 4-4-0's, the later *Eton* and the short lived *Princess Elizabeth,* as well as the full range of Bassett-Lowke, Leeds Model Co and Milbro models of a superior nature. Space was no problem; one simply went into the garden, where, even in the smallest of terraced houses, there was room to spare for a decent main line run. Indoors OO gauge was beginning to take hold. The Trix system was cheap but not very realistic, Marklin HO imports were decidedly Germanic, but in 1938 came Hornby Dublo, which not only introduced the first really authentic new British models for years, but finally settled the pronounciation of the gauge letters, "doubleowe" not "oh-oh".

It is important to stress that during the inter-war period there was virtually no real co-ordination between British and German manufacturers, chauvinism was rife and no-one wished to co-operate.

Top: An era now passed: Hornby gauge O tinplate trains of the 1930s. *B Monaghan*

Centre: A large Hornby 4-4-4T of the 1920s. These engines were supplied in red, green and black in LMS, LNER and GW colours. Each' model of this series carried the number "4-4-4". *J Joyce*

Bottom: O gauge in clockwork: the "Sherwood Section of the LMS" belonging to Norman Eagles. *P J Kelly*

EARLY GERMAN TOYMAKERS

Bing and Carette

Only alphabetical order is possible for the three greatest names in tinplate. Each was supreme in some aspect of commercial model making, and this short article deals above all with the best achievements of each. The great firm of Märklin is still in full production, of course, and now over a century old, but tinplate is no longer the predominant material in their models, and we are here definitely concerned with the past.

Tinplate—tinned steel plate—is light, strong, and crisp to work. It can be soldered easily. It is ideal for stamping out shapes in a press, folds, or rolls into a boiler barrel, cleanly and precisely. But it is not an easy material for the amateur. In a factory, the right tools and jigs ensure the quality of the product, but they

are expensive and their cost has to be covered by a large quantity of goods, so the essence of "tinplate"—in the collector's sense—is the catalogued production item.

Cheap lines were obviously made in larger quantities than expensive ones, and for that reason more money was spent on their tooling. Typically, carriages and wagons, like the cheapest locomotives, were assembled without solder, by means of small lugs passing through slots. This had the important advantage that the finished livery could be printed directly onto the flat tinplate sheet, or, in some instances, transferred onto it. In either case, the resources of colour printing were available to provide a faithful copy of a real livery, to simulate planking, strapping, works plates (and

even, in the cheapest carriages, passengers' faces pressed against the solid tinplate windows).

Carette

When W J Bassett-Lowke and Henry Greenly first commissioned realistic models of British prototypes, it was to Georges Carette, the French proprietor of a Nuremberg toy factory, that they turned. Carette made all kinds of mechanical and scientific toys, from electroplating sets to steam engines, including toy trains. The pre-Bassett-Lowke toy

Above : An externally fired Great Western Railway 4-4-0 "County" Class by Bing with Carette coach – 1909.
(J T van Riemsdijk Collection) Richard Sharpe Studios

train has often been derided as a visual travesty of the real thing, incapable also of any reasonable performance, but this was certainly not true of the products of Bing or Carette. Both produced tinplate steam locomotives in gauges from 1 to 4 (as they later became known) which ran well and were, though not scale models, elegant copies of the style of some German locomotives of the second half of the nineteenth century. Of the two makers, Bing made things which were marginally more robust, while Carette's were slightly more elegant.

The "Bassett-Lowke Era" was inaugurated by two locomotives, both built by Carette. The "Lady of the Lake" was the well known Ramsbottom 2-2-2, as fitted with a Webb cab, and was made, steam only, in gauges 1 and 2. Two oscillating cylinders were largely concealed by the all-enveloping smokebox and cylinder wrapper. They were single acting, so the cranks were set at 180 degrees on the two sides of the engine. A slim boiler was externally fired, the flames being guarded by side sheets, and there was a reversing block. A touch of refinement was the fitting of engraved name plates. At seventy years old, one of these engines still ran fast with a light train round the writer's garden. The working parts are the Carette standards of the time, and the whole appearance, though very faithful to the British prototype, is unmistakeably Carette, even without taking account of the embossed maker's emblem right in the middle of the smokebox door.

The other model was a 0-4-0 Peckett saddle tank, with a clockwork motor, made in O, 1, and 2 gauges. This was no less unmistakeably Carette, and bore the same emblem in the same place, but it was perfectly proportioned (except for the wheels in the O gauge model). This model was catalogued by Bassett-

Lowke 25 years after the Carette firm had ceased to exist, but in a much inferior version first produced by Bing from Carette tools. The distinguishing mark of the original Carette product (in gauge one, at least) is the correct small size of the driving wheels, and small splashers. But the general Carette "look" is rather hard to describe. It is really a certain delicacy of surface detail which is very much more realistic than the over-emphasis usually found on models, let alone toys, and it reached its height in the very refined livery of the British coaches in gauges O, 1, 2 and 3.

The later story of Carette locomotives for the British market was not entirely happy. After a Gauge 3 Stirling eight footer successfully made in the tinplate style, Carette was persuaded to attempt something nearer to the model engineer's style of the period (and the model engineers of the period generally built locomotives which, though often handsome enough, performed exceedingly poorly). There followed an incongruous gauge 1 version of the GER "Claud Hamilton", in which a body built largely of castings was superimposed upon a tinplate type *outside* cylinder chassis. This was accompanied by a gauge 3 model of NER 4-4-0 No 1619—the first Smith three cylinder compound—again built of castings, fully sprung, and fitted with a Smithies boiler. Neither of these engines would steam well enough to pull their heavy superstructures plus a reasonable load, but the NER engine certainly showed the characteristic elegance of its maker.

Reverting to tinplate, and to clockwork, Carette produced, in gauges O, 1, and 2, a really magnificent model of an American 4-4-0 Vauclain compound, which was not exclusive to Bassett-Lowke, and for the British firm, a model in O and 1 of Ivatt's GNR No 251. This last

locomotive marked the end of locomotive building for Bassett-Lowke, though not of carriage and wagon manufacture. It seems probable that by this time Bassett-Lowke had decided that Bing were better able to make locomotives to suit their requirements, and it must be admitted that the Bing GNR Atlantic which immediately followed was better than the Carette one, especially in the quality of its clockwork motor. But all the Carette locomotives had an artistic quality which is now highly appreciated and accounts for their status among collectors.

The Carette locomotives belong to the beginnings of realistic commercial modelling, but Carette carriages and wagons persisted with but slight alterations in the catalogues of the 'thirties. This is because, though the firm disappeared when its proprietor was expropriated and expelled from Germany in 1914 (in somewhat melodramatic and absurd circumstances) the tooling and printing plates were not lost. After 1918, the products reappeared on the market from the great Bing factory, and figured once more in the Bassett-Lowke catalogue.

The range of carriages consisted of full passenger brakes, and coaches with five compartments and two lavatories, in the liveries of the LNWR, the GNR, the GWR, the LSWR and the Midland, plus NER examples in gauge 3 only (originally to run with the model of 1619). LNWR coaches were made in gauge 3 also. Only LNWR and GWR were made in gauge 2, but the full range appeared in O and 1. GWR and Midland coaches had clerestoreys. There were also shortened versions of some, with either six or eight wheels, and a full length clerestory coach in dark blue which was simply lettered "GC&CN", and another similarly lettered but with elliptical roof and finished in a lightish red.

Below: Great Central Railway locomotive: "Sir Alexander" by Bing for Bassett-Lowke, Gauge 1 clockwork—1903. (*R McCrindell Collection*) *Richard Sharpe Studios*

It was in this range that a LNWR travelling post office coach, complete with working net and pick up arm to engage with lineside apparatus, made its most sophisticated appearance; and to crown the whole achievement a LNWR 12-wheeled diner of greater length than the standard coach, and again finished with the greatest refinement of livery, was added.

To this day, a train of these vehicles in motion on a good track—preferably outdoors—looks more realistic and more attractive than almost any of the finest hand-built stock. This is entirely due to the perfection of the livery, for they are really only lightly embossed tin boxes on wheels. However, they truly represent the appearance of the pregrouping

coaches of 1909, the year of their first manufacture, and are more or less historical documents in their own right.

In 1921, a range of corridor vehicles was produced for Bassett-Lowke by Bing, and after the grouping of the railways in 1923 these appeared in the new liveries, but most of the Carette coaches did not. Exception was made for the 12-wheeled diner and the TPO however. For these, Bassett-Lowke had new transfers of LMS livery prepared, and the result was scarcely less fine than the original LNWR style.

If these coaches represent the finest achievement of Carette, the enormous range of tinplate wagons, with the same fine texture printing of surface detail, is scarcely less astonishing. There were

open and closed wagons of all the main pregrouping railways; special wagons for gunpowder, bananas, lime, and tar; bogie well wagons and long loco coal gondolas; and private owner wagons including the superb yellow Colman's Mustard and Colman's Starch vans, adorned with the noble heads of bullocks, in full colour.

Bing

To understand the special place which the Bing concern (Gebruder Bing, Nuremberg—commonly GBN, marked on

Above: Great Central Railway locomotive: "Sir Sam Fay" by Bing for Bassett-Lowke, Gauge 1 clockwork—1913 (*R McCrindell Collection*) *Richard Sharpe Studios*

goods not made exclusively for Bassett-Lowke) came to occupy in the plans of Bassett-Lowke it is only necessary to compare their "official" model of the Great Central 4-4-0 "Sir Alexander", made in 1903, with their 4-6-0 "Sir Sam Fay" of the same railway, made ten years later. The first, (called "official" because the GCR commissioned Bassett-Lowke to have the model made in the first place, both as a prize in a competition, and for ordinary sale), was a dignified toy, with none of the elegance of the prototype, and a good deal of the lumpishness of early German clockwork toys. Nevertheless, it was very well painted, had a good clockwork motor, and like the GWR "Atbara" class model of similar vintage,

held promise. Neither model could compare visually with the Carette productions. But the "Sir Sam Fay" is quite another matter—between these two models Bing has passed from caricature to portraiture.

A good deal of the credit for this transformation must go to Henry Greenly, whose artistic eye judged extremely well the fine adjustments of proportion made necessary by the use of standard clockwork motors or steam cylinders. Greenly also well knew the English preoccupation with the profile of a chimney or a dome, and the authenticity conferred by well modelled tender axleguards, and wheels with a great number of spokes. As a result, Bing embarked upon a magnifi-

cent series of model locomotives for Bassett-Lowke in which the visual artistry was married to excellent craftsmanship and a detail of finish which reached its peak in the South Eastern and Chatham 4-4-0, in gauge 1 only, made in 1913. 1913.

But if the SECR represents the peak, many other models are almost as fine, though the prototype livery may be simpler. The "Sir Sam Fay" was the most massive of the whole range, the great scope of which can be indicated by listing the models available for just one railway, the GNR. There were: the Ivatt 4-2-2, large 4-4-0, large Atlantic and 0-6-2 tank, and the first Gresley 2-6-0. The last was made in steam only, gauge 1

and sold through Gamages, not Bassett-Lowke, but is identical in style and quality with the others. The large Atlantic was also made in steam, its appearance scarcely distinguishable from that of the clockwork version. This whole GNR range existed in gauge 1, and some of the models were also made in O and 2.

The Bing steam locomotives had externally fired boilers and piston or slide valve cylinders, with a reversing block to interchange steam and exhaust passages. Their performance was curiously variable, possibly as a result of partial blocking of some steam passages by solder during assembly. When good, they were and still are very good. The

writer has a GNR 2-6-0 which easily hauls five heavy scale coaches on an outdoor track, and a GWR "County" 4-4-0 which runs for a long time with four.

The Bing clockwork motors were very much better than those of Carette or Märklin. The gauge O six coupled motor was made in quite recent years by Bassett-Lowke, the late Stefan Bing having brought the tools to England when, as a Jew, he felt obliged to abandon the great Nuremberg factory and take refuge in London. The motors for gauges 1 and 2 were of splendid quality, mostly with two speeds, and put together like the movements of grandfather clocks, but these large gauges are not really suitable for clockwork—at least

not for children. They take too much winding up. The "Sir Sam Fay", like the GNR 0-6-2T and the LYR 4-6-0, was fitted with a large motor—in fact the gauge 2 motor reduced in width by $\frac{1}{8}$in would by means of a crank handle and reduction gearing. "Sir Sam Fay" could run 170 feet with half a dozen tin-plate coaches, but winding up was a tedious process. Yet the motor used up little of the available space in the bodywork and when the writer modified one of these engines to take the largest possible spring, a similar load could be taken 350 feet. In the gauge O engines all the available space could be used without making winding an impossible chore.

Bing produced a standard permanent magnet electric motor, with spur gearing onto two axles, which ran smoothly enough but necessitated a bulge on the side of the tender engine models to accommodate the brush gear. For this reason the electric versions were generally less attractive than the clockwork or steam ones.

There can be little doubt that this was the finest range of tinplate locomotives ever built. Before 1914, outside cylinder locomotives were not very common, and outside valve gearing virtually unknown on British locomotives. Within the price at which a model would sell, the care could be lavished on the hand painted livery—and what splendid liveries there were to be copied! Models of continental and American prototypes were never so successful (apart from the Carette Vauclain compound) because of the mass of detail on the prototypes. Even so, Bing very definitely improved the style of their products for the home market, most notably in a series of steam driven models of the Maffei-built locomotives of the Bavarian Railways. There were two series of 4-4-0, 4-4-2, and 4-6-2 locomotives, and a notable version of the famous Maffei high speed 4-4-4. None of these was a scale model of the accuracy of the British types, but they were beautiful and efficient little machines, and their wheels were not too small or lacking in sufficient spokes. Today, they are all highly desirable collector's items.

Right: Coaches by Carette. Top two are London and South Western Railway coaches for Bassett-Lowke made to Gauge O and Gauge 1. (*R McCrindell Collection*) Beneath is a London and North Western 12 wheel diner together with its LMS version. (*J T van Riemsdijk Collection*)   *Richard Sharpe Studios*

Below: London & North Western Railway 4-4-2 "Precurser" tanks by Bing (left) and Märklin (right). (*R McCrindell Collection*) *Richard Sharpe Studios*

Facing page: Bing (for Bassett-Lowke) LNWR 4-4-0.

The great firm of Märklin never had any close ties with Bassett-Lowke, but made many models for the British market. All Märklin products were very strongly made, and the firm showed great ingenuity in developing all aspects of the model railway to a very high technological standard. The present day range of remotely controlled traffic movements, level crossings, signals, lights, cranes, whistles and everything else was brought into being by Märklin at a very early date. The steam locomotives mostly had internally fired boilers with a sloping central flue, large piston valve cylinders with reversing by block—but all provided with much larger steam ways than those in the Bing Models—and ran excellently.

The trouble with the earlier Märklin models was that they were remarkably ugly, and though things improved after 1918, there was never a model of a British prototype which could equal those made by Bing. One has only to compare one of the very best of Märklin's—the LNWR 4-4-2T—with its Bing equivalent, to appreciate the difference. So, as we are here concerned with the finest of tinplate, it is to Märklin's continental models that we must turn to appreciate why this maker is so revered by the collectors.

There was a long series of Märklin Pacifics, all but the last of which were made clockwork, steam, or electric. The first of these appeared in 1909, the same year as its prototype, which was Eugen Kittel's 4 cylinder compound Pacific of the Württemberg State Railway. Märklin tended to copy the locomotives of their home state of Württemberg, as Bing did those of Bavaria, and perhaps it is unfair to blame Märklin for the ugliness of their early models when the real villain was Kittel's predecessor, Adolf Klose. However, Kittel's Pacific was an unusual and graceful looking engine, and the Märklin version, though somewhat out of proportion and coarse in detail, was a tolerably good likeness and a very attractive little locomotive. The drive from the cylinders in the steam version was onto fly cranks. All the coupled wheels had these, to take the coupling rods, and the eccentrics were sandwiched between them and the face of the wheel, the frames being inside. All Märklin steam Pacifics except the last kept this curious arrangement, which somehow conveyed the fussiness of outside valve gear without resembling real practice at all.

The Württemberg Pacific was soon followed by a PLM, perfectly hideous in the steam version, and in some examples built upon a cast iron bedplate. Even more dreadful were the models of "The Great Bear", but in the twenties Märklin Pacifics reverted to the charm of the Württemberg model, and an inaccurate but pleasing Gresley Pacific (sometimes named Flying Fox but sometimes Great Bear) emerged from the Göppingen factory, as did the first attempt at a Reichsbahn Pacific. These engines, in O and 1, ran very well indeed, and it began to be apparent that the Märklin steam system, though not the clockwork motor, was superior to that of Bing. Moreover, these two models, though not yet portraits of their prototypes, were at least beginning to catch a likeness.

The finest of all Märklin tinplate locomotives appeared in the middle thirties. There was an extraordinary brief explosion of exciting new models in O and 1. The gauge 1 models were not all catalogued, so brief was their season, and some collectors are unaware that they were ever made. There was a gauge O New York Central "Hudson", and, in O and 1, the streamlined "Commodore Vanderbilt", electric only. There was the LNER "Cock o' the North", and the unique Etat 4-8-2, both electric and both made in O and 1 (though very few of the gauge 1 versions are known to the writer). Lastly, there was a new Reichsbahn Pacific, in O and 1, steam and electric, and a Reichsbahn 4-6-4 trailing tank (DR series 62) in both gauges, electric only.

Of this series of models, the Reichsbahn engines achieved a standard of realism never before reached by Märklin; in which, at last, a fineness of surface detail, especially in the electric models, provided the illusion of size. The steam Pacific in gauge 1 was only in the catalogue for one season, which was a pity, because this was the finest Märklin steam locomotive. Gone were the fly cranks, replaced by a simulation of Walschaerts gear. The whole thing was brought into proportion, and though such things as steam pipes were inevitably overscale, the model achieved a massive

Above: Märklin "Gotthard" Bo-Bo. Made in gauges O and 1, 1920. (R McCrindell Collection) *Richard Sharpe Studios*

Below: A Märklin primitive gauge 1 train, circa 1900. (R McCrindell Collection) *Richard Sharpe Studios*

elegance just like that of its prototype. Moreover, nearly forty years later, one of these will still pull eight of the heaviest Märklin coaches with the greatest of ease.

Märklin was the first manufacturer to lavish as much care on a model of an electric locomotive as on the steam types. Before 1914 the prototypes were few and far between, but both Bing and Märklin produced double bogie electric types (the Märklin one being based on the Central London locos) as well as four wheelers and such things as trams and the Paris Métro. After 1918, the Swiss Gotthard electrification inspired Märklin to make a fine, dramatic looking, version of the big Gotthard locomotives. It was shortened, and lacked the pony wheels at the ends, as it lacked the jackshaft drive, but it caught the likeness of its

original, was well engineered and powerful, and liberally provided with lights outside and in.

The Gotthard Bo-Bo set the style for all subsequent elaborate Märklin electric locomotives, and it must be said that these remained very much in the style of the twenties, and never achieved the excellence of the last Märklin steam outline types. There were 2 B 1 and 2 C 1 types, and there was the culminating splendour of the articulated "Crocodile", but none of these was anything like a scale model. The "Crocodile", for instance, was four-coupled at each end, instead of six-coupled, and had a jack-shaft arrangement quite unlike its alleged prototype but very like that of the original Gotthard locomotive. It was really a pity that the "upper works" was not based on that locomotive, because the result might

have been a good scale model. However, the gauge 1 version of the "Crocodile" had two motors, and was Märklin's most expensive production. It was also a very splendid toy, and these reasons have sufficed to make it perhaps the most desired of all items in the tinplate collector's shopping list.

The last topic for which we have space is the Märklin coach. Except for the British types and some small, cheap lines, Märklin coaches were soldered together and finished by hand painting and transfers. They also were usually provided with elaborate interiors, with dreadful vertical spikes upon the seats for the location of drilled out plaster passengers. In the early days they were short but elaborately detailed. With time they became better proportioned, and they culminated, in the twenties and thirties,

Top: A gauge 1 Märklin steam Gresley Pacific. *(J T van Riemsdijk Collection)* *Richard Sharpe Studios*

Centre: Märklin 53cm gauge 1 coaches. The bogies of the Brake are substitutes. *(J T van Riemsdijk Collection)* *Richard Sharpe Studios*

Far left: Märklin's last gauge 1 steam locomotive at work out of doors. *(J T van Riemsdijk Collection) Ron Burrell*

in two series of quite remarkable quality, available in gauges O and 1. The second series is commonly found in O, but was so rare in 1 that it has recently been exactly copied in Switzerland by Wilag A. G. and marketed by Fulgurex. Though slightly underscale, these coaches match in realism the last Märklin steam type locomotives. In O gauge tinplate, they have been equalled in recent years only by the products of the Italian firm of Elettren, and only ever surpassed by the now rare but incomparably realistic Etat coaches of Marescot.

The immediately preceding Märklin series appeared in 1920 in the catalogues though some seem to have been made before 1914, and were last listed in the late thirties. In gauge 1 they were 53cm long, and taller than the final series. At first they had tall clerestoreys, cut back at the ends, and trumpet like ventilators along the top. Later the clerestoreys were lower and full length, but still turned down at the ends. The last versions had elliptical roofs with ventilators, end tanks and walkways. Their liveries were many: red, green and yellow with black on the

PLM versions, teak or blue for the Wagons-Lits, teak or red for Mitropa, and standard green. The long guard's vans had birdcage lookouts and sliding side doors. These coaches, though perhaps less realistic than the final series, had decidedly more character, and every train made up with them was a veritable Orient Express—a romantic evocation of the days before 1914, when every international train seemed to serve half Europe, the days of "Grand European Expresses".

Overleaf: Early model locomotives (about 1896) from the collection of Gustavo Reder, Madrid.

Top left: Märklin wine wagon.
(J T van Riemsdijk Collection) Richard Sharpe Studios

Top right: Märklin gauge 1 53cm sleeping car, circa 1930. There was also an identical gauge O version. (R McCrindell Collection) Richard Sharpe Studios

Centre left: Märklin British Pullman car, circa 1930. (R McCrindell Collection) Richard Sharpe Studios

Centre right: Märklin banana van.
(J T van Riemsdijk Collection) Richard Sharpe Studios

Far left: Interior view of a Märklin coach, circa 1905. (R McCrindell Collection) Richard Sharpe Studios

Near left: Märklin accessories: A turnstile.
(R McCrindell collection) Richard Sharpe Studios

SLEEPING - CAR

39

FRENCH MODEL MANUFACTURERS

Gauge O JEP layout of the 1930s : 2-4-0 electric locomotive with 4-wheel luggage van and short express coaches.
Collection Gustavo Reder

It is true to say that until recent years the French model railway manufacturers have always lagged behind their German counterparts, possibly because the Germans flooded the market with their products leaving little space for the native article. One must also remember that the French never seemed to be so railway conscious until the 1930s and they have had to survive the upheaval caused by two wars.

The first model locomotive manufactured in France is believed to have been built by Radiguet, who instigated a small firm of that name in Paris in 1872, making stationary model steam engines and odd small toys as well as instructional models for students of physics and early electrical engineering. It is thought that the first model was put on the market around 1885 and looked somewhat like a very early Crampton 2-2-2 locomotive with the rear wheels having a larger diameter than the others, and these were coupled to a cylinder in the accepted position; the model was fired by a methylated spirits burner.

Later Radiguet went into partnership with Massiot who had been manufacturing a few metal toys. A shop was opened in Paris, which was quite apart from their works, but their existence in the 1900s is obscure and it appears that they failed to survive the competition from other firms entering the market.

One such competitor must have been Brianne who also opened a business in Paris around 1889 specialising in electrical toys, but doing good business by importing the model railway products of both Bing and Carette of Germany. Brianne manufactured some accessories for the railway items and concentrated on and developed a large range of tinplate station buildings which were continued for many years. The range included some prototypical Parisian stations, which were uncommonly good for their time, although they may have been gaudily painted; and there were differing styles from small halts to large terminii. Brianne also produced a small working tramway system.

In the range of larger models Brianne produced in 1910 or 1911 an electrically driven 5½in gauge (140mm) "Train Géart" (Giant Train). The locomotive was modelled on the PLM 4-6-0 type and the model weighed 44lb and with corridor coaches measuring some 3½ft to 4ft in length it was obviously designed for outdoor operation (or in a baronial hall!). A range of goods stock was also offered. The firm did not enter the market of the smaller gauges and vanished during the 1914-18 War.

A similar casualty of the first World War was Maltete, who had been making general toys from as early as 1869 and although in the early part of the century he turned his attention to railways, his models were not to be compared quality-wise with those of his rivals, for they were very toylike in appearance and were designed to be run straight on the floor without rails or track. All were powered by very simple clockwork mechanisms.

One of the leading French manufacturers was JEP (the initials standing for the full title—"Le Jouet de Paris"), an organisation founded in 1899 for the production of toys and having four or five different works throughout France. In 1902 they were producing eight different model railway sets complete with rails, as well as thirteen pure toy trains with no rails or mechanisms, which were of the push-along variety for the very young. Their incursion into model railways proper at first suffered from competition from the German toy industry, but after World War I the JEP organisation seemed to find their feet.

Up to this time the firm had aimed more at the toy market, but this changed during the next few years and they became the French equivalent of our own Hornby products. Production continued in gauge O with quite an extensive range, the alternative of electric traction being offered and more models being added rapidly. Gauge 1 was also marketed with clockwork or electric propulsion.

JEP always seemed to have favoured the Nord railway of France and introduced a Nord Pacific as a 4-6-0 (Hornby did the same but as a 4-4-2), but later JEP improved their model to make it with the correct wheel notation and it was a passably good model for the price and the time. They also produced some Wagon-Lits Pullman coaches which were like the English Hornby (the more expensive ones), plus a range of four wheeled coaches. One must remember that the French Railways had many four and six wheeled coaches still in service in the 1950s. In 1930 a fourgon was added to the Wagon-Lit range, although this was only 7½in long and thus rather short. JEP produced a good range of freight stock, although they had narrow bodies and somewhat flat sides for there seemed to be little embossing on their tinplate stampings, as compared to other contemporary makes. Much of the stock was painted in gaudy colours, but then they were not alone in this aspect. The JEP catalogue was not short of accessories for their O gauge system for they had a good range of tinplate signals, loco sheds, stations and other items.

In 1925, JEP made a landmark in the history of French model railways by producing the first HO scale trains, both clockwork and electric, the latter having the then normal third rail pick-up. The models appeared to be slightly larger than some of the German manufacturers who followed, although they could be run on the same track for the gauge was the same. They all had lithographed tin-plate bodies and the four wheeled coaches had imitation vertical planking which was finished in brown wood colour. The tinplate stamped track had very deep sleepers, three to a length of about 1ft. The first loco was a 2-4-0T with inside frames which allowed as much room as possible for the motor. The electric models were run on AC current direct from the domestic mains supply via a lamp resistance and it was possible to have relays on the locomotive for remotely controlled reversing, a feature which was something of a novelty at that time, although it had been introduced by Marklin.

Shortly after their introduction of HO gauge, JEP produced another locomotive, this time an electric outline model of a type 1-B-1 which could be worked from a pantograph in contact with an overhead catenary; possibly this was the first small scale model to work from this form of current collection. Later a main-line 4-4-0 loco and bogie coaches were introduced still using mains electricity via a lamp resistance. Accessories such as signals (vastly overscale) and station buildings—all tinplate—were introduced. However, these "Mignon Trains", as JEP called them, never proved to be as popular as the manufacturer had hoped and after being in production for eight years they were withdrawn in 1933. Possibly they were slightly ahead of their time, but JEP made no further advances in the smaller scales until they again entered the HO market in 1950, despite the fact that only 5 years after they stopped the smaller scales became universally accepted. Meanwhile in the ensuing years they continued to concentrate on their gauge O products which were produced to better standards.

In the early 1920's, Louis Rouissy—a grandson of one of the Swiss Nestlé chocolate founders—commenced a business in Paris for the manufacture of model railways called LR (the abbreviation for "Le Rapide"), in both clockwork

and electric gauge O. Their advertisements claimed them as "the fastest model trains in the World", which was achieved by good electric motors and high gearing. The firm could never be considered as one of the "greats" in model railway traditions for they adopted a scale slightly lower in height than JEP and

they looked odd when their rolling stock was in a train of other makers items. The electric models were operated at 20V DC and they had automatic couplings. A variety of locomotive models were produced including a Nord super Pacific with correct wheel arrangement, and some other steam and electric outline prototypes. A varied selection of freight stock of both 4 wheel and bogie types were produced, some of them quite good models in their own right. Coaches of Wagon-Lits type and blue corridor coaches supposedly purporting to make up a "Blue Train" were introduced. Le Rapide were taken over by another firm in 1954.

Another old firm was Rossignol who

made some gauge O and gauge 1 locos for running straight on the floor without rails in the early part of this century. One model was of a fireless steam tram loco, which, with its trailers, was like many to be seen in several French towns including Versailles. In 1914 the firm made some track for their gauge O models and after the War they had trains available with either clockwork or electric propulsion, but the latter models were very simple and not as accurate in likeness to prototype as their earlier examples.

The top quality pre-War French model railway items were manufactured by Marescot who in 1920 was producing models of French trains for gauge O. Models like the de Glehn Compound Pacific with full working Heusinger radial valve gear and some beautiful vestibule corridor coaches which were quite light in weight, nearer scale and more closely resembled the prototypes than many other products. The electric model locos picked up from the centre third rail via a mains transformer. Marescot had actually commenced his operations in 1915 with a close liaison with Bassett-Lowke. Marescot did not have a separate existence for any great length of time for within ten years they were taken over by Fournereau in 1928 and the range was then rapidly increased and split into two types of models—the simple and the more ambitious or scale models.

The "scale" range brought out some wonderful gauge O models of PLM pacifics, the great 4-8-2 express locos and the ubiquitous 4-8-4Ts of the PLM. The Paris-Orleans Railway was represented by the Chapelon 4-8-0 and the Est by 2-8-0 freight locos. Coach and goods stock was also not lacking and production did not stop at the steam outline prototypes for the range also gave some prominence to the electric traction of the era in the shape of the Midi Railways 2-D-2 types and the smaller B-B of the Paris-Orleans section. Such models were in the Bassett-Lowke class and represented some of the finest examples of proprietary or commercial models. Production of such models continued until the beginning of the Second World War, and even after this they introduced a small loco—a delightful model of the 0-6-0T of the Ouest lines which was rather reminiscent of the old Prussian class T3.

In 1937 M. Fournereau founded the very successful magazine "Loco Revue" but kept the publishing side apart from the model business until 1951 when the two organisations split to go their separate ways. The model business was carried on by Fournereau's two sons as JFJ (the founders initials), but after a short time the great influx of the smaller HO gauge, plus perhaps more scale models being produced by other manufacturers caused them to fold in 1958.

Top Left: A Dribbler made by Radiguet & Massiot of Paris (1875–1890). Although 3in gauge it was not intended for use on track. The front wheels swivel to allow it to be run in a circle on a smooth floor. Fitted with safety valve and whistle. It was called a "Dribbler" because of the trail of water and oil from the cylinders. Steam driven fired by methylated spirits. *K A C Melvin*

Above: Comparison of German and French models of the early twentieth century. Märklin 4-4-0 of 1904 for Gamages (top), Planck "Lord of the Isles" (left) of 1904 and a Carette four-wheeler of 1909. *P E Randall*

Left: Carette gauge 1 clockwork loco, tender and coach in Great Northern Railway colours, dating from about 1910. *P E Randall*

For three-quarters of a century now, the name of Bassett-Lowke has been known all over the world in connection with the manufacture of fine models. In the early years of the century it meant, in particular, model railways of a very special quality, and even for those who could never aspire to the ownership of a Bassett-Lowke model railway but had to be content with poring over the beautifully illustrated catalogues, the name Bassett-Lowke had a peculiar magic to it.

Wenman Joseph Bassett-Lowke, born in 1877, came on both sides of his family from engineering stock. His father's business of J. T. Lowke & Sons made boilers and steam engine equipment, and his mother belonged to another Northampton family, the Bassetts, on the front of whose premises was the inscription "Bassett & Sons, Engineers and Boilermakers, Iron and Brass Founders (Gas engines and shoe machinery erected and repaired)". When he eventually entered business on his own account, the young man adopted both his family names, hyphenated them, and produced a marque the glamour of which has remained, amongst all those interested in models, to this day.

On leaving school he served an engineering apprenticeship in his father's works, and there he met and made friends with a contemporary, Harry Franklin, who worked as a book-keeper in the office. Their friendship was based on a mutual love of models, and led to a business connection which lasted the rest of their lives.

At that time, in the 1890s, model engineering, encouraged by Percival

Marshall's new publication "Model Engineer", was rapidly becoming a national pastime. To meet the growing demand, Bassett-Lowke and Franklin went into business on their own, supplying castings, boiler fittings and other parts which they manufactured in the family works. Mention of their products occurs in the first edition of the "Model Engineer" where it was stated that in addition to working model pressure gauges, they also supplied dummy ones for model engineers to hang on their watch-chains —typical of the way in which Bassett-Lowke, all through his business life, never missed a chance to keep his products in the public eye.

BASSETT-LOWKE

A member of the editorial staff of the "Model Engineer" at that time was Henry Greenly, who later made a name for himself as a designer of locomotives for the 15in gauge. He had begun his professional career in the drawing office of the Metropolitan Railway, but being more interested in model engineering, had changed over to the latter. Bassett-Lowke was quick to appreciate his gift for designing model locomotives and engaged him as his consulting engineer, an association which continued for many years.

In 1900, Bassett-Lowke and Greenly visited the Paris Exposition and were fascinated by the model steam and clockwork locomotives and railway equipment produced by the German manufacturers Bing, Märklin and Carette, all working in Nuremberg. These products were being made to recognised standards and with a precision and realism unknown in Britain, where anything resembling an accurate model could only be obtained from firms who built to order, at prohibitive prices and in gauges as large as 3¼ or 4in, though the models were intended for indoor use. The only models available at a reasonable price were steam locomotives of the "Birmingham Piddler" type, antedeluvian in design, in unpainted brass, built to no recognised standards and having no

track, rolling stock or other equipment.

Bassett-Lowke determined to introduce into Britian the small-scale, prototype-modelled railway equipment that continental firms were making, and with this in mind and with the help of Harry Franklin, he set up his own firm and went into business from an address in Kingswell Street, Northampton.

To begin with, they had the models made by the firm of Bing Brothers, Nuremberg, to their own designs (supplied, no doubt, by Henry Greenly). The first models came on the market in 1902 and the catalogue of that year listed one steam locomotive in Gauge 1 (1¾in), no less than six in Gauge 2 (2in) and three in Gauge 3 (2½in). In addition there were three clockwork locomotives which were available in either Gauge 1 or 2 and were probably standard lines of the Bing factory, including as they did Continental and American types. Those made to the design of Bassett-Lowke were modelled on English prototypes and were

Above left: Cover of a 1920s Bassett-Lowke catalogue. *Courtesy R McCrindell Collection.*

Top: Bing for Bassett-Lowke O Gauge. Ex-GNR 4-4-0 as LNER No 4390, produced 1925. *Courtesy Caroline and Andrew Collection. B Monaghan*

Top left: A rare model: The 1915 catalogue showed this nice model of the then new Lancashire & Yorkshire 4-6-0. *R McCrindell Collection. B Sharpe*

Left: Popular tank engine: In 1915 The London & South Western Railway was represented by this model in gauge 1 clockwork. *R McCrindell Collection.   B Sharpe*

Above: Money spinner: The free-lance "Duke of York" was introduced in 1927 in connection with a cigarette coupon scheme. The model was O gauge and could be purchased in clockwork or electric in red or green. The number on the tender varied with the date of manufacture. Some hundred thousand were made. *Courtesy Caroline and Andrew Collection.   B Monaghan*

Below left: Boyhood treasure: Gauge 1 clockwork London & North Western "Precursor" 4-4-0 given as a welcome birthday present in 1907.
J Francis Parker Collection

obviously meant for the home market.
  The sole Gauge 1 engine was a replica of a Midland Railway 4-4-0 goods loco-motive with outside cylinders. At that time the interest of railway amateurs was centred almost exclusively on passenger express engines (the liking for branch lines and obscure narrow-gauge railways is a phenomenon of recent years). But the difficulty was that in 1902 almost all

passenger express locomotives had inside cylinders, a form of motion which it is not easy to reproduce in the confines of a Gauge 1 model. Hence the choice of a goods engine for a prototype. Although the model was of quite good outline and correctly painted, the effect was spoiled by the fact that the outside oscillating cylinders drove only one pair of wheels, there being no coupling rods. To be strictly accurate, the model was really a 4-2-2. It also had a number of typical Bing features which detracted from a realistic appearance, these being the steam pipes which wandered down the outside of the boiler from the dome to the cylinders (permissible on Continental locomotives, but quite out of place on an English engine), and the two large wooden-handled taps, for whistle and regulator, which were mounted on top of the boiler. A four-wheeled tender was supplied.

The Midland goods was a sort of halfway house between the brass "Piddlers" and the later Bassett-Lowke coarse scale models, but nevertheless it represented quite an advance in that it tried to reproduce a real, existing, locomotive. It was 15in long, 5½in high, and cost 21s 6d (£1.07½).

The Gauge 2 engines were rather better. In this size it was possible to put the cylinders inside the frames, though oscillating cylinders were still used, and

three of the models were manufactured in this way. One of them, based on a Midland Railway Johnson 4-2-2 single made quite a convincing model, but the other two (basically alike, but in detail representing Lancashire & Yorkshire and Great Central prototypes) suffered from the same defect as the Gauge 1 loco, for though ostensibly 4-4-0 engines, the lack of coupling rods reduced them to 4-2-2s. However, at the price of £2.00 for the "four-coupled" and £2 7s 6d (£2.37½) for the single, one could hardly complain.

The other three in this gauge were outside cylinder types, with fixed cylinders and inside valve gear. There was a Great Northern 4-2-2 with bogie tender at £3 3s 0d (£3.15), and two 4-4-0 tank engines, one representing a Metropolitan type and named *Pilot*, which sold at £2 10s 0d (£2.50) and the other a rather better version of the same engine in North London colours, at £2 15s 6d (£2.77½).

Although the Gauge 3 (2½in) models are really outside the scope of this article, one of them deserves mention as it was the forerunner of one of the most popular and best-known Bassett-Lowke models. This was the so-called "scale model" of the London North Western 4-4-0 *Black Prince*, 23½in long, 7in high and selling at £3 15s 6d. Of this engine the "Model Engineer" remarked that it

was "deserving of great praise as a genuine step in the direction of more realistic model locos than have often been supplied by professional model makers". (Evidently Bassett-Lowke was regarded still as a supplier of toys). A purchaser of the model was quoted as saying that "with four burners going, and running light with only tender, it ran non-stop for 40 minutes and covered 3,000 yards". It is perhaps necessary to mention here that all the locomotives mentioned so far, even in 2½in gauge, had pot boilers.

To go with these engines Bing also supplied, to the designs of Bassett-Lowke, a tin-plate model with brass wheels of a LNWR bogie corridor coach with clerestory roof. It had opening doors and a corridor partition and was correctly painted and lined. Prices varied from 14s (70p) in Gauge 1 to 40s (£2.00) in Gauge 3. For an extra 1s 3d one could have "Sleeping Car" or "Dining Car" painted on the sides. A LNWR bogie brake was also available, but there was no concession to devotees of other companies. Bassett-Lowke always had a partiality for the "Premier Line" which, at Northampton, was understandable.

From Bing's own standard lines, however, there was available non-corridor bogie stock in both LNWR and Midland livery, at slightly higher prices. Exterior detail (always a strong point with Bing models) included such things as polished brass door handles, foot boards and embossed window frames, while the hinged roof could be opened to reveal compartments with seats and luggage racks.

Tinplate trackwork, including points, was also available for all gauges, and, again to the design of Bassett-Lowke, an English country station, embellished with appropriate advertisements. At last someone had produced, at a reasonable price, a model railway system which was not unlike a real railway and which *worked.*

In passing, it may be noted that at that early date Bassett-Lowke supplied a wide range of Bing products, including some very realistic clockwork motorcars (Veteran Car Club types, of course), ships, submarines and even a "Plunging Pike" which was the submarine disguised as a fish. Steam stationary engines, steamrollers, cranes and other equipment made up a tremendous variety of very realistic toys. In the railway section perhaps the most ingenious item was a passenger coach held together by springs which could be arranged to disintegrate in a railway accident situation!

Bassett-Lowke and Franklin, however, were not content merely to supply the products of other people. Their aim was to be their own producers, and as soon as the factory in Kingswell Street was ready they began to do this. In 1903 they produced the first model locomotive of their own, the result of the teamwork of Bassett-Lowke, Greenly and Franklin, and the forerunner of a long line extending over the next sixty years. It was a Gauge 1 steam model of the LNWR 2-2-2 "Problem" class *Lady of the Lake*. Although still employed on main-line duties, it was not a very up-to-date prototype, but was one of the few passenger locomotives with outside cylinders. The model was quite a good-looking engine, faithful in outline and in such details as the typical LNWR cab, chimney and tender and correctly painted in LNWR colours. As with the cheaper Bing models, it had oscillating cylinders with reversing motion, but they were partly hidden by the ingenious device of fitting them inside larger fixed cylinder casings which merged into the smokebox in true Ramsbottom style. *Lady of the Lake* was 20in long with tender, and 6in high. It sold at 31s (£1.55). On test by "Model Engineer" it was found to steam well and

Above: Gauge 1 in the garden: An early steam model of a GWR County complete with German-built tinplate clerestory coaches passes a later Great Northern Atlantic in LNER colours. *Courtesy J van Riemsdijk Collection. B Sharpe*

Left: Later near-scale model: Towards the end of the 1930s the company produced O gauge models of some of the better known modern classes. One of the smaller production batches was this LNER Sandringham Class 4-6-0. *G Brown*

Right: Midland model: A German-manufactured near-scale model in O gauge of the then-new "999" Class. First marketed in 1911. *G Brown*

hauled two heavy bogie coaches at a good speed. Although no figures of the number produced are available, it was sufficiently popular for it to appear in Gauge 2 as well.

After *Lady of the Lake* Bassett-Lowke produced, in 1904, his own version of the North London 4-4-0 tank, in Gauges 1, 2

and 3. These were better detailed than the Bing engines; for example the steam pipes no longer strayed down the outside of the boiler but were brought through the smokebox, enabling the handwheel of the smokebox door to be used as the regulator. This not only looked better, but was also handier to use than a

control in the cab. At £2 10s 0d (£2.50) for the Gauge 1 version, this was a very good buy. It also represented, under the guiding hand of Greenly, a further step towards the aim of scale realism.

All the locomotives described so far had pot boilers, heated by a row of burners underneath—not by any means

and-water drum on the underside of which was a downcomer and three water tubes. Thus more heating surface was provided and the flames sheltered from draughts, while there was no unsightly lamp burner below the boiler to spoil the appearance. The Smithies boiler was adopted by Bassett-Lowke for gauges above Gauge 1, and was a considerable improvement.

The years before the first World War were the Golden Age of Bassett-Lowke model railways. There is no space here to mention all the locomotives produced, but certain of them have achieved a niche in model railway history. Probably the best-known model of this period was the 4-4-0 express locomotive of the LNWR, *Black Prince,* which began, as we have seen, as a Gauge 3 model produced by Bing, in 1902. By 1911 it was being made in Gauges O (1¾in), 1, 2 and 3. Of the first series some 2,500 were made, with another 300 in liveries other than that of the LNWR (Bassett-Lowkes would do this to order). The second series in 1909 ran to some 1,500 before production stopped with the war. The Gauge 3 version of this series was a particularly fine model, accurate in scale and appearance and having such refinements as water space in the tender with a hand feed pump, bell whistle, spring buffers and head lamps.

Another popular model was the Great Northern Atlantic type of 1898. Bassett-Lowke modelled this in practically every gauge from 1¼ inches to 9½ inches, beginning with a Gauge 2 model in 1905. In the smaller gauges it appeared with steam, clockwork, and electricity as motive power. At the other end of the scale they produced, in 1906, a Peckett 0-4-0 saddle tank industrial type locomotive which began with a Gauge 2 clockwork version at 24s 6d (£1.22½p) and developed into Gauge O and 1. It continued in production as long as Bassett-Lowke went on producing model railways, a period of nearly sixty years.

Rolling stock and accessories developed from the tin-plate toys of the Bing Brothers to beautifully made coaches, trucks, stations and signals in wood and metal. Scale trackwork in brass bullhead rail in cast chairs on wooden sleepers could be had in place of tinplate, though a better version of tinplate was produced with wooden sleepers and pressed chairs under the name of "Lowko"—a neat play on its maker's second name.

The 1915 catalogue showed no less than 19 model locomotives. By this time Gauge O was becoming popular, and in this size there was a clockwork Caledonian "Dunalastair", a Great Northern "Atlantic" and a Midland 4-4-0 compound, all selling at two guineas (£2.10). They were also available in Gauge 1, and in addition there was a very nice London South Western 0-4-4 tank, a South Eastern and Chatham Class E 4-4-0 express, a Lancashire & Yorkshire 4-6-0, a Great Northern 4-2-2, and a six-coupled goods in either LNWR or Midland colours. Prices ranged between £2.00 and £6.00. Gauge 2 still retained its popularity at this time and was represented by a Great Northern six-coupled tank, a Great Central 4-4-2 tank and a LNWR "Precursor" tank of the same wheel arrangement. The LNWR was also represented by a *George the Fifth* 4-4-0. All these were available with clockwork or electric motion. Steam in this gauge was available in the form of a London, Brighton & South Coast 4-6-2 tank *Abergavenny.*

But by the time the 1915 catalogue was

the most efficient way of raising steam, especially out of doors, unless in a dead calm. Even the Gauge 3 models had these boilers, a far cry from the solid fuel, internally-fired types later used in this gauge. A change was on its way, however, for the firm of Bassett-Lowke received a visit from a Mr Fred Smithies, an amateur model engineer of some repute, and inventor of the Smithies boiler, which is still known by his name. It consisted of an outer shell which could be made in the form of the prototype boiler, and contained both the heater (usually a spirit lamp) and also the boiler proper. This was a cylindrical steam-

BASSETT-LOWKE MODEL RAILWAYS

GAUGE O

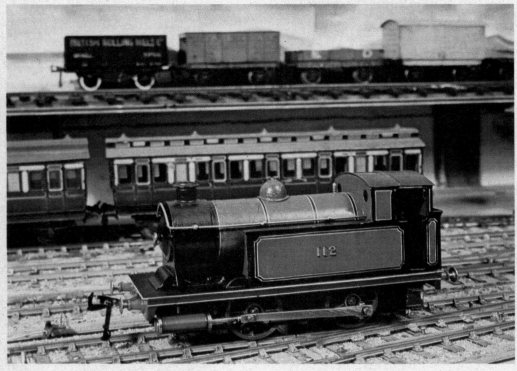

coat of arms and each with its own standards of service. Perhaps the most evocative reminder of those far-off days is an item in the 1902 catalogue—a station refreshment trolley (surely for first class only!) complete with glass decanters, wine glasses and two miniature bottles of hock—a far cry from the plastic cups and pork pies of today.

Bassett-Lowke resumed production of model railways in 1920, but with a difference. By that time Gauge 2 had almost disappeared, and Gauge 1 played a very minor and declining role. Gauge O was now the predominate scale. An interesting example of this trend is shown in the production figures for one of the most popular models introduced at this period, the Bassett-Lowke Mogul. This 2-6-0 tender locomotive was made in steam, clockwork and electric versions, and in Gauge O it was available as a model based on prototypes of all four of the new groups—London North Eastern, London Midland and Scottish, Great Western and Southern. Some 10,000 LMS models were produced, 4,000 LNER, and 1,000 each of the other two.

By comparison, the figures for the Gauge 1 Mogul (available only in LMS and LNE colours) were a mere 750, an indication of the changing trend of things. Obviously, too, in order to compete in the growing market for Gauge O, Bassett-Lowke had found it necessary to adopt mass production methods.

In the years between the wars two of the best known express locomotives in service were the LMS 4-6-0 *Royal Scot* and the LNE Pacific *Flying Scotsman,* operating respectively on the west coast and east coast routes to Scotland. Bassett-Lowke modelled both in Gauge O and sold nearly 15,000 of each. For sheer numbers, however, the palm must go to a freelance type, the 4-4-0 *Duke of*

published Britain was at war, and the Bassett-Lowke works had turned over to making gauges for munition factories. After the existing stocks had been sold there was to be a gap of five years before Bassett-Lowke railway models came on the market again.

A word about the catalogues might not be out of place here. The first one was published in 1899, in a very small edition. It was illustrated with photographic prints, taken by Bassett-Lowke himself and pasted in. Photography was one of his hobbies, a fact that has been a boon to historians of model and miniature railways. The first catalogue illustrated with blocks came out in 1902, and thereafter they were published annually,

except for war years, until 1939. After the second World War they were resumed at intervals, and the last one was published in 1963.

The early catalogues owed much to their illustrator and designer, Ernest Twining, who made a name for himself in the field of small locomotive design and worked for Bassett-Lowke as well as doing much freelance work. He was another of the gifted team which Bassett-Lowke collected around him.

Looking through the catalogues of the early days a picture emerges of a kind of railway travel very different from that of today, an era when more than a hundred railway companies, large and small, existed, each with its own colours and

The New
2-6-0 Type Model Locomotives
for No. 0 Gauge.

THE illustrations on this page showing examples of this splendid range of new locomotives are all actual *photographs of the models* themselves.

OBSERVE the almost supernatural resemblance to the real engines of the respective railway groups.

EACH model is supplied for three different forms of power—clockwork, steam and electricity. Full particulars of these models, with prices, are given in this catalogue.

Opposite top: Catalogue cover from the 1950s. *Courtesy R McCrindell Collection. D Rudkin*

Opposite below: Steam tank engine: This model was carried as a standard product for many years in gauges 1 and O powered by clockwork, electric or steam. The number on the locomotive was that of the firm's premises in High Holborn, London. Note tinplate coaches and wagons in background. *J Francis Parker Collection*

Above: Variety in vans: Sandwiched between Lancashire, Yorkshire and Great Northern open wagons, this gauge 1 lithographed tin LNWR gunpowder van shows something of the wide choice available to Bassett-Lowke customers. *Courtesy J van Riemsdijk Collection. B Sharpe*

Left: Moguls galore: One of Bassett-Lowke's most popular models produced in clockwork, electric and steam was the British 2-6-0 of the 1920s. This was produced in gauges O and 1. **A page from the 1928 catalogue.** *Courtesy R McCrindell Collection. D Rudkin*

Below: Lithographed tinplate coach: Vehicle from the company's standard range circa 1927. *G Brown*

Bottom: Self advertisement: The private owner wagon was prominent on the railways of Britain up to 1948; these were produced in lithographed tinplate. *J van Riemsdijk Collection. B Sharpe*

York, produced in 1927 in connection with the BDV coupon scheme. It could be acquired by smoking large quantities of BDV cigarettes or tobacco and saving the accompanying coupons, or by purchase from Bassett-Lowke for 25s (£1.25). This engine continued in production up to 1939, the name changed in due course to *Princess Elizabeth,* and altogether 100,000 were made. After the war it reappeared in a modernised version and in British Railways colours under the name of *Prince Charles,* and a further 60,000 were produced. By this time the price had risen to £5 5s 0d £(5.25)—an interesting example of the effects of inflation.

As well as these models Bassett-Lowke continued to produce fine scale models in the larger gauges to order. As already mentioned, however, the last catalogue was published in 1963, and thereafter the firm of Bassett-Lowke began to specialise in the manufacture of industrial models. In 1968 a separate concern, Bassett-Lowke Railways, 1968, Ltd, was formed to carry on the model railway tradition and today operates from 59, Cadogan Street London SW3. Their shop provides a place where old Bassett-Lowke models can be bought and sold— a fascinating meeting place for the "Black Princes", "Titley Courts", "Sir Gilbert Claughtons", "Royal Scots" and their attendant coaches and accessories that have been rescued from their retirement in somebody's attic.

MODEL RAILWAYS BETWEEN THE TWO WORLDS WARS

Facing page: Hornby No. 2 Special clockwork locomotive in the form of LMS Compound No 1185, from the C M Whitehouse collection. *Peter Williams*

Overleaf: Another Hornby No 2 Special, this time masquerading as an L1 class 4-4-0 of the Southern Railway. *Richard Sharpe Studios*

HORNBY-MECCANO

There is a story told of how a shipping clerk, named Frank Hornby, walking to his office in Victorian Liverpool, looked up and saw a large crane, and in that moment Meccano was born! Mr Hornby himself, later suggested the process was a more gradual one, but certainly from this, and other of his experiences, grew the vast Meccano Hornby empire.

By World War I, Meccano was well established as a constructional toy and Frank Hornby was already turning his attention to producing clockwork trains in gauge O. Some historians say the first Hornby train set was actually put on the market in 1915 while others claim that it was made by, designed by or, at least, copied from the model trains of the German firm, Bing. The writer has no proof either way, but tends to disbelieve the story, if only because Frank Hornby's links over the years were with Märklin rather than Bing. However, well-documented in catalogues of the period, without any doubt, is the introduction in 1920 of the first Hornby train made in Liverpool.

This set differed from those made by other firms in that the locomotive and wagons were standard parts which, being held together by nuts and bolts,

could be dismantled and rebuilt in the same fashion as Meccano. This historic set consisted of an 0-4-0 locomotive, tender and one open wagon plus an oval of tinplate track. The loco was supplied in black, red, green or blue but was not lettered. A brass plate bearing the number 2710 (reputedly Meccano Ltd's telephone number!) was attached to the cabside and the tender carried a motif incorporating the letters "M Ltd L". The wagon had white metal letters attached to its sides and was available in LNWR, GN, MR, CR or LBSC styles to go with an appropriately coloured locomotive. A very strange feature was that, in addition to the normal places, buffers and couplings were provided between engine and tender, the former of brass and the three-link couplings of over-scale proportions. The writer has had the opportunity to examine several of these locomotives and can see in them the features that ensured the later success of the Hornby range, namely the high quality of engineering and finish.

By the end of 1923 the Hornby series had been considerably enlarged. The original engine was now called No 1 as a larger loco, No 2 had been produced.

This was a 4-4-0 of typical LNWR outline, but was numbered 2711 on its cabside and was finished in the same style as the No 1 locomotive. Four wheeled passenger coaches and bogie Pullmans were now available also, the former in brown with various Railway Company crests and the latter in cream and green, also crested and carrying the words "Pullman" or "Dining Saloon" on their sides.

In 1924 the "Zulu" trains appeared, so called apparently because the locos in them were finished entirely in black! They were virtually cheaper, non-reversing versions of the No 1 series. That year also saw the introduction of two tank engines, one an 0-4-0 and the other a 4-4-4. These were tank versions of the existing tender engines but the larger one appeared just after the Grouping on the real railways and was, as far as can be ascertained, the first Hornby engine to be painted in post-grouping colours. The version illustrated in contemporary catalogues carries on its tank sides the number 1019 with "L M & S R" in large letters underneath.

In 1925 Hornby produced the first of

Above: An early Hornby electric train box (Caroline & Andrew collection). *B Monaghan*

their famous coloured "Book of Trains" which appeared in every subsequent year up to 1940, occasionally combined with catalogues of other Meccano products. These are a great source of information to present day historians and the one of 1925 reveals that many changes and additions to the system had occurred during the first five years.

Browsing through the catalogue today, we find the No 1 and No 2 locomotives, now resplendent in the lined goods and passenger liveries of the LMS and LNER companies. It was some years before Hornby recognised the existence of the GW or the SR! Couplings have now been standardised as the large single link type, interchangeable with other makes, and both locos carry large headlamps fixed in the "express passenger" position. Also shown are the tank locomotives, now known as the No 1 and No 2 and they are also pictured in the goods and passenger liveries of the LMS and LNER, but for some whimsical reason their tank sides carry the legends "0-4-0" and "4-4-4" in place of numbers. A very interesting appearance in the 1925 catalogue are the old tinprinted train sets of 1915 design. Looking remarkably like contemporary German sets, they consist of a simple toy loco, tender and two minute box-like coaches. The illustration shows Midland, GNR, and LNWR styles, the latter with the engine named "George V". Rolling stock was quite extensive by 1925, all now having large single link couplings and pressed tin wheels, both with a nickel finish. Bogie coaches in the original green and cream have now been joined by a new four wheeled type with clerestory roof and opening doors. Goods rolling stock is here in plenty, four wheeled and bogie, including some that were to become firm favourites like the breakdown van and crane, biscuit vans and petrol tankers. Also shown is a good assortment of accessories including the famous "Windsor" station which in modified form was to be produced for several decades to come. An interesting point is that the catalogue showed both clockwork and electric track although at that time there were no Hornby electric trains.

The second five years of the Hornby story, taking us up to 1930, were years of consolidation rather than expansion, although several important introductions were made during that time.

Hornby always marketed a cheaper line for younger boys and this, from 1927, was called the "M" series. Replacing the old "George V" set came the M1 loco and coaches, which were simple but very sturdy toys. The 1915 loco was re-vamped, fitted with a new tender and was designated the M3 loco but it disappeared from the lists as soon as stocks of the bodies were used up. The No 1 and No 2 locomotives continued until the end of the nineteen twenties, the former being also available without reverse and known as the No 0. By 1929 all these engines including the tank varieties could at last be had in the colours of all four railway companies and numbers of real locos had replaced the "2710" "0-4-0" etc.

The year 1927 brought an interesting new locomotive known as No 3. This was of French design and may have originally been made in Hornby's French factory. A freelance 4-4-2, which could run at speed on two foot radius track curves, this loco was supplied in French or British railway colours, the latter being somewhat "anglicised" in appear-

ance and bearing names and numbers of famous British engines like *Royal Scot* and *Flying Scotsman*. These locos have since been much criticised because they were obviously so Continental in style and yet carried prestige British names. It should be remembered, however, that at the time, Hornby trains did not pretend to be other than well-made reliable toys.

The first Hornby electric train was a model of Metropolitan stock powered by a high voltage motor operated from the mains and including a carbon filament lamp in the circuit. Due probably to the inherent dangers of this device, a low voltage motor for use with accumulators was later substituted and this was also supplied in the electric versions of the No 3 loco.

In 1929 the "special" series of loco-

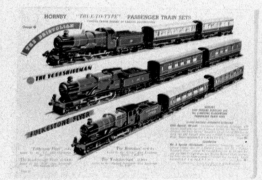

motives was introduced. The No 1 specials were large 0-4-0 toy engines, but the No 2 specials were Hornby's first attempt at scale models.

A different design was produced for each of the four groups and these were, respectively, an LMS "Compound", and LNER "Shire", a GW "County" and an SR "L1".

Other changes and improvements were made during the period up to 1930 and these included the re-design of the large tank engine as a 4-4-2 of more modern design and the fitting of separate lamps

Top: A Hornby "Zulu" O gauge clockwork train set (early 1920s). *P E Randall*

Top left: Pages from Hornby Book of Trains of the 1930s. *D Rudkin*

Above: Hornby No 1 and No 2 locomotives in 1925 styles. *P E Randall*

Top centre: A selection of gauge O Hornby cattle trucks (Caroline & Andrew collection). *B Monaghan*

Top right: Gauge O wagons and breakdown crane outside No 2 engine shed (Caroline & Andrew collection). *B Monaghan*

Right: Gauge O No 2 special tank with level crossing and platelayers hut (Jack Steer collection). *B Monaghan*

and lamp brackets to some engines as well as modified liveries which kept up to date with those on the real railways.

Although locomotives are the main appeal of any railway system to most enthusiasts, Hornby never neglected their rolling stock and accessories. The Hornby Control system was introduced which enabled points, signals and the mechanisms of locos to be controlled from the signal cabin by a system of levers and wires. Some attractive accessories like large engine sheds were added to the system, and the range of rolling stock was increased by new four-wheel and bogie coaches and some interesting special purpose wagons.

In 1930 the first major deletion took place, when the old No 2 locomotive was discontinued. No doubt sales had dropped once the No 2 Special loco was available. At the other end of the scale the original "M" series engines had been replaced by ones of more up-to-date design, the larger one having a reversing mechanism, an unusual feature in a cheap toy engine.

The year 1931 was a landmark in Hornby history for many changes and new introductions were announced in September for the Christmas season. The main changes were the fitting of automatic couplings throughout the series and the introduction of new, lowered bases for all four-wheel goods vehicles. The old No 1 tank and tender locos, whose appearance had changed little since the early nineteen twenties, were replaced by modern looking engines with high boilers, squat chimneys and domes, and a decided LNER flavour. A cheaper version of the tank engine, the M3, was to survive to be the last locomotive to be made by Hornby in gauge O in the nineteen sixties. Back in 1931 new introductions included a series of tinprinted vans which not only looked realistic but were cheaper than the standard enamelled ones.

The Hornby Control system appears to have been withdrawn about 1932 as it ceased to be mentioned in catalogues. The 1934 catalogue drew attention to another development, the introduction of 20 volt electric trains. For several years after that, Hornby made 6 volt and 20 volt trains, side by side, the former for accumulator working and the latter, whose big advantage was automatic reversing, to be operated from the mains via a transformer. Hornby 20 volt engines carried a large electric headlamp in the front of the boiler, scarcely realistic, but

an attractive feature for children! With the 20 volt system becoming standard, a range of illuminated accessories was introduced.

The scenic side of Hornby trains was given attention at this time. Countryside sections which were large representations of fields and hedges made a brief appearance, but were soon withdrawn, presumably not proving popular. Other items, called "modelled miniatures" introduced as lineside effects, were later to develop into a large and separate range called "Dinky Toys". The first ones were human and animal figures and a set of road vehicles.

The years from 1934 to 1937 were again mainly years of consolidation. The introduction of "complete model railways" was presumably a move to interest the younger enthusiast (and to commit him to Hornby!) Attractively boxed, these sets were made up from the "M" series and included scenic items in addition to the usual loco, vehicles and oval of rails.

An introduction of some significance was the bogie passenger coach, available in the colours of all four groups because, up to that time, only Pullmans, and LMS and LNER saloons were made. By 1938 both suburban and corridor coaches were available in tinprinted style, representing the latest designs of the actual railways. In this year too, Hornby introduced several items at the "scale" end

of the range. Apart from the No 2 specials (which they called "true-to-type" locomotives) Hornby trains had always been freelance toy trains with no pretentions to scale. The introduction of 4-6-2 *Princess Elizabeth* locomotive and solid steel track brought real scale models into the system.

What must have been a sales promotion idea, which seems strange in retrospect, happened in the late nineteen thirties when the roofs and bases of many vehicles were painted in gay colours like red, blue, cream and green, instead of the more usual black or grey. This seems to indicate that the thinking at Binns Road in the years just before 1939, embraced both the scale model market and the production of gaily coloured toys for children.

Not surprisingly, no new items appeared after 1940 and Government restrictions from 1942 forbade the making of any Hornby trains. It seems a few may have been assembled or fetched out of stock for export and possibly for the home market at Christmas time, but it was not until 1946 that Hornby trains were again distributed to the toy shops, and then in very small quantities. Postwar shortages affected most goods and in the late nineteen forties people actually queued for Hornby trains and items being kept "under the counter" were not unknown!

The 1949 catalogue lists the smaller locomotives plus a few four wheeled and some bogie vehicles but the latter were soon withdrawn and were probably old pre-war stocks. The growing interest in Dublo must have made Hornby O gauge a "poor relation" in the early nineteen fifties for, between 1949 and 1952, the O gauge range actually contracted. Nevertheless about 1956 all items were repainted in British Railways style and in the next year some new vehicles were added, having realistic die cast bases and brake levers, which were called the No 50 series. Another policy change must have been made at Binns Road because these vehicles had a very short life and by the nineteen sixties the once vast range had shrunk to a mere shadow of its former glory. A few "M" type sets, then known as No 20, were distributed to dealers in 1967, but by the next year, manufacture of the Hornby Gauge "O" series came to an end.

Hornby's French factory made similar trains in pre-war times plus a few special

lines in Continental style. After the war a large independent range of clockwork and electric trains was produced which continued up to the end of the nineteen sixties when this range also ceased.

Through the Hornby Railway Company, a club for boys with local branches, Frank Hornby fostered a spirit of comradeship among owners of Hornby trains and Binns Road always gave an excellent after-sales service. Dealers were appointed with great care and to be allowed to sell Meccano products was an honour in days gone by!

Because Hornby meant so much to so many boys a great nostalgia has developed around it and a club called the Hornby Railway Collectors' Association now flourishes. Items once bought for the nursery are now treated almost like works of art and sometimes change hands at corresponding prices!

To list accurately all the detail and variation in the Hornby range alone through the years would need the space of a large volume, so this is only a survey of the main features of a system now claiming the attention of several historians.

Top: Hornby platform and accessories (Caroline & Andrew collection). *B Monaghan*

Above: The "Princess Elizabeth" locomotive, the pride of the pre-1939 Hornby range. *P E Randall*

Above: One of Hornby's best: The No 2 Special series were the only really life-like engines produced by the company. This is the LNER version No 234 "Yorkshire". *Collection P B Whitehouse Peter Williams*

Below: Hornby Gauge O electric layout: In the foreground Hornby LNER "Flying Scotsman" and Hornby accessories. **Collection and photograph** *William Osborn*

Picture overleaf: Hornby Gauge O electric layout: Left track: goods train being pulled by a Hornby SR 4-4-2T.
Middle left; Hornby LNER "Flying Scotsman" pulling one Pullman coach.
Right Centre; Hornby No 1 Special tender locomotive in LNER livery.
Right; Hornby E120 Tank locomotive in LNER livery.
Far right; No 2 engine shed.
Collection and photograph *William Osborn*

A gauge 1 electric locomotive made about 1913
by Karl Bub of Nuremberg for the American
market.   *K A C Melvin*

Bread and Butter Lines to 1939

Some people might say that it lowered the dignity of a model locomotive to be given away for a handful of cigarette coupons. Yet that was how the Duke of York came on the scene. Perhaps its unorthodox debut was symbolic of the spread of "models for the masses" during this inter-war period, for the Duke became a best seller, both in its original guise and in later incarnations under different regal names.

This was the sort of item that the manufacturers depended on to keep selling for a long time, in a variety of colours, and possibly with a few minor changes now and then. They were the makers' bread-and-butter lines. They were also the staple fare of generations of railway modellers, not only newcomers to the hobby but those of modest means who were thus enabled to enjoy the thrills of railway operation in miniature.

Among these popular O gauge ranges there were few better known examples of the British-built long-runner than the Hornby No 1 locomotive, which in one form or another spanned almost the entire lifetime of Hornby O gauge railways. Inevitably it was a moderately priced four-wheeler, the type of engine with which so many youngsters began the hobby. It was the simple kind of loco which could stand up to any amount of rough handling and cling to the sharpest curves with no stray bogie wheels to jump off the rails.

Frank Hornby's aim was to beat foreign competition, and his advertisements stressed the "British made" appeal. His first train set in 1920 included the loco in its initial form as No 2710, a characterful machine with its small splashers over the rear wheels, nicely rounded cab and glorious brass dome. In its early life it was described as available in "four colours to represent the L&NW, Midland, Great Northern and Caledonian systems", while LMS and LNER colours were announced by the end of 1923, when it was priced at 16s plus 3s 6d for the tender.

An intriguing feature of this loco was that it was "built on the Meccano principle". This meant that it was held together with nuts and bolts instead of the usual bent-over tabs. "All the parts are standardised, and locomotives, coaches and wagons may be taken entirely to pieces and rebuilt." However, unlike Meccano proper, this did not imply that they could be put together again in different forms.

After a few years this constructional method was given up and everything was fixed together permanently. During the 1920s the No 1 loco underwent numerous changes in detail, such as the fitting of headlamps and alterations in the style of painting and numbering. It was also joined by cheaper variations such as the exotically-named Zulu and the more prosaic No O.

Models in GWR colours were adver-

tised in 1926 and Southern colours in 1928, Great Western locos enjoying the distinction of a "brass" safety valve casing instead of the dome. An intermediate design came in 1929, followed in 1931 by a further change to a new design of body that was to remain familiar from then until the end of its production.

This had a more up-to-date "big engine" look about it, with squat boiler mountings, side-window cab and curved footplate. As an added attraction detachable headlamps could be fitted to brackets to show the correct train headcode—and get quickly lost on the floor! The tender also was redesigned, with raised side sheets in place of the coal rails of the old one.

In 1934 electric versions of the loco were available, complete with the delight of an electric headlamp. The No 1 clockwork model returned after the war as the No 501, though it was little changed from its pre-war counterpart. In 1954 it underwent a colour change into British Railways livery, to emerge as two models, the No 50 in lined black and the No 51 in green.

Meanwhile, those enthusiasts who wanted—and could afford—something larger and more elaborate with a "real" wheel arrangement might go for one of the 4-4-0s produced over a lengthy period by Bassett-Lowke, following the tradition

Above: On a very rural branch line! Childhood memories of Hornby O gauge in the garden. *J Joyce*

of the renowned George the Fifth.

Nowadays it might seem out of place to advertise cigarettes in a boys' paper, especially in the "Magnet", for at Greyfriars smoking was one of the cardinal sins. But in this famous weekly the followers of Billy Bunter and Co could have had their attention caught by a picture of a train speeding along an embankment, beneath which they could have read as follows:

"Free. Splendid Bassett-Lowke scale model express locomotive. Yours for 375 coupons. An ideal gift for every boy".

Introduced in 1927 this gift locomotive was the Duke of York, which had been specially designed and constructed by Bassett-Lowke for Godfrey Phillips Ltd in connection with that company's BDV cigarette coupon gift scheme. Advertised as "entirely Northampton-made throughout", Duke of York No 1927, was a 4-4-0 of lithographed tinplate and of freelance design, though "based on the standard practice of the LMS". It was available in the colours of the Big Four railways.

Bassett-Lowke described it as a replacement for the long-popular George the Fifth, on which it was "a great improvement". Apart from the gift scheme, it could also be "purchased in the ordinary way", its price in 1927 being given as 27s. It had an overall length of 14¾in and a weight of 2lb 9oz.

The Duke's clockwork mechanism was "fitted with the latest pattern governor, reversing motion and brake actuated from rail or cab; also additional 'gadget' to enable the locomotive to be started from the track when our special brake rail is used". It was also made available with an electric mechanism; "our new Junior Permag, an entirely new design

and of simpler construction than the standard Permag motor". This was for operation on 4-6 volts, and incorporated spur gearing, a three-pole armature, and spoon-type collectors. This electric model was advertised in 1928 at 36s.

Duke of York was later metamorphosed into Princess Elizabeth (not to be confused with the LMS Pacific of the same name) with side-window cab and paddlebox splashers. Meanwhile those who required a goods engine for their layout could obtain an 0-6-0 tender loco of similar basic character as well as an 0-6-0 tank for local traffic.

However, this was still the age of Euston-Crewe in 8ft by 6ft, so most enthusiasts naturally wanted a big express engine on their lines. This need was met by the Hornby No 3 locomotive, which certainly did look impressive with its massive boiler and outside cylinders. Further it performed well, its suitably flexible 4-4-2 wheelbase enabling it to rush round those drastic 2ft radius tinplate curves.

The No 3 first appeared as a "foreign" engine in the shape of a French Nord with two domes and a bogie tender. In 1927 it was anglicised with three new versions, each with a famous name; as the advertisement said:

"Each locomotive carries the name of a famous British locomotive on the front wheel guard at each side".

They were respectively LMS Royal Scot, LNER Flying Scotsman, and GWR Caerphilly Castle. These were joined in 1928 by a Southern Lord Nelson. They were available with either clockwork or electric mechanism, and priced originally at 27s 6d and 37s 6d respectively, plus 4s 6d for the tender.

In spite of their different names and colours, the No 3 locos were all in reality basically the same model, though again the GWR one had its brass safety valve casing. Later, too, the Nord, LMS and SR locos were each fitted with smoke deflectors of correct pattern. Though to the expert the No 3 bore little obvious resemblance to any of its full-size namesakes, it had definite appeal, and it must have been produced in substantial quantities to judge by the numbers still to be found.

The No 3 was not reintroduced after the war, when the Hornby range was limited to the smaller models. There was thus scope during the earlier post-war period for a larger O gauge loco, and this became the realm of Prince Charles. The direct descendant of Bassett-Lowke's Duke of York and Princess Elizabeth, Prince Charles came in the British Railways liveries of both blue and green.

"Though," said Bassett-Lowke, "the locomotive is not a British Railways prototype, it incorporates many features based on standard British loco design". It again had a side-window cab, round-topped firebox and paddlebox splashers, while the tender was of the LMS high side pattern.

Prince Charles was constructed of the traditional lithographed tinplate, was 16in long overall and weighed 3lb. It was supplied with either clockwork or electric mechanism, the latter being of the spur-drive type. The price of the clockwork

Above: The popular Hornby No 2 Special
Tank locomotive in Southern Railway livery.
J Joyce

Above right: An early Southern Railway
0-4-4-T from Leeds Model Co.   *J Joyce*

Below: A Hornby 4-4-0 No 1 locomotive in
LMS livery and numbered 2711.
C M Whitehouse

Bottom: The Bassett-Lowke 4-4-0 "Princess
Elizabeth".   *J Joyce*

model at the end of the 1950s was £5, while the ordinary electric three-rail one was priced at £6 2s 6d. Unique among the models we have looked at, the electric model was also made available for two-rail operation, at the higher price of £9 17s 6d.

"Here is an inexpensive loco that will satisfy the most critical", claimed Bassett-Lowke. "It is well built and of sturdy construction throughout. For the beginner to model railways it is particularly recommended, not only on the grounds of economy, but because of its pleasing appearance and reliability".

With the large Hornby locos now clear of the field, and although the Bassett-Lowke 0-6-0 and 0-6-0T were reintroduced, Prince Charles must rank as the culmination of this species of low-priced "big" engine. Indeed its makers specially angled the Prince to the juvenile market, with a tear-jerking page in their catalogue:

"A model railway for Junior. Must I wait for Daddy? A heartfelt plea from one too young for electric or perhaps too boisterous for the miniature sizes. With this set you can say No, Son, this is your model railway".

What Daddy could resist that appeal? The set in question included the clock-work Prince Charles, plus four wagons and an oval of track so that operations could begin right away.

As to the scale of production of their popular 4-4-0s Bassett-Lowke estimated that their output of the Prince Charles totalled 50-60,000, while the earlier Duke of York amounted to 100,000.

A contrast in numbers, though none-the-less classics in their own right, came a series of tank locos produced by the Leeds Model Company. "Model Railway News" described them as "an astonishing range" and they do merit a closer look.

There were locomotives for LMS, LNER and SR, but the surprising thing was that they were not just the same carcass dressed up in different colours. These were different models well representing actual engines of varying wheel arrangements, and it is an interesting exercise to see how standardised parts were employed as far as possible while retaining the essential character of each prototype.

The LMC tanks made their debut in 1935 and several of them returned after the war. There was, for example, an LNER 0-6-2T of class N5 of ex-Great Central origin, the well-known LMS 2-4-2T of Lancashire and Yorkshire parentage, and a typically Southern 0-4-4T of ex-LSWR T1 class, all vener-able engines of considerable character. As LMC described them: "Each model is hand-built of finest tinned iron, with every joint skilfully soldered, is painted and hand-lined as per prototype".

Though still at a reasonable price, these LMC tanks were designed for the more discerning enthusiast. They more nearly bordered on the true category of the scale model than the conventional mass-produced ranges like the Duke or the No 3.

Such then were a few of the varied bread-and-butter lines. Thanks to their original prolific numbers, even today most of them are not too difficult to find, but they are all nevertheless deserving of a place in any collection that aims to represent the typical model railway of yesterday. Their character and appeal can be well summed up by a quotation from one of the advertisements: "Richly finished and capable of any amount of hard work". Surely no model could want a better testimonial.

Below: A Hornby engine shed and 0-4-0T locomotive as they appeared in an early book of trains (1928-29). *K A C Melvin*

True Scale or Popular

The pioneer modeller in OO gauge needed to be a man of dedication and determination. He had to keep a clear head through a maze of scales and gauges, and bring infinite patience to solving problems inherent in a new venture during the years when it was establishing itself. Contemporary comments in "Model Railway News" of the mid 1920s hint at the situation:

"Making OO gauge track is a proposition which has yet to be solved. There are already many brains actively engaged on the problem."

"The demand for a well-made HO gauge electric mechanism, with scale wheels and coupling rods, is still ignored by the trade".

Even the fundamental question of scale and gauge had not been settled; this was a controversy that rumbled on throughout the 1920's and 1930's. There were at least six different possibilities to choose from: ⅝in gauge to 4mm scale; 16.5mm gauge to 3.5mm scale; 16.5mm gauge to 3.75mm scale; 16.5mm gauge to 4mm scale; 18mm gauge to 4mm scale; and 19mm gauge to 4mm scale. Little wonder if the newcomer was confused!

By the late 1920's, HO had generally come to indicate 3.5mm scale, against OO for 4mm scale, and "Model Railway News" was referring to them as "true scale" and "popular" sizes respectively. HO scale, in which the firm of Marshall Stewart set an early lead in the fixing of standards and the supply of equipment, was the initial favourite, but 4mm scale,

Top: A Bing for Bassett-Lowke table-top clockwork train set representing the Midland Railway. The signal box is also visible.
W Metzelaar

Bottom: A table-top electric train set produced by Bing for the European market. The roller type collector shoe and reversing trip lever can be seen, also the Bingwerke trademark on the (clockwork) track. *W Metzelaar*

favoured by Henry Greenly, was to sweep the board by the late 1930's, by which time OO gauge had effectively consolidated its position. The admittedly disproportionate combination of 16.5mm gauge and 4mm scale was widely adopted by the trade; although it might offend the purist, it was held to allow more space for mechanisms and for out-of-scale wheel flanges and treads, as well as clearance for outside cylinders and rods on sharp curves.

Though this compromise helped to answer some of the questions raised by the tiny scales, new techniques and methods were still called for. In the wider view, OO encouraged the creation of the complete picture; the small scale enabled the modeller to visualise a railway in its full scenic setting. In detail, the small size made the human hand even more unwieldy, thus stimulating the search for full remote control. Automatic couplings, for example, appeared early on OO; A R Walkley was using them in 1925, while in 1931 Allan Lake Rice published details of an automatic coupling that the present-day modeller will recognise as bearing a remarkable resemblance to today's Peco type.

Motive power also had to respond to miniaturisation, and it took time before the standard permanent magnet mechanism evolved to give the complete remote control demanded in OO. Probably the heritage of the larger gauges may be discerned in the experiments with clockwork and steam power in OO, though in both cases the tiny size was the limiting factor. A few enthusiasts proved that OO steam locos could be built, and it seems that for a time a live steam coal-fired Pacific was actually marketed!

Clockwork was a more practical proposition. Its use was stimulated by the existence of the Bing Table Railway locomotives, which at the cost of a few shillings provided a serviceable mechanism. This found its way into numerous conversions, from 0-4-0 shunters to Pacifics. A limitation was that it was non-reversible, a fact which tended to inhibit railwaylike working, even with turntables installed at strategic locations.

For electric operation, the normal supply was 6 volts from battery or accumulator. Again, in earlier years the Bing electric mechanism was much resorted to; this was reversible by a lever, and further impetus to its employment was given in 1928 when Bonds introduced a permanent magnet which could be fitted to replace the original field winding.

A new mechanism introduced by Bonds in 1930 symbolised the perfection sought by the enthusiast only a few years earlier (and incidentally it forms an interesting comparison with the mechanisms of today). Here is how Bonds described it:

"An entirely new type of permanent magnet has been specially made of 35% cobalt steel and fits between the frames, while the ½in diameter armature works in a tunnel machined in the magnet itself, and so dispensing with the inefficient pole pieces. A worm drive fitted on the armature shaft drives the middle pair of wheels, which are cast brass and spoked. The brushes are of the round gauze type and spring loaded".

The price of a six-coupled mechanism of this type, with 23mm wheels, was 42s 6d, while the four-coupled version was 37s 6d.

Bodywork still left scope for originality, and among one modelmaker's ingredients for a loco were brass tube for the

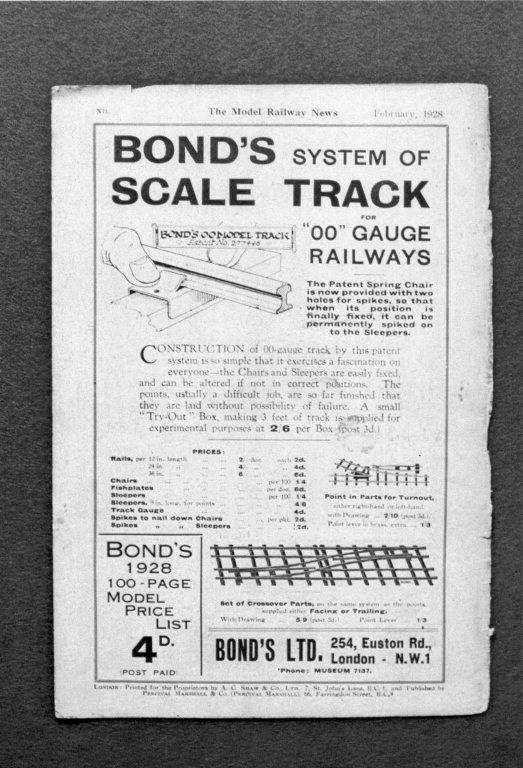

boiler, a 3d piece (a small silver coin in those days) for the boiler end, and a .22 cartridge case for the chimney.

Those who wanted to buy a ready-to-run OO electric loco more true to scale than the "Bavarian toy" (as the Bing range was commonly referred to by the precise modeller) might be interested in the model put on the market in 1927 by Holtzapffel. They claimed it as "the first real attempt to place before the public an attractive model at a reasonable price". It was an 0-6-0 tank, finished in black and operating on 4-6 volts, and it was priced at £3.

This little model was notable in having not only coupled wheels, but spoked wheels. This was worthy of special mention at this period, since many OO locos had to be content with solid disc driving wheels, though the patient modeller could of course use O gauge wagon wheels, filed down in thickness and fitted with extra spokes. As late as 1930, Holtzapffel when advertising a new range of OO spoked loco wheels, illustrated a model loco fitted with them "to show the realistic effect of these wheels over the solid type previously fitted".

Other OO locos available around this time included an 0-6-2 tank by Bonds, "a real model at a popular price" (it was 50s post paid), and an 0-6-0 tender goods loco by Walkers and Holtzapffel (the two names came together in 1931) at £6 6s. For passenger traffic, the Hampstead Model Company offered a 4-4-0 tender loco at £3 5s, while Bonds had a "freelance main line express locomotive", again a 4-4-0, with "many refinements", at £4 17s 6d.

This is Bonds' specification of their new model in 1929:

"Of the standard 0-6-2 goods tank locomotive, or with extended smokebox similar to the Lancashire and Yorkshire locomotives, painted black and numbered, length 5⅝in, height 2in, width 1⅜in, the mechanism is specially made for this model and is fitted with our well-known Permanent Magnet and very low gearing, which increases its hauling power and also gives a more realistic running speed. Twin outside collectors are fitted as standard. The driving and bogie wheels are of CAST BRASS and SPOKED, the Drivers having balance weights cast in. The brass buffers and boiler mountings, which include handrails, are all in keeping with the prototype, and draw hooks are fitted at the front and rear."

For the more affluent, Stewart-Reidpath (which came into existence taking over Marshall Stewart in 1931) could supply a detailed scale GWR 0-6-2 tank at £6 6s, or an SR U1 Class Mogul at £13. The choice of models available by the early thirties was surprisingly wide, even if the prices were correspondingly high; it was possible to obtain a Sentinel shunter or a Southern Electric, a GER Decapod or a Beyer-Garrett articulated.

As a comparison of prices with larger scales, it may be noted that at this time Bassett-Lowke's Royal Scot locomotive in O gauge was priced at £3 15s though admittedly this was basically a mass-produced tinplate model for a larger market than could be expected in OO.

A popular and inexpensive innovation for the OO loco builder of the later 1930's was the Stewart-Reidpath cast body 0-6-0 tank. A heavy metal casting, the body came in two versions, one having a Belpaire firebox and taper boiler in GWR style, and the enthusiast could add appropriate boiler mountings to taste. With a little ingenuity the body could be adapted to various other forms; Edward Beal demonstrated that it could be transformed into almost anything from an 0-4-0 shunter to an 0-8-4 tank!

For rolling stock needs, the Bing items again often formed the basis of conversions. The ordinary four-wheel coaches could be repainted, or mounted in pairs on a new underframe to make bogie coaches, while the goods wagons could also be altered to cattle vans or brake vans.

One of the improvements for the scale modeller using made-up track was the replacement of the ordinary tinplate wheels by new wheels. In 1925 Bonds advertised this innovation with no little enthusiasm:

"Important introduction to owners of Gauge OO Railways. Perfectly-turned Brass Wheels on fine, smooth Steel Axles, 4d pair; 3s 9d dozen. Replace the Pressed Wheels with these, and your Locomotive will pull twice the Load, run 25% longer, and derailments will not occur."

For coaches ready to roll, take a look at what was on the market in 1930.

Bonds were advertising a new range of rolling stock, including 4mm scale coaches. These were fitted with metal roofs, sides and ends, had cut out windows, and were hand painted. The bogies were all brass, and were fitted with large round brass buffers and automatic couplings. The finished vehicles had a length of 9¼in, and the price was 12s 6d.

Something more elaborate was offered by Holtzapffel:

"These coaches are a wonderful

Top Left: LNER tank locomotive body by Bond's; provide your own mechanism with the wheel arrangement you want! *J Joyce*

Far Left: Advertisement for Bond's new "OO" scale track of 1928. *J Joyce*

Left: Advertisement for Bond's new 0-6-2 tank loco of 1929. *J Joyce*

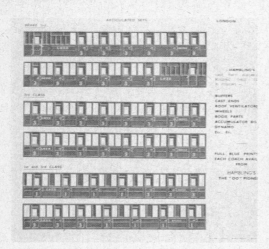

production at the price, glazed windows, weatherboards on roof, and the underframe includes step, tie rods and accumulator boxes, brass buffers and automatic couplings; lining faithfully reproduced in practically any group colouring. Length about 8¼in."

Non-corridor coaches were priced at 25s, corridor coaches and dining cars at 28s, while a Pullman car (9in long) was 40s. The *pièce de résistance* of the range was the Pullman car with interior fittings, which sold at 55s.

Both firms also produced corresponding goods rolling stock. The Bonds wagons, for example, had all-brass chassis, brass wheels and buffers, and automatic couplings. The bodies were of wood, hand painted. Open wagons cost 5s 9d, vans and a tank wagon 7s 6d. The Holtzapffel range included bogie vans such as an LMS milk and a GWR Siphon at 14s 6d.

A useful aid to the rolling stock builder during the 1930s was the "Merco" series of lithographed papers for coach and wagon sides by Miniature Exhibition Railways of Dundee. These were designed by a group of modellers including Edward Beal and Sir Eric Hutchison, and are still familiar to the present day.

Permanent way in OO gauge was generally soldered together from metal components, since for most enthusiasts there was no worry about insulated track for two-rail working. In 1925, Marshall Stewart were advertising made-up track, of all brass construction, straight or curved, in 9in lengths with 23 sleepers, at 10½d per length, while points were priced from 7s 6d.

Something novel in trackmaking was introduced by Bonds in 1926. The rail was of brass and of bull-head section, while the chairs were pressed out of spring steel and had wings to clip over the sides of the sleepers, which were made of wood. A different type of track was introduced in 1927 by Marshall Stewart; this again had brass rail, but the chair clips formed part of the sleepers, which were pressed from spring steel.

A somewhat similar type of track was also available from Holtzapffel, who also supplied parts for the home builder at the following prices: rail in 9in lengths was 3d a yard, sleepers with chairs were 3s 6d for 100, fishplates were 3d a dozen, and pins 3d a packet. Brass strip suitable for the conductor rail was 1½d a yard.

Three-rail operation, with the third rail either outside or between the running rails, was the accepted method of electrification, but the more venturesome were already experimenting in the 1920s with two rail—or the "insulated wheels and rails system", as it was then known.

One of these pioneers was A R Walkley, whose 3.5mm scale models were

well-known at exhibitions in the mid-1920s. His experimental two-rail track was composed of rails and sleepers of brass strip soldered together; then the sleepers were cut along the centre line, the separate parts being pinned or screwed to gauge on battens. Plastic wood or similar material was used to fill in the cracks in the centre of the sleepers. In a working layout, he used a different method; the rails were still brass strip, but the sleepers were of cardboard, the rails being soldered to brass pins in the baseboard, while roofing felt gave the effect of ballast.

This was the type of track Walkley employed in his celebrated "railway in a suitcase" of 1925. This was a remarkable little layout, which apart from the use of two-rail operation, incorporated many features which are regarded as "modern" today. It was a portable layout mounted in a box measuring 6ft by 11in when open, and hinged at the middle so that it could be folded and closed.

The actual track represented a single line emerging from a tunnel and opening out into a three-road goods yard, with another line leading to a small loco shed. Each of the turnouts controlled the current supply to the line for which it was set. Full scenic effects were provided, including a cottage with a wireless aerial, and the whole was given a "weathered" appearance — another "modern" touch.

An SR 0-4-4 tank represented the motive power on the layout. Its driving wheels were insulated by means of a bush between the wheel and the axle, while the bogie wheels had split axles fitted into an ebonite rod. Automatic couplings consisted of a hook and loop, and there was a track ramp for uncoupling.

But not all OO gauge layouts were small. Walkley himself, though an exponent of the tiny (he was also working in 2mm scale in the 1920's), recognised the potentiality of OO from the space point of view. He wrote in 1925: "The construction of a model line through an actual section of 'country' is rendered possible by the area advantage of OO gauge". Perhaps for the first time it was practicable for the modeller with limited space to attempt to reproduce a comprehensive system.

As early as 1923 Ernest F Carter records that he constructed a OO gauge scale model layout representing Slough, GWR, with all trackwork and sidings, while the work of Edward Beal achieved justifiable fame. The typical Beal layout owed little to the "table railway" concept!

Less well remembered is the layout of the Rev H A Turner. This was originally built as a sideshow at a bazaar in 1925, but was later re-erected in an attic some 20ft by 11ft. It deserves to be classed as one of the earliest OO layouts to take advantage of the small scale to construct an extensive railway; moreover, it was a non-continuous layout with the feature of full correct signalling, which not all present-day layouts can boast!

There was a total of 39 signals and 41

points, including a scissors crossover and catch points interlocked with signals. The end to end run was some 70ft, and the five stations rejoiced in the names of High Poggleton, Dwiggle Junction, Swoshby, Little Biffham and Tillywhympleton! Motive power was originally clockwork, but the line was later electrified and christened the "South Midland Railway".

The work of such enthusiasts illustrates their interest in the complete picture; their field of view extended beyond the tracks to the full scenic setting that could now be visualised with OO gauge.

Scenery itself was another do-it-yourself challenge. There was ample scope for such simple commodities as crumpled and stained newspapers for basic contours, and dyed sawdust for grass. Some of the finer details called for more delicate work. One enthusiast used gramophone needles for fence posts; another used matchsticks, which also served for signal posts. Another patient modeller made his telegraph poles from basket withies, fitted with cross bars of galvanised wire and insulators of minute brass beads—even he had to admit it was a "tiresome job"!

In 1938 "Model Railway Constructor" published an article under the title "O or OO?" to help the beginner to the hobby to decide which scale to adopt. It concluded:

"As regards actual cost, there is not much difference between O and OO, nor is there nowadays a greater selection of raw materials, parts, or finished models. So the problem is hardly a financial one, but one dependent entirely upon the space at one's disposal."

Though OO was still not a "cheap option", the advantages it offered to the space-starved modeller were making it increasingly popular, while the range of equipment available showed that it was past the pioneering stage.

Perhaps one of its less obvious advantages was foreseen as far back as 1925 by A Stewart-Reidpath. Because of its small size and portability, he believed, "it should be the means of making the model railway hobbyist a much more sociable person. Imagine one's fellow model railwayac arriving one evening for an hour or two's timetable running with a miniature Feltham yard in an attache case. One could become a veritable perambulating Swindon with a small Gladstone bag or a suit case."

Top Left: Merco lithographed coach sides. *J Joyce*

Top Right: The "Reidmere" cast-body 0-6-0 tank locomotive in its Great Western version. *J Joyce*

Bottom: Examples of private owner's wagons using Merco lithographed paper sides and cast underframe parts. *J Joyce*

'A RAILWAY ON YOUR DINING TABLE!'

The early years of proprietary OO gauge

"Which of us has not yearned to be an engine driver?" exclaims the Bing catalogue. "But there is a first-class substitute for driving an engine, and one which needs no lifetime of preparation and training. And that is to run your own railway. 'How can that be done?' you ask. 'Our garden isn't big enough. And where's the money coming from?' That is where we come to your aid. We have produced the clever Table Railway. The best thing about this railway is that you can begin to own your own railway system, complete with engine, coaches and track, by spending no more than a few shillings."

Here in a few words were the attractions of the minimum-size model railway. Nowadays, of course, OO gauge looks enormous compared with N or Z, but in the days when gauge 1 was still popular and O was considered the smallest worth noticing, OO gauge was almost untried and insignificant. But the pressure was on to make model railways smaller and yet smaller, and the result was such famous names as the Bing Table Railway, Trix Twin and Hornby Dublo.

W J Bassett-Lowke recognised the changing situation as he recalled the

Top: Bing table-top railway showing tender locomotive with passenger stock.
B Monaghan

introduction of commercial OO gauge into Britain:
"When builders were steadily putting up more compact houses, with smaller rooms, I visualised the demand for a still

narrower gauge than O, and I brought over from Germany the first model railway outfit of just half that size, on a gauge of 5/8 inch. It was a crude affair made of tin, but this introduction to Great Britain of gauge OO marked an important milestone in model railway history".

Though the Table Railway had been conceived as early as 1914, it was not until 1921 that conditions made it possible to bring it to reality. Designs were prepared by Henry Greenly, and the models were manufactured at the famous Bing Works in Nuremberg, the first "Bing Miniature Table Railway" sets being advertised on the British market late in 1922. Construction was basically of lithographed tinplate, and the sets were packed in boxes with the most delightful labels—a perfect period piece of paterfamilias and children around a literal "table railway".

The trains were just in time to appear in genuine pregrouping liveries; as the catalogue tells us, "engines may be bought painted in the black colours of the London and North Western Railway, or in 'Midland Red'." The locomotive itself was a 2-4-0 tank—or perhaps more

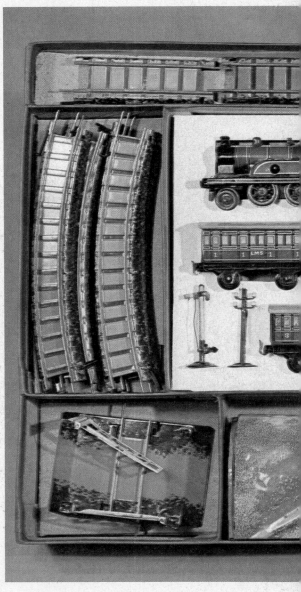

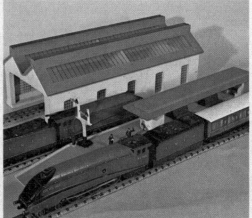

Top right: Bing table-top train set.
B Monaghan

Top left: Early Trix-Twin 0-4-0 tank in LMS
black. *B Monaghan*

Right: Bing table-top engines in various
liveries. *B Monaghan*

Above: Hornby Dublo system: early models
of the A4 Pacific "Sir Nigel Gresley" made in
clockwork and electric. (Courtesy Caroline &
Andrew Collection) *B Monaghan*

correctly speaking it should be 2-2-2-0 since the driving wheels were not coupled. Like so many contemporary railway models, it bore a decided LNWR character, with a marked resemblance to the little "Chopper" tanks of that company, except that the boiler was necessarily pitched higher to allow room for the clockwork mechanism. The black loco was lettered "L & N W R", while the red one sported the MR crest on the tank side. Appropriate four-wheel coaches were also supplied in both companies' colours.

Later trains were available in the liveries of the LMS and LNER, as well as the GWR, and here may be found variations in lettering and numbering to gladden the heart of the avid collector. There were also differences in mechanisms; early models had the brake lever protruding from the cab door, while later ones had the brake lever sticking up through the top of the bunker with a trip by which the loco could be braked from the track.

Rolling stock was also diversified by the addition of goods vehicles. At first these comprised only open wagons and vans, but later they included a fish van and a Shell tank wagon.

By 1925 electric operation was possible. The electric version of the locomotive incorporated a nicely-made mechanism with a wound field (apparently a permanent magnet motor was experimented with but not found satisfactory). It had the important advantage over its clockwork counterpart in that it was reversible, with a drum-type reversing switch at the rear, operated by a lever which could also be actuated from the lineside by a special trip attached to the track. Pick

up from the third rail was by two sprung roller collectors. The motor worked on 4-6 volts from a battery via a control rail, while later a "reducer" and a transformer were introduced for operation from the mains supply.

Another welcome innovation was a tender locomotive. This showed some family likeness to the tank version, with the same wheel arrangement and the same type of clockwork mechanism, but it had a lengthy side-window cab and large "paddle box" splashers over the driving wheels.

To make up a complete railway, there was a good choice of track and accessories. These included points and crossings, buffer stops, a station and halt platform, signal box, engine shed, turntable, level crossing and tunnel, as well as signals and telegraph poles. A sensible feature of many of the accessories was that they were fitted with lugs which could be inserted into slots in the track to prevent them being knocked over.

Perhaps the most attractive accessory was the station, and the more nostalgic enthusiast can spend happy moments studying its tiny advertisement posters; some names are familiar (for example, Bovril and Lux) but how many people remember Pinks Jams or Pat A Cake Biscuits? Further, not all models had the same advertisements or the same arrangements of posters, while to add to the permutations there were differences in the colours of the "brickwork" and the platforms.

A few prices will give an idea of the economics of Table Railway construction in those days. The clockwork tank loco was priced at 4s, the electric loco at 14s. Coaches and wagons were 8d each. Sections of clockwork track cost 4d each, while a station was 1s 4d and a signal box 8d.

When Bing ceased production after 1933, the Table Railway was continued for a time in similar form by Karl Büb, and items were advertised at least until 1938.

Meanwhile, in 1935 Bassett-Lowke was instrumental in introducing into Britain another OO gauge model railway system, which again originated in Germany and which employed a unique feature. It was advertised as "The Bassett-Lowke Twin Train Table Railway" (shades of Bing!), but was afterwards to become well known as the "Trix Twin Railway" or simply TTR. It was described as "Something entirely new and far ahead of anything of the kind ever attempted before". "Two electric trains running on the same line at different speeds, in the same or opposite directions, forwards or backwards, fast or slow! These are some of the outstanding features of the Bassett-Lowke Twin Table Electric Railway which has astonished the experts and sent thousands of boys wild with delight".

Initially the system comprised models brought over from the German "Trix Express" range, but such was the reception given to the "Twins" that Bassett-Lowke soon made arrangements for the manufacture in this country of British-style trains, and these were announced in 1936:
"Meet the new 'Twins'. British made this year! Better than ever come the new sets, finished in either LMS or LNER colours, true to English standard types and made in Northampton!"

The passenger train set was priced at 45s, the goods train set at 42s, and the suburban set at 35s. Models in Southern Railway colours were soon added. Motive

power comprised perky little 0-4-0s in both tender and tank versions, with cast metal bodies, and of freelance design although carrying such illustrious numbers as 4472 and 6200.

"Twin" was the key to the unique feature of the railway: two trains could be operated on the same track under completely separate control. There were two controllers, one for each loco, and the apparent miracle was accomplished by means of a three-rail system that was in effect a double two-rail system. All wheels and rails were insulated; one loco was arranged to pick up current from one running rail, and the other loco from the other running rail, while the centre rail was used for the common return. So with two locos in service there was no need for any sectionalising of the track, and all kinds of intricate manoeuvres were possible—even if the more youthful enthusiast could not resist the temptation of spectacular head-on collisions!

The locomotive mechanism incorporated a wound field motor, with a sequence reverser, and it operated on either 14 volts ac or 12 volts dc, the standard Trix transformer supplying 14 volts. Pick up on both running rail and centre rail was by collector shoes; the running rail collectors could be changed round to pick up on either side as required for the appropriate "twin" running.

A distinctive piece of equipment was the controller, which had a red push button to activate the loco reverser (and also reset the overload cutout when it popped up). This button was in the middle of a speed control dial that suggested the tuning knob of a contemporary wireless receiver. Track was of a similarly novel design. The actual rails were of tinplate, but since they had to be insulated for "twin" needs, they were mounted on a black bakelite base. Sections of track were joined by unusual snap fastenings.

"Twin" working, together with the complete remote control of the locomotives, brought operating possibilities hitherto unattained in ordinary commercial OO gauge. The picture was completed by the addition of remotely controlled points and signals, as well as by automatic couplings consisting of a cast metal hook and wire link. The later addition of a stirrup to the coupling and a ramp to the track gave the extra thrill of remote control uncoupling.

Other attractions of the Twins included coaches with windows cut out and glazed with "celastoid"; there were both bogie coaches and four wheelers. Among goods rolling stock, particularly attractive were the tank wagons and the private owner wagons, the latter including models lettered respectively TRIX and BASSETT-LOWKE. Among the modernistic lineside accessories, the "Many-ways" station sets were outstanding; they comprised prefabricated units of wood and metal enabling almost any type or size of station to be assembled.

Motive power possibilities were enhanced by a London Transport electric locomotive, while in 1937 a better known electric-outline model made its debut. This was a representation of the Southern Railway's new multiple-unit trains for the Portsmouth main line electric services inaugurated in that year—indeed, the model seems to have been on sale even before the real trains were in full service!

The miniature Southern Electric was the first Trix Twin train to be based on an actual prototype, and it was also the first "scale model" to be specially designed for the new system by Bassett-

Lowke. It included a motor coach, necessarily foreshortened to enable it to negotiate the standard Trix 13½-inch radius curves, plus two ordinary coaches, the whole set being offered in a box decorated with a special label designed by the Southern Railway.

The Trix Southern Electric was the centre of displays arranged by the SR to publicise the new electric train services, an instance of the good publicity the Twins enjoyed. Twin trains were also an attraction at the British Industries Fair, while on a more modest scale displays at Toy Fairs in department stores fascinated a younger generation of potential owners! Another instrument of TTR publicity was the "TTR Gazette", introduced in 1937 and sent free to registered owners of Twin trains.

In 1938 came an important step forward with the introduction of models that proved that commercial OO gauge could appeal to the scale enthusiast. A German-style Pacific had been made available on the British market in the previous year, but now came two Pacifics based on British prototypes, the LNER 4472 "Scotsman" and the LMS 6201 "Princess", again both being scale models designed by Bassett-Lowke. The six-coupled mechanism was complete with valve gear, while a remote control uncoupling device in the tender enabled the loco to be uncoupled from its train anywhere on the track simply by pressing the button on the controller. A new range of scale-length coaches went with the Pacifics, while the whole train was packed in a special presentation case.

More motive power appeared in 1939, with the start of a series of 4-4-0s, including an LMS Compound. But perhaps the apotheosis of the entire Trix range was the new model of the LMS streamlined "Coronation Scot", one of the high-speed trains popular at this time. The loco represented 6220 "Coronation" in its distinctive livery and complete with nameplate and crown, as well as the headlamp and bell which it had acquired for an American visit, while its coaches were in matching style.

By this time, though, Trix had a strong British rival. Hornby, a name long familiar in O gauge, entered the field of OO in 1938 with the introduction of Hornby-Dublo. Once again the domesticity of this small scale was made a selling point:

"The Perfect Gauge OO Table Railway arrives! The introduction of the Hornby-Dublo system marks a notable advance towards the ideal home railway. It is the ideal system for the development of a miniature railway where space is limited."

Hornby-Dublo was almost as different from Trix as it could have been; the two systems were quite incompatible. Even the gauge and scale were different! While Trix advertised itself as 16mm gauge to a scale of 3.5 mm to the foot, Dublo was described as 16.5mm gauge to a scale of 4 mm to the foot. Moreover, there were vital differences in the mechanism, the electrics, and the wheel profiles, while perhaps most striking of all, in view of the "toy" nature of much of Hornby's O gauge, was the "scale" character of the Dublo trains.

The passenger train included a replica of the LNER streamlined Pacific No 4498 *Sir Nigel Gresley,* complete with eight-wheel tender and a two-coach articulated unit. The goods train comprised an 0-6-2 tank, hauling an open wagon, a van and a brake van, in the liveries of the LMS, LNER, GWR and SR. The tank

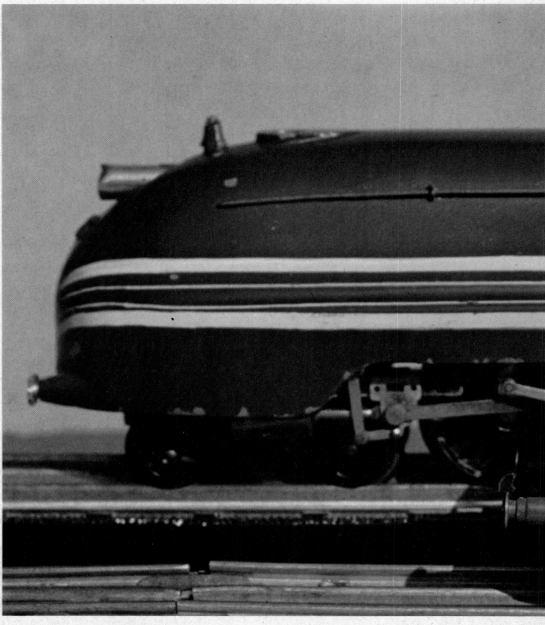

Above: Table-top streamliners: Trix "Coronation" Pacific alongside Hornby "Sir Nigel Gresley". *J Joyce*

Right: Early Trix-Twin "Flying Scotsman". *J Joyce*

Overleaf: A Hornby No 1 LMS clockwork tank locomotive with No 2 suburban coach. (Courtesy Caroline and Andrew Collection). *Brian Monaghan*

loco was based on the LNER N2 class, but it looked happy enough in the other companies' styles, the Great Western version being the odd one out in having a domeless boiler with the characteristic "brass" safety valve casing.

The locomotives had cast metal bodies, while the rolling stock had tinplate bodies on cast underframes or bogies. Automatic couplings were fitted, these being of the simplest design, merely a one-piece spring strip with loop and notches stamped out.

Locomotives were available with either electric or clockwork mechanisms, the latter notably having reversing gear. The electric mechanism, in contrast to Trix, was of the permanent magnet type, working at 12 volts and on normal three-rail. Operation from the mains was via a transformer and a controller with a rectifier incorporated to supply the necessary dc. The positive direction control possible with the permanent magnet motor was made another selling point: "The remote control of the Hornby-Dublo Electric Locomotives is the most perfect ever devised. Starting, stopping, reversing, and regulation of speed are all carried out by the movement of one lever. The control is positive. Move the lever to 'Forward' and the train goes forward; move it to 'Backward' and the train goes backward—every time! There is never the slightest hesitation!"

The general simplicity of this type of mechanism, in contrast to the complexity of the Trix counterpart, was doubtless a significant factor in the lower price of the Hornby locomotives; the Dublo "Gresley", for example, was only £1 9s 6d against £4 7s 6d for the rival Trix Pacific. Moreover, the Dublo models were sufficiently "fine" to satisfy even the scale enthusiast. Not only were the locos good representations of particular real life engines, but the wheel profiles were much finer; they are of a standard still acceptable today. The Dublo track, too, although on a tinplate base, employed solid-drawn brass rails of correct section.

During its first year or so the Dublo range extended quite rapidly, with additions announced almost monthly in "Meccano Magazine". These items included more goods rolling stock of such varieties as tank wagons and a bogie brick wagon, and accessories such as remote control points and signals and an impressive "City Station".

Sadly, wartime conditions were soon to bring disruption to model railways as to other peaceful occupations. Although for a time it was "business as usual", new projects not already well advanced had to be deferred, while some planned innovations did not see the light of day. Trix, for example, proposed to introduce a 2-4-2 tank locomotive, in LMS, LNER and SR colours and with remote control uncoupling at both ends; during the war they advertised this as "the double ender loco we didn't make" (they were never to make it). Better known was the Dublo "Duchess of Atholl" LMS train set, which got as far as being included in the late 1939 catalogues but which did not reach the production stage (in this case, it did appear after the war).

Nevertheless, during these interwar years proprietary OO gauge had established itself as a contender for popularity with the larger sizes, especially for those enthusiasts with limited space. It had developed from a parlour toy to a respectable model railway system—even if it still retained something of the "dining table" image!

Overleaf: Great Western in miniature. A 4mm scale 0-6-0 pannier tank takes a freight train into the sidings on Mr Ken Ball's layout in Macclesfield. *Brian Monaghan*

Porters and Passengers

An amusing novelty in the old Karl Büb range was the "Whatsamatter-train", in which the driver kept popping his head up through the cab roof to see what was going on. This was one of the rare exceptions to the rule that the small scale people on a model railway were not imbued with movement. Yet even though these figures necessarily remained static, they were essential to the illusion of reality that the modeller attempted to create. Hence it is worth glancing at a few of the vintage figures that graced the model railway platforms of the past and are now sought after by collectors.

Model railway figures appear to date from at least the earliest days of the mass-produced ranges; certainly Märklin had people on their stations in the 1890s. In Britain the provision of suitable railway figures owed much to the makers of model soldiers.

With the growth of model railways, the established toy soldier makers naturally diversified into this expanding market. The best known manufacturers of model soldiers were William Britain and Sons, who had been producing these toys since 1893. Turning their attention to civilian subjects, they introduced in 1908 a range of railway miniatures, including staff, passengers, luggage and barrows.

Britains' figures continued in production for many years to enliven the stations of successive generations of railway modellers. They were of the same size as the standard lead soldiers; this meant they were just right for railways in 1 gauge, which at the time of their introduction was one of the most popular scales. To today's eyes these Britains' people have a period charm which makes

them particularly attractive to the collector of vintage models.

The items were available individually as well as in sets. Here is how sets were being advertised during the mid-1920s:

"Railway Station Staff for Model Railway Stations. This set of figures is made throughout in white metal and consists of:

No 1—Small Set consisting of 1 Station Master, 1 Ticket Collector, 4 Porters, 4 pieces of luggage, 2 Porter's barrows. Price 1s 9d.

No 2—Large Set consisting of 1 Station Master, 1 Ticket Collector, 1 Day Guard, 1 Night Guard, 1 Policeman, 2 Passengers, 2 Platelayers, 4 Porters, 10 pieces of luggage, 2 Porter's barrows. Price 4s."

At the undisputed peak of this hierarchy of staff stood the Station Master, a personage redolent of the military traditions of his makers. A tall top-coated bearded dignitary, he had the mien of a general and the air of a talisman strong enough to ward off all the evils that could befall a model railway.

His minions were no less characters in their own right. Surely the Ticket Collector could never miss a snip of one ticket? And the Porters, though their caps were set at a surprisingly saucy angle, must have been equally dutiful men; one was bent forward in the act of pushing his barrow, while the other was literally open-handed to grasp the separate items of luggage with which he could be burdened. The Guards too were ever vigilant, whether armed with flag or lamp, while in the background stood the Policeman, though one could not imagine that his services were much needed in this well ordered community.

As to the Passengers, there could be no doubt that they were first-class travellers; but then of course at this time all model trains were first class, if not Pullman. The gentleman in the bowler hat carried a coat on one arm. His other arm was of the movable type favoured for model soldiers; not only could a different appendage make a different model, it could also allow for "movement". Thus, one specimen had an arm with a paper or book in his hand, another a pipe which could be raised to his mouth. Both versions of this gentleman were equally stately; surely he must be an Army officer in mufti?

And his lady? Here there was scope for more variation over the years as fashions changed from the Edwardian ground-sweeping skirts to the later calf-length styles. She was a tall, angular, haughty looking woman; yes, definitely the Colonel's lady!

Even the catalogue listing of the individual items had its own period atmosphere. For example, one found not just men and women but "Lady Passengers" and "Gentlemen Passengers", while a further note of distinction was given by the appearance of the "Yachtsmen". Their appurtenances also had an old-world touch; there were Trunks, Dress Baskets, Portmanteaux, Golf Sticks, Rugs and Sticks, hints of all the paraphernalia required in the days when no one would dream of travelling light.

Model railway figures were also produced by one of Britains' major rivals, John Hill and Co. Under the name

Above: A Hornby station with an array of Dinky Toy figures and Hornby station accessories. *J Joyce*

Johillco, they were probably the largest producers of toy soldiers after Britains, and their range of model railway staff, passengers and station items was just as distinctive.

Though, like his Britains contemporary, Hill's Station Master wore a cap and a long coat with shiny buttons, one felt that his personality was quite different. He was rather a rotund figure, with a round face and with a sheaf of papers (or perhaps the rule book?) in his hand. Whereas Britains' Station Master would have fitted perfectly into a miniature Paddington or Euston, the Hill counterpart looked the ideal dignitary for the country junction.

His porter also seemed to have sprung from the bucolic life; he was a jovial looking character, in blue uniform and carrying an outsize suitcase. The guard, with his green flag and whistle at the ready, seemed just right for the all-stations local train. The passengers included ladies in 1920s dress, such as a woman in blue and another in a white coat and long blue skirt, both of them topped by a cloche hat.

Again the Hill figures were to the same scale as Britains, but with the growing popularity of O gauge there was a demand for smaller individuals who would not tower above the trains. Britains therefore introduced a series for O gauge; these were generally similar in character to those of the larger size, though one could not help feeling that they looked less upper-class and rather more democratic—clearly the social structure was changing!

The Britains O gauge range included ticket collector and porter, the latter being a diminished edition of his 1 gauge brother, engaged in the energetic pushing of his barrow loaded with right-size luggage. There was also a guard with his flag. The passengers included a woman in a natty two-piece, and a golfer with movable arm, dressed smartly in grey plus-fours and a yellow waistcoat.

A further range suitable for O gauge was introduced by Hornby, starting in 1931 with a set of railway staff. Designated "Modelled Miniatures No. 1" they were later to become members of the famous series of Dinky Toys. This first set included station master, ticket collector, guard, driver and two porters.

Tommy Dodd's description of these functionaries in "Meccano Magazine" can hardly be bettered. The station master had "the dignity that is peculiar to his rank. He is an imposing personage in a long coat, and his gilt buttons and

gold braided cap are visible signs of authority. Surveying the scene with calmness, he is an impressive figure".

The ticket collector had "a business-like appearance", while the guard had his whistle to his mouth and was about to wave his flag. The two porters were "energetic looking men", one of them carrying a suit case and a hat box.

These lively officials were soon augmented by three further sets, respectively Engineering Staff, Train and Hotel Staff, and Passengers. Some members of the staff possessed a remarkable versatility in that they consisted of the same basic figure adorned in different colours; the porter, for example, doubled as a fitter and as a Pullman car waiter.

The Engineering Staff consisted of six utilitarian figures, representing such esoteric occupations as fitter, greaser, electrician, store keeper and engine room attendant. The five members of the Train and Hotel Staff, by contrast, were more glamorous personages; they comprised Pullman car conductor and waiters, and hotel porters. The chief car attendant, dressed in white coat and blue trousers, "is a responsible official and has quite an important appearance", wrote Tommy Dodd. "His subordinates are similarly dressed, but they have shorter coats and

different caps, showing their inferior rank".

But no doubt the passengers were the most colourful set, and again one cannot do better than quote Tommy Dodd. There was a woman and child together on one casting; the child "is possibly a future railway enthusiast, although at the moment a teddy bear is tightly clutched under one arm. The lady is smartly dressed in a green coat with fur collar and has a green hat". A separate woman passenger carried a mackintosh over her left arm and a small case in her right hand.

Above: Dinky Toy figures, including mother and child, hiker, newsboy and porter.
D Salisbury

Above right: A station scene: The bearded stationmaster is by Britains, the porter and lady passenger by Hill; the two seated figures and the barrow are also probably by Hill. The station is 1930s vintage tinplate of unknown make. *J Joyce*

Centre right: Definitely "First Class"! Britain's passengers board their train, with stationmaster and porter in attendance. The coach is by Bowman, the station Hornby and the chocolate machine by Hill. *J Joyce*

Bottom right: On the famous Windsor station, a Dinky Toy man contemplates a heavy Hornby trunk. Hornby posters are on the fence. *J Joyce*

The hikers, a man and a woman, were "typical representations in miniature of the modern open air enthusiasts. Both are dressed in regular hiking kit. They have stout sticks, and their rucksacks are carried on their backs in the orthodox manner". The newsboy was wearing "a brown suit and a very rakish-looking cap. His haste is well shown by his attitude".

Most imposing of all was the gentleman. "He wears a blue suit of the latest cut and the usual bowler hat, and has the appearance of being a successful man of business. With his cane, spats and gloves, he looks decidedly smart, and is obviously a first-class passenger". First-class he certainly was, but it is not too fanciful to imagine that he and his fellow-travellers were much more middle-class than their Edwardian forebears.

Anyway, the democratising process seemed to have been carried a stage further by 1938 when these Dinky Toy people had been replaced by smaller and slightly different figures. The woman, for example, looked to have been on a slimming course and now wore a dark green coat while her child was now standing on her other side. At the same time, the business man sported a full length coat, and the newsboy had become a more dignified figure with a tray of periodicals.

For the rising OO gauge came a range of even smaller figures during the late 1930s. The Trix Twin Railway included scale-size passengers, personnel, platform equipment and merchandise. These were made for TTR by Britains, and were "of exact dimensions and finished in good taste". The passengers included a woman and child, a standing woman, a man reading a newspaper, and a golfer (funny how many golfers there must have been on the trains in those days), while the staff included porters struggling under bags or pushing barrows.

Hornby also produced a range of scale figures to go with their new OO gauge Dublo railways in 1938. Again there was a golfer, as well as a man reading a newspaper, and three women. The railway staff included a driver, a porter, a ticket collector, station master, guard, and an unusual figure of a shunter complete with his long pole.

All these figures, whatever their make or scale, were surrounded by a plethora of miscellaneous equipment; not only luggage of all shapes and kinds, but seats, nameboards, platform ticket machines, chocolate machines, nameplate-making machines, weighing machines, milk cans and barrows.

Nowadays, as with model soldiers so with railway figures, metal has given way to plastics, leaving these earlier lead passengers and porters to inhabit the world of the collector. For not only are they essential to the vintage railway scene; they are also fascinating in their own right. Attractive in form and colouring, they are a mirror of bygone times in dress, fashion and class structure. What images are conjured up by the bearded station master, the first-class passengers and yachtsmen, the hikers and the hotel porters! Almost the entire social scene of yesterday is epitomised in these tiny human figures. They represent, in short, a miniature study in social history.

Above: On the way to the station: Vintage Dinky Toy figures and vehicles make a lively scene outside a Hornby station; the vintage tinprinted cars are worthy of study! *J Joyce*

Below: Britain's OO gauge figures for the Twin Trix Railway on a Manyways station. *J Joyce*

POST-WAR MODELS

Overleaf: A fine model of a "Castle" Class locomotive on Anthony Murray's 7mm scale layout. *B Monaghan*

Scales and Gauges Since 1945

World War II was less destructive of life than the previous conflict, but far more damaging to civilian affairs. In a total war model railways were a dispensible luxury. Manufacture in Europe ceased, but the spark was kept alive by dedicated enthusiasts in the black-out at home, in billets, behind the battle lines and even under adverse conditions in prisoner of war camps.

In Britain, it was decided that the virtually complete shut-down provided a unique opportunity to tidy up the whole business of scale and gauge. Under the patronage of J. N. Maskelyne, editor of "Model Railway News" and R. J. Raymond, editor of "Model Railway Constructor", the British Railway Modelling Standards Bureau (BRMSB) was formed. The object was simple, to determine wheel and track standards that would be made uniform in the post-war era.

Unfortunately, while the Bureau contained many outstanding modellers, it had three serious deficiencies. It did not have any direct link with the club movement, it met at irregular intervals in unpublicised places and then delivered its lofty deliberations as though engraved from on high on tablets of stone. The final and most telling disadvantage of the BRMSB was its lack of teeth. It was never able to influence the major toy firms at all and many minor firms, while claiming to manufacture to its standards, paid little more than lip service to them. The American NMRA issues "Conformance Warrants" and carries out regular checks to see that the quality is being maintained; the weight they carry is such that the fear of losing his "conformance warrant" publicly is sufficient to keep a manufacturer in line. The BRMSB has not met for many years. In recent years their standards have been condemned as unworkable. This is rather a sweeping statement, because a surprisingly large number of railway modellers managed to make perfectly

Above: Gauge O in the garden: J. Wheldon's layout runs clockwork and steam. Hornby and Bassett-Lowke clockwork trains shown in action. J Wheldon

Centre: Comparison of gauges and scales in general use. Drawing by Stuart Hine.

Below: Rare model: Carette Gauge 3 North Eastern Railway 4-4-0 and lithographed tinplate coaches (R. McCrindell Collection.) B Sharpe

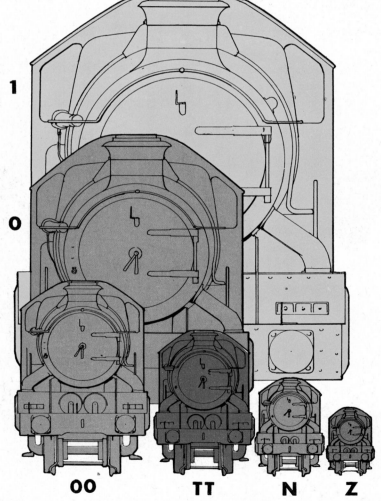

1

O

OO TT N Z

good working layouts using them. However, the rather remote academic approach of the Bureau did ensure that neither the organised clubs nor the Trade felt any loyalty towards it.

Even so the Bureau did a lot of good work. It established standards for gauges 1, O and OO. It inaugurated the more accurate gauge of 18mm for 4mm scale, originally called Scale OO, but later termed EM. Originally the Bureau stipulated a narrow tread for EM, which looked rather pretty, but fell off the track with annoying regularity for no discernable reason. The problem was solved by adopting the same wheel profile as used in OO.

In the post-war era, there were two distinct trends. First of all, serious modellers were more concerned with scale than gauge. In the USA there arose a peculiar habit of referring to O scale, HO scale, which is imprecise. In Britain the practice was to say 7mm scale or 4mm scale—or whatever one thought. Whereas in the past, near enough was good enough, now it was considered important to make models within at least 1mm of their true scale size. It also became important that models should be accurate replicas of their prototypes.

The second change was that 4mm scale overtook 7mm in popularity, so much so that for some ten to fifteen years, the question of scale was virtually settled. In Britain it was 4mm to the foot, in the USA 3.5mm to the foot, and in the rest of the world 1:87. Furthermore it was

taken as axiomatic that 16.5mm gauge was quite unsuitable for outdoor use— as indeed it was for all intents and purposes at that particular time. In the USA this was of little importance; many homes had large basements where a worthwhile HO empire could be built, but in Britain and Europe it was difficult enough, in post war days, to find a home, let alone a place for a layout.

The British solved this problem by a radical and revolutionary step. First, layouts were made portable, built in small sections so they could be carried about, second, many layouts were based on country branch prototypes. This is a subject in itself, but the principle certainly made it possible for anyone who had just a single room, or even who lived in a caravan or trailer, to own a working layout.

The post war years saw the emergence of two new gauges from the USA. S gauge ($\frac{7}{8}$in gauge, $\frac{3}{16}$in scale) was known in Britain for a while as H1—it is half the size of 1 gauge, but it has never been very popular once the American Flyer S gauge system ceased production. The other gauge was TT—Table Top. It enjoyed a short-lived vogue in the USA, as the answer for the man who lived in an apartment. With a track gauge of 12mm and a scale of 1/10in it was commendably compact. TT was introduced in Britain, with a scale of 3mm to the foot. It came in with a bang, but dwindled in support once Triang ceased production. Although TT buffs on both sides of

the Atlantic kept the flag flying, the market is now confined to a relatively limited range of kits. A little ready-to-run equipment is still manufactured in East Germany.

The next introduction was N gauge. Various experiments with 2mm scale, sometimes called OOO, were carried out by amateurs from the early 1920s onwards, and finally a gauge of 9.5mm was standardised. This scale has never been developed commercially. A short-lived British range by Lone Star used approximately 2mm scale diecast bodies on 9mm gauge track. The stock was heavy, and the diesel locomotives, which had a rubber band drive, somewhat erratic. It was left to the Germans to produce a reliable 9mm gauge system. The European Standards body called the new gauge N, since in most European languages 9 starts with that letter. The scale in Europe and the USA is 1:160, but with the wheels and other fittings adopted as standard, models of this scale are considered by some to be impractical within the smaller British loading gauge, so once again the British models are built to 1:148 scale ($2\frac{1}{16}$mm to the foot). There

is a 2mm Scale Association which claims enough know how to model at 1:152 or 1:160.

Finally, Marklin have evolved a new gauge Z, 6.5mm gauge, 1:220 scale. It works well, but it is too early yet to say how it will develop.

The post-war period also saw the introduction of narrow gauge modelling on an organised system. Since the prototype comes in a variety of sizes, a wide selection of combinations is possible. In the USA the two most popular combinations are HOn3, 3.5mm scale and 10.5mm gauge, and On2, $\frac{1}{4}$in scale, $\frac{1}{2}$in gauge, both using non-standard gauges. In Britain the practice is to use an accepted gauge and either fiddle the scale or take advantage of the fact that narrow gauge prototypes come in so many sizes that whatever you do must more or less fit. There are at present three popular combinations, in order of descending size, 16mm scale on 32mm gauge track, true 2ft scale on O gauge. This is a neat combination, permitting very solid engineering work with a wealth of detail. There is no common gauge letter. Next there is OOn3, 4mm scale on 12mm

Top Left: Gauge O indoors: the York O Gauge Group's "Jubilee" 4-6-0 stands in their Holgate St. Paul's station. *B Monaghan*

Below: OO 16·5 mm gauge: Alan Lawson's model railway. *B Monaghan*

gauge, used almost exclusively for models of Irish or Isle of Man prototypes. Finally there is 009 4mm scale on 9mm gauge track (or if one favours Continental HO9 the same thing, but we say the scale differs). It is used to represent 2ft 0in, 2ft 3in and 2ft 6in prototypes with complete impartiality.

One must also mention in this connection the LGB system, 1:22 scale on 45mm gauge track. There is again no common nomenclature in use in Britain, largely because the serious narrow gauge worker is apt to define both scale and gauge, and leave it at that.

Mention has been made of the inaccurate gauge of 4mm scale. An attempt has been made to improve it in EM, but this is still underscale. Recently a group of modellers have defined P4, which has a track gauge of 18.83mm. Many claims have been made, but it is significant that the few small systems so far exhibited are, at their best, virtually

indistinguishable at first glance from EM, or in some cases, very accurate OO layouts. It is still early days, but published statements suggest that the same difficulties that bedevilled the narrow wheels in post-war EM gauge are arising, and the old hands some of whom have seen this twice before are poised to say "I told you so!" We can only wait and see. There are many things to command in the P4 approach, an emphasis on precision can never fail to be of value, but whether it will prove thoroughly reliable for general adoption remains to be seen. At least one worker who has tried it has claimed that unless one models an actual station layout, the exercise seems pointless. And here one comes up against the great problem in scale. A small station, modelled accurately to 4mm scale, requires some fifteen to sixteen feet in length—the length of a normal garage. It is worth keeping a sense of proportion. In OO the gauge

scales out at only 4ft 1½in, but for all that it is still far more accurate than measurements along the track.

What of the future? Having gone as far as one can in miniaturisation—a sub Z gauge is theoretically possible, there have been 4mm gauge models built, the practicability is in question since few people could put the stock onto the track! There is indeed, a sign that the process of reduction in size may be reversing. The LGB narrow gauge has been mentioned, there is also a new line of Gauge 1 models by Marklin. More than that, it is established that ground level 5in gauge is practicable, and one or two people are experimenting with the old 5 gauge and above, not for simple passenger haulage, but as a serious railway with signals, signal boxes and stations, operating in accordance with strict prototype practice. In O gauge, steam traction is making a come-back.

This is where we came in!

Left: Early new-standard gauge: A Bing Gauge 4 (3½ in gauge) steam engine of 1895. This has been repainted and is as shown in the film "The Railway Children". (R. McCrindell Collection.) *Richard Sharpe Studios*

Below: TT Gauge 3 mm scale model of Worsted Station on J. G. Raymond's Gable End and Worsted Railway. *N F W Dykhoff*

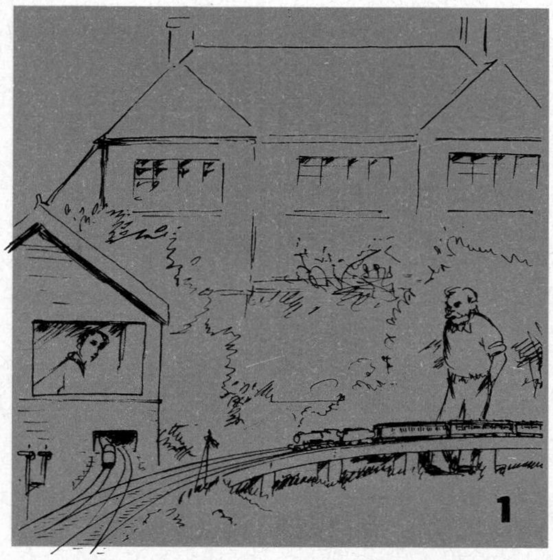

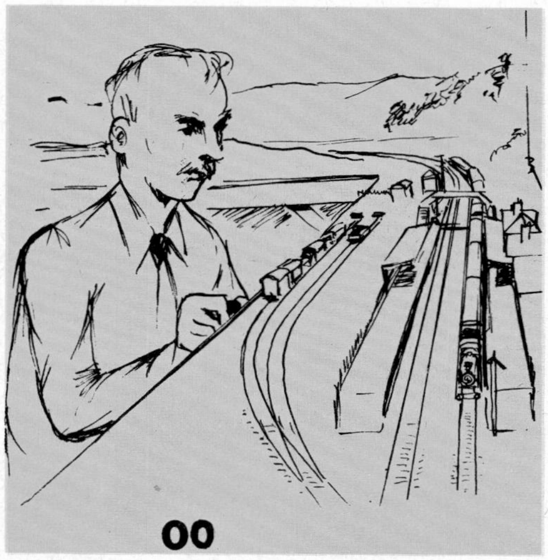

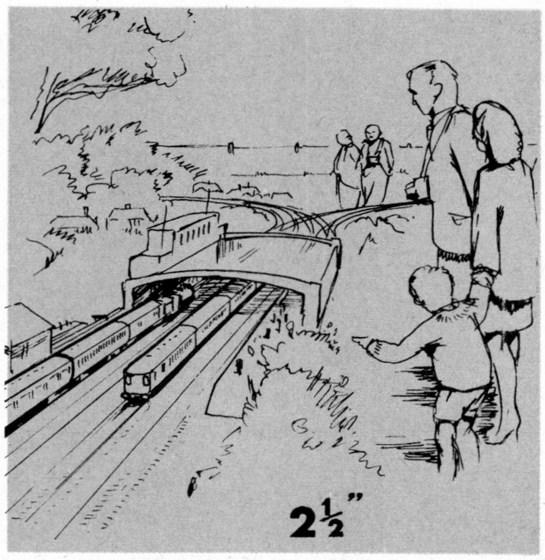

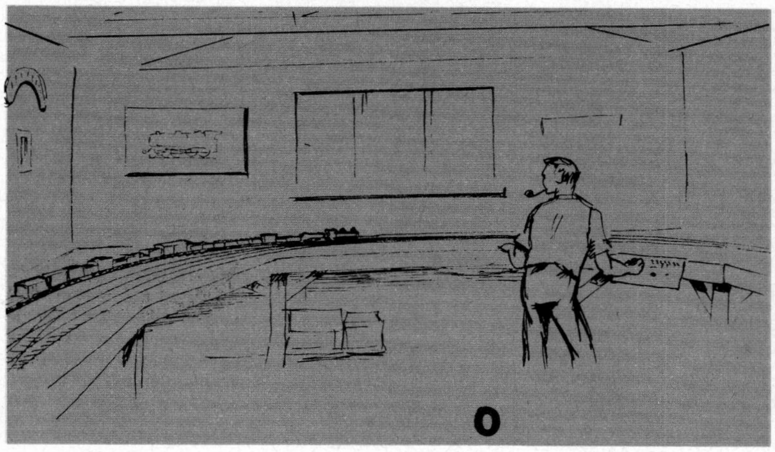

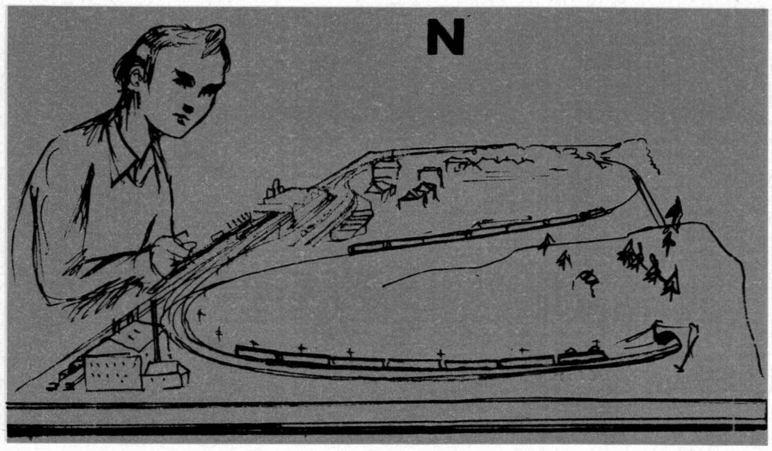

Name	Gauge	Description
1	2½ins (63.50mm)	In 1902 the first commercial models appeared built to gauge. Three scales are used: ½in, $\frac{17}{32}$in, or 14mm to the foot.
Standard	2⅛ins (53.97mm)	Much in vogue before 1938, this American gauge used a scale of ⅜in to the foot, or sometimes $\frac{7}{16}$in.
2	2ins (50.97mm)	Not much used. The scale used was normally $\frac{7}{16}$in to the foot, and the scale ratio was 1:26 or 1:27.
1F	45mm	A fine scale version of a gauge ideal for use in garden railways. The scale is 10mm to the foot. The ratio is 1:30.5.
1	1¾ins (44.45mm)	Britain uses a scale of 10mm to the foot; Germany and the USA have a scale of ⅜in and a scale ratio of 1:32.
O_{17}	1¼ins (31.75mm)	Using English instead of metric measurements, this rarely used gauge uses a scale of $\frac{17}{64}$in to the foot.
O	32mm	Appearing before the First World War, the British O Gauge is still popular. The scale is 7mm to the foot.
OF	32mm	Also with a scale of 7mm to the foot, this gauge uses much finer measurements; the rail height, for example, is only half that of O. Ratio: 1:43.5.
O	1¼ins	In America a scale of ¼in to the foot is normal, and a ratio of 1:48, as opposed to the 1:45.2 ratio of O_{17}.
Gm	45mm	LBM are huge German models. Using Gauge 1 track, the scale is 22.5mm to the foot.
O*n*	32mm	Rolling stock for 2⅞ins Gauge, Gauge 3 and Gauge 1 use scales of 16mm, 14mm, and 10mm to the foot representing 2ft, 2ft 3ins and 3ft prototypes.
O*n*3	19mm	One of the three standard American narrow gauge models, with a scale of ¼ inch to the foot and a ratio of 1:48.

Name	Gauge	Description
O	1⅛ins	A number of Continental models have appeared using this gauge, built to a scale of 2cm to 1 metre.
Q	1$\frac{3}{16}$ins	Also referred to as a gauge of 1.188ins, this American gauge uses a scale of ¼in to the foot. It has been replaced by O.
HI	⅞in	Literally half of Gauge 1, this gauge was superseded by S Gauge. It has a scale of $\frac{3}{15}$in to the foot.
S	⅞in	Quite common in the USA, with a scale of $\frac{3}{16}$in to the foot and a ratio of 1:64; Europe prefers to express the gauge as 22.2mm and the ratio as 1:65.
OO	¾in (19mm)	Much confusion derives from the use by America of a 19mm gauge with a scale of 4mm to the foot and a ratio of 1:76.2.
EEM	18.83mm	Originally called EMF Gauge, this was a British fine scale attempt, superseded by the Protofour group, using a scale of 4mm/1ft and a 1:76.2 ratio.
EM	18mm	Since the gauge/scale relationship of the British OO Gauge is inaccurate, quite a number of modellers use 18mm as a gauge with a 4mm scale.
OO	16.5mm	The most common British gauge, with a scale of 4mm to the foot (giving a top-heavy overscale appearance but useful for including large motors in small locos).
HO	16.5mm	The most widely used gauge. The scale is normally 3.5mm to the foot and the ratio 1:87.1. Some models have used a 3.8mm scale.
O*n*2½	16.5mm	The scale used is ¼in to the foot, and this enables HO items to be used to represent both 2ft 3ins and 2ft 6ins prototypes.
O*n*2	½in	The second standard American narrow gauge uses ¼ inch scale models, and has a ratio of 1:48.

Name	Gauge	Description
OO*n*	16.5mm	Using 7mm scale models—that is, those normally built for Gauge O—on trackwork half the size will represent 2ft 3ins and 2ft 6ins prototypes.
OOE	16.5	There are still a number of French and German models using this gauge with a scale of 1cm to the metre, and a scale ratio of 1:91.
HOE	16mm	Rarely used, this gauge was replaced by HO Gauge. It had a scale of 3.5mm to the foot.
E	$\frac{19}{32}$in	Another rare gauge, also replaced by HO gauge with a scale of ⅛in to the foot. The gauge is also called 15mm.
QO	0.6in	This is a very rare American gauge, in which the models are built to a scale of ⅛in to the foot.
OOC	14.3mm	This Continental scale aims to obtain a perfect scale ratio of 1:100 with a scale of 1cm to 1 metre.
TM	13.5mm	A British fine scale/gauge ratio of TT Gauge, using the standard British scale of 3mm to the foot.
TT-3	12mm	The commonly used British table-top gauge with a scale of 3mm to the foot, giving an oversized effect. The ratio is 1:101.6.
TT	12mm	The original table-top gauge of 0.471in, with a scale of 2.5mm (European) or $\frac{1}{10}$ in (USA) to the foot, and a ratio of 1:120.
TT-X	12mm	A few British modellers decided to scale down the British TT-3 Gauge, and use a scale of $\frac{1}{9}$ in to the foot.
TT3*n*	12mm	One British manufacturer makes models of Welsh narrow gauge railway locomotives and cars to a scale of 5½mm to the foot.
OO*n*3	12mm	To represent a 3ft gauge prototype, one British manufacturer issues Isle of Man models to a scale of 4mm to the foot.

Name	Gauge	Description
HOO	10mm	Known as *centimetrico*, or micro-gauge. It is in use in Sweden, with a scale of 2mm to the foot and a ratio of 1:144.
OOO	9.5mm	Fifty years ago the first models appeared for this gauge. The scale is 2mm to the foot and there is an active Scale Association. Ratio: 1:152.4.
N	9mm	The British modeller uses a scale of 2.06mm to the foot, which is a ratio of 1:148, and gives a slightly overscale effect.
N	9mm	On the Continent of Europe, the ratio used to be 1:150, but in 1960 was standardized at 1:160, with a scale of 1.9mm to the foot.
K	8mm	Only in Europe are there models to this small gauge, with a scale of 1.75mm to the foot and a ratio of 1:180.
QOO	7.62mm	Rarely used, except for special purposes at exhibitions, this is an American gauge with a scale of 1.75mm to the foot.
Z	6.5mm	Introduced in Germany in 1972, this minute gauge is likely to be the smallest commercially. The ratio is 1:220 and the scale 1.51mm to the foot.
X	$\frac{3}{16}$in (4.5mm)	In 1935 Mr Reg Walkley produced a scale model of an 0-4-0T tank locomotive to a scale of 1mm to the foot. It operated perfectly.
TT*n*	12mm	An East German company markets a number of models of German and Austrian equipment to a scale of 3.5mm to the foot.
HO*n*3	10.5mm	On 0.413 inch gauge, many Americans model to a scale of 3.5mm and a ratio of 1:87.1 to represent 3ft gauge prototypes.
OO9	9mm	Strictly speaking, this is OO*n*2.25 Gauge, using a scale of 4mm to the foot to represent 2ft 3in prototypes.
HO*n*2½	9mm	The smallest scale for narrow gauges in common use is 3.5mm to the foot to represent 2ft 6ins prototypes. It is also called HO*n*9.

7mm scale model of a Midland Railway double-framed Kirtley 0-6-0 goods engine No 594. *B Monaghan (Courtesy Derby Municipal Museum).*

SMALL SCALE READY TO RUN

The Meccano factory in Liverpool began to remanufacture its toy trains soon after the end of the second world war, but O gauge was largely ignored. A basic clockwork system was reintroduced with a simple choice of tank or tender 0-4-0s and a selection of four wheel stock. An item good for the youngster, but of no interest to the serious enthusiast. No moves were made to reintroduce electric traction, or to revive the No 2 special series of reasonably accurate 4-4-0s or the *Eton* and *Princess Elizabeth* super models. Those were casualties of war.

Instead, production was geared to the Hornby Dublo system. To the casual observer, it was a case of starting where it had left off, but the more observant noted certain significant changes. First, the A4 appeared without valances, in its strict post-war condition. This was a harbinger: from now on the toy aspect was receding. Mechanically, there were considerable changes. The motor was improved, in place of the early cast magnet a new design, with steel pole pieces and a slug magnet, was introduced. The successful large-diameter, vertical armature continued, with the relatively low ratio 18:1 worm reduction. A new pattern coupling, designed by S C Pritchard, was adopted in place of the somewhat ineffective spring steel pre-war version. Clockwork traction, for Dublo as available pre-war, was not reintroduced; three rail traction continued, with 12V DC supply from the same basic power equipment, a combined controller-rectifier with a separate mains transformer giving 16V AC supply.

Trix got off to a much slower start. The old AC system, with its unpredictable sequence reverser, apt to function when

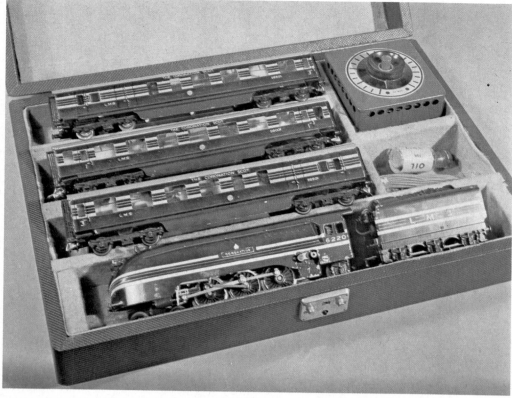

one least required it, continued, but the free-lance 0-4-0s and disproportioned rolling stock made little impact on the more sophisticated post-war purchaser. The rather neat HO 4-4-0s reappeared, as did the A3 and "Coronation" class Pacifics, now both collector's items. The "Coronation Scot" set had superior coaches finished in the distinctive blue striped livery; later versions had coaches in red. Other improvements were the introduction of fibre based track and the adoption of the Hornby pattern coupling.

The reintroduction of AC equipment was only a stop-gap; by the early fifties Trix introduced a range of top quality locomotives operating on 12V DC. Supplied for their unique twin running system, these could run on two rail, and later locomotives were arranged for easy conversion to the finer scale flanges in place of the heavy Trix pattern, a legacy of the pre-war bakelite insulated wheel. These locomotives were die cast, with

Above: Trix-Twin "Coronation" Pacific set. *B Monaghan*

Below: Hornby Royal Mail T.P.O. with mail bag collector. (Courtesy Caroline & Andrew) *B Monaghan*

excellent detail and a first class tunnel magnet motor, soundly designed and powerful. Their only fault lay in the use of 1:80 scale. Lying between HO (1:87) and OO (1:76) this produced a pleasing model which was, sadly, too big for 3½mm scale and too small for 4mm.

With British Railways standard classes now coming into service, the accent was on modern stock: BR "Brittania" and Class 5 (oddly described as Class V) locos, an excellent model of the LNER EM1 class BoBo electric locomotives for the Manchester-Sheffield 1500V DC electrification, and later, a Warship class B-B diesel hydraulic completed the modern motive power. A small Ruston-Hornby 0-6-0 diesel-mechanical locomotive also

appeared, partnered with a GWR pattern shunter's truck. The final new locomotive was a GWR 56XX class 0-6-2 tank. Unfortunately the promising beginning was not immediately followed up with corresponding rolling stock, and British Trix became involved in the first of the take-over crises that were to bedevil its future.

Meantime, in the late 1940s a new name appeared, Graham Farish. This concern, with plenty of experience in the electrical and electronic field, decided to enter the model railway business. Their first locomotive was chosen to appeal to the serious modeller, the familiar LMS Stanier "Black Five". The model was to 4mm scale, two rail pick-up was adopted from the start, and although the wheels were not precisely to BRMSB scale standards, they were the finest that had appeared on a ready-to-run model in Britain. Unfortunately, an ingenious, but rather unpredictable motor of unconventional design was adopted, while the

use of plastic wheels was, at that stage, premature. The material used was brittle, and chipped flanges were commonplace.

Farish persevered and further locomotives appeared: a GWR 64XX 2-6-2 tank, originally supplied in kit form, and a Bulleid streamlined Pacific, available in a variety of liveries as either "Merchant Navy", "West Country" or "Battle of Britain" classes. Another innovation was a GWR "King" which somehow did not quite convince. All these locomotives were fitted with the original motor, and sadly the erratic performance of this device did much to prevent what could have been a highly successful line, gaining general acceptance. Therefore when the HO scale New York Central "Hudson" was introduced in an attempt to tap the profitable American market, it was soon fitted with an excellent tunnel magnet motor.

Farish also introduced two excellent Pullman cars, based on the old pattern vehicles with vertical matchboarded lower panels. These very distinctive models have recently been reintroduced. Goods stock, with detailed die-cast bodies, was both heavy and slightly disproportioned. Nevertheless it was the first modern British goods stock in 4mm scale. The track was an odd mixture: it was sold in flexible yard lengths, clearly aimed at the serious enthusiast. How-

ever, the thick fibre sleepers and the very heavy section steel rail did nothing to attract the scale modeller, while the complete absence of pointwork dissuaded most others.

In the early '50s two ready-to-run locomotives appeared, the Gaiety pannier tank, and 0-6-2 LNER N2, substantially similar to the Hornby Dublo version. These models were nicely proportioned, indeed the 57XX pannier was well received by serious GWR modellers. The mechanisms were unusual in that the motors were long and slim, and instead of driving with a single worm and wheel, had a crown and pinion first gear coupled to a double reduction spur drive which, in theory, should have been fairly noisy, but was in fact relatively quiet. The worst feature of these models was a tendency towards wobbly wheels.

Another entry in the train set field about this date was Ever Ready Ltd. Before the invention of the transistor this company was seeking fresh markets for its batteries, and with this in mind produced a small low voltage motor with considerable application in the toy market. They produced a neat 3-car version based on the 1933 standard tube stock, roughly to 4mm scale. The use of a low voltage prevented scale modellers from considering these, very few were manufactured and those that survive are collector's items. It was a sterile development, but it is worth recording, as the only attempt since the War to model the distinctive London Transport stock in ready to run form.

During the early 1950's a new firm entered the toy train market—Rovex Ltd. The original sets, intended for sale in department and chain stores were, on the

face of it, nothing special. The track, steel rail in a grey acetate plastic base, looked, and was crude. What was more the sectional system was single-ended, the rails could not be linked in reverse order. The coaches were somewhat of a caricature. The locomotive however, was better. It was a reasonably well-proportioned model of a "Princess Elizabeth" class 4-6-2, devoid of valve gear and most frills. It was powered by a motor designed by Jack Hefford of Zenith Models, which was powerful and efficient and could be run from batteries. The whole set was so cheap, that one could afford to throw away the track and coaches and keep what was a remarkably sound little locomotive.

The Rovex system used two-rail traction, and as no points were envisaged at the start, there was no objection to using thick flanges, necessitated by the use of the soft, weak acetate plastics of the period. It was just a cheap toy train for a child's present. And there it might have stayed had not Lines Brothers decided to enter the model railway field. One of the then largest toymakers in Europe, they had almost everything in their extensive range except a good train system. They bought out the Rovex firm, and began development.

The first changes were something of a stop gap. The grey-base track was modified to be double ended, and simple turnouts were provided so that the user could assemble a system with loops and sidings. A slightly improved, but still basically crude coupling was introduced. But the majority of the parts still showed their cheap toy trainset origin. Then came the "Jinty", an excellent model of the LMS 3F 0-6-0 tank. This was a reasonably

good 4mm scale model, moulded in the newer polystyrene, giving a better finish and greater strength, as well as freedom from warping. The chassis was simple, a solid diecasting separating two sheet steel sideframes, the basic motor was slightly improved: diecast wheels with a spoke effect and a thick flange provided the only serious fault. The best point of all was the price—29/6d! Improved coaches followed, shortened versions of the new BR standard classes, then came better goods stock. The new track had black open sleepers slightly short, rather too thin and too wide apart for scale, but for all that a distinct improvement. A new pattern coupling, called tension-lock, but in fact a properly engineered version of a design introduced in the 1920's by A R Walkley, a pioneer of accurate small scale modelling, was also applied. Further locomotives appeared. At first there were a number of variations on a theme, using the "Jinty" chassis, but as confidence grew new designs, using their own chassis arrived. (Each new introduction was a significant improvement on the old, while as opportunity offered, old models were upgraded.) A new factory was built at Margate; production began in earnest.

Meccano Ltd reacted to the threat. To date their only significant change had been to abandon the rather pleasing matt pre-nationalisation liveries in favour of a glossy version of British Railways colours, which was supposed to appeal in the toy market. The company also introduced a new locomotive, the British Railways 4MT 2-6-4 tank. This, the last new model to incorporate the original vertical large armature motor, was without doubt one of the best engineered models produced. Performance and appearance went hand in hand, it was a sound reliable workhorse, and so far as the serious modeller was concerned the only fault lay in the use of three rail traction.

Meantime, Triang-Rovex were accelerating. A simple, reliable power bogie was developed, and from it a whole range of modern equipment followed. A Southern Electric set, curiously dated, with the obsolete pointed nose of the original LSWR design appeared plus a modern two-car diesel railcar set. After a brief flirtation with American style designs which had little appeal, the basic bogie

design was modified and a small range of British diesels followed. More important from the serious enthusiast's viewpoint, the new steam-outline locomotives were getting better.

Model railways were in a boom period. After various financial re-arrangements in the parent companies, British Trix emerged from the doldrums, introduced an excellent range of 1:80 scale BR standard coaches and a matching inter-city diesel railcar set, taking advantage of the fact that the trailer cars in these rakes were standard BR stock, suitably modified. Mettoy introduced a range of French made models to approximately British outline, but unfortunately more or less to HO scale, and incompatible with existing 4mm scale stock. These models were incredibly cheap and certainly got many schoolboys interested in the hobby.

Meccano Ltd began to move decisively. They introduced the new SD series goods stock, plastic bodies on diecast underframes. Having learned their lesson these models were matt finished and, a pointer to the future, fitted with spoked

nylon wheels. They could be used on two rail systems without alteration. A new steam locomotive appeared, an excellent model of the Stanier 8F 2-8-0, followed by a GWR "Castle" spoilt only by the inexplicable error in the coupled wheelbase. Both were fitted with a new tunnel magnet motor and their chassis had a significant recess. New, improved tinplate coaches, with plastic roofs and ends were produced. An excellent Class 1 BoBo diesel electric locomotive appeared. Then came the bombshell. Hornby and Dublo went two-rail. This was done thoroughly: a new low priced 0-6-0, based on the SECR R1 class appeared, and bit by bit all the existing locomotives, with the exception of the LNER N2 0-6-2T first introduced in 1938, were to be made available in two rail. (The challenge was clear, the attack was well thought out.) Further locomotives were coming along, fitted with a new pattern motor, using a large diameter armature in a ring-field magnet. There was a fine model of a Deltic class diesel, extremely powerful and capable of astounding feats of

Top: Two favourite Triang models: "Evening Star" and the Caledonian Single. *P E Randall*

Above: An A1A-A1A Diesel Electric by Triang.

Left: Hornby Dublo Stanier 8F 2-8-0 and E3002 electric. *B Monaghan*

Overleaf: Caledonian "Oban Bogie" in 7mm scale by George Ure.

haulage, a model of the ill-fated Metrovick CoBo diesels, which were withdrawn so rapidly that the Hornby model was very nearly the first example of a historic diesel ever produced. A very good standard 0-6-0 diesel mechanical, with outside frames as on the prototype followed, and last of all, a model of the modified "West Country" Bulleid Pacific.

Meantime Triang were moving themselves. They introduced a range of TT gauge models, scale 3mm to the foot, track gauge 12mm, but although well designed and reliable, these never really caught the public taste, possibly because while smaller, they were not small enough to make an appreciable

difference. However, the availability of smaller motors turned the Triang designers' thoughts to historic models. First of all came a Dean 4-2-2, *Lord of the Isles,* and matching clerestory coaches, then a Caledonian 4-2-2 (using the same chassis) plus two Caledonian coaches. Finally Triang produced a model of Stephenson's *Rocket* and a Liverpool & Manchester coach.

The short-lived craze for slotcar racing was then at its height, and in Triang there were those who believed that it would oust railway modelling in a year or so. This was serious, but worse was to come: there was financial trouble in Binns Road, and Meccano Ltd were taken over by Triang.

Triang set out to reorganise the Meccano empire. The two systems were technically merged, but once the existing stocks of Hornby-Dublo equipment were disposed of, all that remained was the new name, Triang-Hornby. Later, some parts of the old Hornby Dublo system were to reappear under the Wrenn label.

Triang-Hornby was now the only complete train set system in development

in Britain. Even here, movement was slow. Gone were the days when one excitedly opened the new catalogue and looked longingly at the range of new locomotives that would be produced in the next year. Instead, one noted with sorrow, that certain features were disappearing. Not that there was no progress – wheel standards were slowly improving, to the point where the reliable series 4 track—probably the most versatile geometry of all sectional trackage systems in the world—was replaced by system 6, with the same geometry but scale sleepering and code 100 rail, to match international standards. The last vestiges of the old Rovex sets had now vanished and though the "Princess" Pacific remained in the catalogue there was virtually no part in common with the original. Fully spoked wheels, valve gear, and where appropriate, the old pre-nationalisation liveries had come in.

Trix had meantime introduced their 4mm scale *Flying Scotsman.* This was an excellent model, available in a range of liveries and even with an extra tender, to correspond with the locomotive as preserved by Alan Pegler. From this a whole range of LNER Pacifics followed, but then British Trix ceased production.

This went almost unnoticed, because in 1972 the whole Lines' Brothers empire foundered. However, unlike the Meccano debacle, one of the few viable parts of this complex toy making concern was the highly efficient Rovex company, now, in addition to the trains, producing the Frog plastic kits and what remained of the slot racing ventures. Rovex became part of the Marx-Dunbo-Combex group, and continued after a brief hiatus to develop along the lines it had already established. Before the crash a fine model of the BR standard 9F 2-10-0 had been produced, incorporating several features new to British practice, a motorised tender with ring-field armature driving the wheels through a spur gear train, a free-running locomotive chassis with all wheels flanged, except the centre pair which, as on the prototype, were blind. An LMS class 5 using similar drive was introduced in late 1973, while the existing BR "Britannia" Pacific is to be brought into line. Goods stock is being improved, and more stock appears in pre-nationalisation colours.

At the same time the Wrenn subsidiary became independent. Holding the Hornby Dublo tools, they are now reintroducing many of the old range that had been dropped. Some confusion has followed. The former Triang system is now known as Hornby, the original Hornby Dublo range is marketed by and as Wrenn. More than that, some decidedly odd colour schemes are being perpetuated. The Wrenn 0-6-2 was produced in LMS colours, the BR 2-6-4 took things one step further by appearing first in LMS red—even the rather similar Stanier 2-6-4T's never sported this bright livery—and later in GWR colours. Oddly, the engine has not yet appeared in Caledonian blue, despite the existence of a preserved tank in this attractive livery on the Lakeside Railway. The former Triang "Hall" appeared in bright red, bearing the name *Lord Westwood* and the phone number of the Rovex factory on the tender. This has infuriated the purists, but the test will come when the year's accounts are drawn up. Too much is made however of the danger of deluding young enthusiasts. The critics seem unaware that the most assiduous seekers of minor errors are schoolboys.

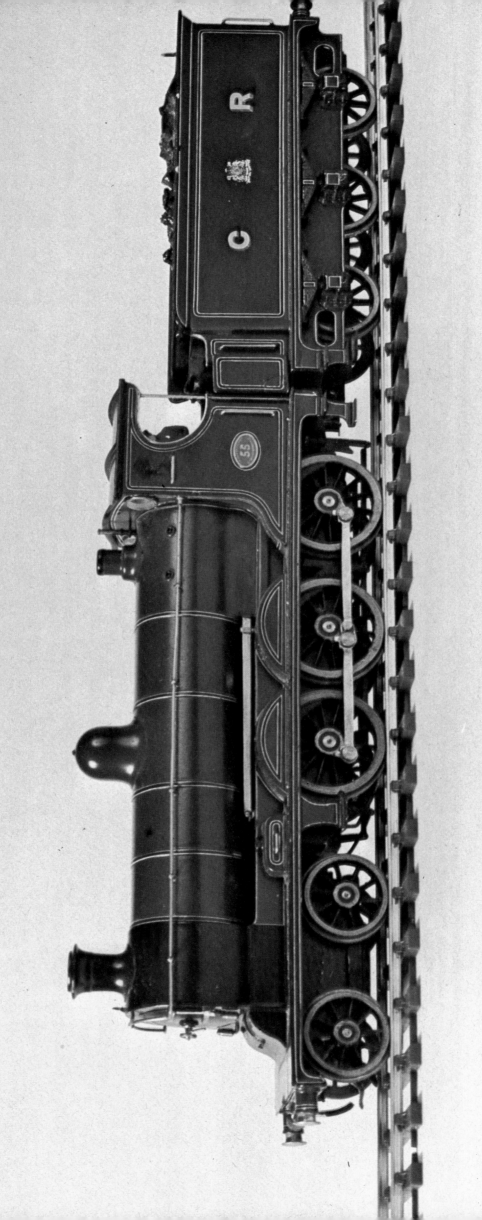

Most of the well-known names in the model railway world were first heard of before 1939, and some of these are, alas, no longer on the scene. The Triang story is different for here is a system which has become, as it were, a legend in its lifetime. The system was entirely a post-war innovation and is, happily, still with us.

In 1949 the model railway enthusiast could find little in the shops of Great Britain. Hornby Dublo and Trix trains were being made again but were in very short supply. Several manufacturers put on the market kits of parts to make loco-

"lantern" type batteries.

At about the same time a firm called Trackmaster brought out some plastic vans and wagons in OO gauge which had much greater detail than similar toys seen previously. These were followed by a die-cast clockwork tank locomotive from the same firm. In the Autumn of 1951, Rovex Plastics Ltd was incorporated into the Lines Bros. Group, makers of Triang Toys, and the manufacturing rights of the Trackmaster items were also acquired. The resulting trains were re-named "Triang Railways", manufacture was centred at a large modern factory at

and a new "series within a series" known as "Transcontinental". These were American and Canadian type steam and diesel locomotives, with matching coaches and wagons produced mainly for export.

The years up to 1964 brought many introductions into the Triang range, some of them "first ever" inventions. The 1963 catalogue showed a total of nineteen British steam and diesel locomotives. The old "Princess" was now available in red or black with optional names and numbers, something quite new in toy trains. A bold step by Triang, welcomed by boys

ROVEX, TRIANG, HORNBY

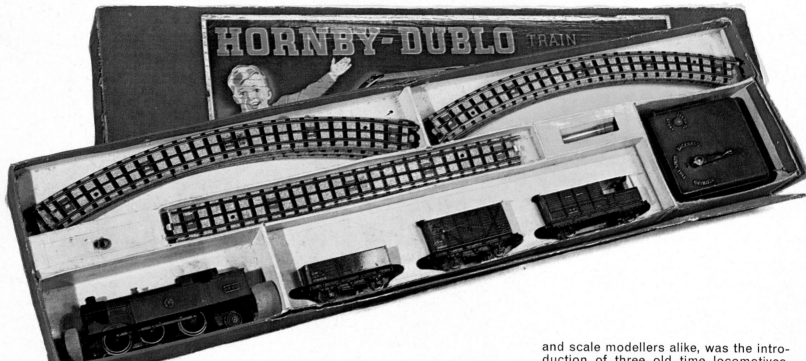

motives or rolling stock items and some of these were good, but many suffered from post-war shortages of materials, time and skill. Second-hand items were also in very short supply and only cheap toy train sets were readily available. Then, during 1950, we began to see a new OO gauge train set in toy shop windows, the engine of which looked more realistic than most others. Closer inspection revealed that the track was "two-rail", that is the current was picked up from one running rail and returned via the other, a system used by scale modellers but not well known in commercial train sets at that time.

The set was, of course, the first Rovex Train Set with a black plastic "Princess" locomotive and two short red plastic coaches. By the standards of the 1970's the set now looks rather crude, but when it appeared, adult enthusiasts as well as children gave it more than a passing glance. From this small beginning the vast range of Triang Trains was to grow during the next ten years. Co-operation between Jack Hefford of Zenith Ltd, the Birmingham firm who made the mechanism, and Rovex Plastics Ltd of Richmond, who made the body, led to the two companies amalgamating in 1951. After minor modifications on the mechanical side the train set was a great success and sold like hot cakes to the train-starved boys of Great Britain. Self-contained with its battery box, the price was very reasonable, even with the extra cost of two

Margate, Kent, and the new company became known as Rovex Scale Models Ltd. Jack Hefford joined the new company and became its Chief Designer in 1954.

Triang Railways were first introduced to the public at the British Industries Fair in 1952. The original items were augmented by a longer coach in BR cream and red, a realistic set of station buildings and an improved track system with metal rails fitted to a grey plastic base.

From this time onward, Triang produced a coloured catalogue early in every new year which has now become an eagerly awaited publication. The issue of 1954 showed that great expansion had taken place in the series since being launched two years before. The "Princess" loco had received a still further improved motor, known as Mark III and a green version of this engine, with Walschaerts valve gear, was now also listed. The clockwork Trackmaster tank engine was still available, and the open and closed wagons had been joined by a brake van, flat truck, bolster wagon and petrol tank. The original red coach was still being made, also the longer one, now in either BR or SR colours. Featured, too, was a Royal Mail Coach which automatically discharged and picked up small mail bags from the lineside. A new locomotive was now available, the famous "Jinty" 0-6-0 tank, the first engine to be produced under the new Triang banner. Accessories of many types were there

and scale modellers alike, was the introduction of three old time locomotives, the *Rocket*, the Great Western *Lord of the Isles* and the famous Caledonian Single No 123. Supplied with appropriate coaches, these handsome examples of Victorian trains were soon to be found in many homes. Triang later deleted these three locos but had to re-introduce the two larger ones to satisfy demand. Inventions referred to previously included an electric smoke unit enabling certain locomotives to "puff" out realistic smoke, and overhead electric wires for operating locos fitted with pantographs.

Coaches were available in many different styles and finishes, together with four-wheel and bogie wagons, reproducing most of the different types seen in Britain. The "Super 4" track, now supplied for the trains, indicated constant improvement in this department, culminating in toy sectional "lines" having the appearance of scale model track. The scenic side had received attention too, for bridges, tunnels, embankments and lineside effects were added to the station buildings to provide the railway setting. By 1964, Triang had achieved, in twelve years, what had taken other manufacturers decades in earlier times, that is a complete model railway assembled from the products of only one maker.

In 1964 a significant event took place in the toy world when the famous firm of Meccano Ltd, makers of Hornby Dublo Trains, was taken into the Triang Group.

Above: A pre-war boxed Great Western Hornby Dublo electric train set.
(*Caroline & Andrew Collection*).   B Monaghan

In May 1965, Triang issued a brochure outlining their policy regarding the two erstwhile competitors, Triang Railways and Hornby Dublo Trains. Although both were two-rail systems (Hornby Dublo had converted to this system not long before) there were differences between the two. The methods of joining track sections were quite different, as were the couplings on the locos and rolling stock. Triang locos were all plastic, whereas the majority of those in the Hornby Dublo range were made of die-cast metal. Duplications also existed especially in accessories such as stations and bridges. Not surprisingly the standards for the new system, to be known as Triang Hornby, were basically those of the existing Triang Railways! Converting track to connect the two types was supplied as were vehicles fitted with a Triang coupling at one end and a Hornby Dublo type at the other

In the 1966 catalogue Dublo stations were still shown, along with two ex-Dublo locos, but all the other Dublo items had presumably been discontinued. However, if we may jump forward to 1971 for a moment, the firm of G and R Wrenn Ltd began to manufacture the original Dublo engines and wagons again and these were included in the Triang catalogue for a few years as Triang-Wrenn. At the time of writing this range is still being made by Wrenn but as an

Above: Hornby Dublo "Castle" with added detail re-painted in Great Western colours. *C M Whitehouse Collection*

Right: British Electric type locomotives. A green EM2 "Electra" and a blue AL1 class. Both by Triang. *Peter Randall*

Below: Just some of the 25 or more variations of the Hornby Dublo 0-6-2T. The picture shows eight of the post-war varieties. *(Caroline & Andrew Collection). B Monaghan*

independent system.

Returning to 1967, we find interesting variations in colours appearing in the Triang catalogue. The 0-6-0 3F locomotive is shown in Midland Railway red with the old crest on the cab side and a large number on the tender—a very pleasing finish. The first Triang Western Region engine also appears in that year's catalogue, a "Hall" class, together with a

Southern Region 0-4-4 Tank locomotive. Transcontinental items are still shown and also another "series within a series" known as Battle Space Combat Units. These are mainly standard items adapted for the use of boys whose tastes run to more war-like games than simply playing trains! Some of these items, such as the ambulance coach and searchlight wagon closely resemble real army equip-

ment, but the Battle Space Turbo Car with its "heavy duty ramming spike" is straight out of a science fiction comic! Presumably the series did not sell well as most items were withdrawn within a fairly short time.

The featured introductions for 1969 were Freightliner items. Seven types of Freightliner wagons were introduced with a working depot crane for transferring containers from rail to road. Probably the most famous of all real engines, the

Above: A 1973 LMS 2P class 4-4-0 alongside an early black "Princess", the latter is similar, except in minor details, to the first Rovex loco. *Peter Randall*

Left: Locos from the Triang Trans-continental series, an overhead electric loco and a diesel. *Peter Randall*

Below: A realistic Triang Pullman Car.

Bottom: An early Rovex/Triang coach in British Railways livery.

Flying Scotsman, now made an appearance in the Triang range, in both LNER and BR liveries. Never at a loss for new ideas, Triang also introduced Assembly Packs which enabled standard items to be assembled by the purchaser with a slight reduction in cost. This year too saw the extension of the range of the Model Land Building Kits which made up into very realistic houses, shops etc, and being already coloured, they needed no painting.

Due, no doubt, to the favourable reception of such models as the *Flying Scotsman* in LNER colours, Triang announced in 1970 that no less than seven locomotives were to be painted in the style of the old "big four" companies. One of these was a new production, the LMS streamlined "Coronation" class engine. The option of BR or pre-nationalisation colours was also extended to the Wrenn locos being produced for Triang, as mentioned earlier. This trend has continued and proves that for both young and old, the appeal of a steam engine is heightened if it is painted in the colours of its heyday rather than the more drab BR uniform finish. Triang have since produced coaches in "big four" colours, some with a very attractive representation of panelling. However, the modern image enthusiast is not neglected, and intercity blue and grey coaches have been introduced with appropriate diesel locos to pull them.

The year 1969 brought another shock to the toy industry when the Triang Group, who had taken over Meccano Ltd only five years before, was itself in difficulties, going into liquidation later in that year. For a time the fortunes of Rovex hung in the balance, and then this part of the group was bought by the Dunbee, Combex, Marx organisation. The firm of Rovex Ltd was set up to operate the Margate factory, and the name of trains changed once more, this time to "Hornby Railways".

In spite of these troubles, the 1971 catalogue announced the best locomotive so far to emerge from Margate, the *Evening Star.* This superb model possesses many revolutionary features, chief of which is the new ring field motor which drives the tender wheels. The wheels on the loco pick up the current but are not powered and this enables "daylight" to be seen under the boiler, as in the real locomotive. The writer has owned one of these locos and can vouch for its amazing hauling power at very low speeds.

By 1972 it was "all systems go" once more at Margate and that year's catalogue had, as usual, many new ideas to tempt the enthusiast. Two locomotives were announced, a GW Pannier Tank and an SR L1 class, the latter being a re-issue in Southern colours. More coaches and also wagons were shown in pre-nationalisation colours, so it seems demands had revealed a bias towards the older finishes. A finer scale track, known as System 6 had now become standard, together with wheels of finer dimensions running, in the case of rolling stock, in low friction bearings.

The younger enthusiast was not forgotten, however, and two novelties appeared in the 1971 catalogue. The first was the "Railway Children" Train Set, based on the contemporary film and consisting of a brown loco in the colours of the fictitious "Great Northern and Southern Railways", pulling two period coaches. The other device was an ingenious control mechanism whereby a train could be made to start and stop by insert-

The eleven main varieties of Post-war tinplate Hornby Dublo tank wagons. *(Caroline & Andrew Collection).   B Monaghan*

ing a ticket in a slot cut in the station roof.

Following the success of the *Evening Star,* two more locos were announced in 1973, with a similar tender drive unit, the LMR "Black Five" and a re-introduced "Britannia" class loco. A still further improved track system became available, known as "Silver Seal" which had rails of nickel silver. Common Market influence can be detected as this track's measurements are listed in metres! The old Rovex battery box had long given way to Triang transformers, but the 1973 season brought a new range of Power Control Units, the largest of which could operate three trains simultaneously.

The modern image market was catered for by the introduction of English Electric Type 37 and Brush Type 31 and 47 diesels, and in addition an excellent model was made of an Ivatt class 2 2-6-0 steam engine, of the type which has been preserved on the Severn Valley Railway and at Steamtown, Carnforth. Indeed, the Hornby range (perhaps rather for-

tuitously) includes numerous models of locomotives which have been retained for preservation: the GWR Pannier Tank, the "Princess", *Flying Scotsman,* the "Hall", the "Black Five" and *Evening Star* for example, whilst the Wrenn range boasts a "Castle", a Stanier 8F and the BR Standard 2-6-4T, all the prototypes of which can still be seen on preserved lines around the country.

In a little over twenty years Triang Trains, now Hornby Railways, have changed from plastic toys to scale models by most people's definition, the change in quality being even more impressive than the growth of the range.

Right: EM gauge model of Aylesbury station by G Williams. *Brian Monaghan*

German Model Railway Manufacturers since the War

The German model railway industry has undergone a complete change since the end of the Second World War. It can now be said to be divorced from the German toy industry, in as much as nearly all the manufacturers are producing very accurate models to exact scale and incorporating all the minute detail. Such models cannot be called "toys", in fact probably the only affinity to the toy trade is the fact that most of the German model railway industry exhibits at the annual Nuremberg Toy Fair in February, for this town is still the centre of that industry.

A further break from the pre-war days, as with other countries, is the question of size, for apart from the gauge 1 LGB system, plus a new Märklin introduction, all the manufacturers have concentrated on the smaller scales.

Another change has been the development of plastics, for gone are the tin-plate creations that were the apple of our father's or grandfather's eye. The plastic age has now been with us for over 25 years and the Germans were soon in the lead in bringing their expertise to the injection moulding techniques, so that locomotive bodies could be moulded in plastic with all the detail added—not only for locos, but for all rolling stock and accessories.

With the introduction of the UIC standard coaches for continental use, it is now easier for the model manufacturer to produce their models in the liveries of other countries, using the same basic mould for the body; thus having a greater variety of rolling stock in many colourful liveries.

One firm which has pre-war roots is Märklin, established in 1859 and who now employ over 2,000 workers in their main factory at Goppingen in Wurttemberg, and they also have two smaller manufacturing plants. In order to consolidate their products and concentrate their production on HO scale, they ceased making O models in 1955 after a period of many years. It is interesting to recall that they stopped making gauge 2 models in 1935. In 1970 they re-introduced gauge 1 models after a lapse of more than 30 years, but now of course, the models in this scale are all plastic mouldings. Within the last two years, Märklin have introduced Z gauge—which they call "Mini-Club". It is the smallest commercially produced model railway system with a scale of 1:220, with a track gauge of 6.5mm ($\frac{17}{64}$in), which means that an express passenger type main line steam locomotive is approx $4\frac{1}{4}$in long, while a main line bogie coach (full length) is approx $4\frac{7}{8}$in long. All the motive power is electrically driven, but at the time of writing no other manufacturer has ventured into this ultra small scale.

At the cessation of hostilities, Märklin re-organised and were soon in production once again, and it was not long before they were producing models of the latest German (DB) locomotives which has continued with the subsequent appearance of diesel and electric locos. One of their successes was the production of an HO scale model of the DB class 44 2-10-0, which in spite of its length would negotiate the sharp curves so often found on a model railway. They

now have an extensive range of German and other European countries' locomotives and rolling stock (including a few examples from the USA).

Märklin continued their use of the pre-war stud-contact system of electrical pick-up using 14V AC, which made their products incompatible with the more universal two-rail 12V DC systems adopted by other manufacturers. However, they purchased the business of A Hannemann (Hamo) of Nuremberg, who had been producing models of diesel locomotives and tramcars, and incorporated some of these products into their catalogue. Later they produced several of their own models for 12V DC operation (two-rail) and marketed these under the Hamo name. In 1967 they introduced a model of a "Warship" class diesel locomotive in the Hamo range, and although the performance of the model was exemplary, it was to the scale of 3.5mm:1ft and thus did not prove popular with the UK modellers.

Fleischmann is now a household name in the model railway world in many countries, but this is not in fact a new firm, for they were established in 1887 and before the last war were well known for their model ships. The two sons of the founder had to virtually start from scratch after the war, as more than half of their factory and machines had been destroyed by allied bombing. They restarted in 1949 with gauge O models, but in 1952 produced their first HO scale model which was their turning point, for this was the first commercially produced two-rail model which, with the realistic track, became so popular that the gauge O models were discontinued and every effort was turned to the manufacture of a complete HO two-rail system. The locomotives and rolling stock have every possible detail incorporated into their plastic injection-moulded bodies, while the motors are extremely powerful, silent and reliable. Track, accessories and electrical equipment have all been added, until today Fleischmann have a very comprehensive range covering the prototypes of many European countries, although of course the majority of their models are of German outline.

The main factory is still at Nuremberg, but others have been built at Heilbronn and Dinkelsbuhl and they are recognised as being one of the largest International manufacturers in their sphere.

A newcomer to the scene is the firm of Arnold Rapido who started making toys in Nuremberg in 1900, but it was not until 1960 that they entered the model railway field by producing what at that time was the almost unheard of N scale. This is approx 2mm:1ft scale, or 1:160 with a track gauge of 9mm. Since then the Arnold range has been rapidly expanded until today they have a comprehensive catalogue featuring the prototypes of many countries and offering a complete railway system. All the bodies are plastic mouldings with metal underframes or chassis. It is true to state that where Arnold Rapido led, others have followed.

The Trix organisation, well known before the war, have had one or two financial changes during the last decade and are now owned by a large German mail order consortium. They have for some reason recently decided to contract their range and are reverting more to their older three-rail system as against the more accepted two-rail which they called "International". Trix have still a number

of the old type prototype German coaches in their range, as well as more modern examples. Trix took over the old established firm of Distler which was founded in 1890 making toy trains mainly in gauge O for clockwork or electric.

Trix also branched out into the N gauge market after the initial success of Arnold-Rapido, and this they called "Minitrix". A good range was soon developed that proved popular in Germany and in the UK where it had an outlet via British Trix, but is now handled by Hornby Railways (Rovex).

Rowa is another new name which came onto the scene in 1969, but were in operation for some years before this as they have been making model railway equipment for Trix and other manufacturers in their factory at Neckar, before they commenced to produce models under their own name in HO and N scales. In 1971, however, they decided to drop the N gauge from their production and to hand this over to Minitrix, taking in its place the Rokal TT scale models, which

have been manufactured since 1953.

The largest model railway system currently being manufactured is the LGB narrow gauge models to gauge 1 size. Lehmann is a firm established in 1881, but it was not until 1967 that they launched the LGB (Lehmann Garden Bahn) system onto the market. The track gauge is 45mm and being of narrow gauge prototype the size of the locomotives and rolling stock is considerably larger. The range is being extended each year and now includes steam and diesel outline models, and many freight vehicles and passenger coaches as well as a range of track, points and accessories.

One aspect of the German model railway industry today is the plethora of kits for model buildings and accessories—all of course, made in polystyrene. It is true to say that Germany has taken the lead in plastic construction kits of houses, shops and all kinds of buildings, from the medieval to the modern in both HO and N scales. Many of the kits contain pre-coloured plastic parts which eliminate the need for painting, and all have the correct embossed brick or stone-work clearly defined. These are the products of such firms as Faller of Gutenbach, Kibri of Boblingen, Vollmer of Stuttgart and Wiad of Wurttemberg who all manufacture a large range of kits for every requirement.

In a similar way the scenic accessories that are now available are vastly different from pre-war, and again it would seem that Germany is in the forefront in the manufacturing of same. The number of firms producing scenic effects such as model trees, cork bark, scenic mats, has trebled with the influx of enthusiasm for model railways that now exists, not only in Germany itself, but on the Continent of Europe. Trees, shrubs, flowers and complete landscape set-pieces are now available in wide profusion at any good model shop counter. Herpa of Nuremberg, Heinrich Kittler and Co (Heki) of Baden, Vau-pe of Kassal and Sommerfeld of Goppingen are the most famous names for scenic accessories, the latter firm also producing some good model overhead catenary for the modern electric locomotives that can take power from the pantograph. The change-over of current collection usually being made by altering the position of a hidden switch on the locomotive.

Preiser of Bavaria, who both make a large variety of models of people in characteristic poses and dresses for all occasions. The range is not merely confined to station staff and passengers, but includes service personnel, sunbathers, wedding groups and even women hanging out washing—an ideal adjunct for the suburban houses made as constructional kits by other concerns.

A further adjunct to the scenic side of the model railway is the model road vehicles produced by Wiking, which are accurate 3.5mm and 2mm models of cars, lorries and buses, the range giving a variety of types for both period and modern layouts. Roskopf of Bavaria is another firm producing a similar range but also including some interesting horse-drawn carts.

The German model railway trade is prosperous and thriving now more than it has ever done in the past, and its products are sought after not only in Germany but throughout the model railway world.

Left: Part of the German "Layout of the Year" by Fleischmann which was displayed at the Model Railway Exhibition 1973. Houses are by Faller and trees by Vau-pe.
Richard Sharpe Studios

While still keeping within the broad sphere of scenery, two German firms are now well known for producing a range of miniature figures in both HO and N scales. These are Merten of Berlin and

Top: An Arnold Rapido N gauge model of a German State Railways Series 01 Pacific locomotive. *David Rudkin. Courtesy W.H. Models Ltd.*

Lower: An Arnold Rapido N gauge model of a German State Railways Express passenger coach. *David Rudkin. Courtesy W.H. Models Ltd.*

Overleaf: Gauge O LMS "Duchess of Sutherland" by Beeson.
Collection Count Antonio Giansanti-Coluzzi

N GAUGE COMMERCIAL

The original clockwork and steam train sets were designed to run on the floor; they were too large for any other site in the normal home. Indeed the only possible support, apart from a purpose built baseboard, was a billiard table. While many of the homes where extensive train set collections were to be found did contain such a table, and it must be admitted that green baize makes an ideal scenic setting, it is doubtful if such a use would be countenanced. But with the advent of OO it appeared that the table was possible, indeed the earliest Bing sets did show this location. But the average dining table had barely room for more than an oval, and even TT, despite the derivation of its name, did not greatly assist. What was needed was something small enough to enable a really interesting system to be built up on a table top.

The answer was obvious, indeed amateur experiments with 2mm scale pointed the way. Furthermore, in the 1920s an attractive tin-printed push along LNWR train was available, but, alas, at that date motive power had to remain the human hand. Commercial motors small enough to fit into this size were still in the future.

Before true N came on the scene, the push-along tiny train reappeared in the form of the Lone Star diecast toys. Later it was provided with quite respectable looking diesel outline locomotives, powered, alas, by the unpredictable rubber band drive that hampered development. Further slowed down by the sheer weight of the diecast rolling stock, the project failed to catch the market.

The first true N gauge, as yet untitled, was made in Germany by Arnold. Here the designers looked at the problem from first principles and came up with a rather unconventional answer. The new line would appeal to people solely because it was small, and because it enabled a superior model train system to be built in a compact space. It would succeed only if the purchaser came back for more, which meant that everything had to be completely reliable and that the locomotives must be able to haul trains as long as one would find on the prototype. The models must be well detailed, accurate and of high quality. In other words, it must not be made down to a price.

As soon as the system was launched, a number of manufacturers took note, and, learning from past mistakes, ensured that track, wheel and coupling standards were fully compatible. While some small deviations have arisen, this has remained the second great advantage of N after its size, the fact that the purchaser does not have to ask himself if X's stock will run on Y's track and couple with Z's locomotives.

So, before we come to discussing N,

let us consider the general characteristics of N gauge equipment. First, the great majority of the products are, within fairly close limits, true scale models with a wealth of detail. Second, the great majority of locomotives, steam- diesel- and electric-outline alike, will haul much longer trains than their prototypes can. 20 coach or 100 wagon trains are possible if the layout is big enough! This is achieved by the use of traction tyres on the locomotives, by the common practice of coupling driving axles by gears, and by the care that is taken to ensure free running rolling stock. Some vehicles can be propelled forty or fifty feet with a single push! There is almost complete interchangeability between makes.

Indeed, the reliability of N is astonishing. Given fair treatment, most N gauge systems will work almost indefinitely; the only serious enemy is dirt on the track, and of course, in the small bearings. For this reason it is definitely not advisable to lay N gauge on a carpet!

Above: The up "Queen of the North" first-class Pullman, headed by Bo.Bo straight-electric "Minerva" crossing Greenbank Viaduct on the Rev. Alan Shone's Wardleworth Line. The locomotive is a Minitrix Bo.Bo chassis and the superstructure is from a Wrenn–Lima BR AL6. The coaches are Wrenn–Lima wagon-lits repainted in the old Pullman umber and cream.
B Monaghan (Courtesy Railway Modeller)

The first major firm to exploit N was Arnold. A German concern, it began by producing German prototypes, diesel and electrically powered, but soon moved into steam outline. The introduction of an 0-6-0 tank to a large extent ensured the success of N, for here was evidence that no reasonable prototype was impossible in this size. This firm had begun to exploit the American market, of which more later.

Fleischmann, with their Piccolo range and Trix (Minitrix) also entered the N gauge market, followed by the Italian firms Lima and Rivarossi. Minitrix, through its British counterpart, and Lima produced British outline stock, and in fact still do. In Britain Peco and Grafar have introduced native lines.

Within a few years eyes were turned towards the American market, and most European manufacturers began to exploit the potential. However, at this point the position becomes a trifle confusing, for although the products were made in Europe, they were marketed under American names, and to confuse the issue still further several manufacturers sub-contracted to supply the American houses, creating a severe "who made what" problem for future collectors. Japan and Hong Kong had also made assaults on the American market, the former in the quality end, the latter in the field of low-priced, but robust standard lines. Regrettably, too much was produced too quickly with the result that the market was temporarily flooded, leading to some degree of uncertainty.

In Europe, where the general shortage of space in the majority of homes had given N gauge a great impetus, the new scale rapidly carved out a respectable slice of the market, encouraging the accessory firms to take up the scale. First and foremost, plastic building kits were introduced, sometimes scaled down versions of popular HO scale models, in others entirely new N gauge designs were introduced. Another popular line, the beautiful plastic figures by Merten and Preiser, are now available additionally in N scale, at least, the most popular sets are so provided. Special N gauge pre-formed scenic bases are very popular in Europe, but to date they have made no impact on the British market.

Here a more important development is the kit. A number of locomotive kits, cast in whitemetal, to fit into existing chassis are now being produced, but at the 1975 Brighton Toy Fair Peco announced a new range based on their own self-contained tender drive unit, giving a wide potential selection of prototypes without too great a difficulty in construction. Initially the popular British 0-6-0 "maid of all work" is to be produced for all four pre-nationalisation companies.

Above: A well produced and finely detailed model of the Jubilee class locomotive of the LMS. This powerful model which will haul 15 or more coaches is produced by Peco in British 'N' scale.

Below: One of the many attractive private owner vans produced in British 'N' scale by Peco.

So, in less than a decade, commercial N gauge has progressed from the "isn't it small, and isn't it wonderful that it works" stage into a well established thoroughly integrated miniature railway system. It is largely orientated towards the serious worker, not necessarily a fanatic, but a man who loves and appreciates miniature trains. It has, so far, largely avoided the toylike gimmicry that has from time to time moved into the larger scales, possibly because its greatest selling point, that of size, is such that it must appeal primarily to the discerning.

N gauge, moreover, has drawn heavily upon experience in the larger scales—the question of interchangeability, mentioned beforehand, is but one case in point. Because the manufacturers realised what models were most likely to appeal to the enthusiast, progress has been rapid and few serious errors have been made. To a large extent N has been instrumental in opening up an entirely new market among those who thought, beforehand, that they simply did not have room for a respectable model railway.

Indeed, such has been the rate of growth that it has been impossible in this short survey to do more than mention the major manufacturers, without going into any details of their extensive ranges. The interested reader is advised to acquire a selection of catalogues and then to gaze longingly at the riches therein.

One criticism levelled against N is that of price. It must be admitted that in many cases, the models do cost more, some-times appreciably more, than their OO or HO counterparts. However this comparison is fundamentally unsound. In any case it is usual for a miniaturised product to cost more, at least in the initial stages if the product is otherwise strictly comparable. This is almost mandatory in the mechanical field, hence a ladies cocktail watch costs more than a gentleman's pocketwatch. In other cases, the N gauge product is technically superior, particularly in all round performance. Most important of all, N gauge can make the difference between owning a worthwhile layout, or just aquiring a collection of locomotives and rolling stock. The flat or apartment dweller will appreciate this point immediately. It must be realised that under present conditions in Europe space in the home is extremely expensive. The whole purpose of N gauge commercial equipment is to provide a valid answer to the space problem.

Above: This minute lime wagon built by Peco in British 'N' scale is barely 1½ ins. long. In spite of its size it incorporates every detail and is very free running.

Above: A typical example of a Peco Streamline item of point work. Peco points are ready for use, being fitted with an over-centre spring device eliminating the need for separate levers. This example shows a 3′ radius point in "N" gauge.

Right: The British international universal trackage system produced by Peco for "N", "HO/OO", "O" and 009 narrow gauge. This finely detailed track is flexible so that it can be laid straight or to curves of any radius. Also available is a foam ballast inlay to add the final touch of realism.

Below: A 'Grafar' "Battle of Britain"/"West Country" class Light Pacific.

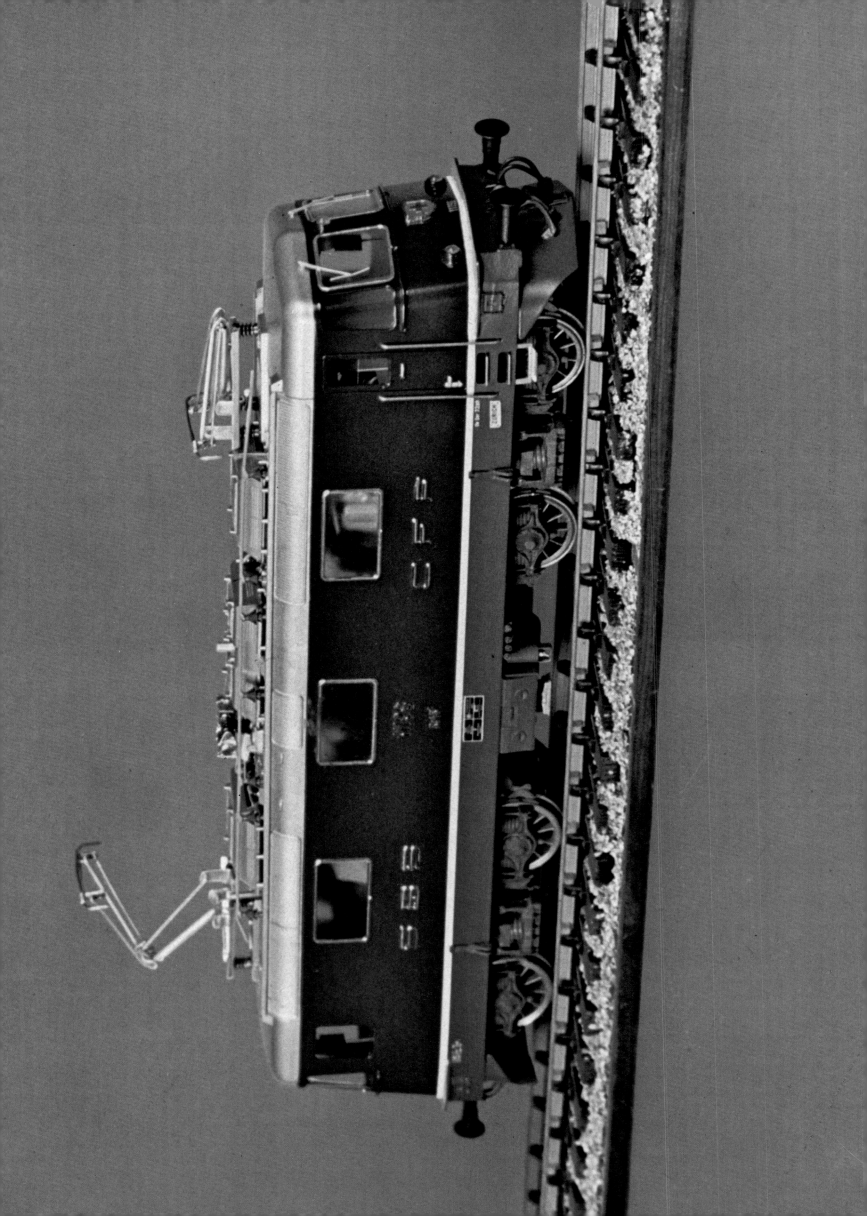

FRENCH TRAINS TODAY

The English firm of Meccano, the manufacturers of Hornby Trains, had a factory at Bobigny near Paris since the end of the first War, producing O gauge models. In 1960 they took over the SMCF (Super Modeles de Chemins de Fer), a smaller concern manufacturing 12V DC two-rail HO gauge models and some of their range was absorbed into the recently introduced Hornby-Acho catalogue. This later product was one of good quality using die-cast metal bodies and plastic coach bodies, and all their items had good detail and were accurate. Generally speaking they seemed to have more detail than their English counterparts and produced some good electric and diesel outline models. A few of the range of SMCF goods vehicles were absorbed into the new range.

A further change took place in 1960, when VB, toy makers who had a factory at Calais, were taken over by the English Tri-ang (Lines Freres SA) they extended the range and introduced some of the English Tri-ang models to the French catalogue. Some confusion arose when Tri-ang took over Hornby in England for it had the obvious repercussions in France with the two factories, and regrettably the Hornby-Acho range is

now finished.

The main proprietary manufacturer in France is now Jouef who in 1949 opened a factory in the Jura mountains to produce HO models at an economical price using plastic injection moulding for all the bodies of both locomotives and rolling stock. Within a couple of years Jouef had changed their track standards to those near to the German Fleischmann but at a much lower price, and at the same time changed their original 6V DC system to the universal 12V DC working. The price and the good quality of these products affected some of the smaller manufacturers such as SMCF and PMP who merged with other firms or closed down.

In 1962 they produced a good model of a Night Ferry Sleeping Car (albeit a trifle short in length) and also made some English outline locomotives and coaches marketed in that Country under the name Playcraft. These items finished in 1970, but the French production has continued unabated and their latest loco-

Top Left: SNCF (Sud-Est) 231 K Ex PLM 4-cylinder, compound Pacific, modernised before the war. Model introduced 1973 by Jouef. *E S Russell*

Left: Model introduced by Jouef in 1970 of **SNCF**-owned restaurant car, staffed by **CIWL**. *E S Russell*

Below Left: Ex Nord 231C locomotive. Model introduced late 50s, early 60s. First attempt by **JOUEF** to produce a life like **HO** loco model. One of the original Playcraft introductions into England; originally, unpainted black plastic body. *E S Russell*

Top Right: SNCF (Ouest) 040TA. Model introduced by **JOUEF** in 1965/66 in versions with side sheeted cab (as photo) or with spectacle plate and cab roof only in green or black. *E S Russell*

Right: SNCF (Sud-Est) Panoramic Autorail for use on "Le Cevenol" service from Marseilles to Clermont Ferrand. Model introduced early 60s by **JOUEF**. *E S Russell*

Below Right: Cast-metal bodied model of Nord region 4-6-4 class 232R. Model dates by **JEP** from early 50s and was originally for 3 rail (centre collector). The model has been fitted with a Triang 2-rail chassis and a tender modified from a Kitmaster 241P kit. The loco body, however, apart from being repainted is original. *E S Russell*

motives are remarkable for their accuracy, attention to detail, performance and low cost. The range now includes the classes 141R, 241P, 231C and 231K for steam outline as well as eight different electric locos and three main line diesel models. An excellent range of coaching stock is now being produced some of them to full scale length. Goods stock and accessories are also manufactured and the range represents the best value for money at the time of writing.

When SMCF were absorbed by the Hornby concern, one of their principals, a M. Gerard, started making superb hand-built models on a limited production basis under the name TAB. These are still being continued, and in the same category are France Train who are reproducing a range of super detailed coaching stock for HO gauge.

Despite the many changes the French model railway industry is probably in a better position now than it has ever been in the past.

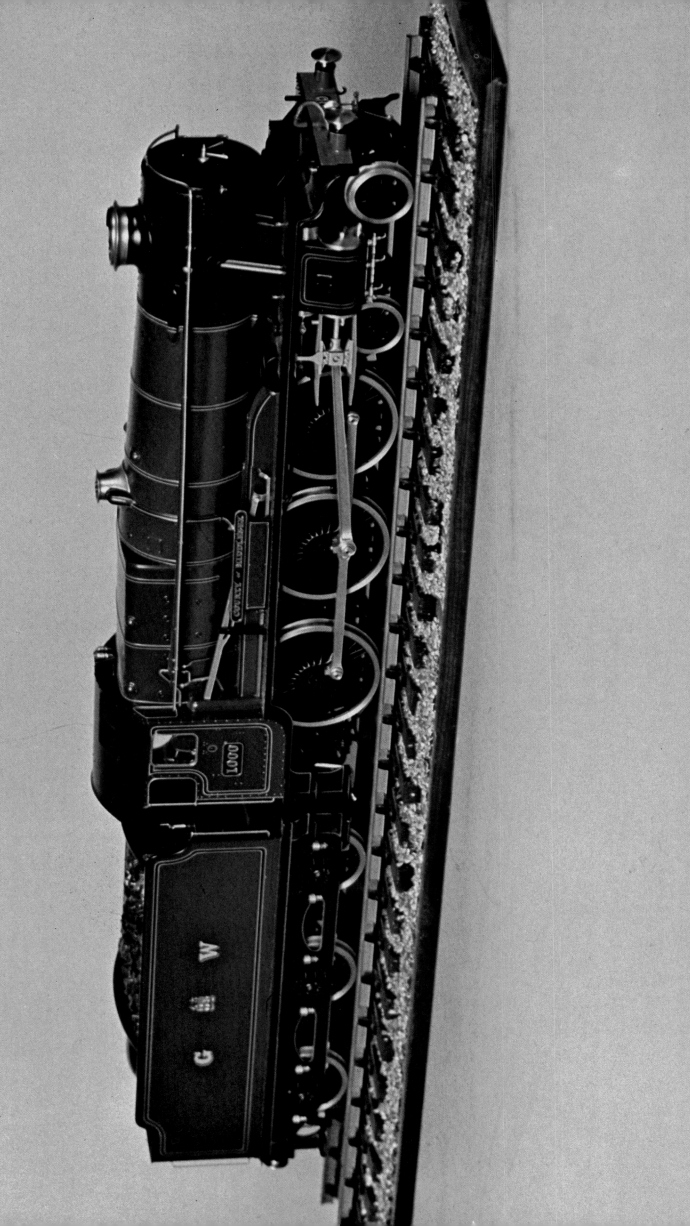

THE MODEL BUILDERS

Facing page : O gauge GWR "County" class
4-6-0, byilt by Beeson in 1955.
Collection Count Antonio Gionsanti-Coluzzi

Roger Guy Williams

On a shelf in the "den" belonging to Guy Williams can be found a very well-worn coverless book inscribed "To Guy, Paddington, 1934". It was a present from a big brother following an outing to London and is the key to the model making which is now the chief activity pursued in this little room.

That well-worn book is a copy of "The Cheltenham Flyer"—a Great Western Railway publication priced one shilling in 1934. To a more critical reader of today, the sentiments expressed are rather nauseating and the obvious inferences that the GWR is, was, and will be the only railway worthy of study are quite naive to anyone whose railway knowledge and enthusiasm goes beyond the confines of God's Wonderful Railway. However, this book, read and absorbed in Guy's early days, set a pattern of thought about the GWR which had to find expression one day in the form most suited to his particular bent.

Guy Williams has made models of one sort or another since he was eight or nine but he is only known to the model railway fraternity through his work at the Pendon Museum and his articles in the "Model Railway Constructor" in which he has discussed the problems of modelling locomotives to a scale of 4 millimetres to the foot.

It may come as a surprise to some to know that "The Cheltenham Flyer" and its successors, "Track Topics" and "The King of Railway Locomotives" lay unopened and gathering mould and dust for many years while his current enthusiasm was for aircraft model-making. While the big brother was making an O gauge system in the attic to do justice to the hauling powers of a Bassett-Lowke "Duke of York", obtained by persuading father to smoke vast quantities of B.D.V. cigarettes for the necessary coupons, Guy was making a collection of one seventy second scale model aircraft from scrap wood and the occasional "Sky-bird" kit. Modelling aircraft to the scale of 1/6th of an inch to the foot became a totally absorbing pastime and, for a schoolboy, was cheap enough to allow a continuous output not relying on birthday presents and Christmas. Plans appeared in a periodical, now alas extinct, "Air Stories". These were studied and a tremendous file of aeroplane photographs was built up to supplement the information. The models would look crude beside today's plastic masterpieces, but a considerable fund of experience in working in this scale was built up and as time went on some of the later models were to a fairly reasonable standard.

All this activity, mixed in with making some flying models, consumed the spare time available after working hard during the early years of the war with the intention of being sufficiently qualified to pass as a pilot trainee. Strangely enough the Navy claimed the enthusiasm, perhaps the West Country influence, and eventually R.G.W. could be found flying a single seat fighter, his favourite type of aeroplane, from a carrier based at Scapa Flow and later Colombo.

Professional training followed the war and then it was that the original influence began to reappear. The aeroplane "bug" had bitten very hard, but achievement of the ultimate ambition seemed to quench the modelling activity somewhat, so that upon seeing for the first time some scale models of rolling stock in 4 millimetres to the foot scale, Guy immediately saw the similarity of scale to the one seventy second scale for aircraft, and the common skills involved. That did it! Out came the "Cheltenham Flyer" and all the other railway books long forgotten. Magazines were obtained and articles on the subject were devoured. A lucky chance led him to a tiny shop in Bristol where Steve Ryan held court for the local enthusiasts. Here he was led along the right lines and absolutely invaluable advice was given. What a service the local retailer gives along with a couple of yards of rail! If he doesn't quite know the right answer he always knows someone who does!

Metal work was a problem. It hardly

Left and above: LMS "Jubilee" class No 5593 "Kolhapur", built by Guy Williams in EM gauge. (Collection P B Whitehouse)

Although trained for Art and Craft teaching, and now a Primary School Headmaster, Guy has kept his hobby out of school and uses it as an escape and relaxation. He seeks to represent in as close accuracy as possible those things which capture his imagination.

Not just engines, but all manner of things. A drawing of a Brunel timber viaduct by Cyril Freezer in the "Railway Modeller" many years ago has a place in the Pendon Museum collection. Roye England and Guy Williams had met sometime before this through Steve Ryan and one or two Pendon engines date from this time. But the viaduct idea came from Roye England seeing a four-span model which Guy had made 'in aeromodelling style, from balsa wood on a pin-jig.

This immediately struck Roye as an ideal way to show off trains to their best advantage—high, eye level viewing with low thin handrails not covering the under detail. A vision came up in Guy's mind of just the kind of railway he wanted. No stations to absorb the space, just a lovely open scene where trains could be really seen and the locomotives could

comes into aeromodelling where the soldering required is very simple. Here was a new technique to learn. Fortunately again, there was a local conjuror, who made his own gear, who naturally was a good miniature mechanic, and he gave very sound lessons on soldering. There was also the good luck that nickel silver was available to replace brass as the recommended sheet metal and after one attempt to assemble an all-brass kit, brass has never found favour in the Guy Williams raw materials box except for turnings.

The first locomotive had to be Great Western, and a "Pannier" Tank as well— what a choice to start with! But it wasn't too bad and on completion was put up as a metal work piece for the craft section of a college course. Imagine Guy's disgust when the craft lecturer took one look, saw it was painted and went on to admire a shiny copper box which some other student had made out of two pieces of metal soldered together. What is art and what is craft? Why should there be this disdain among those who like to admire so called art for a representative scale model or picture?

haul scale length trains at scale speeds.

There also began a new drive for authenticity. More and more information was sought and obtained, drawings from Swindon works, visits with the camera to railway yards and depots for data then available, personal contacts and so on. The quest for better and more realistic models for Pendon was on.

John Ahern's book on model locomotives was a very valuable acquisition in the early days and the articles by Roche in the "Model Railway Constructor" proved very valuable as a source of new ideas and authentic drawings. At this time there was a very select group of

Top: Guy Williams' favourite model: the Great Western's only Pacific, No 111 "Great Bear". *Peter Williams*

Centre: GWR double-framed 4-4-0 No 8 "Gooch", the Armstrong 4-coupled express engine thought by many to be even more handsome than the famous "Dean Singles". *Peter Williams*

Left: Named after its designer "C. J. Bowen Cooke", this magnificent model represents the final design of London & North Western Railway express engines. (*Collection P B Whitehouse*). *Peter Williams*

Great Western modellers known as the "Great Western Four Millimetre Circle". This group had some very able members, and they invited Guy to join them. As they remarked—"His models *look* like Great Western Engines." Some of his early work was exhibited in the Great Western case at the Easter exhibition of the Model Railway Club.

It would be wrong to think that only Great Western engines came out of the workshop, since Guy Williams worked closely with Jack Newton of Bristol on a project to supply engines to portray the traffic at Bath Green Park station in the 1950s and produced several LMS, LNWR and SR models at that time. There were also other friends who succeeded in persuading Guy to make models of non-Great Western prototypes so that he began to have a much wider interest than before.

Making a good model demands a deal of research into the design history of the original and this delving into railway lore enables Guy to hold his own in railway circles although he is in no sense an engineer. Much to his astonishment, (but only his) he was elected Chairman of the Bath Railway Society in 1971.

All this model making naturally takes up space and the Williams household has long since given up the idea of having a second living room. His wife would like a separate dining room, but she has never been able to convince Guy that model making should be done in an outhouse or an attic! There has recently been a room available near the kitchen which is too small for anything other than a model makers' den and so to that Guy resolutely clings, claiming that he really *has* to have it to house all his books and gear.

As the history is revealed it becomes clear how Guy has progressed as far as he has in this craft of portraying locomotives in 4 millimetre scale. It is strange to find however, that he owns but one model engine—*The Great Bear* and that runs at Pendon. He feels that once the model is made that it should go somewhere where it can give pleasure to those who appreciate what it tries to say. These models are really an expression of the maker's admiration for the original and the organisations which created them.

If by making a careful authentic model, Guy Williams can recreate the thrill which the original gave to its admirers, he is more than content; and because the *Great Bear*, which he never saw, even from his pram, conjures up for him a very special feeling, it's the only model locomotive which he wants to own, of all the seventy or so engines which he has so much enjoyed making.

All models illustrated in this article are 4mm scale-EM gauge.

Below: Constructed from a kit, but with added detail, this LMS coach of the pre-steel panel era is one of a representative train of the early 1930s. (*Collection P B Whitehouse*).   *Peter Williams*

Bottom: In early LMS livery with the company's coat of arms on the bunker, No 6655 is one of Webb's 5ft 6in passenger tank engines built for the L&NWR at the close of the last century. (*Collection P B Whitehouse*). *Peter Williams*

All his life Roye has been what his mother used to call "an odd fish": original, artistic, quite indifferent to success as most people see it, and though for years unknown, an ardent pioneer and exemplifier of high-grade modelling.

He has always had many interests, but he was pointed toward his greatest one, the future Pendon, as a child in Western Australia when he was given some tinplate trains of English outline, followed by the Wonder Book of Railways. Together they gripped him for nearly ten years, fixing his mind irrevocably on the far-away railways of England. So much so that when he was eighteen he gave up a good (but frustrating) insurance job in Perth for what he rightly believed to be the more important call—to see the English railways at first hand and to model them. One day he would build a layout here which would be really great. . . .

Roye's first railway loyalty was to the London & North Western, but this line had recently been overtaken and submerged by the LMS, and when, not long after arriving in England, he went to live with relatives near Swindon it was inevitable that the Great Western should begin to steal his allegiance.

Not only the railway, however; living in the hill village of Wanborough beside the Vale of White Horse he discovered the other thatched villages of that most beautiful area—rolling downs behind them, richly treed meadows and farmlands in front, and the main line in the midst of the Vale with its long primrose-panelled expresses which slid by but never stopped. The country remained as peaceful then as before Brunel first went there, and many of the villages almost as unspoilt.

This was a new and unexpected allegiance—an essential part of the Great Western scene which must not be separated from it in the model that was now shaping in Roye's mind. But though railway models had often been made realistically, could he reproduce such a countryside at all convincingly?

Just at that time an old thatched cottage in Wanborough, supposed once to have been an inn, was cruelly "restored" with roughcasting spread over its mellowed walls and a roof of pink asbestos. If this were the sort of sacrilege that the future might bring, it was also a phase that Roye might reverse in his model, and he began building experimentally, working out a technique as he went. He had never done any modelling before and no-one, as far as he knew, had attempted work of this kind or of the standard he was setting himself. Even the start of John Ahern's pioneer Madder Valley layout lay several years ahead. Roye was entirely alone, and everything he did had to be proved by trial and error. But it shaped well, though very slowly owing to an unavoidable exam, followed by a return to Australia for a couple of years. He was building this try-out model in the form of the inn which it might once have been, and he finished it in Australia in 1936, having thatched it with human hair. But there was no thatch out there to copy, and years later a member of the Pendon team re-thatched it more convincingly.

The inn had shown that realistic village modelling was possible, and that Roye would be able to do it. But his temperament was purely artistic and he knew he would never build the railway. For that and for all the bigger work others must be brought in to join him. In such a project a vast amount of effort would be en-

Roye England-fo

tailed and it would be wasted unless people could see what was made. This meant aiming at an exhibition model, perhaps portable, which would bring in money to meet its obviously great cost. On the principle that it is better to give than to gain, Roye took it for granted that the work would be voluntary; and this, of course, would make possible a far higher standard than could be attained by commercial means. Any profits would be devoted to charity.

Here, already, was the basis of Roye's life work, and it has changed very little from that day to this. He was an optimist, to say the least, for he was then doing only a part-time job with literally no money behind him, he had no particular training to fall back on, and he knew no-one who was likely to be interested in such a

specialised and demanding venture. His friends told him it would be a miracle if ever he got it under way, but Roye was not to be put off, and with nothing more to bring to it than faith, enthusiasm and some modelling skill, he pressed ahead.

By now he was living near Bristol, and since he is a Christian his first attempt was in the form of a Church guild—the Guild of Saint Aidan. Its slogan was "Miniature Reproduction in the Service of Missions". With the farcical sum of 3s 5d in hand (17p) he founded it on St Aidan's Day, 31st August, 1939. Britain became embroiled in the Second World War three days later.

A more disastrous time to float a new scheme could hardly be imagined, but he persisted and despite all difficulties it prospered for several years, with an

Dusk at Pendon Parva. *Peter Williams*

under of Pendon

sive programme of research, making notes of hundreds of coaching and goods vehicles and taking literally thousands of photographs of them. In the Vale, too, he was systematically recording buildings for his village, and also had begun modelling the chapel group from Badbury, later to become famed for its flowers and its rabbits.

But finance was again threatening to run low. If ever he were going to get a home for the future Pendon he must do it now while something was left. Early in 1954 he more or less stumbled on the "Three Poplars" ex-pub at Long Wittenham, between Wallingford and Abingdon in Berkshire, and converted it into a Youth Hostel. This gave Pendon a ready-made public. In a large hut put up by hostellers, the Dartmoor scene was begun by Guy, and the same year visitors from outside also started coming on weekends. Pendon has been open to the public every weekend since that time.

Over the years Roye fitted in a large number of cycling trips to continue his photographing and measuring in the Vale. Change was now greatly accelerating and it was fortunate indeed that he was able to record so much precious material which, in another few years, would have been lost for ever.

But data for Pendon had to be changed into three dimensions and it may be helpful here to give a few notes on Roye's methods in modelling.

Almost the whole of his architectural work is done in card—white pasteboard from 0-5mm to 0-75mm thick—and his usual adhesive is White PVA. Walls are made in one piece, with a V-groove on the back at each corner to allow folding, and they always extend 30mm or more below the ground. This gives something to hold without fingering the watercolour, and if building on a slope there is no problem, as the ground can be added at any angle, the building actually sitting in it as it would do in the original. While still flat the walls are scored with a blunt point to represent the outline of stones or bricks—freehand for stones, ruled for brick—and are given an all-over coat of watercolour to represent mortar. The individual stones or bricks are then painted in, using different blends of colour, and often more than one coat, to give the necessary variety—a tedious job, but in the end well worth the trouble. Windows are glazed with mica (obtainable from ironmongers), the frames, which extend behind the walls, being cut from paper or very thin card. Glazing bars can also be made from the latter or from No 60 cotton dipped in watercolour and stretched when dry across the frames

Inner floors and walls must be put in for strength whether they will be seen or not. If braced sufficiently card will not warp. Roye lights his buildings with a torch bulb or similar on a stalk made of its own leads, which is inserted into a shaft of card with an aperture at the top. It can be withdrawn to renew the bulb. The shaft must be carefully placed, both to conceal the bulb and to give the lighting a natural effect, and considerable experiment (in the dark) is often needed. For this, the filament of a gas-lighter can be replaced with a 2.5 volt bulb, which gives a most useful light for testing, since its stem is thin and long enough to go up the shaft. Furniture is generally made from card about 0.3mm thick, and is painted, as usual, with watercolour. For things like tablecloths, washing on the line, the leaves and petals of flowers, and much else, Roye finds paper tissue

eventual membership of nearly 400. Roye is a pacifist—with his outlook on life he could hardly be anything else—so during the War he worked on the land, running the Guild as best he could in spare time. Its members were drawn from 32 counties of Britain, and with the help of Esperanto, which Roye speaks, from 30 countries of the world. It was hopelessly scattered and far too ambitious. All its energies went in merely keeping itself going, and worst of all, for various reasons beyond control, no modelling was being done. The War had been over for three years when Roye finally realised he had taken the wrong road, and that the Guild would have to go. Modelling must come first, and organisation follow only when really necessary.

It was 1951 when he started again,

once more completely alone with his ambitions, but as determined as ever to make a go of them. Owing to a legacy he did now have some money to spend on them, and from Steve Ryan's model shop in Bristol he bought his first engine, a Collett 0-6-2T No 5624. After this he commissioned several others and it was not till a couple of years later that he discovered they were being built by Guy Williams. This was the start of an enduring friendship and of a partnership in their respective fields of modelling which was to put Pendon on the map.

Roye now moved to Swindon, so was once more on the threshold of the White Horse Vale and at the hub of the Great Western. Everything on wheels that was GWR sooner or later came to Swindon, and for 2½ years he undertook an inten-

such as Kleenex invaluable. He paints it, in its double form, on both sides, with watercolour, hangs it up to dry, and it is then quite strong and can be cut or bent as required.

Roofs may be of tile, slate, stone or thatch, and in each case the visible roof is laid on a card under-roof supported by card partitions placed like rafters beneath it; but if sagging tiles and so on are needed, instead of fitting card beneath them strips of paper are stretched loosely between the rafter partitions, and the tiles laid on these, giving a very realistic wave. The tiles themselves are cut and laid in strips made from 0.3mm. card (almost a scale $\frac{1}{8}$in), each tile being cut and painted separately but not detached from the strip unless a very dilapidated roof is being modelled. Slates are made similarly but from paper instead of card, and stone tiles from thicker card cut with irregular edges. The finished roof must be weathered with watercolour on a brush that is no more than moist (or the existing colour will come off and ruin the effect). For thatching Roye formerly used human hair, but Paddy Burridge of the Pendon team has recently evolved an improved and very much cheaper method using tow (plumbers' hemp, regularly stocked by ironmongers) and this is now standard at Pendon. It is put on much as in the prototype—small bundles of "straw" laid from the bottom upwards, trimmed (with curved scissors held vertically), and runners added (of linen thread or wire pegged with bent entomological pins). Weathering is with Humbrol matt paint somewhat diluted, and moss can be grown on it using small lumps of either Polyfilla or wood flour mixed with watercolour.

For ground contours expanded polystyrene was tried, but it was rejected owing to its getting brittle, warping and disappearing under Humbrol paint. The Pendon technique is now a box-work of card with the contours cut in the top, mutton cloth or butter muslin over this to give continuity, Polyfilla mixed with sawdust to give strength and texture, and then the scenery. It is slow, but good, and it never moves. As to colouring, almost all scenic work is done with matt oil paints.

Trees are twisted from copper wire, painted with matt Humbrol and wrapped while wet, with paper tissue which absorbs the paint and gives the appearance of bark. The under foliage is generally of rubberized horsehair, the upper foliage varying according to the type of tree—sawdust for elms, but for oaks rubber sponge put through the mincer. The problem of chestnut leaves still remains to be solved! Final painting is done with a spray. Shrubs, bushes and smaller vegetation, as well as flowers and vegetables, are made of foam rubber, rubber sponge, rubberized horsehair, lichen, moss or paper tissue, sometimes

Top left: Primitive Methodist Chapel and Little Chapel Cottage. 7,000 bricks are individually modelled on the Chapel walls.
Peter Williams

Top right: A row of cottages modelled from Bradbury, Wiltshire. They stand about 4in high and were modelled by Roye England.
Peter Williams

Right: Holburn Farm in a new setting. Pendon Parva is a composite village, and this farm from Letcombe Bassett here adjoins a cottage from Uffington. The surroundings had not been fully modelled when the photographs were taken.
Peter Williams

with sawdust added! And for the stems of flowers Roye uses cotton, small feathers, cat's whisker, or a strand of hair. Gardens, made to Roye's standard, are the most tedious work of all, and the one in front of his Chapel group took him ten weeks working about five hours a day.

Finally, the success of all architectural and scenic modelling depends on colour. You *must* get your colour right, and this, perhaps more than anything else, is where Roye has scored, and Pendon's team with him. No hard and fast rules can be given but Roye's advice is to look consciously at colour, which is everywhere —see it critically, and when you paint don't rest till you're sure its like the real thing.

If the hostel had been less popular Roye's modelling would have gone ahead quicker, but again true to form, he had made it different from the general run of hostels, giving more freedom, much appreciated friendliness, and the added interest of Pendon. Even so, it was a struggle financially to keep going and after six years, having put up nearly 17,000 hostellers, he closed it, with regret, and took a clerical job at the M.G. car factory in Abingdon.

From Pendon's start on a bench-top in the hostel in 1954 to the showings of the mid-sixties, Roye had conducted each and every one alone but as attendances grew, particularly after the advent of the new building, a rota was formed. In 1970 Roye accepted voluntary redundancy at M.G's and thankfully began giving the whole of his time to Pendon—still, of course, unpaid, but as he sees it, no less rewarding for that. Without his increased help the conduct of the ever-more-demanding Museum would be a serious problem.

Besides his lifelong preoccupation with Pendon, Roye has a variety of side interests, and some of these have a bearing on his modelling. Cycling is a case in point, making easy his data expeditions in the Vale where very little other transport exists. Incidentally, he has covered more than 100,000 miles on his present bike and about another 20,000 on others. A very different interest of his which has furthered the model cause is writing. He is at present engaged on a "Saga of Pendon" which will tell its story from the tinplate trains of the beginning to the expanding Museum of today, with its preparations for the 70-foot Vale landscape. No-one else could write this work for Roye is the only member of the team who has known Pendon from the start and who has been intimately in touch with every phase of it since.

To sum up, apart from the actual conceiving, founding and nursing of Pendon, Roye's main contributions have been fourfold: the setting of a superlative standard and the evolving of a rural modelling technique to reach it; the documenting both of the unspoilt Vale of 1930 and of coaching and wagon stock of the same era; the designing of the composite but typical Pendon Parva village and its surrounding countryside and railways; and, at the time of writing the lifelike and very detailed construction of between a quarter and a third of its total completed buildings. No-one else had attempted such realism in scenic modelling until Roye led the way, and it is very doubtful whether anyone, apart from the Pendon team, has done so since to any notable extent—certainly not for exhibition. If you want to see Pendon's work the Museum is open from 2 p.m. to 6 p.m. every Saturday and Sunday throughout the year.

Overleaf: 7mm "Castle" class locomotive on Andrew Murray's Dean Bridge layout.
Brian Monaghan

Michael Longridge

Michael Longridge was a perfectionist. All his life he had been interested in railways, particularly in the old Great Western. He was a member of the Model Railway Club for many years, as well as the Wimbledon MRC and the Historical Model Railway Society. He also assisted in the formation of the Standards Bureau. As a craftsman he built many superb $3\frac{1}{2}$mm scale models before the war, which gained awards at the Model Engineer exhibitions, and it was through these initial models of Great Western freight stock that his reputation as a top rank model maker became known.

He wrote an article on the building of the $3\frac{1}{2}$mm rolling stock in 1938, which was published in the October issue of the "Model Railway News", and the sheer excellence of the workmanship attracted much attention from modellers and enthusiasts alike. So much so, that many were inspired to try the new art of cardboard wagon construction for themselves. This was the secret material that Michael used for his models; it consisted of $\frac{3}{4}$mm fine cardboard, impregnated with shellac varnish, which gave the material the necessary strength and permanence. The resulting tough sheet was used for the sides and ends of vehicles, whilst satin walnut wood was chosen for the roofs and floors. The long life of this material can be judged from the fact that several of these early models are still running today—25 years after building, a fact which also must reflect great credit on the master craftsman himself.

In 1945, several like-minded enthusiasts gathered together to discuss the possi-

Top: O gauge GWR 2-6-2T No 4523.
J H Russell

Centre: Open C. O gauge. Courtesy of
C.G. Bennett. *David Rudkin*

Bottom: 1914 Brake 3rd Corridor. O gauge.
J H Russell

bility of forming the GW 4mm Circle. This was another Longridge idea, in that a few chosen acquaintances, whose aims and ideals concentrated on the modelling of the Great Western items to a scale of 4mm to 1 foot, should meet regularly, have discussions, swop ideas, and eventually produce a postal portfolio for their mutual benefit. Suffice it to say, that the scheme was brought to fruition by his endeavours, and some of those enthusiasts involved became lifelong friends, still corresponding with one another, enthusing about the hobby after two decades.

Although primarily interested in HO scale, before the war Michael finally switched to the 4mm, EM track gauge, and with these fine scale standards, set to work, after the cessation of hostilities, to construct a layout based on Kingsbridge in South Devon. Knowing the area well through holidays taken at Salcombe, he made a detailed study of the complete branch line which ran from Brent to Kingsbridge, and with his usual thoroughness eventually produced what was one of the first fine-scale 4mm layouts, that are so familiar today.

He was one of the earliest to try ½mm flanges on the running wheels but as the majority of fittings in those days had to be made by hand, the running left much to be desired, and derailments were many, so much so that Michael eventually sold all his EM rolling stock, and indeed even the Kingsbridge layout complete, and started anew in 7mm fine scale.

This change was probably due to the influence of Geoffrey Mann, who owns and runs a superb outdoor O gauge line. Michael set to and produced a really wonderful model of a Great Western 2-6-2T locomotive of the 55XX class. This

engine was operated by electricity with the stud contact principle, and was a real collectors' piece. This was followed by a series of 7mm scale rolling stock, some of the finest examples of this class of work in the hobby that have ever been made.

Naturally enough, Michael became very well known in the model railway fraternity, and could always be relied upon to pass on the results of his experiments and research to other would-be serious modellers. The many photographs of his work, which appeared in the model press of 1945-47 created such favourable comment and impressed so many people, that he was frequently asked to put his methods into print in book form. R J Raymond, who in 1947 was the Editor of the "Model Rail Constructor" also prevailed upon him, and a small volume was produced in 1948 entitled "Modelling 4mm Scale Rolling Stock". It was published by Rayler of Cricklewood; copies are very difficult to obtain today, but if it is possible to locate one second-hand, it will be seen how valuable it was twenty five years ago. It opened up a completely new field of modelling opportunity, and showed the average man that fine vehicle building in the very small scales was not only feasible, but quite practical. In Michael's own words "You never know what you can do until you try, and never never say 'that's good enough' ".

Just after the war, several disciples could often been seen on summer Sundays, prowling around Great Western carriage yards and loco depots, and always in the lead with notebook, tape measure and camera would be Michael. Many pictures taken at that time just happen to get a glimpse of his

tall bespectacled figure, slightly balding, perched up on top of a locomotive tender, or crouched underneath the solebar of a dining car. When on field days, Michael was indefatigable, always first to start recording and last away. Coupled with his skill as a model maker and draughtsman, was a very comprehensive knowledge of miniature photography and armed with his Leica, he used this expertise to compile a superb collection of coaching stock pictures. Concentrating on the vehicles of the old Great Western Railway in general, and in the passenger carriages in particular, he not only photographed them, but made first class working drawings of many.

Michael was an extremely methodical man, and his coaching register is a model of precise detail. Every negative in the library is given its code number, and information is recorded, not only relevant to the vehicle pictures, but also date, place and film used are annotated. First started in 1933, the register goes on through until 1956, with a gap for the war years, and more than 900 negatives have been left for posterity. Unfortunately the first 194 are missing from the collection. If anyone can trace their whereabouts, it would be a pleasure to restore them to their rightful place.

Those who knew Michael well, were shocked and completely shattered when his sudden death was announced, in January 1958. The hobby has missed him sorely, but through his energy and farsightedness, there still remains a fund of information in the "Register" which he produced jointly with his friend and colleague, John Binney. So much so that all seekers after details of GWR carriages can still be sure of authentic data from this comprehensive source.

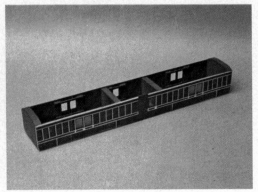

Top: Great Western Railway, clerestory corridor brake third. 4mm scale EM gauge. *Collection P B Whitehouse*

All Six pictures courtesy David Lee

Far Left: Body of a Bloater-Fish Van, unpainted and without framing irons. *David Rudkin*

Left: 6ft 6in Dean Bogie (without suspension links). *David Rudkin*

Far Left: 25ft 0¾in 4-wheeled Parcels Van body, sides completed with all mouldings, lining out and lettering. Roof to be fitted. *David Rudkin*

Left: 8ft 6in Dean Bogie. *David Rudkin*

Far Left: 48ft 6¾in Parcels Brake Van body showing mouldings applied in thick card. *David Rudkin*

Left: 40ft 0¾in Parcels Brake Van showing body shellacked ready for mouldings to be applied. *David Rudkin*

Overleaf: Bing O gauge LNWR No 819 "Prince of Wales". *(Collection P Whitehouse) Peter Williams*

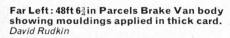

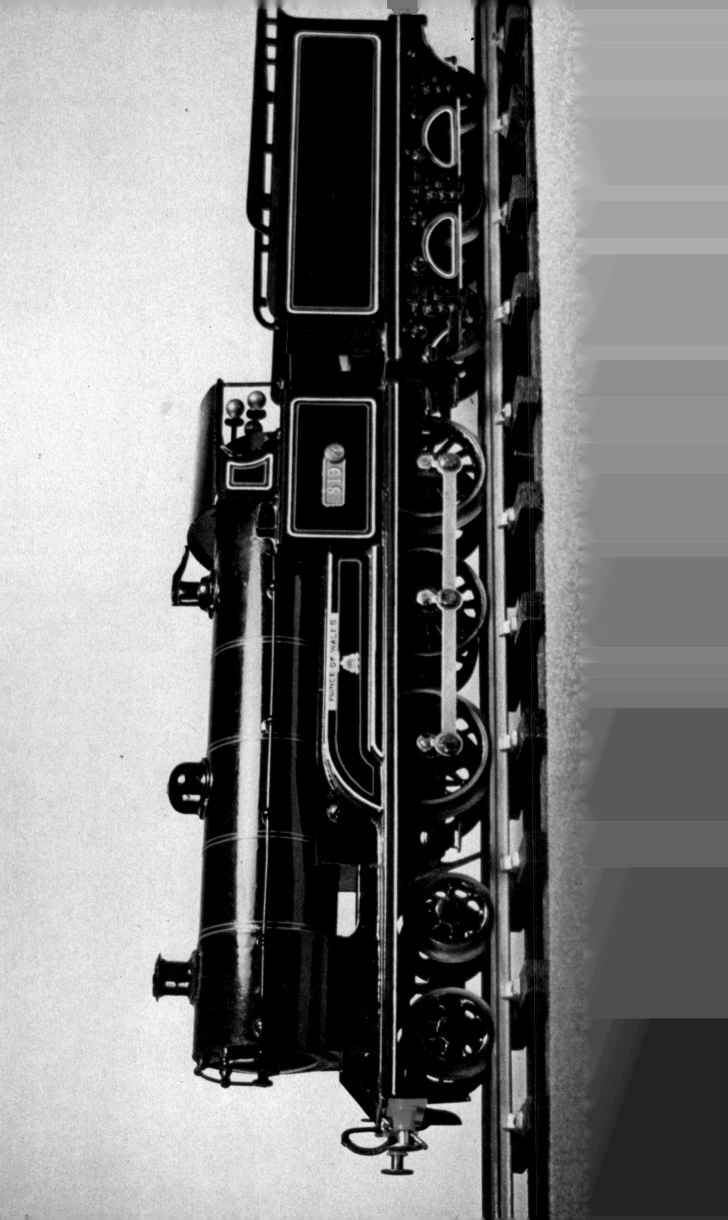

The Groves Family

H H Groves. *B Groves*

Herbert Harry Groves was born in 1882 in Chelsea, and next to his family, the delight of his life was the making of small things that worked. Before the first World War he was already well-known in model engineering circles due to the record-breaking successes of his "Irene" series of flash-steam hydroplanes, and through his articles as "H.H.G." in "The Model Engineer and Electrician" he introduced countless readers to the pleasures of model-making. Although not the first to fly a model aircraft in Britain, he was certainly among the pioneers. In those days, model aeroplanes were typically biplanes of some 6ft wingspan, built of cane and Jap silk (balsawood being then unknown) and powered by flash-steam engines; the testing of these somewhat alarming "flying blowlamps" had to be carried out on Blackheath at 5am. before the parkkeepers were about! It was during a flying competition at Hendon in these early days that he met a director of the world-famous engineering company in which he later made his career.

In 1924 electricity came to the Groves household, and for the first time the round-bed Drummond lathe, previously treadle-powered, acquired an electric motor. This lathe, incidentally, is still in the family's possession and still in first-class working order. H.H.G. quickly realised the potential of this new source of power and allied it to his other engineering skills, to the benefit of both his work and his hobby. By this time the family had progressed from a motorcycle (belt driven) to a car, paid for out of the proceeds of his writing at a time when few in his position could afford one.

The next field to be conquered was live steam. H.H.G. built locomotives in both $2\frac{1}{2}$in and 5in gauges, running them on a 130-foot track in his back garden, complete with a bridge over the stream which ran through it. The family now included a daughter and two sons, of whom Bert was particularly keen on model engineering and spent a great deal of time with his father in the workshop.

In 1937 H.H.G. retired from business due to ill-health. His definition of retirement was, however, somewhat different from that which most of us would give, for next year we find him acquiring an International 14-foot sailing dinghy—considered to be one of the tougher types to sail—and racing it successfully at Elstree and Teddington, proving just as meticulous a sailor as he was an engineer. He continued to sail it until he was 72—possibly a record age for this class of boat.

At the outbreak of the second World War, although officially in retirement, he turned his skill and machines to the war effort in the manufacture of specialised components. After the war he developed the "walking toy", whose cunningly articulated legs would swing forward in turn as it marched down a sloping surface with a wheelbarrow, on all fours or even on roller-skates. Later he returned to model aircraft and the newly-discovered compression-ignition engine, of which he built several; in the early 1950's he built the first powered model helicopter, the mechanism of which is now in a national model aircraft museum. Around this time he also made three 35mm cameras, though he never achieved one of his lifetime goals, the design of the perfect camera shutter. As if all this were not enough, he was also a talented artist, and many of his water-colour landscapes and studies of horses still survive.

But it is as a modeller of railways in sub-miniature scale that H.H.G. will really be remembered, and as so often happens, his entry into this field was the result of chance. Bert, flat on his back after a surfing accident, read through a great pile of back issues of "Model Railway News" and "Model Railway Constructor", in which he found several references to the newly-popular 2mm scale and the work of H B Whall. At the end of his enforced four weeks of idleness, Bert was itching to build a working locomotive in this scale, and at once designed what was virtually a half-scale model of the standard Tri-ang chassis to fit into the Lone Star cast model of the LMS "Jinty" 0-6-0 tank. H.H.G. agreed to make the spoked driving wheels for this; in the event, he made two sets, and himself built a second "Jinty", but this time with a mechanism based on H B Whall's design and a completely hand-built body. Both locos worked well, and still do.

At this time (the late 1950s) 2mm scale was still generally regarded as a gimmick: something on which an exceptional model engineer could demonstrate his skill rather than a serious scale for the railway modeller. H.H.G. and Bert got down to the task of getting the remaining bugs out of the scale, Bert tending to concentrate on track and other matters requiring careful handwork, and H.H.G. on the machine work at which he was so skilled.

H.H.G.'s experience of electricity told him that the smaller a motor is, the faster it must run to develop power. The locomotive chassis, therefore, had noticeably higher gear ratios than were usual in OO gauge; they also had ball-bearings for the armature shafts and other precautions to minimise friction at the high-speed end of the system. He also wisely avoided rubbing contacts for electrical pick-up; each chassis had thick phosphor-bronze frames insulated by plastic spacers, the axles being split and fitted into nylon

Below: Bert Groves holds one of his father's locomotives. *B Groves*

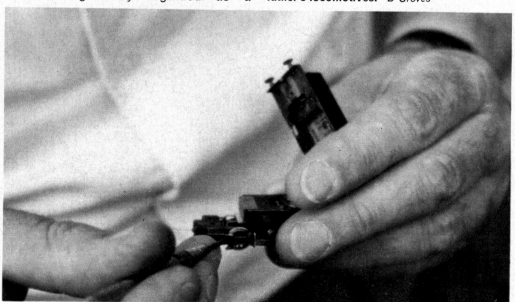

muffs so that current was collected directly from the wheels. The result of combining these features with his superb workmanship was a dozen tiny locomotives, mostly under two inches long, with a degree of realism, controllability and reliability in service seldom equalled by models, either hand-built or commercial, in OO gauge. Regrettably, it has to be said that although a few Continental manufacturers have adopted some of his design features, to the great benefit of their products' reputation, in Britain H.H.G. remains very much a prophet without honour.

Bert, meanwhile, tackled the problem of permanent way. Starting from H B Whall's well-tried system, in which the rails were soldered to rows of brass pins driven into the baseboard, Bert refined the rail section and carefully calculated the clearances to produce a set of measurements which gave not only reliable running but also complete compatibility between layouts, so that a modeller using these standards could run his stock on anyone else's railway. He also painted and assembled the rolling stock, using many parts moulded in plastic by his father using home-made dies and injector, and a half-scale version of the "Alex Jackson" auto-uncoupler developed by H.H.G. using phosphor-bronze wire .006in in diameter.

The pinnacle of the Groves' locomotive development was a BR Class 3 2-6-2T, No 82024. During a holiday in Bude they took some 60 photographs of this locomotive, and Bert spent an hour on top of it noting details of pipework which did not show in ground-level shots. A further source of information was a $1\frac{1}{2}$in:1ft works print of the prototype. The finished model, so detailed that in a photograph it is almost impossible to guess its true size, is a faultless performer, with ample hauling power and able to run reliably at any speed from a scale walking pace to

over 70mph.

All this development took place on a fairly large sectional layout which father and son built between them. The speed at which it took place is the more remarkable as, at this time, Bert was living away from home and any joint work had to be concentrated into his fortnightly visits to his parents. Feeling a need for a separate small layout for testing, Bert bought, through a small-ad in "Model Railway News", a second layout which was to become one of the most famous in Britain, if not the world. This little line represented a typical country branch terminus and was laid with early flat-bottom rail; Bert got it working and modified the turnouts to suit the finer wheel standards. On taking this layout, which had really only been intended as a test track, to Keen House (headquarters of the Model Railway Club) they were immediately invited to show it at the next Easter exhibition.

Thus committed, Bert and his father began a race against time. The whole of the track was relaid to fine scale standards, based directly on the Platelayers' Manual, for improved appearance, and a new section, incorporating an engine shed and a goods yard, was added. Working signals, with incredibly fine lattice posts made up from wire, and telegraph poles were added, and H.H.G. built two automatic turntables, one of normal size for the loco depot and the other, large enough to turn a complete train as a unit, concealed under a hill at the "country" end of the layout. The first words Bert remembers being able to read

were "Rydes Hill" on the label of the old Drummond lathe, and in their honour the layout was named Rydes Vale.

The layout was exhibited in 1961 and again in 1962, the two again dividing the work between them according to their skills. Bert ran the layout, giving a series of 20-minute performances each including some 300 movements, while H.H.G. serviced the locos and explained their constructional methods to the public. Both found the week's duty at the show exhausting but immensely enjoyable; H.H.G., though normally quite a shy person, could be seen chatting with the animation of one half his age under the influence of so many kindred spirits, and Bert, already more extrovert than his father, developed a skilled showman's patter using each time a selected small boy in the middle of the audience to concentrate attention, and involving such tricks as a moving shunter who "uncoupled" wagons in the yard and a whistle at each end to draw the audience's attention to the appearance of the next train (or, occasionally, away from a malfunction!).

Running such a small railway at a public exhibition has, naturally, its special hazards. Hairy tweed jackets in particular are sudden death to small locos, the moulted hairs causing electrical contact troubles and occasionally getting wound round the gearing or commutators. However, once a problem is defined, one is half-way to solving it; Bert's regular cleaning of the track kept the reliability good and typically captured enough "tiffle" in a week to fill a 100-

Far left: Bert Groves and a crowd of young enthusiasts at the Model Railway Club Exhibition at Central Hall, Westminster.
B Groves

Below: "H.H.G." and Bert operating the "Ryde Vale" layout at the Model Railway Club at Central Hall, Westminster.
B Groves

Bottom: A shed scene on the "Ryde Vale" railway. On the turntable is the famous BR 2-6-2T.

cigarette box! Know thine enemy!

The success of the model's showing was so exceptional that the Groves were invited to give a return showing in 1965. H.H.G. died in January of that year, but Bert ran the layout solo—on the last day he was so tired he had forgotten which switch to throw to start his car to get the layout home. Few model railways achieve the distinction of being asked to appear three times at an M.R.C. exhibition, and fewer still that of being talked about eight years after their last appearance; the Rydes Vale line has become something of a legend, not only because of its exquisite detail but because it *worked*, destroying once and for all the hoary old myth that a small, fine-scale layout cannot stand up reliably to continuous working.

Many professional railwaymen visit the MRC show during their off-duty hours, often straight off the footplate and still in their working clothes and Bert still remembers with pleasure the days of chatting with such a knowledgeable and receptive audience. The general public's most frequent question was "Are you a watchmaker by trade?" "No," smiles Bert (who is actually a Post Office engineer) "I put up telegraph poles".

Right: The 2-6-2T halts at a scale lattice-post signal. *B Groves*

Below: A scene on the "Ryde Vale" railway. *B Groves*

OUTSHOPPED FROM ONSLOW WORKS

Almost since the inception of real railways, there have been model railways and normally model design has kept pace with prototype design, often in a simplified and schematic way, until a degree of sophistication has been reached. Visitors to most railway museums will see simple steam locos (piddlers) and highly sophisticated models, coal fired and almost precise replicas of the real thing.

Electric locos have also been built, more or less like the working prototype but because of the available size of the electric motors their actual drive was anything but prototypical.

Shunting the Type 4 is very easy, using the plug-in manual control box.   *Stewart Hine*

131

Diesel locomotives have been treated in a much more cavalier fashion. In the small scales, of course, they are just boxes with electric propulsion, some of them superbly detailed and some of them with even a desultory attempt to make them sound like diesels. In the bigger scales, alas, they are really mainly lawn-mower engines, driving the wheels through sprockets, gears and clutches. One or two valiant efforts have been made by French model makers to reproduce an internal combustion locomotive using small petrol engines. This was again designed for the larger scales. The first attempt ever of producing a scale model diesel hydraulic locomotive was made in 1962. A very different approach was needed as there were virtually no drawings and very little information about the behaviour of small scale hydraulics transmitting quite considerable powers. The Onslow Works team, which has now specialised in the original design of small model diesels, has varied in composition. Experts in all fields have joined

and subsequently left the team according to their own interests. Since its inception this team has now produced two distinctly different types of diesel locomotives, using the criterion of a genuine diesel motor propulsion. The scale decided upon was gauge 1 (1/32) full scale. Originally a start was made with a Hymek type 3 locomotive. Although it would appear logical to make a diesel electric loco, it was thought that electric efficiency and transmission problems were at that time too difficult to deal with.

The design team found itself unable to fit the motors of the right size into the bogies or produce a generating set of adequate power. Diesel mechanical transmission was thought unrealistic because of gear box and clutch problems and so the only avenue open at that time was to design a diesel hydraulic locomotive.

The Hymeks of the Western Region, made extinct in late 1975, were the smallest and most attractively designed locomotives to choose as a prototype. The first choice of a diesel (model diesel, of course) motor was the Taplin Twin Marine Motor; water cooled, it delivers well over .75 of an hp with a revs range of between 500 and 10,000rpm, and it could easily be accommodated inside a gauge 1 body. A bread board mock up was then made of all the relevant working parts: the motor, a Plessey FP3 torch igniter pump and a RM gun turret actuator, which is in fact a revolver barrel ball motor and was used as the final drive.

On trial, it was found that the mismatch between pump and hydraulic motor produced just about the right reduction but a further reduction gear was needed between engine and pump to stop the transmission fluid cavitation at high speed. This section of the design was simple; totally empirical and successful. But the translation of a schematic working system into a proper locomotive took over three years. The design of an adequate cooling system for the motor and the design of the reversing valve took a long time. The valve itself turned out to be rather more sophisticated than its designers had originally imagined, as it involves laminar flow principles.

The whole structure was assembled and proved totally unworkable. Hydraulic resistance in the pipes was so severe that no power was transmitted and the whole model finally disintegrated with a spectacular bang at about four thousand pounds per square inch. Most items left after this explosion were about the size of a thumb nail. Nothing daunted, another model was built and this time the piping system was radically redesigned. An efficient silencer was fitted to the motor, the cooling improved, a much better reduction box was made, the control valve redesigned with larger porting and the loco tried again. It performed adequately, but of course more work had to be done to fit it all into a locomotive. Cardan shafts to drive both bogies, adequate fuel tanks and a simple and efficient starting method had to be devised. The starting relies on an electric drill with a dog turning the diesel motor until it fires. A body was made of brass, properly painted and the loco put into service. And that's where the interesting phenomenon occurred. Despite its good performance, being a diesel, it was very unpopular with most Gauge 1 Society members. It stinks prototypically, drips oil from time to time and is a trifle noisy.

According to the log for the locomotive it requires good maintenance but

proves to have a ninety-nine per cent availability factor. At the time of writing, it has completed fifteen hundred actual working hours and is in the shops for reconstruction. Its internal appearance has always been a bit messy and as a great deal has been learned by the Onslow Works team, they are now planning to redesign certain sections of the loco incorporating such refinements as prototypical springing, self starting and simpler and better pipe work, a completely clean and drip free exhaust and a non-leaking hydraulic system.

After this locomotive had been exhibited at a model railway exhibition where it had aroused considerable interest, a new recruit to the Onslow Team queried the lack of interest in electrical transmission. A challenge was immediately issued for him to help with the design, or admit that it was impossible. This technique has always produced new recruits to the team and did not fail here! However, the resultant locomotive underwent an even longer gestation period than the Type 3. It was decided in this case to make no compromises to model bashing at all but produce a small prototype locomotive. So the most attractive prototype, the Brush Type 4 was selected, partly because of its good looks and partly of its space.

The first problem was to find motors which could be axle hung and nose suspended. The search for these motors was world wide, going from Switzerland to the United States and Japan. Eventually it was found that a Strombecker Dragster Motor could be made to fit between the wheels if it were modified and fitted with ball races. Its power

characteristics multiplied by six would be adequate for the locomotive and so it was decided that at least the bogies would be no major problem. This is where the design pattern of the Type 4 radically differs from the design of the Type 3, because no empirical work was done but every single parameter was calculated and every single component was drawn before being made. The bogies and their suspension, including primary and secondary springing, were copied from the Brush Type 4 drawings, and even the motor suspension was scaled down. But there the work rested for some time because no suitable generator came to mind. Eventually a member of the Onslow Team suggested a motor-cycle generator, which could also be used as a dyno starter. So a generator was acquired. It just fitted into the loading gauge but the electrical design had to be carefully calculated. It was then decided to use an (A/C) alternator to excite the field windings via a rectifier bridge and to couple the motor permanently to the generator and thus produce a self supporting "power egg". With this in mind, the whole unit was drawn out and all the bits and pieces for it made.

Refinements such as an integral water-pump, a bell housing containing a fan unit for the radiator, a silencer detuner which also acts as an oil separator were designed. The whole power egg was to be suspended on anti-vibration mountings in the frame. A complete assembly drawing, tank mountings drawings and frame drawings were prepared. From these drawings it was possible to decide which parts would have to be fabricated

Opposite page top: The Brush Type 4: the body still requires detailing and painting.
Stewart Hine

Left: The first gauge 1 diesel: the Hymek on a goods train passing Onslow East Junction.
Stewart Hine

Opposite page bottom: "Works photograph" of the Brush Type 4 with the covers removed.
Stewart Hine

and which parts would have to be cast. Wooden models were made of the pump and the bell-housing and the end plates to the generator. The pump impeller was made and fitted to the motor. The bell-housing and outrigger mountings for the engine were cast and fitted, the generator end plate was prepared and an extra winding fitted for starting and a three phase alternator was made from a speedometer drive (ex military) by fitting two button magnets as a rotor.

But before the assembly, the generator was tried out with one bogie and seemed to meet the specifications which had been calculated. Once the power egg was assembled, the only remaining problem was to produce an adequate coupling between motor and generator. As there was to be no separate fly wheel but the kinetic energy stored in the mass of the shaft and rotors was deemed adequate

Below: Not all the Onslow locomotives are diesel: "King James I" being steamed ready for a run. *Stewart Hine*

for the purpose, a coupling, which allowed for minute misalignment on one hand, and on the other hand, was able to transmit a reciprocating load, proved extremely difficult to make. Several designs were tried and failed almost immediately, until finally a Fiat wheel hub and spline shaft were tried out and met with instant success. The power egg produced sufficient output and the circulating pump worked very well. All that remained now was to design the water system and the fan unit. Here again calculations alone proved inadequate and finally the fourth radiator showed signs of promise. An in line impeller was tried on the generator shaft but did not produce enough draught. Finally, an impeller wheel was made, a special nose was fitted to the bell housing and there again, only the third one really worked. The whole unit was then fitted on to the frames. The silencer detuner was connected to the exhaust manifold and a split tank provided to take the fuel and the overflow oil from the silencer which could be dumped at will instead spreading over the track. The locomotive was ready for its first test and performed superbly.

The next step was to design and fit the control gear together with a wandering lead for shunting. So far the actual speed control is very simple and depends on throttle settings but it is planned to fit electronic controls, a battery for lighting automatic reversing and other refinements in due course. Both cabs were prefabricated from brass and fitted on to the frame. The body shell was bent up from one single sheet of aluminium. Before the roof apertures were cut, the design team visited a British Railways depot to measure up one specific engine —the number of which this Type 4 will carry. As a result of this visit the overflow tank venting was fitted to where the train heating boiler's exhaust normally goes and all the louvers and doors were sketched and incorporated in a line drawing. The next step is to cast brake blocks, sanding gear and many of the other small fittings in white metal so that the locomotive will be as near a copy of the prototype as possible. Painting will be done by spraying, makers' plates have

already been etched and so a diesel locomotive "comme il faut" will join the stud.

Meanwhile, test runs are being made continuously and it looks as if the cooling system may still need some attention but the Onslow Team already have an engine which will start at the push of a button and haul continuously 1.5kgs on the draw bar, without fuss and without slipping. What is more, when using the remote controller or driving the loco on its throttle, its behaviour is remarkably like that of its big sister—probably the only model that will inch away keeping full power.

It is felt that pioneering in this field is necessary because with forthcoming electrifications the diesel locomotive will disappear and it would be a pity if this development of railway engineering remained unmodelled.

The Onslow Team challenges all of the many railway modellers to produce working diesel locomotives. The ground work has now been done and it is really no more difficult to make one of these exciting machines than it is to make a steam locomotive. Not satisfied with

original design, the Onslow Team also converted two commercially available "diesel" locomotives, ie Marklin and Lehmann Diesel Outline Locomotives, into accumulator electric locomotives. That means genuine prime movers. The German member of the Onslow Team, an electronics specialist, provided an elegant solid state chopper circuit which will allow the locos to crawl at 10mm per minute, or to run freely at scale 50kph. The accumulators were either SAFT or DEACS and have proved extremely competent. For the young diesel driver, these locos represent a simple first stage to driving. From there on it is not very difficult to drive a genuine Diesel locomotive.

And now a word about the line. The track mileage is about 300ft most of it double track with considerable gradients (ie 1 in 70) which tend to stress most engines to the full. There are two main stations and a high viaduct to complete an oval. Block instruments, ex GWR, and telephones are needed for full scale operation. Normally each engine is allocated a driver who has to run his train in accordance with the signalman's instructions and continuous train movements are logged and monitored. But the line can also provide an excellent test bed when operated under the one engine in steam principle. The rolling stock is varied and although there are ten shells of SP coaches available they have not yet been made up. Onslow works will go into mass production of bogies in due course. There are about thirty goods vehicles of every type and vintage, from modern UIC stock to ancient GW and NE stock. It has been found that with rolling stock, as with locos, sprung vehicles ride very much better than unsprung and that a heavier train seems to give an altogether better performance though it makes the locomotives work harder. The biggest problem on the line, however, is maintaining the alignment and recently a laser has been found extremely useful and time saving.

It's even in the field of steam locomotives that the Onslow Team has been able to produce exciting innovations. Super efficient boilers designed and calculated for maximum heat transfer and minimum heat leakage have been constructed. A new type of "Scharfenberg" coupling between tender and locomotive has been devised to allow instant coupling of draw bar and liquid connections without unions and screw fittings. A new type of gas firing, using a flameless combustion is being experimented with and Onslow Works have a GW steam railcar on the stocks.

But the next step in development of modern motive power which occupies the "think tank" is the design of a small but efficient gas turbine which could be made to drive an alternator. Although this sounds very far fetched it is by no means impossible and it's just exactly here where model engineering and real engineering once more meet, because if a three horse power gas turbine with all its ancillary gear can be produced in this small scale, it will surely have considerable industrial and commercial applications. The lesson learned from all this is that *a team* is necessary to produce innovations and if Onslow Works had a coat of arms the motto would be borrowed from the Austrian Coat of Arms: viribus unitis—with united effort!

ARCHANGEL MODELS

When, at some date remote in the future, the social habits of the 20th century are investigated and written down, the development of model railways will have its share of scholarly attention. In this connection some eagle-eyed historian will doubtless comment upon the extent to which so many model railway enthusiasts, while professing to worship the steam locomotive, in fact, restricted their attention to their idol's outward appearance. They count the rivets in his skin, and make sure that the same number appear on their model, yet when it comes to his insides, they rip out all the hot, wet, messy guts, and replace them with a tidy little electric motor. Not for them the loud exhaust and shrieking whistle, the touch of hot metal and damp drifts of steam, the glare of the fire and the array of levers.

Many railway modellers sincerely regret this, and blame it on necessity, "It's the steam itself that's difficult," they say. "We can scale most things in OO and O and 1; You can pick up our ballast with tweezers, and you'll find each piece just right. But we can't make scale steam. Steam at sixty pounds to the square inch has just as much urgent energy in a model as it has in a full size locomotive,

and when you try to let it out in the form of rotary motion, it just goes mad. It's all or nothing—and you can't run a railway like that. Your timetable can't be worked, and your best rolling stock gets involved in dreadful catastrophes . . . No, you can't have small-scale steam . . .".

Yet the basic fact remains that a model of a steam locomotive should be driven by steam; and indeed the sight of a modern small scale live steamer behaving itself, and running to time, and leaving a delicious smell behind it, never fails to stir the modeller with a desire to run the Real Thing. If only, he says . . . If only they all went like that. If only I could afford it. Well, the modern small scale steamer does go like that. And it doesn't cost more than good quality electrical gear, either.

The trouble with small scale steam is that it is overshadowed by the ghosts of the Age of Tinplate. Bing and Marklin, Greenly, Bassett-Lowke and Bowman. These, the great model builders of the old days, left several serious problems unsolved in the design of steam locos for Gauge O and Gauge 1. The first concerned steam-raising within an internally-fired boiler. A boiler for Gauge O can be as small as 5½in (140mm) in length

by 1¼in (35mm) in diameter, and a fire confined in a tiny box at one end of it and led through to the smokebox along narrow copper pipes, will not get much air. If it burns solid fuel, it will give up the unequal struggle and die. If it uses methylated spirit fed via a valve, it will drip down and burn on the track. Today, this problem is easily solved by using a miniature low-voltage electric motor to drive a fan. The spigot of the fan is inserted in the chimney top; the fan draws the fire; and when steam is raised, the blower valve or the exhaust blast takes over, exactly as on a full size engine.

But miniature electric motors were not available to the commercial model-builders of the Age of Tinplate, and so they gave up internal firing except on their largest models, and for the general market that bought Gauge O and Gauge 1 models, they supplied externally fired engines, which in most cases retained

Bottom: Great Northern Railway Stirling 0-4-2 after painting. *J Wheldon*

135

'fifties, Bassett-Lowke listed but one, their well-known 2-6-0. This was a curious mixture of soft-soldered tinplate superstructure, a pot-type boiler, and steam-roller wheels devoid of axle bearings. It was not very efficient; it was unreliable out of doors. It was certainly not a 'modern' design.

If you wanted a live steam engine that was internally fired and of excellent material quality, you had two choices. You could build it for yourself—but this took a long time (even supposing you possessed the necessary skills), and unless you could guarantee your workmanship, you might end up with something rather immobile—very nice in the showcase, but not quite the thing to put on your best express on the day friends have called to see your railway. Generally speaking, people who build locomotives as a hobby, and do it well, have insufficient time to develop their railways. You could order a machine from a professional engineer. It would be unique, and it would also be very expensive; so much so that you might find yourself querying whether the sight and the smell were really worth ten years of your pocket money. And, dare it be said, some very expensive professionally hand-built steamers have actually needed coaxing to keep them going . . .

This was the small scale steam situation until 1968, when Archangel Models of High Wycombe decided to intervene, and make the Real Thing work like—the Real Thing. Archangel worked out designs for quantity-produced live steamers in Gauge O and Gauge 1 that would satisfy three basic requirements: They would make abundant steam under all conditions. They would use it with economic efficiency. And—equally important—they would look as handsome and well-proportioned, in steel, brass and copper, as any electric powered model. And this they have done. The designs have proved eminently successful. The locomotives are beautiful to behold, they run like watches, and are now to be found in action all over the world.   ·

the character of simple toys.

With the fire burning in a row of wicks below the boiler there is never a shortage of air. On the other hand there is often too much—and this time the fire can die of exposure. Externally fired toy engines have long been known as "pot-boilers", and the boiling of their pots was ever uncertain. One can stand beside a toy pot-boiler out-of-doors, and see the flames flaring out horizontally, trying to fry the leaves on the nearby hedge. The breeze may be only moderate, yet, coming from the side, it can be enough to prevent that locomotive from moving itself.

With those earlier models, matters were not helped by the unrealistic wheel-treads in general use, and the tendency to use track having excessively tight curves. 2ft 0in radius in Gauge 1 was not unknown! It was inevitable that with steam-roller wheel treads, sharp corners, and primitive water-boiling equipment, steam powered model railways of the old days seemed to oscillate wildly between hysterical speed culminating in overturn, wheels whizzing in the air and spreading pools of burning meths; and engines that fumed and sulked in corners, reluctantly moving an inch or so when poked, while making rude sucking noises and spitting hot water from their cylinders.

So model railway operators turned to clockwork and electricity, for if the former was of restricted circuit, at least it was regular; and while the latter started off quite dangerously with toys that went (bang?) when you plugged them straight into the electric mains, they soon settled down to safe voltages and utter reliability, and graduated to the rank of Scale Model.

Steam thus languished. From its true status of the Real Thing it descended to that of uncertain toy, and after World War Two, the rise to popularity of the tiny scales OO, TT and N, and the perfection of two-rail electric operation, led to its near-complete eclipse. By the end of the

Archangel Models is the creation of Stewart Browne, still in his twenties at the time of writing. His interest in railways has been virtually lifelong; he began to model railways at about the age of 12, running a variety of lines in OO and O, and always in the garden. His first visit to North Wales came in 1963, and there, at Towyn, he encountered the narrow gauge. There, at home in a beautiful landscape, was a steam engine one could make a pet of; there was a machine with a sense of place and local service; a friendly, sympathetic thing. As the larger railways became remote and changed, Stewart began to think of the narrow gauge as the most interesting subject for modelling, and when he set up his own light engineering concern, and decided to make the renaissance of small-scale steam one of its objectives, he determined to give it a friendly, narrow gauge character. His first design was in 16mm/ft scale, to run on O gauge track; a 2-4-0T based on the locomotive *Rheidol,* which was used on the Hafan and Vale of Rheidol railways early in the century. The prototype was fired with butane, but this was abandoned in favour of methylated spirit, and subsequent variations aimed at getting yet more heat-transfer from the fire have all used this fuel.

The most striking thing about Stewart's designs, which are all his own, is the amount of working steam he can get out of a small boiler. The balance of fire, boiler capacity and cylinder dimension is a tricky business, and by no means all engineers hit it off, in either full-size or miniature practice. Indeed, some miniature steamers will pull a house for a dozen yards and then stop breathless. Others may have a more reasonable endurance, yet cannot take advantage of it because of being virtually unmanageable. But Stewart's designs work. They pull great weights; they run great

distances on small quantities of water and a reasonable fuel consumption; they are withal docile, and responsive to the controls. They look like high-quality hand-made models, exquisitely beautiful in brass and copper and polished steel, and they come on the market at reasonable prices. Customers calling at Archangel Models to collect their models may see their own, or some other newly-completed machine, being road tested; and if they are newcomers to live steam, they will be given steam-raising and driving lessons. Perhaps a Stirling 0-4-2 and a Caledonian Single are about to make their first journey. Unpainted, they stand glittering in their natural metallic colours, and the rapidity with which they raise steam never fails to surprise, as does the regularity with which they haul their test train 450 yards or so without attention, running with watch-like precision. The safety valve tell-tale indicates the state of the boiler; and at the end of the run, attention to the hand-pump quickly lifts feed-water through the clack-valve into the boiler.

Gauge O is Stewart's favourite; it enables him to design both standard and narrow-gauge for one track—and of course the narrow-gauge locos, built to a scale of 16mm to the foot, are happy on curves as sharp as $4\frac{1}{2}$ft radius, despite their size. It is undeniable that the Welsh narrow-gauge lines are the only ones surviving complete and entire as steam railways, and this, plus the large size of the models, gives the latter a powerful attraction. These engines, you feel, are very real work-ponies.

His first design, the Rheidol 2-4-0T, while still exceedingly popular in its several variant forms, side-tank, tender-tank, saddle-tank, has since been joined by other designs; Dolgoch and Prince of Wales. They can be seen trundling around garden railways in places as far

apart as New Zealand, South America, France and Switzerland, beside England, Scotland, Ireland and Wales. The greatest endurance recorded is 9 scale miles with a train of 2 bogie coaches and a pair of four-wheelers. These tall-chimneyed engines, the outside-framed ones with flashing fly-cranks, appear indescribably charming as they bring their trains into view through a rock garden; they wear the livery of their owner's choice, and their own name on a brass plate; they have real whistles that perfectly reproduce those still to be heard among the mountains of North Wales; and you can tell the state of the boiler by the needle on the pressure-gauge.

Now, one of the characteristics of the steam engine is that it has to be tended; it doesn't like to run a very long way without feeling a reassuring hand on its controls, and this characteristic is undoubtedly reproduced in the miniature loco. Archangel engines can be "set", and relied upon to do their 450 yards or so—but it is necessary to keep an eye on the boiler and pump in more water when it is needed. Stewart began to cogitate the idea of an externally-fired engine, a super pot-boiler that would not let its fire blow out in a breeze; that could run literally all day with but the minimum of attention; that would not—as with the earlier, soft-soldered commercial pot-boilers—suffer

Top Left: Pre-Archangel: Earlier externally fired small steam engines did not work happily out of doors—the wind blew the fire out! Here is a Bassett-Lowke Mogul with additional side plate to keep the wind out and the fire in. *J Wheldon*

Bottom Left: Stewart Browne with the GNR Stirling 0-4-2. *J Wheldon*

Top Right: Ready for the "Right Away". An Archangel narrow gauge type model on Jack Wheldon's O gauge garden railway. *Robin Butterell*

disastrous damage if it chanced to boil dry. The result was *Brick*, a 0-4-0T based on a Bagnall-designed industrial works locomotive. *Brick* does all the things required of him. He will run in a gale of wind, haul more than prototypical loads, shunt at a scale walking pace, take a train of tourist coaches at a scale 20mph. Above all, he is the perfect complement to the internally-fired engine, for he needs so little tending that he allows the single-handed operator to run two in steam with perfect safety. His only drawback is that until the paint manufacturers come up with coloured heat-resistant paints, he must wear black-and-brass livery. *Brick* has proved so successful and so popular that Stewart has taken his mechanical characteristics and fireproof construction to power a new design; a two-cylinder six-coupled loco. This, believe it or not, is a single-Fairlie based on the old Welsh Highland *Snowdon Ranger*, with a swivelling steam bogie, and a carrying truck under the bunker. It looks, and performs very well at the head of a mixed "tourist train" of Festiniog, Talylyn, Welshpool, Corris, Rheidol and Lynton and Barnstaple wooden rolling stock – vans, coaches and trucks, which are turned out to order from another department of Archangel Models.

Are there any secrets to this uniquely successful combination of appearance, quality and performance in commercial live steam? How does Stewart Browne manage to keep the "hand-made" style, with goods produced in quantity?

So far, this expertise has given us a rich variety of locomotive type; a Victorian single, mixed traffic workhorses, industrial potboilers, and Welsh mountaineers, including that single, Fairlie. Whatever will be the next new locomotive to emerge from the Archangel shops we cannot say, but it will continue the Archangel tradition of putting live steam on the practical working roster of modern small-scale railways.

Stewart served his apprenticeship with a firm specialising in all-round prototype, one-off and batch production, and perforce he acquired expertise—speed with accuracy—in every aspect of the work. Fine instrument work, brazing, welding, silver-soldering, engraving, sheet-metal work, tinsmithing, machine tool setting up and operation, jig-making, pattern-making and casting. And, equally important, he acquired a sound understanding of the economics governing light engineering. He could work out a design, programme its manufacturing sequences, and cost it accurately, and so, when he made his decision to launch himself as a professional engineer, he was able to realise his concept of what a commercial live steam model should be, and put it on a sound industrial basis. It is a shrewd, highly-professional balance, that gives much of the refinement associated with the individually ordered model, with the low costing of the quantity-produced model; a balance that can be maintained only by expertise in design and production techniques.

Below: Steam in the garden: a Stewart Browne live steamer with narrow gauge type wagons. *J Wheldon*

Right: "Rosemarie" another Stewart Browne live steamer. *J Wheldon*

Bottom Right: "Prince of Wales": inspired by the Vale of Rheidol engine. *J Wheldon*

**EM gauge LNWR "George the Fifth" class
4-4-0 "Dovedale" built by Guy Williams.**
P B Whitehouse Collection

MINIATURE RAILWAYS AND THEIR BUILDERS

Henry Greenly

(1876-1947)
Ernest A Steel

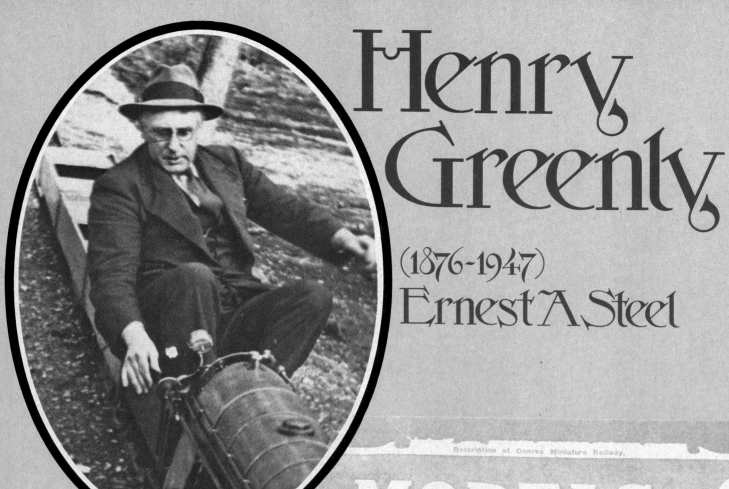

As the result of a meeting of student apprentices at the Royal Aircraft Establishment, Farnborough, early in 1919, a model engineering club was formed. Henry Greenly had come along to give a talk and to display a number of working models of steam engines and aircraft—a model aeroplane club was already in existance, it having been established in 1915. Having been employed at the RAE during the 1914-18 war, Greenly returned to private practice, working freelance again at home and editing his magazine "Models, Railways and Locomotives" now that the war was ended.

The year 1919 can be said to have been the midway course of Greenly's career. It began in 1895 when he was nineteen years of age and an engineering student already participating in a scheme to establish a national railway museum—he was elected on to the committee—and concluded on his enforced retirement due to ill health during the second World War, thus spanning a period of nearly half a century.

It was perhaps inevitable that Greenly should turn to locomotives and railways for a career, due mainly to other Greenly's having been closely associated with railways since their early days and particularly with the Great Western Railway. Indeed the young Henry had come to familiarise himself with railway practice in and around Paddington Station and the works at Westbourne Park, his home being but a few minutes walk to Queen's Park.

Following both an engineering and architectural course at the Regent Street Polytechnic, London, Greenly joined the

Right: A typical front cover of Greenly's magazine (the colour was changed monthly), and an advertisement of the period.

Above: Henry Greenly on a test run of a LNER Pacific locomotive on the 7¼-in. gauge railway at Kenton, Middlesex in 1936.

Far Right: The 15-in. gauge "Little Giant" at Eaton (1905). Standing from left to right: Messrs. W. J. Bassett-Lowke, Green (works' foreman) H. Greenly, Henry Lea (on engine), F. Smithies, and the driver's apprentice.

Right: Greenly's 7¼-in. gauge 4-6-2 American type locomotive at Kenton, Middlesex.

Right Below: "Count Louis" (Fairbourne Railway) designed by Henry Greenly and built by Bassett-Lowke in 1924 – final version of the "Little Giant" class.

Circle: Ravenglass and Eskdale 2-8-2 "River Esk", built in 1923 by Davey Paxman & Co.
E S Russell

Far Right Below: Romney, Hythe & Dymchurch Light Railway No 2 "Northern Chief". Built to ⅓ full size for the 15-in. gauge in 1925 by Davey Paxman & Co.
C M Whitehouse

Metropolitan Railway in February 1897. The next four years were to prove of considerable value to the young man in both the Company's locomotive and Surveyor's departments. There is no doubt that, if he had pursued a railway career, he might well have established himself as a competent engineer of some renown among his contemporaries. But it was not to be. Having assimilated all that he considered essential in full-size practice, he set out on an entirely new venture; one that, although totally untried in that age of individual enterprises, did subsequently enable him to work independently without being confined to a "nine-to-five" outlook for almost the remainder of his working life. From full-size engineering practice he turned to models and miniature railways.

Henry Greenly's interest in model railways and locomotives was engendered partly by the appearance of the "Model Engineer" in 1898 and partly by his frequent visits to the Science Museum, South Kensington. It was not long before he began to participate in that magazine's competitions and then later—in 1900—he met Percival Marshall, founder and editor. Then events began to move rather more quickly. Early in 1901 the young man was appointed by Marshall as technical assistant and later as technical editor. Soon he was writing articles on model locomotive construction.

Greenly's association with the "Model Engineer" continued until 1908, and it was during this period that he became well known among an ever-growing model engineering fraternity of the day: Dr J Bradbury Winter, James Crebbin, W J Tennant and many others. Whilst working with Marshall he had almost complete freedom of action in so far as he was able to work to some extent on his own account as well as for the magazine. His terms of employment were almost comparable to those one would expect today, the Victorian era having only recently ended! In this way he met many well-known personalities, names that have never really faded: Bassett-Lowke, Stuart Turner, Arthur Bond and Arthur Drummond of lathe fame. Then followed visits to Europe to meet well-known model and toy manufacturers, especially those in Germany: Marklin,

Bing, Carette and others.

In 1904 Marshall published Greenly's first book, "The Model Locomotive". Then that same year Greenly's first large-scale design of locomotive *Little Giant* was built by Bassett-Lowke at Northampton. The engine was given its trials on the Duke of Westminster's 15-in. gauge railway at Eaton, near Chester, before being put into service at Blackpool. Then followed pioneer miniature railways at Rhyl, Halifax and Great Staughton, Huntingdonshire; the last being both the 9½in and 15in gauge railways on John Howey's estate. Other locomotives were being built at Northampton for various gauges; one in particular being Greenly's heavier-type 15in gauge Atlantic of the "Sans Pareil" class.

In Europe prior to 1914 Greenly was associated with miniature railways in Belgium, France, Italy and Switzerland. Perhaps his best known project was the Lunar Park Railway in Geneva where an extensive system was laid down to include deep cuttings, tunnels and a five-span bridge over an ornamental lake.

In January 1909 the first number of Greenly's monthly magazine "Models, Railways and Locomotives" appeared. In this he was ably assisted by W J Bassett-Lowke. From time to time Bassett-Lowke would add a commercial supplement under the title of "The Oil Can". Editorially Greenly had complete freedom of action and the magazine survived down to the early 1920's when it was incorporated in a new venture, "Everyday Science".

In 1904 Greenly, now married and with

a family, moved to Watford. Here he set up his drawing office and workshop in a large house on the edge of the town. He now employed an apprentice draughtsman and in those years before the war a number of young men came to be so employed. One, who joined him in 1910, was Adrian Brough who, in later years was appointed chief engineer of a well-known engineering company in the South of England. Adrian Brough is now retired and residing in the Isle of Man where he is still engaged on making model locomotives.

It was in 1911 that Greenly first became acquainted with John Howey when attending the trials of his 9½in gauge Atlantic. This was prior to Howey laying down a 15in gauge line on which to run his "Pacific" locomotive *Gigantic*—another

Greenly design built at Northampton. Later Greenly was responsible for the design of a "Forth" bridge of timber construction for the 9½in gauge trains to run over. The bridge spanned an ornamental lake in front of the manor house. A war was to intervene before the two men were to meet again; this time to plan a project that went far to establish nationally a miniature railway system known so well today: the Romney, Hythe and Dymchurch Railway in Kent.

With the outbreak of the 1914-18 war Greenly soon switched from miniature railways to aeroplanes. Early 1915 found the family settled in Farnborough Park, Hampshire. His daily trek—either on foot or on a bicycle to the RAE—reminded him of those earlier days when he had to keep to a strict time schedule!

In spite of prevailing war conditions interest in models and railways never flagged so that, even with limited leisure at his disposal, Greenly managed to edit and publish his monthly magazine without missing a single issue throughout the war. With the appearance of the hundredth issue in April 1917, Greenly observed in an editorial that "with this issue . . . although published under the most trying conditions that could ever be imagined, we still retain the good will of nearly all our readers . . .". Already in 1915 Cassell had published Greenly's "Model Engineering".

At the conclusion of hostilities in November 1918 Greenly, together with a number of his colleagues made haste to return to private practice and to resume work that had had to be abandoned four years earlier. In this he was largely successful.

Having been settled in Farnborough Park for close on four years, the family had no desire to move nearer to London. Following the success of his last book, Greenly now set about producing three more works for Cassell: "Model Steam Locomotives" (1922), "Model Electric Locomotives and Railways" (1922) and "Model Railways" (1924). In so far as practical work was concerned, in 1920 Greenly was engaged on a 15in gauge project at Dreamland Park, Margate. As the new engines were not ready at the works, the locomotive Prince Edward of Wales was brought from Rhyl, North Wales, and put into service.

In 1921 Greenly paid his first visit to the Ravenglass and Eskdale Railway, Cumberland where Sans Pareil, together

with the Heywood locomotives, was employed. (The last occasion he had seen the Heywood engines at work was at Eaton in 1905.) A year later Greenly was appointed engineer to the R & ER, a post he held for eighteen months during which time he designed the 2-8-2 locomotive River Esk which was built by Davy Paxman & Co, Colchester.

It was during this period that Greenly renewed acquaintance with John Howey at Ravenglass. Howey was now searching for a site for a 15in gauge public railway and had made an offer to purchase the R & ER but the owners were unwilling to sell. From the North West of England Howey moved to the South East where, at New Romney, he purchased a plot of land as a first step in his great scheme: the laying down of a line across Romney Marsh to Hythe, a distance of eight miles (13 km). In this project he was joined by Greenly who, in the years from 1924 until the official opening in August 1926, attended to the negotiations with the Southern Railway, the Ministry of Transport, local authorities and landowners. There was also the design of the locomotives to be considered and attendance at the works of Davey Paxman and Company at Colchester where the engines were being built.

The histories of both the Ravenglass and Eskdale Railway and the Romney, Hythe and Dymchurch Railway have been well-documented elsewhere and so need not be recorded here. In so far as Greenly was concerned, however, his work at New Romney continued until February 1929 when by that time the extension to Dungeness had been completed. This extension made the system the longest in Britain for so small a gauge, it being no less than 13 miles (21 km.)

This writer's introduction to the little railway was in August 1927 when he met Greenly for the second time. The meeting was at Dymchurch where Greenly was attending to a fault that had developed on a locomotive hauling a passenger train to New Romney (Littlestone). The trouble having been located he mounted the footplate and accompanied the driver on the remainder of the journey. It was not until a year later that, as a guest of the Greenly's, the writer was able to travel over the whole system and inspect the workshops. Perhaps his most interesting experience was to ride on the footplate of Green Goddess to Dungeness prior to the official opening of that section of the line.

With the completion of the Dungeness extension there remained little for Greenly to do other than maintenance duties; an important task but one that proved not entirely satisfactory when dealing with other members of the staff. However, Howey had other plans for extending the line still farther: one to Sandling Junction, a distance of 1½ miles (2¼ km) from Hythe, and another beyond Dungeness in order to link up with the Rye and Camber Railway which would have extended the line another 7½ miles (12 km). However, both schemes had to be abandoned. Howey would have dearly desired to have a railway some 22 miles long whereby he could perhaps have driven his locomotives non-stop from one end of the system to the other.

Thus it came about that early in 1929 Greenly left New Romney to settle in London again. Here he rented a flat in Torrington Square, close by the British Museum and University College, until such time as he could purchase a suitable property that would provide a work-

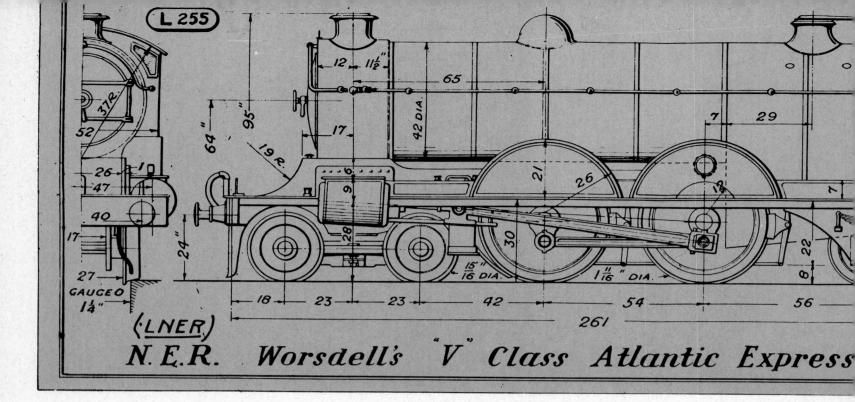

(·LNER·)

N.E.R. Worsdell's "V" Class Atlantic Express

shop and drawing office. Almost at once he was engaged on a full-size railway project for a company in West London. The work involved the re-planning of a private siding with all the essential railway equipment including a turntable. By mid-summer of that year the family was settled in Heston, Middlesex; a house that overlooked the broad acres of Osterley Park.

Greenly was now joined by his son, Kenneth, down from University College, Southampton, with an honour's degree in mechanical engineering. Later Kenneth was appointed to the Surveyor's Department of the Southern Railway, thus maintaining a tradition of Greenlys being associated with railways.

Now that Greenly was working on his own account, he re-introduced his "apprenticeship" scheme; one that had been suspended for fifteen years. The apprentice was Aubrey Smith, whose home was nearby. Smith remained with Greenly for several years and later was appointed secretary to his private limited company established in 1935. Indeed Smith became a staunch friend of the family and a great help to Mrs Greenly during her widowhood after 1947. He was an excellent draughtsman with a capacity for making fine details.

With the final crisis of 1930 and soaring unemployment Greenly reverted to his literary work and to publish articles for the model and technical press. Yet at the same time there was still a demand for his services in a field that went beyond model engineering both at home and overseas. Contact was still maintained with his old friend Bassett-Lowke who was producing model locomotives for 7¼in and 10¼in gauges. There were also several new books being published by Marshall among them being Greenly's "Planning and Layout," "Walschaerts' Valve Gear," "Signals and Signalling" and other titles. Among the Cassell "Model Maker Series" Greenly also produced "Model Steam Locomotive Construction", "Model Electric Railway Construction" and "Model Railway Construction". To further the popularity of the new "double-O" gauge (at that time fixed at ⅝in) Greenly produced the "TTR Permanent Way Manual" for Trix Limited in 1937.

Whilst Greenly's prime interest was still with locomotives and railways, he did not neglect other aspects of the model engineering hobby. Almost from the very early days attention was given to the design of stationary and marine steam engines. Thus he had assisted Bassett-Lowke and Stuart Turner. There were also his numerous articles in the "Model Engineer" on the history and development of the steam traction engine. His interest in the internal combustion engine—including the oil and gas engine for modelling—goes back to about 1909.

During the 1930s and up to the outbreak of the war in 1939, Greenly became engaged upon a number of industrial projects. Perhaps his best-known was a patent automatic train control (ATC) system for railways. In 1938 the system was given official trials on a section of LMSR track. The Westinghouse Company being interested in the system, world-wide patents were applied for, but the intervention of another war caused the project to be shelved. Arising out of his commercial patents Greenly formed a private limited company in 1934 which did not go into voluntary liquidation until twenty years later.

It was about 1934 that Greenly acted as consulting engineer to Field Place development scheme near Worthing, Sussex. Apart from the planning of the new estate, the work involved the construction of a hundred-foot span road bridge over the Southern Railway, the laying down of roads, a drainage system and the conversion of an old country house to a country club. For such a comprehensive scheme the SR agreed upon the construction of a station near the site—now Durrington Station. By 1938 the new bridge and approach road was almost completed, but further development seemed to hang-fire with the crisis of September and threat of war. Indeed, as things developed, the bridge proved to be the last of Greenly's major projects before the outbreak of war in 1939.

With the outbreak of war, Greenly once again abandoned his professional and model work and set out daily to work in an engineering drawing office in Hayes. However, due to ill-health early in 1940 he had to retire. He was now sixty-three years of age, but he did not give up entirely: once again he turned to his pen and occasionally to the drawing board. Indeed early in 1940 he received an enquiry for the design of a 15in gauge locomotive suitable for running on a continuous track with steep gradients and sharp curves. Greenly's choice turned to that of a 2-6-0 and in fact the stage was reached for the design to be discussed in detail, but now the war had taken a more serious turn with Dunkirk and the Battle of Britain. Suddenly the project was shelved.

Yet in spite of the war, enquiries continued to be received at Heston on matters concerning models in general and locomotives in particular. Evidently model makers were as keen as ever to make plans for making models at the earliest opportunity after the war was over and when materials would once again be readily available. The postponement of their plans proved to be of long duration.

Such was the state of Greenly's health by 1942, it was imperative that he should move into the country; away from his beloved drawing board—in spite of the bombings around him—and where he and his wife could obtain complete rest at their daughter's home until the end of the war.

In 1947—the year of Greenly's death—model engineering was progressing again and it was mainly due to the efforts of Mrs Lilley Greenly, with the help of members of the family that Greenly's work was kept on the main-line track. The demand for his drawings was remarkable at that period of austerity, and so it continues down to the present day. It was on the initiative of Mrs Greenly that it was decided to exhibit her husband's work at the Model Engineer Exhibition in September of that year. It was then that she took over the management of the firm until 1967, the year of her death.

What of the character of the man, Greenly, himself? In his work there was nothing he enjoyed more than being on the shop floor with the men. This was particularly noticeable whenever he was at Northampton, Colchester—and on one occasion at the GWR Swindon works—or wherever his large-scale locomotives were being built. His architectural training made him a charming companion when on a tour of the City of London and visiting its churches. The same could be said when travelling with him in Europe;

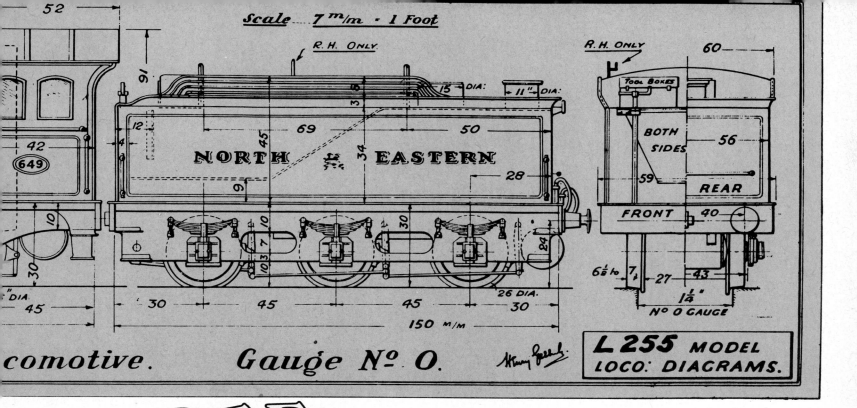

Scale 7 m/m - 1 Foot

R.H. ONLY

R.H. ONLY

NORTH EASTERN

BOTH SIDES

REAR

FRONT

TOOL BOXES

No O GAUGE

comotive. Gauge N<u>o</u>. O.

L255 MODEL LOCO: DIAGRAMS.

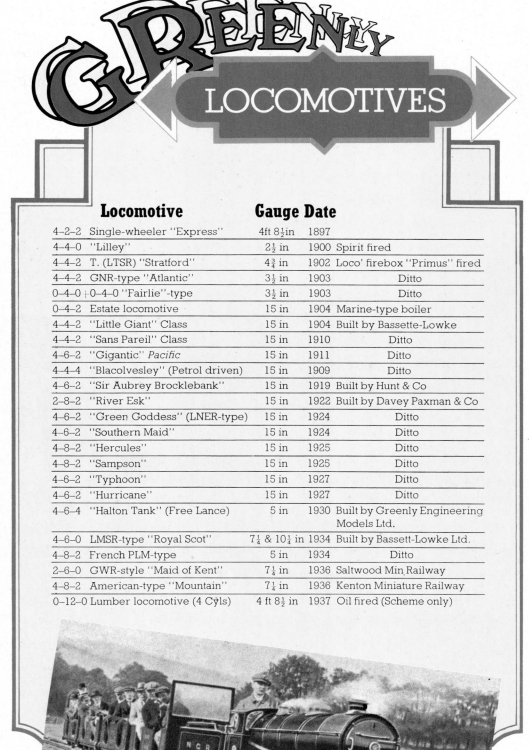

GREENLY LOCOMOTIVES

Locomotive		Gauge	Date	
4–2–2	Single-wheeler "Express"	4ft 8½in	1897	
4–4–0	"Lilley"	2½ in	1900	Spirit fired
4–4–2	T. (LTSR) "Stratford"	4¾ in	1902	Loco' firebox "Primus" fired
4–4–2	GNR-type "Atlantic"	3½ in	1903	Ditto
0–4–0 ⊢ 0–4–0	"Fairlie"-type	3½ in	1903	Ditto
0–4–2	Estate locomotive	15 in	1904	Marine-type boiler
4–4–2	"Little Giant" Class	15 in	1904	Built by Bassette-Lowke
4–4–2	"Sans Pareil" Class	15 in	1910	Ditto
4–6–2	"Gigantic" *Pacific*	15 in	1911	Ditto
4–4–4	"Blacolvesley" (Petrol driven)	15 in	1909	Ditto
4–6–2	"Sir Aubrey Brocklebank"	15 in	1919	Built by Hunt & Co
2–8–2	"River Esk"	15 in	1922	Built by Davey Paxman & Co
4–6–2	"Green Goddess" (LNER-type)	15 in	1924	Ditto
4–6–2	"Southern Maid"	15 in	1924	Ditto
4–8–2	"Hercules"	15 in	1925	Ditto
4–8–2	"Sampson"	15 in	1925	Ditto
4–6–2	"Typhoon"	15 in	1927	Ditto
4–6–2	"Hurricane"	15 in	1927	Ditto
4–6–4	"Halton Tank" (Free Lance)	5 in	1930	Built by Greenly Engineering Models Ltd.
4–6–0	LMSR-type "Royal Scot"	7¼ & 10¼ in	1934	Built by Bassett-Lowke Ltd.
4–8–2	French PLM-type	5 in	1934	Ditto
2–6–0	GWR-style "Maid of Kent"	7¼ in	1936	Saltwood Min Railway
4–8–2	American-type "Mountain"	7¼ in	1936	Kenton Miniature Railway
0–12–0	Lumber locomotive (4 Cyls)	4 ft 8½ in	1937	Oil fired (Scheme only)

historic church architecture would immediately attract his attention so that such an appeal would be induced in his companion.

When writing articles on the subject of his model work, Greenly was bound to prove controversial concerning certain aspects of design. (His smokebox-type superheaters and methylated-fired water-tube boilers for small models were cases in point; the former he abandoned at a later stage.) Yet he could hardly be accused of being dogmatic in his opinions as there was that degree of versatility in his make-up that would permit a different approach to a problem. He was ready to admit his own limitations as had been demonstrated in his lectures and articles. "It is with considerable temerity that I approach this subject" were his opening remarks at a lecture on one occasion, but it would be left to his listeners to make the final judgement. Whilst he had his supporters, there were bound to be his detractors too; a perusal of correspondence in the early magazines and journals show the extent to which controversies tended to prevail.

Greenly possessed what can only be described as an Edwardian sense of fun and good humour. He had his particular generation's enthusiasm for practical jokes which were directed not only against friends, but also against those who presumed to be the appointed authorities of particular subjects under discussion. His daughter once observed that "if there was one thing he abhorred it was pretentiousness and technical pretentiousness most of all."

To work with him was indeed a pleasure and an experience to remember —although this did not always prove to be the case with a dour Scots mechanic Greenly once employed!—as there was always a strong atmosphere of enthusiasm for the particular job on hand.

Below: Eskdale narrow gauge railway. One of the summer service trains hauled by Atlantic Type locomotive "Sans Pareil", built 1910 by Bassett-Lowke.

Early Miniature Railways

Facts about passenger carrying miniature railways in the 19th century are woefully meagre. It is known that models of locomotives began to appear very soon after the full sized prototypes had come into existence. Some of these were built as static exhibits sitting in glass cases, while others were used as demonstration models by the locomotive manufacturers themselves to illustrate their products in countries abroad where the railway was still an unknown quantity. There have always been modelmakers who have been quick to portray man's latest technological advances in miniature form, so it can have been only a short time before the models were put to practical use pulling trains on layouts inside the house and eventually out of doors.

Who made the first tempting step to actually ride behind his model locomotive will probably never be known, but one of the earliest lines that it has been possible to trace belonged to a Mr Noble who built quite an ambitious miniature railway in Argyllshire in 1852. This railway, which was built to a gauge of about 15in, ran from his house through the grounds to an artificial lake, passing through a tunnel en route. On the lake was a miniature paddle steamer to complete the picture (rather like the existing line of Lord Gretton's at Stapleford Park). It is understood that the line was in existence until the turn of the century, but nothing remains of it today.

Another early builder was Peter Brotherhood who constructed the first recorded 15in gauge locomotive, a 2-2-2 called "Pearl". The design appears to be based on a standard gauge tender engine built by Robert Stephenson for the Midland Railway. The tender no longer exists, but the locomotive has been restored as a static model and it now stands on display at Kings College, London. By the 1880s accounts began to appear of a number of private lines, mostly laid down by wealthy landowners for the amusement of their children, their friends and themselves. At this time no "standard" miniature gauges had been established so scale and workmanship varied widely.

Another interesting sideline appearing at this time was the construction of showmen's miniature railways, one or two of which have survived to the present day. Savage & Company of Kings Lynn built a number of these, the gauge being quite large, about 2ft 6in, although the circumference of the track would be under 300ft. As the curves were so sharp the locomotive was constructed with wheels smaller on the inside of the circle than on the outside. This helped to reduce wear on the treads and flanges which, otherwise, would have been considerable.

The history of the larger gauges really starts with the work of Arthur Heywood, later Sir Arthur. He lived in Derbyshire and had always wanted to become a pro-

fessional engineer, but his family, obviously considering that this was not a suitable occupation for a gentleman, dissuaded him and as a result he started work as an amateur. He set out to determine the smallest possible gauge for a railway to provide alternative transport to the horse and cart, both on large estates and for the army. Having built his own workshops at Duffield Bank in 1873, he began the construction of a railway line. His early experiments had been on the 9in gauge, which was quite satisfactory for moving fairly heavy loads, but was too narrow for carrying human passengers, because any vehicle would inevitably have a high centre of gravity and could become unstable. 15in appeared to be the minimum gauge on which it is possible for two adults to sit side by side; as a result, his line was built to this gauge. The ground was anything but flat and in the course of the continuous

run, there was a 90ft high wooden viaduct and three tunnels; the gradient and curves were extreme, the line from the workshops having a slope of 1 in 10 and at one point a 25ft radius curve.

The locomotives were very basic types, being of the 0-4-0 and 0-6-0 wheel arrangements. Although simple, they incorporated a number of interesting design points which Heywood had worked out, the most notable being a radial gear which enables the coupled driving wheels to conform to the curves of the line. Most were built with outside frames and all had launch type boilers. The latter proved to be effective on short lines when there was plenty of time to "blow-up" at the end of the run, but inadequate when used on a railway of any length, as was found later on the Ravenglass & Eskdale Railway. Much interest was engendered by the line and a number of open days were held so that

members of the public could see the railway running.

One of the people who visited the line was the Duke of Westminster's Agent from Eaton Hall near Chester. The nearest railway station to the Hall was at Balderton, three miles away, and the Duke was looking for some way of conveying coal and other materials to the estate. As a result Heywood was commissioned to provide a 15in gauge line for this purpose. The work was completed in less than a year and the route included a branch to the estate works, which rejoiced in the name of Cuckoo's Nest. Heywood gave careful consideration to his permanent way and the flat bottomed rail was laid on cast iron sleepers with integral chairs, the rail being secured with a spring steel key. The line worked until 1947 and although, by this date, the locomotives had been superseded by internal combustion en-

Left: At Broome in Worcestershire, J A Holder's 10¼in gauge Atlantic halts at Tennis Court with a train load of guests. The driver is Terence Holder. *Sport & General*

Below: Peter Brotherhood's 15in gauge locomotive "Pearl" which is now at King's College, London. *Richard Sharpe Studio*

gines, a number of pieces of rolling stock and much of the track went to the Romney, Hythe & Dymchurch Railway or to private collectors. Even though, as it has been pointed out, Heywood's railways were not miniatures in the true sense of the word, they formed the basis for many of the principles which have been perpetuated on the 15in gauge down to the present day. The Eaton Railway, as mentioned in another article, provided an admirable testing ground for the early Bassett-Lowke 15in gauge locomotives.

The Americans were ahead of us in the production of large scale passenger hauling locomotives and several built by the Cagney Brothers were imported into this country. The best known examples ran on a line at Blakesly Hall owned by Mr C W Bartholomew, the railway fulfilling a similar function to that for the Duke of Westminster by connecting Bartholomew's house with the nearby station.

In 1909 a new monthly magazine appeared known as "Model Railways and Locomotives", edited by Henry Greenly and W J Bassett-Lowke. This publication gave descriptions of many of the lines in existence at that time and is a valuable source of information on the contemporary scene. One of the first railways to be described was that of Mr J A Holder at Broome, near Stourbridge. It had formerly been at Pitmaston Moor Green, on the outskirts of Birmingham, where Holder and his brother had laid a line which, though short, was complete in every detail: at Broome the opportunity was taken to increase the length and realism. The railway skirted the lake and passed through several well-wooded sections of the grounds. Greenly and Bassett-Lowke gave a vivid account of a day spent inspecting the railway following an invitation from Holder, whom they

met at the Model Engineering Exhibition in London. Even the luncheon table was decorated with stationary engines and pieces of locomotive under construction, the centrepiece being a $\frac{3}{4}$in scale model Caledonian locomotive of the Dunalastair Class, the tender surmounted by a working model of the *Rocket*. After lunch the party went out to inspect Holder's latest locomotive which was a 10$\frac{1}{4}$in gauge GNR "Atlantic". This was built by his engineer, Grimshaw, it being interesting to note that the engine was started very soon after the prototypes had first appeared and when it was still difficult to get working drawings. As on the original Pitmaston Moor Green Railway, most of the vehicles on the line were in scale with the locomotive, passengers sitting either in the wagons or on top of the vans.

The next issue of "Model Railways and Locomotives" described a locomotive which had run on the Pitmaston line, a model of an American 4-4-0 built by the Holder Brothers with Grimshaw. This was somewhat basic in design and nothing like as professional a model as the Great Northern "Atlantic"; obviously the standard improved with the passage of time.

The Broome line operated successfully until the 1930s when Holder moved to a house near Beaulieu in the New Forest. The railway was laid down here again operating spasmodically until Sir John Holder's death when most of the locomotives and rolling stock were sold. It is interesting to note that Terence Holder, who appears in many of the photographs of the early lines as a small boy, has become a wellknown figure in the railway enthusiast world having been associated with Ian Allan and the Dart Valley Railway in Devon and at one time

General Manager of the Romney, Hythe & Dymchurch Railway.

Another line described in Greenly's publication was a remarkable railway built by Mr Guy Mitchell in Sheffield. Known as the Brook House Model Railway it was a 7¼in gauge line, but part of it was laid with two gauges, a 3½in gauge line running on the inside of the 7¼in with a third rail. There is a graphic description of a run which Mr Mitchell carried out on the 3½in gauge (nowadays rarely laid on the ground) in which he performed a continuous run of three miles, including 1¼ miles non-stop on one firing with an 0-4-2 tank locomotive built by himself in six weeks. Jugs of water were passed to him to replenish

the water supply and the run was only terminated by the fact that he eventually overbalanced.

When Greenly visited the railway it had only been recently completed, but from the photographs and drawings accompanying the article it is obvious that great attention had been paid to detail. The bull head rail in cast iron chairs was attached to creosoted oak sleepers at 11in centres, the whole being finished with a ballast of limestone chips. After leaving the engine shed, the line joined the main circuit at a junction, then passing through a 25yd long tunnel which was built of brick throughout on correct wooden centring giving a height of 4ft and a width of 3ft. On completion, about

200 tons of earth were laid on top of it. Other line-side details included full semaphore signalling controlled from a scale signal box, gradient posts and mile posts. Even the signals were lighted at night with Bullseye lanterns fired by paraffin; evidently Mr Mitchell tried nightlights initially, but these were not successful.

The 7¼in gauge line was operated by a "Precursor" L&NW engine which was purchased from Bassett-Lowke, being built to a design by Henry Greenly. One suspects that the 7¼in gauge L&NW locomotive which Bassett-Lowke offered for a number of years was based on this prototype. Greenly gave a detailed description of all the equipment, the article

Left: Local school children helping out by turning one of the engines on the Holder Railway at Broome. *Sport & General*

Right: The locomotive "Synolda", which was the first of the Class 30 "Little Giants" to be built by Bassett-Lowke to the designs of Henry Greenly in 1912. It was named after Sir Robert Walker's wife and he is seen driving the locomotive. The engine is still in existance after having operated in several locations and is now at Belle Vue, Manchester. *The Locomotive Publishing Co*

Below: The Holder Atlantic at Broome with W J Bassett-Lowke driving piloting a North Eastern style 4-4-0 probably built by Grimshaw, Holder's engineer, who is sitting on it. *Courtesy J T Holder*

being accompanied by black and white photographs showing the line in operation. It would be interesting to know if any trace of the railway still exists.

Shortly after this there was an account of Mr J E P Howey's (later Captain) 9½in gauge railway at Staughton Manor. To run the railway Bassett-Lowke supplied the first of their 2in scale GNR "Atlantics" numbered 1442 and beautifully lined out with Howey's initials, JEPH, on the tender. Initially the track was quite short, but this was eventually extended in 1913 to about ¾ mile, the most interesting feature being a 20ft span model of the Forth Bridge. This was all constructed of timber sections bolted together with ⅜in bolts, but designed on the same principle as the prototype. There is a delightful photograph accompanying the article showing Greenly and one of the estate workmen illustrating the principle of the cantilever system, complete with Howey's dog suspended from the centre section in a sack. Howey subsequently decided to enlarge the gauge to 15in, commissioning Bassett-Lowke to build him a 4-6-2 which was based on the design of the latest "Little Giants", the standard 4-4-2 engine produced by Bassett-Lowke for lines all over the country. Later photographs show that the model of the Forth Bridge had to be strengthened by vertical supports under the centre span. There is no doubt that this 15in gauge railway at Staughton Manor whetted Howey's appetite and brought about the construction of the Romney, Hythe & Dymchurch Railway.

Although the standard of construction and design of the model locomotives was improving all the time, some of them still appeared somewhat crude in outline. One of these so described was built by Mr C Herbert C Waller, being a 4-4-0 tender locomotive which was obviously intended as a worker, it appearance being somewhat marred by an overscale steam pump fitted to the outside of the cab with the accompanying collection of pipes necessary for efficient operation. No gauge is given for this railway, but Mr Waller, as seemed typical of the times, gave his address at the end of the article saying that he would be only too pleased to show readers his locomotive at any time. Presumably in those days there must have been fewer enthusiasts than there are now.

Another well known name at the time was Mr Spriggs who built an outside framed locomotive for the 7¼in gauge thereby setting a trend which has been adopted since by many others to provide stability for a larger locomotive on the smaller gauges. This particular engine eventually found its way to the Downs School near Colwall, Worcs., where the gauge was widened to 9½in and it became an inside frame locomotive.

During the next few years, apart from the description of readers' locomotives and railways, there were often photographs showing the latest progress on the lines already described, most of which had been carefully posed to include the owner's family and friends.

A line similar to Mr Mitchell's in Sheffield was one built by Mr Tom Foster at his home in Manchester for his son Elliot. This 7¼in line was known as the Burnage Model Railway and used a Bassett-Lowke 4-4-2 tank, designed by Greenly, as motive power. This became another of the standard types of locomotive produced by the firm and is very similar to the 10¼in gauge locomotive operated at Northampton, immediately

preceding the design of the 15in gauge "Little Giants". One of the most delightful features of the railway was the terminus station which was roofed over and was complete with ticket office and window in scale with the children who were the principal passengers on the line. Once again the contemporary photographs give us a vivid picture of the time.

The issue of "Models, Railways and Locomotives" (as the magazine had become) describing Mr Foster's railway was dated June 1914; soon after this the first World War broke out, the result being a considerable curtailment in the enthusiasts' activities. Greenly's magazine continued, but there was much more accent on model aeroplanes and electric model railways and it finally ceased publication at the end of the war. In a way this marked the end of the era of

enthusiastic amateurs and the whole history of miniature railways entered a new and more professional phase. No doubt some of the lines described existed for many more years, but most have now vanished without trace and it is only by leafing through the pages of the early magazines, such as "Models, Railways and Locomotives", that one can get some idea of the work which pioneered the many miniature lines that operate in the country today.

Above: Circular fairground railway in Paris similar in type to those built by Savage and mentioned in this article. *R C U Corbett*

Below: HRH Duke of York, later King George VI driving Holder's 10¼in gauge GN "Atlantic" at an exhibition at Dudley in the 1920's. *Daily Mirror*

Bassett-Lowke

Model Engineer

As we have already described in these pages, the name of Bassett-Lowke was a household word (both literally and metaphorically!) as a manufacturer of model railways in Gauges O, 1, 2 and 3, during the early years of this century. But there was another side to his work which attracted just as much attention from the general public, and this was the manufacture and operation of miniature railways.

The term "miniature railways" is used to describe passenger-carrying railways with gauges of between $7\frac{1}{4}$ and 18 inches. In general, the locomotives of a miniature railway differ from those of narrow gauge systems in being modelled on standard gauge prototypes, though not always to scale. Passengers are generally carried for pleasure, and so one tends to find miniature railways at seaside resorts and pleasure grounds, though there are lines such as the Ravenglass & Eskdale and the Romney, Hythe & Dymchurch, which combine the job of carrying for pleasure with serious work.

In the 1890s miniature railways of this kind became popular in the United States, largely because of four Irish-American brothers named Cagney who in 1894 formed a company, the Miniature Railway Co, to supply miniature railways to amusement parks. The locomotives and equipment for these lines were manufactured by their uncle, Peter McGarigle, who owned the McGarigle Machine Co of Niagara Falls.

In 1901 Cagney Brothers supplied one of their miniature railways for an exhibition at Earl's Court, London, and later in the same year this was transferred to an exhibition at Glasgow. Probably as a result of the publicity received, in the following year Cagney's had an order for two of their locomotives and other equipment from a Mr C W Bartholomew, of Blakesley Hall, near Towcester, Northants.

Mr Bartholomew used this equipment to build himself a 15 inch gauge line from his home at Blakesley Hall to Blakesley station on the Stratford & Midland Junction Railway. As a director of the latter railway company he was able to use his influence to obtain running powers into Blakesley station itself, where he had his own private platform and waiting room.

The motive power for his line consisted of two Cagney 4-4-0 American type locomotives. They were replicas of a standard gauge engine, the famous No 999 of the New York Central Railroad, which in 1893 had achieved much publicity by reaching a speed of $112\frac{1}{2}$ miles an hour. They were by no means scale models, however, for like all Cagney engines they were made for hard wear, and many parts were oversize. Simplicity of construction was carried almost to the point of crudity, bearing in mind the kind of maintenance one can expect

The Miniature Railway, South Shore, Blackpool. Train entering Station.

A. N. Co.

Round She Goes

Southsea Rly.

Llewelyn's Miniature Railway, Southport

Centre: The original Southsea $9\frac{1}{2}$in gauge line with standard Bassett-Lowke $9\frac{1}{2}$in gauge Great Northern Railway "Atlantic" (the railway is now $10\frac{1}{4}$in gauge). This locomotive was recently in the ownership of W H Dorman. It originally ran at the home of Sir Edward Nicholl. *Arnold Wood Collection*

Top: The Miniature Railway, South Shore, Blackpool in the early 1900s. This was the original Bassett-Lowke line at Blackpool—the first built by Miniature Railways (Great Britain) Ltd. Locomotive "Little Giant". *Arnold Wood Collection*

Bottom: Llewelyn's Miniature Railway, Southport, Lakeside Station in the early 1900s (railway later known as Lakeside Railway). Class 10 Little Giant. "George the Fifth". This engine is now jointly owned by Robin Butterell and W H McAlpine and is being rebuilt. *Robin Butterell Collection*

LAKESIDE MINIATURE RAILWAY, SOUTHPORT

on a fairground or amusement park. As a result, one of the two engines is still running today, seventy years later.

Even the simplest of steam locomotives still requires periodic maintenance however, and for this Mr Bartholomew went to his friend W J Bassett-Lowke of Northampton.

Thus Bassett-Lowke acquired a first-hand knowledge of the products of the Miniature Railroad Company, and as a result decided to enter the same market in Britain.

For this purpose he formed a separate company, Miniature Railways (Great Britain) Ltd, with the help of a number of Northampton businessmen. He himself was Managing Director and Henry Greenly was Engineer.

Greenly had been designing small model locomotives for Bassett-Lowke for the past two years. He had received his training at the Regent Street Polytechnic, and in the drawing office of the Metropolitan Railway. While at college he had assisted in the construction of an 18 inch gauge model of a 4-2-2 locomotive from castings provided by Bagnalls of Stafford, and his interest in model railways had persuaded him to leave the Metropolitan Railway for a post on the editorial staff of the "Model Engineer". As a freelance designer he produced a rather fine model of a London, Tilbury and Southend 4-4-2 tank loco for W Martin & Co of West Ham, and shortly afterwards became consulting engineer to Bassett-Lowke. As Engineer of Miniature Railways, (Great Britain), Ltd he not only designed locomotives but also laid out the lines they ran on. The firm operated the lines themselves, as well as supplying all the equipment.

Miniature Railways, (Great Britain), Ltd was formed in the Autumn of 1904, and in December work began on the first locomotive in the Bassett-Lowke works. For this purpose a new workshop, the Large Scale Model Shop, was set up under Mr James Mackenzie, an enthusiast for model locomotives and an experienced mechanical engineer. Under him was a staff of four.

Greenly's first design was the famous *Little Giant*, which gave its name to three succeeding classes. It was an Atlantic (4-4-2), of free-lance design, but most nearly resembling a North Eastern "649" class.

The inside frames were made of $\frac{1}{4}$in steel plates, cut out by hand with drill, hacksaw and cold chisel, and then finished off with hand files—a month's hard labour for one man. Cylinders were $3\frac{1}{4}$in by 6in, the driving wheels 18in in diameter and the trailing and tender wheels 11in. The Adams type bogie had $9\frac{1}{2}$in wheels.

The boiler was made by the family firm of J T Lowke and was 3ft 5in long by 1ft 3in in diameter. It had 37 brass tubes, a grate area of 204sq in and a heating surface of 5,270. Working pressure was 110psi.

Stephenson's valve gear was used, and wheel reversing gear. A steam brake of Greenly's design was fitted to the locomotive, acting on the driving and trailing wheels.

The tender was six-wheeled, the frames being of oak with the axleguards bolted to them. It had a drivers seat and a well for his feet, with a pedal-operated brake. It could hold 56 pounds of coal (though coke was the fuel usually employed).

Above: Lakeside Miniature Railway. Class 20 Little Giant "Princess Elizabeth" at Southport. This locomotive was extensively rebuilt by Harry Barlow in the 1930s after a fire in the works. (Now elsewhere – no steam at Southport today!). *Arnold Wood Collection*

Below: The very popular and much photographed "Count Louis" on the Fairbourne Miniature Railway. *N R Knight*

In designing *Little Giant* Greenly followed in several ways the practice employed in Mr Bartholomew's Cagney locomotives, especially in the use of steel and iron castings. The former were used for wheels, crossheads, connecting rods, frame stretchers and hornblocks, and the latter for the wheel splashers, cab sides and the axleguards and dummy springs of the tender.

The proportion and finish of *Little Giant* was of a much higher standard, however, than that of the Cagney engines, and maintained the high traditions already set by Bassett-Lowke in other fields.

By Wednesday, April 25th, 1905, *Little Giant* was ready for shop trials. Meanwhile, work had been going ahead on what was intended to be the first enterprise of Miniature Railways (Great Britain) Ltd. This was to be a 15in gauge line situated on the South Shore at Blackpool, near to the giant roller coaster. It was a good position as far as traffic potential was concerned, but a bad one from the point of view of locomotive maintenance, for the line was laid on the sand, and this found its way into axleboxes and motion and caused much additional wear and tear.

The line was a single-track irregular circle of 433 yards laid with flat-bottomed steel rail bolted to steel sleepers. The weight of the rail was 12lb per yard. There was one station with a raised wooden platform, a wooden booking office, an engine house and a water tower. Enamelled iron advertisements for Virol, Coleman's Starch and Nestlé's Milk, together with a cast-iron slot machine dispensing chocolate, gave the correct Edwardian railway station atmosphere. The line was all ready and everything was set for the opening on Whit Monday 1905.

It had been planned to make Blackpool the first Miniature Railways project, but events decided otherwise. Early in 1904,

while work on the railway and locomotive was still in progress, Bassett-Lowke received a visit from a Mr Fred Smithies. Smithies, whose name is familiar to most model engineers as the inventor of the model locomotive boiler which bears his name, had been involved during the previous summer in operating a 10¼in gauge line at Bricket Wood, near St Albans, in association with George Flooks, a motor engineer. The place at Bricket Wood where they operated was a field used for Sunday School treats for London children, and they laid down a short, straight "up and down" length of track on which they operated a 0-4-4 tank engine built by Flooks from one of Henry Greenly's designs and known as *Nipper.*

Following an accident in which he broke a leg, Flooks became disenchanted with miniature railways (only temporarily, it should be added, for he built another line at Bricket Wood later) and so Smithies was now calling on Bassett-Lowke to see if he was interested in purchasing *Nipper* and its equipment.

The offer provided a good opportunity for Miniature Railways Ltd to operate a miniature railway locally as a sort of pilot scheme for Blackpool, and so they purchased the engine, rolling stock and track and applied to Northampton Borough Council for permission to operate it in Abington Park, one of the town's public parks. The Council turned down the idea, which they considered frivolous, but fortunately some private land was available just outside the park, and on this a track was laid down in time to open on Easter Saturday, April 20th 1905. W J Bassett-Lowke himself drove the first train; the fare was twopence and in spite of the cold weather a good time was had by all.

At Whitsun the Blackpool line was opened to the public. The train consisted of *Little Giant* and four twelve-

seater, open type bogie coaches. The project was a great success, and in the first week carried 3,000 passengers, adults paying threepence and children twopence. On the busiest day *Little Giant* made 120 circuits of the track, a total distance of 30 miles.

Among the teething troubles experienced on the new line was a rather peculiar hazard—damage to the hats of lady passengers. At that time the fashion was to wear huge wide-brimmed hats with a profusion of artificial flowers adorning them. These made splendid receptacles for the sparks thrown up by the engine, and in consequence the company received many claims for compensation for damage. There is even one recorded case of a hat catching fire on its owner's head! Because of this, roofs were fitted to the carriages before very long.

The Blackpool Railway lasted for five years, at the end of which the concession from Blackpool Corporation expired, and the railway was removed to Halifax Zoo.

In the meantime, Miniature Railways Ltd had opened another line at Sutton Park, near Birmingham. To begin with it consisted of George Flooks' *Nipper* and the 10¼in gauge railway, operating a straight up-and-down run of about 400 yards. It must have proved successful, for the following year, 1908, it was replaced by a 15in gauge line on which ran a locomotive named *Mighty Atom*, the second of the "Little Giant" class. The line was extended and a loop formed at one end so that there was a straight-forward run out and back. At the terminus the engine was turned on a turntable and ran around the train.

In 1909 Miniature Railways (Great Britain) Ltd launched their first venture abroad when they built a 15in gauge line at the Exposition Internationale de l'Est de France, at Nancy. This was an industrial exhibition at which most of the leading continental builders of locomotives exhibited. The miniature railway was a circular one, about a mile long, with stations at each of the entrances to the exhibition, and halts at intervals, so that it served as a means of transport as well as an amusement. To work it, Bassett-Lowke built a third locomotive of the same type and named it *Entente Cordiale.* On its arrival at Nancy it attracted much attention from the French railwaymen, and the railway proved very popular with the public, so much so that additional locomotive power was urgently needed. To meet this need *Mighty Atom* was withdrawn from Sutton Park and after a quick overhaul and repaint was re-named *Ville de Nancy* and sent out to join *Entente Cordiale.* Between them, they operated a longer train, which they double-headed, *Entente Cordiale* running in the dark yellow livery of the LBSCR and *Ville de Nancy* in the apple green colour of the GNR.

Between 1909 and 1912 Miniature Railways (Great Britain) Ltd operated similar exhibition lines on the continent at Roubaix, in Belgium, Brussels, Cologne and Breslau, while at home they ran a line at the 1909 exhibition at the White City, London. In addition they built two permanent lines to order, one at Rhyl, in North Wales, which opened in 1911 and the other at Southport (the Llewelyn Miniature Railway) which opened in the same year.

Miniature Railways Ltd was wound up in 1912, and soon afterwards Bassett-Lowke initiated another enterprise under the title of Narrow Gauge Railways Ltd. Before looking at this, however, we ought to take a closer look at the Bassett-Lowke locomotives.

Up to 1912 eight of these had been constructed, all belonging to what was known as Class 10. The first, as we have seen, was *Little Giant*, which had a very chequered career before reaching the private railway of Mr Tate at Haswell, County Durham, in 1964. It still runs

there to this day, carefully restored and cherished as an historic locomotive. The second, *Mighty Atom*, after running at Southport and Yarmouth, returned to Sutton Coldfield in 1937 and ran there until it was last steamed in 1957, since when it has been kept by its owner in store. *Entente Cordiale,* the third, ran at the Brussels exhibition in 1911, after which nothing further was heard of it. The fourth one, *Red Dragon*, was built in 1909 for the White City exhibition and ran subsequently at Rhyl and Margate; it is now in private hands. Also built for the White City was *Green Dragon*, the fifth, but it was not required as the expected traffic did not materialise. It was one of those which operated abroad, and like the others was last heard of at the Brussels exhibition. For this occasion Bassett-Lowke built another new locomotive, the sixth, the name of which is not known.

The last two were built to order, the seventh, *George the Fifth*, going to the Llewelyn Railway at Southport. This, too, is still in existence in private hands. Finally, number eight was an export order. Named *Hungaria*, it went to the Angol Park in Budapest.

As we have seen in the case of *Mighty Atom*, Bassett-Lowke locomotives were sometimes renamed and renumbered, a fact which makes for some difficulty in tracing their history.

The new Bassett-Lowke enterprise, Narrow Gauge Railways Ltd was formed in 1912. Its policy was to develop former narrow gauge lines as miniature railways, with a view to using them commercially rather than as amusements, though to begin with the new company opened two exhibition lines abroad in the old style.

Henry Greenly realised that the Class 10 locomotives, good as they were, were too small for the new form of miniature railway, and so he had set about designing two new classes, the first examples of which appeared in 1912.

Class 20 was a larger version of the Class 10, with a bigger boiler and increased cylinder bore. Otherwise it was

Above: "Little Giants" class loco at Breslau, Germany 1909. *Author's Collection*

Below: Restored 15in gauge Cagney (from Blakesley Hall) at New Romney in 1970. *Author's Collection*

much the same, though some details, such as the wheel splashers were altered. Whereas a Class 10 weighed 1ton 12cwt, the Class 20 weighed 1ton 15cwt, and boiler pressure was raised from 120psi to 125psi. Three of this new class were built, one going to the King of Siam who had a 15in gauge line at his palace at Bangkok (with a Cagney 4-4-0 which was entirely nickle-plated!). The second was supplied to the Llewelyn Railway at Southport where it ran under the name of *Prince Edward of Wales.* It is still in existence, though much rebuilt. So too is the third engine, *Prince of Wales,* built in 1914 for one of Narrow Gauge Railways' own lines at Fairbourne.

At the same time Greenly designed a third and entirely new class, known as Class 30. Although still of the 4-4-2 or Atlantic type, they were bigger in every way (boilers, cylinders and driving wheels), weighed another half ton, and were obviously intended for the more serious work required by Narrow Gauge Railways Ltd.

The first one was completed in 1912. Known as *Synolda,* it was made for Sir Robert Hutton's private line at Sand Hutton in Yorkshire. Two more were made, *Sans Pareil* in 1913, and *Count Louis* in 1923.

The first line to be opened by Narrow Gauge Railways Ltd was at Geneva, in the Parc des Eaux-Vives, a pleasure ground on the south side of Lake Geneva in what had formerly been the home of Louis Favre, builder of the St Gotthard tunnel. It was quite an ambitious line, with a 150ft tunnel, a five-span bridge over a small lake, cuttings and embankments and a station with passing loop. The line was correctly signalled and points and signals were worked from a small signal box.

To work the line for its opening in early summer 1912, Bassett-Lowke supplied one of the Class 10 engines, though which one is not known. It was joined shortly afterwards by *Sans Pareil,* the second of the Class 30 locomotives, which was specially built for this purpose. An interesting feature of this engine was the fact that it was the first Bassett-Lowke model to be fitted with continuous vacuum brakes. The four wheeled coaches were, of course, also so fitted, thus introducing a new element into miniature railway operation. It was one which fitted into the new policy of Narrow Gauge Railways Ltd. The coaches, incidentally, carried the inscription "Lunar Park Express" on their sides in brass letters plated in gold.

Sans Pareil ran for two seasons at Lunar Park and then returned to Northampton for overhaul before going to Norway for work on an exhibition line at Christiania (now Oslo) which was Narrow Gauge Railways' second enterprise. For this occasion the engine was renamed *Prins Olaf,* after the then Crown Prince of Norway.

The exhibition was held in the summer of 1914, and before it had ended, war had broken out. *Prins Olaf* and the rest of the railway were stranded in Norway, and did not get back to Britain for nearly a year.

In the meantime Narrow Gauge Railways Ltd had found an opportunity to put into practice their policy of taking over a narrow gauge line and turning it into 15in gauge. At Ravenglass in Cumberland was the terminus of the Ravenglass and Eskdale Railway, a 3ft gauge line built in 1875 to carry iron ore from Boot, seven miles away, and to act as a general

carrier for the district. It had had a precarious existence until it had finally closed in 1908, and was now derelict. In spite of wartime restrictions, the directors of NGR decided to go ahead with their scheme, and took a three-year lease on the line. Work started immediately on re-gauging the track, and in August 1915 the first mile had been completed in time for the arrival of *Prins Olaf* and its train from Oslo. It reverted to its old name of *Sans Pareil* and was set to work immediately.

Before long it was joined by another, and even more famous, Bassett-Lowke engine—the Pacific *John Anthony* which had been built in 1914 for Captain J E P Howey.

This was the one and only example of another new class of locomotive which Henry Greenly had designed in 1911. Known as the Class 60, or "Colossus" Class; it was really a lengthened version of a Class 30. It weighed 3ton, was 18ft 2in long and worked at a boiler pressure of 150psi.

John Anthony, named after Howey's son, appeared early in 1914 and ran on its owner's garden railway at Staughton Manor in Huntingdonshire. During the summer it was taken to the Duke of Westminster's line at Eaton Hall, Chester, for trials, and was there when war broke out in August. Its owner left to join the forces, and the engine remained in store at Eaton Hall where it was seen the following year by one of the directors of Narrow Gauge Railways Ltd and purchased for that line. It arrived at Ravenglass in time for the summer season of 1916 and was renamed *Colossus.*

It was the only Pacific locomotive ever built by Bassett-Lowke, and at the time of its appearance was hailed by its builders as "the second Pacific locomo-

tive to run in Great Britain" (the Great Western loco *Great Bear* was the first).

1916 saw the start of another Narrow Gauge Railways' enterprise. Continuing the policy of rejuvenating derelict narrow gauge lines, the company took over a tramway at Fairbourne on the south side of the Mawddach estuary in Merioneth. Originally a 2ft gauge horse tramway, it ran from Fairbourne station to the ferry across the river to Barmouth. It was regauged to 15in and Bassett-Lowke supplied a Class 20 engine which they had built the previous year. It was named *Prince of Wales,* and remained in use at Fairbourne until it was sold to the Llewelyn Railway at Southport in 1922. It was replaced by the last 15in gauge engine to be built by Bassett-Lowke, a Class 30 built just after the war for Count Louis Zborowski, the famous racing driver. He was killed in an accident while racing, and the locomotive came to Fairbourne unused, and it remains there to this day. It was named *Count Louis* in his memory.

Bassett-Lowke gave up most of their miniature railway work at this time, but they continued to produce models in $10\frac{1}{4}$ and $7\frac{1}{4}$ gauges up to the second World War. In both these gauges they produced models of the LMS *Royal Scot,* which took the place of the GN Atlantic which they had made in $9\frac{1}{2}$in gauge previously. The golden age of Bassett-Lowke miniature railways was, however, undoubtedly the period before the first World War, when their fame and their products spread over the whole world.

Top: 4-6-2 "Colossus" at Staughton Manor in 1914 with Jack Howey driving. *Author's Collection*

Bottom: $10\frac{1}{4}$in gauge "Nipper" and train at Abington Park, Northampton, Easter 1905 with W J Bassett-Lowke driving *Author's Collection*

THE HUDSWELL CLARKE DIESELS

The miniature railway at Scarborough, opened in 1931, has operated continuously in the holiday season apart from a break during the war years. Attractively laid out at this well known seaside resort, the North Bay Railway runs for just under a mile through the Northstead Manor Gardens with views of the sea at the upper end of the line. When the Corporation decided that a miniature railway was a desirable attraction they investigated various forms of motive power to determine which would be the most satisfactory. Among the firms presenting quotations were Bassett-Lowke of Northampton, Baguley of Burton-on-Trent and Hudswell Clarke of Leeds. Bassett-Lowke, whose largest engines had been for the 15in gauge suggested a railway using ¼ full size steam locomotives; Baguley suggested internal combustion or steam on 20in gauge and Hudswell Clarke, the successful contractors, proposed diesel locomotives with a steam outline, also on the 20in gauge.

Well known for their standard and narrow gauge locomotives of all types which still operate in many parts of the world, this was a new venture for Hudswell Clarke, but was to be the start of the building of several similar types of locomotive. Enthusiasts tend to decry internal combustion engines dressed up to look like steam locomotives, but the Hudswell Clarke engines are probably unique in that the standard of construction and general overall appearance were the outcome of considerable research. Too often miniature railways running today employ diesel or petrol locomotives which have but rudimentary appendages to disguise them somewhat thinly as steam locomotives. With the introduction of diesel locomotives on British Rail there are plenty of attractive prototypes on which miniature versions could be modelled. The internal combustion engine has the added advantage of being instantly available and not requiring a highly skilled driver.

The Scarborough line, designed and laid out by the Borough Engineer, was opened by the Lord Mayor who drove the

first train in May 1931: the track for the line was supplied by another well known firm of light railway engineers, Robert Hudson of Leeds. The careful planting of trees and shrubs carried out when the line was built has now come to fruition and today's passengers reap the benefit of this work. Leaving the main station, known as Peasholm, the line passes a signal box, under the water chute and then skirts the boating lake in the middle of which is an island with a stage for the open air theatre. Passing through a short tunnel, followed by an attractively wooded area, the train enters Beach Station which acts as a passing loop when two trains are operating. From here on the line runs above chalet high above the bay and eventually

reaches Scalby Mills station at the upper end of the line. Here the locomotive runs round the train on a loop and at one time passed through a short tunnel, but this has now been removed. A similar procedure takes place at the main station which cuts out the necessity of providing turntables. Both locomotives are shedded off the loop at Peasholm and the two trains of open coaches normally stand in the station when not in use.

The first locomotive was delivered for the opening of the line in 1931. Named *Neptune* the design was based on the Gresley Pacifics of the LNER, the shortness of the tender and the greater length of cab being the most noticeable differences in appearance. Motive power was a 32bhp Dorman diesel engine which was

Above: Maker's original photograph of **No. 6203 "Princess Margaret Rose"**, sold to Butlins. *Hudswell Clarke & Co. Ltd.*

Bottom left: "The Princess Royal" at Blackpool Pleasure Beach. *Robin Butterell*

Bottom right: "Neptune" at Scalby Mills Station at Scarborough. *Robin Butterell*

situated in the tender. The exhaust from the engine actually passed up the chimney, thereby achieving a greater sense of realism. An interesting feature was the Vickers Coates converter which eliminated gears and clutch and gave a 3½:1 torque multiplication initially thus ensuring an extremely smooth start with no jerking. In the following year, the second locomotive, *Triton*, was delivered. Over 400,000 passengers were carried in the first season, confirming the Corporation's wisdom in providing this new attraction. With an overall length of 26ft and a total weight in full working order of just over 10tons, it can be seen that these were extremely substantial engines.

Having established this new design, other operators became interested and in 1932 another 20in gauge railway was opened at Golden Acre Park, Leeds. Two engines were supplied, the first being of similar mechanical arrangements, but in design a 4-6-4T of freelance appearance: this was named *Robin Hood*. In the follow-

ing year a further engine, identical to those at Scarborough, was supplied and named *May Thompson*. The line here was laid out as a continuous run in the park where there was a lake and other lineside attractions. During the winter months the 4-6-4T used to stand on exhibition at Leeds station. Eventually the park changed hands, the railway was removed and the locomotives sent to Blackpool Pleasure beach in 1949.

In 1953 a line was opened at Morecambe using the Golden Acre railway track and rolling stock in an amusement park operated by the same organisation as the Blackpool line. Trains run out under the Big Dipper through a reverse curve and round a loop at the end, being turned after each trip on a 25ft turntable.

The railway at Blackpool Pleasure beach had been opened in 1934, running round the funfair under the Big Dipper and in and out of various sideshows, part of the line crossing an ornamental lake on a wooden replica of the Forth Bridge:

Top left: "May Thompson" (formerly at Leeds) now at Morecambe. *Robin Butterell*

Centre left: Train at Scalby Mills Station with "Neptune". *Robin Butterell*

Below left: Train at Scarborough drawn by "Neptune". *Robin Butterell*

for some unknown reason the gauge was 21in. The total length at Blackpool was 1200yds. It is interesting to note that the first public 15in gauge railway ran a short distance away from the present site for a year in 1904, before being moved to Halifax. New Hudswell Clarke locomotives were built in 1933, *Mary Louise* being once again identical to the Scarborough locomotives and *Carol Jean* another 4-6-4T like *Robin Hood*. These were followed in 1935 by Hudswell Clarke's most impressive design of miniature locomotive, a 4-6-2 based on the LMS "Princess" class. Initially named *Carol Jean II* it is now called *The Princess Royal*. The first two engines were painted in green, but the "Princess" was painted in the correct LMS maroon. The line continues in operation today, the only alteration being that the ornamental lake is now dry, having become a car park.

In 1938 the Empire Exhibition was held in Glasgow on the outskirts of the city and among the attractions was a large funfair which could be described as a forerunner to the Festival Gardens at Battersea which complemented the Festival of Britain in 1951. The amusement park was provided by Butlins who built a 21in gauge railway that ran round three sides of the perimeter. The line was point to point with stations at either end where the locomotives ran round their train via loops similar to the arrangement at Scarborough. Two "Princess" type diesels were supplied by Hudswell Clarke, *Princess Elizabeth* and *Princess Margaret Rose*. The former was in the correct LMS maroon with "Skegness Special" painted on the smoke box, but *Princess Margaret Rose* was in NE green and was called "Clacton Express"; on the tenders were the words BUTLIN'S RAILWAY. The names on the smoke boxes were pointers to their ultimate destinations as after the exhibition closed, railways were laid down at Clacton and Skegness, the first two Butlin Holiday Camps. With the opening of further camps, all of which now have miniature railways of one type or another, there was considerable interchange of stock. *Princess Elizabeth* went to Minehead and subsequently to Pwllheli. *Princess Margaret Rose* was re-named *Queen Elizabeth* and also went to Pwllheli from Clacton. Both these latter locomotives have now been sold to a firm in Lincolnshire and as yet are not running again.

Evidence of the excellent workmanship of these nine locomotives is given by the fact that they have all covered many hundreds of miles and have proved extremely efficient and trouble-free in service. The following table lists the locomotives in chronological order with the Hudswell Clarke Works numbers and dates of building:—

Top right: "Neptune" at Scalby Mills Station. *Penny Butterell*

Centre: "Robin Hood" (formerly at Leeds) now at Morecambe. *Robin Butterell*

North Bay Railway, Scarborough	D565	*Neptune*	NE	4-6-2	1931
	D573	*Triton*	NE	4-6-2	1932
Golden Acre Park, Leeds (subsequently Morecambe)	D570	*Robin Hood*		4-6-4T	1932
	D582	*May Thompson*	NE	4-6-2	1933
Pleasure Beach, Blackpool	D578	*Mary Louise*	NE	4-6-2	1933
	D579	*Carol Jean*		4-6-4T	1933
	D586	*Carol Jean II* (Later *The Princess Royal*)	LMS	4-6-2	1935
Empire Exhibition Glasgow (Butlins) (Later Skegness, Minehead and Pwllheli)	D611	*Princess Elizabeth*	LMS	4-6-2	1938
(Later Clacton, and Pwllheli)	D612	*Princess Margaret Rose* (Later *Queen Elizabeth*)	LMS	4-6-2	1938

7¼" GAUGE

Miniature railways have often been regarded as the prerogative of the well-to-do, and the larger scales have particularly been seen in this light, but the number of tracks and the quantity of equipment built for these lines has greatly increased of late. It must be admitted, however, that not many can indulge their fancy to create miniature railways on the scale of the Romney, Hythe and Dymchurch Railway or the Ravenglass and Eskdale Railway, and between these outstanding examples and the much more common 3½in and 5in gauge railways is a range of ground level lines of 7¼in, 9½in and 10¼in gauge. It is to present the virtues of the 7¼in gauge that this article has been prepared.

While efficient and interesting, 5in gauge ground level lines in existence and operated in many districts suffer from a limiting factor of stability. The adult human frame comes in many sizes, but its basic "across the hips" measurement dictates that on a ground-level line of less than 7¼in gauge a certain lack of

stability and confidence is detectable and this, of course, reduces as the gauge increases. Therefore, the advantage apparently lies with the larger gauges—the larger the better. Unfortunately, other factors are involved: the disadvantages of the larger scales are that they require more money, more space and more workshop equipment to build. In these days of escalating material costs the heavier the rail section required, the larger the diameter of copper tube required for the boiler and the greater acreage for laying out curves, the greater the finance required.

Whilst nobody could argue that the 7¼in gauge can handle loads and passengers as well as the 9½in or 10¼in gauge, it can provide a practical compromise.

Normally built to a scale of 1½in to the foot, the smaller engines and rolling stock of a 7¼in gauge railway can be built on a 3½in centre lathe of the type owned by many model engineers, and with this, and a pillar drill of ½in capacity,

excellent 1½in scale locomotives have been built. Larger types of locomotives with larger diameter driving wheels will require more robust equipment for their construction.

It is uncertain who first pioneered railway models of a scale of 1½in to the foot, but the first steps were probably taken at about the turn of the century, and it is known that a London company produced models for a gauge of 7in at that time.

Traditionally, a Mr Mitchel, of Nottingham, is credited with the first 7¼in gauge layout in 1906, and not long after this Bassett-Lowke Ltd entered the field and by the time of the 1914-18 war had a LNWR "George the Fifth" in production as a standard design. This continued as a stock product, which in 1936 was selling at £250. Later, a GC "Immingham" was produced, but by the late 1930's this was "to order" only. Between the wars, Bassett-Lowke also advertised a 7¼in gauge "Royal Scot", the envy of several generations who pored avidly, and en-

viously, over their catalogues and wished beyond everything for the £500 which would make it theirs. Alas, that sum of money which, even in these inflationary times seems huge, was in 1930 beyond the reach of most. This engine, introduced in 1934, was designed by Henry Greenly.

Bassett-Lowke also produced permanent way for miniature railways and an attractive cast-iron chair held the rail down: This was produced as a single chair and in double form for check rails. The popularity of 1½in scale grew only slowly between the wars and might well have been forgotten had it not been for an enterprising partnership between the model engineer, George Gentry and Bonds, for in 1935-6 the "Model Engineer" described the construction of a 7¼in gauge locomotive designed by Gentry, for which the famous model supply firm of Euston Road provided castings and materials. This 0-4-0 locomotive was christened "Midge" and it appealed widely to those preferring a ground level track with tight curves, and who had limited workshop equipment. It would be wrong to describe it as a simple design although with four driving wheels, outside cylinders and accessible valve gear it had much to recommend it in this respect, but it also had Walschaerts valve gear with its curved slides and many parts, making for complication. It is uncertain how many of these locomotives were built, and are, indeed, still being built, for even nowadays occasional incomplete locomotives come into the market and recently a new boiler design was described for this engine in the "Model Engineer". It can be said that the number runs into dozens and the basic design received the accolade of popularity by being completed with a variety of cabs and side tanks, and an equal variety of colours. The chimney height was adapted to the builder's idea of a suitable prototype and it became the basis of a breed of narrow gauge engines about which more will be said later.

Perusal of Bond's catalogue for 1936 reveals interesting facts and figures about the "Midge" design. It was based on a GWR Dock Tank and was designed to haul up to 12 adults round small radius curves. The cylinders were 1½in diameter x 2½in stroke. The working pressure was 100lb/sq in and the tractive effort 80lb. Length overall was 38in and height 17¾in. In 1936 the drawings cost a mere 9/3d and a set of castings £10 7s 6d—it was indeed a very different world from today!

Henry Greenly had not neglected the 7¼in gauge and produced, in addition to the "Royal Scot", a 2-6-0 GWR Mogul design of which the original locomotive, built in 1940, operated the Saltwood Miniature Railway at Hythe in Kent, and was known as "Maid of Kent". This line, owned by Mr A Schwab, was laid down round his garden to a very high standard and the running was always excellent. It was Mr Schwab who described the Greenly Mogul as "one of Greenly's finest works". Also in Kent, Mr J Liversidge had been running a 7¼in gauge. Pier Railway at Herne Bay; at the same time he was building 7¼in gauge locomotives, amongst those of other gauges.

Meanwhile, there had been a divergence of opinion within the hobby, and

Above: Hilton Valley Railway No. 1 "Lorna Doone" with a busy summer train at Stratford Brook.

Below: The author driving his locomotive "Penrhyn", built by Roger Marsh at Stoneleigh Abbey.

our Transatlantic friends in the USA had standardised on a gauge of 7½in. The history of model and miniature railways has been bedeviled by the difficulties of getting agreement on gauge and wheel standards, and the 1½in scale is no exception. One of the best known lines in America was that owned by Walt Disney and a film documentary exists of the Disney studios in Hollywood, in which the continuity between one department in the studios and another was bridged by showing Disney travelling on a 7¼in gauge train. Disney's Carolwood-Pacific Railroad was about half a mile in length and on it ran a model of a Central Pacific Railroad 4-4-0 of 1872. Track was laid to most exacting standards, which was just as well when one sees photographs of the train on a massive trestle bridge about 10 feet high and with no guard rails!

Another well-known modeller in 1½in scale between, and since, the wars is C R H Simpson who has built a large number of 1½in scale locomotives. Two of these can currently be seen in the Birmingham Museum of Science and Industry, and well repay a visit to inspect them. Many other builders were also active.

After the 1939-45 war, the difficult conditions and shortage of supplies of all kinds dictated a slow return to modelling and at the same time seaside miniature railways, which had had no maintenance for many years and upon which beach defences and gun emplacements had been constructed were in no condition to re-open. Nevertheless, by 1948, a new 7¼in gauge line had been opened in Llandudno and later moved to Bridlington operated by a Southern 4-4-0. Model Engineering Societies had been slow to appreciate the advantages of ground level tracks, but an exception was the Brighouse Society whose Chairman, Douglas Miller, was an enthusiast, and he had built a magnificent LMS Pacific which formed the nucleus of the club's 7¼in gauge line outside the raised track of the 3½in and 5in gauge.

Shortly after the war a new type of 7¼in gauge venture began to take shape at Walton-on-Thames, where the Greywood Central Railway was begun. It aimed to be, and eventually became, probably the most complete miniature railway system in the world. For its success it depended upon the willing co-operation of a number of enthusiasts, each giving the time and expertise to construct and run the railway and, what is more important, to turn out on winter weekends to re-align track and shovel ballast—often in inclement weather. The track was basically a continuous run arranged in a spiral with a superimposed branch and a couple of passing loops. Extensive carriage and locomotive storage was provided, and complete signalling and interlocking was gradually installed.

In 1957, the well-known Hilton Valley Railway, near Wolverhampton, was opened by the late M C Lloyd, and this is described elsewhere in this book. Here again a number of enthusiastic helpers have rallied round the railway, and on summer Sundays they can be found operating the intensive train service which carries thousands of passengers each year.

When the Greywood Central had to close down recently, its equipment and "goodwill" were taken over by Ian Allan and a site was found near Chertsey. Here an even more comprehensive and complex layout than the Greywood was

commenced, and is now operational in an attractively rural setting.

The Derwent Valley Line in Durham is a further example of co-operative effort by enthusiasts, whereas at Dobwalls, in the Duchy of Cornwall, the Forest Railway is a mainly commercial undertaking.

Following the "Midge" there had been no well-publicised designs and no descriptions in the journals of the construction of any 7¼in gauge locomotive until in 1965 Martin Evans, Editor of "Model Engineer", described, in a series of articles, the construction of a Stanier Black 5 for 7¼in gauge. "Highlander" was a large engine for the amateur builder to tackle, and it is a tribute to the designer that so many have accepted the challenge. An engine to this design operates on the line at Great Cockrow near Chertsey, and there is a beautiful model completed by a Belgian model engineer. Though "Highlander" was described some time ago, many are still under construction and eventually they may outnumber the "Midges"; and, with the increasing number of club tracks where

curves are more tolerant to a 6-wheel rigid wheelbase locomotive than on most garden lines, they will endear themselves to a generation who never knew the ubiquitous originals in service on the Midland lines.

It was in the post-war era that a general interest developed in narrow gauge railways, and the reasons for this are difficult to determine; certainly the nationalisation of the standard gauge lines and the ensuing standardisation of the nationalised lines had some bearing on this, but suddenly people became aware of an infrastructure of delightful independent characterful lines, usually in isolated and often pleasantly rural areas, and most of these were operated by ancient, very diverse, types of steam locomotives. As the main line networks of the world contracted, masses of people turned to the narrow gauge as a source of interest and modelling prototype.

In 1948 J N Liversidge at Herne Bay had constructed two 7¼in gauge locomotives based on a colonial narrow gauge design. These were attractive

Above left: "Bendigo" at Porters Hill Farm.
K Blackham

Above right: Ken Blackham driving his Roger Marsh-built 4-4-0 "Zebedelia" on the track at Stoneleigh Abbey which is operated by the Midland members of the 7¼in Gauge Society.

powerful units and the ability to put one's feet inside the tender and the benefits of increased width seemed attractive. One of these locomotives now operates at Hilton as "Hilton Queen". It was at Hilton that the stability and comfort of 7¼in gauge passenger vehicles was studied, and a heavy design of bogie vehicle having roller bearings and swing link suspension was developed.

Slowly the idea of following the precepts of Spooner for the two foot gauge and Sir Arthur Heywood for 15in gauge spread to the smaller scale and a number of people began to build 7¼in gauge lines to narrow gauge scales and the concept of the maximum size of locomotive and rolling stock which could safely use the gauge.

Whereas the strictly model scale for the gauge is 1½in to a foot, a two foot gauge locomotive would be built to a scale of 3½in to one foot. The advantages of this increased size are that a more powerful locomotive can be constructed and rolling stock can be heavier and more comfortable and commodious. Covered stock is quite practical, and has been in service. The line must be drawn somewhere and dining cars are not feasible. The feeling of driving a larger scale locomotive is one of increased stability and of being in or behind rather than on top of the locomotive.

Wagons which are about 21in wide will carry 5cwt so that even short trains will pull a ton of sand, gravel or bricks. Some railways built in this way are already operating as farm railways and do a useful job on a day to day basis. One line now being built is intended as the access to an area of forestry and will be the means of extracting the thinnings in due course, special timber bolster wagons being used for this purpose.

Where the prototype used is a 3ft or metre gauge railway, the scale alters again to approximately 2in/foot and at the Forest Railway, Denver and Rio Grande prototypes have been reduced to 7¼in gauge. These, some 13ft in length must be some of the most powerful 7¼in gauge locomotives ever built. Further advantages are that by choosing short wheelbase stock, fairly sharp curves can be used and the usual narrow gauge

devices such as wagon turntables, stub points and temporary points are practical. Of the disadvantages, the most obvious are the increased size and weight of the vehicles which require special handling devices and workshop equipment to suit them. It is a fortunate hobby that provides unlimited material for thought, ingenuity and variety of opinion. Some will be inclined to develop the gauge in one way and others in quite a different direction. One of the more recent developments has been an increasing interest in internal combustion and battery locomotives. Some beautiful examples, both scale and freelance, are running and provide a challenge to their designers, quite different to the steam man's, though no less intense. Again, the increased scale of the narrow gauge idea gives room for larger internal combustion units with a consequent increase in power. Many lines, such as those at Hilton and Dobwalls have large internal combustion units which take turns on their passenger hauling and are useful for immediate use. The multiplicity of compact internal combustion motors from garden mowers and the like has taxed and stimulated the ingenuity of many to produce small, powerful, easily portable petrol locomotives near to scale. Diversity of this kind is healthy for the hobby and for this gauge in particular, but it has its danger. There are certain basic standards which should be maintained and this can best be achieved by providing a forum for discussion. Such a forum has been provided by the recent formation of a $7\frac{1}{4}$in Gauge Society, and it is hoped that one of its functions will be to inform members of the activities of other workers in the field and to achieve, if possible, a concensus on such basic standards as will permit interchange of rolling stock between one line and another. The importance of track and wheel standards in this respect is paramount, and in this context it is essential when it is considered that the $7\frac{1}{4}$in gauge Society hopes soon to have its own railway which will be available for the use of all its members. The Society looks forward to the day when it can entertain enthusiasts from all over the country and give them the opportunity to experience the pleasure of intensive running on this most fascinating and adaptable gauge of railway.

The range of supplies for these scales has increased and widened. Several manufacturers are now specialising in the construction of locomotives and the popularity of the gauge increases—it is perhaps a sign of this that at the Model Engineer Exhibition in 1974, the Championship Cup was won by a $7\frac{1}{4}$in gauge locomotive built by the Secretary of the $7\frac{1}{4}$in Gauge Society.

Above left: A L & SWR 4-6-0 S15 and train at Great Cockrow.

Below left: The practical side of $7\frac{1}{4}$" Gauge: "Tinkerbelle" (R Marsh) pulls a construction train with about a ton of building material.
K Blackham

Above right: Ken Blackham's "Dolbadarn" built by Roger Marsh being coupled to a train at Stoneleigh Abbey.

Below right: The Rheidol Valley model owned by Dennis Bates pulling away from a terminal station at Stoneleigh Abbey.

DAVID CURWEN

As a designer and builder of small-gauge locomotives England's David Curwen has a reputation second to none. At many a "stately home" or seaside pleasure park, Curwen locomotives are to be found hard at work all summer long and one or two of them are now twenty-five years old. He has no exact record of how many locomotives he has made to date, but reckons he must be well into his second fifty. This may not at first thought seem a large number until you remember that each locomotive is virtually a "one-off" job.

The term "small-gauge" rather than "miniature" is used deliberately to describe David Curwen's locomotives because the term miniature suggests an exact scaled-down version of some existing prototype. Such a miniature may be a superb piece of craftmanship and look magnificent, but owing to what is known as "scale effect" it is usually insufficiently robust to continue to work reliably and hard over a period of years. Henry Greenly was the classical advocate of the miniature, while the equally celebrated "LBSC" of the "Model Engineer" championed the more robust, free-lance small gauge locomotive designed for the job. David Curwen undoubtedly belongs to the second school of thought. Here he is explaining how he formulated his locomotive building policy at the outset: "I had a look at several other locos at this time and decided that they were really far too flimsy for hard work and that, if it was to be successful, building as a model was out and locos to work must be built as

small narrow gauge locos in their own right—robust, good engineering, using commercial parts where possible". This practical, down-to-earth approach combined with good engineering explains why Curwen locomotives continue to live such long and hard lives when their contemporaries have either been scrapped or confined to glass cases.

David Curwen remembers watching the trains go by from the warmth and comfort of his pram, while his interest in narrow gauge was first aroused by the sight of a decauville railway laid by prisoners of war through the Buckinghamshire beechwoods near High Wycombe. At school, like myself and so many of our contemporaries, the current Bassett-Lowke catalogue was his bible. We were usually content with clockwork as a motive power in those days, but the young David thought in steam from the beginning and his first locomotive was an O gauge 0-4-0 steam tender engine. His parents indulged him to the extent of dedicating a spare room for his exclusive railway use, but they jibbed when he proposed buying a secondhand, primusfired 5in gauge steam locomotive from Gamages, and it was not until many years had passed that young Curwen's dream of bigger and better steam locomotives became a reality.

From 1936 until the end of the war, David Curwen was employed by Shorts, the Rochester aircraft builders where before war broke out he worked on flying boats of different types. It was towards the end of the war after a long spell of

Above: Longleat No 6 "Dougal", a 15in gauge 0-6-0T. *Robin Butterell*

Top right: A Curwen Atlantic. A model of No 4433 for the Audley End Railway. *Robin Butterell*

Right: "Queen of Colorado", new from the makers, swings on the table at White's Hill, Buckinghamshire. *Brian Hollingsworth*

Below: David Curwen with his little 0-4-2ST now on his private test track. *Robin Butterell*

work on Stirling bombers, that David Curwen had the idea of building himself a locomotive for his own amusement and the time to carry it out. Owing to the use of the wrong materials—most of the right ones were in extremely short supply at this time—combined with his own lack of experience, he prefers to draw a kindly veil over this episode. Nevertheless, nothing daunted, he joined with an older war-time friend in starting a business,

David Curwen Ltd, with the intention of building locomotives commercially.

The first enquiry the new firm received was from a man who intended to revive the Hillsea Lido Miniature Railway and required a 10¼in gauge steam locomotive as motive power. Sticking his neck out, as he puts it, David undertook to build him a 4-6-2 based on the design of the LNER A2 Thompson Pacific. The little firm built two of these Pacifics in 1947 and very successful and long-lived they proved to be. The prototype, after some years at Hillsea, went to the Drayton Manor railway, near Tamworth. The second Pacific was run by David himself with two partners on a track at Weymouth, and it continued to work there until two years ago when it was purchased by a friend of the Hon. Robin

Neville for service on the railway at Audley End. It carried its original boiler for twenty years.

Following these two Pacifics, David designed what he now considers an ugly locomotive, an Atlantic of free-lance American outline. But handsome is as handsome does, for these ugly ducklings proved equal to all the work that could be given to them on the 10¼in gauge and to be remarkably reliable and long-lasting. Ten or twelve of these Atlantics were built between 1947 and 1949, mostly for seaside pleasure gardens, one going as far afield as Durban.

At this time Curwen locomotives were built in a little village high on the Wiltshire downs near the village of Baydon and it was here in 1948 that the writer first met him. The reason for this en-

counter was that we were already interested in saving the Talyllyn Railway in Merioneth, but considered it financially out of the question to relay the whole line to its original gauge of 2ft. 3in. David's opinion was sought on the practicability of converting the gauge to 10¼in and still being able to haul a useful payload of passengers. It was thought that a large locomotive of narrow gauge outline could do just this, and some of David's subsequent designs have since proved this point although the scheme was abandoned.

In 1951, David Curwen worked as Chief Mechanical Engineer at Pendre shops during the first year's running of the Talyllyn Railway under the auspices of the Talyllyn Railway Preservation Society. David is a mechanical engineer who combines a flair for simple and straight forward design with first class practical ability and versatility. He has a great sense of humour and is completely unflappable. The General Manager at Towyn during that first critical season of running could not have wished for a better right-hand man. There were practically no tools or equipment in the shops at that time, yet David succeeded in producing a new smoke-box door for *Dolgoch,* the old one having become paper-thin.

Following this Welsh excursion, David Curwen, with the late A E Newbury as a partner, took over a small general engineering business in Devizes. Over the next few years the little firm was preoccupied with other projects and only one new locomotive was built. This was a small 0-4-0 diesel for the late Sir Thomas Salt's private railway (which he used to feed his pigs) at Shillingstone, Dorset. Meanwhile, however, the idea that a small gauge railway was an essential property for any enterprising stately home owner was being noised abroad and it was thanks to the longevity and reliability of his Baydon-built locomotives that David found himself in on the ground floor of this new "stately home" market. It was Lord Gretton who pioneered the new movement when he laid down a 10¼in gauge line in the grounds of Stapleford Park in Leicestershire. To provide motive power for this he purchased second hand two of David's "ugly duckling" Atlantics which had originally been supplied to Bognor Regis. As a result, the new owner was soon in touch with their builder who was commissioned to build for him (sign of the changing times) a 10¼in gauge version of a Western Region "Warship" class diesel. This was propelled by a 1,200cc petrol engine with mechanical drive.

With infinite faith in David's versatility as an engineer, Lord Gretton then ordered from him a 40-seater miniature liner *Northern Star* to ply on his lake in conjuction with the railway. Despite the fact that he had never built a ship in his life and the lake concerned was extremely shallow and weedy, the result was a complete success. A single paddlewheel was concealed in the stern and driven by a Ford engine using hydraulic transmission.

Following this excursion into shipbuilding, three 7¼in gauge "Warship" class diesels were built, two with hydraulic drive for the Lanark County Council and one mechanical for Gillingham. Next came two locomotives for the Hon. Robin Neville's line at Audley End. The first of these, which the writer had the delightful experience of driving, is both in appearance and sweet running performance, David's finest achievement. It is a Great Northern Ivatt Atlantic built to heavier proportions than true scale, yet retaining the graceful lines and character of the prototype. The second locomotive for Audley End was a "Western" class diesel *Western Enterprise.* This proved

a popular prototype and was the first of many similar locomotives, some with mechanical and some with hydraulic drive, for 7¼in, 10¼in and 15in gauges to be built over the next few years. For obvious reasons, commercial operators prefer diesel locomotives to steamers and steam enthusiasts may be saddened to hear that this change is accompanied by no falling off in youthful passengers. Some operators, backing it both ways, order a locomotive of steam outline driven by an i.c. engine concealed in the tender. David does not boast about such "mock ups", but the customer must always be right.

In 1966, David left the firm of Curwen & Newbury following a takeover and started an engineering design and consultancy practice in Devizes. Although this is by no means confined to locomotives and railways, they continue to occupy quite a fair share of his time. In the first year of this new practice he designed the 0-6-0 narrow gauge outline tender engine *Muffin* for the 15in gauge railway at Longleat. This was built for him by the Berwyn Engineering Company of Thickwood, but shortly afterward he entered into a highly successful arrangement with Severn-Lamb Ltd, model engineers of Stratford-upon-Avon, whose activities will be the subject of an article in a forthcoming part of this History. It was Severn-Lamb who built *Dougal,* an 0-6-0T companion for *Muffin* at Longleat.

Meanwhile, at his home in Wiltshire, David Curwen has his own workshop where he builds locomotives up to 7¼in gauge as a hobby, leaving the larger sizes to be built at Stratford. It should not be thought, however, that the locomotives which emerge from this home workshop are all tiddlers. They have included two Denver & Rio Grande 2-8-2 steamers on the 7¼in gauge which are as large and as powerful as many locomotives of much wider gauges. One of these went to a private owner and the other to John Southern's Forest Railway at Liskeard, one of the most attractive 7¼in gauge layouts in public use in this country. There it has recently been joined by a small 0-6-0 Plantation engine which rejoices in the name of *David Curwen.*

In the garden outside David's workshop there is a circuit of 7¼in gauge track where new locomotives are steamed for the first time. Its only resident motive power, so to speak, is an 0-4-2 saddle tank, a model of the Kerr Stuart No. 4 *Edward Thomas* of the Talyllyn Railway which David built purely for his own amusement. It is a reminder of a never-to-be-forgotten pioneering summer in Wales. It also provided the writer with a much more forceful reminder in the shape of a permanent bump on the top of his head. This was caused by making contact with the roof of David's tunnel while driving this spirited little engine round his track.

Top right: One of David Curwen's free-lance Atlantics: No 750 "Blanchel of Lancaster" at Stapleford Park.

Right: 2-8-2 Denver & Rio Grande built by David Curwen 1972 and 0-6-0 built 1973 and named "David Curwen", both on the Forest Railway, Liskeard. *Robin Butterell*

Left: "Western Enterprise": Western Class diesel built 1963 for the Audley End Railway. *Robin Butterell*

Above left: Atlantic Type Locomotive of 194? design built in 1965 for Lowestoft Corporation. *Robin Butterell*

PETER LAMB

Stratford-upon-Avon is known throughout every country in the world as the birthplace of William Shakespeare. Each year thousands of people go to see and hear his plays performed in the theatre beside the river Avon and wander through the streets to admire the mediaeval architecture. Not far from the centre of the town the firm of Severn-Lamb Limited is gaining international recognition in a very different field. In a small office near the main entrance you will find the man who started it all, Peter Severn Lamb—that is assuming that he is not rushing off to some far-flung corner of the globe accompanying his latest creation. For not only is he an excellent modelmaker himself, but he has the ability to grasp the problem quickly and come up with the right solution. Most of the highly skilled members of his small staff have been with him from the early days of the organisation and it is a fair indication of their loyalty and en-thusiasm that one of them has been there for 20 years and another for 17.

Peter Lamb wanted to be a model-maker from an early age and his first engine was started at Ackworth, a Quaker boarding school in Yorkshire. As did many of his contemporaries, he came under the influence of LBSC who wrote for years in "The Model Engineer" and whose articles have been the starting point of a large number of small scale locomotives running today. As so often happens, this first engine was never completed, but at least it is still with him now. When he left Ackworth, Lamb was apprenticed to the engineering firm of Priestman Brothers Limited at Hull serving in various departments, including the drawing office. He was with this firm from 1938 to 1942 and continued his model making interest by constructing models of the Priestman Brothers' grabs, selling his first commercial model to them in 1941. Priestmans also commissioned him to develop a grab for cutting seaweed from the sea bed; this he carried out in his own workshop. By now the 2nd World War was into its third year and Peter Lamb joined the RAF, serving as a pilot

in Coastal and Transport Command until 1946. When he left the Air Force his parents were in the process of starting an hotel in Stratford-upon-Avon called "The Fold", and he joined them there in this enterprise. Although there had been little time for models in the Service his interest in such things had not abated and he started once again making model railway engines, completing his first freelance 0-6-0 based on LNER practice in a workshop at the back of "The Fold" in 1947. The present location of this locomotive is unknown although photographs of it exist and it would be interesting to know of its whereabouts.

About the same time he started to advertise in "The Model Engineer" for modelling work and from this obtained one or two small commissions. Resulting from a contact with the RAFVR, in 1948 Messrs Prodorite commissioned him to build a model of a cold steel strip pickling mill for the Abbey Works at Port Talbot. This was exhibited at the British Industries Fair in 1949 and is still in existence. At the same time Lamb received an order from Metropolitan Vickers Ltd., for a model of a power station and water turbine.

He then decided that the moment had come to leave "The Fold" hotel and devote all his time to the making and supplying of models.

In the early days it was often necessary to work up to 20 hours a day, but the business expanded and further commissions for models of different types came rolling in. These included many

kinds of electrical switchgear and models of the first diesel electric locomotives for British Railways which were being supplied by Metropolitan Vickers Beyer-Peacock Limited and built in their works at Stockton-on-Tees. These were followed by models of locomotives for the future electrification of the Liverpool/Manchester/Euston lines. Other jobs included models of turbines and associated equipment in this and the electrical field. By this time the original workshop had expanded into more and more of the garages at the rear of the hotel until it was apparent that new permanent premises were required. It was, therefore, decided to design and build suitable accommodation in Western Road and the firm of Severn-Lamb Limited commenced operations here on the 13th August 1958.

It was not long after this, in 1960, that a major turning point occurred for Peter Lamb's firm which was to set him on the road to international recognition. Bassett-Lowke Limited of Northampton who, in the early part of the 20th Century, were probably the best known modelmakers in the world, had received an enquiry for a model of the Westinghouse Allis Chalmers double compound steam engine for driving the New York subway. At that time they were unable to accommodate the order and Peter Lamb's name was put forward to the Smithsonian Institution in Washington DC as a possible alternative.

As he was comparatively unknown at this time outside the UK, the Smithsonian Institution requested that he should prove his workmanship by supplying a part of the model before they gave him the full commission. He proceeded to construct one of the HP cylinders, borrowed the air fare from his mother and flew direct to Washington with the cylinder. The Institution was suitably impressed with the quality of his work and, as a result, the complete engine was constructed and became the first model by an English modelmaker ever to appear in the Institution. Following this he received an order for the supply of the Union Pacific "Big Boy" 4-8-8-4 steam locomotive to a scale of $\frac{1}{2}$in to the ft. Since then Severn-Lamb Limited have supplied 17 non-working locomotive models to the same scale including Stephenson's *Rocket,* a Consolidation 2-8-0, a Pennsylvania K-4 Pacific, a New York Central "Hudson", an Atcheson Topeka and Santa Fe Compound, a Budd Stainless Steel Car, an electric Street Car and a Horse-drawn Street Car. Apart from these locomotives, the Company has also supplied the Smithsonian with models of stationary steam engines and other pieces of engineering, making a grand total of 37 exhibits. Since the setting up of the firm in Western Road, models of many shapes and sizes have come from the workshops and these include the Globe at the Boy Scouts' Jamboree in Sutton Park and a scale model liner, the *Southern*

Above: A 3½in gauge "County of Warwick": GWR 4-4-0 County class built for a private collector

Centre right: Longleat engine: an 0-6-2T locomotive supplied to the order of Mini-Rail Limited in 1969.

Centre left: ½in : 1 foot scale model of Stephenson's "Rocket" built for the United States National Museum in Washington. *William J Clouser*

Bottom: A show-case model of "Talyllyn" the original 1865 locomotive of the Talyllyn Railway in Wales.

Opposite page : Peter Lamb.
Robin Butterell

Right: Western diesel: 10¼in gauge model (petrol driven) "Western Comet".

Top: Rio Grande steam outline petrol driven locomotive. *Robin Butterell*

Above: A Union Pacific 4-8-8-4 "Big Boy" model built to ½in scale, which is now in the United States National Museum in Washington. The result of 3,000 man hours. *William J Clouser*

Cross, which seats 40 people and plies the lake of Stapleford Park where it connects with the 10¼in gauge miniature railway. Another significant date in the organisation was when Peter Lamb was introduced to David Curwen by L T C Rolt, the well known author and instigator of the preservation of the Talyllyn Railway. Curwen is best known as a designer of model locomotives for the 7¼in, 10¼in and 15in gauges and provided consultant services for passenger-carrying model locomotives built by the Company. The first model to emerge from the partnership was a 10¼in gauge petrol locomotive based on the Western Class diesels of British Railways; this was to operate on the Brooklands Railway at Worthing. Two similar models soon followed, running at St Albans and Luton, and a further machine was sent to Ayr Corporation in Scotland.

David Curwen had tended to specialise in 7¼in gauge locomotives as these were of a size which could be constructed in his own small workshop in Wiltshire, but with the engineering skill and facilities of Severn-Lamb Limited he was able to embark on larger locomotives. In 1969 an 0-6-2 Tank Locomotive was supplied to the order of Mini-Rail Limited to operate on the railway running at Longleat, the home of Lord Bath. It is difficult to decide whether this interesting locomotive is really a miniature or a narrow gauge type as, although based on many typical

narrow gauge details which have been scaled down, it is possible for the driver to actually sit in the cab as he would do with a full-sized locomotive. This locomotive "Dougal" has proved to be extremely powerful and capable of pulling heavy loads over long distances.

Later, the Ravenglass and Eskdale Railway Company, which operates the wellknown line in Cumberland, ordered a 15in gauge diesel hydrostatic locomotive which had to be suitable for hauling passenger trains on their stiffly graded line. This has proved to be a most successful addition to the railway and has the advantage of always being instantly available if the traffic should so demand it. Since then Severn-Lamb have built both 10¼in gauge and 15in gauge locomotives for a number of railways in Great Britain. Many of these have been produced in association with David Curwen, but others have been completely designed and constructed within their own works. Many of these engines are illustrated in other chapters, and this will show the wide range of models that have been produced to date.

The largest and most ambitious locomotives have been produced in 1973 for two new railways, one at Bala Lake and the other on Southport Pier. These are both of 60cm gauge, the former line being laid on part of the track bed of the old GWR line which runs for part of its distance along the shore of the lake.

Severn-Lamb Limited had already built two coaches for the railway and although this diesel hydrostatic Bo-Bo locomotive is obviously going to be very successful, its true potential really has not yet been assessed. There are plans for the production of a small 60cm gauge 0-4-0 saddle tank locomotive based on the diminutive designs produced many years ago for industrial and mining railways in many parts of the world.

In case one might think that work is now concentrated only on large scale locomotives, it is worth noting that at the present time about half of the firm's production is engaged on the smaller railway models. In addition, orders include models of many pieces of engineering equipment used not only for exhibition, but for training technicians in the highly skilled work of maintaining and operating modern machinery. Nor have the smaller gauges been forgotten and here recent work has included the construction of a run of 3½in gauge Great Western locomotives for a private customer. This has so far included a "King", a "City", an original "County", a "Dean Single", a "Castle", a "Star", a "Hall" and a "Saint".

Obviously the future for Severn-Lamb Limited is bright and it is difficult not to be envious of this man who, by his skill and determination, has turned a schoolboy hobby into a thriving international business.

TREVOR GUEST

A H Guest Limited are well established in the Stourbridge area of Worcestershire as a firm of building contractors, but probably many people do not know that Mr Trevor Guest, one of the Directors, is also recognised in the model engineering world as a distinguished builder of miniature railway locomotives. Trevor Guest, like most schoolboys, was interested in model railways, but when he joined the family firm in 1921 he had no thoughts of pursuing this hobby as a possible sideline to his chosen career. In 1935 he discovered that a near neighbour, one R K Saunders who was a Naval Engineer and also a Captain RN, was in the process of building a $2\frac{1}{2}$in gauge "Schools" locomotive. As Trevor Guest says, they soon got fed up with fiddling about with the minute parts of such a locomotive and decided to build something bigger. Saunders suggested contacting J N Maskylene, who was for many years editor of the Model Railway News. They felt he might be able to produce a suitable design for a passenger carrying locomotive and there were also ideas about laying a miniature railway on the site of the old Kinver Light Railway.

Maskylene duly arrived clad in his usual attire of wing collar, black tail coat and carrying a Gladstone bag. Meeting him at Dudley Port Station Guest and Saunders were somewhat apprehensive, but he turned out to be a delightful companion and they had a fascinating weekend discussing the possibilities of a locomotive and the projected railway. Unfortunately it was not feasible, due to the ownership of part of the track bed of the old light railway, to pursue the idea of the miniature line, but Maskylene duly came up with a design for a freelance 4-4-2 Atlantic locomotive and the firm of G & S Light Engineering was born, the name of the firm being taken from the initial letters of Guest and Saunders. For economic reasons they decided to complete two identical locomotives as there could be a saving on castings for such items as wheels and cylinders.

About this time when having a drink one evening at the "Crown Hotel", Wychbold, near Droitwich, the proprietor, hearing of their venture, suggested that they should lay a track through the pub garden and into a neighbouring field. The railway ran its first season here in 1937. About the same time the building of Dudley Zoo had just started and one of the Directors, who knew Trevor Guest, saw the railway at the "Crown" and said that this was the very thing needed at the Zoo. As a result, the complete railway, which now consisted of the two locomotives, passenger rolling stock and track, was moved to Dudley and ran there until the outbreak of the 2nd World War.

Trevor Guest had already started on a third $10\frac{1}{4}$in gauge locomotive based on a Great Western *Saint* Class which was fitted with a Goodhand boiler, as were the two previous locomotives. It was not possible to get coal for running a miniature railway during the war so a rail car

Top: Trevor Guest with drawing of "Katie".
Robin Butterell

Centre: Dudley Zoo railway in its early days.
Robin Butterell Collection

Centre and Bottom: The two faces of "Ernest Twining": Trevor Guest's Pacific, named after the designer, as existing at Fairbourne in 1962 and 1972. *(upper) Robin Butterell*

was built from an old Singer engine with fluid flywheel, and the railway kept operating with this. When conditions improved Trevor Guest felt that the 10¼in gauge was really too small for the number of passengers that could be carried and that the 15in gauge was the obvious answer. As a result, agreement was reached with the Zoo to relay the line to the wider gauge. At this time Guest was in the process of building a fourth 10¼in gauge locomotive based on an LMS Class 5 type so he completed it, lending the machine to run on a short railway at Rhyl (on the other side of the road from the well known 15in gauge railway). Badly treated and left outside for a whole winter, it was brought back to Stourbridge and overhauled and then, quite by chance, the Borough Engineer of Lowestoft, who was looking for a suitable locomotive for a miniature railway there, arrived and bought it. This locomotive ran at Lowestoft for a number of years before passing into the hands of a private owner in Worcestershire where it now operates on half a mile of track.

The other 10¼in gauge locomotives, now also redundant, were sold—the two original Atlantics going to an operator on the South Coast where they ran for many years and are still in existence, although both now in private hands. The *Saint* went ultimately to the miniature railway at Hastings where it was running until very recently.

At this time Trevor Guest had been building a 7¼in gauge locomotive which had been seen by the late Michael Lloyd, operator of the Hilton Valley Railway. This was completed in Lloyd's engineering works and now runs on the Hilton Valley Railway as *Francis Henry Lloyd*. Guest had also constructed a locomotive for the late Sir Thomas Salt to run on his line at Shillingstone in Dorset. This is powered by a Petter diesel engine and has done a great deal of work over the past 20 years. Two 10¼in diesel locomotives built for the Dudley Zoo line were also disposed of at this time.

For the 15in gauge it was decided to build two 4-6-0 Class 5 locomotives and Maskylene was approached for suitable drawings. At the time, due to pressure of work, he was not able to proceed so Guest and Saunders contacted Ernest Twining, who had an engineering firm in Northampton, to see if he could carry out the commission. He quickly prepared a general arrangement drawing and this was followed by the other detailed drawings while the boilers were ordered from Goodhand. When the first locomotive was completed, the narrowness of the fire box, some 8½in, became apparent, so it was decided to construct the second locomotive as a 4-6-2. Twining soon produced revised drawings and construction of the second locomotive went ahead. Both these locomotives then went into service on the Dudley Zoo Railway.

One day Trevor Guest received a drawing from Twining with a note saying "this is the locomotive I would like to build". It was based on Great Western practise although generally a freelance design. The locomotive was duly built and went to run on the line at Dudley Zoo where it proved to be very successful and was named *Katie*. One afternoon, a man leaning on the fence watching the trains asked if he could drive the engine. Casual strangers were not, as a rule, allowed the privilege of travelling on the footplate, but as he appeared to be seriously interested the rules were bent.

It was obvious that he had a fair working knowledge of the steam locomotive and within an hour he was driving *Katie* up and down the line. He then announced that he wished to buy the locomotive and after some discussion the price was agreed and the cheque promised in the post the next day. When the cheque arrived the accompanying letter asked Trevor Guest to store the locomotive until the new owner was ready for it.

Apparently Captain Hewitt owned seven islands in the West Indies and the locomotive was to go to one of the larger of these where he had a coconut plantation. The railway would be laid out to collect the coconuts and transport them to the harbour for loading on board ship; the coconut shells would be burnt by the locomotive as fuel. Trevor Guest heard nothing more from Hewitt for a year, but, getting short of space, he wrote to ask if he could take delivery; the locomotive was despatched to Anglesey where Hewitt lived on the north side of the island.

Many stories have now come to light about this man who was probably one of the last great eccentrics. Being extremely wealthy he was able to indulge a number of his whims and, apart from being a collector of fine models he was also very interested in the habits of sea birds. At his home on Anglesey he built a high red brick wall which was not only to maintain his privacy from curious visitors, but also to funnel the birds up the estuary at dusk. Apart from his extensive collection of model locomotives, most of which had never been out of their packing cases, Hewitt had also knocked a row of seven Welsh cottages into one and these were filled inside with the largest collection of birds' eggs known in the country. He also owned seven traction engines, a £40,000 lifeboat and two 2-man submarines.

Shortly after *Katie* had been completed and was running at Dudley Zoo, Trevor Guest made the acquaintance of John Wilkins, the owner of the Fairbourne Railway in Wales. Wilkins had taken over the railway in a run–down state and urgently needed new motive power. He commissioned a second *Katie*, which was to be named *Sian* and while this was building the first Class 5 from Dudley Zoo, now named *Prince Charles* was loaned to Fairbourne for two years. The second original Twining locomotive, built as a 4-6-2, also eventually found its

Top: The first of Trevor Guest's 2-4-2s "Katie" as now running on the Fairbourne railway.

Right: The Pacific "Prince Charles", now belonging to W H McAlpine, at New Romney.
C M Whitehouse

Far Right: Hilton Valley Railway: 4-8-4 No 3 "Francis Henry Lloyd" painted in East African railways maroon. Built in 1959.

way to Fairbourne when the Dudley Zoo line abandoned steam traction. It now runs at Fairbourne regularly and at John Wilkins' request it is named *Ernest Twining* after its designer, who died about five years ago. When *Sian* was completed, *Prince Charles* was returned to Stourbridge to be rebuilt as a 4-6-2; it was recently sold to Bill McAlpine and now runs occasionally on the RH & DR, but more often on a special portable track at steam fairs up and down the country.

Another interesting locomotive constructed by Trevor Guest for the 15in gauge is a model based on the narrow gauge locomotives running on the British Rail line from Aberystwyth to Devils Bridge. Although having a steam outline and with fully working motion and valve gear is actually operated by a Daimler Scout car engine mounted in the dummy boiler. If fitted with a normal boiler, it could be operated as a steam locomotive. This locomotive has also been acquired by Bill McAlpine and is at New Romney where it is used mainly for yard shunting. The locomotive is named *Tracy Jo* after Trevor Guest's grand-

When Captain Hewitt died a few years ago his remarkable collection of models came on the market and *Katie,* which had been languishing in her packing case for some time, was acquired by John Wilkins and has joined her sister engine *Sian* on the Fairbourne Railway. Most of the remainder of Captain Hewitt's collection was bought by Bill McAlpine, who will be the subject of a later article in this book. Trevor Guest is now building for his grandson what he claims will be his last locomotive; he has gone back to the $7\frac{1}{4}$in gauge and his favourite Class 5 type. Although it is sad to think that there may not be any more 15in gauge locomotives from Trevor Guest's workshop, it is evident that those in existence will continue to give many years of excellent service and could form no better tribute to this skilled, but modest locomotive builder.

Top: Daimler Scout Car engined locomotive "Tracey Jo". Built to imitate the Vale of Rheidol locomotives. *C M Whitehouse*

Centre: "Prince Charles" running on a portable 15in gauge track at a steam fair. *Robin Butterell*

Bottom: The Petter powered diesel on the late Sir Thomas Salt's line at Shillingstone, Dorset. *Robin Butterell Collection*

daughter.

Trevor Guest has also built a number of petrol and diesel locomotives both for Dudley Zoo and the Fairbourne railway. Most of these are still operating and have run many thousands of miles. One of the principal problems at Fairbourne is that the line is laid for a great part of its length through sand dunes and the strong westerly winds encourage the sand to find its way into all the moving parts. This has necessitated the provision of specially enclosed bearings for all the locomotives and rolling stock. Brake blocks also tended to wear out more quickly due to the scouring action of the sand, so one of the Guest petrol locomotives called *Sylvia* and operated by a $3\frac{1}{2}$ litre engine was fitted with disc brakes. These are similar in type to those fitted to Mini-Cooper cars and have been entirely successful in that the discs on *Sylvia* have only been changed once in 12 years. It is interesting that pioneering work in this field should have been carried out on a small gauge railway. The disc brakes have also been fitted to the bogie coaches and are Westinghouse operated.

LINES FOR LIVE STEAM

Beetle-size model trains or N-gauge as we call it are small enough to allow us to portray a railway landscape. As we progress upwards in size through the scales our attention must more and more be concentrated; in mouse-size (HO) it is the railway itself, in O and 1 gauge it is the trains. With some notable exceptions layouts in these scales take up too much room for anything else.

Above this size, and before we reach commercially exploitable gauges, 7¼in and above, it is the locomotive itself upon which model makers must concentrate. Model railways in gauges 2½in, 3½in and 5in are now almost unknown but locomotives for these exist in their thousands.

The majority are real steam puffers burning real coal on tiny grates just like big sister and their construction and operation has occupied and fascinated a large fraternity who on the whole remain quite distinct and separate from both the "electric mice" people below and the miniature railway "ride-through-your-park" people above.

Control is no problem because in these sizes you drive yourself, generally sitting astride on a flat car with footrests. The track would be raised, multigauge and usually arranged in an oval to give runs of any length for which the locomotive (and its driver) has the stamina.

The building and operation of these locomotives is no rich man's pastime and therefore, because the tracks are costly both in space and material, clubs have been formed and now exist in most parts of Britain. Some have bought or leased land and built a track, clubroom and workshop, others operate in public parks, giving rides to children in return for their accommodation.

Perhaps one should add that outside countries where the Anglo-Saxon influence operates the hobby is almost but not quite unknown. In USA its growth and extent is comparable with that in Great Britain, as indicated.

The steady development of the hobby has been curiously but completely unaffected by the end of steam on the world's railways. The only detectable effect seems to be just that those who preferred an up-to-the-minute new pro-

duct as a prototype have either to join the rest who anyway liked miniatures with historic significance or alternatively design and build a model of a locomotive that might have been developed in full-size, had steam continued.

In this respect a challenge was recently thrown down to the live steamers in an article in the Feb 1973 American "Trains" magazine. The Americans had the largest engines ever built, and, with the Mallet-style articulated arrangement used for these giants, they had reached the maximum power possible with this configuration, having regard to the various physical constraints of weight and size. However, even more power was desirable from an operating point of view, and could have been provided if they had adopted the British "Garratt" arrangement, which in its greatest development had far from reached its limit. A possible 4-8-8-4 + 4-8-8-4, a "double Big Boy", if you like, was sketched out, with the suggestion that it would make an excellent subject for a model.

Perhaps a British Model Engineer will be the one who carries the development of the steam locomotive out beyond the furthest limit yet reached!

Coming back to the tracks themselves, there are two main schools of thought

Above: Tingley. A visiting 3½in gauge rebuilt "Royal Scot" from the Huddersfield Society of Model Engineers, waits to move on the massive welded steel track of the West Riding Small Locomotive Society at Blackgates. Note the numerous running gauges provided.
J B Hollingsworth

in respect of construction. The first is the more expensive and involves spiking or screwing non-ferrous near-scale flat-bottom rail to cross sleepers supported 30in above ground level by timber, steel or concrete longitudinals resting on concrete pillars. In essence, this type of track follows the design of the legendary POLAR route, the line which belonged to that high-priest of live steam, L Lawrence or "LBSC". He described all its stages from survey to operation in his inimitable and charming style in the "Model Engineer" back in 1934-1936. Until his death in 1967, the track was visible next to the Brighton main line on the upside just south of Purley Oaks Station.

The second school follows an qually hallowed example, that of the track belonging to the Society of Model and Experimental Engineers, which, in portable form, has been the principal feature of most Model Engineer exhibitions since before World War I. Here, steel flats are set on edge and spaced with tie bolts and spacing pieces, cross sleepers being dispensed with. In some cases the track so formed is strong enough to be self supporting between uprights, in others independent longitudinals are used. The advantage is either that of cheapness or the ability to provide easily gauges additional to the normal $2\frac{1}{2}$in, $3\frac{1}{2}$in and 5in. The disadvantage of steel strip tracks is that the hard sharp-edged flats are unkind to cast-iron locomotive wheels. Steel tyres, as used in full size, are unusual in small practice.

As with most types of monorail, points are a problem and usually some form of turntable or traverser is used. Running connections would just be feasible but no one in Britain seems to have achieved them. Neither, apparently, have any appeared in recent years in the USA although the New England Live Steamers' Club at Danvers, Massachusetts had them at one time. A few clubs, notably Derby and Ickenham, have ground level tracks, but this involves certain problems both with stability because of the narrowness of the gauge and also with comfort because of the inevitable lowness of the seats. Yoga training is an essential for riding ground-level passenger tracks in this size, but, of course, points and crossings, even though mixed gauge, can reasonably easily be provided.

conveniences, is important, since, if conditions are right and safety is adequately covered, club funds can be augmented by offering rides to the public. In fact, many sites have been made available by local authorities on condition that this amenity is provided.

One Club, the North London, whose track is at Colney Heath, has gone so far as to fit water troughs and, in spite of very different hydro-dynamics in the smaller scale, they function satisfactorily. Elsewhere, when a long non-stop run is operated, cans of water are exchanged on the fly like mail-bags or single-line tokens in full-size.

On English tracks, rolling stock is almost invariably confined to the flat trucks with foot-boards which carry the passengers. In America this is not so; many live steam buffs hang some scale box cars and a caboose or perhaps some varnish, ie passenger cars, on to the couplers of their driving car, making up a caboose hop, limited, drag or hotshot as appropriate.

So, unless he lives in the very wild and remote parts of Britain anyone having a steam locomotive is within reach of a type of model railroading which is very different. More realistic in some ways, because you have real steam and coal and drive your own train; less in others, because the track layout is usually of elemental simplicity as described.

What is it like to have a day out on one of these lines? First, the locomotive; this, according to the attitude of the domestic authorities, has either to be taken down from its pedestal or else extracted from its hiding place, cleaned and carried out to the car. A 3½in gauge 4-6-0, weighing without tender, say 70lb can nicely be lifted by one man; 5in gauge locomotives, unless very small, need more than one. Next, all the paraphernalia of a miniature running shed, fire-irons, coal, kindling, two kinds of oil, tool-box, steam-raising blower, a few spare parts; then, away to the track.

Most live steam clubs provide steam raising sidings connected to the main line by a traverser or turntable and it is on one of these that operations begin. Perhaps the most amazing thing about these little locomotives is the way coal will burn on a tiny grate which may be as small as 1½in x 2½in and produce sufficient energy to drive them along hauling loads several times greater than scale. However, one effect that cannot be reproduced is the natural draught upon which full-size locomotives depend for raising steam; so, we have to provide forced draught, either by an electrically driven blower adapted to suck from the chimney, or by compressed air applied to a nozzle in an extension chimney.

After a crucial check to see if there is water in the boiler, we set up the blower, switch on, ignite the system with a scrap of paraffin-soaked rag and feed in first wood or charcoal, then coal to build up a fire. The fuel has previously been broken up into pieces which will enter a scale fire-hole door.

Raising steam in 3½in gauge is a fairly rapid operation, boilers are almost invariably 100% copper with excellent conductivity and the volume of water is 4,096 times less than full size. Where in full size steam raising one allows hours, in miniature one allows the same number of minutes, perhaps seven or eight, in fact barely time to get around the bearings with an oil can and fill the cylinder lubricator with that strange treacly sub-

Because points are so difficult the typical layout is of elemental simplicity, ovals or hour-glasses. Double ovals with a fly-over are a variation, Malden and St Mellons (Cardiff) are examples, exciting because the vertical clearance at the bridge must be sufficient for footboards below rail level to clear heads well above.

Other railway features can be more easily provided signalling is important when several locomotives may be out on the track at once and here we run the gamut of full-size practice from "permissive block" (a euphemism for being without signalling) to automatic four-aspect colour-light signalling with track circuits.

A station complete with platforms, footbridge and, hopefully, the usual

Top left: Stapleford Miniature Railway No 750 "Blanche of Lancaster" waits at Lakeside station.

Top: Kinver. A superbly finished 5in gauge LMS Jubilee, handled by a most professional looking driver, awaits entry to the station. *J B Hollingsworth*

Left: Haywards Heath. A 3½in gauge GWR County/Castle No 3052 "Stormy Petrel" blows off while waiting for passengers on the Sussex Locomotive Society's track. *J B Hollingsworth*

Above: Hilton Valley Railway No 7. A Great Western style 2-6-2 on the well known 7¼in. gauge line near Bridgnorth, Shropshire.

stance known as superheated steam oil.

There then comes perhaps the best moment, when the needle of the pressure gauge lifts off the zero stop pin, the artificial draught can be dispensed with and the engine's own blower turned on. Then and there she comes alive with a strong personality all her own.

A word with the track steward to check that all is clear and a short warming-up run in the sidings to clear condensed steam out of the cylinders completes the preparations. The locomotive is then moved on to the main line and coupled up to the flat cars which form the train. You and your passengers can now clamber on.

The mechanical lubricator will take care of the oiling and all you have to do is to judge how often to fire her and keep her to a safe speed. As you will realise, driving and firing of these little machines is no sinecure. First, you are doing tasks which in full size are allotted to two men. Second, with such a relatively minute volume of fire and water present, the steam production cycle can deteriorate very quickly. George Barlow, Operating Manager of the Romney, Hythe & Dymchurch Railway whose locomotives, one-third full size, come half way between the little ones we have been discussing and full size, finds that handling them comes easier to drivers with miniature experience than to those with full-size.

Every pleasure has its price and after the run there are the chores to carry out, drop the fire, clear the smokebox, sweep the tubes, and clean up. But there are other locomotives and their running to observe, endless discussions to be engaged in on the relative merits of Churchward and Gresley, Walschearts and Stephenson, compounds and simples, Welsh steam coal and Yorkshire hards, and so on and so on.

An annual competition is a feature of

Tingley. "Lion", a perfect gem of an old-timer attracts admiration.   *J B Hollingsworth*

Below: Brighouse. A 7¼in gauge model of an un-rebuilt "Royal Scot", kept busy by the crowds at an open day.   *J B Hollingsworth*

Left: R F Hanks' 5in gauge "Castle".

the clubs' year; one particular club acts as host and, with the aid of a dynamometer car, entrants run against one another and their performance is measured on the basis of coal consumed for the amount of work done, whilst performing a normal task for the locomotive concerned. The winners tend to have thermal efficiencies in the 2% region, compared with 6% for a good full size steam locomotive. This is, of course, fully accounted for by scale effects, some simplification, eg no exhaust steam injectors, and the smaller working pressure, say 100lb instead of 225lb and hence the lower temperature of the steam.

Ah, you may say, it is all very well to

describe the delights available to the lucky owner of a live-steam locomotive but nothing is said about how you become one. One can only say that a good first step is to join one of the clubs; most welcome new members, particularly anyone willing to lend a hand with the chores. Another is to take in the one and only periodical which deals with live steam, "The Model Engineer". The risk is not that you will find insufficient advice from these two sources, but rather there will be too much, and some of it contradictory.

Purchasing a second-hand locomotive is only barely less hazardous than horse dealing, and one can only emphasise rule one, which is to say, however nice she looks, do not part with money until she has been demonstrated in steam. Nevertheless there are good buys to be had, but few bargains, owners of good locomotives being only too aware of their value.

The alternative is to make your own; the cost, including equipping a workshop with machine tools, will be comparable with buying, except that, at the end of the day, one will have not only a locomotive, but a well equipped workshop and a considerable modicum of engineering skill. The chief hazard is the persistence and virulence of the bites of the locomotive building bug, incurable but rarely fatal; indeed, the therapy of making things with one's own hands is on the whole beneficial.

The "Model Engineer" carries serial articles on building live steam locomotives from A to Z and a number of these have been serialised as books. A fairly simple locomotive, say a 4-4-0 or 4-4-2, is suitable as a starter. Beware the too simple ones, they are sometimes a bit too plain to continue to inspire through the long construction period, perhaps two years or more.

The Rhyl Miniature Railway

This 15in gauge line round a small lake at Rhyl on the North Wales coast, opened in 1911, was unique in that for many years it held the record for continuous service. Regrettably, due to a change of ownership of the line and the land, it closed in 1970 after nearly 60 years. At the moment, the whole of the track, together with locomotives and rolling stock, is in storage, but enthusiasts hope that another site may be found before too long. Apart from its long-term existence the railway remained in almost original form for the whole of its period of operation and the trains were pulled by locomotives designed by Henry Greenly. The later types were specially designed for the railway and built in Rhyl, four of them worked for nearly 50 years and are still in excellent condition today.

Rhyl has always been a holiday resort for the Midlanders, being within easy reach by road and situated on the main London to Holyhead railway. The Local Council, mindful of this fact, concentrated on attractions to be enjoyed by visitors. At the west end of the town by the mouth of the river Clwyd some ground had been reclaimed for the purpose of forming an artificial lake; the area was laid out as a park with boats on the lake and other attractions operated by Rhyl Amusements Limited. In 1910 Miniature Railways of Great Britain Limited (the company formed by Bassett-Lowke and Henry Greenly and mentioned in other articles) approached the Council for a concession to run a miniature railway round the lake. The Council, seeing this as a further attraction for visitors, readily agreed and in December of that year Henry Greenly visited the site to survey it. He was very enthusiastic and

Above: A scene by Marine Lake, Rhyl, with a train in the 1920s. *A. Wood Collection*

plans were put in hand without delay for the construction of the line.

The track was to be a simple single line around the lake with the station in the north corner adjoining the road and a siding on the opposite side where the locomotive and coaches would be shedded. Only one train was envisaged at the outset, running clockwise round the circuit, and the construction presented few problems, the ruling gradient being 1 in 220 in a cutting of just over 100 yards on the west side. Progress was regularly reported in Greenly's magazine, "Models, Railways and Locomotives" and the April issue included a note to say that the plans had been passed by the Council: the line would be just a mile long and the gradients very favourable. The locomotive was to be of the standard "Little Giant" type named "Prince Edward of Wales" and a train of six cars was being specially built for the line; further details were promised in the next issue.

What Greenly failed to mention was that the locomotive was not in actual fact a new production, but "Little Giant" No 15, which had been built for the White City Exhibition of 1909 and named "Red Dragon". This practice was carried out on several occasions and obviously served to impress prospective customers with the number of locomotives built by the company. The locomotive in question was overhauled at Northampton and re-painted in Caledonian Blue before being despatched to Rhyl. The most interesting fact is that the original nameplates were re-used with the new name engraved on the other side and these are now in the

possession of the author. When attempting to trace lineage of a class of locomotives, failure to possess such information makes the task even more difficult!

Work on the site started in March 1911 and was completed ready for opening by the 1st May, a remarkable achievement, which it is unlikely would be emulated today, although few engineering problems were presented. The six new cars were the standard Bassett-Lowke four-wheeled eight-seaters and were painted in GWR chocolate and cream. Greenly hurried off to Southport to superintend the construction of another 15in gauge railway, which is now the oldest line running in this country. Everything was in the railway's favour and it was a great success. Evidently the summer of 1911 was a particularly good one as far as the weather was concerned, so many people decided to go to the seaside for their holidays and Rhyl had one of its best seasons.

Among the people who crowded on to the railway were many who wanted to ride on the tender, so footplate passes were issued at 1/- for adults and 6d for children. The Earl of Grosvenor, son of the Duke of Westminster, was one of many who enjoyed this experience. The July issue of "Models, Railways and Locomotives" reported that on Whit Monday, 5th June, 3,630 passengers were carried, 99 trains ran with the result that the locomotive travelled just over 100 miles in the 12 hours that the railway had been open. Better things were still to come for it was decided to make a supreme effort on the Bank Holiday Monday, 7th August. By this time gradient and mile posts had been fixed round the line and two extra cars had been supplied. The proprietors came from Northampton in force: as well as Bassett-Lowke there was Proctor Mitchell, who was soon to have much to do with the re-opening of the Ravenglass & Eskdale Railway, Henry Greenly, of course, and Fred Green who was the Works Manager from Northampton. The local members of the staff included Albert Barnes, the Manager, and Fred Smithies, who had been driving "Little Giants" ever since the first one was built, the assistant driver, aptly named Jones, and Kelly, the railway dog that appears in all the contemporary photographs sitting on the tender.

Another improvement was the fitting of simple vacuum brakes and Fred Green had spent the weekend installing the vacuum brake ejector on the locomotive. The contemporary account in the September issue of "Models, Railways and Locomotives", although short and to the point, captures the atmosphere of what must have been a very exciting day. At 9 o'clock the first train pulled out and immediately there was a small fault in that the joint on the steam brake pipe gave out. Not wishing to anticipate further trouble and as the vacuum brake was working well, the steam brake was removed from the locomotive: Fred Green dealt with this in 40 minutes and the second train left at 9.45 am. Details are given in the article of all the 93 trains that ran until the last at 10.15 pm. These include times of departure and numbers of passengers carried, together with who drove which train. The fastest trip was train No 69, achieved in six minutes and the greatest number of passengers carried on one trip was 74 on train 33; during the busiest period of the day all trains carried over 60 passengers.

"Prince Edward of Wales" performed splendidly and at the end of the day a total of 5,003 passengers had been carried, the ratio of adults to children being 3:2. It was finally noted that although the "Little Giant" had been quite successful "a new engine of larger dimensions is to be put in hand for the next season so as to have two trains available during the busy times".

In the following year the line was taken over by Rhyl Amusements Limited who, it will be remembered, were already the operators of the Lake Amusement Park. They continued to operate it until its closure in 1970. The extra locomotive which was acquired was in fact virtually identical to "Prince Edward of Wales" and came from the new line at Southport, which was opened shortly after the Rhyl line. Named "George the Fifth" it pulled a new train of six bogie coaches built at the Company's works at Rhyl. All the seats faced the same way because the trains always ran in the same direction, clockwise round the lake. A loop was provided in the station so that two trains could stand there at once. A dummy tunnel was built where the railway passed under the big dipper, this was also for storing rolling stock when not in use.

Mr Albert Barnes, the Manager, was the person responsible for these improvements and he soon had even more ambitious ideas. The "Little Giants" were not really man enough to handle the traffic that the railway might expect, so Greenly was asked to design a new type of locomotive. Greenly himself had always felt that the "Little Giants" were probably too small and so set to with enthusiasm. No doubt his experiences at Rhyl stood him in good stead for his designs for the Ravenglass & Eskdale and the Romney, Hythe & Dymchurch railways when he changed from the $\frac{1}{4}$ scale of the "Little Giants" to the $\frac{1}{3}$ scale. Greenly stuck to the "Atlantic" 4-4-2 wheel arrangement, but virtually all dimensions were enlarged; the width of the engine went up by $4\frac{1}{2}$in, cylinders from $3\frac{3}{8}$in x 6in to $4\frac{1}{4}$in x 7in, coupled wheels from 1ft 6in in diameter to 1ft 8in and the overall length increased by over a foot. The boiler pressure remained the same at 120 psi.

War broke out soon after the new locomotive was designed and it was not until 1919 that construction started. Albert Barnes was connected with the

family business in Rhyl that built the engines; over the years six of the type were built, numbered from 101 to 106 and named after the children of one of the Directors. There were three "Billies", together with "Joan", "John" and "Michael". Four engines worked at Rhyl and two were sold, one going to Manchester to the line at Belle Vue and the other to Dreamland at Margate. Both are still running satisfactorily although the one at Belle Vue, Manchester appeared for a time in North American disguise. When the Rhyl line was operating normally, three locomotives hauled two trains in rotation seven days a week from Whitsun to September and at Easter weekend. The fourth locomotive was the one undergoing a major overhaul, which took place every fourth year.

Apart from minor alterations to the line and the building of a new locomotive shed near the station in the 1920s, the pattern of operation remained the same until it was closed in 1970.

Below: The Barnes Locomotive at the main station. *N R Knight*

The Seaside,

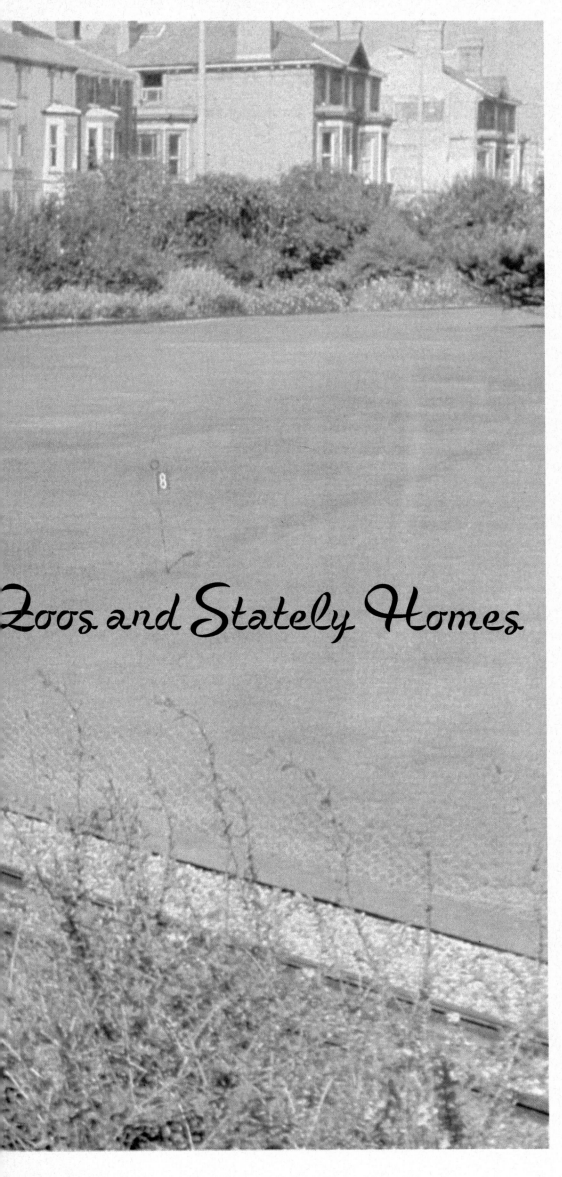

Zoos and Stately Homes

Public miniature railways operating commercially tend to be situated in established leisure areas. As a result, many are to be found at seaside resorts around Britain, a large number of them having been in operation for some years. Zoos also have their fair share, mostly with lines operating as an additional attraction for visitors. Since the war, with the opening of many stately homes to the public, a number have built miniature railways enabling visitors to see their grounds in comfort. This article does not cover every existing line in these three fields, but describes a cross section of those which are open to the public.

Dealing with the seaside first, there are a few lines which have been open since before the First World War. The Lakeside Miniature Railway, a 15in gauge line at Southport, commenced operation in 1911 equipped with Bassett-Lowke locomotives and rolling stock. The controlling interest was held for a number of years by Mr Llewellyn who was a local postman and called it the Llewellyn Miniature Railway. In the early thirties it passed to Harry Barlow who renamed it the Lakeside Miniature Railway. The two Bassett-Lowke Little Giant engines were extensively damaged in a fire and were rebuilt by Barlow. The precise formation of the track has changed from time to time, but it now runs alongside the lake from Pleasureland under the pier and then towards the sea to Peter Pan's Pool.

As with so many of the older lines described in this article, the steam locomotives have been sold and diesel engines of steam outline have taken their place. Mr Barlow built a number of these for lines in various parts of the country, probably his best known being those that operated in the Far Tottering and Oyster Creek Railway at Battersea Park in connection with the 1951 South Bank Exhibition; these were produced to the design of Mr Roland Emmett.

Another well established 15in gauge line is at Dreamland Park, Margate, where it is part of the amusement area of the Margate Estates Company. The original line was opened in the 1920s, designed and supervised by Henry Greenly. For many years the motive power consisted of two steam locomotives, one being a Bassett-Lowke Little Giant *Prince Edward of Wales* and the other a Greenly design called *Billie* built by Albert Barnes of Rhyl. Both these engines were of the 4-4-2 wheel arrangement. A petrol locomotive was added to the stock at a later date, *Prince Edward of Wales* having been sold. The line runs round the edge of the amusement park with a dummy tunnel used to store the stock in the winter and when trains are not in service. This is a favourite device on a number of miniature railways as a tunnel is considered to be an added attraction and the doubling up as a storage shed saves money. Often these tunnels are constructed of corrugated iron sheets of the type used as shuttering for air raid shelters in the last war.

The 12¼in line at Littlehampton is unique in that no other railways of this gauge exist in the country. It is believed that the locomotives were constructed from castings and parts designed by the late Mr Bullock who built a number of

Left: Lowestoft 10¼in gauge pleasure line. 4-4-2 No 1865, built by David Curwen.
Robin Butterell

10¼in gauge engines in the 1930s. The original owner of the railway thought that the extra 2in on the gauge would give additional stability. Two handsome 4-6-4 locomotives operate the line, which is about 900yds in length. Part of the route runs alongside a putting green and the locomotive shed and turntable are situated by the main station.

The remainder of the seaside lines described are all built to the 10¼in gauge, which is by far the most popular for passenger carrying at the present time and superseded the 9½in gauge which is now little used.

At Hastings there is a most ambitious 600yds line which operates at the East end of the town, close to the seashore. Controlled by the Ian Allan organisation, steam locomotives have been used for a number of years, but these have now been superseded by diesels. One of the

steam engines was a Royal Scot built by Bassett-Lowke in 1938 for a private line at Easthampstead Park: there was also a GWR 4-6-0 *Hampton Court* built by Trevor Guest to work on the original 10¼in gauge at Dudley Zoo Railway. The present line opened in 1948, having run for a season previously at St Leonards;

Right: Hastings. A 22 hp diesel on the 10¼in gauge line. *C J Gammell*

Below: Belle Vue Zoo, Manchester. The 15in gauge 4-4-2 "Railway Queen", built by Albert Barnes. *N R Knight*

Bottom: Newby Hall. The 10¼in gauge "Royal Scot". *N R Knight*

there are loops at either end with a passing loop in the middle. When two trains are running a five minute service is maintained.

In the late 1940s three lines on the south coast were owned by an organisation known as Southern Miniature Railways.

Left: Minehead Miniature Railway. 10¼in gauge Western Region type diesel "Exmore Enterprise", built by Curwen & Newbury in 1965. *F Pugh*

Below: Chessington Zoo Railway. 4-4-0 "Princess Margaret", built by Barnard & Co (1937) to 12in gauge. *Richard Sharpe Studios*

Bottom: Longleat Light Railway. No 6 "Dougal", a 15in gauge 0-6-0T locomotive built by Severn-Lamb in 1970. *F Pugh*

Situated at Bognor Regis, Southsea and Poole, they operated identical steam locomotives, the design being based on the original 4-4-2s built by Trevor Guest for the Dudley Zoo Railway. The Bognor Regis line has since disappeared with the building of a holiday camp on the site, but the lines at Southsea and Poole still run. That at Southsea was previously to the 9½in gauge, the motive power being one of the standard Bassett-Lowke GN Atlantics. The Poole line runs for about ¾ mile round the lake in Poole Park, a particularly attractive location. Both these railways are now making increasing use of petrol locomotives.

Another old established line is at Christchurch, operating in close proximity to a holiday camp. It is attractively laid out and has unusual motive power in a 4-6-2 Coronation Scot, which is a type rarely modelled in the larger gauges.

A number of railways are now running using petrol hydraulic models designed by David Curwen. These are replicas of the "Western" class diesel locomotives which have been in use for some time on the Western region of British Rail. They are now built by Severn-Lamb Limited of Stratford-upon-Avon. Two lines which use these engines are at Minehead and Brooklands, near Worthing. Both were opened in 1965, the Minehead line being about 400yds in length. Here the locomotive is called *Exmoor Enterprise* and operates on the continuous track which is laid immediately adjoining the seafront. There is an attractive station with signal box and overbridge, while at one point the line runs through a tunnel adjacent to the one-time British Rail branch. The Brooklands line runs round an ornamental lake, but was originally (when 9½in gauge) a point to point run.

The westernmost line in England is at Hayle on the North coast of Cornwall where the line is in the form of a balloon loop operated by Cromar White rolling stock, the firm supplying the complete railway. The track is situated in the sand dunes close to the beach.

At Lowestoft, the Borough has a short continuous line round a putting green near the seafront. The present motive power is a Freelance North American type 4-4-2 which is one of David Curwen's standard designs.

Colwyn Bay has a short line close to the seafront run by the Corporation; this adjacent to the main British Rail line to Holyhead. The locomotive named *Prince Charles* is based on the "Royal Scot" class of locomotive.

Turning to the lines operating at zoos, the oldest and most interesting is that at Belle Vue, Manchester. This 15in gauge line was opened in 1928, but the present formation is the third that has existed within the grounds, being relaid in 1964 as a continuous run. Chief interest centres around the two steam locomotives, one of which is the original Bassett-Lowke *Little Giant* (in its most advanced form) built in 1912 to run on a private railway at Sand Hutton in Yorkshire. Still in running order after a somewhat chequered career in a variety of locations, *Prince Charles* as it is now named, has been dressed up in North American disguise to be in character with the "Sante Fe Miniature Railway" as the line is now called. The other engine, similarly treated, called *Railway Queen*, is another Barnes 4-4-2 similar to the one operating at Margate. Another old established line is at Chessington Zoo, built to the unusual gauge of 12in, with motive power of steam outline petrol locomotives, the design being based

somewhat loosely on Great Western practice. A further line has been built recently entirely separate from this one with a model of the *Rocket*, regrettably powered by internal combustion.

The Dudley Zoo line started out in 1938 to the 10¼in gauge, as detailed in the profile of Trevor Guest, but was converted to 15in gauge after the last war. Worked by steam locomotives for a number of years, this attractively laid out line through the woods now relies on petrol locomotives, one of which is a steam outline 0-4-2T called *Clara*.

Paignton Zoo's 10¼in gauge line enables visitors to see an interesting selection of animals and birds on its continuous line round a lake. Motive power is petrol and diesel; *Pride of California* having been built by Trevor Guest for the original Dudley Zoo Railway. At one time, when this zoo was in association with Chessington, the line was 12in gauge.

The two most recently opened railways are at Blackpool and Twycross in Leicestershire. That at Blackpool Zoo has a distinctly North American flavour with locomotives, rolling stock and names to match. Two 15in gauge Severn-Lamb steam outline petrol locomotives pull trains from Wells Fargo to Dodge City. When two trains are operating from either end, they pass at a loop at the half-way point named Injun Creek. Both open and closed coaches are in use on the line.

Twycross Zoo has a 7¼in gauge rail-

way with Cromar White equipment consisting of a Hymek locomotive pulling a train of sit astride coaches. The track is laid in the form of a figure eight with a bridge crossing the line at the centre. The stock is kept in a "tunnel" type shed when not in operation.

With stately homes, the role of the miniature railway has now come full circle. In the early years of this century wealthy landowners built miniature railways either as a means of communication between their homes and the nearest station, or to provide amusement for themselves and their friends. Today,

with the economic problem of maintaining large buildings on dwindling budgets, many have thrown their doors open to the public, new miniature railways being built this time as a paying attraction for the visitors.

Longleat in Wiltshire, the home of the Marquis of Bath, has had a 15in gauge line for some years running alongside the lake towards the lions' enclosure, the railway being operated with steam, petrol, and electric locomotives. The steam engines, designed by David Curwen, are difficult to define as either miniature or narrow gauge locomotives because, although small in scale, they are not models of any particular prototype and could, therefore, be better classed as narrow gauge locomotives in their own right. A regular service is maintained at weekends and during the week in the holiday season, the terminus being situated next to the Children's Zoo.

At Thoresby Hall in the East Midlands, a 10¼in gauge line runs for about ½ mile in the grounds. Opened in 1969 it has unusual motive power in the shape of a model of *Sir Nigel Gresley,* one of the streamlined LNER pacifics. These are rarely modelled and it is interesting to see one built to such a large gauge.

Mr Kirkland, the builder, also operates a 7¼in gauge line on heath land near Ollerton at weekends from Easter to September.

At Newby Hall, near Ripon, there is a ½ mile line running along the banks of the river Ure with a lifting steel bridge. This 10¼in gauge line has a Royal Scot and a recently built Severn-Lamb diesel locomotive.

The well-known line at Stapleford will be described on the following pages.

One of the most attractive 10¼in gauge railways is situated at Audley End adjoining the entrance to Audley End

House, run by the Honourable Robin Neville. It has three Curwen designed locomotives, the first being one of the standard North American type 4-4-2s originally built in 1948. The second is a Great Northern 4-4-2 built in 1965 and is particularly robust and workmanlike. The other locomotive is one of the standard Western Class *Western Thunderer,* which are now built by Severn-Lamb. Stirling Moss opened the line in 1964 and since then several additional attractions have been added. The main station is well laid out with a signal box which is a model of the one nearby, being named Audley End Junction. The line takes passengers through woodland, over the river and then through gardens, making a total run of about ¾ mile.

The main conclusion to be drawn from observing the running of all these lines is the decline of the steam locomotive in favour of petrol or diesel motive power. This is largely for two reasons—a steam locomotive is very expensive to build and drivers for them are becoming increasingly difficult to find. An internal combustion engine has the advantage of immediate availability and does not require a skilled man to drive it.

It is hoped that there will always be a few at least who will be able to keep steam powered miniature railways in operation.

**Left: Margate. A 15in gauge 4-4-2 "Billie",
built by Albert Barnes, on the traverser.**
Robin Butterell

**Below: Audley End Miniature Railway. A
10¼in gauge David Curwen "Atlantic" No
3548 "Bobbie".** *N R Knight*

STAPLEFORD MINIATURE RAILWAY

The home of Lord and Lady Gretton is at Stapleford Park near Melton Mowbray in Leicestershire and the grounds have been open to the public for some years. A desire to provide more entertainment for children and the knowledge that a complete 10¼" gauge railway was available for disposal prompted the purchase of this equipment and construction was started in 1957. It was intended that the railway should not be just a gimmick, but correct, as far as possible, in every detail and performing a transport service within the park.

The original equipment consisted of two 4-4-2 locomotives built by David Curwen to his North American design, six coaches and sufficient track for a line from the cark park near the stables to a point adjacent to the Hall. The track was laid with the assistance of the late Mr W T Clark of Whissendine who had recently retired after 45 years' service as a platelayer with the Midland Region of British Rail. The first station, complete with platform shelter, situated near the car park was called Stable Hill. The opening ceremony was performed by the late Earl of Northesk on the 18th May 1958, in the presence of the late James Harrison MP, who had at one time been a driver on the London to Leeds expresses; Mr George Dow, then Commercial Officer, London Midland Region; Mr W B Carter, District Commercial

Manager, Derby, and David Curwen, the builder of the locomotives. During the course of his speech Lord Northesk reminded listeners that it was just over 100 years since the sixth and last Lord Harborough fought the battle of Saxby with the intention of preventing the Midland Railway from coming through this Park. There had been a full turn of the wheel and, as a result, it was to be hoped that the Stapleford Miniature Railway would be the means of giving pleasure to a large number of people for many years to come.

During the first season more than 8,000 tickets were sold to passengers travelling to and from the Hall. The only disappointment was the shortness of the run. The announcement that the railway would be extended down to the lake was, therefore, greeted with enthusiasm. This, however, presented a problem, the difference in the levels between the site for the Central Station and Lakeside accounted for a drop of no less than 17½ft. It thus became evident that a deep cutting would have to be made and the length of the route extended to ease the gradients on the return journey to the Central Station.

A Priestman Dragline Excavator was hired and by the beginning of September, a cutting 350yds in length had been completed. Some 2,150 tons of soil had been excavated and the cutting at the

deepest point was 12 feet below the surface of the ground. The next task was to build a concrete bridge across the cutting for the conveyance of farm tractors, the driving of cattle and the use of the shepherd on his rounds. The rails used for the extension consisted mainly of 14lb per yard continental section mounted on steel sleepers. These had to be broken down and the rails re-set on 2' x 4" wooden sleepers. The work of laying the track continued throughout the autumn and was resumed again in the spring. It was a hard struggle, but nevertheless the line was ready for the trains to travel down to the lake during the first week of May 1959.

It was during the course of this year that the Central Station was provided with a cantilever roof supported by metal columns. A turntable was installed near the engine shed and at Lakeside the platform was provided with a shelter, a Waiting Room and a Booking Office.

Top: No 6100 "Royal Scot" runs out of the replica Midland Railway tunnel entrance with a down train to Lakeside.

Below Right: The driver's controls of No 6100 "Royal Scot".

Below Far Right: SS "Northern Star" on the lake at Stapleford Park.

Above Right Centre: No 750 "Blanche of Lancaster".

Above Far Right: D100 "White Heron".

The major project planned for the season of 1960 was the construction of a train operated automatic level crossing at the point where lakeside trains cross a drive shortly after leaving the Central Station. This was accomplished by means of a track circuit and a sequence of micro switches which in turn control a road traffic light signal, a warning bell, the lowering and raising of the barriers across the roadway and lastly, the railway light signals. This improvement was not only popular with visitors, but it also eliminated the need to have a flagman on duty for the safety of all concerned. At Lakeside the interior of a small stone building, formerly used as a power house for making electricity and pumping water to the Hall, was converted into a railway Refreshment Room for the benefit of visitors desiring teas at the lake. At the close of the 1961 season, the railway had carried 20,000 passengers. The time had now come to obtain a third locomotive and to increase the coaching stock. An order was accordingly placed with David Curwen for a model of a Western Region diesel and six coaches. It also followed that an additional platform would have to be built at Lakeside for the accommodation of the new train which came into service on the 2nd June 1962.

The decision to build a ship was made in response to a desire by visitors to hire boats on the lake. This, it was felt could be dangerous because if anyone got into difficulty out of sight they would then be beyond the reach of help.

It was during a voyage from Southampton to Las Palmas on board ss *Southern Cross* that the idea first occurred to Lord Gretton that with the engine room in the stern it would be possible to make a model of an ocean-going liner since the central part of the ship could be used for the accommodation of passengers. Messrs Shaw Savill very kindly agreed to send drawings of their sister ship, the ss *Northern Star* and to give advice with regard to technical detail. As a result, David Curwen was approached and, after overcoming many difficulties, the first miniature passenger carrying liner came into being during the summer of 1963.

On Thursday, 27th June, the wife of the Chairman of the Shaw Savill Line performed the christening ceremony, which by coincidence took place two years later to the actual day upon which the parent ship was launched by the Queen Mother. The *Northern Star* is 45ft long with an 8ft beam and the single multi-blade paddle wheel is driven by a Ford 10hp engine through a pump and hydraulic motor. The ship draws 12″ and has a speed of about 4 knots. This new feature was so popular that a second vessel was commissioned to be built by Severn-Lamb Limited and to be called the ss *Southern Cross.* This vessel, fitted with a Ford Cortina engine came into service in June 1968, and in the same year took part in the Lord Mayor's Show in London, representing the Furness-Withy Group.

The locomotive stock on the railway now numbers five and a table showing the technical details appears at the end of this article. As already mentioned, the first two locomotives were built by David Curwen and are named *Blanche of Lancaster* and *John of Gaunt.* Although a number of refinements have been made to these locomotives, as will be seen from the table, they are substantially built and have carried the lion's share of the passengers since the railway came into being. The modifications have enabled the payloads on the lakeside trains to be increased where gradients between 1 in 50 and 1 in 100 have to be climbed. *John of Gaunt* has had the distinction of also featuring in films for the television series "The Avengers" and "Mrs Thursday" and is now able to haul a maximum of eight coaches on the lakeside route, although the average train load is about six coaches, with twelve passengers on each. In 1962 David Curwen produced one of his Western Region diesels to be called *White Heron* and powered by a Ford Cortina engine. As with the other locos, the technical statistics are given later, but it is interesting to note that this locomotive travels at a speed of 12 miles per hour at a maximum load of 5 tons. Originally the locomotive was fitted with a Vauxhall Viva engine and was the first one to be built by David Curwen after closing his works at Baydon in 1949. Normally this locomotive deals with all mid-week operations on Wednesdays and Thursdays and is second engine on the Lakeside run on Sundays.

In 1972 a scale model of the 4-6-0 *Royal Scot* arrived at Stapleford. This locomotive has an interesting history and belongs to a friend of Hon John Gretton, Lord Gretton's son, Mr G E Milligen and is currently on loan to the railway. The locomotive was built between 1966/72 and a number of people contributed to the work. Most of the work on *Royal Scot* was carried out by Mr William Whiteley and the locomotive is fitted with a

Gower boiler. The tender was the joint work of John Gretton, Mr G C Nicholson and Mr J Pickaver. Some of the parts used in its construction were salvaged from a previous *Royal Scot* belonging to Mr Milligen. Apart from these cylinders, wheels and a few small castings, the remainder of the locomotive is new. Although the external appearance of the engine is remarkably accurate, it only has two cylinders instead of three on the prototype. It has proved a very successful addition to the motive power and is considered to be an improvement on the original Bassett-Lowke *Royal Scot* design produced by Henry Greenly, on which it is based. The locomotive is also provided with scale tender coal plates, lockers and cab floor for exhibition purposes. It normally works from the lake with a maximum of four coaches, but cannot run to Stable Hill as the wheelbase is too long to take the curve after leaving Central Station.

The latest addition to the railway is a scale model of an American type 2-8-4 locomotive "Berkshire". It was built in 1970/71 by Coleby-Simkins and exhibited at the Model Engineer Exhibition in 1972 before starting work on the line. It has a welded steel boiler constructed by Michael Lugg and is 18' 9" long overall and weighs $4\frac{1}{2}$ tons. It has several interesting features which are noted later and is also equipped with a number of scale fittings for exhibition purposes.

During the winter of 1972/73 the Central Station has been enlarged so that trains approaching from opposite directions will not have to share the same platform. The solution adopted has been to retain the through line for the use of the local train to and from the car park and then create two bay platforms to accommodate the boat trains. An electrically operated traverser has been installed to provide for run-round facilities.

A further major work has been the construction of a landscaped tunnel (believed to be the first of its kind on $10\frac{1}{4}$" gauge railway) and in response to

requests from visitors that it would be "really quite dark inside", it has been sited on the bend in the cutting going down to the lake. From the point of view of safety, a "Magic Eye" has been fixed near the entrance to the tunnel. If trespassers should wander inside an alarm comes into operation and at the same time the interior is illuminated by overhead lights. The portals are the unique feature of the tunnel. At the east end a Midland Railway elliptical arch type of entrance, made with 12,000 scale size blue bricks is nearing completion. At the north end will be a replica of Brunel's famous Box Tunnel made of stone. This fine structure was finished during 1974. No doubt there will be further developments on this interesting line in the future which will keep it in the forefront of the most attractive miniature railways in England.

Top: No 752 "The Lady Margaret" waits for the right away with a trainload of visitors from Lakeside Station.

Above: No 6100 "Royal Scot" at Lakeside.

Top Right: No 752 "The Lady Margaret" with the Hon John Gretton awaits the next load of visitors at Lakeside Station.

Right centre: No 752 "The Lady Margaret" at Lakeside.

THE LOCOMOTIVES
No 750 *Blanche of Lancaster*
4-4-2 Atlantic

Designed by David Curwen and built in 1948 at Marlborough. Purchased 1958 from the Mablethorpe Railway, Lincs.

Original boiler made by Goodhand, Baker Valve Gear and Slide Valves.

Cylinders	$4\frac{1}{16}$" x $4\frac{7}{8}$"
Driving Wheel diameter	1' 1"
Bogie and trailing wheels dia	$7\frac{1}{4}$"
Wheelbase coupled	1' $4\frac{1}{4}$"
Engine total	7' $1\frac{1}{2}$"
Engine and tender	12' $3\frac{1}{2}$"
Width over footplate	1' 10"
Chimney to rail	2' $10\frac{1}{2}$"
Grate area	1.5 sq ft
Working pressure (non-superheated)	100 psi
Weight in working order Engine	16cwt
Tender	4cwt

Also fitted with:—

(1) Steam pressure differential cylinder drain cocks
(2) Enlarged brake blocks with Ferodo linings
(3) A double lapped brake valve (steam) (Berkshire pattern)
(4) Front engine bogie side control
(5) Lubricator fitted to brake cylinder
(6) Steam chest pressure gauge

No 751 *John of Gaunt* 4-4-2 Atlantic

Designed by David Curwen and built 1948 at Marlborough. Purchased 1958 from the Mablethorpe Railway, Lincs.

Locomotive dimensions as for *Blanche of Lancaster* (see above). New boiler 1970 by Gower of Bedford. Weight of engine increased to 19cwt.

Additional work carried out includes:—

(1) Fitting of larger steam pipes to each cylinder
(2) Fitting of larger exhaust and blast pipe
(3) Widening of main boiler steam pipe from the regulator
(4) Modified tapered slide valves in the cylinders
(5) Large poppet valve regulator
(6) An increase of weight of 3cwt and improved engine balancing
(7) Frame strengthened
(8) Larger firebox with greater water space and improved drafting
(9) Modified and chromed valve gear
(10) Pressure differential steam cylinder

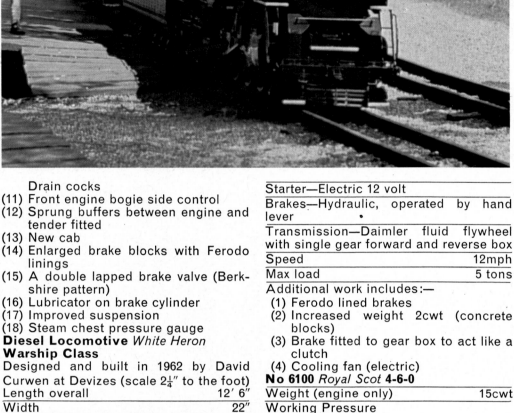

Drain cocks
(11) Front engine bogie side control
(12) Sprung buffers between engine and tender fitted
(13) New cab
(14) Enlarged brake blocks with Ferodo linings
(15) A double lapped brake valve (Berkshire pattern)
(16) Lubricator on brake cylinder
(17) Improved suspension
(18) Steam chest pressure gauge

Diesel Locomotive *White Heron* Warship Class

Designed and built in 1962 by David Curwen at Devizes (scale $2\frac{1}{4}$" to the foot)

Length overall	12' 6"
Width	22"
Height	36"
Engine—Ford Cortina 1600 (cross flow) (4 cylinder)	

Drive—Drive shafts with universal couplings and totally enclosed gears to all 8 wheels

Starter—Electric 12 volt	
Brakes—Hydraulic, operated by hand lever	
Transmission—Daimler fluid flywheel with single gear forward and reverse box	
Speed	12mph
Max load	5 tons

Additional work includes:—

(1) Ferodo lined brakes
(2) Increased weight 2cwt (concrete blocks)
(3) Brake fitted to gear box to act like a clutch
(4) Cooling fan (electric)

No 6100 *Royal Scot* 4-6-0

Weight (engine only)	15cwt
Working Pressure (Non-superheated)	150psi
Driving wheel diameter	1' $2\frac{1}{2}$"
Walschearts valve gear with piston valves	
Cylinders (2)	$3\frac{1}{2}$" x 6"

Additional features include:—

Right: No 751 "John of Gaunt" with No 6100 "Royal Scot" in the background on the shed at Central Station. *N R Knight*

Overleaf Top: A fine impression of power given by the motion of No 752 "The Lady Margaret".

Overleaf below: The engine sheds at the Central Station showing, left to right, No 6100 "Royal Scot", No 752 "The Lady Margaret", D100 "White Heron".

(1) Increased engine and tender weight for good adhesion
(2) High Boiler pressure, 150psi (original was 100psi)
(3) Steam brakes with Ferodo linings on engine and tender
(4) Steam pressure differential cylinder drain cocks
(5) Steam operated ashpan rake to clear pans to avoid manual cleaning (2 flat bottomed ashpans)
(6) Steam chest pressure gauge

No 752 *The Lady Margaret*
2-8-4 "Berkshire"

Scale	$2\frac{1}{4}$' to 1ft
Length (Engine and tender)	18' 9"
Height	3' 0"
Width	2' 0"
Weight	$4\frac{1}{2}$tons
Cylinders (2)	$4\frac{1}{2}$" x $7\frac{1}{2}$"
Baker valve gear	
Working pressure	150psi
Driving wheels	1' 1"

Interesting features include:—
(1) Tipping grate and self-emptying ash-pans
(2) Mechanised stoker, steam operated (2 cylinder steam engine)
(3) 2 Electric turbines for headlights and water gauge lights
(4) All round mechanical lubrication (26 pumps)
(5) 3 valve poppet regulator on super-heater header
(6) Feed water pump
(7) Heating coils on lubricators
(8) 2 Twin cylinder air compressors
(9) Woodward drive system
(10) 2 "Buckeye" tender trucks (6 wheels)
(11) Air operated brakes throughout engine and tender. Auxiliary steam brakes on the engine only
(12) Air operated fire hole door
(13) Air operated firing jets, for coal distribution in the firebox
(14) Air operated sanding equipment

HILTON VALLEY RAILWAY

Bridgnorth in Shropshire has come into prominence recently as the headquarters and terminus of the Severn Valley Railway, which runs south alongside the river and is one of the better known preserved standard gauge lines in the country. Not far away, adjoining the road from Wolverhampton, in the small village of Hilton, is a 7¼in gauge railway which provides all the elements of mainline operation in miniature. Together with the Forest Railway in Cornwall and the Great Cockrow Railway in Surrey, it is one of the three most ambitious lines in this gauge in the country. The late Michael Lloyd, who conceived and built the railway, was originally interested in trams and trolley buses, but also had an extensive O gauge railway which he started at the age of 14. This was a three rail electric line operating items of Bassett-Lowke rolling stock. In 1955, when passing through Leicester, he saw a miniature railway advertised for sale and, following further investigation, purchased the locomotive, together with some track and coaches for £300, which formed the nucleus of the present railway.

This first engine, named "Lorna Doone" is a 4-6-2 built in 1925 by Lewis

Shaw which operated pre-war on the Mablethorpe Miniature Railway. This veteran locomotive which has since been extensively overhauled by Mr A J Glaze, is fitted with Stephenson link valve gear and two 2in x 3in outside cylinders.

The railway was opened to the public for the first time in 1956; other motive power at that time being a Royal Scot, later sold, and a battery electric locomotive originally built for the 10¼in gauge, but subsequently converted to the narrower gauge. The railway was an immediate success and over the past

18 years the line has been extended, extra rolling stock added and many other improvements made. In 1963, extensive flooding washed away part of the track, so careful thought was given to its relaying. The ash ballast, previously used, has been replaced by crushed slag and most of the sleepers are now tanalised elm. Half the 1963 season was lost because of the flooding, but since then the line has operated most Sundays and Bank Holidays between Easter and September in the afternoons; at busy times a train can be expected to depart at approximately five minute intervals. A mixture of 9lb and 14lb per yard flat bottom rail is used on the main line whilst some of the original lighter section is laid in the sidings. The points are spring loaded, the line being controlled by colour light signals which divide it into two main sections. Single line staffs are used, coloured red and blue to avoid confusion. The method of picking up and putting down the staff is ingenious in that a catcher is used so that as the staff is dropped over a counter balanced

Above: A busy Sunday afternoon train hauled by 4-8-4 American-type loco No 3 "Francis Henry Lloyd" approaching Lawn Pastures.

peg, an electric change-over switch is operated which changes the aspect light to green. Using this system it is possible for four trains to be in operation on the railway at the same time.

The permanent steam locomotive stud consists of the original "Lorna Doone", which is No 1, with two other engines. No 2, based on a freelance narrow gauge prototype, is a 2-6-0 built by Jos N Liversage who operated it on Herne Bay Pier for a number of years where it was called "Teddy". This locomotive, now named "Hilton Queen", has also been extensively rebuilt and reboilered since it was acquired. Locomotive No 3 is a freelance Canadian type which was started by Trevor Guest to be completed by the apprentices at the training school of the firm of which Michael Lloyd was chairman. This powerful 4-8-4, named "Francis Henry Lloyd", is able to cope with the heaviest trains on the line. It is fitted with Baker valve gear and screw reverse. Other engines operate on the railway from time to time, a 2-6-2 of Great Western outline running regularly in recent seasons. Although steam is the major attraction on the railway there are interesting battery electric and petrol locomotives which augment the stock at busy times, also being used on maintenance and works trains.

The most interesting of these was originally a petrol-mechanical locomotive numbered 6, but this has now been completely re-built as petrol-electric. In its original form it must have been one of the most remarkable 7¼in gauge locomotives in existence as it had a totally enclosed driver's cab enabling the operator to travel in great comfort, but with the high centre of gravity there were problems with stability and the re-building has improved this.

A new steam locomotive came into service in 1974 and became one of the largest and most powerful 7¼in gauge engines in the country. Based on a 2ft 6in gauge Bolivian engine, this 2-8-0 features two 4¼in diameter cylinders. It was being built by Mr A J Glaze to drawings prepared by Mr Levie, who has designed the extremely efficient roller bearing bogies for all the stock on the railway and which are noted for their very smooth running. The main station on the railway, known as Hilton, adjoins the car park where the locomotives and rolling stock are also shedded. The station itself consists of an island-platform with an overall roof and from here a track runs to the turntable, from which nine lines now radiate. Three of these run into the latest building, which contains an inspection pit, another branch from the station leading to the carriage sheds. An ingenious device exists outside the sheds to assist with raising steam, this being a movable arm on which the blowers are situated to be placed over whichever track is appropriate. The locomotive water supply tank is fed from the adjoining trout stream.

The route of the line is particularly attractive as for the whole of the distance it is within a few feet of the local brooks and is also thickly wooded in parts. Leaving Hilton, the line runs over two small culverts and then reaches the original terminus known as Lawn Pastures. The loop here is now a passing place, the line continuing on to Bradney Bridge. Trains pass on the loop at Lawn Pastures, the movement being controlled by the staff system already mentioned. Bradney Bridge again acted as the terminus of the line for a time with a pas-

sing loop and turntable which are still in situ, but this is now only used as a relief siding as trains cannot pass each other here. This means there is only one section from Lawn Pastures to the end of the line.

After leaving Bradney Bridge, the line passes over a cattle grid, then into a deep cutting, swinging round the loop at Stratford Brook where trains pause before starting the return journey. When four trains are running at once, Stratford Brook, like Lawn Pastures, is used as a passing place. It also gives the driver an opportunity to service his locomotive during the halt, which lasts about three minutes, while the passengers can enjoy the rural scenery. On the return trip the train passes round the opposite side of the loop at Lawn Pastures before running back into Hilton station. Twelve minutes is the approximate duration of a trip and, on an average Sunday afternoon upwards of 1,000 passengers may be carried in the five hours that the railway is open

After each trip, the locomotive, detached from its train, moves on to the turntable and is positioned ready for the next run. Everything is organised on the railway to keep operational procedure to a minimum while ensuring that the safety of all trains is fully protected. The total part-time staff numbers about twelve, but often there will be a working party of half a dozen people carrying out maintenance work on the track.

The rolling stock on the line which consists of open and closed vehicles, remarkable on so small a gauge, has been the subject of very careful design. The main object was to achieve a very low centre of gravity so that any tendency to overbalance with passengers leaning out was virtually impossible. Obviously the overturning risk on a $7\frac{1}{4}$in gauge railway is considerably greater than on the larger gauges even when passengers are exhorted to sit up as straight as possible. The temptation to lean out, especially when going round a curve, to get a better view of the locomotive at the head of the train can be irresistible. The average number of passengers carried is around 30,000 a year, an excellent figure for so small a line, all the profits going to charity.

Since Michael Lloyd's tragic death, the railway has been operated by his son, Daniel, also a keen enthusiast, and it is obviously appropriate that the Hilton Valley Railway should continue to operate as a fitting memorial to this kindly and generous man.

Top left: Locomotive No 2 "Hilton Queen" waits at Stratford Brook for clearance to return to Hilton.

Top right: Petrol locomotive No 6 with a lightly loaded train approaches Lawn Pastures.

Centre left: The driver placing the staff on catcher as No 1 "Lorna Doone" passes Lawn Pasture Junction with a down train.

Centre right: Michael Lloyd with No 1 "Lorna Doone" waits for a clear road at Stratford Brook.

Far left: Diesel locomotive No 8 with a down train mid-way between Hilton and Lawn Pasture. Hilton House is seen in the background.

Left: Happy travellers on the Hilton Valley Railway.

These three railways are the major existing lines built to the 15in gauge in the British Isles. Although widely separated from each other they share certain characteristics and their histories are largely linked by personalities common to them all. They have passed through periods of depression when their futures were in doubt, but all are now happily in the ascendant; two of them were at one time operated by the same company, having been adapted from derelict narrow gauge lines and have also exchanged motive power. All three use locomotives designed by Henry Greenly, acknowledged as the most famous of miniature railway engineers.

The pioneer of 15in gauge railways, Sir Arthur Heywood built a private line on his estate at Duffield Bank near Derby to demonstrate the practical applications of the gauge and some of his equipment was inherited by all of the lines. More will be said about him in an article dealing with early miniature railways.

In the early 1900's Greenly was associated with W J Bassett-Lowke, founder of the wellknown model firm, in a venture to build and run 15in gauge passenger carrying railways. This company, originally known as "Miniature Railways of

Great Britain", was followed by another known as "Narrow Gauge Railways Limited". The latter operated railways at Geneva and Oslo, but was looking for suitable sites in the British Isles. In due course NGR came upon the Ravenglass & Eskdale Railway in Cumberland, built to the 3ft 0in gauge in 1875 to carry iron ore down to the coast. This railway, during a somewhat chequered career, had limped along over the years from one financial crisis to another until it finally expired in 1913. When Bassett-Lowke discovered it, the line was in a very run down state, but a lease was negotiated with the former owners and work immediately started on narrowing the gauge. Half the new railway was opened by the end of 1915 and the full length of 7 miles in the following year.

To work the line the company used a Bassett-Lowke 4-4-2 *Sans Pareil* and some rolling stock which had worked previously at Oslo and augmented this

Left: RHDR "Southern Maid". *C M Whitehouse*
Above: The cab interior of "River Mite".
N R Knight
Below: Ravenglass & Eskdale Railway:
Ravenglass shed with "River Mite" in the
foreground and "River Esk" and "River Irt"
in the shed. *N R Knight*

The Ravenglass & Eskdale, Fairbourne and Romney, Hythe Dymchurch Railways

with extra stock from Duffield Bank, plus another Heywood locomotive which had run on the railway at Eaton Hall built for the Duke of Westminster and named *Katie.* As the railway prospered, still more stock was added from Duffield Bank after Sir Arthur Heywood's death, including two locomotives, an 0-6-0T *Ella* and an 0-8-0T *Muriel.* A further Bassett-Lowke locomotive came via Eaton Hall where it had been on trial. This was a 4-6-2 designed by Greenly and built for Captain Howey to run on his private line at Staughton Manor, who was at this time a prisoner-of-war in Germany. Named *Colossus* it was joined shortly by another Pacific of very similar design, by Hunt of Bournemouth, called *Sir Aubrey Brockle-bank* after the local landowner who had an interest in the railway.

The Ravenglass & Eskdale Railway continued to operate through the twenties and thirties in a reasonably prosperous state until the outbreak of the second World War, especially as the company opened up a large granite quarry served by the line. During this period considerable modifications were made to the locomotives. *Colossus* and *Sir Aubrey* were re-built as a single locomotive called *River Mite*; *Sans Pareil* was scrapped, *Muriel* was re-built as a tender locomotive of miniature outline and called *River Irt.* A new locomotive *River Esk,* designed by Henry Greenly and built by Davey Paxman of Colchester, was added to the line in 1923. With this 2-8-2 Greenly produced a design of locomotive that was in essence one-third full size running on one-quarter full size track. Visually this was quite acceptable and gave a more practical and commercial result.

Top: "River Esk" outside the shed at Ravenglass. *N R Knight*

Right: "River Mite" on the turntable at Dalegarth. *N R Knight*

Below: "River Irt" complete with tall chimney waits on the shed at Ravenglass. *N R Knight*

had been part of an experimental steam operated tender for *River Esk. River Irt* has reverted to a more narrow gauge appearance by being fitted with a larger cab, chimney and dome and a new tender. Much new covered rolling stock has been built and this is very necessary in a situation where it is possible to leave Ravenglass in bright sunshine only to arrive at the other end of the line in mist and pouring rain.

The station buildings have all had attention and at Ravenglass there is now an impressive awning which came from the old BR station at Millom. Each winter about 600yds of track is re-laid with new rail on Jarrah sleepers and by Easter 1974 there will be enough new covered coaches to cater for all passengers. The railway also claims to be the first line to be sprayed with Asulam weedkiller from the air to help keep the bracken at bay. 24 acres were dealt with in this way in the autumn of 1973.

There are also plans for a new steam locomotive and a possible extension of the line at the Ravenglass end. Happily the Ravenglass & Eskdale Railway now continues to prosper not only because it is a line situated in one of the most attractive parts of the country, but also due to the efforts of a small body of dedicated enthusiasts.

The Fairbourne Railway, like the Ravenglass & Eskdale, was adapted from an existing line. As the standard gauge railway reached the Welsh coast, the nucleus of many of the existing seaside resorts was born, as the Victorian middle classes from Birmingham made their first visits to the seaside. A 2ft gauge horse-drawn tramway had been opened here in 1890, originally as a mineral line from a brickyard to Penrhyn Point. As the houses were built, passenger cars were added to the tramway and the line was operating in this way when Narrow Gauge Railways Limited arrived on the scene in 1916, at the same time as they were re-opening the Ravenglass & Eskdale Railway, and once again reduced the gauge to 15in.

A new Bassett-Lowke 4-4-2 locomotive (not quite as advanced as *Sans Pareil*) was supplied, together with a number of 4 wheel passenger cars of Bassett-Lowke standard type, the route being virtually identical to the original tramway and 1½ miles in length.

In 1924, Narrow Gauge Railways Limited sold the line. Two years previously *Katie*, the Heywood locomotive of the Ravenglass & Eskdale, was exchanged for *Prince Edward of Wales* with the miniature railway at Southport. This curious transaction, when *Katie's* days were already numbered, seemed an odd move and under its new owners the line went steadily downhill. *Katie* finally succumbed and her frames lay in the sand dunes for many years until students of the Heywood era, realising her place in history, persuaded the present owner to allow them to be displayed at the Narrow Gauge Railway Museum at Towyn.

In 1925 the owners of the line, the Fairbourne Estate & Development Company, without any motive power approached Bassett-Lowke and were offered a 4-4-2 similar to *Sans Pareil* of the Ravenglass & Eskdale Railway, which had recently been completed for Count Louis Zborowski, who had just been killed motor racing at Monza. In the following year the company acquired a 4-2-2 Stirling Single built to the 18in gauge and originally constructed at the

Top: Fairbourne Miniature Railway: "Count Louis" and train of holiday makers waits at Bathing Beach Halt.

Above: "Katie" waiting with her train in the Golf Course passing loop.

Left: "Dingo" one of the petrol driven engines running through the sand dunes after leaving Penrhyn Point.

society had been formed, but had only raised £5,000. Mr Colin Gilbert, a Midlands stockbroker who had already considered buying the line, agreed to back the society for any necessary balance and it was bought at the auction for £12,000. Following this, the Ravenglass & Eskdale Railway Company Limited was formed to operate the line with Mr Gilbert as the major shareholder. Douglas Ferreira was appointed General Manager and Tom Jones returned as Engineer. Since then, the line has gone from strength to strength and the past ten years have been a period of steady improvement. Two new diesel locomotives have been added to the stock, known as *Royal Anchor* and *Shelagh of Eskdale* and in due course a new steam locomotive, a 2-8-2 called *River Mite*, was built by Clarksons of York, paid for by the Preservation Society supporting the railway. This utilised a chassis which

Passenger traffic ceased during the war, but the carriage of stone continued. When matters returned to normal, the passenger service resumed, but the mineral traffic gradually deteriorated and as this was really the mainstay of the line, the Keswick Granite Company, the operator at that time, decided to offer it for sale in 1958. The asking price was £22,500, but as no bids approaching this were received it was decided to offer the whole at auction in 1960. A preservation

Regent Street Polytechnic by the students (one of whom was Henry Greenly) from castings supplied by W G Bagnall Limited in 1898. Undaunted by the difference in gauge, the operators laid a third rail to accommodate this locomotive, but this never reached beyond the half way point on the line and was removed in 1938. The locomotive had been sold to the Jaywick Railway in 1936. Recently restored, it will shortly be running again on a private railway.

In 1927 the line changed hands yet again and from then on the railway went into a decline. By 1939 *Count Louis,* the Bassett-Lowke locomotive named after its original owner, was in trouble and in 1940 after the outbreak of the second World War the line closed completely.

After the war most people thought that the Fairbourne Railway was finished. Much of the track had been displaced by storms and in places where the wind had drifted the sand dunes it was completely buried, but a new operating company led by John Wilkins, a Midlands industrialist, decided to salvage it.

Apart from *Count Louis,* the only other motive power was a Lister petrol locomotive, so both engines were taken away and in 1946 the Lister returned to begin reconstruction of the line. In the following year the line was completely reopened and *Count Louis* also returned. Since then a number of new locomotives and rolling stock have been added to the line and at Fairbourne a considerably enlarged terminus was built on the other side of the stream that runs alongside the railway for a short distance. Apart from the diesel and petrol locomotives, steam engines were supplied by Trevor Guest, as mentioned in a previous article. Two Stanier type locomotives, *Prince Charles* and *Ernest Twining* came from Dudley Zoo and these and *Count Louis* were eventually joined by two 2-4-2 locomotives with a more narrow gauge outline and named *Sian* and *Katie.*

The railway now operates a published timetable and provides a useful public service by connecting with the ferry to Barmouth. As in the case of the Ravenglass & Eskdale Railway, having passed through a period of decline, the line now appears to have an assured future.

The Romney, Hythe & Dymchurch Railway has always been known as the world's smallest public railway and is internationally famous for a number of remarkable features. One being that it is now the only privately owned railway in the British Isles where it is possible to travel non-stop for 27 miles behind a steam locomotive—and this is on the 15in gauge. Captain Howey, who, as it will be remembered, had a private line at Staughton Manor and whose 15in gauge Pacific went ultimately to the Ravenglass & Eskdale Railway, had long entertained the idea of an ambitious 15in gauge railway which would fulfil a public service. He looked at several possible sites in the country and even considered purchasing the Ravenglass & Eskdale Railway before deciding on a line from Hythe to Dungeness in Kent. He was joined by Count Louis Zborowski, already mentioned in connection with the Fairbourne Railway, and plans for the line were well advanced when Zborowski was killed. Howey continued alone and the first part of the railway was opened In 1927 with the extension to Dungeness completed two years later.

Top left: Romney, Hythe and Dymchurch Light Railway: "Northern Chief" and train leaving St. Mary's Bay. *C M Whitehouse*

Left: "Typhoon" leaves Hythe with a heavy train. *C M Whitehouse*

Top right: "Hercules" about to leave Dymchurch. *C M Whitehouse*

Right: The Davy Paxman makers plate which is on "Southern Maid". *C M Whitehouse*

Below: Fairbourne Railways *Ernest Twining* arrives at Penrhyn Point with an afternoon train.

The steam locomotives for this line were designed by Henry Greenly soon after *River Esk* had started working on the Eskdale Line and were constructed by Davey Paxman of Colchester. Howey wanted miniature versions of Sir Nigel Gresley's new Pacific locomotives on the LNER and Greenly designed them to one-third full size, as with *River Esk*. Five were built, together with two 4-8-2s, similar in general outline and intended for goods traffic. Later two North American type 4-6-2's, also designed by Greenly, were built by the Yorkshire Engine Company in 1931. One additional steam locomotive, an 0-4-0 tender engine built by Krauss of Munich in 1926, was used extensively during the building of the railway. Not really suitable for regular passenger traffic it was sold in 1934 to run on a railway in Belfast and lay derelict in a scrapyard for 25 years; it is now back at New Romney being re-built.

The line presented few engineering

problems apart from crossing a number of dykes and several roads, most of the latter having ungated level crossings, but two major roads are carried over the line on bridges. Covered rolling stock is used throughout and these coaches have been augmented and improved over the years with the experience gained in their operation.

The railway had a fairly uneventful life until the outbreak of the second World War, when it was taken over by the army and an armoured train operated on the line. Its most interesting role was to carry sections of the pipeline known as PLUTO, which ran from Dungeness to Northern France forming a vital link in carrying fuel supplies after the invasion. After the war the track was in very bad repair and it was some time before things were fully operational again. Luckily the locomotives have always been well cared for and in the post war years this has been largely due to the expert maintenance supervised by George Barlow, who joined the railway in 1947, was for many years the chief driver, and is now the operating manager of the line.

Although the railway has always operated a regular passenger service for most of the year, its continuation mainly depended on the enthusiasm of its owner, Captain Howey. When he died in 1963 there was much speculation about the future of the line, but it was eventually acquired by Mr S H Collins who hoped to keep it running in much the same way. However, various problems arose and the new directors put the line up for sale in 1971.

Fortunately a group of railway enthusiasts led by W H McAlpine got together and raised enough money to take over the line and keep it running. The new organisation took over at the beginning of 1972 and McAlpine became Chairman of the Company.

The past two years have been a time of taking stock and planning for the future. The railway needs almost complete renewal apart from the locomotives which, although over 40 years old, are still in good heart and most were re-boilered in the 1950/60s. Between one and two miles of track will be re-laid each winter. All the station buildings need urgent attention and there are plans for a major re-development of Hythe Station. New rolling stock is also urgently re-

quired and, over the next ten years, almost all of the coaches will have to be replaced. Fifteen have been re-built so far, using the original frames, bogies and brake gear although the 16ft frames are being extended to 24ft in length. Unlike the new Eskdale coaches, with aluminium bodies and sliding doors on one side only, the new RH&DR 20 seater saloons have wooden bodies finished with a hardwood veneer, which is varnished, and with sliding doors on both sides.

The General Manager, Peter Hawkins, the Operating Manager, George Barlow and the Traffic Manager and Engineer, Tony Crowhurst, look after the day to day running of the railway with John Snell as the resident Managing Director. The railway is also supported by an active association, members carrying out voluntary duties under the guidance of the permanent staff.

Interesting matters which have occurred recently include the renaming of the pub at New Romney as the "Captain Howey" at the instigation of Peter Hawkins and with the whole-hearted co-operation of the Brewery; another is the improvement to the layout at New Romney which, together with a new passing loop at Maddisons Camp enabled the RH&DR in 1974 to be the first British steam "preserved" line to offer a regular interval service with trains every 20 minutes from Hythe to New Romney and hourly to Dungeness.

It can be seen that these three railways, as stated at the outset, although bedevilled by problems at various times during their history, are now all faced with an assured future because they are controlled and operated by people who basically put pure commercial consideration second to the main aim of preservation.

Right: "Typhoon" ready for the off.
C M Whitehouse

Below: "Southern Maid" on the down "Marshlander" at Hythe in 1958.

Forest Miniature Railway

The Forest Railway really began with a 5in gauge line for the Southern family's private use, but the acquisition of two fine Duchess class Pacifics in 7¼in gauge sowed the seeds for the future. Although at this stage it was never intended that the railway should be open to the public, every time steam was raised friends (and strangers) would appear, seemingly out of the ground, and ask for rides. Realising the potential of the railway as a tourist attraction, it was decided to "go public" in 1970. Since then the railway has not only extended to its present length of one mile, but has also achieved a standard of businesslike efficiency which could be an example to many other privately owned railways of considerably larger size in England.

The 7¼in gauge layout was started in 1967; when the ingenious plan had been worked out, the ground surveyed and the route pegged out, work started with bulldozers and diggers. As there were to be cuttings and embankments, the rough earthworks were left to settle for six months before the final grading took place. Over 100tons of ballast were laid from two 5cwt trucks followed by the first sections of track. These consisted of 15ft lengths of aluminium alloy rail, screwed to timber sleepers.

The first layout of just over ½ mile took two years to complete and in March 1968 3,000 trees were planted to enhance the scenic appearance of the line. These are now well established, some having grown to a height of 15ft, making the run much more attractive. Once the railway was open to the public, a car park, station building, ticket office, lavatories and a cafe were all provided. Now there are footbridges over the line to picnic areas with rustic tables and seats where visitors can bring their own food and watch the trains go by.

The locomotive power on the railway is now extremely interesting. One of the Duchesses was sold soon after acquisition, the other, 6233 *Duchess of Sutherland*, working almost alone for the first two years; a scale locomotive more than 30 years old, it covered 1,500 miles in the initial season without any mechanical troubles—a firm tribute to its maker, the famous Harry Powell of Crewe. It was in the second year that the railway took on the North American flavour which it now has. This began with the arrival of a model of one of the Denver and Rio Grande locomotives, designed and built by David Curwen. This 2-8-2 based on narrow gauge practice is a model of surprisingly large dimensions for the 7¼in gauge; the locomotive and tender are 13ft 6in overall, 2ft 1in in width and stand 2ft 8in high from rail level to top of chimney. In fact it is almost the same size as some of the diminutive 15in gauge locomotives which were built in America at the turn of the century by Cagney. On the severe gradients on the line, this locomotive has found no difficulty in pulling sixty adults up 1 in 25 and has

hauled more than 50,000 passengers in one season. Apart from weighing 1 ton in full working order it has a tractive effort approaching 1,000lbs.

A diesel locomotive was added to the stud about the same time as the D & RG *General Palmer* was acquired; this is based on an English Electric type shunting engine. It is a useful standby for works trains and if a sudden influx of visitors requires an additional train at short notice. For a short time also, one of David Curwen's Western Region diesels, named *Western Warrior,* ran on the line, but this has now been sold. During 1973 *General Palmer* was joined by a sister engine *Queen of Colorado* belonging to another steam enthusiast and is on loan to the line as a standby engine.

The latest permanent acquisition is a further Curwen locomotive, an 0-6-0 tender engine with outside frames, in appearance an imaginary locomotive running on a plantation in the Scilly Isles with distinctly Great Western characteristics. This engine, which is finished in blue livery and equipped with a large headlight and cow catcher, has proved to be a most useful and reliable addition to the stud. Although originally planned to be called "Daffodil", it has been named *David Curwen* after its builder—a tribute to this well-known model locomotive engineer.

Future plans include a GWR "Castle" begun by Harry Powell and now being completed by Lewis Raper. Also under construction is a Union Pacific 800 Class 4-8-4. When this project is complete it will be fair to claim that it will be the most powerful $7\frac{1}{4}$in gauge locomotive in the world.

The first train of the day, carrying 30 people, leaves at 10.30 am during the season. Before this departs over an hour is spent each day on checking over the whole track to ensure that everything is in satisfactory operational order.

General Palmer stands at the head of the six coach train, consisting of sit astride vehicles with padded foam seats. These are extremely comfortable and ride very well. They are also fitted with a continuous air brake, which is rare on a line of this size. The main station, Forest Central, is a simple timber building with overhanging awning containing the cafe at platform level with lavatories beneath. Passengers wait behind white painted railings until the previous loaded train

Previous page: Holiday Train: Denver & Rio Grande No 488 "General Palmer" drifts into Forest Central from Lost Souls Canyon. *John Southern*

Above: Owner driver: John Southern at the controls of his 2-8-2 No 488 "General Palmer". *Robin Butterell*

Below: Duchess Pacific: One of the late Harry Powell's masterpieces No 6233 "Duchess of Sutherland". *John Southern*

Centre: Small and large Curwen's: 0-6-0 "Plantation" type side-by-side with the Rio Grande engine at Forest Central station: the small engine is named in honour of it's maker. *Robin Butterell*

Far right: Gunnison Tunnel: as with the prototype in Colorado the railway abounds in steep gradients sharp curves and tunnels. *Robin Butterell*

has left the platform and are then admitted by the guard to take their seats. There are now three running lines through the station, one adjoining the platform and two through roads. The whole railway is fully protected by colour light signals. A scale signal box and water tower complete the equipment at the station. When ready to depart there is a shout from the guard to keep your feet on the boards and arms and legs in, a blast on the whistle, an answering hoot from *General Palmer* and the train is away up a 1 in 25 gradient.

Climbing up the outside of the circuit the line passes under a gantry, across another track on the level by a diamond

crossing, under a footbridge and into Cumbres Pass. Curving to the left into a cutting and entering the 60ft Toltec tunnel the line continues, curving to the left as it leaves the tunnel and passes another track at a slightly higher level. Entering Toltec Gorge on a falling gradient of 1 in 50 the train passes non-stop through Chattanooga Station. Passengers may well see another train travelling in the opposite direction at this point. Still falling, it curves away to the right above the Lost Souls Canyon and drops down to run through Forest Central on the outside road. Passing a diesel standing in a siding and curving away to the right under another footbridge the train then climbs a 1 in 100 gradient into Horseshoe Pass. From here it levels out on to the heights of Windy Ridge embankment and, passing the half-mile post, climbs to a point where the track is level with the roof of the main station. Curving to the left it traverses the high level line above Chattanooga Station and

shortly enters Gunnison tunnel. Reaching the summit at the ¾ mile post the line then falls at 1 in 30 and shortly afterwards passes the branch to the locomotive sheds and carriage sidings on the right. Then the Horseshoe Pass is seen again on the left and the train travels for the second time through Forest Central on the centre road. Crossing the Diamond again, it drops down on to the new section of line into Echo Canyon. Curving now away to the left through nearly 20ft of shale it enters Sherman tunnel, the longest on the line, and emerges into a deep natural rock cutting, which is probably the most spectacular feature of the railway. Passing under a girder bridge which carries the siding to the sheds, the train emerges on the outside of the circuit, passes under the footbridge once again and returns to Forest Central after a trip of one mile.

This new part of the line was constructed during the winter months of 1972/73 and was brought into use at Easter. Most of the work was carried out with a digger, but some of the more stubborn pieces of rock required removal by blasting. In fact, several thousand tons of shale and rock were moved and at the deepest point the cutting measures 12ft. Sherman tunnel is 85ft long and with its restricted loading gauge gives a most realistic impression as the train passes through, particularly as the blast from *General Palmer* echoes back from the walls. This new section of line alone cost £17,000 to complete and John Southern reckons that the railway has now cost him well in excess of £50,000. This gives some indication of the amount of work that has been carried out.

The greatest number of passengers that have been carried in a day is around the 2,000 mark and this has been achieved by running from 10.30 am to 6 pm. Next year it is hoped that special late trains will operate on certain occasions and the locomotives will have headlights and all the coloured light signalling will be seen to its best advantage.

As well as this, plans have already been made to add further American type locomotives to the motive power department and this may well be at the rate of one a year. One of the unique features of the line is the fact that it is possible to see three trains passing through the main station simultaneously if the particular schedule permits it—two travelling in one direction and one in the other. Probably the most lasting impression of the Forest Railway is the fact that it has a more steeply graded route than any other of its type. It is extremely arduous and as a result drivers need to conserve their steam to enable them to tackle the various banks when they occur. It would have been all too easy to bulldoze the earth into a level site which would have made life much simpler from the operational point of view, but the resultant line would not have been nearly so interesting for the passenger.

John Southern is supported and helped considerably with his railway by his wife, Barbara, and there is no doubt that their ambitious plans for the future will continue to make this line one of the most outstanding 7¼in gauge miniature railways in the country.

Above: Double-header: Brian Hollingsworth's No 487 "Queen of Colorado" pilots John Southern's No 488. Both models are based on prototypes the Denver & Rio Grande Western's narrow gauge lines in Colorado. *Robin Butterell*

Left: Diesel in reserve. *Robin Butterell*

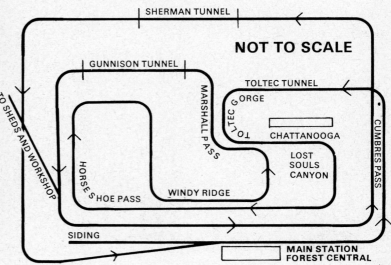

THE SUTTON MINIATURE RAILWAY

Sutton Park, 2,400 acres of unspoilt heath and woodland just north of Birmingham, England, is a favourite recreational haunt with the industrial population of the Midlands. It was here, on an adjacent area of land close to the park's main gate that a fun-fair was established in 1906. It became known as the Crystal Palace because of the large wintergarden type of building which formed its central feature. News of this venture must have quickly reached Mr W J Bassett-Lowke, miniature railway pioneer, for in the following June he relayed at the Crystal Palace the 10¼in gauge line which had previously operated at Abington Park, Northampton. The complete railway was transferred, including the Flooks 0-4-4T *Nipper* and six 4-

wheel passenger coaches. The line was approximately 1,000ft in length and ran in an almost straight line parallel to the park boundary from the Crystal Palace to Wyndley park gate. The only major engineering feature was a bridge of some 30ft length over a stream which flowed through the grounds.

The enterprise was clearly a success with the public, judging by accounts in the current number of "The Model Engineer and Electrician", and during the winter of 1907/8 the line was re-gauged to 15in and brand new rolling-stock constructed by Bassett-Lowke in his workshops at Northampton. The locomotive

Above: No 2 "Sutton Flyer" entering Sutton Park Station. *W T Hunt*

was the second of Henry Greenly's now legendary "Little Giant" class—Works No 11—named *Mighty Atom,* and weighing 1ton 12cwts.

It was finished in Midland Railway red livery and carried on the tender sides the initials of the Bassett-Lowke company which operated the line—Miniature Railways of Great Britain Ltd. Passengers rode in three open bogie coaches of the standard type then being produced for MRGB lines, each seating twelve passengers. The single fare from one end of the line to the other was 1d.

The line followed the same route as the original 10¼in gauge railway, and was provided with a loop at either end. So that the driver could perform run-round operations without leaving the footplate, the points were self-acting and the couplings on locomotive and tender could be operated from the cab. At the Crystal Palace end there was also a two-road engine shed.

The line opened at Easter 1908 and ran in this form until the First World War years.

An unfortunate accident occurred during this early period which resulted in the only fatality in the line's history. The bridge already referred to was only just wide enough for the train and had low parapets either side. It is not clear exactly what happened, but a small boy was either caught by a train or fell from one while on the bridge, and later succumbed to his injuries in hospital. Not long afterwards the bridge was considerably widened to take a cart-track as well as the railway, and the parapets disappeared.

For a short time in 1909 an interesting change in motive power took place. To meet a heavy increase in traffic on the 15in gauge railway Bassett-Lowke had laid down for the Exposition Internationale de l'Est de la France at Nancy, *Mighty Atom* was transferred from Sutton, re-named *Ville de Nancy* and painted in standard GNR livery for the occasion. In her place at Sutton, one of the little American Cagney 4-4-0 locomotives was borrowed from the Blakesley Hall railway near Towcester, Northamptonshire.

The story of the railway during and immediately after the First World War is veiled in mystery, but in 1920 *Mighty Atom* was bought by the Llewellyn Miniature Railway at Southport, who completely overhauled it the following year. Visually the only change was the fitting of continuous splashers over the driving wheels which bore the locomotive's new name—*Prince of Wales.* In this form, and immaculately finished in the ornately lined-out green livery of the line, it ran at this seaside resort for the next eight years. Meanwhile at Sutton, the railway had been taken over by Pat Collins, the well-known Showman and lessee of the Crystal Palace fairground. It was in operation at certain times during 1922 and 1923 but the identity of the engine involved is now unknown. The idea of

Top: The American type locomotive on loan from Blakesley Hall in 1909. *J Tidmarsh Collection*

Right: Early days at Sutton Coldfield: "Nipper" and train in 1907. *J Tidmarsh Collection*

Below: Immediate post-war: "Prince of Wales" pilots No 1 "Sutton Belle" on the enlarged track in 1949. *J Tidmarsh Collection*

Below: The Great Western railcar purchased from Dudley Zoo in 1957. *J Tidmarsh*

Below centre: No 2 "Sutton Flyer" with a train of modern stock. *J Tidmarsh*

Below right: "Prince of Wales" in the works at Oldbury. *J Tidmarsh*

retaining a miniature railway as one of the "novel attractions at the Crystal Palace" (as the local Press described the fair at the time) was evidently not popular with the new management who probably had little experience in operating this type of amusement. At any rate, the line was never used again in its original 1908 form, and although left in situ, became completely derelict over the next fourteen years. Incidentally, the three open coaches remained at Sutton, locked up in their shed all this time, until being scrapped in 1938.

Our attention must now be turned to Yarmouth where, in the years around 1930, Mr (later Commander, MBE, RNVR) Nigel Parkinson and his father laid down a very extensive 15in gauge railway. Most of the rolling-stock was built in his own workshop, and included a set of

magnificent totally enclosed bogie coaches. Later, a two-car self-propelled petrol-electric set was added, similar in appearance to the loco hauled vehicles, and powered by an Austin Seven car engine. These vehicles were constructed to a scale of one third full size (whereas 15in gauge is approximately one quarter full size), and therefore always looked somewhat oversize when hauled by scaled 15in gauge locomotives. Each coach was 18ft 6in long and held twelve passengers. They were fitted with doors and end corridor connections.

The locomotive fleet for the line consisted of a B-B "electric" outline petrol loco powered by a 10hp Chapuis Dornier engine, and, our old friend *Prince of Wales* purchased from Southport in 1929. Mr Parkinson soon set about rebuilding

the steam locomotive, and in 1930 it reappeared, once more in Midland Lake livery and numbered 53. Smoke deflectors had been added, and outside bearings fitted to the trailing pony truck because of trouble with firebox ashes falling onto the inside bearings originally fitted. During the 1930's Mr Parkinson also operated a 15in gauge line at Southend-on-Sea and *Prince of Wales* saw service there too.

In 1937 the Yarmouth Miniature Railway closed, and by a strange turn of events the much-travelled *Prince of Wales* came back to its original home—Sutton Coldfield! It is quite certain however that no-one at this time, or for many years to come, ever identified the little engine with the old *Mighty Atom*. Pat Collins had evidently decided to make a second essay into the miniature railway field, for in that year he purchased the Yarmouth line and most of the rolling-stock from the Parkinsons. The old Bassett-Lowke line at Sutton, still extant, was incorporated into a completely new and lengthened layout, laid down for Collins by Mr Parkinson Snr. early in 1938.

The terminus complex consisted of a covered station, which also acted as engine and carriage shed, and contained a platform road and an engine release loop. As in previous days, the points were of the spring-loaded self-acting type. At the "terminus" end of the station was a turntable and an engine spur road. At the "country" end, the departure and return roads ran parallel for some 300ft before separating and making a large "balloon". The total journey distance was approximately 3,000 ft. Following Yarmouth practice, the trains originally ran in an anti-clockwise direction, but this was quickly reversed due to the heavy gradients on the new line, which was of quite a scenic nature and ran through very pleasant countryside. There were two level crossings (over a cart track), two major bridges over the stream, 1 in 60 falling and 1 in 80 rising gradients, 3ft embankments and cuttings, and curves of 100ft radius. The turntable was rarely used and quickly fell into dis-repair so that alternate trains ran with the engine tender-first.

Stock for the new line, which was called the Crystal Palace Railway, consisted of *Prince of Wales*, the Yarmouth B-B petrol locomotive, and three of the closed coaches already mentioned. The livery was brick red lined out in yellow. Although the petrol engine arrived before

the steamer and operated the initial service over the new line, it never saw much activity at Sutton and by 1941 had become derelict, being finally cut up in the early 1950's. For the remaining stock it was a very different story. The train continued to operate up to, and even at certain times during the Second World War when people were encouraged to take their holidays at home and such attractions were kept open.

In time however, the war years and general lack of proper rolling-stock maintenance facilities took their toll. The addition of a long and unsightly stovepipe to the elegant chimney of the *Prince* told its own tale of poor steaming, and by 1946 the railway had taken on a very run-down appearance. So it was that at this juncture a meeting took place which was destined to affect the whole future of the line. Mrs Collins, who had come to view the little train with some affection, called in Mr T G Hunt, a Black Country industrialist and miniature railway enthusiast, to examine and carry out necessary repairs to the ageing "Atlantic". As a direct result the locomotive underwent a major overhaul at Mr Hunt's works at Oldbury, Worcestershire, which included the fitting of a new firebox. But more basic moves were afoot, for in 1948 Mr Hunt acquired the entire railway from Collins, and the stage was thus set for a renaissance on the grand scale.

First of all the line was given a new name—the Sutton Miniature Railway. The most urgent need was to improve the rolling-stock and this became Mr Hunt's first priority. At the same time as he acquired the SMR, he also purchased the track and equipment of a private 15in gauge line at Hardwicke Manor, near Tewkesbury. This included three open toast-rack type bogie coaches, one "Atlantic" steam locomotive and some parts for a second. In view of the history of the *Prince of Wales,* the origin of these new engines is of considerable interest.

Prior to the First World War, Mr Douglas Clayton, a director of the (then) Cannon Ironfoundries, Bilston, Staffordshire, and a miniature railway enthusiast, purchased from Henry Greenly/Bassett-Lowke plans and castings for a Class 30 "Sanspareil" type "Atlantic", itself a development of the original *Little Giant.* Assembly commenced in Mr Clayton's own workshop with the assistance of apprentices from the works. Then came the war and work ceased, not to be recommenced until 1930, by which time all

the original drawings had been lost. So the locomotive was completed at the works in 1933 as a very handsome freelance model weighing 3tons. Complete with the inscription "Great Western" on the tender sides, the locomotive was turned out in Brunswick Green and named *Douglas Clayton.* The second locomotive was started in 1938, but once again a war intervened, and this time the work was not completed because in 1946 Mr Clayton died suddenly and the whole of the layout at his home, Hardwicke Manor, disposed of in the way already described. Thus it was that, completely unknowingly, the SMR became the home of both a first and a (modified) third generation *Little Giant!*

Douglas Clayton arrived at Sutton in August 1948, but because of superstitious misgivings on the part of the fairground management, was not allowed to enter service until its green livery had been replaced by a less "unlucky" colour! The locomotive was therefore hurriedly repainted brown as a temporary measure.

A siding was laid in for the new stock, and during the following winter a roomy two-road engine shed and workshop constructed on the site of the old turntable. This building had a sunken floor with the tracks supported on columns, giving easy access to wheels and motion. At the same time, *Douglas Clayton* was completely overhauled at Oldbury, and renamed *Sutton Belle,* becoming No 1 in the SMR fleet. Over the next few winters also, an extensive programme of track re-alignment and relaying was carried out using heavier rail laid on ex-BR sleepers cut into three. The opportunity was taken of easing a number of curves and also raising the lowest part of the line by a substantial amount in order to reduce the adverse gradients facing the trains.

Now that two locomotives and six coaches were available for traffic, it became possible to operate a service with two trains at peak weekends and Bank Holidays—one making its journey while the other was being turned round at the station. Some very slick operating was necessitated by this pattern, since the journey only took 4-4½ minutes. In this short space of time the second train had to run into the platform road, disgorge its 36 passengers and re-load, while the engine was being run round the train and coupled to the other end. Any locomotive servicing also had to be carried out in this time. Finally, the train had to depart and clear the platform road before the other train could return! This sequence was executed with the greatest precision throughout peak periods, sometimes lasting 5-6 hours at a stretch.

One curious feature of two-train operation, which incidentally provided a most successful train regulator, was caused by the presence of restricted lateral clearance between tracks at the point where departure and arrival roads diverged some 100yds beyond the station. As a result, it was not possible for two trains to pass at this point. Because returning trains were travelling at speed just here, and around a blind curve, they were always given right of way, the out-going train being held back until the line was clear. In this way, not only were collisions avoided, but also there was no possibility of one train catching up the other! Although signals and signal box featured in the Sutton landscape, they were only dummies to give authentic background, and the above regulating feature was the only means of train control ever employed. Nevertheless there is no record of any accident other than the bridge incident mentioned earlier.

Other improvements followed. Locomotive No 2, *Sutton Flyer,* was quickly completed in readiness for Easter 1952. Similar in appearance to No 1, but finished in Royal Blue livery, there were a number of important differences. In particular, the driving wheels were 1in less in diameter than on No 1—an important factor in wet-weather operation. Neither engine was fitted with sanding gear and No 1 could be very light on its feet on a greasy rail.

Attention was next turned towards developing the carriage fleet. The closed coaches had been completely overhauled in the late 1940's. The corridor connections had been blanked off, it being far too easy for high-spirited passengers to lean over and split a train in two (!), and the compartment doors removed. This latter modification, while certainly improving station turn-round time, unfortunately marred the otherwise superb appearance of these vehicles. All the axles ran in Skefko bearings and although each vehicle weighed approximately one ton tare there was never any real haulage problem. On the other hand the three Hardwicke open coaches, each of only 12cwt tare, ran on plain bearings and were heavy to pull on the steeply graded Sutton line. So, between 1952 and 1956 they were transferred to the Fairbourne Railway and four new 18ft 6in long light-weight open bogie coaches were built for the SMR, all running on Skefco bearings and each holding 14 passengers. Finally a further three closed coaches were built, virtually identical to the original Yarmouth set.

One of the Yarmouth coaches was provided with an "observation" end compartment, having at one time been used as a driving-trailer for the two-car petrol-electric set mentioned previously. The Austin Motor Company was highly delighted at the use of one of its engines for this train, and as well as featuring the unit in one of its publicity films (appropriately entitled "The Mighty Atom"!), presented Mr Parkinson with a set of Austin "wings" which were mounted prominently over the end driving cab windows of each vehicle. When the coach was transferred to Sutton and throughout its life there, the emblem was retained, resulting in many questions from curious passengers! A similar observation end

was provided in one of the new coaches built for the SMR, but of course, there were no "wings" this time.

Three significant events took place in 1953. Firstly, *Sutton Belle* was completely rebuilt, the work including provision of new firebox and boiler tubes, driving wheels and axles. A significant visual improvement resulted from slightly raised running-boards over the driving wheels and fitting of GWR "Hall" type cylinder covers. The effect was so pleasing that in time, *Sutton Flyer* was also treated in the same way. Then at Easter, and after 45 years of almost continuous service, the veteran *Prince of Wales* was finally retired to await preservation. Finally in June, the coronation of Queen Elizabeth II provided the occasion for a change in rolling-stock livery. Crimson was chosen, lined out in white and yellow with blue bands above and below the coach windows. Coach roofs were always painted cream. With the exception of the blue bands, this livery was also applied to *Sutton Belle,* but *Sutton Flyer* retained its Royal Blue livery.

Thus the little trains, which were always maintained in immaculate condition, presented a most attractive sight. The locomotives in particular, with their polished brass chimney caps, domes and safety valve covers, burnished smokebox door fittings and handrails, and distinctive chime whistles, helped draw the crowds who flocked to the railway throughout the season. This began at Easter and continued until September, the railway being open every day from Whitsun onwards. Normally a three-coach train was adequate for traffic, strengthened to four or even five when necessary, choice of open or closed stock depending on the weather.

Of course the sun did not shine all the time, and many were the days when a locomotive would be steamed in the morning only to spend the whole afternoon with its smokebox poking out of the shed into the pouring rain, and never turning a wheel. So in 1957 a B-B petrol locomotive was purchased from the Dudley Zoo line. The machine was styled to resemble one of the pre-war GWR diesel railcars and was powered by a 20hp Morris Commercial engine with fluid flywheel transmission. It was built by Messrs G & S Light Engineering Co Ltd, Stourbridge.

Internal combustion engines were no strangers to Sutton, for in 1951 the line had been host to *Dingo,* the then new B-B petrol locomotive for the Fairbourne Railway, which underwent extensive trials at the Crystal Palace.

Locomotive trials of another sort took place in 1959 when *Sutton Flyer* visited New Romney. Because of the nature of the Sutton line, it was never possible to extend the engines fully and discover their potential for sustained high speed—15mph being about the maximum achieved. On the flat and level RH&DR main line, and hauling a load of three coaches, a speed of 27mph was reached but insufficient lateral stability at the front end prevented anything higher being attempted. Certain other deficiencies were also revealed by these trials. Because *Sutton Flyer* was not fitted with vacuum brake equipment there was no possibility of its working regular service trains while in Kent.

With three powerful locomotives now available for traffic, it was possible to extend the peak service once more—this time to two five-coach trains. The length of the engine release loop at the station limited trains to four coaches. So longer trains were only possible if the principle of running the engine round its train was abandoned and the points at the shed end of the station clipped out of use. The need for a third engine then becomes obvious, and the station operating pattern was as follows:

Train A arrived at the station behind loco No 1; loco No 2, waiting at the country end backed onto the train in readiness for the next trip. After departure, loco No 1 followed it out of the station to clear the platform road and await arrival of train B behind loco No 3.

In this way, and with the journey time now reduced to 3½ minutes as a result of the various improvements, it was possible to deal with passenger flows of up to 1,500 per hour. During a good Bank Holiday anything between 6,000 and 8,000 passengers were carried per day, and the all-time record was achieved on Whit Monday 1960 when the almost unbelievable number of just over 12,000 people were carried during an 11-hour period.

To cope with such crowds, and in preparation for the World Scout Jamboree which was held in the park in 1957, the old Parkinson station was replaced in that year with a new and enlarged structure giving covered accommodation for the longer trains being handled. In addition, a bay platform was provided for special workings and extra stabling sidings for the coaches.

Development of the SMR was now complete and the line seemed set for a sunny future, with annual passenger figures of around 100,000 and all equipment in first-class condition. However, the writing was already on the wall, for it was known that the ground lease for the whole of the Crystal Palace site would expire at the end of the 1962 season and would not be renewed by Sutton Town Council who now held the freehold. Efforts to avert this tragedy were fruitless, and so, after a life of 55 years, the little line's existence came to an abrupt end on October 7th, 1962. Within four months, the track had been lifted, buildings dismantled, and all equipment moved into store. No longer do the surrounding woods and hills of Sutton Park echo to the rapid chatter and shrill whistles of the little engines, or the happy laughter of passengers. Overgrown cuttings and empty embarkments are all that remain to remind one that here ran a line of some significance in the history of the 15in gauge railway. And yet one must remember that once before there was a gap of 14 years in the Sutton story. With growing demands for restrictions on the use of the motor car in the park, who is to say that the story of the Sutton Miniature Railway is, even now, complete?

L N E R

4433

The 'Liliputbahn' Lucerne

Near the Lucerne Transport Museum, in which the model railway of the Gotthard line featured in a later chapter of this book is situated, are several blocks of flats. Only a few years ago, from among the tall grass and foliage which then grew on the site and above the buzz of summer insects, could be detected smoke, steam and the sound of locomotives at work.

Entering the area by the "Liliputbahn" ticket desk, one soon arrived at the locomotive shed. Around the turntable roads several locomotives would be sizzling gently in the sunlight; the nostrils would dilate to the tang of smoke, steam and hot oil. Further down the path were the carriage sheds—tunnels with doors in which stock was stored away from the weather—and finally one reached the station. Here it would be found that not one, but two working steam railways were in operation.

This was the realm of the Brast brothers, where coal, steam, oil and ash held sway, and visitors were carried behind working steam locomotives on circuits of the area.

The larger line was one quarter scale with a track gauge of 36cm, nearly 15in. It was worked by two really magnificent steam locomotives, working correct-scale models of Swiss prototypes, fully detailed and finished to perfection. Their capabilities must have been greatly in excess of the loads they were called upon to carry, and even the extensive line they operated was somewhat restrictive.

No 182 was an inside-cylindered 4-4-0 with a six-wheeled tender, built for the Swiss Federal Railways in 1904. The model faithfully portrayed the domeless boiler, inside-valved cylinders with outside return crank, and rather gaunt aspect of the original.

If No 182 was a very good model, No 781 was superb. This was a scale reproduction of the original 4-6-0 compound express locomotive built for the Swiss Federal Railways in 1908. It was a genuine compound, and the reversing rod was knuckled to connect the two sets of valve gears. The boiler carried both a dome and sandbox, and the loco was equipped with bogie brakes, a most unusual feature. It would appear that de Glehn and F W Webb were not unknown in Switzerland in 1908.

For British visitors, though, the more fascinating of the two lines was the smaller one. Built to 1:8 scale ratio (1½in/ft) the track gauge was nominally 7¼in. The smallest locomotive of the five in stock was a model of an elderly 0-4-0 locomotive with a four-wheeled tender, the *Esslinger* of the Original Nord-Ost Bahn. It reminded one of something out of Hornby, and the remainder reminded one of Bassett-Lowke, for the other four locomotives were all of British prototypes and were built from Bassett-Lowke castings.

The eldest of these was the famous

Below: The elderly Ex LNWR No 513 "George the Fifth" painted in early LMS crimson livery. *Robin Butterell*

Top: A shed scene on the Liliputbahn with
Nord-Ost Bahn 0-4-0 No 2176 on the turntable.
D Trevor Rowe

Above: BR No 60072 "Sunstar" an A3 Pacific.
D Trevor Rowe

Opposite page. Above: LMS 4-6-0 No 6100
"Royal Scot".   *Robin Butterell*

Below: Swiss Federal Railways 4-4-0 No 182
out in the "country" with a train.
D Trevor Rowe

George the Fifth of the LNWR, painted in early LMS crimson, which heat and exposure had weathered to oxide; there was a "Royal Scot", a "Flying Scotsman" and a BR A3 Pacific named *Sunstar.* All were coal-fired.

The Brast Brothers made all the locomotives themselves, and one supposes that they had a whale of a time doing it. More's the pity, therefore, to relate that the line no longer exists. Long negotiations to incorporate it within the Transport Museum were frustrated by an intervening landowner, and so this ideal project has been committed to limbo. Following the demise of the elder Brast, the site was sold and the equipment was purchased in toto by a factory owner in Grenchen, where, for the time being, it is inaccessible to the public.

Near the site of the line there is a funicular railway, which leads from the lakeside roadway to the Dietschiberg. At the summit is to be found a further open-air model railway, hand-built by one A Oswald from 1934 onward. The track gauge of this line is 5 21/32in, which translates to 143.5mm, or 1:10 scale ratio. It is a very robust line, the rails being inverted "tee" section, spiked to wooden sleepers laid in ballast. The line is almost unique in its genre in incorporating correct superelevation. The stock is of Swiss and German types and is run "on the right" unlike Swiss railways.

The loss of the Brast line has not dampened the enthusiasm of the Lucerne model railway fraternity; quite the reverse. The group that built the Gotthard line in the Verkehrshaus is planning a new HO layout to be housed in special quarters owned by the Club. There will be plenty of railway interest in Lucerne for the future.

Below: A scene on the Dietschiberg line.
Photo Courtesy Mrs P P Jones

Right: No 781, a fine model of a Swiss Federal Railways 4-6-0 compound. *W R Jones*

Bottom right: "George the Fifth" over the ash pit. Whilst the livery is supposedly LMS the lettering L&NWR appears on the tender. *Robin Butterell*

Miniature Railways World Wide

Although English supremacy in such matters as naval strength or industrial power has long since passed away, one must confess to an impression that, as regards miniature railways, foreigners are still just nowhere, except perhaps for a few enthusiasts in America. Is this borne out by a study of the facts?

Certainly no nation other than the British has actually gone so far as to have a miniature railway with statutory or common carrier status, as Captain Howey did with the Romney, Hythe and Dymchurch Railway. The RH&D, without doubt the premier line in the miniature world, might be said to be the standard by which all miniature railways should be judged.

In this article we are attempting to range world-wide so a definition of what constitutes a miniature railway would be in order. In the narrow context of these words, therefore, a miniature railway is defined as one where, first, motive power is a reasonable representation, to half size or less, of something that runs, did run, or could have run on full-size

railways. Second, it is of such a size that passengers can ride inside the cars, which really excludes gauges below $7\frac{1}{4}$in. Third, just to prevent the author having to dip his pen in vitriol, there is no mention of any that depend on pseudo motive-power, that is, diesel masquerading as steam or, perhaps, electric as diesel.

If one begins, therefore, by taking the aristocrats of the miniature railway world, ie. those which run from place A to place B and, against our existing three (Romney, Ravenglass, Fairbourne) plus two under construction (Lyme Regis, Manifold Valley), the rest of the world can only muster one sole example, Sandley & Son's Riverside & Great Northern in Wisconsin Dells, USA.

Sandley senior was an engineer on the Great Northern ("Big G") Railroad, who found the means on retirement to set up a workshop to build miniature locomotives of a very high order of perfection and, after a false start elsewhere, found an abandoned grade of the GN. In 1959 he was able to acquire title to a

3-mile stretch, which has operated ever since, his son Norman Sandley taking over as Superintendent of the Line and Master Mechanic after his death.

Operation is on a small scale and normally one locomotive in steam suffices. Interest is sustained, however, since newly constructed locomotives from the Sandley Works have their running trials on the R&GN, before going out to whichever Park or Zoo has decided to order a real precision-built authentic miniature steam locomotive to delight its patrons. However, the usual performer is a neat modern Atlantic whose most interesting feature is an unconventional boiler having a single fire tube with cross water-tubes to extract the heat from combustion in the firebox. Currently a batch of three Pacifics is being built in the R&GN Shops.

Left and above: Pinconning and Blind River No 5661 at the water tower.   *Emery J Gulash*

At this point it is worth recording a near miss that might have resulted in something that would have made our Romney, Hythe & Dymchurch look like a Hornby train set. Unworldly but wealthy young Louis McDermot constructed the excellent 19in gauge "Overfair" miniature railway to carry people 1½ miles from one end of the 1912 San Francisco exposition to the other. Four superb Pacifics and one 2-6-0T were built, still believed to be in existence at Los Gatos, California, but, alas through a certain lack of experience of the world, he was cheated right and left and, consequently, lost a fortune in the enterprise.

The late Captain Frederick Shaw in his delightful book, "Little Railways of the World", recently reprinted, tells how McDermot considered afterwards using this equipment to rebuild the defunct 3ft gauge North Pacific Coast Railway to miniature size, Eskdale fashion, as a holiday and picnic line, over a fair part of its 75-mile line and how this nearly came about.

But, perhaps, like Alexander Kinloch who conceived and executed the superb but equally financially disastrous pre-war Surrey Border and Camberley Railway— 4 miles of 10¼in gauge double track main —by the time it was over he had had enough.

Coming down several rungs in the social scale, we come to miniature railways which provide something less than transport from A to B but still cater for public demand in a park, zoo, or recreation area. Their numbers are legion and there can be few big cities without

one. So many, in fact, that one must really look at the manufacturers rather than the operators. There were at one time hundreds of such railways in America, but they were stopped dead in the twenties when arbitrary legislation provided that all steam locomotives in public service must have a crew of two. A firm called Cagney of New York was the principal supplier of motive power and produced a flood of crude but sturdy and effective 4-4-0s to cope with

the demand. Their successors Crown Metal Products of Wyano, Pennsylvania, still provide a similar product now that steam is again fashionable and single-man operation legitimate. Like Cagney they cover a wide range of gauges and sizes from 12in to 36in.

Bassett-Lowke provided equipment for a few miniature railways in Europe, notably Geneva and Nancy, but on a temporary basis only, although there is a mystery in that the "Little Giant" 4-4-2s

Left: Pinconning and Blind River. The "Hudson" on the trestle and the "Shay" below. *Emery J Gulash*

Below right: Pinconning and Blind River. No 5661 threads its way through the forest. *Emery J Gulash*

Bottom left: Pinconning and Blind River. Owner and builder Carrington Eddy superintends permanent way operations. *Emery J Gulash*

Bottom right: Pinconning and Blind River. The "Shay" locomotive in the snow. *Emery J Gulash*

supplied for these railways have not quite been completely accounted for on their return. Is there a Sherlock Holmes amongst us that will follow up the meagre clues that are available and perhaps find a long-lost Bassett-Lowke 4-4-2 under a

Greenly's were intended for the previously mentioned RH&D Railway, whereas Martens' were for a Munich exhibition. In addition to a gauge in common, one other fundamental similarity was that they were both 1/3 full size on 1/4 full-size track, almost narrow-gauge, if you like, and consequently were able to be given much more robust-than-scale wheels and motion. Without doubt this practical feature made the locomotives relatively easy to maintain, and led to the survival of all the Greenly locomotives (9 at New Romney, 1 at Ravenglass) and such of the Krauss locomotives that survived the destruction in Germany after the war.

A surprising number of similar locomotives were built by both Krauss and Krupp, 18 at least, of which over half can be traced over a wide swathe from Bressingham, Norfolk to as far afield as India. All were intended to work and

limited usage of the Prater Gardens steam locomotives, together with an apparent absence of outcry when Alan Bloom of Bressingham brought two others to England from Cologne last year, do seem to indicate a rather less extravagent passion for steam than is found in Britain.

In addition to the above, other German-built 15in gauge steam locomotives are believed to operate in Dresden, Stuttgart, Leipzig, Madrid, Seville and Bombay. One in Delhi was a gift to the people of India on Independence, no doubt intended as a reminder that locomotive suppliers existed, other than those of their former masters. A recent report indicated it was still operating in the Indian Capital, but, alas, a sad caricature of its pristine self.

Speaking of India, yet another mystery exists in that one of the locomotives of

pile of scrap in a European back-yard like Robin Butterell did a few years back at Manchester?

Henry Greenly, who was associated as the professional engineer with Bassett-Lowke in these pre-1914 enterprises, had an indirect influence on the post-1918 European miniature railway scene. He and a German Engineer called Roland Martens, who was employed by the loco-building firm of Krauss, co-operated in the design of 15in gauge Pacifics.

most do work on park railways. A particularly nice Krauss line is that in the Prater Gardens, Vienna, where two Pacifics can be found plus a third which has been rebuilt as a diesel. The steam locomotives only operate on 'summer Sunday afternoons but, at such times, since part of the line is double track, we have the only place in the world other than Romney Marsh where 15in Pacifics pass one another at speed.

Regarded as straws in the wind, the

the extensive 10¼in gauge Surrey Border & Camberley Railway is believed to have been sent there when the SB&CR was closed in 1939. This was an 0-6-0 side tank—but with India being so immense and the locomotive so small the task of finding it is outside the range of the possible. Just for the record, the rumour that one of the SB&CR Garratts followed it is certainly incorrect, since both exist in England to this day.

One Indian miniature system, existing in the days of "the Raj", has, however, been very fully written up, in as professional a style as that in which it was constructed and operated. The Jhansi miniature railway, 9½in gauge, described in the "Model Engineer" during 1936, not only had everything from a beautiful Bassett-Lowke two cylinder Midland-style 4-4-0 to full signalling, but also was fully staffed when in operation and worked according to a very strict interpretation of the Indian Railways standard rule book. Mr R Horsfield, who owned the line, was a senior railway officer on the Indian Railways. However, this line properly belongs in our next category.

We have now dealt with miniature railways that try to be real railways; with miniature railways that are, if you like, side-shows. There remain those that are just themselves. The problem of a World Survey is that so many hide their lights under bushels. Take the very fine railroad which is illustrated in this article—a perfect example of the very highest quality of miniature but yet never publicised and only known to the author through a chance acquaintanceship. How many more are there like the Pinconning and Blind River RR? The P&BRR, situated in Northern Michigan, was built by a lumber-man, Mr Carrington Eddy, for his own pleasure, which he likes to share by opening to the public at week-ends. It is 12in gauge and has straight steam, Shay and diesel motive power, all of very fine and authentic construction and, incidentally, homebuilt.

America has many well-known lines—two which particularly stand out are Erich Thomsen's Redwood Valley RR in the hills above Oakland Bay, San Francisco and Seymour Johnson's Goleta Valley Railroad near Santa Barbara, California.

The Redwood Valley line is 5in scale, that is, 3ft-gauge type equipment running on 15in gauge track, and perhaps the best thing about this scale and this line is that the passenger cars can be and are accurate scale models of narrow gauge freight cars. As one might expect, so often the rolling stock of a miniature railway is its Achilles heel when realism

Below left: Ankara Youth Park Railway. TCCD No 46001 in action. *John Blyth*

Top centre: Ankara Youth Park Railway. 60cm gauge 2-8-2 with Turkish State Railways crew. *John Blyth*

Top right: 15in gauge Swiss Federal Railways 4-6-0 and 7¼in "Flying Scotsman" side by side at Lucerne. *M S Cross*

Bottom centre: Close to the Transport Museum at Lucerne was a delightful vintage miniature railway originally built to 7¼in gauge. Later a 15in gauge track was added. The 7¼in gauge "Flying Scotsman" is seen raising steam. *M S Cross*

Bottom right: A 1:5 scale SNCF 141R built by Monsieur Anelair, on the line at Eaubonne, France, owned by Doctor Froger. *G Anelair*

is considered. "4-spot", the Wild West style 2-4-2, which alone protects the operation, is a delight.

What can we say about the Goleta Valley Line? It covers a great tract of country, with four track main lines and two great roundhouses (7¼in and 15in gauge) amongst its immense trackage. On operating days a great conclave of miniature locomotive men bring their iron ponies from all parts of the state and the facilities, among the world's finest, are utilised to the full. All this is due to the generosity of Mr Johnston.

Perhaps one further special mention should be made of a nameless line in Boulder, Colorado, where ½ mile of 14⅛in gauge track has been laid as a test bed for a 2-8-8-4 Mallet being built by a Mr McAllister. It will be over 28 foot long and weigh 9 tons.

Other recorded miniature railways in North America are listed below:

Paradise & Pacific RR—Scottsdale, Arizona. 15in gauge, 5in scale. Rio Grande style equipment.
Centreville & South Western RR—Roseland, New Jersey. 9½in gauge. Recently advertised for sale.
Little Tuesday RR—Alexandria, Louisiana. 12in gauge. Named after the owner's daughter.
Wildcat RR—Los Gatos, California. 19in gauge. Houses the McDermot "Overfair" locomotives.
†*Carolwood & Pacific RR*—Hollywood, California. 7½in gauge. Walt Disney's own line.
Mesa Grande Western—Peach Blossom, California. 9in gauge, 3in scale. Rio Grande style equipment.
McConnell Island Narrow Gauge—Anacortes, Washington State. 9in gauge, 3in scale.
House of David Railroad—Benton, Michigan. 15in gauge. A miniature railroad within a religious community.

Byron Railroad—Creston, Iowa. 24in gauge. A "big little" railroad.
*Currently offered for sale.
†Continued existence uncertain.

In addition to the foregoing there are many North American miniature railways run not by individuals but by clubs.

A meagre selection in England has to stand comparison with a vast nationwide network of miniature-gauge clubs in America and Canada. The magazine "Live Steam" lists 43 with a staggering 75,000ft of track in gauges between 7¼in and 15in.

A further 29,000ft is listed as "planned", being an indication of the rapid expansion which this hobby is undergoing in North America. Titles range from the slightly prosaic "Los Angeles Live Steamers" (5,779ft of 7½in gauge) to the amusingly named "Cinder Sniffers Inc." of Cincinatti (1,350ft of 7½in). Geographically the continent is covered from Alaska to Florida.

Salt Lake City, Utah, has long been noted for unusual social customs. We must now include amongst these the 1,000ft of 17in gauge operated by the Utah Live Steamers.

Steam locomotives listed as available to run on these lines are as follows:

	Operating	Under Construction
17in gauge	4	—
15in gauge	15	6
12in gauge	9	2
9in gauge	2	2
7½in gauge	325	245
7¼in gauge	67	52

(Note that 7¼in is the USA standard in the East, 7½in in the West).

A reasonable collection for a country that, during the heyday of the steam locomotive, produced 170,000 full-size ones.

From the rest of the world comes very little information but sparks of interest can be observed in various countries. Some time ago a M Georges Auclair of Beauchamp, France, advertised an SNCF 141R Mikado in 1:5 full size, 11¼in gauge—illustrations of a partially completed example appeared in both "La Vie du Rail" and "Loco-Revue".

In Switzerland the brothers Brast after some time developing their 7¼in gauge network, graduating from British designs by Greenly to their own superb Swiss models, went still further to ¼ full size (14½in gauge) for public operation at a site near Lucerne: sadly this has now closed.

There were some real vintage items like a 7¼in gauge LNWR "George the Fifth" 4-4-0, which, in pre-war Bassett-Lowke catalogues, to older enthusiasts like the writer meant the ultimate disintegration of the tenth commandment. The queen of the wider gauge was a magnificent dead-to-scale miniature of the standard Swiss Federal 4-6-0 Class A3/5—no doubt the skill and devotion of the Brast brothers maintained what must be, in comparison with many 15in gauge locomotives, a watchmaker's job.

Germany seems only able to offer a club installation, that of the Dampfbahnfreunde at Friedrichsruhe. A fairly complex layout in a pleasant situation seems to attract some interesting locomotives and their builders, on special occasions not only from Germany, but also from Holland, Switzerland, Denmark and even Britain.

Belgium holds a considerable mystery in that the six 1ft 11½in gauge Pacifics, constructed for the Brussels Exhibition by Ateliers Nivelles of Tubize in 1935, have vanished without trace.

Moving further East, in Turkey there exists, in the capital city of Ankara, a line apparently in the fairly common ruck of park amusements, but which on further examination is so remarkable as to require a category by itself. It is this, that the locomotives are excellent miniature steam 2-8-2s constructed by State Railways at their works at Eshekedir. Furthermore, believe it or not, operation is provided by a rostered turn at Ankara shed. The gauge is 60mm, so the locomotives are amongst the extremely rare group of good "big miniatures", if such an ambiguous term can be permitted.

Imagine our BR running a miniature line in Hyde Park and building some half-size "Britannias" at Crewe to work it! The line at Ankara is in the Youth Park and consists of simple continuous track with two stations, one below ground flanked by two tunnels. There is a similar line at Izmir.

It is a long way now between halts for our next is Castledare, Western Australia, where there is a rapidly developing and extensive 7¼in system. The scenery along the Canning River, where the line is located, is described as real Huckleberry Finn country and the line includes some quite elaborate engineering features including a multi-span truss girder bridge over a lake and an artificial tunnel or so. There were some problems recently in respect of earth moving operations and the line's management can now boast it is the only railway in the world to have lost a tunnel!

Left: Prater Park Railway. Driver waits for the "right-away". *I P Hunter*

Bottom left: Vienna. The Prater Park Railway. Train stops to pick up passengers. *I P Hunter*

Bottom right: Prater Park Railway. With blower on the locomotive waits for the signal. *J R Batts*

A line in the State of Victoria, owned by a Dr Bush and built to the odd gauge of 10½in, described in the "Model Engineer" during 1936, must now be defunct; for his Pacific now works on Mr Hamblin's line at Houghton-on-the-Hill near Leicester.

Further systems, in other Australian States, exist or will exist down under. There is one in a Bird Sanctuary at Carrumbim in Queensland. It is to 11in gauge and steam operated with a neat steam American-style 2-8-2 providing power on a half-mile circle.

Also in Queensland, at Strathpine, 10 miles or so North of Brisbane, and still under construction, is a little ¼ mile enterprise, for which a 12in gauge 2-4-0 is now nearing completion.

Even nearer to completion is the Smokey Mountain and Grizzly Flats RR at Gosford, New South Wales, 60 miles North of Sydney. It is to be an ambitious affair, with a mile of 12in gauge and two excellent steamers, a 2-6-2 and a 4-4-2 T. The two locomotives have previously operated on a smaller line, at Reptile Park (The Woodham's Barry sidings of the Dinosaur age) some miles away.

Lastly, 15,000 miles from home, we note the delightfully named Toot & Whistle Railway at Rotorua, New Zealand where the legend of an "old country" that now no longer exists is perpetuated by a 9½in gauge Great Northern Atlantic drawing happy crowds of children round its thousand foot length.

We should, perhaps, consider whether there is a possibility that whole miniature rail empires exist in other countries, and not publicised in England or the States because of the language barrier? No doubt there are some such systems; for example, a delightful 15in gauge tank locomotive recently appeared at New Romney built by a Mr Heiden of Rotterdam. Is it the tip of a Dutch iceberg? Japan is another question mark. Certainly, an unmatched passion for steam trains exists there, but so far there have not been reports of replicas larger than the so-called live-steam sizes. No doubt they will come.

On the other hand, railway enthusiasts are fundamentally travellers, and, with increasing rarity of that rarest of all wild game, the steam locomotive, they are ranging further and further to find even more remote hunting grounds. On return, they are only too eager to rush into print with any new discoveries. So, with this negative evidence, we may conclude with a fair degree of certainty, that Britannia and Uncle Sam do between them rule the miniature rails, at least today.

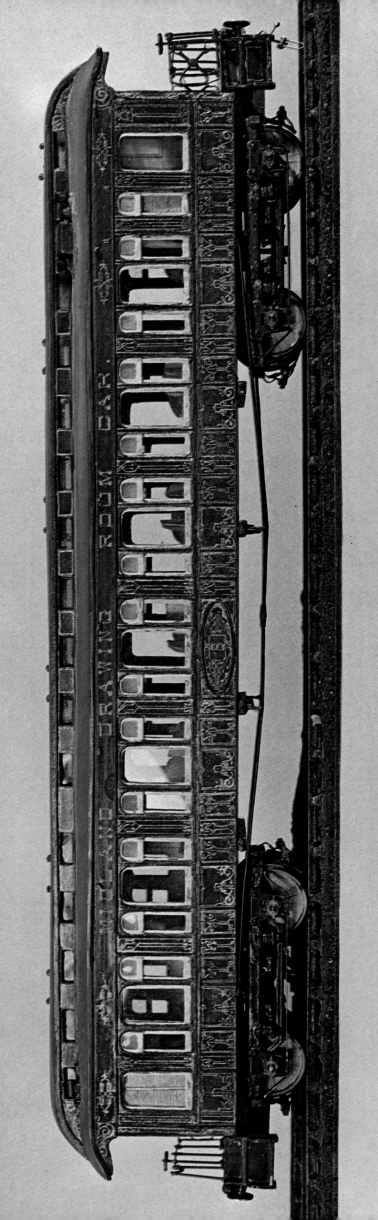

DRAWING ROOM CAR

COLLECTORS AND COLLECTING

BILL McALPINE

Most railway enthusiasts or those associated with a Railway Preservation movement seem to intensify their interest as they pass from adolescence into maturity. In the case of W H (Bill) McAlpine, involvement with railway matters has only come to fruition in the last ten years. As a boy he was interested in model railways, like most small boys, at one time running a 2in gauge line, but there was little practical application of note until he acquired his first traction engine in partnership with his brother Alistair. Road locomotives and their associated equipment were his first love and since taking over Alistair's share he has acquired many more. These cover a variety of types including traction and showmens engines and a living van, the latter being used at rallies from time to time by Bill McAlpine and his wife Jill

Above: A general view of Mr W H McAlpine's private museum. Among the exhibits on show can be seen two of the 9½in gauge L&NW locomotives built by Harry Powell: on the left the 2-4-0 ''Hardwicke'' and in the centre the 2-2-2 ''Lady of the Lake''. The 4-4-0 ''Alfred the Great'' which normally stands on the right was being repainted when the photograph was taken. A collection of GWR locomotive nameplates can be seen and on the back wall are two original oil paintings by Terence Cuneo. In the foreground stands Prince, an alsatian formerly owned by the late Mr Francis, a signalman at East Croydon station. When alive Prince collected money in the box on his back on East Croydon station for the Southern Railwaymen's Home for Children at Woking. After Prince died he was stuffed and continued to collect money standing on the station. *Richard Sharpe Studios*

Left: W H McAlpine. *Richard Sharpe Studios*

who takes a keen interest in his steam activities.

The most interesting engines include a Burrell Showman's engine built in 1925, a Burrell single crank compound traction engine built in 1908, and a Garrett tractor built in 1906 which is the last surviving engine of its type in existence.

When he married he built his present home on a very beautiful site at the head of a small valley. By this time his collection was growing; in 1964 he acquired the major part of a fine group of model locomotives belonging to the late Captain Hewitt, to whom reference was made in the profile on Trevor Guest. Among these were three of the best that have been seen in this country, models of famous London and North Western locomotives in 9½in gauge by the late Harry Powell: these are in showroom condition having only been steamed once. Also included in the collection are 3½in gauge models of the *Great Bear* and No 6028 *King George VI*, a 7¼in gauge Powell *Midge* 0-4-0T No 1106 and a 9½in gauge 0-4-0ST built by the legendary H T (Father) Brown.

Around the same time McAlpine was able to acquire one of the original Company locomotives used by the firm of which he is a member on major contracts in various parts of the British Isles. Before more sophisticated machinery became available for earth movement many major contracts were serviced by temporary light railway lines for which the larger contractors kept a stud of steam locomotives to be used as motive power. When contracts were complete, the lines were lifted and the stock returned to the main depot which, in this case, was at Hayes. To enable this locomotive to run at his home, a length of standard gauge line was laid at the "bottom of the garden", now extending to about a mile. Due to the topography of the ground there are some extreme gradients, the steepest of which is 1 in 15.

Motive power includes a Hudswell Clarke 0-6-0 tank engine built in 1913, which was the McAlpine works engine No 31, Aveling and Porter 0-4-0 traction tram "Sirapite" and a Fowler crane engine capable of lifting 10 tons.

The Midland signal box from Shobnall Maltings has been re-erected at the end of the line whilst a dummy tunnel has been built into the side of the hill to store locomotives and rolling stock. Nearby a large building has been erected to accommodate the traction engines while at first floor level, the Hewitt collection and many other pieces of Railwayana are on display.

Bill McAlpine's first contact with a major standard gauge locomotive was when he became joint owner of *Pendennis Castle* with John Gretton, son of Lord Gretton who operates the miniature railway at Stapleford Park. This was housed for some time at the GWR Society Headquarters at Didcot.

The possibility of operating a narrow gauge railway at Whipsnade decided McAlpine to form a small company, known as Pleasurerail Limited, to be responsible for the construction and operation of this line, of which most of the directors are railway enthusiasts. Since the opening of the Whipsnade

A close up view of the L&NW 2-2-2 "Lady of the Lake" (9½in gauge). *Richard Sharpe Studios*

Above: An 'O' Gauge GWR '1361' Class 0-6-0 Saddle tank painted in pre 1936 livery. Now owned by W. H. McAlpine. *Richard Sharpe Studios*

Left: 3½in gauge model of GWR 4-6-2 "The Great Bear". *Richard Sharpe Studios*

Line, another has been built at Knebworth Park to the 2ft gauge and they are also in the process of developing a monorail for pleasure and practical use. Other sites are being actively investigated for narrow gauge or miniature railways. The line at Whipsnade, after an experimental point to point run, has now been extended to form a complete circuit being opened by H.R.H. Princess Margaret in 1973. The original motive power consists of ex Bowater's locomotives owned by McAlpine.

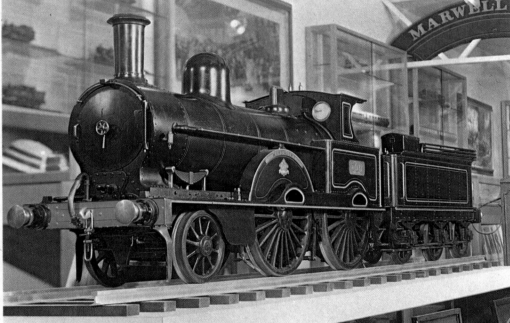

As already mentioned in a previous article, the Romney, Hythe & Dymchurch Railway in Kent was in danger of being split up and sold by auction towards the end of 1971. Bill McAlpine gathered a small group of enthusiasts together and formed a consortium to raise enough money to take over the line in the early part of 1972. He is now Chairman of the Company which operates the railway so, with an assured future, many improvements are planned to be carried out during the next few years.

McAlpine is also joint owner with the author of two Bassett-Lowke "Little Giants". As mentioned in previous articles the "Little Giant" was a standard class of 15in gauge locomotive, the first of which was built in 1905. Over twenty were constructed during a period of some twenty years, the last and most advanced version being built in 1923. Several are still in existence, including the original locomotive which now, fully

restored, runs on a line at Haswell in County Durham. The two under discussion were Nos 15 and 18 respectively: No 15 was built in 1909 for an exhibition at the White City and named *Red Dragon*. It ran subsequently at Rhyl where it was re-named *Prince Edward of Wales* and in 1920 was transferred to a line at Margate. It was sold out of service in a derelict state in 1968. No 18 was built as *George the Fifth* in 1911 and during a somewhat chequered career ran at Southport, Rhyl, Skegness, Southend and finally, Belle Vue, Manchester, where it lay derelict for a number of years until acquired by the author in 1964. *George the Fifth* is at present being re-built by Roger Marsh and it is hoped it will be in service again very shortly. Although the locomotive presented a very sad appearance, when examined many of the mechanical parts were found to be in excellent order, a tribute to Henry Greenly's design and Bassett-Lowke workmanship.

Top Right: A Harry Powell locomotive, a 7¼in gauge "Midge" 0-4-0T No 1106. *Richard Sharpe Studios*

Above: A close up view of one of the L&NW locomotives, the 2-4-0 "Hardwicke", also shows the excellently detailed work of Harry Powell.

Overleaf: LNWR "Mabel", built by the famous "LBSC", on R F Hanks' garden line near Oxford. *B Jones*

The enterprise for which Bill McAlpine is most famous is, without doubt, his acquisition of the locomotive *Flying Scotsman*. It is currently based at Steamtown, Carnforth, and can often be seen on railfans' specials in the summer. Mr McAlpine is also the owner of *Pendennis Castle* and evidence of his seniority amongst railway preservationists can be drawn from the fact that he has been elected to the advisory committee of the National Railway Museum at York.

LOCOMOTIVE MODELS IN THE SCIENCE MUSEUM LONDON

The Science Museum in South Kensington, London, has been in existence, though not always under that name, for well over a century and for most of that period has been able to add to its collections without serious competition from other museums or private collectors. This good fortune has been offset by the traditional difficulty that all museums seem to have in finding enough space to display their collections, and the Science Museum has some fifty subjects to deal with. Although railways occupy about a twentieth of the floor space of the building, much of this is taken up by full size exhibits, so the number of locomotive models on view is necessarily small, generally between fifty and sixty.

To merit inclusion in the permanent display, a model must be of unusual interest. If it is there to represent its prototype it must be of the finest quality available, but there are some models which have no prototypes in the strict sense and yet are of extraordinary historical interest in their own right. Two such are the model which Timothy Hackworth made to present the idea for a six coupled engine which eventually resulted in the *Royal George* of 1827; and the small four wheeled demonstration engine used by the Stephensons. This last has an interesting automatic reverser, which allows the little engine to run backwards and forwards across the floor, covering about ten feet each way. The firing of this, as of many early models, was achieved by inserting an iron rod into a domestic fire until it was red hot, and then sliding it into a blind ended "flue" in the boiler.

However, this kind of personal relic of the great pioneers is scarcely what we nowadays think of as a model, and it was not until the great age of railway building had begun—after about 1835—that scale models began to be made.

Really fine models of this period were equal to anything built today, but they are exceedingly few in number, and the Science Museum seems to house most of the British examples.

There can be no finer locomotive model in existence than the $8\frac{1}{2}$in gauge Crampton locomotive which T R Crampton himself provided for the Museum in 1876. This model was made much earlier, not long after its prototype which was one of the French (Nord) Cramptons built by Derosne and Cail of Paris in 1849. The curious gauge of this model makes sense in the context of the metric system, because the full size dimensions had only to be reduced to one tenth and then increased by half, to give a scale of 3/20. In this large model of a small locomotive every detail is strictly to scale. This model works as well: when the button below the case is pressed, air at a pressure of 7lb/sq in is admitted to the cylinders, with a soft sigh the great driving wheels are set in smooth motion, and one can study the elegant movements of the connecting rods and the outside Stephenson's link motion of this graceful old design. From a Museum point of view this model has everything. It is a perfect model of an important historic type, and a personal memento of one of the great railway engineers of early days.

Another model with strong personal associations is the GWR broad gauge 2-2-2 which came to the Museum from the Gooch family. It represents the "Ixion" class, close forerunners of the *Iron Duke,* and there is an old photograph of Sir Daniel Gooch, then a comparatively young man, with this model, which must have been taken in the 1840s. In this case some liberties have been taken with the prototype, in order to make the model more attractive. It is finished largely in brass and copper, where it should be painted iron, but its proportions are excellent.

Also from this early period, and scarcely less fine than the Crampton model, is the one sixth scale model of a Norris 4-2-0 locomotive. Norris of Philadelphia exported engines of this type to several European countries in the late 1830s. For a time they worked the Lickey incline outside Birmingham, but this model is of one of the Austrian engines built in 1838, and was made by Philipp Wolf in 1843. It too works on compressed air and is a further proof that the highest standards in model engineering were attained a very long time ago.

Below: Model of Crampton locomotive of the Northern Railway of France. 1849. (3/20 scale) *Science Museum, London*

Models of compound locomotives are not common in this country, unless one counts the very numerous models of the Midland and LMS express engines. Most of these are two cylinder simple versions anyway, and it seems a pity that a really good model of one of these admirable and long lasting machines has not yet been built, especially as they formed the most numerous class of British 4-4-0. However, the notorious compound locomotives of F W Webb have been perpetuated in more than one model which actually represents the compound principle, and the Science Museum has a one sixth scale model of one the 2-2-2-0 variety, *Marchioness of Stafford.* This is the only locomotive model which has its wheels turned by an electric motor. Even the sectioned Adams 4-4-0 of the LSWR manages to keep going all day long on its one complete cylinder, but Webb compounds were notoriously bad starters! Perhaps a more scientific view of the matter is that compound expansion of compressed air at a pressure of half an atmosphere is simply impossible unless the exhaust passes into a vacuum pump —and the electric motor at least enables one to watch the behaviour of the external Joy gear which is an unusual feature of the design.

There is another compound model in the Museum: the 4 cylinder 4-6-0 of the Western Railway of France built in 1901 and modelled by P Regnard. This is a twin of a model by the same maker in the Museum of the Conservatoire des Arts et Métiers in Paris, and its acquisition by the Museum in 1903 serves as a reminder that the Science Museum is not a museum of British science and engineering, but has always tried to fulfil its educational function by taking a world wide view of its various topics. The Regnard model is of superb quality. It seems almost a pity that it is sectioned right down the middle, but this is the only way in which the visitor can appreciate exactly what goes into a de Glehn/du Bousquet compound. The prototype was designed by Clérault as a close copy of du Bousquet's celebrated Nord 4-4-2 design, which it resembles in all the main features (though not having so deep a firebox, nor such well proportioned steam passages).

A very long time can be spent in studying this model and noticing the many refinements of this classic type of locomotive, such as the arrangements for independent control of high and low pressure valve gears, the lightness of the four sets of motion, the surprising ease of access to the inside valve gear and the enormous low pressure slide valves. Such a perfect sectioned model is a three dimensional textbook, and it is interesting to compare this one with another of equal quality, though showing an earlier and simpler engine: the Adams seven foot 4-4-0 express engine of the LSWR, modelled by the Coates brothers between 1896 and 1899. This is probably the best known of all the locomotive models in the Science Museum, photographs of

Top right: A 1/6 scale model of a 4-2-0 locomotive introduced in 1837 by William Norris of Philadelphia USA for working on lines having steep inclines and sharp curves. This is a model of a locomotive built in 1838 for Austria. *Science Museum. Crown Copyright*

Bottom right: Great Western Railway broad gauge locomotive of 1840. 2-2-2 "Ixion" class of 1840 designed by Daniel Gooch. (1/8 scale) *Lent to Science Museum, London by Lady M H Gooch*

both sides having been published in countless books for three quarters of a century. As already mentioned, this engine, to one eighth scale, runs slowly all day long on its one "good" cylinder. Of particular interest in this model is the excellent design of the cylinders and valves, much more generously proportioned than in most designs of the period, and the annular blastpipe which equalised the draught over all the firetubes and made it unnecessary to fit long smokeboxes on any of Adams' locomotives.

Adams was the most progressive British designer in the latter part of the nineteenth century, and this model is of a prototype which summed up his long experience with remarkable beauty and efficiency. Both these sectioned models thus represent locomotive types of the highest importance, with the greatest possible accuracy and completeness. Nothing of this kind has been made for very many years. Even though some superb models are made today, with every attention to external fidelity to the prototype, these are made to be capable of running under their own steam, so their internal details are quite unlike those of the full sized machine. By actually steaming, they perhaps achieve a different kind of realism, but this is artistic rather than scientific.

There is a widespread misconception about what goes on in the basement of the Science Museum. It seems to be commonly believed that the workshops are a hive of modelling activity. It would be nice if they were, but the fact is that the maintenance of working exhibits and creation of new displays dealing with all

those fifty or so subjects, to say nothing of the effects of two million visitors per year, keep most of the technicians busy in quite other ways. All the same, a few models are made, usually by a single craftsman and usually, on and off, over several years. Among the locomotive models the outstanding example is the model of the *Planet* 2-2-0 of the Liverpool and Manchester Railway built recently by W Hodges.

The *Planet* was the first of the Stephenson inside cylinder locomotives, and so the precursor of what was for so many years the typical British railway engine. It had double frames, too, and was the basis of the later 2-2-2 "Patentee" design which was to be the first railway engine in so many countries. No good model of this locomotive, or any closely similar, was known to exist, but very complete details were available, so, as a long term project, the model was built in the Museum. Of special interest is the complicated drive to the valves, arranged on the front of the smokebox.

There are some locomotives so famous and important that one expects to find models of them in any collection which has claims to being representative. Such a one is the *Rocket,* represented "in person" in South Kensington and also by a full size replica showing the condition when new, and a large scale model. An-

Above: Compound locomotive: LNWR 2-2-2-0 No 2798 "Marchioness of Stafford".
A 3-cylinder compound locomotive of Francis Webb's "Dreadnought" class of 1885. (Scale 1/6)
Science Museum. Crown Copyright

Below: Sectioned model of London & South Western Railway 4-4-0 express locomotive by William Adams, 1890. (1/8 scale)
Science Museum. Crown Copyright

Right: Liverpool and Manchester Railway 2-2-0 locomotive "Planet" of 1830. (1/8 scale)
Science Museum. Crown Copyright

Below centre: Model of 2-4-0 passenger locomotive of the Taff Vale Railway. 1864 (1/8 scale). *Science Museum. Crown Copyright*

Bottom: Great Northern Railway 4-4-2 Atlantic No 1442 built in 1908 to the design of H A Ivatt. (1/6 scale)
Science Museum. Crown Copyright

Far right: Great Northern Railway 4-2-2 Stirling single of 1887. (1/8 scale).
Science Museum. Crown Copyright.

other is the Stirling eight-foot single driver of the Great Northern, the subject of a superb model to one eighth full size, built by the Baines brothers, in the correct materials, left unpainted, and most unusually left without a tender. The scientific interest of a tender is after all not very great, and one tender is much like another of the same period. Yet another famous locomotive is H A Ivatt's large boilered "Atlantic" for the same railway, of which the Museum has the one sixth full size model made by Bassett-Lowke for the GNR, and subsequently repeated by them for various possessors of extensive garden railways to 9½in gauge. The original model has such refinements as a full set of scale cab fittings. Careful scrutiny of the tender side reveals that this was lettered LNER for many years, but since nationalisation it has been repainted with the letters GNR.

So much for some of the models one expects to find, but what of the ones that take one by surprise? What, for instance, is one of the overworked and undersized Taff Vale 2-4-0s of the 1860s doing here? This is perhaps one of the few models which is here solely on its merits as a

model, but even this one can be regarded as representative of the whole class of double framed, six wheeled engines which were once so common and which had their finest and most durable form in the productions of Matthew Kirtley of the Midland. The Taff Vale engine was built in 1864, during the heyday of Kirtley's ideas at Derby, but was much smaller than the Midland engines. All the same, this type did excellent work on heavy trains and heavy gradients, and is not unworthy of commemoration in distinguished company. The model is a gem. It is one of those labours of love, rare in the 1860s and long after: an exact model of a real engine, built by a railwayman who knew it intimately. The railwayman was Thomas Hopkins, and he built his model between 1865 and 1870, the tender being added later. The original livery, now rather faded, is still on the model, and adds to its charm, but charm is too sentimental a word to describe this magnificent piece of work. One has only to look at the pipe unions to perceive that this is a model of the very highest class. One only need let air into the cylinders to realise that it actually sounds right as

well. To anyone who remembers the sensations of driving or riding on a small inside cylinder locomotive it is quite extraordinary to put an ear against the glass of the case and hear again the gentle rhythmic thumping of axleboxes and big ends, and the quieter murmurs of the valve gear. This engine was just about the size of a Stroudley 0-4-2 tank, but without side tanks or bunker, and the writer drove one of these a few times, during the war. This model has often vividly reawakened the memory of that little old engine.

A museum man often reflects on the fine models which ought to be built, and regrets that so much patience and skill is nowadays lavished on yet more models of frequently modelled prototypes. Has there ever been a good model of the first modern British four cylinder engine, Manson's No 11 of the Glasgow and South Western, which lasted a quarter of a century before being altered beyond recognition as *Lord Glenarthur*? And though quite a few models of the *Decapod* have been made, what about the first practical three cylinder simple design, Robinson's 0-8-4 tank? One would wel-

**Above: London Tilbury and Southend Railway
4-6-4T No 94 "Arthur Lewis Stride" 1912.
(1/12 scale).** *Science Museum. Crown Copyright*

**Below: North Eastern Railway 4-4-0 class "M"
express locomotive No 1620 (1/16 scale)**
Science Museum. Crown Copyright

come a model of the first British Atlantic to put beside its much modelled big boilered brother, and also one of NER No 1619, in the three cylinder compound form in which it served as prototype for the Midland engines—and served the NER and LNER for thirty two years. 1898 was a vintage year, not only for the rebuilding of 1619 with three cylinders, but also for Manson's No 11 and for *Henry Oakley,* and the reader can no doubt add his own favourite to the list.

The Science Museum does possess one model which provides a tenuous link with No 1619. This engine was originally a two cylinder compound, the sole compound in Wilson Worsdell's class M. Its inside cylinders were much the same as those of the large singles of class J, one of which produced over 1000 horsepower while hauling more than 300 tons at 86mph—a phenomenal feat for 1890. The rest of class M were built as simples, with provision for possible alteration into compounds. They were the first express engines in this country to exceed 90 tons weight with their tenders, and were sometimes called "rail crushers". In their original form they had outside steam chests giving a very free path for the steam, and this no doubt helped them to

perform their celebrated feats in the 1895 race to Aberdeen. The Museum possesses a 1/16 full size model of one of these engines, actually built for Worsdell himself. The original paintwork, though authentic Gateshead finish, is not quite delicate enough for so small a model, and the cab roof has a large window to give a better view of the cab details. These features slightly detract from the appearance of what is in fact an extremely good model, but the fine proportions are not lost.

To end what is really a personal anthology of favourites selected from the most distinguished collection of locomotive models in the country, we will have a look at the large model of the London, Tilbury and Southend Railway 4-6-4 tank locomotive. This was the first "Baltic" tank design to run on a British main line, and also perhaps the most attractive—though those who can only remember pictures of these engines with Midland chimneys and smokebox doors will certainly not agree until they have looked at the illustration of the model. It is an irony of history that the best contemporary evidence we possess for the lavish LT&SR livery should be a model of a locomotive which never bore those

colours, for the real engines were delivered in 1912, just after the takeover by the Midland, and were in Midland red.

This model was built in Plaistow works, to be tried out on models of certain pieces of trackwork, so that this long machine would cause no special problems. Sadly, this precaution did not suffice, for the Great Eastern, which had raised no objections to these locomotives running into Fenchurch Street station (into which the LTSR had running powers) when the design was submitted to them, was so incensed at the Midland takeover that it excluded the Baltics from its metals. So, good engines though they were, they became white elephants, and the small engine policies of the Midland ensured their unpopularity at St Pancras. The LMS scrapped them as soon as new 2-6-4 tanks were built, but their designer, Robert Whitelegg (who was also to see the premature scrapping of his larger Baltic tanks for the Glasgow and South Western) preserved the model and eventually presented it to the Science Museum, where its splendid livery, flush fitted chimney, and brass beaded dome remind us of the loving care devoted to the aesthetics of the locomotive in the distant days before 1914.

Overleaf: A sectioned model (1/10 scale) of a 4-cylinder 4-6-0 compound locomotive of the Western Railway of France. Designed by de Glehn/du Bousquet in 1901.
Science Museum. Crown Copyright

A Superb Swiss Collection

Count Antonio Giansanti-Coluzzi's Museum of Commercial Models

If you are fortunate enough to obtain a copy of the Fulgurex catalogue you will find that the address of the manufacturer and distributor is Lausanne, Switzerland —the home town of Count Antonio Giansanti-Coluzzi, a genial and generous man whose love of old models is deep and whose collection of them must rival almost any others in the world. Fulgurex specialises in the manufacture and distribution of superb scale models in HO, O and 1 gauges, its subjects ranging from a Swiss Federal Railways electric locomotive to a German Maffei Pacific, and from a Union Pacific four truck diesel to a Great Western Railway Castle 4-6-0. The larger models are obtainable in steam and electric and the HO masterpieces in brass with electric traction. Fulgurex is the Count's brainchild and

one of his companies—set up to produce commercially, mainly in small batches, for the man who wants a super model. On the whole Fulgurex have concentrated on what they term "the glorious yesteryears of railways" and the Count will tell you that he is far from alone in wanting to capture memories of childhood and youth in these fine models; he feels a periodic need for peace of mind and reminiscence in the past and a love for the things our ancestors enjoyed, such as veteran motor cars, antique furniture and methods of railway locomotion. He is modest about it, but it was Count Antonio who purchased a French 241 P—one of France's finest steam locomotives—for preservation and display on the French-Swiss border at Vallorbe. In particular it is the 1930s

which seem to have caught the Count's memories and imagination and it is this period that he has striven to recapture in miniature.

But it is not only Fulgurex which makes the Count both famous and respected, he has also made it his business to gather together a unique collection of commercial models from the very early days to the present time—all are virtually in mint condition, and the displays on his shelves are reminiscent of Gamages toy shop, London, in the early 1930s. Virtually every European and most American makers of the pre second world war era are represented—Bing, Märklin, Bubb, Carette, JEP, Bassett-Lowke, Hornby, Lionel, Marescot and Fournereau—they are all there in gauges O and 1. Among these treasures (sought and collected

Right: Bing and Märklin Gauge 1 rolling stock.
Courtesy Count Antonio Giansanti-Coluzzi

Below: A Märklin Maffei Pacific in Gauge 1.
Courtesy Count Antonio Giansanti-Coluzzi

Bottom: A collection of Märklin Gauge 1 wagons. *Collection Count Antonio Giansanti-Coluzzi*

Overleaf: A collection of Gauge 1 locomotives by Bing, Märklin, and Bassett-Lowke including an Ivatt Atlantic, a GC "Sir Sam Fay" and the famous Bassett-Lowke Moguls.
Courtesy Count Antonio Giansanti-Coluzzi

long before tinplate collecting became a serious hobby in England) are such rarities as the Märklin *Cock o' the North* and the famous LBSCR 4-6-4 tank, to name but two. Not only the museum rooms, but the Count's office too contain these magnificent examples of the toymakers art in printed tinplate. His office has models in gauges 2 and 3 of old German, French and British manufacture, his showcases house not only locomotives but every variety of coach, wagon, station and accessory. Maurice Debrokra's "Maddonne of Sleeping" may well have immortalised the famous Blue Train from Paris to Ventimiglia, Count Antonio Giansanti-Coluzzi has seen to it that this era of railway modelling has been similarly treated in his own collection. Through his own love of beautiful old things he has been able to recognise and preserve mint and working examples of the tin printer's art—the toys of yesteryear and collectors' pieces of today. In addition, through Fulgurex, newer collectors' pieces have arisen where models based on skilled workmanship are turned out (and often sold out prior to production) for the real connoisseur.

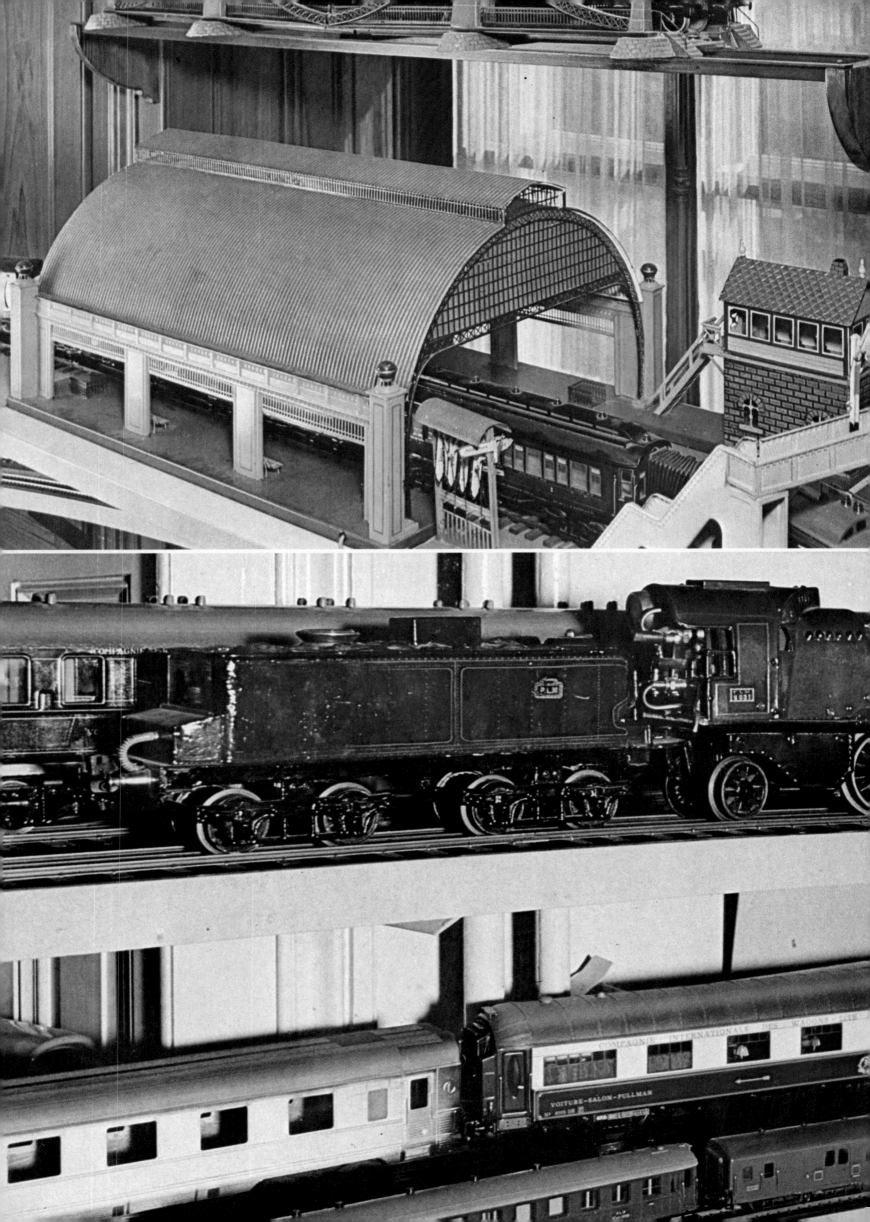

73
FULGUREX—

Far left: **Märklin station and accessories.**
Courtesy Count Antonio Giansanti-Coluzzi

Bottom: **Live Steam Märklin Gauge 1 PLM Pacific on top shelf. Below are Elettress scale coaches in 0 gauge.** *Courtesy Count Antonio Giansanti-Coluzzi*

Left: **The Fulgurex Catalogue.**

Overleaf: **A model of a Midland Railway implement wagon carrying a horse-drawn furniture van.**
B Monaghan (Courtesy Derby Museum)

The first proposal to build a railway between London and Bristol was put forward by a group of Bristol merchants in the autumn of 1824. John Loudon McAdam, the prominent highway engineer who was then the Surveyor of Bristol Roads, was to have contributed to the new venture by surveying the route, but the project was abandoned for no apparent reason. No further schemes were proposed until the autumn of 1832. The Reform Bill had precipitated a violent outburst of rioting and destruction in Bristol and it was clear that the star of economic prosperity which had burnt brightly over the town during the 18th century was beginning to dim.

The railways provided fresh impetus for the tremendous growth of the city in the second half of the nineteenth century. The epic story of the building of the Great Western Railway Company's main line to Bristol and the West of England has been told many times, and both the company and its brilliant engineer, Isambard Brunel, have now become part of the folk-lore of a city that takes its history very seriously indeed. Any museum of Bristol should, therefore, reflect this vital stage in the development of the region and it is fitting that the City Museum and Art Gallery have recently acquired three important collections of models, plans and photographs to illustrate many aspects of the history of the Great Western Railway Company. It should not be forgotten, of course, that the Midland Railway also played a decisive role in the growth of the transport system of the area, but it would seem that most Bristolians prefer to swear their allegiance in historical matters, to the Great Western Railway. Be that as it may, there are plans to add to the existing

Above: A third class, low roof carriage built in 1848 for the Monmouthshire Railway and Canal Co. The model, the smallest in the collection, shows the carriage as GWR stock number 1184 in 1880. It was withdrawn in 1889. *Blissard-Barnes Collection*

Below: "Metro" class 2-4-0 locomotive No 457 by A E Davis. *Blissard-Barnes Collection*

collections of Great Western material some record of the other railway companies which served the Bristol region, but as yet, no ready-made collections comparable to those dealing with "God's Wonderful Railway" have been found.

A new department of technology was set up in the museum in 1964. The initial aim of this department was to build up a substantial collection of industrial and transport exhibits from the region, to be displayed in a new museum and art gallery complex that was to have been built in the centre of the city, near Bristol bridge. Unfortunately, this project, like many a railway company in the last century, foundered on the financial rocks and most of the exhibits which were acquired by the department have since

been relegated to secondary stores until finance for a new industrial and maritime museum can be found.

Over 100 O gauge historical GWR models were first offered to the museum by John Blissard-Barnes in 1969, at a cost of £7,500. The collection, including a smaller selection of models by the late Col G Templer of St Martin, Guernsey, was purchased in 1971-73 with the aid of a 50% grant from the Victoria and Albert Museum. During the same period a massive collection of 20,000 GWR drawings and photographs made by the late R Woodfin of Tewkesbury, was presented to the museum by his family, so that Bristol museum now holds probably one of the best collections of GWR models and photographs in the country. Limitations of staff and finance impose some restrictions on the number of enquiries that can be dealt with by the curator in charge of the technology collections, but the museum is pleased to help as far as possible with bona fide requests from students of GWR history to see the collections. A small selection of the O gauge models is now a permanent and popular feature of the displays in the present museum in Queens Road.

It is difficult, of course, within the limitations of a short article to give an accurate impression of a collection of scores of models which were made to be seen as a complete series rather than described individually. John Blissard-Barnes had set out after the second World War to create more than just another collection of GWR models, in what has become an "old fashioned" scale. He deliberately chose to model a period which enabled him to record all the delightful qualities and idiosyn-

crasies which distinguished the Great Western Railway Company from its contemporaries. Excellent though the photographs are, they only show individual carriages or locomotives and therefore do not convey the full effect of seeing for the first time say the "Dean Goods" coping with its mixed bag of carriages on a through train to Dolgelly in 1897. As Blissard-Barnes records in his introduction to the catalogue of the collection, the main object of the models was "to show the gradual evolution of the GWR standard gauge railway carriage from the short, light four-wheeler of the 1850s to the beginnings of the corridor coach era and also, to record as many as possible of the Great Western carriage livery variations which took place during the 93 years the company operated standard gauge lines".

Above: Joseph Armstrong's locomotive of 1873, "Queen", modelled by A E Davis. The Queen's Royal Saloon shown with this model was built in 1848-50 for Queen Victoria. It was never coupled directly to the locomotive as in this photograph—royal trains were invariably marshalled according to a strict protocol. *Blissard-Barnes Collection*

Below: 2-2-2 locomotive No 55 "Queen" was used regularly on GWR royal trains until the mid-1890s. The model was constructed by A E Davis and painted and lined by J Blissard-Barnes. *Blissard-Barnes Collection*

Right: The Queen's Carriage, built at Swindon in 1873 for Queen Victoria. The model shows the carriage in 1893. The Queen travelled in the central saloon, her dressers in the larger end saloon and her footman, John Brown, in the smaller one. Part of the carriage has been preserved in the national railway museum collections. *Blissard-Barnes Collection*

Bottom right: The old broad gauge eight-wheel GWR Royal Saloon of 1848-50 after it had been converted to run on the standard gauge in 1889. This was probably the first railway carriage in the world to be fitted with a lavatory. *Blissard-Barnes Collection*

Above: A 4-wheel passenger brake van No 471, as running on the GWR Royal train in 1893. Built in 1877, the last examples of these vans were withdrawn in 1929.
Blissard-Barnes Collection

Top right: A finely detailed 2-6-2 tank locomotive No 4555 by Beeson. The prototype was built in 1924 and bought for preservation by the author.
Blissard-Barnes Collection

Right: A beautifully detailed model of "633" class 0-6-0 tank locomotive No 638. The model shows the engine after it was fitted with a Belpair boiler in 1923. *Blissard-Barnes Collection*

The models are based on photographs of actual trains which included a variety of historically interesting vehicles. Any duplicates were systematically eliminated so that the final collection of some 70 carriages are all based on different prototypes ranging from a third class 4-wheel carriage of 1848 to a bow-ended corridor coach of 1926. The locomotives were chosen to head a selected rake of carriages and the collection includes some interesting models of early engines such as the handsome 2-2-2 locomotive, *Queen*, designed by Joseph Armstrong at Swindon in 1873 and used to head the Great Western's Royal Trains of the 1880s and early '90s. In fact, the GWR Royal Train of 1893 is the only "excursion into the unusual". The rest of the models were generally chosen to reflect more prosaic characteristics of the company and its rolling stock, and therefore incorporate a wealth of purely technical information. They are, however, a unique visual record of changing social attitudes and customs. For example, family carriages figure prominently amongst the earlier four and six wheeled stock, but disappear during the Edwardian era when some of the truly magnificent 60 and 70ft corridor coaches and restaurant cars were introduced.

Immense improvements were made in providing for the creature comforts of the traveller—both human and animal—for one can also trace the extinction of the barbarous habit of confining household

pets to "dog boxes" in the passenger brake vans.

One aspect of Mr Blissard-Barnes' modelling which should not be overlooked is the fascinating set of detailed notes which he produced as a descriptive catalogue of the collection. It reflects his dedicated and scholarly approach to his subject and clearly summarises many original conclusions based on his own research and observations. Every model in the collection is carefully listed, in chronological order according to the building date of the original prototype. Every scrap of relevant data the author could find about each prototype was carefully recorded—the serial number, stock number, dimensions, changes of livery, and details of alterations. The fact that the rainstrips of some vehicles were moved nearer to the edges of the roof at some point in their career becomes a crucial piece of information. Seemingly trivial facts of this nature were consistently incorporated in the models and many of the carriages were rebuilt and repainted several times as new information about their livery or condition at a particular point in time became available. The process of "revision" was still in progress when John Blissard-Barnes died in 1971. A number of plans for new rakes of carriages were not completed, but it is again

Above: 42XX class 2-8-0 tank locomotive No 4274; a model by G E Mann of the heavy freight engines designed in 1910 by Churchward for use in the Welsh coalfields. *Bristol City Museum*

Left: A "brown" goods vehicle classified as suitable for use with passenger stock. It is in fact, a fish van, code name "Bloater", No 2177. *Blissard-Barnes Collection*

typical of this modeller's concern for accuracy and continuity that he left a detailed series of notes describing his future plans for the collections together with suggestions about likely sources of information.

Broad gauge enthusiasts will be disappointed to find no broad gauge models, as such, since the collection was meant to illustrate only standard gauge practice. As so little really accurate or consistent information about the carriages and rolling stock used on the broad gauge seems to be available, this would seem to have been a sensible choice. However, some models of the broad gauge "convertible" stock were included and they reflect the difficult years when the broad gauge had become little more than a millstone round the neck of the GWR shareholders. Broad gauge history is clearly an area where the museum can add to the collection from time to time with specially commissioned models and Mr G E Mann, of Guildford, who built a number of the locomotives featured in the collection is now research-

Above: A working model by G E Mann of "Saint" class 4-6-0 No 2939 "Croome Court".
Bristol City Museum

Right: One of the high quality goods vehicles in the collection, a 20 ton brake van.
Blissard-Barnes Collection

Below: "Dean Goods" No 2463 as running in the 1920s. The original prototype had a fascinating career, serving in France in World War 1 and Tunisia and Italy in World War 2. The model is by G E Mann.
Blissard-Barnes Collection

ing a model of a typical broad gauge express train of the 1850s.

On balance, some criticism of the detailed finish could be made of some of the earlier, unrevised models and John Blissard-Barnes was always ready to point out that he had built the carriages but not the locomotives. The latter were not within his area of interest or skills, although most of the better locomotive models featured in the collection were built to his instructions, often using drawings by the late Colonel G G Templer of St Martins, Guernsey, whose work is also illustrated. Certainly, the collection will not appeal to some on the grounds that it was always intentionally a static, "museum piece" in which robust working qualities were sacrificed for the sake of incorporating authentic historical details. It could be argued, however, that few, if any, modellers concerned with working layouts have achieved such a consistent standard of historical accuracy. There are inevitable sacrifices that have to be made if a model is to be used on a working layout, and by deliberately choosing not to make these sacrifices, John Blissard-Barnes produc-

ed a museum standard collection of the highest order.

What are the future plans for the museum's GWR models? Clearly restrictions in the present building prevent any large scale developments, but it is envisaged that the additional working models acquired from Colonel G Templer and G E Mann will one day be demonstrated regularly on a working layout. It is surely not too much to ask for Bristol to finance the GWR equivalent of Derby Museum's popular Midland layout. The Blissard-Barnes collection would also be displayed in its complete form as a series

of ten or more trains. Less than a third of the total number of models is on show at present.

Finally, a published version of Blissard-Barnes catalogue, perhaps incorporating the relevant locomotive drawings by Templer and appropriate carriage drawings, would make a useful addition to any GWR enthusiasts' library. It was unfortunate that John Blissard-Barnes was unable to complete his plans, but his catalogue, together with the models, must form one of the best and most unusual collections of historical Great Western material to be found anywhere.

Cab view of Harry Powell's exquisite model of L & NWR 'Lady of the Lake'. Now in the McAlpine collection. *Richard Sharpe Studios*

COLLECTING TINPLATE MODEL TRAINS

Although the "collecting" hobby has long been established as a medium for relaxation and pleasure, there is little doubt that in recent years the number of its devotees and the level of interest has increased enormously, possibly due to an ever widening range of subjects, not to mention more leisure time and pocket money. The collector who specialises in

weighing 15tons each. A coating of tin is then applied to both surfaces of the steel strip by an electro-tinning process (virtually a huge plating plant) and the resultant "tinplate" is then ready for processing into toys of various shape and colour, limited only by the designer's imagination. The choice of tin as a coating on the base metal has many advantages. It has strong resistance to corrosion and is non-toxic in small quantities—important with a toy. Its surface properties also offer very strong adherent qualities for the printers' ink; this is vital because the litho printing, for ease of production, is applied to the tinplate whilst it is in its flat sheet state—thus the subsequent bending and forming operations (to produce the toy) inflict considerable stress on all ingredients, and it is essential that the ink and tin do not part company Finally, for quality of finish and colour, a tinned surface can rival even the best art paper.

The electro-tinning principle of applying tin to strip, only emerged on a big scale during the last war. This was to conserve tin, as it is possible, with this process to apply a coating only one third as thick as the previous method, known as "hot dip tinning" where the strip was simply dipped into a hot tin bath. Fortun-

design skill and thought. One hopes that these may be the collectors' pieces of tomorrow.

Oh yes, the collector! He looks as normal as the next fellow and probably is. Almost certainly a male (though one or two of the ladies are known to indulge) with an age, occupation and salary bracket as varied as the subject matter he collects. Why he starts collecting old tinplate and railway items in particular, he probably will not know himself with any clarity. It's a deeply individual question, but undoubtedly many people feel attracted to any miniature reproduction of a familiar and long-established object like a train and its associated equipment, especially when it appears in the bright colours and decorative livery of the early railway companies. Accidental contact with an old catalogue is sometimes sufficient to sow the initial seed, or perhaps a casual meeting with a friend who is already committed to the hobby. Nostalgia and a link with one's early childhood (when life seemed unruffled and all sunshine) is probably another good and sane reason.

Collecting generally also feeds a strong human passion for search, acquisition and possession. The serious collector also gets involved with historical research

tinplate model trains and associated accessories may well be one of the "new boys" in this field (compared, for example, with the more familiar stamp collector), but this can be an advantage if you care to think about it.

But what precisely is tinplate which has been the toy manufacturers' first choice raw material from about 1875 to comparatively recent times? Basically it is steel strip produced in widths of up to 3ft, available in various thicknesses between .005in and .015in and delivered in large coils (not unlike a giant clockwork spring) containing up to 3 miles of strip and

ately for the collector, most of the very old tinplate toys were hot dip tinned, thus acquiring a more permanent protection against the ravages of time, neglect and damp storage conditions. It might be thought that the application of plastics and modern die-casting techniques to toy making has completely superseded the use of tinplate. This is not so. Some countries, notably Japan, still produce a big range of tinplate toys, from locomotives and fire engines to motor cars and mechanical figures. Many of them incorporate ingenious mechanisms and gimmicks which reflect considerable

Above and left: Early Hornby railway equipment. *Richard Sharpe Studios*

which has its own special appeal and frequently leads to the making of new friends with a common interest. The number of variants on a particular model introduced at different dates in its production span often poses problems to the historian, but equally adds spice and interest to the hobby. As one might expect with the human element involved, the range of items collected varies considerably. Some will concentrate solely on Hornby model railway products which were introduced in 1920 by the late Frank Hornby (still this country's most famous and best loved toy firm in the opinion of many). Others will perhaps confine their collection solely to Bassett-Lowke or German built locomotives with no interest in rolling stock and accessories.

The question of gauge is another variant. Although gauge O offers the biggest survival rate, and is certainly the most popular in the tinplate collecting field, many people also collect the early OO gauge items introduced to this country by Bassett-Lowke, eg. the Bing Table Top Railway in 1924 and the novel Trix Twin Railway in 1935. Rivalling these, and perhaps setting new standards of quality and design, was the British Hornby "Dublo" series introduced just before the war. Strictly speaking, Trix and Dublo "stretch the rules" a little, as only their freight and passenger stock were genuine tinplate based, the loco bodies being rather finely detailed die-castings. However, they were metal and so well made—who could resist them? At the other end of the scale, gauge 1 still has its adherents, though of more limited number, probably because of the rather scarce supply. Even larger and more scarce are items in gauges 2, 3 and 4 which are really majestic and solid looking examples

of tinplate railway toys of the 1910 era, usually manufactured by Bing for Bassett-Lowke. Hardly suitable for an indoor model railway layout in a modern house, but a rake of these monsters rolling round a garden railway would be worth going a long way to see.

As already mentioned, many collectors specialise in one type or make which has much to commend it. Though obviously more restrictive, it does lead to a more balanced collection and avoids the serious problem of storage space which is sometimes the penalty of a collection of all types of make and gauge. It is often overlooked that a gauge O item will occupy eight times the volume of a OO gauge equivalent. Even so, some collectors, like magpies, cannot resist certain pieces of tinplate and are prepared to accept each item on its merits, irrespective of the gauge, manufacturer, age or value. Perhaps its overall shape and presentation brings a warm glow of pleasure or even a smile to the face? Maybe its combination of colours has a special appeal to the eye?—a long-forgotten memory resurrected? Under these circumstances it is difficult to walk away and ignore it, especially if the price is reasonable. Like a painting, it will give pleasure for years to come and not just

Below: One of Frank Hornby's masterpieces, the O gauge "Metropolitan" High Voltage Locomotive with appropriate controller. Produced in the mid-1920's, it was Hornby's first venture into electrically powered locomotives and set a high standard of performance and appearance. A classic toy with an unusual amount of detail for the period. *B Monaghan*

Centre: This Hornby O gauge LNWR "set" comprising the clockwork "2710" loco and a solitary open wagon was issued along with a circle of track in the early 1920's, housed in the now rare chocolate brown box. These particular examples have luckily survived unscathed for over 50 years. *B Monaghan*

Far Right: A delicious example of O gauge tinplate by Karl Bub of Nuremberg (early 1900's). A 4-4-0 clockwork loco in Midland Railway livery, complete with the typical "steam roller" wheels and ornamental key. A rare specimen, fortunately surviving intact to give pleasure to anyone with an eye for colour and character. *B Monaghan*

confined to its owner.

In the course of time, a representative selection of some of the more famous toy makers over the last 50 years or more may well be assembled dependent on the amount of zeal exercised (luck also plays a part) and the amount of money available. One will get familiar with nostalgic names like Marklin, Bing, Carette, Kraus and Bub of Europe, Lionel and Ives of America and, nearer home, our own Bassett-Lowke and Hornby. A typical example of the latter marque could be a gauge O "2710" clockwork 0-4-0 goods locomotive in LNWR livery with its associated open wagon. This "set", along with a circle of tinplate track was issued by Hornby in the early 1920's, housed in the now coveted dark brown box with an embossed design on the lid. At this period, and indeed up to about 1925, all the major components on the locos and rolling stock were assembled on the nut and bolt principle reminiscent of the associated Meccano products which is understandable. Certainly an attractive, if expensive, method in contrast to the subsequent tab and slot principle of assembly now firmly associated with nearly all types of tinplate toy.

If your allegiance was not to the LNWR, Frank Hornby, in these early days,

battleship. Plenty of detail is evident, including the distinctive roof, brass handrails all round the loco, masses of lining on the body panels and even the "Metro" coat of arms resplendent in full colour. The loco's running qualities were up to the same high standards. It rolled along the track under perfect control wih a steady ponderous gait just like its big brother—a quality not at all common with some of today's toys.

The cost to tool up and produce such a toy, even in 1925, must have deterred all but the bravest. Surely a collector's piece-de-resistance? Locomotives, however, must not be allowed to take all the glory. Hornby produced a bewildering range of O gauge freight and passenger stock, both 4-wheel and bogie versions, based on the big four railway companies formed in 1923, in addition to the earlier companies already mentioned. Many private owner vehicles were also available, bearing familiar names like Crawford's Biscuits, Cadbury's Chocolate, Fyffes Bananas and amongst the Tank Wagons, Castrol and Shell—all now much sought after by collectors. Not all the liveries and colours, however, were produced by the lithographic printing process and some of these wagons illustrate the results of a less complex

safe home for them and, for some samples, dig deeply into their pockets for the privilege.

No review of tinplate collecting, however brief, could avoid reference to Nuremberg, home of so many toy firms, some of which were household names all over the world. At least 150 firms were reputed to be in the Nuremberg area around 1890 and the Bing factory would undoubtedly take pride of place, at least in variety and output.

This firm would even manufacture a specific requirement solely for one of the big stores like Gamages of London, (usually described as a "Bing for Gamages" model) and surviving toys of this type are regarded by some collectors as being rather special.

A typical example of a Bing toy would be one of their vast range of "short" bogie coaches which were invariably well-built and beautifully lithographed in full colour and lining and often featured opening doors and internal fittings. The latter comprised tables and chairs, made from tin, of course, and they are delicate works of art in themselves. The chairs are copied from the familiar kitchen bentwood design, even simulating the round legs and back rest. They are obviously blanked out in one piece, involving

also catered for other preferences, namely the Great Northern, Midland, Caledonian, and London Brighton & South Coast Railways, though samples of the last two are rare indeed. Still with the same stable, another historic toy worthy of a place in any tinplate collection is the O gauge "Metropolitan" loco. This was the very first electrically powered loco produced by Hornby in the mid 1920s and it is unique in that it was designed to run on a high voltage supply to the track—reputedly around the 70-90 volt mark. This may well have been motivated by a desire to eliminate the expensive transformer between mains supply and track. All that was needed was a simple variable resistance controller, wired in series with a 60 watt lamp which served as a voltage dropper—a method not uncommon with other European manufacturers. Second thoughts must have prevailed, however, in the interests of safety. Lower voltage models were soon introduced (4 volt and later 6 volt) before adopting the even later 20v motor with automatic reverse. A clockwork version of the loco was also available. Some collectors regard this "Metropolitan" as one of the best, if not the best, of Frank Hornby's model locomotives; in terms of strength, it was built like a

method. The main body was simply enamelled with the basic colour required and the lettering and decorations added separately, usually with transfers. This principle also applied to many of the locomotives. The full process of the lithographic printing technique appeared to be more often used when plenty of detail and several colours were required, eg., a box van with plenty of planking, louvres, ventilators and outside framed doors etc. with letters and markings in various colours. Although each individual colour required a separate printing process (followed by a separate oven treatment to dry out the ink which the tinned surface will not absorb) the whole process was fast enough to produce a selling price acceptable to the often shallow pockets of pre-war days. Very small detail like bolt heads and door handles were incorporated without any extra cost once the master die had been made, which all added to the overall character and appeal of the finished model, in spite of its often crude scale proportions.

One might need imagination to accept, say, a model of Cock o' the North or a streamlined A4 with an 0-4-0 wheel arrangement, but they are such little charmers—most collectors readily find a

piercing, embossing and bending operations, resulting in a fascinating sample of painstaking endeavour in toy design and manufacture. The tables are given the same treatment and the total cost of press tools must have frightened the accounts department, bearing in mind that these components represent only a fraction of the total cost of the coach and are virtually out of sight too! But not quite; the coach roof is hinged down one side and can be lifted to examine these enchanting reminders of a bygone age and, indeed, of a bygone firm. Regrettably, Bing no longer survive.

When it comes to extravagant use of materials, with a consequent immense solidarity, some of the early American made Lionel models are unsurpassed. The author has a Metro-type 0-4-0 loco which is typical. Built from heavy gauge metal and lavishly covered with thick coats of paint, it needs quite an effort to lift the loco with one hand and "designed for a lifetime's use" is written all over it. No wonder samples survive in such good condition. Many of the loco's body components, such as windows, doors, steps, springs and axle boxes were produced as completely separate units and assembled to the body and chassis on the tab and slot principle. The alternative and more normal method (ie. a simple lithographic print) could incorporate the same detail at considerably less cost in press tools and assembly work, but wouldn't approach the Lionel presentation of elegant brute strength. The tiny pantograph and the grossly overscale handrails fitted to similar locos of this era may well look ludicrous to the "dead scale" enthusiast, but this is the essence of many tinplate models (built for rough handling) and for reasons perhaps indefinable even to a collector, adds enormously to the charm and character of a toy.

A few examples of lineside accessories might be appropriate at this point. The range is far-reaching, many of them portraying lithographic tin-printing at its finest (sometimes involving up to ten different colours) and offering plenty of nostalgic detail in the way of advertisements no longer with us in their original form, and other impedimenta now departed from the railway scene. The

Right: These Hornby O gauge tank wagons illustrate the colourful nature of tinplate toys. The "Shell" and "Colas" wagons were issued in the mid-1920's, followed by dozens of other varieties and colours. It would be a lucky man who has the full set of tankers. *B Monaghan*

Below: A massive gauge 3 First/Third Compo Coach in LNWR livery, probably manufactured by Carette for Bassett-Lowke some 65 years ago. A commendable amount of detail is evident, including gas cylinders, opening doors, end steps, and correct Mansell type wheels. *B Monaghan*

Above centre: A near mint example of the famous Hornby "Windsor" Station, now approaching its 50th year of survival. This item had many subsequent variants, including alternative station names and is a firm favourite with most collectors. The "trees" could be purchased separately and were designed to clip on to the fencing for added realism. *B Monaghan*

Centre Below: American Lionel O gauge locomotive circa 1930. In terms of sheer weight, power and lavish use of materials, it is probably in a class of its own for an 0-4-0 loco. Although not a steam outline model, few collectors would refute its attractive brute strength and character. *B Monaghan*

Far Right: Typical Hornby O gauge accessories. The miniature "K" type oil can, in copper and brass, is a working model intended for lubricating the locos and rolling stock and now a coveted collectors' piece. The famous Hall's Distemper "twins", so long associated with main line journeys, indicate Hornby's imagination and thoroughness in the toy field. *B Monaghan*

famous Hornby "Windsor" station which started its long production run in 1923 (with many subsequent variants) is an ideal example. Colourfully designed to generous proportions, the early version featured opening doors and two candle holders slotted into the base inside the building and positioned just under the two chimneys. The joy of seeing smoke emerge from the chimneys had to be measured against burning the roof tiles! Most of the advertisements on "Windsor" relate to Hornby trains, and some of the statements can hardly be regarded as modest. "Perfect mechanism" and "They last for ever" are typical but, in fairness, one must concede that most of the Hornby range was ruggedly built, and these claims could well have a fighting chance of passing the Trades Descriptions Act of today.

The back face of the station features two delicious litho prints of early motor cars—a tiny taxi with pram type hood and a sedan of the same period. Some of the early German made examples of British stations are equally interesting. Usually built to smaller proportions than "Windsor" they feature several advertisements of old and famous British companies, some of them positively oozing nostalgia. A particularly delightful sample is "Hud-

son's Soap" which is shown illuminated in the beam of an old oil lamp and another intriguing one is "Singer Machines" with the latter word spelt "Mashines". The particular station featuring these advertisements (maker unknown, but the trade mark is a thistle with a leaf on either side of it) proudly proclaims "Central Station" on its roof canopy, in spite of being a good copy of a wayside halt. As mentioned before, one needs imagination in this hobby!

A close look at a selection of the smaller Hornby O gauge accessories will reveal an assortment of luggage ranging from a wicker basket to a heavy chest with a porter's barrow and a four wheel truck for transporting them. Other items include a platform ticket machine, fire equipment box, and the now virtually extinct machine which would print one's name on aluminium strip, all for one penny. The latter is a special favourite with many collectors; with typical Hornby thoroughness all the letters of the alphabet are clearly printed on the tiny dial. All these items, including the platform seats, milk churns and passengers, help to bring the station platform scene to life, and must have delighted scores of children and grown ups over the years.

It would be unpardonable not to men-

tion a few samples of OO gauge tinplate items. Although starting off rather shakily in the early 1920's, OO gauge eventually developed into the most popular gauge to date in terms of model railway layouts and amount of equipment manufactured. Except for the early Bing series of 1924 to 1926, the OO locos have mostly been produced in die cast metal or plastic form, but the freight and passenger stock had a long production run in tinplate from both Trix and Dublo, and some fine examples have emerged over the years.

Few of the post-war issues would be regarded as rare collectors' items at the moment, but the pre-war items are much sought after, especially the "Dublo" LNER articulated twin coach set in teak finish, complete with the streamlined Pacific loco *Sir Nigel Gresley* with low valanced body (unlike the post-war version whose body line was altered, exposing all the valve gear). This loco, along with the 0-6-2 tank series, was available with either electric or clockwork drive, though the clockwork version was not re-introduced after the war.

Some casting deterioration is often evident after all these years, usually on the wheels and wagon chassis and axleguards, and one would be extremely

fortunate to pick up a mint model of either the loco or rolling stock today.

As regards tin printing, however, it is doubtful whether the quality of finish on some of the post-war "Dublo" series has ever been surpassed. The various Western Region coaches in cream and chocolate and the BR maroon 6-wheel and passenger brake vans are typical examples of the tin-printers art at its finest, and the LNER teak coaches (non-articulated after the war) were little masterpieces, considering the difficulties of reproducing the teak finish and the finely detailed body mouldings all over the coach sides. Honest endeavour towards a good scale reproduction is evident at a glance on most of the Hornby Dublo series, and in the tinplate field they are likely to be regarded with affection as long as tinplate is collected.

Trix items were perhaps not so fastidious about scale reproduction, but nevertheless have an appeal all their own. Their freight stock appeared before the war and for some time after, with the chassis and axleguards manufactured from tinplate (unlike the Dublo series which used die-castings) and this accounted for their distinctive and perhaps more toy-like appearance, the latter being an irresistible feature to some collectors,

including the author. On the same theme, and possibly unique to Trix in this period was the fact that all their rolling stock carried the information (in bold print and on both ends of the vehicle), "TTR Patents Pending" and "Made in England".

Many of the larger gauge toys described earlier, are unlikely to be ever manufactured again; thus the collector (apart from his own personal enjoyment) is providing a unique and historical store of toys which, one hopes, will give pleasure to many people yet unborn. Undeniably, toys do play an important part in most people's lives and if one accepts the recently reported annual "toy" spend of around £200 million in this country alone, its influence is still a major one.

Obtaining some of the older and rarer items of tinplate can be a slow and sometimes rather expensive exercise, but by keeping in touch with established dealers now catering specifically for this market, it's surprising how often one can locate the particular wagon or loco tender to fill a vital gap in one's collection. Antique shops occasionally produce a pleasant surprise and the local jumble sales and auctions shouldn't be overlooked.

To learn more about the subject and

the various price brackets, it is advisable to join one of the established model railway clubs. Not all, but quite a number of such clubs, feature a small band of tinplate collectors who can muster a fund of advice and information for a willing pupil. Equally important, these contacts can sometimes augment one's collection, either on a sale or swap basis as, almost inevitably, duplicate items will accumulate in the course of time.

Finally, one may well be wondering what the collector does with all his tinplate trains when he has acquired a fair sized collection. Again, its a question of individual taste and no one should quarrel with that. Some enthusiasts will arrange them in display cabinets (well illuminated to bring out the full detail and colour) to give pleasure and talking points to the many friends and visitors with similar interests. Other collections will be put to work, running through track and scenery permanently assembled in the attic, or if one is fortunate enough, a large spare room, or even in the garden. Many of the locomotives and rolling stock are also given an "airing" at meetings organised during the year throughout the country, and this provides a unique opportunity of seeing some of the really rare items that many collectors can only dream about. Some people will call it "playing with trains", but what of it? It's great fun and anyone blessed with a little imagination will know that it also goes much deeper than that.

Tinplate Restoration

Before dealing with the practical side of tinplate restoration, perhaps a brief reference to the ethics of restoration would not be out of place. Undoubtedly, some tinplate collectors will be dismayed even with the title of this article; their unswerving policy would be to "leave well alone" however battered and scratched the tinplate item might be when purchased. Indeed, some would regard the attempt to transform an old damaged relic into something approaching its former condition as a rather misleading exercise and a completely wrong approach to the tinplate collecting hobby; that the use of a paint brush, however limited, would reduce the value of their "relic". These people may well have a point; at least one can respect their opinion and integrity. A "middle of the road" approach, however, is steadily gaining favour with some collectors, provided that certain basic principles are respected—eg:

(1) The workmanship involved in the restoration must be of a high level.

(2) A flexible approach, taking into account the respective condition and rarity of each particular model, is essential.

(3) Retention of as much as possible of the original paintwork and components should always be sought, however painstaking the task involved, eg a "touching up" exercise is invariably preferable to a complete re-paint, unless absolutely impracticable.

(4) Evidence of validity and manufacturing of a model (eg trade marks and transfers etc) should never be obliterated in any restoration exercise.

(5) Some collectors advocate the special marking of any model that has been restored in the interest of fair play and to avoid possible confusion to the future historian. An expert would doubtless spot "non-original" work, but the novice collector might easily be persuaded to pay a mint-level price for what is, in fact, a nicely restored toy. This is a question of individual conscience.

Most collectors, of course, prefer a mint item in original condition, both structurally and paintwise. Ideally, it would be in exactly the same condition as when it left the factory and complete with instruction sheet, guarantee label, wrapping paper and the original box. It would be very expensive too! A "find" of this nature would be extremely rare, especially if one is thinking in terms of older toys of 30 to 40 years ago, so at the outset one is faced with the decision: accept some form of restoration or allow a very wide variation of condition in one's collection. It is hoped that this article will outline the possibilities of restoration and help collectors to decide their own outlook towards this problem. As already mentioned, each restoration job should be individually considered in the light of condition and rarity of model, but the following modus operandi represents a broad basis of attack.

Facing page: One of the earliest attempts at true-scale modelling: a Great Central 4-0 of 1903 by Bing. From the R McCrindell collection. *B Sharpe*

This page: Hornby "0" gauge N.E. Refrigerator Van. Before restoration, almost the whole of the bottom edge of the body was rusted to a height of about ¼". After removing the rust and touching up the body with matching paint, the plankwork and door framing etc., was restored using Indian Ink. *B Monaghan*

(1) If the model is in a particularly filthy condition, the body and all accessible areas should be wiped with a rag. A dry ¾in soft brush is also useful for removing dust and dirt from inaccessible areas and, preferably, these operations should be performed outside the house for obvious reasons.

(2) The next operation is a simple but vital one. Obtain a strong cardboard box to safeguard all the bits and pieces associated with a strip-down. If a loco is involved, the mechanism is normally the first item to be removed from the body—usually a simple operation involving a few nuts and washers—place it aside in the box for later attention. The body is then stripped down to its basic components or

Large picture: **G.N. version of the Hornby "0" gauge "2710" loco c.1922. The loco had suffered many dents and scratches on the boiler with the footplate sides severely bent and in a rusty state. The latter were the only areas completely repainted; all the other areas were touched up, thus preserving about 95% of the original paintwork. The connecting rods and couplings had to be made from nickel silver strip and rod, as the originals had not survived the loco's ill-treatment.** B Monaghan

Right: Jim Whittaker at work. B Monaghan

Right below: A sample of the less expensive litho-tinplate locos, but proof that character and charm is not necessarily linked with high cost. So cleverly and simply designed, the complete loco was stripped down in minutes and the battered cab and boiler restored in little longer. Incredibly, the whole tender comprises but two stampings and these even incorporate imitation coal and "couplings" at front and back. The fixed winding key and uncommon "side" brake add to the overall charm (to some collectors) and just take a close look at that chimney! B Monaghan

to a level that is considered necessary to do a thorough job. Most units are stripped down very quickly and easily, especially the early Hornby series which used simple nut and bolt construction, so there is little time lost in stripping down to very small units—it facilitates the subsequent metal straightening and painting operations.

More frequently, one will encounter the tab and slot principle of construction which has been associated with tinplate toys for over 100 years. This is almost as simple to dis-assemble as the nut and bolt method, though there is the additional risk of the tabs breaking off when disturbed by further re-bending. The following technique

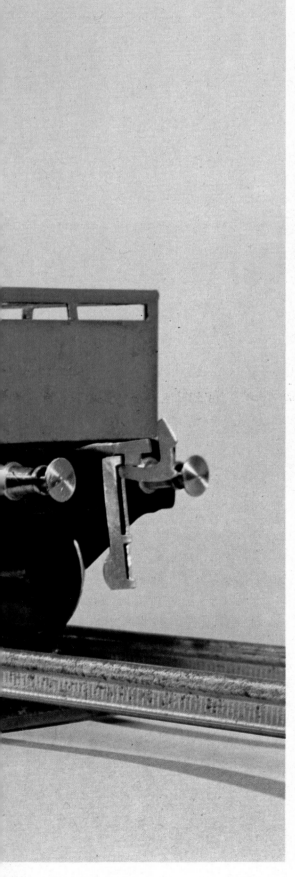

will minimise this risk almost to zero, provided the tab has not been attacked by rust.

A fine-bladed pinion driver is inserted just under the front edge of the tab and used to lever it away from the surface to an angle of about 15° from its former position. This is the maximum movement advised, using the levering action as the tab is under severe strain at this stage. The resultant gap will be sufficient to insert a pair of pliers provided they are of appropriate shape—ie slender, flat-nosed type, tapering almost to a fine edge. The tab is then gripped by the pliers (pressing the latter well into the gap and as near the original bend in the tab as possible) and the tab

very firmly bent into the full 90° position ready for withdrawal from its associated slot. The author has fractured very few tabs using this method. If a fracture does occur, a replacer can quickly be made from suitable tin sheet and soldered in position, but any collector worthy of the name will want to retain as much of the original toy as possible. Another method of assembly features the common eyelet, particularly for attaching couplings to the chassis. Eyelets can be removed by levering up the "riveted" edge of the eyelet with a pinion driver to a position where round-nosed pliers can take over to complete the full bend and restore the body of the eyelet to its original shape. This then permits the eyelet to be removed and, equally important, allows it to be used again on re-assembly.

(3) Some locomotives carry a fair amount of "brass ware" such as domes, hand rail knobs and pipes etc. and these should also be removed for separate treatment (described later) unless firmly riveted in position.

(4) When the stripping is complete, each component (eg boiler, cab and foot-plate etc.) is thoroughly washed with soap and cold water (applied with the fingers using a circular motion or even a soft stumpy paint brush) then thoroughly rinsed clean under the tap before wiping dry with a clean cloth and placing on a warm radiator to dry out the inaccessible areas. There are other cleaning agents, of course, but soap and water involve low risk in terms of safeguarding the paintwork, lining and transfers. Even with this method, most transfers are rather vulnerable and in these areas a little less finger pressure is advised during the cleaning process. If the above treatment does not produce something approaching the original colour of the loco, some collectors will apply one of the polishing agents to really attack the top grime. As this involves a slightly abrasive action, considerable care should be exercised and preferably a "practise run" on a hidden area, eg a portion of the cab front, hidden by the boiler. When all the parts are nice and clean to handle, the full extent of the damage can be more readily assessed.

The main faults will be a combination of chipped paintwork, dents, rust, missing parts and components bent out of shape. Removing rust from some areas (eg embossed rivet heads) can be rather laborious, but is quite practicable using a combination of emery paper, scraping tool, smooth file and a small wire brush, whichever is appropriate. Dents usually appear to congregate around a loco boiler, but fortunately they can quickly be removed once the necessary, but modest, equipment has been acquired, ie a hard rubber mallet and a 2in long piece of wood whose outside diameter permits it to fit inside the boiler. This diameter isn't critical, as most boilers are slit along the bottom edge allowing considerable movement to accommodate the wood. The author uses a wooden roller, originally intended for use by decorators. In use the wooden roller is simply pushed into the boiler and positioned under the dent. Holding firmly in the left hand, place on the upper part of the right leg whilst in a sitting position and firmly hit all round the dent with the rubber mallet until it disappears. The combination of a rubber mallet and the soft rebound cushion of one's leg permits this operation to be performed without damaging the paintwork or lithograph. In stubborn cases it can be a little painful, but this is a small price to pay to restore a lovely old toy which might be admired and treasured by one's grandchildren perhaps 50 years hence. Dents on flat pieces of tinplate may be removed on the same principle, but using, of course, rectangular blocks of wood to suit the particular component. For dealing with components bent out of shape, one's fingers are ideal for coping with minor bends. For more substantial bending (eg buffer beams) a pair of smooth-nosed pliers can deal with almost any problem once the knack has been acquired.

It helps to place the component to an angle of light which clearly reflects the exact position of the kink at which the finger or plier pressure should be applied. None of these operations should tax the patience or skill of the average enthusiast. Painting or touching up will require rather more of these virtues, but surprisingly good results can be obtained by practice and the observation of a few basic principles.

Firstly one must decide (according to the damage) which areas to "touch up" and which to completely repaint, avoiding the latter unless absolutely essential. To give an example, a rare Hornby O gauge "2710" loco in Great Northern Livery was presented to the author in a condition which reflected almost malicious treatment. Paint was missing in about 60 different places on the loco and tender bodies. The affected areas were mostly small in size (scratches) so a "touching up" technique was considered the best approach, as it allowed at least 95% of the original paintwork to be retained. The footplate sides, originally painted vermilion had, however, lost all their paint, except for odd patches here and there and rust spots had formed as a result. In these circumstances, the alternative approach was used—ie clean the surface down to bare metal and repaint completely.

To continue with the basic principles referred to earlier. On painted tinplate (as distinct from a litho finish) the more important points are as follows.:

(1) When mixing the paints to the desired shade of colour, always prepare sufficient for the complete job in hand in one exercise.

(2) Add plenty of turps so that the paint runs freely. The brush is virtually used to spread rather than brush the paint on.

With this thin paint approach, it is possible to obtain a near spray finish with no sign of brush marks. Begin thin, it is necessary to apply the paint in copious quantities (a sort of "flood" which finds its own level) rather than repeated brushings, otherwise the paint won't cover the bare surface. This principle applies to both touching up exercises and complete repaints. The thin paint is particularly useful when touching up small irregular shaped patches, as it is not necessary to apply the brush into every nook and cranny; the paint is merely coaxed towards the existing paint line to which it will be drawn by a form of capillary attraction, but without going beyond it, which is vital, and time saving. For these small areas, a pointed sable brush is normally used. For larger, regular areas, a larger flat section brush is advised.

(3) Mixing the right shade of colour is the most difficult part of the exercise, at least to the author! People with a good eye for colour will start with an advantage. It's really a question of trial and error, from which experience will be gained in the course of time. As paint usually dries out darker than in the wet state, it is necessary to wait until it is dry before comparing with the colour sought. The colour mix is usually applied to a piece of scrap tinplate for comparison with the model, but for easier and more critical offering a better "match", the author applies it directly to a typical bare patch on the actual toy being restored. When dry, the result can be examined from all angles and, if considered unsatisfactory, the offending paint can easily be removed with a rag dipped in turps without affecting the original paintwork.

Obtaining a perfect match with paint which could be 40 years old or more is probably not possible, but at least the obvious pitfalls should be avoided, eg. if the new paint is too glossy, add a suitable matting agent. If varnish is to be avoided, in the interest of "playing it safe" (some varnishes can affect colours dramatically) a second coat of paint is advised, especially in areas where the model is repeatedly handled with one's fingers.

(4) Nothing makes a model look more tatty than damaged transfers, lining, and railway insignia generally—possibly because of their bright, contrasting colours, eg red and gold. Using the vast range of modern paints, these can be touched in with a fine-pointed brush with virtually no evidence of their intrusion, making a vast improvement to the overall appearance of locomotives or rolling stock. For delicate brush work of this kind, improved results can be obtained by using a "two eye" magnifier which has an adjustable headband for clamping to the head, thus leaving both hands free for useful work.

Turning now to a proper lithographed finish as distinct from the painted tinplate just described. Obviously the whole character of a lithographed toy would be

lost if large areas were completely repainted, so touching up is the main weapon of restoration and a standard Hornby van can be used as an example of the possibilities. These vans, like any piece of tinplate, are prone to rust at any spot where the ink has been scratched off and will further deteriorate if not attended to. The normal procedure is as follows:

(1) Remove the rust using fine emery-paper, being careful not to scratch the areas which are in good condition.

(2) Paint the bare patches exposed by the emery paper with the basic body colour of the vehicle, using a paint mix which needs brushing on (not free flowing as described earlier). There will be no positive edge to paint up to in this case, as litho printing ink is so thin, so to blend the paint into the existing litho, the outer edge of the area of paint being applied should be stroked into the litho with a dry brush (a kind of tapering action) to minimise the effect of joining paint with ink.

(3) The next stage is to restore the lines of planking, door frames and ventilators etc which were lost with the rust removal. Many of these lines are printed in black, so it is a simple matter to restore them using Indian Ink, a draughtsman's bow pen, and a 6in rule (provided one has a steady hand). The question of varnishing is again left to individual discretion. Any litho toy 25 years old or more is worth a fight to save and would be studied from all angles by any serious collector. The author recently obtained a Hornby van with the body daubed all over with a ghastly blue paint. (There are vandals everywhere!). Although apparently a dustbin job (except for spares) it was essential to see what was under the paint and a clean soft rag loaded with Polyclens was soon put to work. A few moments work in one area produced a familiar chocolate brown colour with yellow lettering—none other than a rarish (lithographed) GWR Fish Van. Three hours further work and the whole body had been restored to its former livery, except for one stubborn area where excess rubbing pressure had removed some of the litho. This needed touching up as described above.

Between bouts of painting it makes a nice change to restore loco mechanisms. They are usually in a dirty state and require a thorough cleaning before examining for damage. Overnight immersion in a cleaning fluid (petrol would do) followed by the application of a stiff brush to all plates and gears etc. will suffice for a clockwork mechanism. Electric mechanisms are preferably stripped down (a simple job) and all parts cleaned individually, especially the commutator, brush holders and reversing contacts. (Locos are almost invariably over-oiled). Except for gear damage (one should always retain old and battered mechanisms for spares) most of the repairs are straightforward enough.

If the mainspring is broken within a couple of turns of the start or finish of the spring, which is frequently the case, it will still give a useful performance and is well worth repairing. To do this, soften at least one and a half turns of the spring using a fine blow torch, so that it can be re-drilled or shaped into an exact copy of the piece broken off.

Electric motors with open circuit windings can usually be repaired using the existing wire. Unsolder the latter from the commutator and unwind carefully from the armature limb. As the wire gets longer with each turn removed, keep pulling it into a straight length along the workshop floor until the source of

Top: This Hornby "0" gauge Breakdown Van & Crane c.1924 gives an indication of the sort of condition one can expect after surviving 50 years, i.e., many paint chippings, followed by rust, with the more fragile areas bent out of shape. A few hours' work will do much to restore its former pride and appearance.
B Monaghan

Above: Hornby "High Voltage" Metro loco in "0" gauge. A rare model, worth many hours of restoration. Nearly half the body was bare of paint and lining; the chassis was pitted with rust and all the brassware covered in green mould. Considerable re-painting was unavoidable, including much of the lining and one of the Metro coat-of-arms. One of the author's early efforts at restoration, taking nearly 100 hours. Virtually 50 years old, the loco motor and drive required no attention beyond cleaning and oiling.
B Monaghan

trouble is found—often a break at the start of the winding and impossible to get at without unwinding the coil. After repair (the loss of an odd turn of wire has no noticeable effect on the performance) ensure that the rewinding of the coil is in the reverse direction to that used when unwinding.

Mention was made earlier about restoring the "brass ware" featured on some locomotives, eg. domes, number plates, handrail knobs and buffers. Nothing improves the smartness of a loco more than a thorough polishing of these components. When received they are usually dulled with old varnish and some even covered in green mould. By intelligent use of very fine emèry paper, or scratch brush or solvent, the bare brass is eventually exposed for "Brasso" or similar treatment, which really brings out a sparkle (in the owner's eye as well as the loco!). A quick-drying varnish can then be applied according to taste, with little or no effect to the natural appearance of brass.

The question of missing or broken components used to be a serious problem, only solved by making difficult cannibalisation decisions. Die-cast wheels (especially on some of the pre-war Hornby models) were a particular headache; many of them would develop cracks and break up completely due, it is thought, to an unsatisfactory mix of metal when cast. The position today is greatly improved, at least in respect of the vast range of Hornby stock. Certain members of the Hornby Railway Collectors' Association (HRCA) now offer a large range of replacement wheels and indeed many other useful castings and turned components which permit many an old relic to "get back on the rails" with something approaching its former appearance and character. Even a range of colourful Hornby transfers is available from the same source and indistinguishable from the original.

Which brings us back again to ethics; which is where we started. Perhaps also a good note on which to conclude!

Below: Bing (believed for Gamages) "O" gauge George the Fifth Class Loco. "Mercury" in L.M.S. livery, partly restored. The tender coal rails and the cab roof had been severely bent out of position and the whole unit had the very tatty appearance associated with rough handling, i.e., paint chippings and bruises all over the body.   *B Monaghan*

CLASSIC
MODEL RAILWAYS

**Facing page : A Kirtley 2-4-0 in its original
Midland Railway green livery, one of the 7mm
scale exhibits at Derby Museum.**
B Monaghan (courtesy Railway Modeller)

This railway came about quite simply as a display for the collection of locomotives which are all pre 1870 vintage, the earliest being the Hackworth of 1838. All of these locomotives were built from scratch, not from kits. The period was attractive mainly because *every* engine was an experiment in those days—wheel size and layout, cylinder position, wildly ornamental liveries, all varied considerably. Also in the small space one usually has available for a model railway, the correct atmosphere can be maintained, as an old engine with four to five tiny four-wheel coaches looks just right.

There are twenty four locomotives in the collection representing twelve different railways, which is only a drop in the ocean when one realises there were about 250 independent railways around this period.

The baseboards are, where possible, made to a standard three foot by two foot unit, as the railway has to be portable, and these units are easy to lift without damaging either one's back or the delicate structures of the layout. The frames are made from two inch by half inch timbers screwed and glued, with the trackbed of half inch balsa sheet glued in position on top. The holes left for the scenery are filled in with scrap materials including plaster of paris, bandage, polyfilla, soft board, hard board, polystyrene and so on.

The trackwork was built up using Peco bullhead rail soldered to pins pushed into balsa sleepers, for the standard gauge, and flat bottomed rail

A Pre 1870 Period Piece in 4mm

Facing page: "Leo" emerges from Bristol No 1 tunnel.

Top: "Leo" was built by the Great Western as a tender engine and converted to a tank engine later to improve its adhesion. She has a lovely round copper firebox and with the seven foot gauge and the short wheelbase "hunts" in an alarming manner when running.

Below: This view is of the curved dock station. The Furness tank hauling a London and Birmingham train by a North Eastern water crane is not prototypical, but the point of the layout is to portray as many aspects of the age as possible.

laid on longitudinal lengths of 3/16 inch square balsa baulks for the broad and mixed gauges. The track route was marked out in ball point pen on the balsa base. The sleeper lengths were then painted with matt black paint and allowed to dry. The next stage was to paint over the markings with a fairly runny mixture of Evostick resin with wood glue, which when settled still left the biro marks showing through. The sleepers were then laid on these marks and the ballast sprinkled over and allowed to dry. When dry this was painted over with a dirty mixture of brushwash and thinners to give the weathering effect, and the rails laid and pinned or soldered down. The final finishing touch after the wiring was to paint the sides of the rails with rust coloured paint.

Spread across the layout are several working models to add to the general atmosphere. The two turntables are semi-automatic, the traverser with its vertical boilered donkey engine works on a similar principle except that the drive is on to a rack laid in the traverser floor

and is stopped by a spring loaded peg dropped into a hole in the side of the rack. To start it again a button is pressed, sending current to a solenoid which withdraws the bolt at the same time making the motor contact, the traverser then runs along until the peg pops into the next hole, and so on.

The beam engine which drives a scratch built milling machine and a lathe provides the power for the works machinery in a workshop of the period. It is a freelance model based on the many low pressure engines operating at that time, and is worked by a motor driving a rubber wheel bearing by spring pressure on to the base of the fly wheel. This keeps all the things which should not be seen neatly out of sight. The drive also produces some very creaky realistic beam engine type noises!

Through the works and out into the country is the narrow gauge feeder system, which, after leaving the works, dives off under the main line and the canal, to appear on the other side where it crosses a working lift bridge over the

river to the base of the incline. The incline has at the top a slate winding house which, having raised the empty wagons passes them over to horse traction for the remainder of their journey to the quarries.

The winding house also works, but strictly under manual control, via yards of cotton, a dozen pulleys, a relay operated double pole changeover switch, plus two weight operated flash contacts! It was intended to be automatic, but having tied all the aforementioned bits into quite complicated knots for the sixth time a halt was called, and it is now manual. It still gives trouble though because while one is operating it one cannot talk to the public to answer questions or—ping!

The swing bridge is the last item of moveable interest, and this is not yet complete. It does swing on a carriage made of little flanged wheels running on a circular rail soldered to the bridge pillars, but the mechanism for the underside has not been built yet. It will probably be by a long screw thread rotating in a nut pivoted to an arm on the base of the bridge pivot. When the thread is turned the arm will move, taking the bridge with it. Limit switches can easily be made to control it by being operated by the swinging arm.

Above: The long boiler No 18 trundles by the works, with "Cornwall" on the traverser in the background.

Left: "Cornwall" is shown here in her original form as built in 1847 by Trevithick for the London & North Western railway. She has, with her 8 foot 6 inch driving wheels, the largest wheels of the standard gauge in Britain. To get the centre of gravity as low as possible the boiler was slung below and between the frames with cutouts for the axles. Needless to say she was rebuilt quite quickly.

Overleaf: "London" leaves the dock station under the raised signal cabin and verandah with "Spey" in the station pilot's bay. The signals are the early London & South Western rotary type.

Right: An aerial view from the footbridge of the two dock platforms with the centre run round line for both tracks. The quay with a sailing ship loading is on the left.

Bottom: This view shows the loco facilities at the workshops end of the layout The Midland Crampton is taking on coal and the little narrow gauge works loco is collecting coal for the beam engine in the works. Some broad gauge track can be seen in the foreground.

Top: London & South Western "Pegasus" on the dual-gauge turntable. She is the most modern of the collection, being built in 1870 by Joseph Beattie.

Left: A bevy of talent sits on shed. Space was so critical when this line was built that the shed was built into a hollowed out cave. The water cranes are London Brighton & South Coast, and the locomotives from left to right are London Chatham & Dover "Xanthus", London & North Western long boiler No 233 and the South Eastern Crampton No 92.

Bottom: This is the only 0-6-0 engine in the collection and is a Kitson built goods engine of 1848 for the Leeds & Thirsk railway. She is shown here in her "Midland Green" livery when she was taken over.

Above: York, Newcastle & Berwick railway "Plews" takes on coal. This engine was built by Hawthorn in 1848. In the background can be seen the two Royal Mail coaches on the tail of the outgoing train.

Right: A very dark Satanic mill type of view this one. The photo was taken through one of the workshop doors with the broad gauge "Sylph" over the pit. Note the overhead pulleys to the machinery and the general clutter.

Below: This little South Eastern Crampton was a rebuild of a Stephenson 2-2-2 long boiler, and was done to improve her stability. With her haystack firebox and outside valve gear she makes an attractive picture.

Buckingham Great Central began as a first attempt in 4mm scale railway modelling in 1946, and two years later it was sufficiently advanced to be exhibited as a working layout at the Model Railway Club Exhibition where it was described in the model press as "perhaps one of the most outstanding exhibits". It was also probably one of the first 18mm gauge 2-rail layouts to be exhibited publicly. The Great Central Railway was chosen for various reasons. It was not the first choice of most modellers; the locomotives and two colour-scheme coaches at the turn of the century appealed; and the wooden signal posts, unlike the lattice girder type, presented fewer modelling problems; the choice, however, was made not because the builder was familiar with the Great Central but since it presented a challenge in undertaking the necessary research work. This original layout was a semi-portable affair with a country terminus called Buckingham and from which the tracks divided, one to serve a smaller country terminus, Stony Stratford, the other, after passing a through station, Tingewick, terminating in hidden storage sidings. Both Stony Stratford and Tingewick won bronze medals at the Model Engineer Exhibitions of 1947 and 1948. Over the years the railway has undergone many changes; the whole layout being rebuilt again and again to suit the domestic conditions in which it found itself until now it is permanently housed in a room of its own. Today the basic principle of the first railway

BUCKINGHAM

remains the same. There is the terminus Buckingham (now an important town station) and a through station, Grandborough Junction, where the tracks divide, one going to a country terminus, Linslade, and the other to hidden storage sidings representing the main Great Central line through Quainton Road and Aylesbury to Marylebone. There is also a small branch line from Grandborough Junction to Verney Junction which again disappears into a hidden siding.

The characteristic feature of this model railway is that nearly everything has been scratch built by the owner, but no attempt has been made to build really super detail models, only sufficient detail being included that can be readily seen. Great care has, however, been taken to see that locomotives, rolling stock and signals are scale models of such as would have appeared on the Great Central in the year 1907. The railway buildings have been inspired by those on various parts of the Great Central and its associate companies. For example, Buckingham Station buildings are based on the arrival side of Marylebone, the overall roof covering the platforms is from Chester Northgate while the goods shed is based on that at Burnley. The non-railway buildings are scale models which have been taken from various places, the gas works being based on Truro, the gateway and adjacent shop on that at Launceston and the chapel and timber framed house on Northleach. No attempt has been made to reproduce an actual piece of

railway; the whole thing is an imaginary branch line that might have been seen in the year 1907. By adopting this principle it has been possible to create a picture in three dimensions, and to design and arrange the various features to present a railway scene that is pleasing to the eye.

The Buckingham Branch Line is, however, more than a pretty picture, above all it is a working model railway. The three stations are separated from each other by breaks in the scenery, each station being a complete unit in itself and which can be under the control of one operator. When there are three or more operators, with at least one at each station, the trains are received and despatched in a railway like manner by the use of bell codes and in accordance with a predetermined timetable. The storage sidings, which incidentally are also a large turntable con-

Top left: Buckingham Central Station with Marylebone train waiting to depart from platform 1 with Pollitt 4-4-0 No 269—circa 1907.

Below left: 2-4-0 Altrincham tank No 23 stands by Buckingham Gas Works, while the driver is having a cup of tea with the signalman!

Below right: A Down Aylesbury stopping passenger train waiting at Grandborough Junction with Pollitt 0-6-2T No 773.

Overleaf: Robinson 4-4-2T No 47 waiting to leave Buckingham Central with a rake of six-wheelers for Aylesbury.

GREAT CENTRAL

taining six roads so that the trains which have been despatched can be turned round for return in due course, are under the control of a home made computer which works in conjunction with a clock on the wall of the railway room. When a train is due to arrive from the storage sidings the attention of the operator at Grandborough Junction is called by one stroke on a bell. On acknowledging this the computer rings the correct code for the train that is due, sets the points for the route out of the storage sidings, and when Grandborough Junction replies that "line is clear" for this particular train the computer rings "train on line". In the same way, when a train is due to be despatched to the storage sidings the computer sets up the correct line and will not accept the train until the correct bell sequence has been given. If any train is over five minutes late arriving or leaving the storage sidings, then the clock stops, but re-starts automatically as soon as the train is run. When there is only one operator then Grandborough

Junction Station is ignored and the operator at Buckingham deals directly with the computer which is really a second operator, so it is possible to enter the Railway Room at any time and run the next few trains on the timetable. The actual timetable represents a day's working of 17 hours and since the clock runs at three times the speed of normal time it takes about six hours to complete a working day. At the present time there are ten locomotives, twenty carriages and some eighty goods vehicles nearly all of which have been scratch built over the years. The pattern of operation is the arrival in the early morning of the mail and stores from Marylebone, followed by a frequent service of local passenger trains to and from Aylesbury. Less frequent are the express passenger trains to Marylebone, while Linsdale is served by a steam rail-car. Goods working includes a daily goods to and from London, a coal train from the North, a pick-up goods to Linslade, a cattle train and a horse and carriage train. Each goods wagon is

marked with a distinctive colour on the solebar and is shunted in accordance with a schedule which varies from day to day. Altogether there are eighty movements on the time-table. The electrical control is arranged so that the operator at the station receiving a train brings it in from the station of departure on his own controller, an arrangement that is effected by the signals. The turntable is operated electrically and can be pre-set to stop at any of the roads leading to it.

The pictures will give some idea of the railway, but its real satisfaction lies in operating something that is not a collection of railway models but a real railway in miniature.

Top: Leighton Buzzard, Linslade Station: Great Central steam rail-car, just arrived from Buckingham.

Above: An Aylesbury train approaching Grandborough Junction with a Pollitt/Robinson 4-2-2 No 971.

At one time too many model railway layouts were designed without sufficient thought having been given to their function when built. Four-track main lines in a continuous oval soon lose their interest and the present popular branch line layout has its limitations. "Haverthwaite" was designed to make use of the combined advantages of both types—that peculiar hybrid a continuous branch line.

The chief considerations behind the planning of "Haverthwaite" were that it had to be typically Furness Railway of about 1890 in character; that the trackwork should be simple, trouble-free and easy to maintain, and take second place to the author's main modelling interest—locomotives and rolling stock of the late Victorian period of the Furness Railway to a scale of 4mm to a foot and 18mm gauge. In other words the layout would serve primarily as a test track and parade ground for rolling stock models.

So Haverthwaite on the Windermere Branch between Ulverston and Lakeside was chosen as a prototype. The branch was a single-line with a passing loop at Haverthwaite Station. There were a few sidings and a long spur to Backbarrow Ironworks. What remains of the track is now the hub of the Lakeside Railway Society.

The model "Haverthwaite" follows fairly closely the basic layout of the prototype but with the sacrifice of a couple of sidings and part of the goods yard area.

There are two platforms each capable of holding a train of 9 six-wheel coaches with locomotive, an end-loading bay and three main sidings with a long spur to the site for Backbarrow with its two sidings. The spur serves as a shunting neck for the yard and is fitted with a magnetic uncoupling spot for the Alex Jackson automatic couplings which are fitted as standard to all my stock. Goods trains can be marshalled; wagons dropped in selected sidings or collected by remote control and without handling.

Drawings for the station buildings were made from measurements and photographs on site and a series of slides records the colours of the yellow brick

Below: An up passenger train hauled by 2-4-2 tank loco No 73 heads over the viaduct, next stop Haverthwaite. The scene is circa 1895. Seven of these engines were converted from 2-4-0 tender engines for branch line duties. *B Monaghan*

Picture overleaf: No 16 was the last of the "Coppernobs" delivered to the Furness Railway. She was built by W. Fairbairn & Sons of Manchester in 1861. The model has a specially designed motor with flywheel in the tender which drives the locomotive wheels by means of a universally jointed cardan shaft. This scene was taken on the layout of Mr. S. Stubbs. *B Monaghan*

⤙ HAVERTHWAITE ⤚

structures with their blue and red brick ornamentation.

The station is the main feature of the layout which takes the form of a figure 8 folded over on itself. The Up and Down single lines from the station drop down gradients of 1 in 60 until they branch out into four storage roads hidden underneath the station section.

The Up and Down lines parallel each other over an estuary. One by means of a plate-girder bridge based on that at Greenodd the other over a viaduct based on the Levens viaduct before rebuilding. Scenery comes rather low down on the modelling priorities and there is still about one-third of the layout to be dealt with. But working signals are virtually complete.

All track and points are scratch-built on shellaced sleepers fitted with chair plates, cemented to ballasted sponge-rubber and mounted on hardboard track-beds. Points are electrically operated by "motors" converted from post office type relays. Signals are operated in the same way.

Sections, points and signals are switched from a pair of ex-RAF bomb release switch boxes. Operation is at present on the principle of "one engine in steam" and is controlled by a simple transistorised unit working on a line voltage of 24. Control is exceptionally smooth and speeds can be regulated from a mere crawl to a realistic prototype speed for the branch.

Seven locomotives handle the traffic—

three passenger and four goods types. All are authentic Furness of the period 1861 to 1890, built from scratch and, with one exception, from photostat copies of the makers' general arrangement drawings. The exception is "Coppernob" No 16 of which no original drawings have survived. However, with a few known dimensions and some good photographs, reasonably accurate drawings were prepared.

All the locomotives have motors fitted with flywheels to assist controlability. Tank engines have flywheels in the bunkers. Tender engines have flywheeled motors in the tenders which drive the locomotive wheels by means of a universally-jointed cardan shaft.

Wheels are turned from brass bar, pierced for the correct number and shape of spokes and then nickel-plated.

Coaching stock consists of nine 6-wheelers of 1894 vintage, a horsebox, some 4-wheeled passenger brake vans and a rake of four outside-framed 4-wheel coaches of 1870 vintage. Most of the 6-wheelers run on Cleminson-type flexible wheelbases.

Goods stock numbers 36 vehicles including five goods brake vans. There is a full train of Furness wagons and vans and a varied selection of pre-group vehicles and private-owner wagons mostly scratch-built but with a few assembled from kits.

In what might be considered blasphemy in some model railway circles, there are no block instruments, no bells and no timetables on the "Haverthwaite" layout. Operation is to a sequence of movements which includes spells of shunting in the yard.

But operation takes second place to construction. It is most frequent when visitors come to view the line and the latest additions to the rolling stock. They also expect to see how the scenery is progressing. There are still plenty of sites for fresh fields and pastures new to say nothing of embankments and cuttings. But they can wait whilst another locomotive is built.

AYLESBURY

Aylesbury High Street station was discovered when out Railway Rambling with the family. Here was a small terminus still absolutely steeped in London & North Western Railway details, and within a reasonable distance of home. In its earlier days there had obviously been sufficient traffic to maintain operational interest in a model. It was small enough for most of the main features to be modelled complete, and it would be a challenge to try to model a real prototype. An end-to-end model was planned, occupying four portable baseboards which could be reasonably stored in a small house. The opportunity was also taken to use EM gauge. Track was of soldered construction using fibre sleepers. It was stuck down to cork with Casco glue and ballasted with Maw seed and coke dust. The cork was fully floating on a sponge rubber sub base in the interest of silence. A reasonably authentic model resulted, but the Casco dried out and warped the cork, twisting the track all over the place. It was a fine old game sorting things out. To produce a model of this kind takes some time. Apart from sundry rolling stock kits, nearly everything had to be built from scratch. During this time the continuous supply of local detail sometimes proved that too many short cuts had been taken. Sometimes the LNW period features had not been included, sometimes space considerations had necessitated some slight modification, which was found later to limit shunting or other train movements seriously. There was also the ever-present track problem—those fibre sleepers. Time went on, and it became frustrating to try to finish features known to be wrong. One day some EM track soldered up with FB3X TT3 rail was seen, and that did it. A fresh start was made. It meant losing several years work, but so much modelling experience had been gained, and so much authentic Aylesbury material collected that it would have been a pity not to have persevered.

Learning from Aylesbury Mark 1's shortcomings, it was decided that this time the track would be right and stay right. This meant ¾in block-board bases on 2in x 1in framing, ⅛in cork underlay stuck down with Evo-stik. Plywood sleepers with brass pins snipped off and riveted over on the underside, then filed flat, stuck down to the cork with Araldite. Casco glue to secure the Peco/Erg ballast and the TT rail soldered to the pin heads after the latter were levelled in. The levelling in was done using a 12in piece of 2in x 1in bevelled off like a punt at each end, covered in fine emery cloth on the underside. Chairs were represented by little fillets of Polyfilla. Great care

Top: "Bassethound" with 42ft 0in brake van standing at platform, Aylesbury Gas Works in background. *B Monaghan*

Bottom: Precursor tank 528 arrives with a motley collection: carriage truck, 21ft 0in horse box, 21ft 0in fruit and milk van, 5-door 6-wheel parcel van, M R horse box and 32ft 0in invalid saloon. *B Monaghan*

Overleaf: Aylesbury box and level crossing. *B Monaghan*

was taken with this track. When it was supposed to be straight it was just that, when it curved, it flowed easily. It was level—most important. It was laid in situ, and all setting out was done very carefully, using templates made from hardboard, straight edge and Railway Curves borrowed from the Drawing Office. The job was not hurried. The gauge was set at 18.2mm, but the EM Society people were not told in case they laughed (this was in 1960, now they do it themselves). No rail length was greater than 9in. Sundry gauges were made to facilitate track laying, but the final "gauge" was the author's eyesight, often using a mirror at rail level. The ultimate test was to run a long wheelbase test trolley fitted with "Manchester" wheels. The time spent on this track has never been regretted, the only snag up to the present is that the firm fixing makes for noisy operation—nasty noise like a tram.

Aylesbury Mark 2 had just started when the family moved into a house with a loft space very suitable for housing the model. The portable baseboards, suitably modified provide an end-to-end run of 34ft, and sufficient width for Aylesbury to be modelled complete even though some of the track and turnouts right at the back in the Goods Yard are dummies. There is a 14ft straight run to represent the dead straight prototype branch, and a train length sector table with 5 roads having a loco length traverser across all roads at the far end. Additional siding length is about to be provided here for storage of stock used only infrequently, such as the Excursion trains etc. The baseboards are supported by 2in x 2in steel angles which span between the roof collars of the house. There are thus no supporting legs. Initial adjustments to align track at the baseboard joints is easily accomplished using metal shims between the angles and the baseboard framework.

Railway buildings are to scale length and the siding capacity at Aylesbury is about 60 wagons without overcrowding. The usual building methods are used and

Top: Light engine passing passenger and goods home signals. *B Monaghan*

Bottom: The overall roof and screen showing period horticultural features. The coach is a 32ft 0in invalid saloon. *B Monaghan*

materials vary depending on the date when the models were built, and what was on the market at the time. For example, the station building is of Ballard brick embossed card stuck to $\frac{1}{16}$in ply, the loco shed is of brick embossed Plastikard. Neither have the correct bond in the brickwork, but otherwise both materials are quite effective. Incidentally, the bricks of the prototype loco shed were different from those of the station, so perhaps it is as well that the card was no longer available when the loco shed was built.

Backgrounds vary enormously, but mostly conventional methods have been used. Plastikard plays a big part in these back scenes as it is so quick and easy to cut and join when experimenting to get the required effect, when the space available necessitates compromise and exaggerated perspectives. An interesting lineside feature just outside Aylesbury is the Prison, a huge building block, looking rather attractive (at least from the outside) but very complicated to produce in model form, even as a flat. Most of the hard work was eliminated by taking a photograph from the Railway fence and enlarging the print to a length

of 18in. This was then coloured and blended into the 3D foreground, using suitable trees and bushes at the transition areas.

Much of the Town back scene has yet to be produced, but this will be 5ft 6in from the normal viewing area so that flat scenes will play a big part. Not so the Gas Works, which is just over the wall immediately behind the station. A start has been made on this, the purifiers and shed, also the oxide storage area has been produced. More has yet to be done, and this is the real challenge. There are 2 frame guided gas holders, one of which is to be 14in diameter—allowing for perspective etc.

Trying to produce the authentic "Aylesbury atmosphere" is a fascinating exercise. It is a slower job than freelancing as one cannot duck out of the difficult bits, also dead scale dimensions are often incorrect due to viewing angle and perspective.

Thanks to the coal merchants and other friendly natives of Aylesbury a very clear picture of the traffic on the Branch has been built up. Details of appropriate private owner wagons have been collected and the type of Railway vehicles used for some of the special traffic has been discovered. Thanks also to people too numerous to mention, but many of whom are members of the Historical Model Railway Society, sufficient information on the various vehicles has been collected for modelling purposes. Building the stock is a never-ending interest. When kits are available these are freely used, sometimes modified to fit in with local ideas—eg. a home-made chassis using finer wheels for the K's Coal Tank and on the Gem *George V,* but some are built up as standard—eg. K's 6-wheel coaches and the various PC coaches. Sometimes added detail is included such as brakes and interior fittings. Other models are scratch built, some using Trevor Charlton's engraved coach sides and ends, and some by the author's son who makes a very nice job in Plastikard. One very attractive 50ft 0in brake compo is by Mike Peascod. Initially most of the stock was originally appropriate to the branch, but eventually the odd misfit appeared, including sundry PO wagons for sentimental reasons.

A simple form of electric interlocking is provided by drilling the H & M point and signal levers to take silver steel rods, on which are Aralited tufnol bobbins. To each of these bobbins is secured a piece of $\frac{1}{4}$in bore copper pipe $\frac{1}{8}$in long. These little contacts thus slide between phosphor bronze blades when the lever is moved. By fitting the required number of bobbins necessary for the circuits controlled by the appropriate levers, conflicting point and signal movements are avoided. Traction current is independent of point and signal operation as this seemed more suitable on a pre-grouping layout. Power is via a Coder controller, and the realistic "steam" handling is extremely satisfying. The prototype branch was opened in 1839 from Cheddington, on the London and Birmingham main line, to Aylesbury, 7 miles distant. Apart from curves at each end it was dead straight throughout. There was an intermediate station at Marston Gate, and despite several attempts to provide a second track, it remained a single line all its life. It was worked by staff and ticket. A new station was opened at Aylesbury in 1899 and this is the subject of the model. The period is a little loose, but is broadly based just prior to 1914.

DEAN BRIDGE

Modellers choose the scale in which they are going to work generally by the cost and the space which they have at their disposal. With larger models we can work more easily to accurate scale proportions and to include full lining and lettering when it comes to painting. Even today the term "scale" must not be taken too literally, especially when it comes to individual components or parts of a model, because it would demand an extremely high degree of skill in some instances to attain satisfactory working. Allowances must be made quite often, and it is in connection with these allowances that the sub-division of the Gauge 0, 7 mm scale into 'standard' or 'fine' dimensions was made by the British Railway Modelling Standards Bureau some years ago. Measurements were finally agreed so as to assist modellers and their suppliers more on the question of uniformity and practicability, especially in the realm of wheel and rail cross-over dimensions rather than to lay down the law for absolute accuracy for the purist. The layout is not built to the finest dimensions which are possible in Gauge 0 and in which others have succeeded, but it was decided to get as near as possible to attain a realistic general appearance, especially in the case of trackwork.

The pictures were taken in the station area of the layout which is housed in an attic, and permanently laid on trestles for continuous running about 4' 6" high which affords a better eye-level view than does ordinary table-top height. Materials used for making locomotives, rolling stock and buildings etc. are brass, nickel silver, wood, card, and lately, plastic sheet. Some models have been made from scratch, some from kits, and some from re-building old commercial models to more accurate proportions and with additional details. But the best are those built to special order by professional model makers. Propulsion is by 12 volt electricity, fed to studs between the rails and earthed through the rails themselves. A skate collector under the engines picks up the current which is controlled remotely, for speed and reversing. Many modellers starting on a new layout today, and who are not committed, obtain greater realism still in having the electric power fed and returned through the two running rails only, but this necessitates all axles on locomotives and rolling stock being insulated to prevent short circuits.

Since the early 1950's this layout has really become a collection in miniature to recall the railway system in this country as it was in the author and builder's lifetime during the steam age, and to preserve as many items of interest as possible which have been provided by the trade during these years, for the hobby.

Until recently every place of any importance, and not even that in some cases, had a railway station, especially in the more populated areas in England. Extremely common with all their Victorian buildings and paraphernalia extant, they

Top: Dean Bridge Station buildings and furniture by Anthony Murray. Great North of Scotland Railway suburban train of the 1897 period by the late Sir Eric Hutchinson. Passengers by Messrs Brittain and G. N. Slater, and the bicycle from Tyldesley & Holbrook, Manchester. Staircase lattice work was cut from a radio speaker grille and the lamp posts are plastic lemonade straws to preserve insulation mounted by perspex globes. Miniature bulbs are amber tinted to resemble gas light when lit. Advertisements have been culled from periodicals and from the paper cut-out range by Messrs Hornby. Through Great Western Railway train service from South Wales and Wessex to Scotland is occasionally observed at Dean Bridge, hence the Brunellian timber frame roof supports! *B Monaghan*

Centre: Locomotive Shed. Caledonian Railway train of high level, Dunalastair locomotive of 1896 built by J. S. Beeson of Ringwood. Coaches by Anthony Murray, as are the yard fittings and completion of shed modelled after that at Blair Athol in Perthshire. Highland

Railway Strath class of 1892 by the late Sir Eric Hutchinson Bart. and the 1900 Midland Railway 4-4-0 is by Messrs Edward Exley. The makers of the CR 60 class of 1916 and the North British Goods of 1890 are unknown. This mixture of engines in such close proximity would have been very unlikely in real life. *B Monaghan*

Overleaf: Perth-bound North British train built by Anthony Murray is representative of the type which ran on the Company's system from the turn of the century, the locomotives of the 633 class being originally built for the NBR's share of the 1895 East Coast Companies London to Aberdeen race against their West Coast rivals. Some of these locomotives survived in rebuilt form until the second world war, whilst many of their contemporary goods engines ran long enough to be nationalised. The vehicle in the foreground is an example of a private coal owners wagon which abounded in thousands all over the country until taken over by the National Coal Board. The maker of the Hansom cabs is obscure – in all probability foreign. *B Monaghan*

were, we thought, an indissoluble part of life in the British Isles, but now they are either completely removed, left derelict, or else rebuilt in stark and characterless modernity. We suddenly find things are just no more, and it is this speed of change and 'development' nowadays which has so encouraged the Industrial Archaeologists in their work, and to the forming of the Historical Model Railway Society, as much as 20 years ago. This society caters for those interested in the study, acquisition and preservation of information relating to all railways of the British Isles, and the construction, operation, and preservation of models of these railways. Nationwide, it has a large membership devoted to photographing and making drawings for posterity of all the aspects of the British railway system which have survived. To it and to specialist firms we have to turn for components, if we want to re-create the old time railways in miniature. Latter day railway models are produced by manufacturing firms to an astonishing degree of perfection and reliability.

Left and right: Dean Bridge Station looking west. The fine examples of North British lattice post signals were for many years on the layout of the late Rev. Moorhouse Johnston of the USA, but there is no record of who made them. The colour light signals are by Bassett-Lowke and are perforce out of scale in depth in order to accommodate the lamps. The Caledonian Railway 4-4-0 No 188 was built by the author. High-level station house is modelled on the original terminus of the Edinburgh & Glasgow Railway; dating from the 1840's it still exists in use. All signals and points on the railway are worked remotely from a lever frame, or electric contact switches from the central control panel *B Monaghan*

Below: Midland Railway No 2607 model by Edward Exley of Bradford, of the large express engines for the Settle & Carlisle Line in 1900. Station buildings and signals by Anthony Murray. The metal advertisements were supplied by Bassett-Lowke between the wars, and were faithful reproductions of the multitudes which used to adorn the walls of railway property before the days of TV commercials. Their descendents still survive on the London Underground, and the old miniatures are now very rare and costly.
B Monaghan

Little Western

A Model Railway in 4 mm. Scale

The Little Western line was begun in 1957 and is an attic railway, built to EM track gauge to a scale of 4mm to 1 foot: it is the fourth model railway the author has constructed. The primary aim of the layout was to achieve a visual record in miniature of the old Great Western Railway, not only as remembered but also to recapture the beauty of old steam trains as they were in the glory of their Edwardian liveries, and even between the Wars. To this end a comprehensive layout was planned, which could handle many trains of not only different classes,

Left: A model of one of the 4-4-2 "Scott" class engines built by the GWR in 1903. This particular locomotive was No 171, named for several months of its existence "The Pirate". Seen in this overhead shot at the head of a train of clerestory coaches.

Below: "Gooch", No 8, one of the famous four "Armstrong" class of 4-4-0 engines, is shown here on the viaduct behind Watchet Jct station. Note the hand built houses running away into the backcloth. The coaches are a set of scratch built four wheelers, at least 20 years old!

but also of varying periods.

To an ex-railwayman, the image of a scale model line, packed with locomotives and rolling stock, did not appeal, as in the full size prototype, station yards and depots were seldom if ever crammed with stock, it was out on the line, earning revenue. Traffic was intended to run between stations, and so could only be seen when in service. To accomplish this effect, it was decided to install eight long hidden loops, into which trains could run, be stored, and emerge again, as required to a set timetable.

Although the room available was quite sizeable, (25ft x 15ft) greater track length was obtained by the use of two levels, one at the baseboard datum, and another level, 5in higher. At one end of the room, a country station (Watchet Junction) was built, which was of the double main line design, and from which extensive siding space radiated. A locomotive depot was constructed in a small alcove, off the main rectangle: this could house at least twelve engines. Apart from the station

plus its attendant yard and loco sidings, all other track would be fully landscaped as open countryside with embankments, cuttings, over and under bridges, etc. to act as a backcloth and setting for the trains themselves.

As the scheme was a long term one, it was vital to lay a type of track which would not warp, twist, or fracture as time went by, otherwise, with upwards of 500 yards of trackage, maintenance would be a major and continuous headache. Remember, this was sixteen years ago, and the availability of reliable 4mm track was not as good as today. Therefore, a scale track was designed by the author, and so with the assistance of Messrs Walkers of Paddington, the "Little Western" track base came into being. The track has given excellent service to date. With four main lines, Up and Down low level, and Up and Down high level, four control channels were necessary to enable trains to run independently. Each of the four was provided with its own 12V DC supply through the usual metal

rectifiers, with four matched controllers of the 100 watt variable resistance type for speed variation, and double-pole double-throw switches for the direction of travel movements. Each channel was colour coded, namely red, green, blue and yellow so that controller, switches and panel lights were all of the same colour for the one particular line. For example, all the train movements on the high level Up line are handled by the red controller, through red switches and indicated by red lamps. This made train control much easier, especially as a colour-light panel was installed to show just which sections of track were electrified and which were isolated.

A system was devised, which arranged for all trains entering the hidden sections via the tunnels to switch themselves off

Overleaf: "Lord of the Isles" No 3046, is seen here standing in the station, on special duties, propelling one of V.I.P's seated in a model of one of the old Royal train stock. Note the clerestories in the Bay platform.

when in their respective loop lines, alter the points for the adjacent track, and energise a thermal delay switch which would, after a delay of several minutes, cut in, and allow the train on the adjoining loop to move off and proceed on its journey to the station. Thus we have the effect of one train entering a double main line tunnel on one side of the room, and not re-appearing, but five minutes later, a totally different train emerges from the other side of the area.

All this electrical magic is achieved by the use of dry-reed switches set into the track, and small bar magnets fixed to the underside of the locomotives. The pulse given out by the reed as the field of the magnet passes over, is used to trigger relays and rotary selectors, through thermal delay switches working on 4 volts AC, and results in an effective automatic train selection and control. This side of model railways is very fascinating, and the majority of the equipment is ex Government spares which can be bought in Lisle Street, London, for very reasonable prices.

The extensive rolling stock on the line is the result of 30 years collecting and building, many are hand-built from scratch, but a number of vehicles have been made up from some of the excellent kits which have appeared from time to

Above: A 2800 class locomotive is seen picking up iron ore traffic from the quarry sidings, behind Moreton Cutting signal box on the low level line, whilst the train is left on the main line.

Below: No 6011, "King James 1" on a West of England up express, passes the down starting signal. This model is a super detailed example of Guy Williams' work.

Left: A superb EM "Claud Hamilton" from the Great Eastern Railway.

time. All vehicles on the "Little Western" have been fitted with pin-point axles, running in coned bearings, and this has enabled full length trains to be handled by the locomotives with ease. The free running qualities so obtained are a revelation, and the result of these fittings repays every minute spent in their installation.

Model locomotives on the system now number 35, and like the rolling stock, the majority are scratch built throughout; a few are half and half, meaning that kits have been used as a basis, and hand-built mechanisms, chassis, boiler fittings added with scale wheels to make a good representation of the prototype. The engines range in type and classification from the early Dean 2-2-2s through the Churchward designs, with several Collett locomotives of the mid-thirties, to just one of the Hawksworth machines, which gives a fair cross section of the GWR

steam development over 50 years.

Scenically the whole layout is set around the perimeter of the room at a height of 3ft 6in with a walk-about space in the centre. From the edge of the baseboard down there are black curtains hiding the wiring channels and storage cupboards, and from the ceiling a black pelmet cloth extends down for 2ft 0in. There is little or no lighting in the room, except that behind the pelmets, and this is concentrated on to the railway scene, making the model landscape stand out in the dark room to good effect, like a diorama. The lighting under the pelmets is alternate neon tube and tungsten bulb, which together give the effect of warm sunlight with little or no shadows. The cuttings and embankments are all profiled in heavy plywood formers and upon these are fixed sections of expanded wire mesh. On top of the wire mesh is laid papier mache, which in turn is covered with a mohair material, to give a representation of the grass and herbage usually found on railway embankments. The mohair is sprayed lightly with greens, yellows and browns, and finally brushed up so that the nap of the material stands erect, this looks like grass, and has stood the test of time, moths being the biggest enemies!

Buildings and trees were made by the skilled Iliffe Stokes, and are masterpieces; the station is a facsimile of Kingham, whilst the locomotive depot was culled from the old wooden shed at Oxford. Cliff faces are constructed from knobs of coal glued together, and all the scenery on the back cloth has been hand-painted from locations photographed of real Great Western sites.

The non-operating signals are all made from the splendid Ratio kits, from which it is possible to construct dozens of different types of GW semaphores. Bushes and hedges along the line of route are made from a mixture of horsehair and Swedish lichen, with dried tea leaves sprinkled on to the branches, and all the retaining walls use the superb rock papers which have been introduced by Messrs Faller.

What more can one say? The layout still continues to give a great deal of pleasure, and especially so in the winter months, when it is possible by retiring to the loft to recapture a small Great Western scene upon which the sun always shines.

The
South Devon Railway Company

The South Devon Model Railway was conceived in 1962 when members of the Castle Railway Circle were invited to exhibit at an exhibition in Knaresborough. The leader of the Circle—whose members, at that time, were between the ages of ten and fourteen years, searched for a prototype which would feature main line trains, simple trackwork and an unusual prototype location. On discussion with a friend the suggestion of Dawlish was made. Thus the seed was sown and a new layout, measuring thirteen feet by eight feet was constructed. This was not a club owned layout as the finance for this and further extensions afterwards was by the leader whose personal layout it is and who, whilst the Circle is in existence, loans it to the members.

The first layout—named "Lyme Bay" —was a double tracked oval representing the two main lines. At the rear, and hidden from public view were storage loops off each "road". The layout was easily transportable—no board had a greater size than six feet by two feet. It was built in four months during the Summer and was exhibited for the first time at the end of August. Several other exhibitions followed, but the size proved rather restrictive—the truth was that the layout's stock had grown to such an

extent—especially the locomotives, and it was felt that some means of displaying the locomotive collection should be found. A plan was formulated to construct a model of Newton Abbot station and yard—complete with locomotive shed. Track plans, photographs and other relevant details of all stations were obtained from British Railways and private sources.

This South Devon was end to end and measured some forty two feet in length. The length was the main drawback as the layout could not be set up in the clubroom. The latter measures only twenty two feet in length. Running at exhibitions was most difficult without practice and grave difficulties were experienced with baseboard height levels. Another drawback was that stock, especially locomotives, suffered greatly from excessive handling. The layout did stay in this form for over two years and was shown at several exhibitions in Yorkshire either as one complete unit or in part. It was at one of these exhibitions — Sheffield — that members met the Macclesfield Group who were exhibiting their TT3 "Longacre" layout. Note was made of their system of operation, that is a looped figure eight arrangement and also of their sub-base method of support for the layout boards.

The South Devon owner and architect returned to the "drawing board" and discovered the idea was possible for South Devon and, what was more, the layout would be able to fit into the clubroom in its entirety and could be completely operational. Thus the first really successful South Devon was born. Dawlish was placed along one of the long sides whilst Newton Abbot was placed on the opposite side. Both were, of course, facing outwards as they would be in this position when viewed by the public. In the centre of the layout was storage for trains plus a branch terminus. This system proved most successful as most of the track was on gradient and all trains had to be "driven" by the operators. There were difficulties, however, as lengths of trains had to be limited to the capacity of the locomotives. Another difficulty was that, despite the interesting operation possible through "block working" the constant concentration needed

Above: No 7007 "Great Western" passes through Totnes station with an Ocean Special whilst 2-8-0T No 4205 hauls a long coal train towards Plymouth. *B Monaghan*

Right: "Clevedon Court" pulls away westwards whilst No 4205 waits its turn. Shunting the milk tankers is 57XX class pannier tank No 7700. *B Monaghan*

by operators at exhibitions was most wearing and often exhaustion caused accidents to happen. The main difficulty was in the setting up and dismantling. For the sub-base, although foolproof regarding levels, took longer to erect than a complete conventionally supported layout.

This layout was, however, a great success with the viewing public. With its variations in trains—at least a dozen could be operated on each of the main lines, and the complicated train movements which were possible at Newton Abbot with the splitting of trains, changing locos etc., plus, of course, the display of all the spare locos on shed, it made an attraction wherever it appeared. It was honoured to be awarded trophies at Sheffield and Harrogate when it appeared. During its existence it travelled widely and also appeared on television but, eventually, it was decided that the layout had been over exposed, the operators were tired of the hard work needed to erect and dismantle it and it was decided to remodel it to fit around the walls of the clubroom as a permanent structure. It made its final appearance at the Circle's own show in 1969.

The plans to make a permanent South Devon did not, however, come to fulfilment. True, Newton Abbot was put in place and storage loops were placed on the other side of the room. Dawlish was never coupled in, however, before a reverse of plans came about.

Work had been concentrated, after the "retirement" on the redecoration of the clubroom and on preparation of a narrow gauge layout and the Emmet layout for an exhibition in Leeds in October. Two things became evident at this exhibition: one was the disappointment expressed by a good percentage of the regular visitors that the South Devon was not on show and, secondly, the frustration of the operators with the lack of interest in the operation of the replacement layouts. So it was that, during the Leeds exhibition of 1969, the plans for a completely new South Devon were begun.

The plan was to model several different stations with the idea that one or more could be exhibited. Thus the over exposure of one section would be limited and the "permutations" of the five stations proposed were quite comprehensive. The stations chosen were Dawlish (favourite from the old layout and for sentimental reasons), Kingswear (unusual in that, as a branch single line terminus, it saw Castle and King class locos and, although compact, also featured a riverside scene), Totnes—an interesting through station with a branch junction though no branch bay, Ashburton—an interesting branch terminus with Brunel overall roof and the terminus of the branch from Totnes and, finally, Exeter St. David's. This was chosen in preference to Newton Abbot as the former gives more interesting working with the possibility of running Southern trains, banking these up to Central Station plus branch trains, a loco shed and several very interesting buildings to model.

But, where to start? Firstly Newton Abbot was ceremoniously destroyed— the large and unwieldy baseboards being used as the basis for a bonfire! The "Company" as the builders now called themselves, decided that, to maintain

Left: "Dartmouth Castle" with an up express passes the old atmospheric pumping station at Totnes. *B Monaghan*

interest Dawlish should be revived first. New storage boards were built and what was good of the original Dawlish layout was re-used. A new Coryton Cove was constructed and new scenery was made for the "northern" end of the layout. In this form it was exhibited and a start was made on Kingswear. The new Dawlish was rather like the first "Lyme Bay" except that the length had increased to twenty feet and the standard of display was improved—as was the modelling. "Kingswear" was made in such a way that it would attach to the "other side" of the Dawlish layout; trains gaining access to the branch by a triangular

of 1972. The scenic work was then begun and this took until Easter 1974 to complete. Most of the scenic work is the author's but with some notable exceptions: the gardens, painting of figures and road vehicles are Steve Malton's work as is the main Goods Shed. Ralph Ashton built the small huts and signal cabin on the down platform and also the footbridge (which took four weeks to complete) and the bridges over the mill leat. As he was also in charge of another project in the club at the same time this was no mean feat. Each of the main buildings on the layout took an average of two weeks to complete mainly being

scratch built, kit built or are rebuilt commercial models. Passenger and goods vehicles are also in these categories. The latest additions to passenger stock are a complete Cornish Riviera Express as running in the Great Western's Centenary year and also a prototype Ocean Special rake.

In a project like the South Devon Railway Company things never stand still for long. Already plans are in hand for future development but, as with all model railway projects, time is the enemy (or lack of time). The whole scheme will, eventually, be completed but it is not anticipated that this will be for several

junction off the down main line. This junction made the turning of locomotives possible when the layout was being operated end to end as a terminus to fiddle sidings layout.

So the second stage of the master plan was completed and stage three began in earnest. This was to be the station of Totnes with the branch to Ashburton.

Once again plans and photographs were sought and, after a great deal of trouble, found. The construction group now numbered three—Steve Malton, Ralph Ashton and the author. They decided that, to make a successful model, standards should be improved as much as possible. Handbuilt trackwork was a necessity with bullhead rail —as opposed to the commercially available flat bottom track used previously. At the same time all buildings were to be scale models of the prototype as in the 1930's. The model was begun in December 1971. Baseboards were built and trackwork laid. In this they had the great assistance of S M P Cleethorpes who constructed the difficult pointwork. Electrical installation was completed and working signals placed in situ by the end

made of Plastikard and other Slater's products. The model of the Atmospheric Pumping Station took slightly longer. In all some ten major structures were built and some sixty sections of fencing were constructed from wire and nickel silver sheet.

A triangular junction on the new boards means that Kingswear can be attached to Totnes as it was to Dawlish. There is not, at the moment, any means for joining the three stations—the "Company" have, in fact, decided to rebuild Dawlish once again as they feel the standard of modelling is not as high as the rest of the layout. First they must complete the construction of the branch from Totnes and a start has already been made on Ashburton.

Running parallel with the development in scenic modelling has been the actual modelling of rolling stock. Early in the layout's existence the owner aimed to collect together a representative of every locomotive class running in the South Devon area in the 1930s. This stud has now grown until it numbers well over 60 locos. As his modelling improves some examples leave to be replaced by better examples. The locomotives are either

Above: "Dartmouth Castle" passes through Totnes with a London bound express. All the buildings are scratch built from plastic sheet. The locomotive is a re-built Wrenn commercial model with Cotswold fittings.
B Monaghan

Right: Activity at Westcott's coalyard. Now completely demolished it was only by the kindness of a contact that this could authentically be modelled. The bridge carries the main road from Totnes to Plymouth.
B Monaghan

years yet. In the meantime stations which have already been completed will be exhibited from time to time and as additions are completed they will be shown to the public either on their own or with one of the sections already displayed. The new sections started well for after "Kingswear's" winning of the Peco Cup at Harrogate in 1972 and the Visitor's Trophy at Pontefract it won the City of York Trophy in 1973. Totnes, at the time of writing, has only been exhibited once and on that occasion won the City of York Trophy, the Peco Cup and came second in the third competition at York Model Railway Show 1974 against some of the stiffest competition in the country. A just reward for the efforts put in by the constructors.

As model railway exhibitions have grown in popularity and the standard of workmanship displayed becomes higher each year, it is worth a glimpse behind the scenes to discover the whys and wherefores of one of the most popular types of exhibit—the working layout. Exhibitions are dull places without movement and fortunately today one finds more and more that the working exhibits often provide a vignette of a section of railway history. So it is with the Yatton Group, who have produced a small piece of yesterday's West Country to entertain and instruct.

Yatton was born of a desire by a group of friends to approach the hobby from a different viewpoint, adopting as their prime aim the wish to entertain exhibition visitors whilst instructing them in a little railway lore. Being Bristol men their natural choice was the Great Western Railway. To meet the situation it was felt that a section of the track incoporating a main line station with one or two branch lines radiating from it was advisable, and it should be local if possible. Yatton Junction, some twelve miles from Bristol (the team's home town) fulfilled all these requirements.

The prototype of Yatton was originally owned by the Bristol & Exeter Railway Company: it had two branches starting from its platforms, the Clevedon line and that serving the Cheddar Valley; the main line itself was very straight and level, allowing high speed running—indeed, *City of Truro*'s famous run of 1904 was made over these metals. The period chosen was the mid nineteen thirties when most of the buildings, signal boxes etc. still maintained their Bristol & Exeter

Below: Many exhibition layouts have a great deal going on at the back which the public never sees. Here is the detailed track layout of Yatton showing the public face and storage yards. *E Harriman*

Right: 0-6-0 saddle tank No 1809 shunts a train of vintage coaches at Yatton station, while an up freight headed by 2-8-2 tank No 7219 passes on the main line. *E Harriman*

Far Right: 2-8-2 tank No 7219 is held at Yatton West Up home signal to allow the passage of pannier tank No 3717 on the Wells goods. *E Harriman*

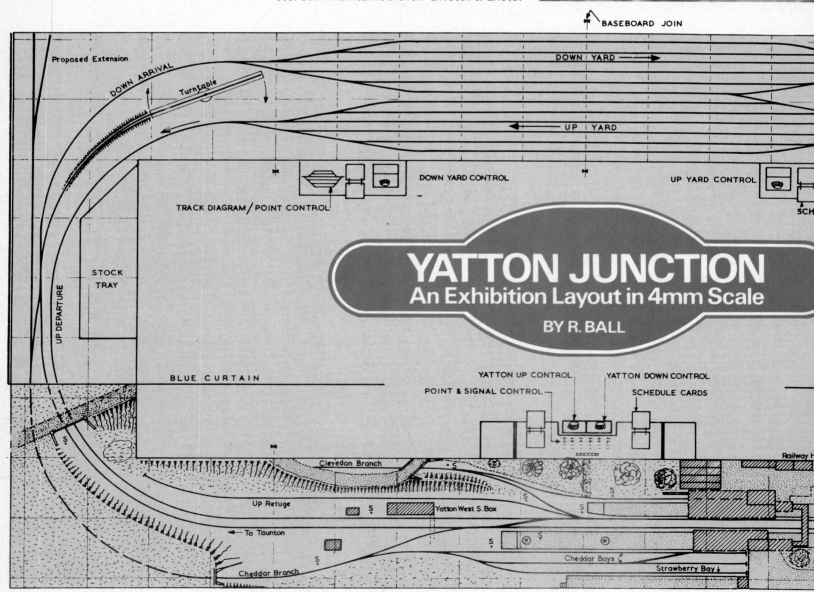

BASEBOARD JOIN

Proposed Extension

DOWN ARRIVAL

Turntable

DOWN YARD

UP YARD

TRACK DIAGRAM / POINT CONTROL

DOWN YARD CONTROL

UP YARD CONTROL

SCH

STOCK TRAY

UP DEPARTURE

YATTON JUNCTION
An Exhibition Layout in 4mm Scale
BY R. BALL

BLUE CURTAIN

YATTON UP CONTROL

YATTON DOWN CONTROL

POINT & SIGNAL CONTROL

SCHEDULE CARDS

Clevedon Branch

Up Refuge

Yatton West S. Box

To Taunton

Cheddar Bays

Strawberry Bay

Cheddar Branch

Railway H

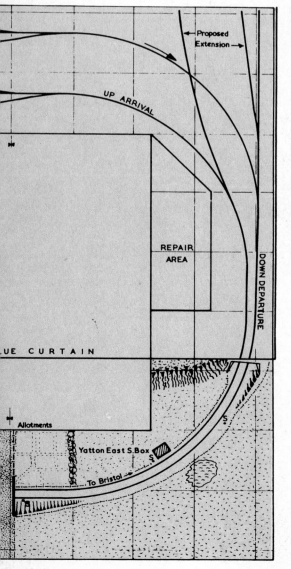

character, and when the Great Western Railway system was at its most interesting. At that time a variety of locomotives and rolling stock, ranging from the mighty "Kings" on the Cornish Riviera Ltd to the humble branch line tanks, were in constant use in the West Country on the main line, whilst the Clevedon branch was monopolised by a typical GWR auto train and the Cheddar Valley branch had strawberry, cheese and more prosaic, some limestone specials. Fruit specials were also a big feature of the landscape, some made up of complete trains and others attached to the rear of calling main line trains. There was plenty to interest everyone.

Because of the obvious limitations of space it was not possible to model the whole area and like so many railway modellers, the Group compromised, choosing to concentrate on the station and its immediate approaches. This way it was possible to provide main line Flyers dashing through the countryside, trundling freights and connecting branch line trains. The tracks at each end are screened by curtains, leaving the station as the living centre piece. Operating Panels are designed so that operators can sit through a long working schedule, and all the unsightly framework is covered to present a complete and tidy unit. Trackwork is made completely from scratch, whilst locomotives and rolling stock are provided by individual members.

To portray the Yatton workings correctly sixteen trains are required, and seventeen locomotives are available, each of these having a reserve ready to replace it in case of failure. Main line,

suburban, and auto stock make up the passenger trains, while on the goods side there are coal, empty wagon, mixed and vacuum trains. The perishable traffic is catered for by parcels, milk, and fruit trains. Locomotive classes represented are "King", "Castle", "County", "Hall", "Saint", "Bulldog", 47XX, 28XX, 52XX, 72XX, 43XX, Dean Goods, Metro tanks, 57XX, 31XX, 48XX, Beyer Peacock No 336, and a GW railcar.

Shunting is carried out on a very limited basis and is in fact restricted to "tail traffic" moves, which up to now have met with the approval of visitors. One of these occasions worthy of mention is the milk tanker which travels up the Cheddar Branch attached to the rear of the local passenger train. On arrival at the station the train loco uncouples from its coaches, runs around to the rear, detaches the milk tank and then moves back over the station throat to await the arrival of the milk train from Taunton. In due course this arrives and stops in the up platform, the waiting milk tank is then placed at the rear of the train to continue its journey to Bristol. The realistic part of this manoeuvre is, that it is carried out "untouched by the human hand". The passenger who alights at Yatton from a main line passenger train is always assured of a connection with the local branch train, likewise those travelling in reverse do not usually have to wait very long. An event particularly pleasing to the eye is the passing of 2822, a 2-8-0 type on a long train of coal for Newton Abbot, and 7219 a 2-8-2 tank on a train of empties for South Wales, both crawling along with the distant signals at "caution". But the children will tell you that the most popular event is the passing of a non-stop express, usually with a "King", "Castle" or "Hall" on, tearing through the station at high speed with whistle screaming. All these happenings are briefly noted on the "Train Describer" so that the interested visitor can get to know the various lines which make up Yatton, and determine the destination of every passing train.

The type of layout, the choice of location portrayed and the method adopted for working the trains has been a very successful combination, judging by the letters and remarks received from past visitors. Frequently Mums and Dads point to certain parts of the layout and explain to their children that when they themselves were small they caught the train to such and such a place from that platform—they have been reminded of those halcyon days of steam.

In addition to those who seek nostalgia, there is the would-be modeller who has had it in mind for a long time to build a model railway but has not yet got around to it, and also in the same category is the young lad who is interested but has not got the knowledge. Both of these, having studied exhibition layouts and possibly discussed the problems with the operators, have been known to receive the extra incentive which is sometimes needed to start a railway of their own, and the hobby is thus extended further, which is the Group's aim.

Running an exhibition layout such as Yatton Junction is not a single handed job, it has been achieved by the members accepting discipline and inconvenience. They enjoy their hobby immensely, and can commend it to those thinking of taking it up. The Yatton Junction Group is comprised of nine members who are:— John Kite, Roy Ball, Tony Reynalds, Dave Weekes, Peter Trigwell, Andy Churchill, Chris Keeler, Eric Harriman, and Brian Chappell.

RAILS IN THE RECTORY

Cadeby Parish Church in Leicestershire, dates from the very early thirteenth century: its register of baptisms, marriages and deaths goes back to 1597, it has a Rector who is a railway enthusiast, and a narrow gauge railway with its terminus only a few yards from the porch. The General Manager of the railway is the Rev E R Boston, MA.

The railway line around the rectory at Cadeby does not fit easily into the pattern of railway preservation in the third quarter of the twentieth century. Owing to constricted space it is not like the "Great Little Trains of Wales" and as it is run entirely by voluntary staff its public operation is limited to one day a month. Its timings are remarkably free and the running time for the main line is even slower than the worst of British Railways. The line is built to the nominal 2′ 0″ gauge and runs with both steam and internal combustion power, using ex quarry locomotives. The objects of the railway are simple. First to provide an opportunity of seeing a steam engine at work without having to travel far from the centre of England. Second, to teach the voluntary staff a little of what real railway work involves—there is more to be learned on permanent way, for example, by holding the business end of a sledge hammer than by sitting in a comfortable chair reading a track manual for three hours! To the educational end (and of course

for pleasure as well) there is housed in a wooden shed some 40′ 0″ x 20′ 0″ of model railway representing an imaginary section of the Great Western Railway in South Devon.

So far the model, where the countryside between Dartmoor and the sea has been faithfully reproduced, has taken some ten years to complete, and it is estimated that at least another five years of intensive work lie ahead. The layout is built to OO scale, ie 4mm to the foot, operating on 16.5mm gauge track with two rail electrification. The total main line run is approximately 55 yards with an overall track length of nearly ⅛ mile. Full size bells and telegraph instruments are provided and there is even a telephone to connect with the more remote parts of the layout. Twenty locomotives are required to maintain the timetable service which is based on the actual GWR one for 1938. The engines are all duplicated by spare locomotives standing at Olton Prior shed adjacent to the main station of that name. The locomotives are mainly modelled on Great Western prototypes: "Kings", "Castles", "Stars", "Halls", "Manors" and "Granges" handle the through traffic, and "Bulldogs", "Dukes" and "Moguls" the local workings. Freight is headed by "Aberdares", "Dean" and "Collett Goods" while pannier and saddle tanks take the station pilot duties. The timetable contains 180 paths and is

**Above: The Reverend Teddy Boston –
General Manager.** *B Monaghan*

**Top: A realistic Great Western scene at Olton
Priors Station.** *B Monaghan*

**Picture overleaf: Branch train at Gotham
Dock: this line is loosely modelled on the
Brixham branch from Churston.** *B Monaghan*

worked against a speeded up clock (ratio 8:1), thus allowing a whole day's work to be completed in the space of three hours. Teddy Boston will tell you that it is only fair to add that this ideal is actually realised on rare occasions.

A narrow gauge railway based on the 3′ 0″ gauge Southwold line, late of Suffolk is also situated in the model shed. This is of 12mm gauge, also to 4mm scale. It is operated by five locomotives (one more than possessed by the prototype!) but at present is not running owing to an extensive reconstruction.

In the rectory itself is a remarkable collection of "railwayana" ranging from nameplates to luggage labels, and also a comprehensive library. Needless to say, books on railways and music, the owner's two main passions, are well represented. Here too are the spare 4mm scale engines, 65 of them are of Great Western prototypes while another 20 or so are from the General Manager's minor companies such as the LNER.

Over the years many people have helped to build and operate both the large and the small lines, and have derived not only pleasure but learning. It is without doubt a corporate and enjoyable piece of social work and its spirit is epitomised by two of the General Manager's rules for the Cadeby Light Railway. "Them as gets it off gets it on" and "Them as makes a suggestion gets given the job".

Left: Twixt Dartmoor and the sea: a 'Bulldog' takes a van and empty stock train down the main line. *B Monaghan.*

Below: Local train and branch goods: a study in 0-6-0 tank engines over 50 years. *B Monaghan.*

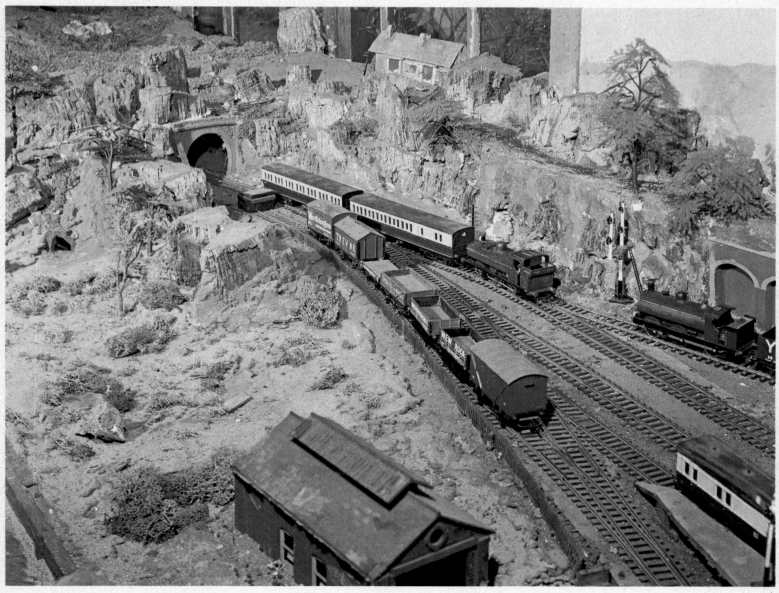

An attractive but uneventful village near the Thames in Berkshire called Long Wittenham has been surprised in recent years to find itself placed very firmly on the map: for something approaching ten thousand visitors from all over the country are being drawn to it each year by Pendon. Long Wittenham lies on by-roads ten miles south of Oxford and five each from Wallingford and Abingdon.

It all started in the early 1930's when the author came to live on the hills beside the Vale of White Horse, between Didcot and Swindon, and fell for the thatched villages as much as for the Great Western mainline that ran near them. Its beauty was too good to last, and the first signs of change were already there, so the idea of their perpetuation in model form was born. From the beginning the standard had to be a superlative one, and as the work would be far too great for one pair of hands or for the skills of one man that meant forming a team of skilled helpers. Guy Williams as CME was the first; Ken Budd followed for coach building, Paul King for track and control, Jim Arnold for scenery, Stewart Hine later applied his electronic know-how to the lighting of coaches, and the author was already under way with the building of the village. These completed the original team, and the project was put on a sound basis in 1961 as The Pendon Museum Trust Limited, a non-profitmaking company and a registered Charity. Including members, modellers and workers in other ways, there are now upwards of fifty helpers involved to a greater or lesser degree.

Although the greater part of this work still remains to be done, there is already the spectacle of full-length mainline trains and pottering branch-line ones working in a stretch of country where the clock has been put back. Yet Pendon, in the ordinary sense, will never be a model railway, any more than it will be a model village: but rather a study in topography aiming to create a countryside where the railways and roads, the hill-set village, even the work of the farms in progress, will form a natural part of the rural setting which surrounds them. In other words the start is with the broad conception of a landscape and man's works take their logical place within it: but always, as well, with the most careful planning to make sure that the viewer sees as much as possible to advantage. Near perfection is the goal, and the team believe it will be worth all the years of effort that must still be put into it. Almost certainly presentation as accurate, as detailed, and as comprehensive as this has been undertaken by no other exhibition in the world.

Pendon's scale is 4mm to the foot (1/76) and the period is the first 15 years of railway grouping, circa 1930, giving a tolerance from 1923 to 1937. These were the best of the inter-war years, when steam on the railways had reached maturity, yet the individuality of pre-grouping days still lingered. Similarly, the countryside had become mature yet remained essentially rural. When change struck the railways it was violent and spectacular, and hardly a single feature from the 1930 period now remains. In the country it has been insidious instead, creeping in so gradually as to be hardly noticed—until comparisons are made with photographs and descriptions of the past, even the recent past, and it is realised what ravages have been inflicted.

This, of course, is where Pendon comes into its own: for while photos give a

PENDON

MUSEUM

somewhat lifeless documentary of former days, Pendon is doing it in the flesh. Two principal areas are being worked on, and at present it is in the first of these

that the trains are running. This is a moorland scene on the edge of Dartmoor. It is 46 feet long, and features a tunnel opening on to the Brunel timber viaduct of 16 piers which has become almost a symbol of Pendon. This was built by Guy Williams in 1955 and installed in a large ex-RAF hut. By the start of the seventies plans were made for a big new building. This was built over the top of the hut, which was pulled down from the inside. The Dartmoor scenery suffered badly, but completion was postponed until it could be glassed in and made both dustproof and fingerproof. So at the moment of writing the scenery is not what the founders would really like to see, and it is the trains that matter.

The railway is built to eighteen millimetre gauge, fine scale, and nine trains are currently running, with five engines in reserve. All locomotives as yet have been built by Guy. There is a mixed freight of

30 odd wagons, behind a Dean Goods No 2323, and this is usually followed by a sandwich push-pull whose 0-4-2T may be either 4837 or *Fair Rosamund* of Wood-stock fame. An impressive *Great Bear* hauls a milk-and-parcels train with stock from three groups out of the four (Pendon apologises for the *Bear*'s presence here until the Swindon mainline can be built) and a Barnum 2-4-0 takes a delightful local stopper made up of brown vehicles, clerestorys, a flat-roofed Dean B-set, and a milk tank at the tail. A foreigner is a Southern M7 0-4-4T with three coaches by Guy from the Atlantic Coast Express (floods on the Southern causing diversion, we presume) and then comes a coal train, built by Tony Smith, behind 2844. This unhurried 2-8-0 emerges from the tunnel and its train continues to do so till all its 86 private-owner wagons and

Above: GWR Barnum 2-4-0 modelled by Guy Williams. *P Williams*

**Picture overleaf:
GWR No. 2921 "Saint Dunstan" with a mixed train of clerestories on the timber viaduct.**

their load have appeared. *Saint Dunstan* passes with a train of stock by Teddy Francis on loan to Pendon: and then Ken Budd's 11 coach Plymouth and Penzance express sweeps round the far curve proudly headed by *King George V.* This magnificent engine, quite recently completed by Guy, will later be transferred to the 10 coach centenary Cornish Riviera Limited at present being built by David Kearsey. Finally, night falls on Dartmoor and a lighted train, the work of Stewart Hine, slows on to the viaduct. The fully-fitted interiors can now be critically seen—the Indian Potentate that many visitors will remember, together with his private detective, the cyclists with their map and bikes, and the ticket collector who now wears a white carnation in his buttonhole—when daylight returns, the engine is seen to be *Sedgemoor,* a curved-frame Bulldog the original of whose combined name and numberplate is in Pendon's relic room. Reserve engines include 4908, *Broome Hall*; an 0-6-2T, 5624; the Prairie tank 4405; and a Pannier 5724.

There is still, of course, a lot to be done to complete the Dartmoor landscape. It will have a station—Pen Tor Road—and this should shortly be put in hand. But though Dartmoor will be finished first, the Vale of White Horse scene remains the major project. Sections of the hill-set village have to be shown for the time being in three showcases, but when finished the scene will occupy the whole of the upper hall of the new building, and will be all but seventy feet long. Its railgauge will be the dead-scale one of 18.83mm though other track and wheel standards will depend on the results of experiments now being carried out.

There is no space here to enlarge on Pendon's village modelling, but this is an art in itself and one which has taken years of craftsmanship. Pendon has a fine collection of railway relics dating from 1812 onwards, and John Ahern's famous Madder Valley layout – to be described in a later chapter–is on permanent loan to Pendon. The Museum is open every Saturday and Sunday throughout the year, and on Bank Holidays except Christmas Day and Boxing Day. It is not open to the public during the week, but special showings can be arranged at most times for clubs or schools.

Above: Part of Pendon's model village.
P Williams

Right: GWR 0-6-0PT No 5402 – another Guy Williams model. *P Williams*

THE NORTH DEVONSHIRE RAILWAY

This model railway was commenced in 1951 and has progressed year by year since then with little modification from the original plans drawn at that time. When space became available for the North Devonshire Railway 23 years ago it was in the form of a floored attic to a bungalow in Edinburgh and was 27 feet long x 18 feet wide with a small extension in one corner of this measuring 7 feet x 4 feet. Plans were drawn and the following aims and objects were borne in mind:

1 The model would be built to OO gauge 16.5mm and scale 4mm to 1 foot.
2 The electrical supply would be 12 volt DC 2 rail.
3 The minimum radius curvature would be 3 feet.
4 The GWR circa 1930 to 1940 would be the inspiration for the models and scenery.
5 No facing gradient would be steeper than 1:80.
6 Forty wagon freight trains and 10 coach passenger trains would be run.
7 Stations and sidings of adequate length for the above trains would be installed.
8 Methods of storing complete trains in hidden sidings should be incorporated.
9 Uncoupling by magnetic means would be used with automatic coupling.
10 The countryside scenery should be like the West Country.
11 Through stations and not terminals would be installed as the prime interest would be the running of the trains and not constant shunting.
12 At least one locomotive shed and turn-table.

It was realised that it was not possible to model a particular section of railway accurately and so a fictitious prototype was imagined. It was assumed that the county of Devon extended north westwards of Barnstaple into the Bristol channel and a railway was built to serve the area in the 1840/50s. This railway followed the river Torrey through the towns of Torreyford and Torreymouth—the latter a small seaport. The geography of the imaginary terrain gave scope for desirable scenic features such as a viaduct across a valley, the river Torrey itself, a low arch bridge across it, rock faces beside the line and tunnels through hills. The stations of Torreyford and Torreymouth are through stations with platforms about 10 feet in length to accommodate long trains. The layout which was planned to incorporate these was arranged in the form of a "dog-bone" (or dumb-bell) with reversing loops at each end. These loops would include sidings in tunnels so that trains could be stored out of sight and brought out later and run right around the track to

the loop sidings at the opposite end. They could then either be stored once more or run right through to emerge in the opposite direction.

The layout plan herewith shows the attempt to achieve the above and construction commenced with baseboards, at an average height from the floor of 3 feet, in April 1951. At that time supply of the present flexible OO gauge track was not obtainable and so nickel silver rail was soldered to rivets in fibre sleeper bases. A considerable amount of track was constructed with cast chairs on cork sleeper bases. All the early points were hand-made and were dimensioned with check rails 14.5mm apart. A gauge of this dimension was made for adjusting the back to back measurements of the wheels of all rolling stock. This has been of great assistance in keeping derailments to a minimum.

Most of the rails are laid on a base of rubber to help lessen noise problems and to enable the track to "float". When the rail heads are notched every 60 scale feet, very realistic "clickety-clicks" are a prominent sound effect by passing trains. The whole of the visible trackwork is

ballasted.

The country scenery of Devonshire has been reproduced by means of surgical lint, dyed various shades of grass green and laid on previously formed contours. The "fluffy" side of the lint uppermost was "teased" with a comb in places to represent long rough grass.

Use was made of various makes of buildings and kits throughout but Torreyford Station was entirely built by hand in balsa wood, Bristol board and building papers. The overbridge, canopies and the retaining wall at the rear are all made

Top: The River Torrey flows beneath the long low brick bridge and the eight arch viaduct which carry the tracks of the North Devonshire Railway over the valley.
The train in the foreground has emerged from the tunnel mouth which conceals the loop storage sidings and is heading for Torreyford. The Mail train on the viaduct is headed by No 2927 "Saint Patrick". *B Monaghan*

Overleaf: Bulldog No 3417 runs on to the turntable at Torreyford engine shed watched by the shed foreman seen in front of the tender. The near loco is No 7902 "Eaton Mascot Hall," hand built and awarded a diploma at the Model Engineer Exhibition of 1953 and still going strong. *B Monaghan*

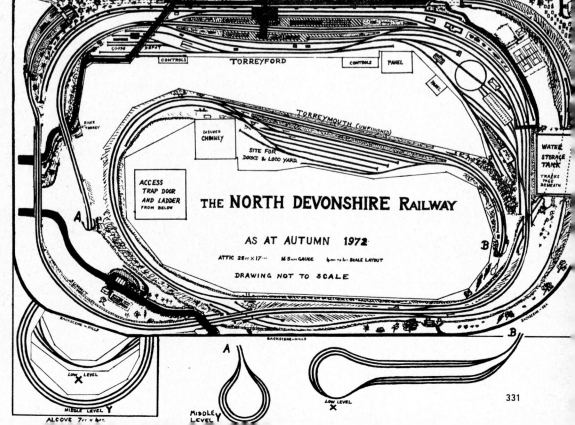

THE **NORTH DEVONSHIRE** RAILWAY

AS AT AUTUMN 1972

ATTIC 28 FT X 17 FT 16.5mm GAUGE 4mm to 1ft SCALE LAYOUT

DRAWING NOT TO SCALE

removable for track maintenance purposes. The eight arch viaduct over the river valley is also made from wood and covered with "Faller" stone paper. Rock outcrops and rock faces are made with cork bark in Polyfilla suitably coloured and embellished with shrubs and lichen.

GW lower quadrant semaphore signals have been placed around the line. At Torreymouth use has been made of Ratio kits and the arms are made to operate by means of threads and lead counterweights. In the Torreyford area the colour light signals and box have been copied from those which were installed at Bristol and Cardiff in the early 1930's.

Over 700 feet of track is now in use on the railway and this needs a substantial amount of rolling stock. The stock book at present declares 237 goods and minerals vehicles, 60 passenger cars and 30 locomotives, many of which are classed as "super detailed". For free running the stock is fitted with pin pointed axles and metal wheels. A simple system of pin-pointing bearings was evolved which was cheap, quick and effective. Wagons with these bearings have no end play in the axles therefore the buffers do not interlock when trains are reversed buffer to buffer. Jackson magnetic couplings are used which can be uncoupled by magnets placed beneath the track. The wagons are an assortment of proprietary models plus kit and hand-built ones. Many have been hand lettered to drawings which have appeared in the Model Railway press. Most of the passenger coaches are Exley's but some kits have been added and some more are

Top: 2-8-0 No 3822 takes a down goods train past Charmans Bridge Junction Box while "Dartington Hall" is in the foreground.
B Monaghan

Below: The coaling stage at Torreyford with a pannier tank receiving attention and a hand built "Castle" awaiting its next turn of express duty. All train lamps on the NDR are painted dark red as were those of the GWR until 1936.
B Monaghan

being constructed.

The locomotives are also of several sources. Some are hand-built but the majority are constructed from metal kits with added details. Gearing is usually 40:1 and Pitman motors have been extensively used. In order to get both good current collection from the rails and good adhesion of the driving wheels, locomotives have been weighted with as much lead as possible. An arrangement with current collection from both tender and loco wheels (five at least on each rail)

enables very steady running to be attained and nullifies problems with dirt on the track.

The railway is controlled from one panel on which the layout is schematically indicated with coloured sections. Ex-Post Office telephone switches are used to connect any one of the four controllers to each section.

The items described above have occupied more than 20 years of hobby time and there is still a lot of work to do especially in the Torreymouth area.

EASTBOURNE

Above: Vivien Thompson
in her workshop.
B Monaghan

Vivien Thompson's Eastbourne

Like so many other modellers, Vivien Thompson's first railway was of the Hornby O gauge tinplate variety. The rather meagre components of this were bought at a bring-and-buy sale in Harrogate during the war—the loco being dredged up from a bran tub! Her male cousins owned a vast layout built up from similar Hornby equipment, but Vivien was not allowed within a scale mile of it.

Her own first, small model railway was sold when she was in her early 'teens; and though she spent many hours, during this part of her life as a music student, in train-spotting—she was even mildly reproved at college for sitting on Blackfriars Station "spotting" London Transport stock, an activity which evidently was felt to be unworthy of a serious music student—she did not return to model railways until the 1960s. After the birth of her son, Richard, she realised she would now be largely tied to the house, and accordingly she cast about for a constructive hobby. She made a start by building Airfix vintage car kits, and then progressed to Kitmaster locomotives. This move re-awakened her dormant interest in railways and prompted her to buy a Triang "Lord of the

Isles" and some clerestory coaches, in addition to sufficient track to provide interesting running, plus the necessary control unit. From this small beginning the layout was expanded until the large spare bedroom in which it was housed was filled with Triang-covered baseboards, and she and her husband found much enjoyment in operating it.

But by now Vivien had delved more deeply into back numbers of the modelling magazines and had discovered that, apart from a few outstanding exceptions, the buildings on other people's layouts were exactly the same as hers. She realised that if she wanted to get more out of the hobby than was possible from merely buying proprietary material and operating the railway, a change in policy must be adopted.

So the proprietary track she already possessed was donated to her son, who was now beginning to require something more reliable than a tinplate railway round the dining room, and thanks to the helpful advice of the man in the local

model shop, she took the plunge and went ahead to purchase flexible track and scale points with a fair idea of what the new layout was to try to achieve. Appreciating that first things must come first and that every new layout starts with baseboards, she began by constructing these with insulation board on 2in x 1in frames, the legs being 6in wide by $\frac{3}{4}$in thick and raising the baseboard to waist-level. Once the foundation work was completed, she began to lay the flexible track and was much impressed by the improvement over the rigid type she had hitherto used.

There were to be two stations on the layout—one LNER, the other SR—and though they were to be given fictitious names, each building was to be a model of a prototype. In those days there were far fewer plans published of railway architecture, and it took her some appreciable time to assemble the required structures. But by dint of much use of cardboard, building papers and glue, the two stations and their satellite buildings

were eventually completed. She also tried to model the locomotives, coaches, goods vehicles and signals correctly, and derived much pleasure from creating, as best she could within the terms of reference, typical scenes on the two railways concerned. She built her first locomotive from a cast metal kit, but in the process she made a ghastly, disastrous mistake: she found that despite a glue manufacturer's instructions about curing their product in an oven, cast metal kits do not take kindly to such treatment... Despite learning one lesson the hard way, she went ahead until the layout was in something like satisfactory shape and was featured in one of the modelling magazines. This was her first work published and, also for the first time, brought some return on the work and money invested in modelling to plough back into her increasingly expensive hobby. Particularly since, after the completion of the layout, she found she was totally "hooked" on railway modelling as an all the year round hobby.

Hitherto she had concentrated most of her spare winter time on modelling, having a sabbatical during the summer months; but her interest in the subject had intensified to a point where henceforth she found herself wanting to continue during most of the spring and summer too. She was, as she herself puts it, "bitten by two bugs"—styrene sheet as a building material, and the concept of modelling a prototype as authentically as possible. By now, her favourite pre-grouping company was unequivocally the London, Brighton and South Coast Railway, and gripped by the challenge of modelling a real station in a set period she decided that what she obviously needed was a south coast terminus. So she hunted through her considerable collection of photographs relating to numerous facets of this company, seeking a suitable station. Brighton itself seemed out of the question, and Bognor lacked appeal; but when she came across the well-known O J Morris photograph of the "Sunny South Special" about to leave Eastbourne in 1905, she knew she had found her station...

The simplicity of the Eastbourne trackwork proved to be deceptive in the sense of making the terminus seem attractive and not too problematic for a modeller. It was true enough that the trackwork was not complicated, but what Vivien did not at first realise was that the station buildings were among the most complex and ornate on the LBSCR system! However, track plans were purchased and pored over for hours so as to decide what would have to be omitted on the model. Even such a relatively simple track layout would be too large to include in its entirety in a room measuring approximately 13ft x 12ft—even allowing for the fact that she intended swinging the main baseboard diagonally across the room in order to provide a longer run.

Having made her decision to model Eastbourne, Vivien faced her first task, which was to clear the room of the existing layout and to construct new baseboards, on the same principles as before, using as much as possible of the old timber, nails and screws. Thanks to an over-ordering error by her father, Vivien found herself in possession of a superior type of insulation board, so that Eastbourne itself could be mounted on a new baseboard. Much of the track from the previous layout could be used for sidings and the fiddleyard, but a large quantity of new track had to be bought

Above: A model of the exterior of Chichester Station on the up side. The original building has now been demolished. *B Monaghan*

Left: Looking towards Eastbourne Station. The Roundhouse is to the right, with the gantry and signal cabin in the background. The Marsh Class J 4-6-2T No 326 "Bessborough" (in grey livery) heads the "Sunny South Special" towards Brighton. *B Monaghan*

for the main lines.

An important question then remained to be resolved: what period should the model represent? She decided on circa 1909 as an ideal "in-between" period. This decision was arrived at on the grounds that when D E Marsh took over as loco superintendent in 1905 on the death of R J Billinton, new locomotive and coach liveries were introduced, replacing the famous Stroudley/Billinton liveries. Vivien reasoned that she could have both liveries without prejudicing the correctness of the effect, since no railway company could completely repaint all its motive power and coaches in a mere four years. It was not only that railway vehicles had to be right, for horse-drawn vehicles, some early motor cars, and all "people" on the platforms and pavements had to be modelled by adapting kits so as to have an Edwardian appearance. A friend, prone to describing herself as a frustrated artist, kindly agreed to paint a backscene for the model, and the result looked most effective.

With the exception of the loco roundhouse, every building was made from styrene sheet. Vivien learned techniques for using this modelling medium as she went along. She worked from ground plans and photographs, working out many of the necessary dimensions by counting bricks to be seen on the photographs. She also made a safari to the station, knowing by this stage which structures were extant in 1909. She received permission to take measurements which enabled her to fill the gaps where plans and photographs failed. The Eastbourne concourse was then modelled, complete with W H Smith bookstall, ornate columns, barrows, excess luggage office, period advertisements and sundry other details. Apart from trackwork, locomotive chassis and all wheels, she constructed the entire model railway

from scratch, mainly using styrene sheet. The resultant layout was published in 1968 and, to her delight, won her the Railway Modeller Cup, voted by readership of the magazine, for that year. A gratifying sidelight of this award was the fact that evidently she had been accepted in a man's hobby.

In 1969 she decided to locate the railway in the loft. Although she would have preferred to continue having a waist-level layout, it was found that by placing the baseboards on the joists, a far larger area became available for operational purposes. After rebuilding in this form, the actual layout extended round three sides of the loft, then behind a water tank which constituted an annoying obstruction, and eventually resolved itself into a fiddleyard of 27 lines. The size of this fiddleyard was necessitated by what had become Vivien's new ambition: she hoped to model an example of every type of train which worked into Eastbourne after about 1860, each hauled by the correct locomotive. The 1909-period layout already possessed approximately a hundred coaching stock vehicles, besides locomotives and goods stock; and since 1967 she had been increasingly concentrating on architectural models, partly for reasons of space, but largely because she was finding this the most satisfying facet of railway modelling. With the completion of the fiddleyard, she was able to return to building coaches.

In the revised version of Eastbourne it is impossible to have the station in the correct period all the time, but to counteract this disadvantage as much as possible, Vivien next decided to update the model to 1912, since which time the trackwork, at least, remained almost the same until electrification in 1935. Fundamentally, her idea is that in years to come it will be possible to have operating sessions in the 1900-1910 period, or in the 1920s, or even the 1950s, by using the appropriate stock and motive power. Over the last two years or so, an appreciable start has been made by building stock ranging from Stroudley 4-wheelers in mahogany livery to an electric 4COR set in BR blue, from LNER (ex GNR) teak 6-wheelers to SR (ex SECR) sets with birdcage lookouts, and to BR GUV (general utility) vans in green or blue.

Young Richard benefited substantially by the transfer of Eastbourne to the loft because he was thereby given the front bedroom—much to his delight, since this meant he could have a much larger model railway of his own. Non-comprehending relatives were completely puzzled to find his bedroom consisting almost entirely of a model railway with a bed in the middle! Consequently, his mother was led to reflect on how difficult it would have been had she produced a daughter instead, and on the inevitability of Richard having inherited an interest in railway modelling. As a result of these changes in domestic arrangements, Vivien was able to commandeer her son's erstwhile bedroom, the smallest in the house, for her modelling workroom, with all her books, photographs, materials and tools comfortably to hand. So as to benefit to the full from her new surroundings, she installed a work table across the window-end of the room and built bookshelves along an entire wall, in addition to further shelves opposite. The remaining wall is taken up by the only non-railway item—gramophone equipment and radio which cater to her fondness for listening to music while she is engaged in modelling. The actual shelves are packed with modelling and prototype magazines, railway books and timetables, completed architectural models, and various railway relics that have been acquired. Vivien

feels herself lucky in that the prospect from her modelling room is so pleasing that she can look out over countryside as far as the eye can see. This vista and music she finds the ideal counterweights to the necessary but more intricate or tedious jobs which have to be done in the process of railway modelling.

Asked about her enthusiasm, Vivien says that she has never regretted taking up the hobby. As a result of it she has met many interesting people and she and her family have acquired some genuine friends. Making models gives her a satisfying feeling, and if the results never quite achieve the standard she hopes for when she contemplates a new undertaking, she always hopes that the next model might be better. She finds, also, that the hobby's many facets guard against staleness: if she tires of a coach-building spree, for example, she has several new buildings to add to the layout, or a station has been promised to a friend, or there are improvements to be effected to the scenery, or there remains the task of assembling all the locomotives required to haul the trains. Then a new loco shed will first require a baseboard, next the trackwork . . .

In addition to her direct practical work, she has devoted much time to writing about railway modelling since the time she finished her original cup-winning version of Eastbourne. The success of

the architectural models on this layout encouraged her to concentrate on modelling railway buildings, especially those on closed lines or those demolished when rebuilding, due mainly to Southern Railway electrification, took place. Several of these, including her drawings, were published in the model press. As a consequence, she was commissioned to write a book on the subject, and this was duly published by Peco Publications in the spring of 1972.

In between modelling activity and operating their respective railways, she and her son visit exhibitions and are to be found utilising BR Railrovers for their holidays, making expeditions to obtain more prototype information, train-spotting on the old GN main line—or, by way of a change, playing cricket in the back garden. And with the layout more complex than ever before, it really requires all three members of the family to operate it. So, to an appreciable extent, it can be said that railway modelling is a family hobby.

Below: A view over the Roundhouse roof at Eastbourne. Marsh, Billington and Stroudley locos are on the shed.   *B Monaghan*

Right: An elevated view from above Eastbourne Station looking towards Ashford Square. No 326 "Bessborough" in on the turntable while the other locomotives wait patiently for their next duty turn.   *B Monaghan*

Overleaf: Johnson "single" No 673 leaves Garsdale Road with a northbound train. The coach is a scratchbuilt MR clerestory and the locomotive is a modified white metal kit. Strictly speaking, the model is "out of period" for the layout, which is set in the late 1930s.
Courtesy Railway Modeller. B Monaghan

Johnson "single" No 673 leaves
Garsdale Road with a northbound train. The
coach is a scratchbuilt MR clerestory and the
locomotive is a modified white metal kit.
Strictly speaking, the model is "out of
period" for the layout, which is set in the
late 1930s.
Courtesy Railway Modeller. B Monaghan

SETTLE TO CARLISLE

David Jenkinson's layout based on the Midland Railway's route to Scotland

When one decides to base a model on a particular railway route, it must be accepted that it is almost impossible to actually achieve the aim of total authenticity—if only because the prototype is usually built on a grander scale than most of us can reproduce in miniature. Nevertheless, in the hope that he might be able to create the sort of layout which at least suggested the Settle and Carlisle more strongly than any other part of the British railway scene, David Jenkinson resolved to make the effort.

At the time he made this decision, in the early 1960s, David Jenkinson was in the armed forces and enjoying the somewhat peripatetic existence of this way of life. Obviously he could not contemplate a permanent system for some time but he could at least gradually build up a collection of authentic locomotives and rolling stock and, possibly, construct a small layout to act as a trial scheme. As things turned out, this proved to be an excellent situation: he was never committed to building something which could not be finished within the foreseeable time scale of any one RAF appointment, and he gained a great deal of valuable modelling experience. As a result of taking the various layouts to several exhibitions, many good friends were made. Furthermore, there is no doubt that these years were important in helping to determine an overall attitude to the hobby.

David cannot give any precise reasons for his final choice of prototype or period but can say that having made the choice, he has never regretted it nor deviated too markedly from the theme first established back in 1962. The long term aim was and is to build a large permanent layout on which authentic length main line trains could run in reasonably accurate settings in a correct and railwaylike way. Accuracy of appearance is important but this must be in the overall context and not confined to one element of the layout. For instance, there would be little point in spending a great deal of time getting a locomotive correct in every detail if, as a result, there was no time left to build a layout on which it could run, or a train for it to pull.

David has always tried to give a reason-

ably balanced amount of time and energy to all aspects of the model railway scene, concentrating on none of them to the exclusion of any other. It is against this background that he would wish his efforts to be judged and certainly not as examples of high quality miniature engineering. Nevertheless, he does try to make his models as correct as possible within his self-imposed constraints and the limitations of his own skill.

The Garsdale Road layout here is, in essence, the second preliminary to the larger scheme on which work has now been started. Marthwaite was the first to appear, built when the only available space was a two foot wide shelf along two walls of the room. A simple terminus seemed inevitable and, at first, threatened to be completely at variance with long term ideas. It would have been easy to build any sort of layout to gain the necessary experience in EM gauge, but this would have involved an almost instant abandonment of the newly defined aims. Consideration was given to the possibilities of a branch off the Settle and Carlisle line; the joys of devising an imaginary but feasible railway in real life geographical settings then became apparent. One could, of course, argue endlessly whether the Midland Railway

would ever have built such a branch line as the chosen route—in fact the company was asked to do so and refused—presumably on economic grounds. So the thesis was and is that if one could, in imagination, slightly re-define the economic potential of the area, then such a line *was* geographically possible: thus the Marthwaite branch was born. The terminus was actually sited on the Ordnance Map and the prominent river and road bridge really do exist. David feels that any success achieved by Marthwaite in creating atmosphere was probably because the line was geographically identifiable, the station approximated to scale proportions and, above all, the layout was operated correctly to a sequence of movements designed to portray connecting services with real main line trains running to a genuine timetable.

Marthwaite lasted for about four years,

during which time David gradually built up a more than adequate collection of locomotives and rolling stock until, at the end, he had to some degree spoiled the overall effect by an over intensive operation of somewhat unsuitable trains for a branch line environment. However, the all-important experience had been gained and he felt that if the opportunity arose, a large main line system was within his capability.

The second layout, Garsdale Road, was built partly by accident. One of the many house moves eventually lodged him in a residence into which Marthwaite would not fit (it was quite long although somewhat narrow). He had anticipated such a happening and had more or less decided that when it took place, he could manage without the layout for a while; without a model impatience takes over! He had a spare room with 13ft x 9ft of useable space and, after some thoughts of rebuilding the terminus, finally decided that he would, in total contrast to Marthwaite, build an ultra-simple main line layout to test whether main line operation was what he really wanted to portray. The scheme adopted represented in reduced form a long term ideal, namely a reasonably authentic passing station to provide the visual interest and fed by as many storage sidings as could be contrived into the available space.

Looking back, David feels that although he had never originally intended to build Garsdale Road, he is glad he did. For one thing, it really did remind him of the real station on which it was based (Dent) and the imagination did not have to work quite so hard to make the scheme believable. It also convinced him that given a little more space, he could get fairly close to the railway scene which he most wanted to create—the impression of trains going from somewhere to somewhere else, giving a fleeting glimpse to the trackside observer as they passed by. It is significant that Garsdale Road and not Marthwaite has been incorporated into the much enlarged final scheme now being built.

Above left: The down "Thames-Clyde Express" passes Garsdale Road signal box behind the original LMS taper boilered "Royal Scot" Class 4-6-0 No 6170 "British Legion"—the author's first ever scratch built locomotive.
Courtesy Railway Modeller. B Monaghan

Above right: Scratchbuilt large boilered "Claughton" Class 4-6-0 No 5946 "Duke of Connaught", fitted with Caprotti valve gear, is shown working south with a Saturday extra train for the LMS Western Division. The two leading coaches are handbuilt models of ex-WCJS 12-wheelers, originally used on the 2pm "Corridor" from Euston to Scotland but now relegated to lesser use as befits a late 1930s scene.
Courtesy Railway Modeller. B Monaghan

Right: A down parcels train headed by Hughes/Fowler 2-6-0 No 2803. In this area of the layout, an attempt was made to include as many Midland Railway lineside features as possible without overcrowding—eg. diagonal fencing, angled station nameboard, water crane, Settle-Carlisle architecture &c.
Courtesy Railway Modeller. B Monaghan

KIRTLEY

A 7mm scale LMS layout in the garden,

Lack of space is often a major difficulty facing those who wish to model in O gauge and very often a garden railway is the answer to the problem. This was the case with the "Kirtley" line although previous experience of running model railways out of doors revealed quite a number of advantages for this type of system over the normal indoor layout. Full-length trains can be run, stations have room to spread, the main line can meander and distances between stations can be more to scale. Above all, there is about most outdoor lines an "atmosphere" difficult to define. Trains appear to be going somewhere, often through quite natural scenery; there is the smell of flowers and the creosote, the jog-trot of coaches over rail joints, the roar of a long train passing over a bridge and the effect of it disappearing from view.

So "Kirtley" was built outdoors. Gauge O was chosen because of its superiority in this field; it is large enough to be seen in a natural background and sufficiently sturdy to withstand the hazards of its environment. On the other hand, it is small enough for the home constructor to manage most jobs without elaborate machinery.

Until comparatively recent times, outdoor model railways have been synonymous with heavy timber baseboards which, while presenting a firm track bed,

often left much to be desired as far as appearance was concerned. "Kirtley" was planned with the object of marrying railway and garden to produce a complete and satisfying picture. The line winds through a rockery laid around three sides of a sunken lawn. This brings what is virtually a ground level line up to a satisfactory working height. The track-base, hidden by the rock garden consists of a 5in thickness of breeze concrete which gives a well-drained bed.

Very little of the 250ft length of route is straight, large sweeping curves being favoured, although in one or two places the radius is down to eight feet. Single track is capable of handling quite a traffic flow; passing loops situated at a junction station half way along the route often have full track occupation. Several bridges and tunnels have been built along the line and the pièce de resistance is a 24ft long concrete viaduct finished to represent a stone built structure.

The railway follows the boundary of the garden fairly close by and the layout, being built on the end-to-end principle, terminates in a greenhouse. One side of the building accommodates the terminus proper while the other side houses the magazine sidings. A sunken floor brings the track base up to an operating height of about 2ft 6in. The baseboard is of $\frac{3}{4}$in plywood, battened track being laid on this

and ballasted in the normal way. This method allows for any layout alterations as may become necessary in the light of operating experience. Such alterations out of doors are a more difficult proposition and often result in wastage of material and garden plants and shrubs.

The terminus can handle 9-coach

Left: Pulling away along a ledge after a short sharp climb out of the terminus, Bowness-on-Windermere, is the afternoon express for St Pancras. Black Stanier 5237 is piloted as far as Hellifield by class 2 No. 579. The granite hillside is beginning to get its summer cladding. *B Monaghan. Courtesy Railway Modeller*

Below: Short freight train heads out over the viaduct towards Bowness-on-Windermere while Stanier 2-6-4 tank in charge of a local passenger drops down the branch. The tank engine began life as a Bassett-Lowke standard model. *B Monaghan Courtesy Railway Modeller*

Picture Overleaf: Heavy freight hauled by 4F No 4278 rumbles over Deeley viaduct while miniscule branch goods passes below. The Jinty hauling this train was the first engine constructed by the owner and like all the others is powered by a Bonds motor. Deeley viaduct is cast in concrete, the moulding box being gouged on the inside to simulate stone construction. *B Monaghan Courtesy Railway Modeller*

trains and a bay is available for shorter sets of vehicles. Normal run-round facilities are provided together with ample coach sidings. The goods yard, now being completed, will offer the usual country-style shed and cattle pens, and have standing space for about 80 wagons. A motive power department will stable three locomotives with standing space for larger engines and will have an 18in turntable. On the other side of the greenhouse, the magazine tracks which feed trains to the terminus and receive traffic in the opposite direction, provide seven roads, several of which are 15ft long. Here is also found the "control centre" of the line with panels feeding over 50 sections of track. Transformer-rectifiers supply power at 20/24V DC. There is also a controller attached to a 60ft long wander lead which enables a "driver" to follow his train around the layout and perform shunting operations at isolated stations.

There are, in all, four stations on the branch which represents a fairly busy LMS (Midland Division) line tapping the Southern Lake District. Because of the paucity of suitable Midland Railway branch terminals, the situation is purely imaginary. It is supposed to end at Bow-ness-on-Windermere and to have been built in opposition to the North Western line from Oxenholme higher up the hill.

Fine scale chaired track is used throughout but wheels are to modern coarse standards having a back-to-back measurement of 28mm. Points are built with a frog angle of 1 in 6 or 1 in 8 and consequently provide very smooth running. Fine chicken flint is used for ballast and on the outdoor sections is fixed with thinned copal varnish or Unibond. This not only keeps the ballast in place but holds the track in line.

Stud contact electrification has proved admirable for out of doors use, an Eastertime cleaning being sufficient to keep the railway in working order for most of the running season. The line is sit-uated on the edge of open country near Kettering and air pollution is not very severe. This may account for the small amount of cleaning required. Half-inch brass No 2 round head screws are used for the contact studs and are set at 3in intervals. In view of the easy angles of the points and crossings a more sub-stantial pick-up skate to that normally used has been designed. Five inches long and $\frac{3}{4}$in wide, they are arranged on the parallelogram principle and have proved highly effective on all stud systems on which they have been tested.

About 30 coaches are required to run the service together with 70 freight wagons. At the moment nine locomo-tives cope with the traffic but another half dozen or so are planned to be built ranging from a Kirtley outside frame 0-6-0

to a Stanier Jubilee. Engine-building is a major job and takes precedence over other branches of the hobby, sometimes resulting in a backlog of work!

A well-fenced garden is essential to ensure privacy and security. Such fenc-ing also helps to protect plants, many varieties being grown. Cupressus trees in many of the miniature varieties along with lime-tolerant heathers and shrubs help to clothe Kirtley in a reasonably attractive garb for most of the year.

Signalling will eventually be a feature of the line. Why not? Remember those anticipatory minutes when the "boards" were pulled off. Those minutes of sheer delight which are perhaps responsible for our models being built. . . . Will it be a Duchess . . . a Scot . . . Jubilee . . . a Patriot . . . ? and out of the bridge hole trundles a scruffy 4F. All part of the thrill then and part of the picture we are all desperately trying to recreate.

Below Left: Ex-Midland Railway 3P 4-4-0 No 726 nearing the summit of the steeply graded branch with a nine-coach train. The coaches are a mixed rake of commercial and home-built wooden models. *B Monaghan Courtesy Railway Modeller*

Below: Flowering thyme, alyssum and aubretia make a colourful foreground as the Black Stanier heads a fast train through a halt. Shunting in the yard is being conducted by the "old faithful" Jinty. *B Monaghan Courtesy Railway Modeller*

The Sherwood section of the LMS

Cyril Freezer, the Editor of the "Railway Modeller", once said that he thought that the ultimate in timetable operation is carried out on the Sherwood Section of the LMS. He stated that the table was highly complex and represented every conceivable working that one could imagine on the prototype railway. When operators had mastered that, they could move on to special workings consequent on breakdowns, excursions and even track maintenance. Mr Freezer thought that this class of work could only be achieved by years of experience.

Norman Eagles always had the ambition to run a line to timetable and indeed, back in 1921, he had a tinplate end to end layout on the floor which was run to a limited timetable. He then started work on a permanent layout which, as with most modellers, has been rebuilt several times, this being the fifth version.

There are many features that make Sherwood an outstanding model layout. These would include the size, even in O gauge, and the excellence of the modelling whether it be locomotives, rolling stock, buildings or scenery. However three features have made Sherwood unique in its 52 years of existence. The first of these is that it is clockwork driven which, although not unusual, is rare. The second is the complex timetable

Below: General view of Bradcaster Loco. Depot with Gretley Colliery in background. On shed are Ex M.R. 2-4-0 No 155 on the turntable; Ex M.R. 4-4-0 No 391 in foreground; Ex M.R. Kirtley 0-6-0 No 2630; Ex M.R. 0-6-4 T No 2002 on down train passing Gretley Colliery. Note the breakdown train and crane.
Richard Sharpe Studios

working and the third is the camaraderie of the group of modellers who operate the line and help model it. Most of these have been working Sherwood for a very long time and consider the meetings to be a social occasion in the calendar.

Mr Eagles feels that one of the biggest attractions of clockwork mechanisms is that any locomotive can be built using them and that there are no size restrictions that could occur to other forms of motive power. Another attraction is that no two locomotives are quite the same even though they could be of the same class. Each mechanism varies slightly giving the locomotives differing power. In this respect an operator has to face the same problems that a locomotive foreman has to face in real life. He has to look at his shed and decide which loco-

motive to use on a particular working bearing in mind the load to be hauled, over what banks and what distance. For instance 5154 is slightly more powerful than 5408; they are both Black Fives but one works more freely than the other. This follows exactly the variation that one finds in prototype locomotives. A further item regarding clockwork mechanisms is that the smaller locomotives are forced to take prototypical loads; for instance the 0-4-0 tanks will only haul a coach or two and cannot be expected to do more. The mechanisms are fully wound before each journey and have to be judged so that they are just running out when they reach the next scheduled stop. This means that the operators must know the locomotives well particularly concerning their performance and their mechanisms.

When it comes to the question of signalling, once the operator has pulled off the advance starter the clockwork driven train will come and nothing can be done to stop it. In this sense an operator is very like a real signalman in that if the points are not right before it is accepted, then there is no chance afterwards. It is not possible to twiddle a knob and stop it halfway and it is not possible to change ones mind after accepting it. There are over 90 signals on the line, each operator working one or more signal boxes which cover each particular section. In practice each station's advance starter is controlled from the next box up the line and it is not until this is pulled off that a train can proceed. Bell signals are installed between Rufford Market and Lincoln North, and between Oxton and Gretley Colliery. Buzzers control shunting movements in and out of Nottingham Castle and its coach sidings. Conversations are therefore completely unnecessary and the visitor can see trains operating in a thoroughly realistic manner.

Before the method of operation and the timetable working and compilation can be dealt with it is necessary to discuss the types of services that operate on the line. The timetable covers a full twenty four hour day with every type of traffic included. The clock is speeded to run 83 minutes in the hour giving realistic frequencies for the services and time to carry out the shunting required.

The passenger trains can be broken down into ten different services varying from the main line and boat specials through branch and suburban services to the Light Railway and push-pulls. The Nottingham Castle to Trent Town service would run approximately every 30 to 40 minutes in the peak periods and approximately every 60 minutes outside this. The Nottingham Castle to Bradcaster trains run every four hours as through trains or a dividing train; alternatively in the four hours there is a local train running between Bradcaster and Rufford Market which makes a connection. This gives a two hourly service between Nottingham Castle and Bradcaster. The Trent Town to Bradcaster and Port Trent to Bradcaster services work rather irregularly but mainly in the peak periods. The Port Trent to Lincoln North Light Railway works three times a day within the twelve hour period and obviously not at night. The suburban services run approximately every twenty-four minutes in the rush hours so that a suburban train reverses at Friars Hollow every twelve minutes. The Royal Mail makes only one up and one down journey a day.

Above: Down Main (Nottingham Castle to Trent Town) train leaving Rufford Market hauled by a re-boilered "Claughton".
Richard Sharpe Studios

Below: General view of Friars Hollow station showing: Fowler 2-6-0 No 2817 standing in the yard having brought an up perishable freight from Trent Town; Ex M.R. 2F 0-6-0 No 3525 standing on down main; Ex M.R. 3F 0-6-0 No 3712 on up parcels; Rufford Dairy and milk tanks in distance. *Richard Sharpe Studios*

The horse boxes work once as a loaded train from Nottingham to Bradcaster with an empty return working. Fish work twice during the day from the docks to Nottingham. The milk work mainly at night but odd vehicles are attached to varying trains throughout the day. The newspaper train works in the early hours of the morning. The Parcels also work mostly at night but odd vehicles are worked throughout the day and occasionally a parcels train will run during the day. The Oxton to Gretley Colliery push-pull service works from approximately 5.30am to 10pm and connects with most of the local services between Nottingham and Friars Hollow working via Oxton.

Trent has a large marshalling yard and will hold up to about 110 wagons; freight trains for all parts of the system are marshalled here. Trains are made up according to the requirements of the timetable and loads carried according to the requirements of the goods agent. If there is no through service to the station required, loads may be sent to an intermediate yard where they will become transferable via a local freight to the station in question. In other words, loads coming down from Nottingham to go to Rufford Market may be on a train going straight through to Trent passing

another to be taken out and emptied; they are brought back to the station and move on continuously. There are well over 100 different varying loads. Empty coal trains run from Trent to Gretley Colliery. They are then loaded with coal loads for the return journey to the various goods depots whilst loco coal is taken to the various locomotive depots on the line.

To make life easier for each operator, each station has a small notebook which contains a summary book of what happens

Below: The timetable book for Friars Hollow. Note the method of fixing onto the signal box, whose levers control the signals in prototype manner. *Richard Sharpe Studios*

parcels, the milks, the milk tanks, the fish, the horseboxes, the cream van and the gas tank; it shows exactly the specific workings throughout the twenty-four hours and the trains to which they are attached. There is also a summary sheet which lists all the sidings and what is in the sidings at any given hour of the day; this prevents the capacity of the siding being exceeded. It is also useful when a new vehicle is being put into service to decide whether it can be scheduled into a particular siding or not. There is a series of sheets which give the position of every piece of rolling stock at 4am which is regarded as the starting point, so that when the stock has been off the line for overhaul, cleaning or maintenance, it can be put back on the line in its correct place. Just to make life a little more complicated special notices are issued to all operators giving information on such things as permanent way work and excursion trains. In fact on the 18th September 1971 when the line had its Golden Jubilee a special circular of ten pages was issued giving details of many excursions and specials including a parade of locomotives and stock. These were not just put in place but had to be worked between normal workings as would happen on the prototype lines.

The first time working starts, the time is

Above: Down local passing Gretley Colliery headed by Ex NSR 0-6-2 T No 2271.
Richard Sharpe Studios

through Rufford Market; it will be re-marshalled on to a local freight returning to Rufford Market. In some ways this is similar to the practice of mainline railways. Loads are considered to originate at or near the stations in question and are such things as castings, gates, wheels, girders all of which are made or produced within the vicinity. These are shifted back between sessions to the point of their origin. Various insulated, furniture and cement containers are deemed to move on from one station to

at that particular station. The operator then does not have to worry about the happenings at the next station and may not even be aware of them. The master working timetable shows the working of every passenger train, every freight train, the number of wagons on each freight train and the number of brake vans on each freight train. It shows the number of vehicles on a parcels train and where a vehicle has to be added or subtracted from a through train; this vehicle could be a parcels van or a carriage truck or a fish van or anything of that nature. There is also a summary sheet which shows the miscellaneous vehicles such as the

taken as 4am. When that session finishes the time is recorded on a diagram—this is the time as it would be at Sherwood. The next session starts at that time and so on. It would give a complete circle covered in about four sessions but there is a fair chance that the time may be overshot to say 5am. If this happens then the next session just picks up from that time. At the start of each session an

Overleaf: Nottingham Castle station. An up express from Trent Town is standing at Platform 2 headed by 4-6-0 "Jubilee" class No 5594 "Bhopal"; up local from Friars Hollow at Platform 4 with Fowler 2-6-2 T No 1.
Richard Sharpe Studios

operator will study his station and the timetable. The Controller will decide on specials such as the Pigeon Special and each man gets ready any trains so that he is not held up when working starts. After a warning the clock is started by the man at Friars Hollow. As with all things there must be a final arbiter and this falls on the lot of the Controller. He also has a position to fill but does not have to despatch many trains. It is up to him to decide if trains may be taken out of order should they start to run late. This can happen on the best regulated railways be they model or real. This is the only time when talking takes place as there is no need for speech to pass trains from one station to another. It is his job to keep things moving and try to regain the lost time. He has to know his timetable well because he may try to put something into an occupied track or cause other unfortunate misfortunes.

The operating does not become boring because there are four sessions to divide up the twenty-four hours and six operating positions. It is highly unlikely that an operator would have the same position and the same time within months or maybe years.

Earlier it was stated that the third outstanding feature of Sherwood was the cameraderie of the people who modelled and operated the line. Norman Eagles acknowledges the debt that he owes to these people in that Sherwood depends on them. One particular feature is a system known as the "Gaffer System". Each particular person involved has his own particular allocation of duties. This developed quite randomly during the building stage and each has continued with this function for the maintenance. It could well be a particular side of modelling that he is good at or interested in. Although he is in charge of that function others may work under his direction. The functions are divided up in such ways as signalling, track, stock painting, wagon building and maintenance, building construction and scenic work. Should there be a disagreement then the problem is taken to Norman Eagles who is the final arbiter. His decision usually comes with a comment "Cor, anybody would think that it was his railway."

Sessions used to take place in the evenings but they now take place once a month on Saturdays. Sessions—in the summer for running and winter for maintenance and rebuilding as required —start about 2.30 when people start gathering and last until about 8.30. The day has developed into a social event on the calendar as quite often the wives come as well and many of the "Gang" meet outside of the sessions even for such things as holidays. As nobody knows exactly who is going to arrive or which wives will be coming there is a chance for a good natter session for the ladies. It is arranged that they have their tea first and then make tea for the operators who have a break from operating. Then after closing down they all get together for coffee prior to leaving for their homes—some of them having quite a journey.

So Sherwood has now existed for 52 years; some of the "Gang" have been coming for years and bring their wives and families with them. One wife who first came as a fiancée of one of the "Gang" and is not only married to him but now a Grandmother, once said that she just couldn't imagine life without Sherwood.

Left: On the Crewe Grammar School LNWR system.

Below: Down local freight approaching Bradcaster, loco Ex L&Y 0-6-0 No 12521. On high level: Down local passing Gretley Colliery, loco Ex NSR 0-6-2 T No 2271.
Richard Sharpe Studios

THE CREWCHESTER MODEL RAILWAY

The Crewchester Model Railway is a mass of compromises, inconsistencies and sheer bluff, for within the confines of a normal suburban garden it attempts to represent a main-line route stretching from London to the Scottish border. The full length of the layout from end to end is some 140 feet, (little over one scale mile) which means that London to Carlisle is crammed into the distance between Euston and the top of Camden Bank. It is of course quite impossible to build a model railway when one remembers that to make a model layout in O gauge of

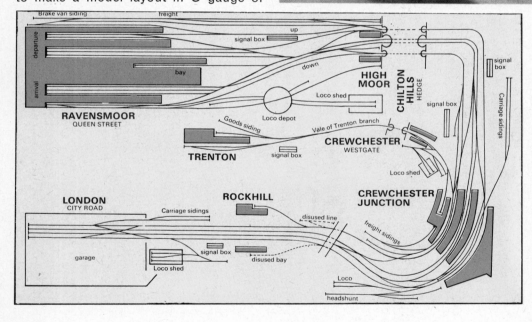

layout whose principal aim was to evoke atmosphere, scenery was an absolute essential. Some very practical considerations had to be borne in mind when deciding the height above ground, not the least of which was comfort. Maintenance of track effected with one's head between one's knees may be fun when one is twenty-one but loses some of its appeal as anno domini begins to make its presence felt. Quite as important as this is the matter of viewpoint. Railways are usually watched from such vantage-points as station-platforms, boundary-fences, embankments, or from the tops of over-bridges; seldom from a heli-copter. Crewchester was designed so that the trains may be viewed side-ways on rather than as a mere row of carriage roofs. Scenery was provided by careful landscaping of the garden, throwing up high embankments, cultivating hedges which isolated sections, and building baseboards sufficiently wide to accommodate lineside effects.

Another decision which was reached

Birmingham (New Street) together with its approaches and freight departments, it would be necessary to use an area the size of a tennis-court.

The reasons and influences which shaped the vital decisions taken when Crewchester was first envisaged are so numerous and complex that it would take many articles to expound them. Jack Ray and John Blair met nearly twenty-five years ago, discovered strong mutual interests including an almost passionate obsession with steam trains, and set about trying to recapture the atmosphere of the days when steam reigned supreme, by means of a gauge O layout.

Jack Ray had already made a few struggling attempts, and, joining forces with John Blair perpetrated one or two more about which the less said the better. With no practical experience, few resources, and less cash, lessons were

learned the hard way, and a succession of undistinguished layouts provided salutory lessons. Perhaps the most striking peculiarity about Crewchester is its unswerving allegiance to spring-drive (clockwork) as its principal motive power. But it must be admitted that the use of spring-driven locomotives was not inspired by some extra-sensory perception or clairvoyancy which foresaw the wonderful developments in this field. It was a visit to the now-defunct Conway model railway in Harrow which really showed the architects of Crewchester just what could be done with spring-drive, and Joe Goadby-Griffiths started more than he dreamt of that evening in 1952 when he entertained Messrs Blair and Ray on his magnificent layout.

It is often stated that a layout built in the open and raised on stilts to table-top height precludes scenic effects. For a

after much heart-searching was to build the entire main line with four tracks, the two fast roads occupying the centre of the baseboard, flanked on either side by the slow roads. This was the result of experience on past layouts where one shunting freight at a way-side station could virtually paralyse the entire layout. Indeed, in the early days when John Blair

Above: Compound on a down express near City Road. *J L Ray*

Right: A4 "Golden Eagle" at Crewchester Junction on a down express. *J L Ray*

Below left: A general view of the interior of Ravensmoor Station looking to the south during a busy morning on the Crewchester Model Railway. *J L Ray*

Overleaf:
LMS "Royal Scot" 4-6-0 No 6113 "Cameronian" leaving the north portal of High Moor Tunnel and approaching Ravensmoor with a down express of early LMS main-line stock. *J L Ray*

wished to do a bit of urgent soldering on something he would accept a stopping passenger train or freight, hold it in a station and refuse to clear the line until the job was completed, knowing he was safe from interruption. Four-track layout meant that slow traffic could be confined to its own road without impeding faster through-traffic. There was a high price to pay for this however in the form of points, for reasonable transfer facilities between slow and fast routes has to be provided.

The present layout was started in 1961 and the original plans have been adhered to remarkably closely, considering how many fresh avenues have been opened. The layout starts in a "fiddle yard" in the garage at the top of the garden, leaves it by means of a tunnel, travels down the side of the garden, swings through a 90-degree curve at the bottom of the garden to enter the principal through-station, Crewchester Junction, moves once more through 90 degrees to travel up the other side of the garden, passing through High Moor Tunnel to emerge into the northern terminus of Ravensmoor. The fiddle-yard in the garage is the London terminal called "City Road", and between this station and Crewchester lies the small country station called Rockhill, served only by the two outer slow roads. Simi-

larly, between Crewchester Junction and Ravensmoor there is another small station served by the slow roads, named "High Moor". From Crewchester Junction on the down side, the Vale of Trenton branch swings away to the west, calling at Crewchester (Westgate) and then running down the middle of the garden to the small country market-town of Trenton. Thus several ambitions have been fulfilled. Here is a layout where crack named expresses may hurtle along, stopping trains may take a more leisurely journey, consuming time at the smaller intermediate stations of Rockhill and High Moor, while the escapist may revel in the peaceful single-track branch line, remote from the busy-ness of the main line.

Operation of the layout is as near to prototype practice as is possible to achieve in the circumstances. Three-position single-pegger block instruments have been salvaged from old signal-cabins, and installed in three separate signal-cabins on the Crewchester layout, one at City Road, another at Crewchester Junction, and the third at Ravensmoor. Block-bells, telephones, and buzzers complete communication, and all trains are offered and accepted by means of these instruments. Timetables are prepared and used whenever possible, although free-lance sessions are not unknown. All engines carry correct headlamp codes and all trains carry the statutory tail-lamp. This layout is an instance of how the railway has been adapted to the locomotives, rather than the more normal converse. The length of the layout is approximately the length of run of a six-coupled express engine, normally loaded, in optimum conditions. Crewchester Junction, being the half-way point, is within the reach of the smaller four-coupled engines.

The baseboard is built up on oak posts which support bearers upon which is laid the final surface—usually 1″ thick planking. Track is brass bull-head section, held in slide-on chairs which are pinned to cedar sleepers at about 42 to the yard-run. The sleepers are in turn pinned to longitudinal battens, each 6′ x 1″ x $\frac{1}{4}$″. A fine flint chick-grit is used as ballast, tamped down and treated with a boiling mixture of creosote and bitumen. This latter serves two main purposes, for not only does it knit the ballast into a rock-hard consistency and provide complete weather-protection, but it also coats the webs of the rails with an extraordinarily realistic rust-colour. Finally, expansion gaps are left so that trains moving along the track do give a thoroughly convincing "diddly-da, diddly-da" sound effect. On really large expanses of baseboard the surface is covered with roofing felt before laying track.

The train-service provided on this railway has evolved over many years and has settled down into a versatile and interesting general pattern. Three crack expresses ply non-stop daily between London (City Road) and Ravensmoor, and as the line is jointly operated by the LMS and LNER, duties are shared. The two LNER trains are "The Raven Pullman" and "The Northerner", while the LMS offers "The Moorlander". The Pullman is naturally enough made up of pre-war Pullman stock, and as the line is intended to operate during the nineteen-thirties, it is not surprising to find the Northerner comprising teak main-line corridor stock. Locomotives normally allotted to these non-stop runs are Gresley Pacifics *Flying Scotsman, Wind-*

sor Lad of the A3 class, Gresley Pacific class A4 *Golden Eagle*, and Thompson Pacific A2/3 class *Edward Thompson*. The LMS usually roster either *Princess Elizabeth, Duchess of Montrose* to the Moorlander, with a couple of Royal Scots available if necessary.

In addition to these non-stop expresses there are two further named trains. The LMS operate "The Crewcastrian" between Crewchester Junction and City Road, complemented to the north by the LNER express plying between Crewchester Junction and Ravensmoor, named "The Fellsman". In direct contrast to these aristocrats is the little push-pull which ambles up and down the branch between the Junction and Trenton. Between these two extremes are all manner of other trains, passenger, parcels, and freight moving about their appointed tasks.

The layout can be operated by four

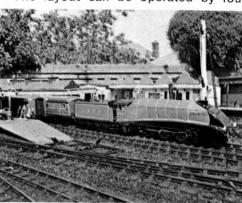

really experienced people who do not mind risking a heart-attack, but it really requires seven or eight to make life comfortable. Crewchester signal-cabin with its four bells and eight instruments —to say nothing of telephones—demands a degree of concentration which allows little relaxation. Ravensmoor must surely take pride of place, for it is possibly one of the most ambitious stations ever attempted in gauge O clockwork. Occupying an area of some 220 square feet, it provides a large covered terminus of seven platforms and two carriage storage roads, with the principal departure platform which is seventeen feet long. A mpd provides accommodation for some fifteen engines if necessary, and the freight yards have space for 150 wagons. Quite naturally the approaches are a mass of points, but the principle is essentially simple. Avoiding scissor crossovers and slips, points provide access to or from any running route to and from any platform or siding.

With nearly one hundred points, such a layout demands a tremendous amount of maintenance, and clean track and clean wheels are essential for the best running.

Started in 1961, the present layout is far from finished. It is huge and complex almost to the point of absurdity, yet its very size and scope offers such a variety of acitivities that boredom or staleness are unlikely to occur. Crewchester has been the proving ground for some startling developments in the realm of spring-dive, and it is hoped, will continue to do so for many years yet. It owes much to a number of people who have shown interest in an extremely generous and tangible way—not with money—but with time and effort, and no small degree of technical skill. And the heart and soul of Crewchester is the band of youngsters who come round week after week to operate, to carry out maintenace, or in fact do anything which requires doing.

LNER
IN THE GARDEN

The present layout, which is 7mm fine scale, was commenced in 1954 by my son and myself; prior to that there had been a coarse scale line also in the garden since 1939 and this survived the war without damage.

The first thing done in 1954 was to erect a shed 14ft x 8ft and in this a four road terminal station was initially put in together with sidings and engine shed after a "bay window" was added at one end. The line at that time left the shed and went out and back round the garden, with a through station at the bottom of the garden together with sidings in a small shed.

Later the terminal station was rebuilt as a four road through station and this involved also changing the approach roads, sidings and engine roads together with new lines and sidings added at the other end of the shed. The lines in the garden were also altered to conform to this through station version. This work was put in hand in 1962 and is now at a fair stage of completion. Scenery in the shed was done in oil paints by my son, representing a typical Scottish town.

It has always been the endeavour to blend the railway with the garden but it must be confessed the reverse was sometimes the case.

The line is based on LNER practice up to the end of the Company's existence, somewhere in Scotland. Buildings have a NBR flavour as do some signals, others are LNER upper quadrant. Signal boxes are fully fitted with levers and the

Above: In foreground LNER 9000 L1 Class 2-6-4T. **Centre:** LNER 4411 C1 Class ex-Great Northern Atlantic, on the Fife Coast Express. *D Rudkin*

Right: LNER 6185 ex-Great Central 2-8-0. *D Rudkin*

Overleaf left to right: LNER 6391 D11 Class "Wizard of the Moor", GNR 1006 Stirling single, LMS 1203 2P Class 2-6-2T, ex-Great Eastern 7374 0-6-0T and ex-NBR 9309 C15 Class. *D Rudkin*

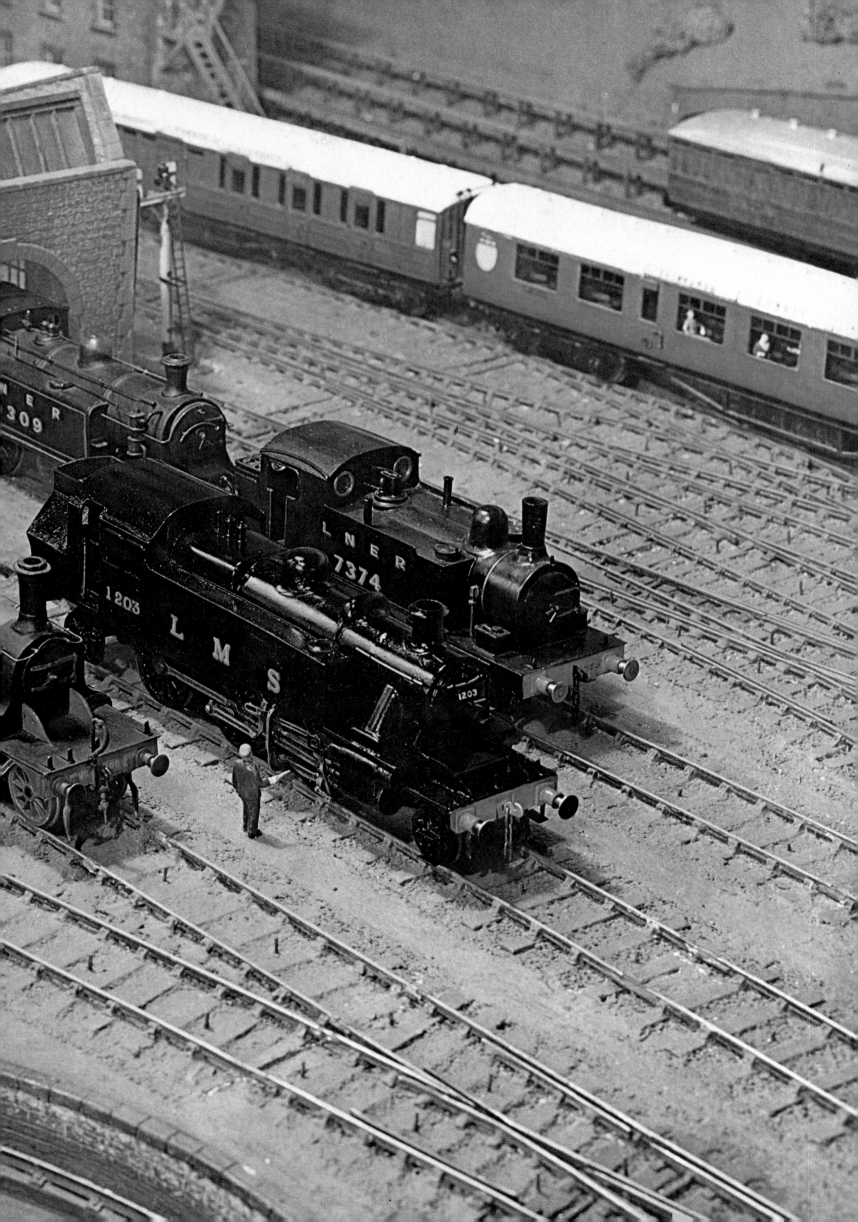

various instruments.

The station names are mythical, it being considered almost impossible to model an actual locality for lack of necessary space. The main station since the re-building having become a junction for what became a branch line was named "Whitelaw Junction" (after the last chairman of NBR and first chairman of LNER and incidentally the grandfather of the former Secretary of State for Northern Ireland). The branch line terminal is "Inverannoch" (a combination of Inverness and Rannoch Moor). As will be seen from the plan the main line is a circle and so that trains can have destination boards as per LNER tradition a mythical terminal was invented to this end. It is Sturroch (a slight corruption of Archibald Sturrock, born in Dundee, and was the first Chief Mechanical Engineer of the GNR). In this way a set train of five Gresley teak coaches are run bearing destination boards "Fife Coast Express. Glasgow-Sturroch".

Practically everything on the railway has been produced in the home workshop. It has been a matter of pride that in the main only raw material has been purchased. In addition to above mentioned train another deserves special mention, it being six coaches of Stirling's six wheeled stock together with large single wheeler engine by the same designer as would have comprised trains for Scotland from Kings Cross in the 1890's. The LNER era concludes with some samples of the last coaches by Thompson. There is also a GNR Royal Saloon of 1908 as a night car refurbished in 1926 as a day saloon and still in use. Another

interesting set are two Gresley Quad articulated suburban sets coupled together thus forming the correct 8 coach rake. To conclude coaching stock there are full bogie luggage and parcels vans of LNER, NER and one LMS theatrical van on through working. In all there are 30 items of coaching stock.

Freight vehicles cover most types of all the constituent companies that made up LNER also other companies and private owners being 47 altogether including an LNER 20ton brake van made in Egypt by my son when on National Service and a 20ton NER wagon by myself on a ship when on voyage round Africa.

There are 9 locomotives at present with one building comprised as follows:— 4-6-2 A3 "Gainsborough" No 2597 (First built 1934 but since rebuilt to fine scale except boiler which is the original, a complete history of prototype is in our possession).

4-4-2 C1 Atlantic No 4411.

4-2-2 8ft Stirling single No 1006 built 1894 was last of the class to be scrapped 1915. (It will be noted these three locos are in lineal descent).

4-4-0 D11 Scottish Director No 6391 "Wizard of the Moor".

4-4-2 C15 No 9309 (was last of class built for NBR by Yorkshire Engine Co. and were known as "Yorkies").

0-6-0 J35 No 9371 (This inside cylinder engine has model motion working between frames with motor in tender).

0-6-0T J69 No 7374 (Ex GER and was stationed at Thornton Junction in Fifeshire).

2-6-4T L1 No 9000 and 2-6-2T LMS No

1203. These are the only items not home built.

2-8-0 04/2 No 6185. Building (Only GCR loco of this type to be cut down for NBR loading gauge).

It is intended that there will eventually be one loco at least of all the companies constituting the LNER.

The railway as described was at Thornton Heath but last year it was necessary to move to Essex where it has been re-erected to the same formation.

All coaches are correctly fitted internally even to passengers, the Royal Saloon has bath, toilets and dressing rooms. Locos have cab fittings and crews and the A3 has fully equipped smoke box with opening door. It is fitted with a corridor tender, this is incorrect as prototype never had one but when the loco was first built in 1934 it was thought it would get one and so it has remained to illustrate how the non-stop runs Kings Cross to Edinburgh were achieved in steam days.

This model LNER is operated electrically on 12 volt stud contact, all wiring beneath the base board or otherwise out of sight, points and signals are worked by solenoid motors also beneath base board. There are four controllers in a large shed and one in a small shed so that five operations can be going on at one time.

*Facing page: **NER 4-4-0 built by Carette for Bassett-Lowke in 1909 to gauge 3.** R McCrindell collection (Richard Sharpe Studios)*

*Below: **LNER 4411 C1 Class ex-Great Northern Atlantic; in background ex-NBR 9309 C15 Class on branch line to Inverannoch.** D Rudkin*

WINTON
An LNER layout in 4mm scale

The author's interest in railways was probably kindled by his maternal grandfather. An afternoon jaunt in his Austin Seven would usually entail a stop near a bridge over the London and North Eastern Railway's main line. In retrospect it was no coincidence that the route often led to a bridge near some water troughs and that the arrival time was invariably just before the Coronation streamlined express was due. These visits contained the ingredients of drama which were not lost on an impressionable five year old—the hope as the signal was raised, the suspense of waiting until a speck of smoke appeared leading rapidly to a climax with that wonderful chime whistle, spray everywhere, a roar that seemed to fill the whole world, followed by silence as the blue blur receded into the distance.

Of course, it all had to be recreated with toys in the form of a Hornby gauge O four wheeled engine and two small coaches; the only concession to realism being the coveted letters LNER, the imagination happily supplying the rest. The gauge O lasted about ten years and provided much fun.

The proceeds from its sale allowed the purchase of a very small quantity of Hornby-Dublo, but at least the engine and coaches had the correct number of wheels. It never gave the enjoyment

expected—the child was growing up. The imagination was being tempered by experience and demanding more accurate models, but had yet to learn how to incorporate items into a model of a working railway.

Twenty years on, helped by many people both inside and outside model railway clubs, the writer thinks he knows what he wants to model even if he is unlikely to achieve it. It has led beyond a study of railways, their history and operation, to topics such as architecture, the English landscape and social history. One also begins to look at things like the form and colour of the surroundings rather than taking them superficially for granted.

The layout had to satisfy several conditions. First and most obvious it was to be based on LNER practice. Ten or twelve years ago this was more easily said than done. Only three or four locomotives were available ready made or as kits. Worse still, there were no LNER coaches on the market and so the first decision made was to hand build some. The first two ended in the dustbin, but the next eight remain and a few can be seen in one of the photographs.

The second aim was to be able to run a wide variety of traffic typical of that on the East coast main line. This is still only partly fulfilled as stock is built up from

the better kits or more often hand built.

Thirdly, a layout was wanted which would provide interesting operation. Trains stop, connect with one another, drop and attach coaches or vans, engines have to be coaled watered and turned, yards must be shunted. The whole thing would be signalled and operated to a timetable.

A bonus in modelling the LNER is that it was financially very weak. Thus locomotives and stock were kept in service long after companies like the Great Western would have sent them to the scrapyard. A rich variety of things ancient and modern can therefore appear on the layout without looking wrong.

Setting a date for the model was easy. The 'thirties had all the excitement of record breaking trains while many ancient monuments were still trundling around. Setting the location was more difficult but also important for setting the atmosphere. It gives great satisfaction when someone not particularly interested in railways can take one look at the buildings and tell you that "it must be Yorkshire or somewhere near". The only really satisfactory way to achieve this is to copy actual structures from the area concerned. Yorkshire gives one the chance to operate locomotives from several constituent companies of the LNER.

And so the imaginary Winton was

Above: David Potter's model of class V2 "The Snapper, The East Yorkshire Regiment, The Duke of York's Own" heads an express through Winton. The coaches were hand built from teak and the water tower in the foreground is a replica of one at Goathland in Yorkshire. *B Monaghan (Courtesy Railway Modeller)*

Far left: A train of coal empties threads through the points from Winton Yard onto the main line. The trucks are mostly kits of which one or two are hand lettered. The locomotive is hand built from brass. Note the Royal Engineer's badge and service stripes on the leading sandbox which indicates service in France during the First World War. *B Monaghan (Courtesy Railway Modeller)*

Left: The **LNER** used Sentinal steam railcars extensively in the 'thirties in an attempt to reduce costs. With their customary eye on publicity, they were named after stage coaches. This particular one "Hark Forward" took its name from a Leeds coach which ran through the Yorkshire Dales in the 1830s. It was seriously damaged when it overturned while racing along the rutted roads. *B Monaghan (Courtesy Railway Modeller)*

Pictures overleaf: Two views of "Hunt" class No 238 "The Burton" being turned. The nameplate is embellished with the figure of a fox. *B Monaghan (Courtesy Railway Modeller)*

created. Due to restrictions on time and space it was initially built as a terminus. The main line element is provided by having double track. The operating potential is enhanced by providing a small yard and a single line branch which is supposed to lead to a small port. The latter not only generates traffic destined for the main line but takes traffic from the main line, thus enabling the limited siding accommodation at Winton to be kept reasonably empty. There was only room for a model of a small country station if one was to keep the illusion of space which railways often have.

Having seen the terminus, several friends in the Oxford Model Railway Club volunteered to build a ten foot extension to turn Winton into a through station for use at exhibitions. This has added a great deal of interest for both operators and spectators. There never seems to be a shortage of club members who are prepared to spend a whole day or more operating to the background of a repetitious tape recorder which describes the trains. Meanwhile the owner can sit back and watch that streamliner pass through —only the Austin Seven and the small boy are missing.

In 1937 John Ahern started to build a model railway. He was a man of great originality as well as of artistic and constructional skill, and it was almost inevitable that what he produced would be different from, and go beyond, anything which had been seen up to that time. In those days there were no kits to fall back on, so almost everything had to be made from scratch, but despite this, the ambitious layout that he gradually evolved included not only the railway but a harbour with shipping, the adjoining seaport town, and two outlying villages set in a realistic countryside.

He called it the Madder Valley—a fictitious name for an imaginary setting, which, however, shows examples of real buildings and rollingstock. They were chosen from widely scattered parts of the country from Dorset to the Isle of Man, from Hampshire to West Wales, and on the railway there was later even a slight American influence due to a holiday in Canada. But he created a layout of the 1920-30 period which became a unity in itself, natural and convincing, and with a charm which has captivated all who have seen it from that day to this.

Above: Gammon End station with the Wantage 0-4-0ST and the tram-type coach quietly waiting for passengers.

Overleaf: Madderport: 0-6-0T "Caledonia" sits in the station with an end balcony bogie saloon.

John Ahern continued the creating of the Madder Valley, on and off, over a period of 25 years, extending it as his ideas shaped, changing, improving it. His photos sometimes show the same building in three different positions, but it all settled down eventually into its present very satisfying form.

The line more or less follows the course of the River Madder, and it starts from a terminal station on high ground in the village of Gammon Magna. This is a pretty spot with the village street curving up a hill and the castle on a small eminence nearby (already in 1930 a museum, admission 6d). The railway runs down the valley through a rock tunnel in the foot-foothills of the Madderhorn(!)—a scene based on the Aberglaslyn Pass on the former Welsh Highland Railway—with a low-level branch from Gammon End running parallel to it on the other side of

the river gorge. The little train which often stands in Gammon End station consists of a tram-type coach headed by one of the 0-4-0 Wantage Tramway engines (not the preserved "Shannon" or "Jane"). In the station yard waits a toast-rack char-a-banc, a hansom cab, and a rather dashing Bugatti. Further down the branch there is a brickworks which shows an early type of kiln and a diminutive engine on a rather fearsome incline, with Gammon Worthy Halt under the cliffs above, and Cuckoo Island lying midstream in the river.

On this island there is a Greek temple said to have been built in the 18th century by the then lord of the manor, Sir Hugo Gammon-Hogg (it's rude to smile). Now of course the folly is a ruin, but they say it looks very fine by moonlight. Just past the island the river bends sharply to the left and the two railway tracks unite as they enter the village of Much Madder—another wonderful name. Here there is a boat-building establishment with a boat under construction on its cradle, and beyond this the village scrapyard, complete with every kind of junk from tin cans, baths, and bedsteads to the re-

mains of early road vehicles, including the chassis of a bull-nosed Morris.

There are some interesting buildings in Much Madder, and a hexagonal one on the station platform. After leaving it the railway passes the Moonraker's Inn with its tea garden and tables under striped umbrellas. There is a lock on the river, the line crosses a lattice bridge, and we are in Madderport. A timber store, a fairly large warehouse, and the ugly but very characteristic China Clipper pub on the corner. The engine shed is situated at this end of the town, and shedded here are an 0-6-0 saddle tank with a tender— "Welsh Pony" from the Festiniog Railway—and an 0-6-0 side tank "Caledonia" from the Isle of Man. John Ahern "stretched" his narrow-gauge engines to make them fit his standard (16.5mm) gauge, but this liberty has very little effect visually.

The sleepy town of Madderport consists of shops and a variety of other buildings, and a two-horse bus may be seen standing there awaiting its passengers. The station, though unimposing, forms the headquarters of the Madder Valley Railway, and is the most important place on the line. Yet there is little doing there as it drowses away each summer afternoon. The train which can often be found lingering at the platform may be taken by a very unexpected engine. This has both its water tank and its coal bunker astride the boiler, and it comes from the far away Darjeeling and Himalayan Railway.

Behind the station is a pillared Harbour Office from Poole, and then comes the seaport proper—steam trawlers beside

Bottom left: Madderport Harbour Offices with the Royal Oak behind.

Left: Madderport High Street on a quiet summer afternoon.

Below: "Caledonia" stands by the water tank at Madderport with Perkins & Viger's timber yard in the background.

the wharves, cranes, harbour lights, goods tranship sheds, and all the paraphernalia of a small coastal port. Here, of course, seamen are specially catered for. There are lodging houses and pubs handy in the town, and behind the quay on the Royal Oak Dining Rooms a placard offers "Three Course Lunches, 1s 9d." The good old days. That would mean a lunch for 9 pence today.

The Madder Valley is a fascinating commentary on life between the wars, and it is a great achievement artistically. Its arrangement especially is masterly, presenting sea, town and country in the space of no more than 17 feet by 10 feet, yet with no suggestion of crowding. In this area it made a U-shape, and this was its form when John Ahern died, comparatively suddenly, in 1962. He left it with one part dismantled for further alteration and the whole cut into sections and packed away in an upstairs room after his having moved house some time before. During the blitz it had been under a glass roof in London, yet astonishingly it survived.

Towards the end of 1962 Mrs Ahern offered the Madder Valley on permanent loan to the Pendon Museum at Long Wittenham in Berkshire, where it arrived like a huge jigsaw puzzle in a thousand pieces. After assembly trains ran again, but when Pendon's new museum building was put up it again had to be dismembered and stored. On re-erection the opportunity was taken, with Mrs Ahern's approval, to open it into an L shape, which makes possible much closer and more effective viewing.

The Madder Valley may be seen at Pendon every Saturday and Sunday afternoon throughout the year (but not during the week except for large prearranged parties). Its craftsmanship may occasionally have been surpassed, but it remains a priceless historical relic, a work of great character, and a permanent memorial to the genius of one of the world's most gifted pioneer modellers.

The Campbeltown & Machrihanish Light Railway

A Scottish Narrow Gauge Railway in 7mm scale

The carriage of coal from a remote corner of Argyllshire in Scotland to the nearest port, Campbeltown, has presented problems for over three centuries: first pack-horses, then crude carts, a canal and finally in 1875 a narrow gauge steam railway.

The railway was built to the somewhat unusual gauge of 2ft 3in from the existing pit at Drumlemble to a coal yard, coal ree in the local parlance, at the rear of the town of Campbeltown. Thence coal was transported by horse drawn carts through the streets to waiting vessels at the quays. Later the railway was extended westward to the then new Argyll Colliery on the shores of the Atlantic. To operate the railway, an 0-4-0 well tank *Pioneer* was purchased. Hutches of coal from the pithead cage were run on to flat four wheeled wagons for conveyance to the port, some thirteen of these each carrying four hutches being employed. *Pioneer* was joined in 1883 by an 0-4-0 saddle tank *Chevalier* built by the Kilmarnock firm A Barclay & Son. Both these engines were later rebuilt as 0-4-2 tanks to improve their riding and when they were joined by *Princess* in 1900, she was delivered with this wheel arrangement. *Princess* was one of Kerr Stuart's *Skylark* class.

By 1906, new fast turbine steamers were running day trips from Glasgow to Campbeltown and horse drawn brakes were plying across the peninsula carrying passengers eager to sample the beach and golf course at Machrihanish. Anxious to capitalise on this traffic, the Campbeltown Coal Co, shipping interests and others formed the Campbeltown & Machrihanish Light Railway Co.

The first action of the new concern was to extend the existing railway to the harbour at the eastern end and to

Machrihanish village at the western, making a total mileage of just under six miles. A passing loop with signals was provided at Lintmill, the halfway mark and sidings were provided at a new depot at the back of the town and on the 200 year old New Quay.

Four long bogie coaches and a big new 0-6-2T *Argyll* were purchased to inaugurate the passenger service and were followed in 1907 by two further coaches and a sister engine *Atlantic*. The two identical locomotives were quite huge for so small a railway and a big improvement on the earlier motive power. They were supplied by Andrew Barclay Sons & Co and from then on were the mainstay of all working. Pickerings of Wishaw built the coaches which had end platforms and tramway tip-over seats. The last coach, No 6, differed by having a luggage van built into its middle.

As the concern got under way, the provision of new pithead gear at the colliery enabled conventional coal wagons to be employed and the coal company hired fifty $4\frac{1}{2}$ and a hundred $3\frac{1}{2}$ ton wagons from the Scottish Wagon Company. These were provided with an end door at one end to allow the entire wagon to be lifted and tipped into waiting colliers. A rail mounted steam crane was provided for this purpose on the New Quay. It is interesting to note that this tiny railway was able to load a 500 ton coaster

Right: "Princess" of 1900 crosses Kilkerran Road carrying coal hutches on flat wagons.
B Monaghan

Above: "Atlantic" runs past the New Quay. The crane in the foreground lifted the coal wagons bodily and tipped them into waiting vessels. *B Monaghan*

Overleaf: "Atlantic" waits in Hall Street for the arrival of the Glasgow steamer.
B Monaghan

in six hours and that sometimes three or four ships would call in one week. During the first World War, the loss of continental suppliers produced a great demand for the fine grade of silicon sand lying immediately above the coal seams and this too was transported by the railway.

The railway served its masters well until the 1928 Coal Strike when coal production ceased, not to be recommenced until 1946. At the same time bus competition was robbing the line of its passenger traffic and early in 1932 the "wee train", as it was known, succumbed to road traffic.

When so much information was being collected about a previously little known railway, what more natural than to model the line? The first model, *Argyll,* was completed some twenty years ago, to be closely followed by the remaining stock, all built to a scale of 7mm to 1 foot or, if you like, Gauge O Narrow Gauge. The actual gauge of 2ft 3in enabled OO-gauge (16.5mm) standards to be used for wheels and track.

A model representing the harbour and depot at Campbeltown was built in the cellar of the house but some years later had to be dismantled due to moving house and a new one built in the loft: "Built in" in the real sense and incorporated in a much larger O-Gauge layout. A few years ago, it was requested that a Campbeltown exhibit be put on at one of the Glasgow exhibitions and eight weeks later a completely new third model of the C&MLR emerged without layout No 2 being disturbed!

Planning

The secret of rapid construction is planning. The model was built on six 8ft x 2ft 6ins section which go together to form a 15ft x 8ft layout. The size was determined by the size of the garage in which the initial work was done and by the lounge where finishing took place and where incidently the accompanying photographs were taken. Work on some of the buildings and on the four trestles were carried out by helpful friends.

As the line was conceived as an exhibition project, no question of "playing trains" was entertained. The track formation follows that of the prototype as shown on the 25in ordnance survey map of the period but only that track required for operating is wired. The layout resolves itself into a continuous oval with two loops and two spurs for storing trains. Although the harbour should be a terminus, the track was extended through the yard of the Royal Hotel so that continuous operating is possible. Even so, because the model can be viewed from either side, the public can only see a train running for half the available time. As each member of the public watches a layout for about 3 minutes, trains must always be on the move.

Foundation and Landscape

Each section of baseboard was constructed from two 2in x ½in longitudinal beams with cross bracing of the same material. The trackbed was cut to shape from 3/16in plywood. At the depot, this was done in one piece to allow continuity of curve in both planes as there are three different levels to contend with. Only four railjoints occur on baseboard joints as these can be sources of derailment on portable lines. On the original railway, on leaving the harbour, the line doubled back on itself, passed the depot, and then headed over the peninsula of Kintyre. This lent itself to modelling very well as it was thus possible to have the

harbour on one side and the depot on the other with the operating space where the town would be. Initially the track laid was obtained commercially but as this wore out, much of it has been replaced by scratch-built formations. All points are hand-operated for reliability but sections are switched on or off by point positions.

The countryside was formed from chicken net covered by newspaper and followed by a plaster/sawdust mix. Trees are either plastic or cuttings from a cupressus tree. The water of the harbour is clear smooth glass, painted thinly brown or grey underneath so that the "bottom" can just be discerned. Craft in the harbour includes a Clyde "puffer" (or steam lighter), some Loch Fyne fishing smacks and a small sailing boat ghosting into the harbour on the flat calm water. Buildings are made from plywood and many are in low relief. As the model is of an actual location, even the smaller details had to be made. Road transport, mainly horsedrawn in 1925, consists of models of carts and lorries actually known to exist in the area. Gas lamp-posts, telegraph poles, bollards, all of which have now changed, had to be individually researched. Particularly difficult were the crane on the New Quay and the gents toilet on the steamer quay: no one seems ever to have photographed the latter. The weighbridge deck at the base of the steamer quay gave problems which were solved by using a wafer biscuit. The joint in the "water" of Campbeltown Loch looked unsightly until it was found that a hitherto unnoticed sewer pipe ran out at just the right place.

Rolling Stock

The most interesting part of any display is the trains and even more so when they are as individual as these. The first model, *Argyll,* was originally a 3-rail locomotive but she is now 2-rail and running on her second set of frames and third set of wheels and motor. Such is the punishment of exhibitions. The big C&MLR engines were originally painted brown but over the years, cleaning with oil gradually darkened this. *Argyll's* finish of near black but clean, tries to catch this. The model *Atlantic* is much newer and is finished ex shops. Even so it has already gone through one motor. At the first showing, this model was not ready, so the body was hurriedly placed on a Hornby Dublo 2-6-4T chassis and temporarily named *Kintyre.* The enormity of this offence was not appreciated until questions appeared about "another C&M engine" from completely different sources. One must be careful not to rewrite history! The colliery engines are represented by *Chevalier* in its as-built condition as an 0-4-0 tank and again in its rebuilt 0-4-2T form with a large overall cab and other changes. *Princess,* which did not have a long life, is modelled as built. There also appears from time to time an ex-WD Baldwin 4-6-0 tank, one of which was considered for the line but never purchased. The remaining locomotive is a diesel hydraulic underground mine locomotive which may have been used had the railway been reopened by the NCB as considered in 1947. After the *Kintyre* episode, the last two are kept in the background. Apart from *Argyll,* all the locomotives operate on the split frame 2-rail system which does away with any need for collectors on the wheels, another source of irritation on hard working stock.

Three of the railway company's six

coaches are modelled including No 6. The sides are made from laminated card but the floors and roofs are wood. The ornate wrought iron work on the platforms is faithfully reproduced. Inside, the coaches are fitted with passengers and tip-over seats. The railway company had but two goods vehicles, a heavy brake van and an open milk wagon, both four-wheeled and there are models of each of these.

But the principal traffic was coal: two loaded rakes of coal wagons and one rake of empties have been modelled. One coal train is made up from six 4-wheeled flat wagons having transverse rails to accommodate four mine hutches each. This train runs behind the original *Chevalier* and represents the 1875-1906

period of operation. These wagons have dumb buffers and chain couplings. The other loaded rake is made up of six $4\frac{1}{2}$ ton wagons. As in real life these have Norwegian centre couplers like the passenger coaches in addition to dumb side buffers. The empties train is made up of eight $3\frac{1}{2}$ ton wagons, chain coupled but with a $4\frac{1}{2}$ tonner at each end to facillitate coupling, a prototype formation. Two of the $3\frac{1}{2}$ ton wagons are built on early underframes as is believed to have happened. In addition, there are one or two wagons of both sizes loaded with sand, and some empties.

All rolling stock is fitted with Jackson wheels which are the only ones tried thus far which stand up to continuous operation. Wagons have false floors of 1/16in

lead sheet to ensure stability and the weight tends to make the wheels run clean. Experience showed that light-weight stock was much more prone to develop black mud on the wheel treads.

Operation

As far as possible the Campbeltown scene is portrayed. Loaded coal trains run anti-clockwise to simulate coal arriving at the harbour and empties run in the opposite direction. The locomotives all face Machrihanish as was generally done and the wagon end doors are all towards the harbour.

An electronic controller is employed which gives slow starting and stopping of the locomotives. At the start of an operating session however, this is switched to direct control until wheels

and rails achieve their working polish.

Throughout an exhibition it is the aim to have the railway running continuously and this has largely been achieved, sometimes for 12 hours non-stop. When trains are changed, one train is run into a loop or siding and immediately the next one moves out. At "peak viewing" times, no train should do more than two laps before being changed.

The railway has been shown extensively over Central Scotland and last year appeared in Manchester. The most stringent test was an appearance in Campbeltown when 10 per cent of the population of 6,000 visited it—and accepted it.

Below: The locomotive depot on a quiet summer afternoon. *B Monaghan*

STRONACHLACHAR

A NARROW GAUGE LAYOUT IN 4MM SCALE

In 1973 one of the outstanding model narrow gauge railways celebrated its 21st birthday. David Mander, its creator, has been interested in railways all his life and at one stage he played around with gauge O and later EM. In 1952 David decided to try an experiment in modelling a two foot narrow gauge line in 4mm scale which was most unusual at that time and meant that he had to work out his own standards and break his own ground. There were others working along the same lines but, at that date, there was little contact between the few people. To start with he built a yard of track, a wagon and began work on one of the Festiniog larger England engines. The idea had been to build the lot including the motor but before the locomotive was finished K's produced a motor that was small enough to fit. This meant that the only items that David had not made himself were the motor and the gears which were of instrument manufacture. Fortunately the experiment was a success as this locomotive has been followed by some nine more, the yard of track to some 130ft of running track and the wagon to 45 wagons and 14 coaches!

The railway is housed in a room in his house together with a small workshop, the latter including a 3½in centre lathe, a ¼in pillar drilling machine and a tool grinder. The room itself measures 21ft by 12ft whilst the base board is 3ft wide all round at a height of 42in.

The line starts at Stronachlachar which has still to be finished. This is an interchange station with standard gauge giving a chance for working transporters. (These are narrow gauge wagons used to carry standard gauge vehicles and were quite common on the Continent but limited to the Leek and Manifold in these islands). The trains leave on mixed gauge over the viaduct where the standard gauge finishes. The narrow gauge then continues for two circuits of the room through mountainous scenery as befitting a line reputedly in the Scottish Highlands. A tunnel leads on to a very fine viaduct which is based on the Monbulk Trestle Bridge, Danegong Hills, Victoria in Australia. It is a timber trestle bridge and was built in the main by Ed Ballard with David Mander doing about a quarter of the work. Built on a radius of 12ft it is made from over 400 pieces of balsa wood stained to give a brownish look. The line then travels through hills and woods (there are over 100 scratch built trees on the layout and many others adapted), over a waterfall and a bridge based on the Festiniog

iron bridge. It then comes to the delightful station called Dearglairig. This has a run round loop with two sidings, one leading to a goods shed, and a short length of standard gauge for the wagons carried by the transporters. Soon after this the line dives into another tunnel—the object of which is to hide the line from the two termini! Soon after going under a viaduct the line comes to Taighantulach. This is a junction with the other line disappearing into a fiddle yard; the station comprises a simple loop and

Above: Strathmoine Hamlet looking down the road to the ungated level crossing. Some of the cottages are scratch built whilst others come from Ballard Bros.

The shops were Triang commercial items adapted to suit the location. On the halt can be seen some locals talking including one with a bicycle. The trees are scratch built. The bridge in the background is based on the Festiniog cast iron bridge at Tan-y-Bwlch. In the halt is locomotive No. 3, based on the larger Festiniog engines built by George England, with two modified Zeuke coaches. On the bridge is No. 4 the Lynton and Barnstable locomotive on a passenger train.

one siding and again a short length of standard gauge. Here also is a siding belonging to the Benbuidhe Quarry Company at the end of which are some staithes with an unloading shoot down which granite chips are unloaded into barges beneath. There are over 300 pieces of balsa wood in the staging.

The line continues through a short tunnel and over a river bridge. It then bursts into Strathmoine Hamlet. As well as a hotel it boasts some little cottages and a level crossing. Loch Moine is crossed by a cob after which the line reaches Beinfhada Yard; this is the main works for the line. Here is a small diesel shed as well as the main locomotive shed and works. The town of Portbanrich has yet to be built but the harbour has all the lines laid to it. That then is the line as one would have travelled down it.

Below: Locomotive No 9, the Darjeeling Himalaya Garratt, crosses the viaduct. This was based on two arches of Dolgoch viaduct. The bridge was built by Ed Ballard on a balsa framework. It was then covered with polystyrene sheet cut into squares before gluing. The guard rail is soldered wire. Cliffs are made from cork bark covered with Polyfilla with flock glued on afterwards. Note the foliage growing out of the cracks in the viaduct and the excellent modelling of the stream water.

Bottom: Taighantulach Station with the Darjeeling Himalaya Class B heading a passenger train. The train comprises the Talyllyn Brake Van (from Mikes Models) and scratch built bogie coach and open and closed toast rack coaches. In the background are cliffs made from cork bark with 'foliage' growing from them. In front of the train may be seen the passing loop and the timber-built water tower. The fir tree is scratch built. The red bar in the foreground is the timber of a single bar gate which is hinged and will open and close; this is the yard gate. The red oxide painted wagon standing on its own is the one built 22 years ago together with locomotive No 3 and a yard of track as an experiment. That this experiment was successful can be seen from the pictures.

Above: A cast iron bridge based on the Festiniog bridge at Tan-y-Bwlch. The cliffs are again cork, Polyfilla and flock. The water under the bridge is flecked with white foam having just fallen down the waterfall behind the bridge. The cottage is built from scraper board and, once again, more scratch built fir trees. The locomotive leading the passenger train is No 4, the Lynton and Barnstable engine.

Left: Taighantulach yard. This view shows the working of the transporter wagons. These were used only on the Leek and Manifold in these islands. The wagon was designed to carry a standard gauge wagon or van which, at the end of its journey, is winched off the wagon and onto a short length of standard gauge track. A standard gauge wagon and a transporter wagon may be seen headed by an Andrew Barclay well tank. This is the only steam locomotive that is not scratch built but is made from a Gem kit. It is No 12 in the stud. The other wagons are scratch built from styrene sheet and are typical of the types found on various British narrow gauge lines. Part of a timber water tower can be seen and the timber trestle bridge which is reached through a tunnel.

Above Right: The trestle bridge crossing Clackan Water is based on the Monbulk Trestle Bridge. The model, constructed by Ed Ballard and David Mander, is made from Balsa wood. The water is made from many layers of varnish with paint mixed in it. "Rocks" are embedded into the water. Cliffs are made from cork and polystyrene with assistance from Polyfilla and flock. Note the crofter's cottage made from one of Ed Ballard's mouldings. The trees are scratch built. Engine No 5 is the GWR built "Vale of Rheidol" engine hauling a passenger train of Egger and Playcraft coaches slightly modified.

Scenics defy description but the photographs give a good idea of how the line looks. The scenery is made from Polyfilla and commercial grass fabric. Rocks are made from cork bark and expanded polystyrene carved to shape. The cob and some bridges are based on wood formers covered with Polyfilla; to give the effect of the stonework, they are scribed when the Polyfilla is dry. The water is made from layer after layer of varnish with varying quantities of the right colour paint underneath.

The buildings are a mixture of scratch built and modified kits. The station building and the crofters cottage at Dearglairig are both scratch built from styrene sheet. The station at Taighantulach is a modified kit. The hotel at Strathmoine is scratch built whilst the cottages are either scratch built or some of the excellent ones that used to be marketed by Ed Ballard.

A portion of the rolling stock is commercial but has been modified in some way. For instance the coaches come from such sources as Egger, Playcraft and Lilliput together with some from Zeuke narrowed down from metre gauge. There are some scratch built and the intention is to replace all the commercial items with scratch built vehicles. Many wagons are scratch built; those that are not, come from the Festiniog kits or Mikes Models.

With the exception of the brief mention of the Festiniog locomotive at the beginning of this description, no mention

has been made of the motive power. The reason for this is not that they should be hidden away, but that they are the climax of superb modelling.

The first locomotive was the larger England locomotive which has been mentioned. The second locomotive appeared in 1954. This was a model of the Lynton and Barnstaple *Exe*—a Manning Wardle 2-6-2T. This loco was chosen because its size would give plenty of room to add weights for extra adhesion. Once again the only commercial parts are the motor and four gears. The third locomotive, built in 1956, was once again chosen for its size and power. One must remember that at that date lightweight plastic bodied rolling stock and pin point axle bearings were unknown. This locomotive was based on the Vale of Rheidol engines built by the GWR and has full Walschaerts gear which is faithfully reproduced in miniature. Comment could be made about the length of time between each locomotive coming off the work-bench but over one hundred hours work goes into each including detail design. All are built with meticulous precision, extreme accuracy being the keynote. For example David built two models of his next locomotive—one for himself and one for a friend—on the basis that it is as easy to do two as one. The two locomotives took him about six months of his leisure time to build and are replicas of the Colonial Sugar Refining Company's locomotive built by Fowler in 1880.

The ubiquitous Baldwin 4-6-0 arrived on the scene a long time before the Festiniog produced their kit. Previously all locomotives had only used commercial motors and occasionally a commercial gear or two. This was the first locomotive to take advantage of the introduction of commercial N scale items and runs on an Arnold chassis with the motor in the smoke-box. Naturally the body, the Walschaerts valve gear and the pony truck are scratch built.

The next locomotive to be produced was also an innovation—a Hibbert four wheel diesel. Regrettably no drawings were available for it at the time so its dimensions were taken from photographs. Once again an Arnold N scale chassis was used. Locomotive number

Overleaf: Waiting for the train to pass by. None of your fancy lifting barriers or level crossing gates, this is a crossing narrow gauge style – just a man holding up the traffic. The traffic on the road consists of a traction engine and a horse and cart waiting for the train which comprises locomotive No 2 and a coach. The locomotive is a John Fowler built for the Colonial Sugar Refining Company Limited and the coach is based on a North Wales Narrow Gauge Railway coach both scratch built. The house, on the edge of Strathmoine Hamlet, in the centre of the picture was made from scraper board – the little white lean-to was added at a later date by another tenant! The other building was made from styrene sheet. The stone walling is made from wood covered with Polyfilla which is scribed, when dry, and painted.

one of the Stronachlachar was the quickest to be built. Having been ill, it was considered to be a bit of physiotherapy whilst convalescing; however David did not feel like the exacting task of an accurate model. It is based on an Anglicised version of the Egger tank scaled up to 4mm scale and runs on a Minitrix chassis. Oh, by the way, it took two days to build! The Darjeeling Himalayan Railway Class B tanks were, in the author's opinion, one of the two most beautiful narrow gauge locomotives ever built; furthermore David Mander considers this model to be his favourite. Although built onto an Arnold N scale chassis the latter had to be heavily modified. A terrific amount of detail work had to be done to this model.

The biggest locomotive of the stud is the Darjeeling Himalayan Beyer Garratt. This model is a masterpiece of miniature model engineering. The commercial items in it are a K's mark 2 motor, driving

wheels and gears from Minitrains. The motor is housed in the firebox and cab; it drives all four axles via a primary 3:1 gear reduction, two propeller shafts, universal joints and then the Minitrains worm and pinion gears. The boiler, power bogies tank and bunker are machined from solid brass whilst the chimney and dome are turned from brass. The remainder was built from nickel silver sheet and wire.

The odd man out of the system was the last to be "built"—modified would probably be the better word as it is an Egger diesel body. It uses a Minitrains mechanism but both the Egger body and the mechanism had to be heavily modified to allow the adaptation. David has more locomotives in mind or already on the drawing board.

That then is 21 years work—much of it spent on the locomotives. Naturally the electrics took a fair amount of time as the central console has two controllers

giving cab control and the switching for the point motors, whilst track, which is scratch built, scenery, rolling stock and research consumed the remainder.

Model Railway Engineering in Perfection. Locomotive No 7 is a Class B 0-4-0 tank of the Darjeeling Himalaya Railway. Shown crossing the "cob", it is difficult to appreciate that this is in 4 mm scale and runs on 9 mm track. Detail that can be seen includes the rerailer bar on its brackets above the boiler, the lamp and bracket in front of the chimney, the sand box above the front buffer beam and the handrails round the front (used when carrying men on the front buffer beam if sanding is required), coal carried in a box above the rear end of the boiler and an electric generator on the footplate (below the SR Emblem). As if this isn't enough the details in the cab have to be seen to be believed. Ed Ballard painted all the locomotives and, as can be seen from this one, made a first-class job of them.

The Story of the Küssnachterseebahn

An H O layout of the Swiss Railways.

Everything is still and dark, save for the red lights from the signals glinting on the rails, when one sees a light go on in the bedroom above Kelleralp station. The station signal room lights come on and before very long the signal changes to green and the Number 5 *Gedeon Thommen* of the narrow gauge Waldenburgerbahn takes its little train down the valley crossing the Feuzbrücke and the Häberliviadukt on its way to Schupplisee station to connect with the main line. On arrival the station staff go about their duties as lamps are lit and the steam railcar makes ready to take the early shift of workers to the Johann Walter brewery. The main line signals fall to green and in the distance one can hear the rumbling noise of a fast approaching train. In seconds there is a flash of mauve and cream coloured coaches with windows all aglow as the "Rheingold" express speeds through the early dawn.

As daylight breaks the local mixed train of one two-axled passenger coach and an SBB K2 van departs hauled by the 0-4-0 *Glaskasten,* which with its unique gravity feed coal hopper needs only the driver as crew. Trains of beer vans from many different breweries in Switzerland keep *Tigerli* the little 0-6-0 WT of the SBB busy during the day trundling them back and forth to the brewery whilst the main station of Schupplisee is kept active with trains picking up and leaving vehicles as well as dealing with the frequent narrow gauge service to Kelleralp. In addition to this several main line passenger expresses are scheduled to stop at the locomotive depot for coaling and watering before the haul over the steep gradients of the pass.

However, this is not some far corner of Switzerland that has lain undiscovered for years by the tourists but a fictional model which has been built to capture the atmosphere of a time long gone when steam was still plentiful in that lovely land.

The whole project came into being some seven years ago during a rail journey over the Gotthard main line when the splendours of the scenery combined with the excellent and interesting railway system of the country made one consider seriously the possibilities of trying to re-create this in model form. At this period in time very little information was available in England about the Swiss Railways and it was indeed fortunate that, as time went by, good friends were made in Switzerland who could supply relevant information about the old steam days of the railways. The time is in the mid nineteen twenties when the main Gotthard route is already electrified although there is still a good deal of steam power being used.

An eight foot by four foot six inches base of chipboard, strengthened by two inch timber and mounted on Dexion legs, was constructed. The basic track area was then laid with 1/8in Balsa wood and Gem track pinned down on top of this. The points used were Marcline powered by Hammant and Morgan motors. These points, with their live frogs, were ideal because of the short wheelbase of several of the engines. The complete track layout was then ballasted using PSM scale-size ballast. This was spooned along the edges and middle of the track and tamped into place. The whole area was then sprayed with a fine mist of water to which had been added a few drops of household detergent. After this had been done a mixture of one part Copydex to five parts water was applied,

Overleaf: **Schupplissee Station where the narrow gauge Waldenburgerbahn meets the Küssnachterseebahn: SBB 4-6-0 No 502 passes on the main line with a freight train.**

Right: **SBB 0-6-0 WT No 8489 on the shed at Schupplissee.** *M Lewis*

by means of an eye dropper as purchased in the large chemists, along the edges and middle of the ballast so that the white liquid would follow the water through the ballast and become quite firm when left overnight.

To power the tracks and points Tony Adam of Stafford built a very complex but functional control board upon which one could set up complete routes and with full cab-control throughout. The lighting for the buildings was also controlled from this panel, so enabling only one operator, if necessary, to run the whole sequence.

The main buildings of the railway, such as Schupplisee and Kelleralp stations are models of Langwies and Küssnacht-am-Rigi stations and have been exquisitely built in all detail by Ron Withers, as was the engine shed, which is based on the locomotive depot at Winterthur. All these towns are, of course, in Switzerland!

Being a Swiss railway, great consideration had to be given to the scenery and in this respect cork bark was used with very good effect for simulating rock outcrops.

This, combined with Polyfilla and flock powders, together with dozens of miniature fir trees and a very good back scene from Faller enabled a truly realistic scene to be made. The whole scene was peopled by the wonderful little miniatures from both Merten and Preiser of Germany.

All of the rolling stock to date, has been bought, and it is hoped now that the layout is virtually complete, time can be found to build some of the more unusual wagons and coaches. The motive power department at present consists of:—

(1) 4-6-0 SBB Nr. 502 Liliput.
(2) 0-6-0 WT SBB Nr. 8489 Fulgurex.
(3) 0-6-0 JS Nr. 413 Rivarossi rebuild.

Bottom: SBB 4-6-0 No 502 being coaled on the shed at Schupplissee. *M Lewis*

Below: The narrow gauge Waldenburgerbahn train crosses the Haberliviadukt on its way down to Schupplissee. *Richard Sharpe Studios*

(4) 0-4-0 SB Nr. 22 Heinzl.
(5) 0-4-0 Railcar SB Heinzl.
(6) 4-6-2- DR Nr. 1847 Marklin.

Being set in the older days one would expect to find items such as clerestory coaches in use and this is so including several belonging to the Compagnie International Wagon-Lits made by Liliput who also were responsible for the complete Rheingold train of the 1928 era. Freight vehicles with the insignia of the Nord Ost Bahn, Gotthardbahn, S.C.B. and Baden Bahn are seen in the yards and brewery sidings.

The KB is operated by means of a planned schedule with the roster of trains made up to simulate a typical day on the railway from early morning to dusk. To facilitate contact between the main control panel operators and the fiddle yard operator a telephone system has been set up so at exhibitions there is no shouting to and fro. This is specially important as the fiddle yard is completely hidden by the drapes of the exhibition unit.

As mentioned earlier, building a model railway of Swiss steam in the 1920's, meant a great deal of research, both from a great variety of books on continental railways, and from several friends in Switzerland itself. All of this has added extra enjoyment to the project and, of course, is an excellent reason for visiting that lovely country each year to look at the latest developments on the railways, and also, to visit wonderful places like the Verkehrshaus (Transport Museum) in Luzern with its up to the minute displays, and finally the many excellent model railways in various parts of the country.

The KB was built by a team of very good friends:— Mike Lewis, Tony Adam, Ron Withers, Brian Brazier, Keith Lewis and John Tranter to try and capture the magic of the old days in Europe and has been a most satisfying and enjoyable exercise but like model railways the world over is not quite finished!

The Gotthard line in Miniature

The working model railway in the Swiss Transport Museum, Lucerne.

The Swiss Transport Museum is situated on the lake shore about a mile from the centre of Lucerne. It consists of a complex of buildings housing transport and communication exhibits, a Planetarium, and restaurant and conference facilities. Its concept, situation, layout, and the quality of its exhibits make it perhaps the world's finest transport museum; visitors to Switzerland should include it in their programme if only to judge this for themselves.

For railway modellers the centre of attraction is certain to be the magnificent working model railway. This occupies an area 40 x 20 feet and represents the route of the Gotthard railway along the western face of the valley of the river Reuss. The particular section modelled incorporates some of the finest scenery and the most interesting engineering features of the line.

The trains are to HO scale (1:87) and are commercial products modified to suit the operating conditions of the layout. The locomotives are powered through the overhead wires as in the prototype, although the provision of a stud contact system between the rails enables steam outline locomotives to be used if desired. The vehicles are appropriate to the traffic of the Gotthard line although unfortunately even a layout as large as this one cannot accept the

length of train normally seen in service conditions. To enable the line to be represented in the form of a free-standing exhibit the scenery has been "folded" around three sides of the unit with the fourth side providing access to the interior of the model.

The layout was built for the Swiss Federal Railways in 1958/9 by the Lucerne Railway Modelling Club and required over 30,000 hours of freely-donated time to complete. Its size, authenticity and wealth of detail, combined with the practical and unusual ideas incorporated into its construction make it an out-

standing achievement in railway modelling. During the season some sixteen trains run simultaneously during the hourly operating sessions. They traverse over 380 yards of line, divided into 18 block sections. The entry and departure of trains into and from the blocks is controlled by relays and their associated colour-light signals. The automatic operation is rendered possible by the double-tracked loop layout on which the trains run permanently 'north' or 'south'.

Non-automatic operations can be controlled from a panel set opposite the layout's station tracks. Whereas the automatic system has 40 relays, this "Integra" panel has 350 and controls 70 turnouts. The panel is built up from "Integra" modules as in full-size Swiss Federal Railways' practice. It is hardly surprising that there is seven miles of wiring in the layout.

The Gotthard route commences in Lucerne and Zurich, and at a junction near Lucerne which gives access to most towns in the Swiss industrial area around Olten and Aarau. These lines converge at Arth-Goldau and continue over the Gotthard to meet the Italian State Railways at Chiasso, near Lugano. After passing Schwyz, the line reaches the upper part of Lake Lucerne at Brunnen and then climbs in the Reuss valley to enter the Gotthard Tunnel at Göschenen.

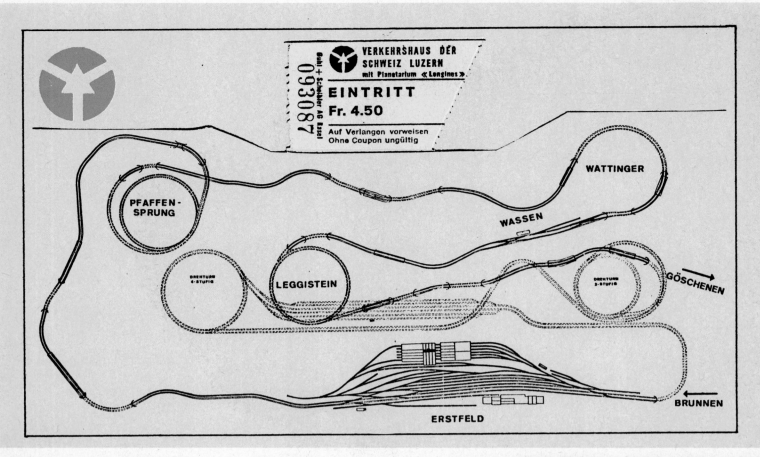

PFAFFEN-
SPRUNG

DREHTURM
4-STUFIG

LEGGISTEIN

WATTINGER

WASSEN

DREHTURM
3-STUFIG

GÖSCHENEN

BRUNNEN

ERSTFELD

In order to gain sufficient height in the distance available, the line spirals in the rock and zigzags across the valley face.

The model portrays the course of the line from the shops and yards at Erstfeld to the mouth of the Naxberg tunnel near Göschenen. The Erstfeld layout occupies one side of the unit; the end contains the tunnels and spectacular bridges near Amsteg. The opposite side portrays the spiral tunnels at Pfaffensprung and the Wassen zizgag between the Wattinger and Leggistein tunnels. All these features, including the Gotthard road and buildings beside the line, are correctly portrayed. In traversing the line the model trains climb and descend nearly seven feet.

The profusion of tunnels, bridges, chasms and rock outcrops ensure that trains constantly enter and leave tunnels, often in unexpected directions and at different levels. "Where do 'ee come from? Where do 'ee go?" said the character in "The Ghost Train", and to find out it is necessary to accompany

Top Right: A train of car transporters at Erstfeld. *M S Cross*

Top Left: Diagram of layout.

Bottom Right: Three levels of railway near **Wassen.** *M S Cross*

Bottom Left: Intgra control panel: Erstfeld Station in the background. *M S Cross*

the uniformed attendant through the access door and to enter the depths of the "mountain". This is even more interesting to the modeller than the external part of the layout, for one is literally in the heart of a great model railway.

The interior of the layout is rather like an attic, with wooden beams supporting the roof. These roof ribs are formed to support the track bases and to provide an approximate contour to the scenery. On them is laid a fine wire mesh, which forms the support for layers of plaster; the final layers are coloured and formed to represent the vegetation and weathered rock, and have trees implanted. Within this scenery "shell" the tracks running in

Above: Trains near approach to Pfaffensprung Tunnels. *Swiss Transport Museum*

Top Right: The Maxon motor mountings and reduction gear drive on locomotives. *M S Cross*

Top Left: Close-up of locomotive coupling. *M S Cross*

Bottom Right: Spirals between the Naxberg and Erstfeld inside the mountain. *M S Cross*

Bottom Left: Typical rolling stock (Ex Liliput) in the ladder sidings. Note overhead power supply rods. *M S Cross*

the tunnels are fully accessible. There are also the spirals which translate the trains from the Naxberg to the approach to Erstfeld station. The lowest level of these is formed into a ladder track so that trains can be taken out of the sequence and replaced by others. Full facilities for minor repair and servicing are to hand, together with relays banks, power supply, lighting fixtures and

"cripple sidings" for stock taken out of service for repair.

The line owes something to Märklin influence, not only for the centre stud-contact system but also for the use of AC power supply. This has been found to be superior to DC in keeping the rails free from dust deposits, and so the transfer to DC for the motors is made in the locomotives themselves. Swiss-made "Maxon" motors are used throughout. These motors differ from the usual type of model railway locomotive motor in that they have the magnet fixed centrally, with the armature wound in the form of a basket rotating around the magnet. The flux return is by means of the motor casing. This system gives far greater efficiency than the standard armature rotating between fixed magnet poles, and it is free from "cogging", or magnetic lock.

The motors should be run at design speed whenever possible, and so the locomotives incorporate a gear cage which matches the optimum locomotive speed to the designed motor speed. Flywheels ensure smooth starting and stopping, and in effect the trains have just two speeds—"stop" and "go". For the purpose of the model this arrangement is ideal; power is supplied at settings between 6v and 12v according to the gradient, and so trains run at a standard speed and progress evenly from one block to another.

The power is supplied from the overhead wires, through the locomotive pantographs. These wires are 0.8mm diameter single-strand copper on the visible parts of the layout; substantial copper rodding is used on the internal sections. The wires are tensioned at about 1 lb per 20ft length, and are laid in zigzag style as on the prototype to give even wear over the bow of the pantographs. The catenaries are faithful reproductions of the originals, and several interesting forms may be seen about the layout.

The track is laid on plywood bases on which cork sheet underlay has been fixed. The track origins are obscure, but the commercial HO-type rails are fixed to sleeper strips by means of small clips every two sleepers. Owing to the use of HO settings, the flangeways and wheels are much overscale, but as the layout is mostly plain line, this discrepancy is not obvious except at the station. What is perhaps a more serious omission is the lack of superelevation on the curves. This is typical of model railways, but in a layout on which curved track abounds, and which otherwise is so faithful to the prototype, superelevation would have given a really authentic touch.

The use of set trains to provide operating interest has brought with it an interesting form of coupling. The commercial couplings fitted to the originally purchased stock have been removed and replaced by a press stud. The two halves of the stud are fitted to wires extending from the respective vehicles, and this enables them to be coupled simply by pressing the two stud halves together, and uncoupled by pulling them apart. When coupled, the vehicles maintain a constant distance from one another, so there is no danger from "buffer locking" and no telescoping when the train stops. The only disadvantage—apart from the use of rather larger studs than necessary—is that vehicles can be fitted only one way round, that is, with the correct relationship of studs to sockets in the couplings.

There is a walkway around the layout which enables the onlooker to view the scene from several angles and levels. This is particularly fascinating near the Wattinger tunnel, where the line runs close to the edge of the layout. Here there is a stone bridge crossing a chasm between two tunnel portals, and one can obtain a natural viewing angle and see the trains and the valley beyond just as if one were standing at the scene. A particularly interesting feature at this point is the provision of a window in the side of the layout through which can be seen the inside of the Wattinger tunnel.

This close examination of the model—and the model is of such excellence that it can accept close inspection—will reveal to the observant visitor a unique feature of Swiss railways. In Continental countries, "driving on the right" is the rule for both roadways and railways. In the model it will be seen that the trains are running on the left, British fashion. In the hall adjoining the layout there is a replica, full-size, of the Crampton locomotive and train from the first Swiss railway between Zurich and Baden. This line was British-built, and Swiss railways have run "on the left" ever since.

From this vantage point the model trains can be followed as they wend their way north and south over the Gotthard. Pride of the line are the Trans-Europe Expresses, the "Gotthardo", (Milan to Basle) the "Ticino", (Milan to Zurich) and the "Roland" (Milan to Bremen). In addition to the TEE's there are some ten expresses daily each way between Lugano and Zurich alone. At Christmas and other holiday times many specials are run for the benefit of the Italian workers who are employed in Switzerland and Central Europe. Swiss passenger cars, in common with most European lines, were painted drab green, but slowly the pattern changed. First came the yellow stripe along the cant rail of first class cars, then the restaurant cars were painted red; now a new orange and white livery has appeared as a probable future standard. Most of the main expresses have a collection of cars from German and Italian railways running as through coaches to various destinations.

Although the passenger service is fairly intensive, it is freight which constitutes the main traffic of the line. Here anything goes, but refrigerator cars, minerals, car transporters and bulk liquids feature more than most other types. The locomotives are deceptive; they look innocuous but in reality are wheeled powerhouses that whisk the heavy trains effortlessly up the gradients at a smart pace. The aged "Crocodiles" are the exception as they both look and are exceptionally powerful machines.

Most of these traffics are featured in the set trains in the yards at Erstfeld. The nature of the model line is such that one can choose many different viewpoints, and look down on the trains or up at them, or see them at eye level both near and far. The scenery is so comprehensive and detailed that the perspective of the trains in their setting is always preserved.

No one has yet established the standards by which model railways should be judged, but when they do so, the presentation of material that appeals to all categories of onlooker will surely loom large among them. That this model railway has operated for thirteen years or more, providing entertainment and instruction for all who visit it, is proof of its quality. And for the Swiss, quality is everything.

Gutland Uzètian Railway

The small town of Uzès lies seven miles from the Pont du Gard, a popular Roman monument in southern France. Standing on a hill, its medieval silhouette can be seen from the winding road lined with plane trees shading the traveller from the summer sun. Here the Romans harnessed the water which supplied the ancient city of Nimes for more than six hundred years via their thirty miles long aqueduct. The Museon di Rodo (the museum of wheels) has been established in Uzès; it contains a large collection of exhibits pertaining to mechanical locomotion, veteran, Edwardian and classic motor cars from 1897 to 1960, bicycles and motor bicycles, prints, posters, clocks and ceramics etc: plus several items of railway interest.

The main railway exhibit consists of scale models, mostly O gauge, a collection of more than 600 pieces apertaining to tinplate railways, mostly Märklin, dating from 1896 to 1937, and an O gauge layout, which is the largest of its kind in France. This model railway is named the Gur-Rug system (Gutland Uzetian Railways—Réseau Uzétien de Gutlande). Traffic is constantly moving on this system, as visitors are always keen to see working exhibits and a layout such as this is an ideal way to promote the hobby. The bilingual title calls for more details of its 50 year old history.

In 1923 William F P Kelly began to build the layout in England. He was a much travelled railway enthusiast, interested both in English and in Continental railways and rolling stock. For this reason his railway was located in an imaginary island somewhere in the Channel, with connecting tunnels to the mainlands of France and Germany. Kelly apparently drafted many intricate track plans. His friends, among them Geoffrey Percy Keen, quickly found the nickname of Gutland for the railway due to its similarity with the digestive system of the higher mammal. It was basically a non-continuous layout, with a terminus station of vast proportions, with six platformed tracks, carriage sidings, shunting yard, and a large engine depot. This station, called Anatomopolis served four tracks, two mainline and two relief, tracks rather like St Pancras in London. Gradients were at a minimum to enable easy operation. During its time in England the Gutland suffered from two or three removals and accordingly went through some alterations of plan.

The Second World War found the Gutland railway in a large garden shed in Hythe, Kent, a most exposed place. However, it did not suffer from any damage by bombing or other kind of military action. Traffic, completely interrupted during these years was resumed after the war.

W F P Kelly's health declined in the late fifties and his death occured after a long illness in 1961. He left all his railway collection to his old friend G P Keen, the late President of the Model Railway Club of Great Britain. It was Keen who presented the entire layout, baseboards, tracks and some rolling stock to the Museon di Rodo. Four metric tonnes of equipment, tidily packed in two large British Railways containers, arrived one day in Uzès. The careful unpacking and re-assembling would have been impossible without the help of David Sinclair of Folkestone, a most skilled modelmaker who, under Keen's guidance, had previously dismantled and packed the layout in England. David Sinclair came to Uzès several times. In fact it was not only a question of re-assembling the original layout but of setting up in a new and unprepared area. The first basic change was to have a continuous layout, ie. a large oval of four tracks with a main through station and the corresponding facilities described above. The late John Mumford, one-time President of the Gauge O Guild and staunch supporter of the Museon, offered many useful suggestions.

The rooms chosen for re-erecting the layout were on the first floor with windows facing south. Uzès has a dry and sunny climate for most of the year, and it seldom freezes, thus eliminating many worries about corrosion; however, it is better to be well above ground level for, when it does rain, it pours. The British timber baseboards have not suffered

Above: Gutland Uzetian Railway. A general view of D'Andoble station from the carriage sidings. *Jean Falaize*

from the change of climate as they were well seasoned. The two rooms proved too small to contain the whole layout, so the main station itself was re-assembled in the larger, and a reinforced concrete gallery was constructed along the front of the building at first floor level to carry the four track mainline to a window leading into the smaller room, and from there back to the west side of the main station.

This enclosed gallery was very strongly built so as to take the weight, not only of the layout but also of the visitors who collect to see the trains. A suburban passing station "Saint Quély" is located in that gallery.

Due to the extensive alteration of the trackwork from the previous Gutland design, the railway's name was changed from Gutland to Gutland Uzetian Railway. The Gur-Rug trackwork consists of one large through station (see sketch) with six platforms (the former terminus) with four continuous tracks, a four track oval mainline 40m (about 130ft) in length, carriage sidings, and engine depot, plus the original Gutland shunting yard. The total length of the track is about 350m (380yds). Scale is 7mm per foot which equals 23mm per metre. Gauge is 0-1¼in which equals 31.75mm. Wheels etc are of coarse scale standard.

Most of the track is laid with brass bullhead rail, with timber sleepers dating from the Twenties. Some, however, is laid with flat bottomed German silver rail (109lb/yd section scale). Traction current is 24 volts DC. Current is supplied to the engines through an outside third rail. The mains current is 220 volts 50 cycles, transformed to 24 volts DC by a rectifier, with an output of 20amps.

There are 6 controllers, which are the large original ones. The layout is divided into sections corresponding with these controllers. The design of the layout is such that practically all points are in the main station area, except for two which are in the suburban station. The present control panel contains a complete interlocking panel controlling the points, and corresponding electrical circuits. The original mechanical interlocked panel will be changed in the near future. Two years ago the points were systematically equipped with electric motors and this programme has now been completed. A new control panel, separate from the baseboards, is being built to house all electrical controls for points and track circuits; it will be connected to the baseboards by a cable, to enable the control panel to be moved for maintenance. The original mechanical interlocking panel, which had suffered from the Hythe sea air during the war, will be kept as a museum piece.

Generally speaking the Museon is too crowded in its present space. For instance, there are 50 motor cars but no room to show them. A new building specially designed for the Museon is planned near the old "Pont des Charrettes" railway station, 2km from the centre of Uzès. It is hoped to re-erect the Gur-Rug on the first floor of this future building. This would not change the basic design of the railway but there will be more room for mainline working. These extended mainlines will allow for concealed tunnels, to store trains so as not to have the visible tracks choc a bloc with trains. The new location of the Gur-Rug will also allow for the introduction of proper scenery, an item not evident on the present layout. The idea being to have a series of "windows" in sections of the main lines to show some

Top: **Nord Railway: A 4-4-2 de Glehn Atlantic with 6-wheel tender. This model was originally built by Munier for the K Lines of G.P. Keen and rebuilt for use on Gur-Rug with Bonds motor.** *Jean Falaize*

Centre: **Paris Orleans Railway: A Forquenot type 2-4-2 of 1880. Model originally built by Jules Baveret, rebuilt for use on Gur-Rug. (Bonds motor).** *Jean Falaize*

Bottom: **PLM Railway: 0-6-2 mixed traffic locomotive of the 3001-3140 class built in 1883. The model shows this type after rebuilding with air brake cylinders on top of the firebox and a large cab. Built for Gur-Rug, partly in England and in France. (Bonds motor).** *Jean Falaize*

Overleaf: **The motive power of Gur-Rug ranged round the turntable at Gare D'Andoble.** *Rene Delon*

Top Left: A free-lance de Glehn small Atlantic. Model originally built by W.F.P. Kelly for his Gutland Railway. Converted and altered by John Mumford for his RENFE system. Reconverted for use on Gur-Rug. *Jean Falaize*

Centre: Paris Orleans Railway. A 1771-1800 class 4-6-0 of 1901. These locomotives were built in USA by Baldwin. This model is built on a Bonds chassis and is fitted with a Hungarian State Railways type bogie tender. *Jean Falaize*

Below: Ouest Railway 2-6-2T 3801-3850 class of 1908. This model came from the Delarue-Nouvelliere collection and has been rebuilt for use on Gur-Rug with Fournereau Motor. *Jean Falaize*

typical aspects of railway practice.

Gur-Rug rolling stock provides examples of trains of various types and periods to give an indication of railway history based on railways of the south of France, like PLM, PO and MIDI. However, no French railway is frowned upon, and those of other countries will not be excluded. There is also no barrier against freelance rolling stock.

The accompanying list of 39 engines at present in service on the Gur-Rug shows their variety; steam, electric, diesel,

French, Swiss, Hungarian, and freelance. The same applies to coaches and wagons. The total number of these is over 100. Gur-Rug passenger trains have to show main line international traffic, suburban traffic and some national traffic. At present these consist of one train of auto-couchettes, two "rapides", (one with a Pullman coach) one international express, a local train, a suburban train, a mail train, a Bugatti autorail, and the necessary saloons for offical use. Goods rolling stock and freight trains

have to deal with local traffic, especially bauxite and international traffic. This means a large variety of rolling stock from the small 10tons to the 50tonnes bauxite wagons, and the special vehicles for carrying heavy loads, trailers, containers for fruit, meat, beer, wine etc: The Gur-Rug has the usual equipment for its own maintenance and operation: an 85tonnes steam crane with a breakdown train, various works wagons, coal wagons, oil wagons, also a special wagon to lay and remove the small girder bridge.

Top Left: Ouest Railway. A 939-998 class 4-4-0 of 1899 built for Gur-Rug. *Jean Falaize*

Centre : A free-lance De Glen 4-6-0 of 1908 vintage built by W.F.P. Kelly for the Gutland Railway. *Jean Falaize*

Below Centre : Paris Orleans Railway 5300 Class 2-8-2T, built between 1911/1923 for mixed traffic in hilly country. Model started by John Mumford for his RENFE layout and completed to Gur-Rug specifications. (Bonds Motor). *Jean Falaize*

Bottom : SNCF 4-8-4, A-1 Class. A rebuild of the Etat Mountain Engine by A. Chapelon. Model rebuilt from a Märklin Etat Mountain Locomotive. (Fournereau Motor.) *Jean Falaize*

All the above means a lot of work for those in charge of the Gur-Rug, and they are as variegated in occupation as its rolling stock. A retired Admiral is head of Mechanical Engineering. An active SNCF officer is in charge of the permanent way. Most of the rolling stock is being built or adapted and maintained in the Gur-Rug shops, but like so many other worthwhile projects, others who do not live locally help out by model building in many varying forms. The Museon di Rodo has become a national institution.

Editions Saincassette: Ste Colline-des-Champs

![SAINTE COLLINE-DES-CHAMPS sign]

SAINTE COLLINE-DES-CHAMPS

A historical French layout in gauge O
by Dennis Allenden

Top left: Since the major purpose of Ste Colline is to form a display background for locomotives, no apologies are made for presenting one of its star performers. This is the front end of French State Railways' No 2616, "St Jean d'Angely," highlighting her unusual Bonnefond valve gear. The 2-4-2 long-boiler express engine was predominant in France between 1875 and 1895, being used in large numbers by Etat, PLM, and Paris-Orleans. This Etat series (2602-2620) was just about the ultimate technical development of the type. 2616 herself was built in 1893 by Cail & Cie of Denain. The livery is the pre 1909 black, relieved only by a yellow border to the buffer beam. The leading wheels are actually spoked in the normal manner; the disc facing is of thin sheet metal, welded to the tyre as a precaution against the tyre breakages which were then one of the most prevalent breakdowns. It will be noted that the valve gear has separate inlet and exhaust valves, which could be independently controlled; the eccentric on the return crank was not technically essential, and arose simply out of standardisation policies.

This closeup brings out one of the main attractions of 7mm scale for the person who likes to build; the sheer amount of detail that can be accommodated without departing from scale.

Left: The railway scene in rural France at the turn of the century is epitomised by this old gravure postcard showing the Ste-Colline to Chancay local trundling out of town alongside the country road. Town marker has had to be located wrong side of the road because the proximity of road and rail is such that it would have fouled the loading gauge if located on the normal side!

Below: Metre gauge 0-6-2T No 3, built by Societe Alsacienne in 1879, and on loan from its home Hermes-Beaumont line, chuffs down the Rue d'Amboise with a train of quarry wagons. Picture catches her passing the 14th century gendarmerie, which advertises its location with a discreet tricouleur. This building, fully at home in Sainte Colline, was transported stone by ancient stone from the corner of the Rue St Lazare in Avallon. (Styrene has revolutionised the building business!) Beside the police station is the office of the metre gauge railway, a tarty building of execrable flamboyance that could have come from any small town in southern Georgia (USA, not USSR). It actually came from Etainhus St Romain in Normandy. Further yet, the eclectic gift shop building is at least in part, Rouennais. On the standard gauge line, awaiting clearance into Ste Colline-Gare is a visiting engine—Este's Flaman boilered Crampton No 604, official world speed record holder (144 km/hr in 1889/90). Various vapid socialisings going on here and there—No 3's fireman waves to his girl friend, officious cop takes suspect vagrant to police station for cheating on ticket, and some protester has been busy on the stonework.

Picture overleaf: A trio of early compounds on shed. In the foreground, a recognisable Webb LNWR "Compound" class with unfamiliar overtones. This is No 500 of the Chemin de Fer de L'Ouest, built by Sharp, Stewart in 1884. No 500 is historic in that (discounting one or two very provisional conversions) she was the first compound to run on a major French railway. Those familiar with the LNWR breed will enjoy picking out the detail differences, and debating whether or not they improve the aspect of a machine which, however controversial in service, was aesthetically first class. At the 1909 date, 500 had only a few months to live—the Etat, who took over the Ouest that year, scrapped her. Beyond, in Etat post 1909 olive, is Baldwin built 4-4-0 No 220-804, a Vauclain compound with seven foot drivers. Etat bought eleven machines in 1909, 5 compounds and six simples, and they were the biggest 4-4-0's ever to run in France. Note the superposed HP and LP cylinders of the Vauclain configuration. In the background is squat powerful looking Est 0-6-0 No 1002, a two cylinder compound built at their Epernay works in 1893. In view of the visibility under the high pitched boiler of 1002, the inside cylinders and valve gear have been reproduced in the model. The Est livery of black, lined liberally in red, and with the boiler bands polished, was quiet and dignified.

Sainte Colline-des-Champs is a perfect example of the adage that the model railway hobby can be anything you want it to be. The author's interest is building historical model locomotives, particularly those of unusual types. Not being content to see such models impotent in glass cases, some sort of authentic setting was necessary, and there would have to be some space to run them. The layout had to be one in which twenty five engines and one flat truck was credible. Out of these criteria came the bare bones of the project; the scale would be 7mm, O gauge, the ideal builder's scale; the fact that the models would be of older engines would mean that space would be less of a problem than with a modern-day layout. Virtually everything would have to be built from scratch (no complaints about that), but it did mean that one would want to centralise the action into a limited space just to make the whole thing capable of realisation. The high engine-to-car ratio virtually dictated that the nucleus of the system be an engine shed or a works. And one's personal quirks specified that the loca-

tion had to be France. (Is there somewhere else?)

Out of all this came Sainte-Colline, an end-to-end layout that begins and ends in the middle. The scenic part, encompassing depot, industry, urban scene, and what-have-you, occupies the twelve-by-four foot middle of a "U" whose verticals are shelf sections of mixed-gauge track, unscenic'd, for running and storage. The total end to end run is about sixty feet.

Southwest of Paris, beyond the race-track flatlands of wheat and beet, beyond les Aubrais' sprawling junction for Orléans, the Loire flows unhurried to the ocean. France's greatest river gathers its tributaries across all a green and silver landscape studded with grey towns old when time was young. Here, in the heart of la Douce France, the wine and the peerless light and the French tongue flow clean and clear as nowhere else. On the river are the big towns—Blois, Tours, Angers. Back from the river, along the sylvan tributaries, are the exquisite little towns—Azay, Chenonceaux, Villandry . . . and Sainte Colline-des-Champs. This latter, belying its name, sits mediaevally

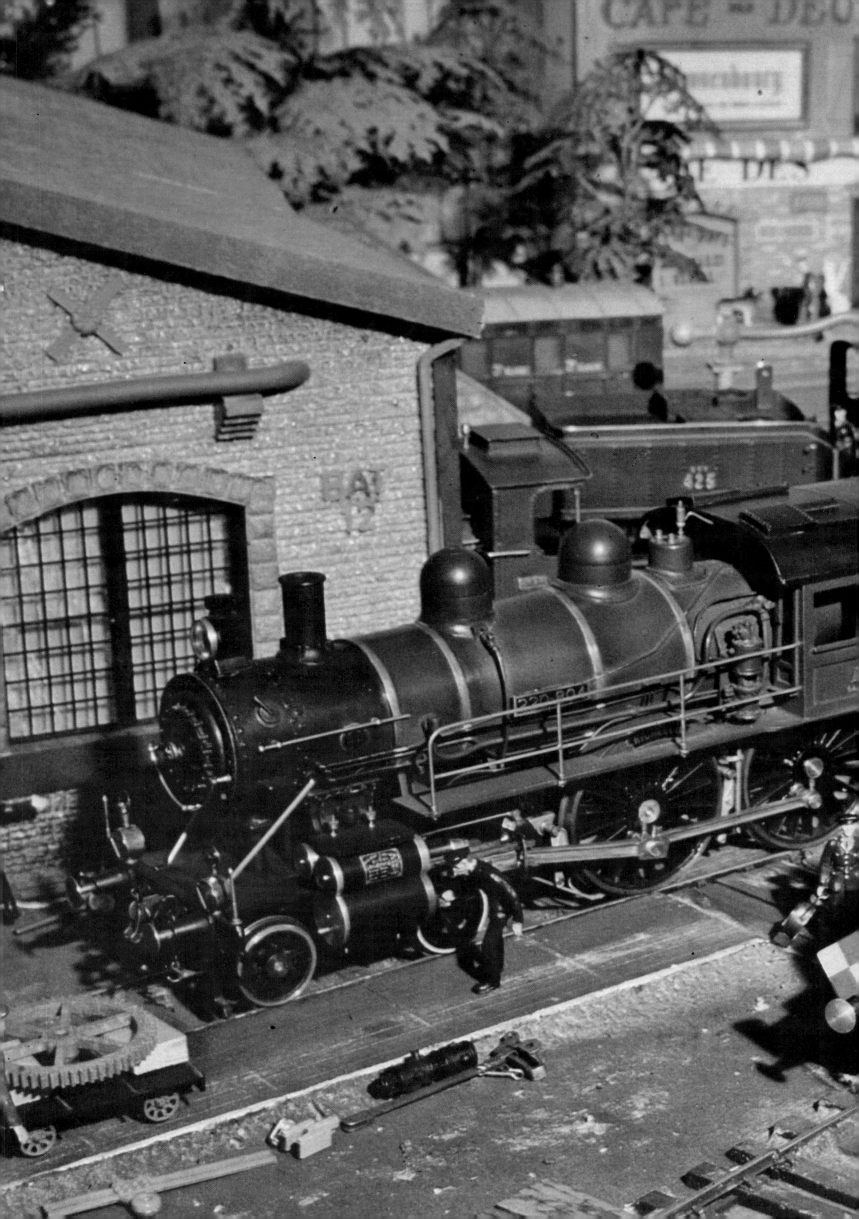

fortified atop a low hill along the Brenne; few remnants of its old walls still exist. Its buildings, too, are mostly old, but there have lately been tasteless encroachments of art-nouveau cast-iron and brash brick. As long as anyone can remember the town's staple business has been wine—the clear deceptively-potent draught named for nearby Vouvray. Like all such towns, Ste Colline advertises itself, in this year of 1909 with gravure postcards which, bearing a five centime stamp, affixed (if you please) on the front, carry the townlet's image the length and breadth of France. Rarely will such cards depict the sylvan beauty of the scene (which doesn't come across in gravure) or the architectural gems (which would). France is on the move—its post cards show the iron bridge—the cement works—the soap factory—or the railway . . .

The railway. Down the Loire valley two great railways jostle frequent shoulders on their separate, but interwined, ways to Bordeaux. One of their spatial coincidences is at Ste. Colline, where the State railways, which owns the depot just outside the old city walls, plays occasional host to motive power from the Paris-Orléans. On shed, engines of the State line can display any of three liveries, for the sober black of the old Etat, relieved by brasswork that sparkles as on no other line on earth, has not yet been completely superseded by the yellow-lined olive green of the Etat-Ouest fusion; while Ouest engines may still show up in their lighter green. As for the P-O, it brings in a livery of grey and black,

sometimes with the whole boiler cladded in polished brass! And this is not all the richness of Ste Colline—the Paris Great Outer Belt line grazes the town, bringing in, from time to time, visting power from the Nord, the Est, the PLM, while the Société Mécanique dumps an occasional real foreigner in the yards for road trials before delivery to Brussels or Cairo or Barranquilla.

If you follow the briquette smoke that rises dark and straight and lazy of a pearly-grey morning, you'll find such a mixture of motive power in the depot yards. Nearly all engines will have short wheelbases, 2-4-0 or 2-4-2 or 0-6-0; they'll have tiny four wheeled tenders, and

the coaches they haul will also be compact four wheelers. And they'll sparkle with an impeccable cleanliness. There'll be variety in the technical sense, too. This is a time of great innovation; some lines are experimenting feverishly with the new compounds, purchased both in France and abroad; others are experimenting equally feverishly to prove that compounds can be bettered without compounding. So there's a plethora of fancy valve gears, way-out boilers, rudimentary superheaters, and all the other gadgetry so dear to the meticulous Gallic mind. To see the on-shed line up at Ste Colline is to see a microcosm of one of the most interesting periods in the annals

of French motive power.

The narrow gauge mania is going full blast in France; every départment has at least one metre gauge local line, usually deficitory and completely dependent on its state guarantee for funds. By roadside ways, by paths through secret greenwood, by dual-gauge incursion through main line tunnels, the little tank engines gather up the peasants and the wine and the cabbages and funnel them to main line stations and country markets. And where the little trains and the big trains meet up, there's a Café des Deux Gares, thriving on the fact that the timetables *never* coincide—there's always a three hour wait! Sainte Colline is served in this respect by the Chemins de Fer Départementaux d'Indre-et-Loire, which runs cheekily down the middle of the Rue d'Amboise. Right now it's having motive power troubles, and has borrowed an 1879 0-6-2T from the Hermés-Beaumont.

A major quarrying enterprise operates in the district, and it too owns considerable metre gauge industrial trackage over which little quarry tubs are jostled by a sparkling blue 0-4-0WT from the Borsig stable. Junctions have recently been made between the two narrow gauge lines, and they've established a tiny joint depot facing the mainline one. Hard by is a ballast plant, which supplies the Etat via a loading track that runs under the crusher house. So the density of ballast and quarry wagons around Ste Colline approaches that of wine wagons.

Ste Colline isn't finished. Won't ever be. But it's reached the state of being complete. What started out as engines, to be surrounded by a corner of rural France, has become a corner of rural France that happens to contain an engine shed. Beyond the old buildings there's not wine and wheat and beet, but corn and tobacco . . . Yet the illusion remains.

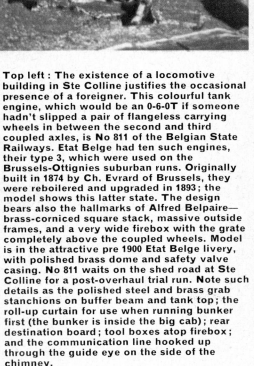

Top left: The existence of a locomotive building in Ste Colline justifies the occasional presence of a foreigner. This colourful tank engine, which would be an 0-6-0T if someone hadn't slipped a pair of flangeless carrying wheels in between the second and third coupled axles, is No 811 of the Belgian State Railways. Etat Belge had ten such engines, their type 3, which were used on the Brussels-Ottignies suburban runs. Originally built in 1874 by Ch. Evrard of Brussels, they were reboilered and upgraded in 1893; the model shows this latter state. The design bears also the hallmarks of Alfred Belpaire—brass-corniced square stack, massive outside frames, and a very wide firebox with the grate completely above the coupled wheels. Model is in the attractive pre 1900 Etat Belge livery, with polished brass dome and safety valve casing. No 811 waits on the shed road at Ste Colline for a post-overhaul trial run. Note such details as the polished steel and brass grab stanchions on buffer beam and tank top; the roll-up curtain for use when running bunker first (the bunker is inside the big cab); rear destination board; tool boxes atop firebox; and the communication line hooked up through the guide eye on the side of the chimney.

Left: Quaint 2-4-0T No 103 of the Western Railway scurries out of Ste Colline with the local for Chancay-en-Touraine. This little engine was the standard Ouest suburban tank for over thirty years. No 103 herself was built in 1882, but the design has been virtually unchanged since 1855. The leading coach, a Ouest third with brake cabin, is also of 1855 vintage, and is followed by a first-saloon. The chef de train makes his nonchalent way along the outside of the train collecting tickets. The train is running alongside the Rue d'Amboise, which marks the line of the old city wall—the gate tower is an intriguing remnant. The Cafe des Deux Gares and the adjoining wine merchant's were stolen virtually as is except for names from the Place d'Armes in Epernay. The year being 1909, Alsace-Lorraine is under German occupation, and we're not too sure about the validity of the Kronenbourg sign! Further away is the cast-iron facade of the Societe Mecanique de l'Indre, an important locomotive builder, stolen from the Place de la Gare in Vierzon to justify the occasional appearance of a foreign locomotive! On shed is a sprinkling of motive power including Est 1002, Est 604 and Etat 2616. Riding the boarded turntable is Webb compound No 500 of the Ouest, Manchester built in 1884.

Top: Ste Colline is a town preoccupied to the point of obsession with wine. A number of major wine merchants are established here; one of them Societe Angevine, does a thriving business exporting the local Vouvray south in return for the rough red of Languedoc. Here Etat 0-6-0 No 030-863 manoeuvres a Ouest flat car under the elevated track at the ballast plant to be offloaded by the metre gauge crane, hauled into position by narrow gauge 0-6-2T No 3. The wine train from which the flat car has been cut stands alongside on the main line. The operation is under supervision from a vantage point on the quarry track, while the consignee stands around to ensure the goods aren't over agitated. Third-Empire hoarding offers no-down-payment credit. The distinctive crane truck was virtually a standard for the French narrow gauge lines. Its lattice sides are fully fabricated from strip metal, the jib rotates on a correct angle roller race, and all items are prototypically functional. Some of the tank cars are a little anachronistic—this is because one of the minor themes of Ste Colline is a historical series depicting the development of wine transportation. Much better than coal!

Above: This picture serves two purposes. It illustrates a very handsome locomotive, and it bears witness to the fact that when one sets out to build a model railway in the larger sense of the term, there is an indefinable point at which the whole thing acquires a life, an entity, of its own. And at the early stage pictured here, Ste Colline does not have it! In spite of fairly complete detailing of the foreground and the placing of a few figures, the impression conveyed is the bare desolate one of a prime factory site in the Essex marshes. Many model railways, it is felt, get prematurely abandoned because the imagination is unable to substitute for the actuality in this critical phase.

The 0-6-0 mixed traffic engine, in the olive green of the post 1909 Ouest-Etat fusion, actually started out at No 2247 of the Ouest built by Societe des Batignolles in 1891. The Ouest had built many, many 0-6-0's to the same dimensions prior to 2247, and ugly brutes they were—big flared stacks, mustard pot domes, massive outside steam pipes, cumbersome link motion, and a whole heap of that miscellaneous gadgetry hung all over the boiler. 2247 and her sisters were the result of a Ouest clean-up programme following the appearance of a number of British engines at the Paris exposition of 1889. Most of these elegant engines lived long enough to become SNCF class 030-D, and were to be seen at sheds in Normandy and Brittany as late as 1952. *All photographs by the author*

LOCOMOTIVES: PROTOTYPE AND MODEL

Facing page: Another scene from Anthony Murray's Dean Bridge layout, with Highland and North British 0-6-0 goods engines.
B Monaghan

ADAMS RADIAL TANKS OF THE SOUTHERN RAILWAY (LSWR)

William Adams was appointed as Locomotive Superintendent of the Southern Railway from the Great Eastern Railway, where his short term of office had not been particularly conspicuous with success, although his previous office with the North London line had seen the introduction of a series of very efficient tank locomotives. Soon after he started his new position at Nine Elms, he designed a 4-4-2T loco, twelve of which were built by Beyer Peacock & Co in 1882. These were a natural development of a 4-6-0 design he had instigated a few years previously. Within three years a total of 71 of the radial tank locos were built—all by outside contractors—the original 12 by Beyer Peacock; 28 by Robert Stephenson's; 11 by Nielson's and 20 by Dubs.

The locos were designed for local suburban services, and they continued in this role for a number of years, first in the London area, and then when ousted by more powerful locos and the beginnings of electrification they saw service on the branch lines in the West Country. They had replaced the Beattie 2-4-0 locos which were not powerful enough to pull the suburban trains and which were also becoming time expired. The trains at that time were mainly made up of a rake of six 6-wheel coaches, which in peak periods and for the special workmans trains were made up into two sets of six-coach rakes.

The first locos in the class, sometimes known as the 415 class, had a very limited water supply, the tanks being at the rear of the bunker, and also in a well tank. Later examples had the water capacity increased from 1,000 gallons to 1,200 gallons by adding a small tank over the splashers of the rear driving wheels, even

so the side tanks were ridiculously short in comparison with other tank locos. In later versions the diameter of the radial truck or pony truck was increased from 3ft to 3ft 6in, with what effect is not really known.

The only troubles with these locos proved to be the adhesion weight, for far too much was carried on the bogie and radial wheels, and not enough on the coupled wheels. Adams realised this and his next design for the LSWR was for an 0-4-4T which were equally as powerful, although considerably smaller in overall dimensions.

After Adams had retired, the locos had some modifications, resulting in an increased boiler pressure, and the substitution of the Adams stove pipe chimneys for the Drummond type on nearly all the locos of the class. The locos were fitted with a single slide motion.

In 1918 four of the locos were loaned to the Highland Railway, where they were employed on some lines with severe gradients and very sharp radius curves which seemed to suit the locos ideally. Two were returned a year later, but two were kept for three years.

Loco No 488 had a very chequered career, for it was built in 1884 and naturally entered service in the livery of the LSWR. It was sold to the War Department in 1917, and they in turn sold it to the Kent & East Sussex Railway in 1919. It was sold to the Southern Railway in 1946 to assist two remaining members of the class which were working the Axminster to Lyme Regis branch, for it was

found that despite several trials with other locos, the old time expired Adams Radials were the only type of loco that was really suited to this line with its heavy gradients and sharp curves. It survived the Nationalisation and wore British Rail livery. It was finally withdrawn in 1961 when it was purchased by the Bluebell Railway Company for preservation and can still be seen on that company's line from Sheffield Park to Horsted Keynes.

The rest of the class were either withdrawn or sold in the early 1920s, by which time they had finished their service in the London area and had been relegated to the branches of the Southern's Western Section, some of the locos having being fitted with apparatus enabling them to work the push-pull trains.

DATA

Cylinders (2):	17½in by 24in
Dia of coupled wheels:	5ft 7in
Dia of bogie and pony wheels:	3ft
	(some 3ft 6in for pony)
Boiler pressure:	160lbs
Overall length (over buffers):	38ft 8½in
Weight in working order:	54ton 2cwt.

Models

It is surprising that no commercial models of this class of loco were made when it was in active service, the Hornby Railways O gauge 4-4-2T being more of a replica of other classes. It is known that some were built by Mills Brothers for special order in the 1920s.

In 4mm scale there is a cast white metal kit manufactured by N & K Keyser of Banbury, which has been quite popular with Southern Railway enthusiasts.

Below: A 4mm Adams tank, built from a K's Kit.

Left: In final BR livery, Adams tank No 30583 rests between turns on the Lyme Regis branch at Axminster.

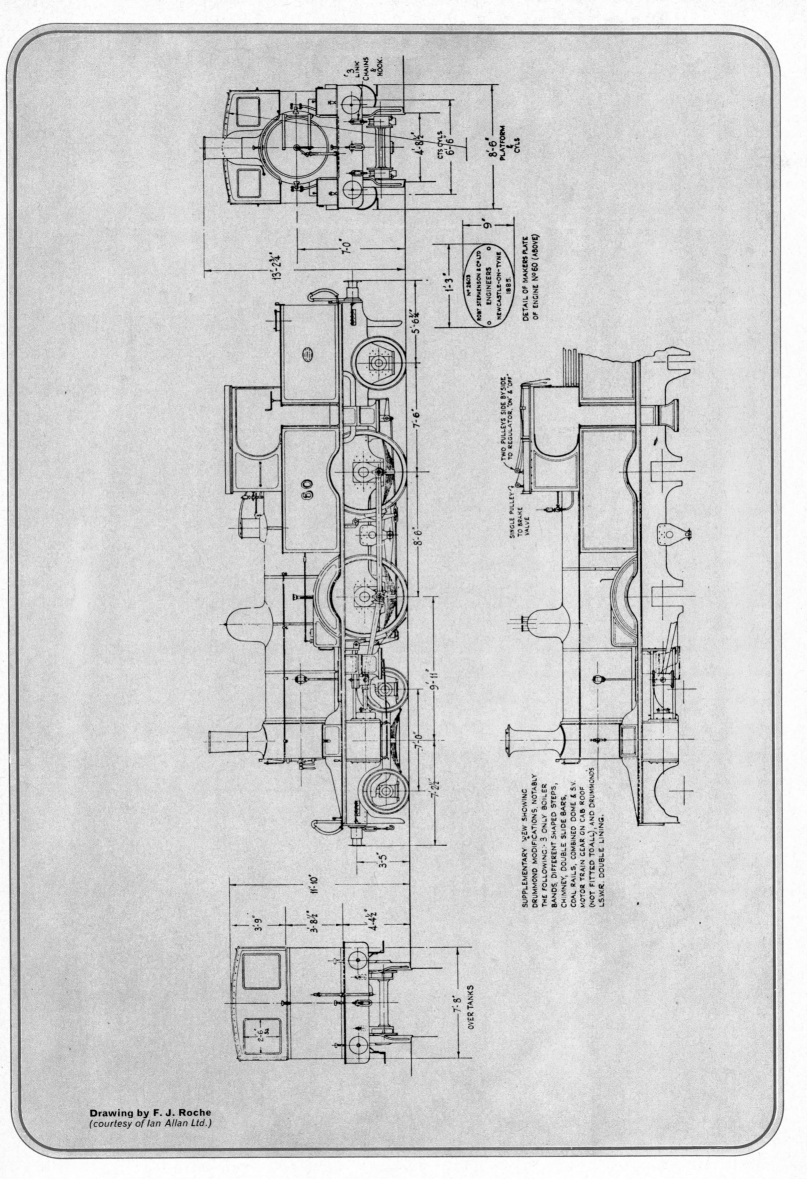

'3 LINK CHAINS & HOOK.

4'-8½"

CTS CYLS 6'-6"

8'-6" PLATFORM & CYLS

13'-2¾"

7'-0"

9'

1'-3"

N° 2603
ROBT STEPHENSON & C° LTD
ENGINEERS
NEWCASTLE-ON-TYNE
1885.

DETAIL OF MAKERS PLATE OF ENGINE N° 60 (ABOVE)

5'-6¼"

60

7'-6"

8'-6"

9'-11"

7'-0"

7'-2¼"

3'-5"

TWO PULLEYS SIDE BYSIDE, TO REGULATOR, 'ON' & 'OFF'

SINGLE PULLEY?, TO BRAKE VALVE

SUPPLEMENTARY VIEW SHOWING DRUMMOND MODIFICATIONS, NOTABLY THE FOLLOWING:- 3 ONLY BOILER BANDS, DIFFERENT SHAPED STEPS, CHIMNEY, DOUBLE SLIDE BARS, COAL RAILS, COMBINED DOME & S.V. MOTOR TRAIN GEAR ON CAB ROOF (NOT FITTED TO ALL) AND DRUMMONDS L.S.W.R. DOUBLE LINING.

3'-9"

3'-8½"

4'-4½"

11'-10"

7'-8" OVER TANKS

2'-6 3∙4

Drawing by F. J. Roche
(courtesy of Ian Allan Ltd.)

The GWR
2301 Class 0-6-0

The most numerous of all locomotive wheel arrangements during the late Victorian and Edwardian eras was the 0-6-0; engines of this type could be found on almost every system hauling most classes of traffic, from trundling local freights to excursion trains with express headlamps. The Great Western Railway was a user of 0-6-0s in considerable numbers, but probably the best known and most long lived was the 2301 class or "Dean Goods" as it was popularly described. The engines were introduced in 1883 and built solidly year by year until 1899 with a total of almost six hundred, their numbers running from 2301 to 2580. The last of the class to be withdrawn was No 2538, in May 1957, and No 2516 is now preserved at Swindon Museum.

The "Dean Goods" could be found at work in all corners of its home system though latterly few were allocated in the South West or in the hilly Newport Division of South Wales. Central Wales, Worcester and Bristol Divisions usually had more "Deans" than most but few GWR sheds were without one as their very simplicity and reliability made them popular wherever they went. After the last War the Central Wales Division cared for most of the class but 1952 saw

the coming of the modern lightweight 2-6-0 which hastened their relegation to branches with special weight restrictions and their general demise.

Of all British locomotive classes the "Deans" went to war more than most: both in the First and Second World Wars engines were sent overseas in the care

of the Railway Operating Department of the Royal Engineers. In May 1917 sixty two engines were taken over and were used in France and Greece: in 1939 a further hundred were requisitioned followed by another eight in 1940. Few ever returned from their last period of active service.

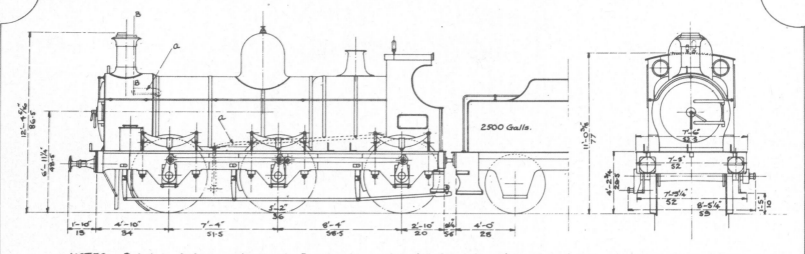

NOTES. Details marked "a" on right side only. Reverse rod passes behind firebox clothing plates. Superheated engines have chimneys positioned as shown: saturated engines have chimneys centred on B–B. Brake rigging is outside wheels. Dimensions in feet (full size), and in millimetres, to nearest half m'metre for Gauge "O". Wheel treads and flanges are drawn to scale: allowances must be made for out-of-scale wheels. Spare lamp irons on left side only.

Some technical details of the 2301 class are as follows:—

Cylinders   Dia 17in Stroke 24in
Boiler   Barrel 10ft 3in
      Outside Dia 4ft 3in
Wheels   Coupled 5ft 0in
Wheelbase 7ft 3in + 8ft 3in total 15ft 6in
Tractive Effort   13,313lb

The standard cast iron chimney which in later years was so familiar began to be fitted from 1919 onwards, and ATC apparatus was carried by a surprisingly large number. A few, six in number, were fitted with tenders with staff exchanging apparatus for the Taunton area.

There was one unusual development—the conversion by Churchward between 1907 and 1910 of 20 engines to 2-6-2 tanks for use in the Birmingham area. Technically these engines were "rebuilds" but in fact, for all practical purposes a new class was built.

The above information can be found (as can information on all classes of GWR locomotives) in that excellent publication "Locomotives of the G.W.R." published by the Railway Correspondence and Travel Society.

Models

Surprising as it may seem with a locomotive so well known and popular, commercial models are rare, though K's have produced an excellent kit in 4mm scale.

Above left: GWR 'Dean' Goods No 2516 at Swindon. This locomotive is now preserved in the Swindon Railway Museum.

Below: GWR 0-6-0 Dean Goods No 2463 in 7 mm scale from the Blizzard Barnes Collection.
Courtesy Bristol Museum

GWR 4·2·2
"Achilles Class"

The 3001, earlier known as the 3031, or "Achilles" class of loco was designed by William Dean in 1890 and were 2-2-2 locos. The first batch were built as "convertibles" so that they could easily be changed from the broad gauge then operating to the now standard gauge which was coming into being. The locos were double framed, so it was not difficult to have the driving wheels outside the frames and then to modify them to the inside position at the time of the conversion in 1892. The locos had a single driving wheel of 7ft 8in diameter and a wheelbase of 18ft 6in, the leading and trailing wheels having underslung springs —that is below the axle boxes.

These locomotives were not particularly steady on the track, even at the speeds of that time, for the long boiler and the uneven weight distribution, particularly at the front end, gave them a fore and aft "pitching" motion which is believed to have been the reason for several derailments, culminating in one right in the middle of Box tunnel, fortunately without fatality. It had been known that up to this time William Dean had not favoured a bogie arrangement, but now obviously something had to be done, thus the first batch of locos were modified to a 4-2-2 wheel arrangnement by the fitting of a front bogie, the frames extended at the front, and the cylinders reduced in diameter by an inch. This all helped to give a better weight distribution and from then onwards the locos became steady riders.

The 30 locomotives that had been converted were distinguished from the rest of the class as they kept the deeper downward sweep of the frames for the trailing wheel spring hangers. The remainder of the class (a further 50 locos) were built for the standard gauge and as 4-2-2s from their inception. There were many rebuilds of these locos for the boilers were changed for Belpaire domeless types, and when C J Churchward succeeded William Dean he made many other changes with both the boilers and the shape and height of the chimneys. Many other alterations were made for such items as the positioning of pipes, and sundry items.

The locomotives were all named, although there is no pattern or theme in the names selected, but many were perpetuated in later classes of locos. The locos became famous and according to reports they looked very smart with gleaming brass and copper parts, the main part of the loco being painted GWR green with Indian red underframes, and orange-black-orange lining. They were originally built for the express trains of the period between London to the West Country, but it was not long before the trains became heavier and a more powerful locomotive was required, and they were replaced on this job by larger 4-4-0 types then being constructed. The class then worked the secondary trains from about 1906, and performed some useful work on the Birmingham line, as well as working some main line relief trains.

As larger and more powerful locomotives became available, so the class was made redundant, thus they had a relatively short life, the last two being scrapped in 1915.

A tender holding 3,000 gallons of water and comparable to the size of the locomotivie was fitted, which ran on six spoked wheels, it being distinguished by its low sides.

Our drawing shows No 3009 *Flying Dutchman*, but it should be noted that there were many detail differences in the class and it has been said that no two locomotives were exactly the same. This may be regarded as an overstatement, but nevertheless there were many variations.

DATA

Two cylinders:	19in by 24in
Diameter of driving wheel:	7ft 8½in
Diameter of leading wheels:	4ft 1in
Diameter of trailing wheel:	4ft 7in
Boiler pressure:	180lb per sq in
Tractive effort:	12,738lb
Weight of loco and tender in working order:	81ton 10cwt

Models

During the early years of model railways many models were made to a 4-2-2 wheel arrangement, but by the beginning of the First World War, most had been re-made to give a passable resemblance to the LNWR and Midland Railway designs, and it seems the GWR 4-2-2s were omitted, probably because of their short working life.

A few gauge O models did appear in the early 1920s produced in tinplate but were not accurate and probably emanated from a foreign source.

In 1971, Tri-ang railways produced a 4mm scale model having a plastic injection moulded body and fitted with the XT60 motor developed for the smaller TT gauge.

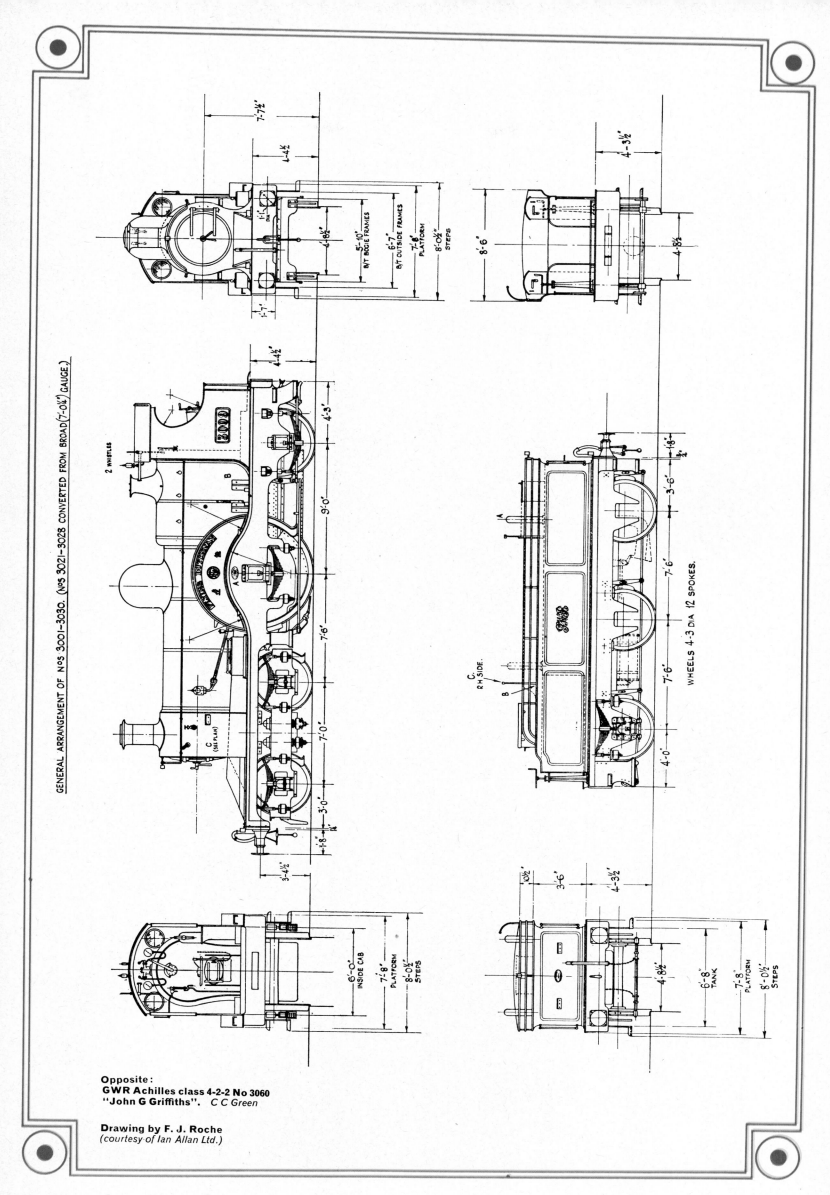

GENERAL ARRANGEMENT OF Nos 3001-3030. (Nos 3021-3028 CONVERTED FROM BROAD (7'-0¼") GAUGE.)

2 WHISTLES

B/T BOGIE FRAMES 5'-10"
B/T OUTSIDE FRAMES 6'-7"
PLATFORM 7'-8"
STEPS 8'-0½"

WHEELS 4'-3 DIA 12 SPOKES.

6'-0" INSIDE CAB
7'-8" PLATFORM
8'-0½" STEPS

6'-8" TANK
7'-8" PLATFORM
8'-0½" STEPS

Opposite:
GWR Achilles class 4-2-2 No 3060
"John G Griffiths".   *C C Green*

Drawing by F. J. Roche
(courtesy of Ian Allan Ltd.)

The history of the LNER class J69 0-6-0T goes back to the year 1890 of the old Great Eastern Railway, for it was in that year that James Holden introduced his class R24 tank locomotives for passenger and shunting work. These new locomotives were in fact a development and modification of the earlier T18 class which were first built in 1886, later to become LNER class J66. In the period from 1890 to 1901 a total of 140 of the class R24 were built. However, by 1904 there was a need for further 0-6-0Ts for passenger work as the early commuter services built up and the coaches became longer to carry more passengers so the need for a slightly more powerful loco became apparent. Twenty similar locomotives were produced but having higher boiler pressures and larger tanks, these were classed as S56.

Meanwhile, between 1902 and 1921, 95 of the earlier class R24 locomotives were rebuilt with new boilers, a larger grate area and firebox, increased boiler pressure and tank capacity. These became known as the class R24 rebuilds.

At the time of the Grouping of the Railway companies the 275 locomotives of these classes became LNER class J69. However, from 1938 onwards many of the locomotives received different boilers, some having a lower boiler pressure which put them into LNER class J67. Later again, in 1946 several of the class J67 were given boilers capable of a higher pressure thus placing them in class J69. This all makes for confusion, especially with the LNER re-numbering scheme which took place. A detailed reference to the whole situation can be found in the Railway Correspondence and Travel Society publication "Locomotives of the LNER. Part 8A".

There were differences in the original class R24 locomotives, for those intended for passenger working were fitted with Westinghouse brakes, screw reversing gear and ten-spoke cast wheels with balance weights. The locos intended for shunting work had hand brakes (later steam), a lever reverse and fifteen-spoke cast iron wheels without balance weights. Some of the class were also fitted with condensing gear and distinguished by the square box fitted on top of each side tank. There were also some detail differences between various members of the class.

The locomotives worked the suburban services from Liverpool Street station and in spite of their small diameter driving wheels (4ft), they attained some fast running between stations. Some observers of those days claiming they reached 55-60mph, but it is thought that these figures were a little optimistic and the sight of the small wheels and coupling rods in fast motion giving a greater impression of speed than was actually being attained. However, there is proof that they could reach 45mph quite easily on certain sections of the old Great Eastern system. In latter LNER days the class could be found in many widely scattered parts of the system, and as far away from the old GER as Scotland. They were employed as carriage siding pilots during the latter part of their life. The first was withdrawn in 1937, but a great many survived and were taken into service by British Railways.

To list all the various modifications is beyond the scope of this article, but our drawing shows the loco in the original GER form. The LNER modified the cab roof which was raised by 6in, it removed

class J69

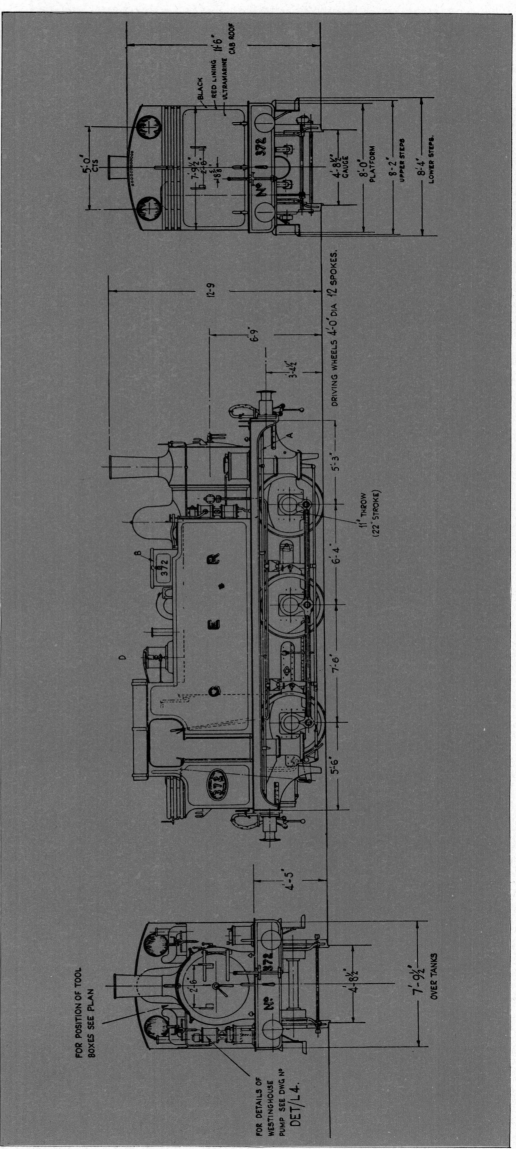

the toolboxes, shown at "B" on the drawing, and an alteration to the positioning of the pipe under the footplate. In addition a variety of chimneys have been fitted to the class.

DATA

Diameter of driving wheels:	4ft
Cylinders:	16½in by 22in
Boiler pressure:	180lb per sq/in
Coal capacity:	2½ton
Water capacity:	1,200gall
Tractive effort:	19,090lb
Weight in working order:	42ton 9cwt (average)

Models

Several of the more "toylike" models of 0-6-0 and 0-4-0 tank locomotives were painted in GER blue or as LNER locomotives and were purported to be class J69s in the period prior to the War. For scale models of this class there is the Wills cast metal kit in 4mm scale which is still available, and in N gauge there is the Grafar model which was introduced in 1972 with a die-cast body and 12V DC motor.

Above: The Grafar N Gauge Model. Courtesy Hamblings.

Left: J69 0-6-0T 68619 employed as Liverpool Street Station pilot in 1957.

Right: From the collection of F. J. Roche (courtesy of Ian Allan Limited).

SOUTHERN RAILWAY M7

Dugald Drummond designed the M7 class 0-4-4T for the London and South Western Railway in 1897, soon after he had been appointed as Mechanical Engineer (later to become Chief Mechanical Engineer). The original intention was for a suburban tank locomotive, but the class proved so powerful that they were used on semi-fast main-line trains.

It has been said that the origins of the design could be traced back to the London Brighton and South Coast Railway, for Drummond was Works Manager at Brighton having dealt with the construction of the Stroudley tank loco *Sydenham* and also two spare 0-4-4Ts. Later Drummond was appointed as Mechanical Engineer for the North British Railway and again the 0-4-4T was introduced and later still while serving with the Caledonian Railway a further type of 0-4-4T was designed and produced. The

latter locos were particularly successful and their outward design shows similarity with the Southern M7s.

From 1897-1911 a total of 105 of the class were built, the later ones having a greater overhang of the frames at the front end, giving an additional overall length of 1ft 3in and adding nearly 6ton to the weight (in working order). These locos also had steam reversing gear. Another variation, later introduced to the earlier constructed batch was the introduction of exhaust pipes being taken into the side tanks to pre-heat the water. All the 105 locos were built at Nine Elms with the exception of the last ten which were constructed at the newly opened Eastleigh Works.

The locos generally remained unaltered throughout their existence and were easily recognisable by their long straight footplate, square fronted tanks,

and straight fronted splashers over the leading drivers, the rear driving wheels having splashers within the side tanks.

One of the class, No 126 was rebuilt by Urie in 1921 with a superheater and an increase of cylinder diameter, but the weight increased and there were doubts as to its stability when running fast. It remained in and around the London area and was withdrawn in 1937.

The locos proved powerful and quite fast runners, so much so that they were put into service on main line semi-fast trains from Waterloo-Portsmouth, and fast trains from Bournemouth-Weymouth and Exeter-Plymouth. However, a derailment in 1898 caused the inspecting officers to criticise the use of such engines on fast trains and the practice ceased, the locos reverting to their original intended use on suburban traffic. However, in the 1930s the locos were

used extensively on semi-fast trains from Waterloo-Basingstoke, Waterloo-Alton and other such duties, frequently requiring speeds of 45mph between stops until ousted by electrification. Many of the locos were fitted for push-pull working and they were ubiquitous in the West Country. They were also used for empty stock workings in and out of Waterloo, often hauling twelve coach corridor trains from such outlying storage sidings as West Weybridge. They also saw service on parts of the central division in Kent and Sussex during the later days of steam.

The whole class, with the exception of No 126, were taken into British Railways ownership and the first was scrapped in 1948, but the remainder were not withdrawn until a start was made in 1958.

DATA

Diameter of driving wheels:	5ft 7in
Diameter of pony wheels:	3ft 7in
Weight in working order:	60ton
Two inside cylinders:	18in by 26in
Boiler pressure:	175lbs per sq in
Tractive effort:	19,755lb
Water capacity and coal capacity:	1,300 gallons and 3ton

Models

In 1915 Bassett-Lowke produced a reasonable scale model in gauge 1 of the M7 class in correct LSWR livery with clockwork mechanism, which in those days retailed at £2 10s (£2.50). Later they produced a gauge O model available as clockwork or electric. The Leeds Model Company also produced an 0-4-4T in 7mm scale, which painted in SR colours purported to be an M7 but was in fact more of a freelance design.

In the 1960's Wills Finecast produced a white metal cast kit for an accurate 4mm scale model of an M7, and in 1970 Tri-ang (Rovex) produced a proprietary model in OO gauge which was quite good, especially if additional detail was added and it was repainted.

Top: An M7 in service: No 30045 at Seaton Junction with the branch line train.

Opposite page bottom: A gauge 1 M7 by Bassett-Lowke. *J Francis Parker Collection*

Drawing by F. J. Roche *(courtesy of Ian Allan Ltd.)*

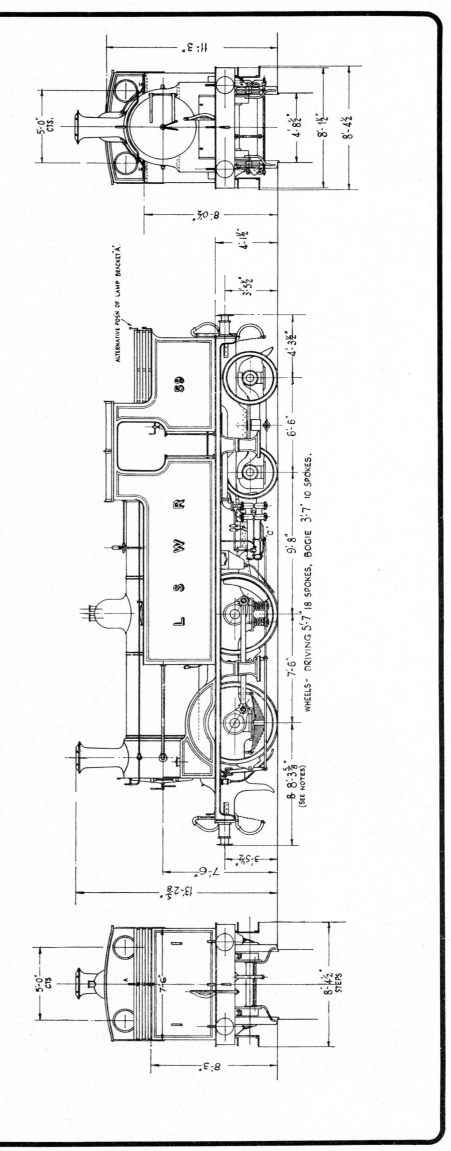

In 1902 the Midland Railway built one of the most successful designs of compound engines ever to run in Britain. They were three cylinder engines—two low-pressure and one high, the latter being between the frames. The first two locomotives, Nos 2631 and 2632 appeared in January 1902 paired with large bogie tenders, as became standard for the Johnson Compounds. They proved an outstanding success and demonstrated their ability to run freely by travelling at speeds of 90mph.

Johnson retired in 1903 and was succeeded by Deeley, who produced his own variation of the Compounds. The external design was radically altered: the straight running plate, small cab and rectangular cab panel of Johnson's engines gave way to a running plate slightly raised over the coupled wheels, a larger cab which was combined with a curved rear splasher, and with the roof extending back over the tender. The engines were paired with a smaller 6-wheel tender after the introduction of water troughs. These alterations, together with the gilt numbers on the tender side replacing the brass cab numerals, were to become the hallmark of the Derby designs.

More important were the mechanical alterations that Deeley made: these included a larger firebox with the largest grate area of 28.4sq ft of any 4-4-0 and an increase in boiler pressure from 195 to 220lb. The class were super-heated in a gradual programme beginning in 1910 which was not completed until 1928 when the last engine, 1022, was converted. The boiler pressure was standardised at 200lb as a result. In 1907 the class were re-numbered in the 1000 series.

The Midland locomotive policy changed during the construction of the Compounds from one of steady progress to one of stagnation, as a result of the practice of running frequent light trains hauled by comparatively small locomotives. Thus the Compounds were not worked to anything approaching the limit of their capacity and their Midland days were confined to working loads of 200-250 tons only.

After the Grouping the power in the LMS came to be held largely by ex-Midland men, and this became apparent in the locomotive policy. In the latter months of 1923 trials were held between a LNWR "Prince of Wales" which was several months out of shops, and Compound 1008 which was in very good condition. Perhaps this was slightly biased but it seems that Derby had already

decided to build more Compounds irrespective of these trials. However, 1008 acquitted herself very well despite hauling a 356ton load over the Settle & Carlisle line—a demonstration of its capability to haul a really heavy train over adverse gradients.

No less than 195 similar engines were built by the LMS and sub-contractors of which all but five were built within 3½ years of the grouping. On the Midland it was merely a case of providing more locos of a well tried design. On the Western division, however, the drivers did not take too kindly to engines that required a wide open regulator and could not be flogged, unlike the LNWR engines. In Scotland the story was much happier. By the middle of 1925 there were twenty Compounds at Kingmoor (Carlisle) for working both the Caledonian and G & SWR trains. The drivers in this part of the country liked their new steeds and much fine running was accomplished. For a brief period Compounds were even found hauling the "Royal Scot" from Polmadie to Carlisle and return. The GSWR section was probably where the Compounds performed their best regular work; though they also settled down with the London to Birmingham trains until superseded by the "Patriots" in the 1930's.

The greatest achievement of the class was perhaps the non-stop run of 1054 from Euston to Edinburgh on the "Royal Scot" on 27th April 1928 which has never been equalled since by a 4-4-0. 1054 had 6 bogies behind her and took 8 hours 11 minutes for the 399.7 miles, consuming only 6¼ton of coal—equal to 35lb per mile.

Stanier's succession to Chief Mechanical Engineer in 1932 had a profound effect on the locomotive policy, for with the construction of his 4-6-0 designs from 1934 onwards the Compounds began to be displaced to secondary work. There was, however, a slight respite for a few years because of the Second World War, but the advent of further Class 5s and 2-6-4Ts and later in the early '50s the BR Standard 4-6-0s relegated the Compounds further, and by June 1948 a start had been made on withdrawals—1002 and 1029 being the first. The Standard Class 4 even took over a considerable amount of their secondary duties as well and thus more Compounds were being withdrawn in increasing numbers. The last Compound to remain active was 40907 of Millhouses which still made occasional trips on the slow lines to Derby and Manchester until the summer of 1960, and

made its last run on the 21st August.

One Compound out of the 240 was saved: 1000 was withdrawn for official preservation in 1951 and restored to 1914 condition in full working order at Derby works, albeit paired with a 1914 SDJR 2-8-0 tender. She emerged in 1959 in the full glory of Midland red livery and worked several enthusiasts' special trains. She was sent to Clapham Museum for display, and has now been moved to the National Railway Museum at York where she has been placed on the possible steaming list. Although the famous Midland trains of gas-lit clerestory coaches have all gone we may yet see a red Compound in full cry once again.

DIMENSIONS OF THE CLASS AS SUPERHEATED

Cylinders HP:	19in dia x 26in stroke
LP:	21in dia x 26in stroke
Wheels Bogie	3ft 6½in dia
Coupled:	7ft 0in dia
Heating surface (total):	1681sq ft
Weight in working order (total):	61ton 14cwt

Some Compound Models

Basset-Lowke sold several varieties of Compound locomotives from the 1920's. There was a gauge 1 version in clockwork numbered 1000 and painted red. In O gauge there were versions of 999 and 1000 in clockwork and 1000 in electric. In 1956 an updated lined black version was brought out in either clockwork or electric.

Hornby produced a Compound in their No 2 Special Series which was not quite so good as Basset-Lowke's, but very good for Hornby.

In OO Trix Twin introduced a 3 rail AC version which captured the atmosphere of the engines quite well although it was not a scale model.

GEM produce white metal kits in OO for both 999 and 1000 classes.

Below left: A late pre-war example of a Bassett-Lowke model of the Midland Compound. These models were still produced into the BR era, unlike the Hornby series which ceased production with the war. *Courtesy Caroline and Andrew collection. Brian Monaghan*

Below right: Midland Compound No 1000 at York on an SLS special in 1960.

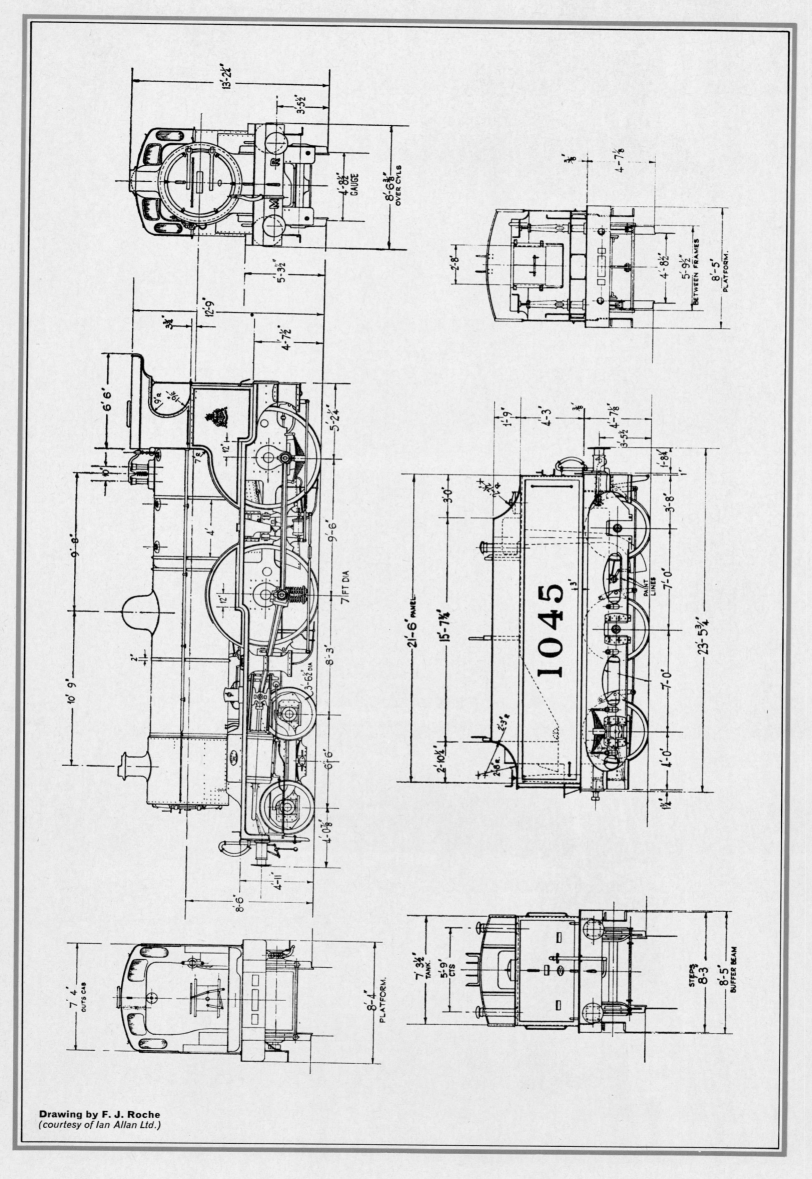

Drawing by F. J. Roche
(courtesy of Ian Allan Ltd.)

Metropolitan Railway electric locomotive

Until recently electric locomotives have not been common on the railways of the British Isles, with one exception—the Metropolitan Railway who had a fleet of 20 working until 1961, and even after this date several were kept for hauling service trains and departmental stock.

The first batch of ten electric locomotives were built in 1905, having British Westinghouse equipment, and they were of the steeple cab type. The second batch which followed two years later had an overall box or square shape with cab at either end; they also differed in their electrical equipment which was manufactured by British Thompson Houston. These twenty locomotives proved quite successful in service, but with the increase in building development along the route, and the prospect of much more property development, later called "Metroland" the Metropolitan Railway decided that longer and heavier trains would have to be run which would severely tax the existing locomotives. Consequently they decided in 1919 to rebuild all the locos with more powerful motors and to give them new and more modern looking bodies.

The first of the virtually new locomotives was delivered from the contractors, Metropolitan Vickers Ltd in 1922 and immediately they became popular with the public and the operating staff alike. They operated the fast and semi-fast trains through the electrified areas for the steam locomotives to take on to their final destination. Until 1925 the changeover point was Harrow-on-the-Hill, but it was then extended to Rickmansworth until the end of the electric loco era in September 1961. From 1960 however the electrified lines had been extended to Amersham and Chesham, and the locos were working over these lines for a few months, before the new electric multiple unit trains were in service.

The locos were of the Bo-Bo type with two 300hp motors driving the axles through single reduction gears. Maintenance was thus an easy task and the arrangement suited the work required of non-stop running at high speed, plus frequent stops with high acceleration and braking, both of which was encountered on the service from Aldgate with all stations to Baker Street and then fast to Harrow-on-the-Hill. Speeds of up to 60mph were necessary on the faster part of the journey to maintain the schedule imposed, and the trains were usually seven bogie vehicles of heavy construction, which when filled with passengers represented a load of approximately 180 tons. Although not a great load for a powerful locomotive the route was not flat, and gradients of 1 in 44 and 1 in 80 existed near Swiss Cottage, as well as some prolonged "drags" on sections

further out. The locos weighed approximately 56 tons in working order, for the frames and cabs were of steel construction and the motors and control gear were of heavy and massive build.

Current was supplied to the locos at 600V DC through the running rails with four shoes on each side of the body, and

another four under the loco for the return via the centre rail. In addition some of the regular passenger stock used with these locos were also fitted with collector shoes, so that the loco would not become isolated at complicated junctions, where there was a break in the conductor rails.

In 1927 the Metropolitan Railway, realising the value of publicity, decided to name all the 20 locos of the class, carefully selecting names of persons connected with the railway, with two exceptions–No 15 *Wembley 1925*, for this loco had been exhibited at the Empire Exhibition of that year, and No 8 *Sherlock Holmes* – but he did live in Baker Street, even if he is fictitious!

DATA

Diameter of wheels:	3ft 7½in
Gear ratio:	23/57
Brakes:	Westinghouse and Vacuum
Weight in working order:	56ton approx.
Length over buffers:	39ft 6in
Height above rail level:	12ft 4¼in
Rating for one hour:	1,200hp at 30mph

Models

A model of one of the original batch of steeple cab locos was made by Bassett-Lowke in 1910, which was for gauge 1 and was for 4-6V DC operation.

Probably the most famous of the models was the Hornby tinplate O gauge loco which they introduced prior to 1927 in three different versions—clockwork, 4V DC (for accumulators) or 100-250V from the mains via a resistance. By 1929 the latter had been discontinued in favour of the lower (and safer) voltage which had been raised to 6V DC. This loco was in reality a four-wheeled mechanism although the bodywork was realistic and typical Metropolitan Railway "Ashbury" type coaches were marketed for this loco.

Top: London Transport No 1 "John Lion" at Neasden.

Above left: An O gauge Hornby model supplied in clockwork and electric. *J Joyce*

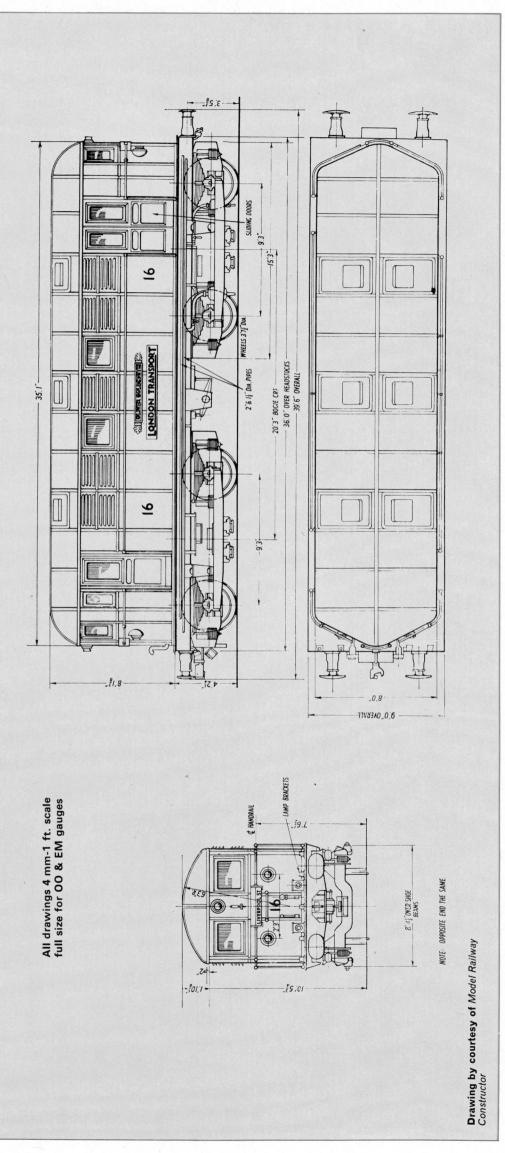

All drawings 4 mm-1 ft. scale
full size for OO & EM gauges

NOTE- OPPOSITE END THE SAME

Drawing by courtesy of *Model Railway Constructor*

DB "MAFFEI" PACIFICS

The four cylinder compound pacific locomotives of the ex-Bavarian State Railways class S3/6 became famous throughout the railway world. Many people considered them to be the most handsome of all German locomotives, with their distinctive appearance and their conical or cone-shaped smokebox door and similarly shaped cylinder and valve covers. They were powerful and technically perfect, so much so, that with only a few modifications, they were still being built after a period of 25 years.

The original locomotives were designed and built by J A Maffei at their works in Munich in 1908—hence the name "Maffei Pacifics". The compound arrangement was ingenious for the locos were started by allowing the high pressure steam into the low pressure steam chest, then as the engine was notched up, valves situated outside by the lower cylinders automatically closed and allowed full compound working.

The class was used for all express passenger workings and handled the early "Rheingold" express train, but in their latter days they became more of a general purpose locomotive. After the 1914-18 War, 19 of the class were sent to Belgium as repatriation locos.

With the reorganisation of classes by the DB they became class BR18 and numbered 18401-435. Some were rebuilt with a larger all-welded boiler as late as 1950. A total of 169 were built with minor modifications, not all by Maffei, but some by Henschal who produced a batch of 18 in 1930/31. The last one was withdrawn from service in 1960. Two have been preserved—one in a Museum at Lucerne and the other in a Museum in Munich.

Strangely, the proprietary model makers seem to have neglected this class of loco in their model building programmes, although Marklin have just produced one for HO scale and there is an Arnold model for N scale.

Top Right: *Top,* **Bavarian Pacific by Bing (1923) live steam gauge 1.** *Middle,* **Bavarian Pacific by Wilag (1973) live steam gauge 1.** *Bottom,* **Bavarian Pacific by Tenshodo (1959) electric gauge Ho.**
Collection Count Antonio Giansanti-Colluzzi

Centre: Gauge 1 Maffei Pacific by Wilag (made by Fulgarex) in steam and electric 1973.
(Collection J. Van Riemsdijk) Richard Sharpe Studios

Right: Gauge 1 German Pacific by Märklin (steam). This is Märklin's last version of a Reichsbahn Pacific made in steam and electric during 1935/36.

(Collection J. Van Riemsdijk) Richard Sharpe Studios

Above: A pair of Maffei Pacifics awaiting scrapping. *D Mackenzie*

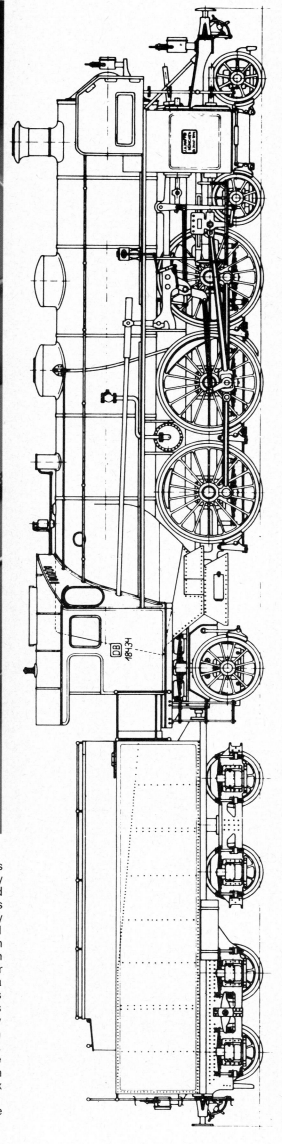

DATA

Diameter of driving/coupled wheels:	1870mm (6ft 2in).
Diameter of bogie wheels:	950mm (3ft 1½in).
Diameter of pony wheels:	1206mm (3ft 11½in).
Overall length:	21,396mm (70ft 2in).
Cylinders:	425/660mm by 610/670mm (16¾in/25in by 23in/26½in).
Maximum speed:	120km/hr (75mph).
Weight in working order:	92ton.

Above: Gauge 1 Maffei Pacific by Wilag (made by Fulgarex) in steam and electric 1973.
Collection Count Antonio Giansanti-Colluzzi

Models

It appears that many examples of this loco class have been built, mainly by model engineers in various scales, and some manufacturers have made models to special order. Among proprietary models is an excellent version in gauge 1 by Wilag marketed by Fulgarex in steam or electric in 1973, while several German firms made models in their pre-War range. Currently, Märklin have made a 3.5mm scale model of the loco which was first featured in their 1973 catalogue. This has a plastic injection moulded body and operates on their 14v AC system with stud contact electrical pickup. A really good example to the same scale is that produced by Tenshodo in 1959 and again marketed by Fulgarex under the title "Bavarian Pacific".

Arnold (West German) have a very nice little model available in N gauge.

THE HOLDEN "1500" CLASS

Up until 1912 the "Claud Hamilton" 4-4-0's were the mainstay of the Great Eastern main line. However, the increasing weight of trains over the difficult Colchester route indicated that a larger type of locomotive was needed. Under S D Holden locomotives with greater adhesive weight and a higher tractive effort were designed and constructed. They were to be the first GER express locomotives with six-coupled wheels, and they were numbered in the 1500 series.

These handsome new engines followed the traditional Stratford ideas and were a logical development from the 4-4-0's. Embellishments included a copper-cap chimney, several strips of brass beading and a brass safety-valve cover. One noticeable feature was the two sets of splashers: the larger being curved in the usual manner, the lower having five perforated holes in them. The engines were provided with an extremely large cab which contrasted sharply with the truncated tender. The reason for the smallness of the tender size was to keep the total wheelbase down to 48ft 3in as there were many turntables of only 50 feet in diameter.

By 1917 forty-one engines of the class had been constructed, but No 1506 was

destined only to have a short life. In July 1913 she was involved in a serious accident at Colchester and being damaged beyond repair she was scrapped within four months of building. Construction temporarily stopped at the end of the war but was recommenced in 1920 with a further twenty engines by William Beardmore & Co of Glasgow; these were the first GER locomotives to be built by contractors since 1884. Ten more were also built at Stratford making 70 in all.

After the Grouping the engines were classed in the LNER lists as B12's. It is a tribute to the design that ten further engines were constructed by Beyer Peacock & Co in 1928; these were fitted with oscillating cam-operated lentz-poppet-valve motion, and the lower splashers were cut away.

Between 1927 and 1934 fifty-five engines were fitted with ACFI apparatus for heating the feed water with exhaust steam. The outward appearance was impaired by the addition of two cylindrical chambers saddling the boiler with several connecting pipes. This was partly responsible for the nickname of "Hikers" which was given to the class.

An allocation of 30 "Sandringham" 4-6-0 engines designed by Gresley and allocated to the GE section displaced some of the B12's and these were sent to the Great North of Scotland section. These engines remained in this area working trains from Aberdeen to Peterhead and Elgin until the mid-50's and were virtually the last of their class extant.

From 1932 Thompson was in charge at Stratford under Gresley, and redesigned the B12's on similar lines to the rebuild of the "Claud Hamiltons" with very satisfactory results. The valve setting was completely re-designed and the piston-valve diameter was reduced from 10in to $9\frac{1}{2}$in. The result was a large cut in coal consumption and a more free-running engine. The Belpaire boiler was replaced with a Gresley type round-topped one

which reduced the total heating surface from 1,919 to 1,874sq ft and enlarged the grate area from 26.5 to 31.0sq ft. This increased the weight of the engine by $6\frac{1}{4}$ tons to $69\frac{1}{4}$ tons and the adhesion weight was increased to 48 tons. Various other Gresley modifications were made including the provision of a new cab, cast chimney, Ross "pop" safety-valves and cut away valances. The engines now appeared much larger, and although their outline had been altered their handsome lines still remained. The rebuilds were classed as B12/3's, painted in LNER passenger livery and lined out with polished beading over the splashers. They proved fast and economical engines.

During the second World War rebuilt B12/3s hauled Ambulance trains in the South and West of England and appeared as far afield as the Somerset & Dorset, Worcester, and Hereford.

The class was repainted in the lined black livery of British Railways. In the early fifties forty-five of the B12's were still active and even the allocation of the "Sandringham" 4-6-0's had not completely removed the class from top express work on the GE. Eventually the last B12, 61572, outlived the newer LNER Gresley engines. 61572 was withdrawn in 1961 having been based at Norwich. She is one of the Beyer-Peacock built engines and has the distinction of being the sole remaining inside cylindered 4-6-0 in the British Isles. 61572 is preserved on the North Norfolk Railway at Sheringham.

DATA

Driving wheel diameter:	6ft 6in
Bogie wheel diameter:	3ft 3in
Length:	57ft 9in
Total weight:	108ton 16cwt
Cylinders (2):	20in x 28in
Tractive effort:	21,969lb

Models

The B12 class has been neglected by the commercial world: the only one produced is by Triang (now Hornby Railways) which is a good reproduction. It is available in LNER lined green, although it used to be in BR lined black. The model is of 61572.

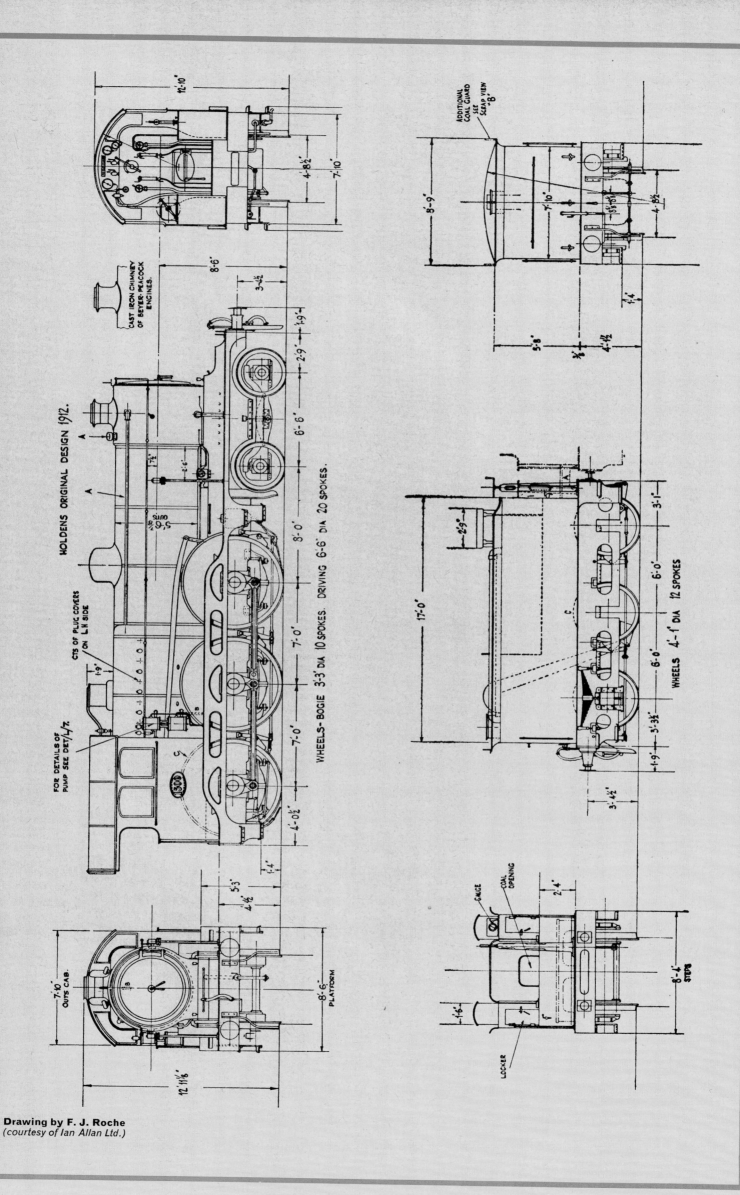

HOLDENS ORIGINAL DESIGN 1912.

CAST IRON CHIMNEY OF BEYER-PEACOCK ENGINES.

WHEELS-BOGIE 3'·3' DIA 10 SPOKES. DRIVING 6'·6' DIA 20 SPOKES.

WHEELS 4'·1' DIA 12 SPOKES

ADDITIONAL COAL GUARD SEE SCRAP VIEW "B"

FOR DETAILS OF PUMP SEE DET/47.

CTS OF PLUG COVERS ON L.H SIDE

OUTS CAB.

PLATFORM

COAL OPENING

GAUGE

LOCKER

STEPS

Drawing by F. J. Roche
(courtesy of Ian Allan Ltd.)

The 51xx & 61xx Class 2-6-2Ts of the GWR

The design of this class of locomotive goes back to 1903, when G J Churchward, then the Locomotive Superintendent of the Great Western Railway, (he was not appointed as Chief Mechanical Engineer until 1916), produced No 99 which was the first of a large number of locos of similar type that were to be one of the most successful designs for general duties over a large part of the system. The first locomotive was thoroughly tested in service and obviously proved to be highly successful for two years later 39 more were built at Swindon without any alterations (Nos 3111-3149). The first loco was renumbered 3100 in December 1912 and this, and a small increase in the bunker capacity were about the only changes made to the whole class of 40 locos. They were all renumbered 5100, 5111-5149 about 1929 and from 1931 onwards all but a couple had their cab roofs lowered, which gave them a more powerful and sleek look. It had been intended to replace these engines by the new 81XX class in 1939, but the War intervened and the class continued until 1947 when the first was withdrawn; the last being scrapped in 1959—having given 53 years of excellent service.

When new this class worked in South Wales and the Severn Tunnel Junction, but could also be seen in Devon and the Midlands on banking and freight duties. Some appeared in London on passenger work and in the later years of their life most were to be found around the Wolverhampton area.

After a lapse of over 20 years, a further 20 locos (Nos 5101-5110 and 5150-5159) were built between 1929-30 and were to the same specification as the earlier type except for a few minor detail differences —surely a tribute to their original designer, that at a time when great progress had been made in the development of steam power, no major changes were necessary. Others followed from 1930-34 (Nos 5160-5199) and again during the period from 1935-1949 (under the Collett

Above right: No 6106 at Didcot.
C M Whitehouse

Right A 4 mm scale plastic model by Kitmaster. *David Rudkin*

regime) another 80 were built at Swindon (Nos 4100-4179) still to the same design.

These locomotives became the mainstay of the suburban passenger services of the Great Western, their life only being cut short by the advent of the diesel multiple unit trains which became widespread in the late 1950s. Even then the locos were performing the duties required for extra peak hour traffic, as well as being used on pick-up goods trains and banking duties in the areas where severe gradients existed—jobs which they had often undertaken in the past.

Between 1931 and 1935, 70 almost identical locos were produced (Nos 6100-6169) which had exactly the same dimensions as the earlier locos, but had a higher boiler pressure (225lb as against 200lb per sq in) and a greater tractive effort. This was necessary for the acceleration of the London passenger services, where the majority of these new locos remained throughout their lives, giving fast times for the heavier commuter trains which often ran non-stop for the first 20 miles or more out of Paddington.

In 1938 a further 10 locos (Nos 8100-8109) were built, which were virtually identical to the 61XX class, with the exception that the diameter of the driving wheels was reduced by 2in to 5ft 6in. These were used on passenger services in the Birmingham and South Wales areas.

Four of the locomotives have now been preserved and can be seen—often in steam—Nos 4164 and 6106 at the Great Western Society, Didcot and Nos 4141 and 5164 at the Severn Valley Railway at Bridgnorth.

If steam was still in operation on British Rail it is more than probable that the later built locos would still be operating for many years to come, and thus it could be said that the class would have been in operation for nearly a Century.

DATA

Cylinders (2):	18in by 30in
Diameter of driving wheels:	5ft 8in
Diameter of pony wheel:	3ft 2in
Diameter of trailing wheels:	3ft 8in
Boiler pressure:	200lb
	(225lb on 61XX class)
Tractive effort:	24,300lb
	(27,340 on 61XX class)
Tank capacity:	2,000 gallons
Weight in working order:	78ton 9cwt
	(slight variation between types)

Models

Bassett-Lowke produced a fine O gauge scale model of No 6105 about 1937 in three versions—clockwork and 6V DC or 20V AC. This was a fine example of pre-War model building in this country on a proprietary basis. After the war it was possible to obtain a sheet metal body kit of the class from Dawson also in gauge O, and these are now being produced by CCW.

In 4mm scale there is a plastic construction kit for making a scale model from Airfix (originally a Kitmaster product), while there is a fine cast metal kit from Wills Finecast which makes up to a perfect scale model with very full detail. In 3mm scale there has been a cast metal kit from N & K C Keyser. There have been many models of this class of loco which have been built to special order in differing scales.

Graham Farish also produced a OO gauge version of the 81XX class with diecast body, but this has now been discontinued for the present.

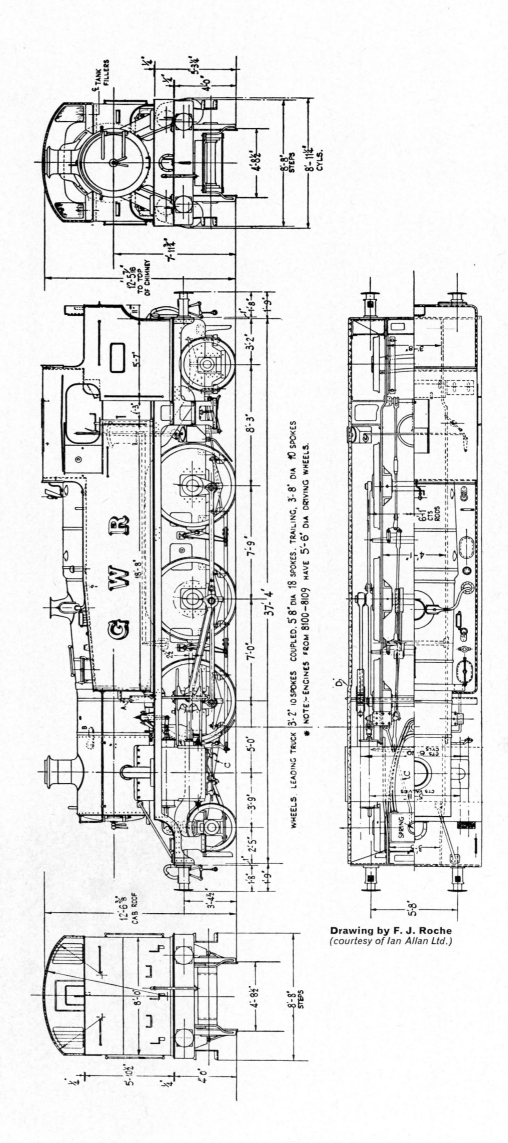

Drawing by F. J. Roche
(courtesy of Ian Allan Ltd.)

THE SOUTHERN RAILWAY MOGULS

In 1914 R E L Maunsell designed two classes of locomotives having similar dimensions and interchangeable parts for the South Eastern and Chatham Railway; the only major difference being the 2-6-0 tender locos (class N) had 5ft 6in driving wheels, whereas the 2-6-4Ts (class K) had 6ft coupled wheels. The locos had tapered boilers, topfeed water supply and smokebox regulators incorporating a superheater, also outside cylinders which were a complete innovation on the SECR locomotives up to that time. The N class tender locos were intended for mixed traffic duties while the K class tanks were to work express passenger services, but not the boat trains.

Due to the first World War, there was a long delay in the construction of the new locos and the tender version was not completed ·until 1917 at the Ashford Works of the SE&CR. It was said that the first of the class (No 810) had a similarity with the 47XX class of the GWR which is possible, but Maunsell had no previous connections with the GWR or Swindon Works. However, the loco proved successful and a further batch (Nos 823-875) were built in 1923, and again in 1933 more were constructed (Nos 1400-1414); both being in the livery of the Southern Railway. Fifty of this type of loco were built at Woolwich Arsenal after the War in order to keep full employment at those premises, and some were sold abroad.

In 1923, Maunsell designed one loco exactly the same externally but it was fitted with three cylinders (16in by 28in). It was numbered 822 and classified as N1. Others followed in 1931, Nos 876-880.

The tank version appeared in 1917 (No 790) and further locos without alteration were produced in 1925 (Nos 791-799) and ten more (Nos 800-809) a year later. Again Maunsell decided that a three cylinder version may be an advantage, thus No 890 was produced in December 1925. These locos were named after Rivers on the Southern Railway system and thus became well known. Unfortunately they received some unwelcome notoriety for the class became involved in a number of derailments, culminating in a very serious one at Sevenoaks in 1927 when 13 passengers were killed and a large number seriously injured. It is now thought that this and some of the other derailments were caused to some degree by bad track alignment, aggravated by water "surging" in the tanks of the loco. One of the class was later tried on the LNER main line, noted for its good and smooth track, where it behaved perfectly even at much higher speeds than were permitted on the Southern. However, at that time public opinion was very much against the stability of the locos and the whole class were converted to the 2-6-0 U class which Maunsell had just designed.

The U class 2-6-0 locos, generally followed Maunsell's earlier design for the N class, but the driving wheels were larger, being 6ft diameter. They were designed for intermediate and semi-fast trains over the heavily graded lines such as Waterloo-Portsmouth and Charing Cross-Hastings, and 30 of the class were built at Brighton Works in 1928 (Nos 620-639).

It seems strange that Maunsell again built some of these locos with three cylinders, thus in 1931 the Eastleigh Works built Nos 890-900 and later Nos 1901-1910.

Some modifications were fitted to all these classes—the Moguls—such as the addition of smoke deflectors etc. The converted River class tanks, now classified in class U and one in class U1 had slightly differing footplate and splashers.

Our drawing shows a U class 2-6-0.

All four classes were fitted with the same type of 6-wheeled tender.

Models

In 1927 the catalogue of Bassett-Lowke showed a very nice O gauge model of an N class which was powered by a 12V electric motor, and we understand that the model proved popular at a cost of £5.5.0d (£5.25).

No further models of the Southern Railway 2-6-0s were produced commercially until the 1960s when Wills Finecast produced a white metal kit in 4mm scale which contained the necessary parts for making up either of the four classes of

Above: Wills Finecast model of "U" class Mogul.
Richard Sharpe Studios

Below: "U" class 2-6-0 No 31797 passing Worting Junction with a fitted freight.

the prototype according to the makers inclination. This kit was designed to fit one of the proprietary Tri-ang chassis and is still available.

DATA

	Class N	Class N1	Class U	Class U1
Cylinders:	19in x 28in (2)	16in x 28in (3)	19in x 28in (3)	16in x 28in (3)
Diameter of drivers:	5ft 6in	5ft 6in	6ft	6ft
Diameter of pony wheel:	3ft 1in	3ft 1in	3ft 1in	3ft 1in
Boiler pressure:	200lb/sq in	200lb/sq in	200lb/sq in	200lb/sq in
Tractive effort:	26,025lb	26,035lb	23,866lb	25,387lb
Weight in working order:	103ton 10cwt	106ton 13cwt.	110ton 14cwt.	107ton 14cwt
Tender capacity water:	4,000gall	4,000gall	4,000gall	4,000gall
Tender capacity coal:	5ton	5ton	5ton	5ton

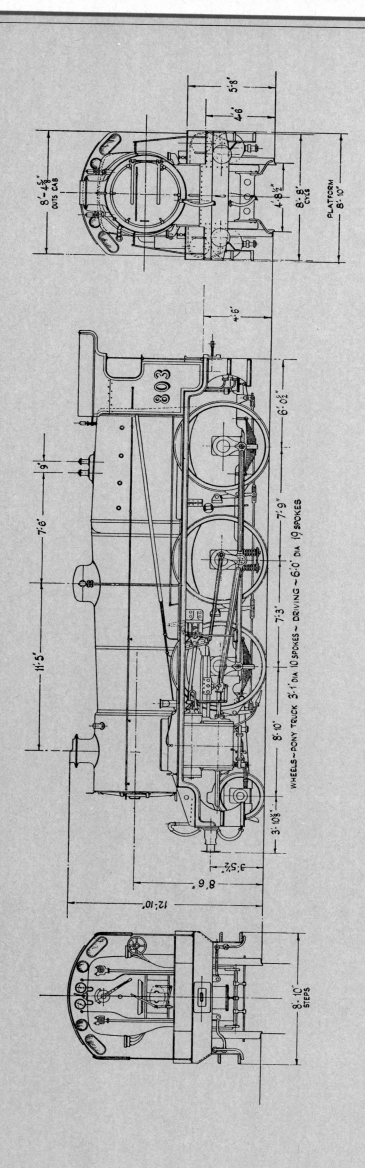

5'-8'

4'-6'

8'-4½"
OUTS CAB

4'-8½"

8'-8'
CYLS

PLATFORM
8'-10"

4'-6'

6'-0½"

7'-9"

9"

7'-6'

7'-3"

11'-5'

8'-10'

WHEELS~PONY TRUCK 3'-1" DIA 10 SPOKES ~ DRIVING ~ 6'-0" DIA 19 SPOKES

3'-10⅝"

3'-5½"

8'-8'

12'-10'

8'-10'
STEPS

LNER CLASS N2 0-6-2T

In 1907 the CME of the Great Northern Railway, H A Ivatt, designed and introduced the first of a series of 56 tank locomotives of the 0-6-2T. wheel arrangement especially for the London suburban services. The locomotivies were designated class N1 and continued their work on the lines radiating from Kings Cross to the outer suburbs, often putting up some good timings. However, the locos were never very fast runners, and with heavier trains and the requirement for more frequent services these locos became somewhat of a liability and were the cause of a lack of progress with the suburban services for the GNR.

In 1920 H N Gresley, who had succeeded Ivatt as CME designed an improved version of the locos which were more powerful and could give the heavy suburban trains a fast acceleration which was so necessary for timekeeping and close headway workings. These were the class N2 locomotives.

Such was the urgency for the locos that Doncaster only built the first ten locos (Nos 1606-1615) and the remaining 50 were built by the North British Loco Co. All the locos had superheaters and

piston valves, and although the boiler was the same size as the earlier class, it was pitched higher on the frames to allow for the piston valves underneath. The locos were fitted with condensing gear for working over the widened lines of the Metropolitan Railway and had vacuum brakes for train and for loco.

These locos proved so successful that further batches were built in 1925, 1928 and 1929 in the works at Doncaster as well as outside contractors—Yorkshire Engine Co, Beyer Peacock, and Hawthorne Leslie. A total of 167 locos finally completed the N2 class. There were some variations in the batches, for some had full chimneys, others had cut-down chimneys for the Metropolitan line loading gauge, and some were equipped with condensing gear and others not. All the LNER built locos were fitted for left-hand drive.

Not all these locos saw service in the London suburbs for some were sent to Scotland, the West Riding of Yorkshire or the old Great Eastern lines from Liverpool Street.

One of these locomotives, now numbered 4744 has been preserved by the

Above right: N2 0-6-2T No 4744 in LNER black livery at Haworth on the Keighley & Worth Valley Railway.

Below: A Hornby 16.5mm gauge model in LNER green.

LOCOMOTIVES

Gresley Society and can be seen working on the Keighley and Worth Valley Railway from Haworth.

DATA

Cylinders:	19in by 26in
Diameter of driving wheels:	5ft 8in
Boiler pressure:	170lb per sq in
Tank capacity:	2000 gallon
Axle load:	19½ton
Tractive effort:	19,945lb
Weight in working order:	71ton 9cwt
	this varied according to batch

Models

Bassett-Lowke produced a clockwork 2½in gauge model of this locomotive class which appears to be a mixture of classes N1 and N2, soon after the end of World War I, while Douglas Models (now dissolved) also produced a fibreglass body kit for these locos in the late '50s. The N2 class was the first of the two locomotives produced by Hornby Dublo when they made their introduction in 1938, the model having a die-cast body and being available for clockwork or electric propulsion, it is still available in 12V DC from Wrenn. There was also a Jamieson metal kit.

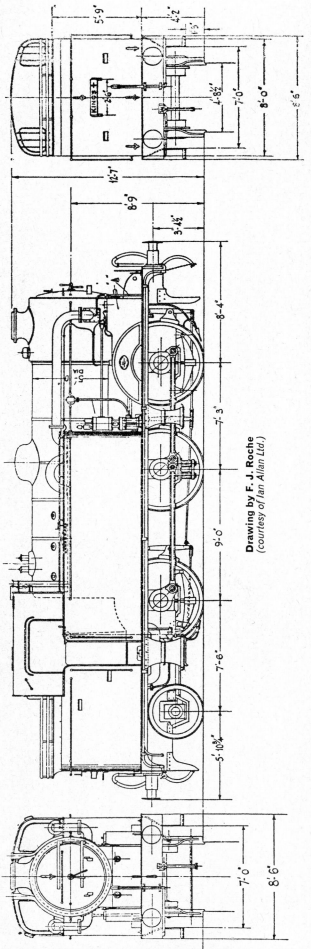

Drawing by **F. J. Roche**
(courtesy of Ian Allan Ltd.)

The LNER class A3 4-6-2 locomotive No 4472 *Flying Scotsman* has achieved world-wide fame, which has been reflected on the whole class of 78 locomotives. From the very first, the name—"Flying Scotsman" captured the public's imagination and with several inaugural runs to its credit and other items of publicity it has become well known. This particular locomotive has been preserved and having returned from a trip to America spent the summer of 1973 regularly working trains on the Torbay Steam Railway between Paignton and Kingswear.

The class, (originally designated class A1) was designed by Sir Nigel Gresley in 1923 and No 1472, (for that was its original number), was the third loco of the class.

On 20th November 1934 the loco was again in the news for, with a special train, it had become the first steam engine to reach a speed of 100mph. (A GWR loco *City of Truro* claimed this in 1904 but it was never officially substantiated and has been the subject of debates ever since).

The A1 class was rebuilt in 1927 by having new boilers raising the steam pressure to 220lbs per sq in and substituting the original dome for the new "banjo" shaped one. In 1941 the class was renumbered; *Flying Scotsman* becoming No 4472, later carrying the No 501, then 103 and at Nationalisation in 1948 it was given the No 60103. During BR regime it was fitted with a double chimney

locomotive exchanges of 1925 and the LNER loco worked the Cornish Riviera Express. Another of the class, No 2750 *Papyrus* reached a speed of 108mph in March 1935, which at the time was a world speed record shared with a French compound locomotive.

The class were constructed as right hand drive locos but after many years they were converted to left hand drive. The class were generally named after race horses and the first to be scrapped was *Solario* in December 1959.

DATA

3 cylinders:	20in by 26in
Diameter of driving wheels:	6ft 8in
Boiler pressure:	220lbs per sq in
Tractive effort:	29,815lbs
Adhesive weight:	60ton
Weight of loco and tender in working order:	148ton 15cwt
Tender capacity:	9ton coal and 5,000 gallons of water.

Bassett-Lowke produced an 0 gauge model of the locomotive around 1925, which was available with clockwork or electric (4–8v DC) propulsion. Later the electric version could be obtained for a 20v AC supply. Prior to this the German firm of Märklin marketed versions of the engine in gauges 1 and 0 – the larger models in steam, clockwork and electric. In 1926 Bassett-Lowke made some 2½ in. gauge live steam models of the prototype.

In 1928, the Hornby Trains 0 gauge tinplate range was extended to include a *Flying Scotsman*. In reality this was a 4–4–2 locomotive based on the company's design for a French "Nord" locomotive. This series was painted and named as appropriate for the four main line railway Companies.

In the early 1930s Bing manufactured a standard 4–6–0 whose L.N.E.R. version was named *Flying Fox*. 1938 saw a Trix Twin version of the locomotive.

There have of course been several hand-built models of the class and special orders executed by many of the model firms.

LNER CLASS A3 4·6·2 'FLYING SCOTSMAN'

the class to be built at Doncaster Works of the LNER. The remaining locos in the class were constructed at Doncaster or the North British Loco Company's works between 1923 and 1924. No 1472 was exhibited at the Wembley Exhibition in 1924 as a showpiece for British engineering.

In 1928, at a time when the LMSR and LNER were rivals for the London to Scotland traffic, the latter company decided to run the whole 392.7 miles from Kings Cross to Edinburgh without a stop. The service started on 1st May and *Flying Scotsman* was at the head of the train of the same name. In order that the crew could be changed half way on their long trip to the North a corridor tender was fitted to the loco and to some others

and smoke deflectors.

The loco was purchased by Alan Pegler in 1963 in whose hands it made many special trips and excursions to lines other than the LNER, but on 1st May 1968 it again undertook a special non-stop trip to Edinburgh. However, it was then carrying a second tender as a supplementary water supply, for the BR had demolished all the water troughs where locos could replenish their tenders.

In September 1969 the loco hauled an Exhibition train on a tour of America and Canada staying there for three years and returning to the UK in 1972 to a new owner—William McAlpine.

Another member of the A3 class, No 4474 *Victor Wild* was involved in the

In 1966, two 4mm scale kits appeared on the market. The first was a Jamieson kit of nickel-silver parts for the body and a special brass chassis; the second was a kit of white metal castings by Wills Finecast kits.

Two ready-to-run 00 gauge models appeared in 1968, one from Triang (Rovex) and one from Trix. Both had plastic injection moulded bodies and were for 12v DC two-rail working. The former model is still obtainable, as are the two kits mentioned.

Above: One of Bassett Lowke's most popular models: a 1930s and later version available in clockwork or electric at 12v DC.
K A C Melvin

Left: "Flying Scotsman" as BR No 60103 backs down from Kings Cross Loco. towards Gasworks Tunnel in 1958.

Far left: A trio of German manufacture from the collection of Count Giansanti Coluzzi. Top: Märklin Gauge 1 Steam LNER Pacific dating from 1928; Left: Märklin Gauge O Steam LNER Pacific dating from 1968; Right: Trix Gauge OO Electric 12v DC dating from 1970s.
Count Giansanti Coluzzi

Right: This is a 4mm: 1ft scale drawing of No 4472 "Flying Scotsman". From the collection of F J Roche (courtesy of Ian Allan Limited).

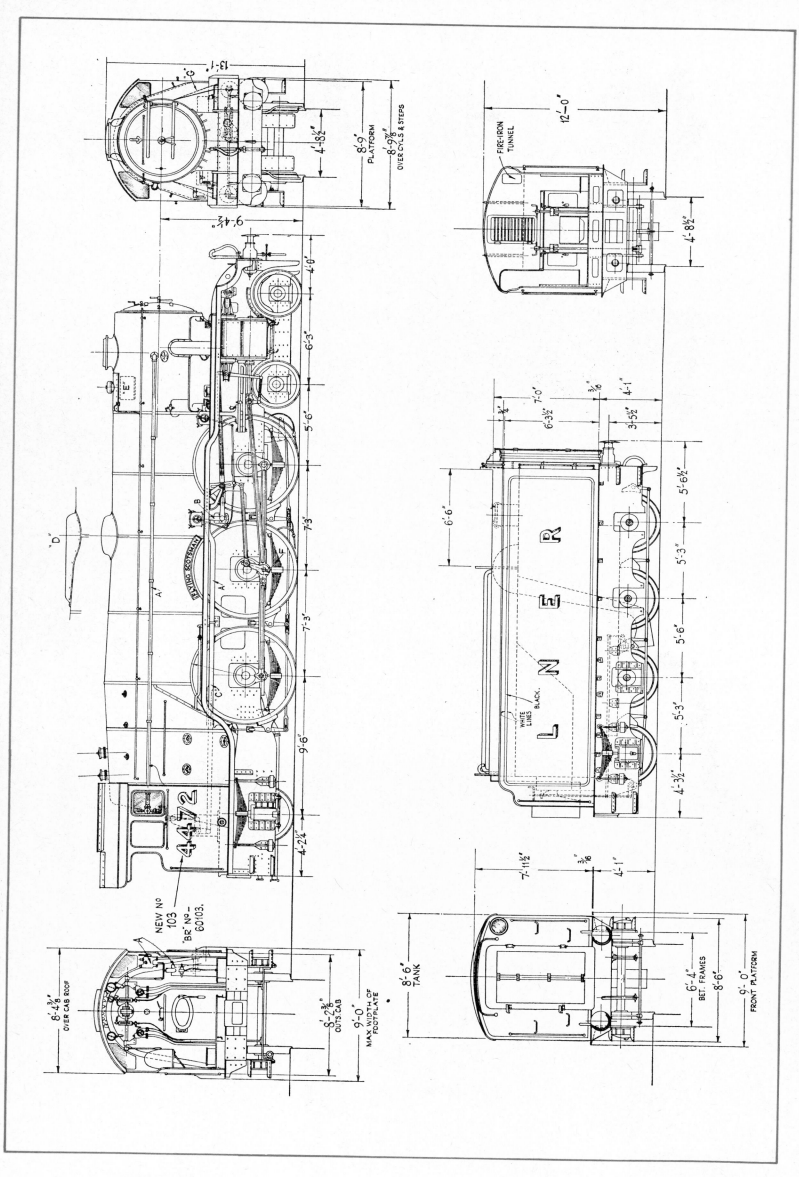

FLYING SCOTSMAN

4472

NEW No 103
"BR" No – 60103.

L N E R
WHITE LINES
BLACK.

FIRE-IRON TUNNEL

SOUTHERN N15 CLASS 4-6-0
THE 'KING ARTHURS'

Left: "Wills Kit of SR King Arthur" in 4mm scale.

Below: Southern railway 739 King Leodegrance. *R M Quinn Collection*

S.R. 'KING ARTHUR'
Designed by Urie in 1918 and rebuilt by Maunsell. Model can be built in either version.

When the Southern Railway was formed in 1923 the management was faced with the problem of a considerable increase in passenger traffic, together with insufficient locomotives of the necessary power to comply with this. The problem was aggravated in that the existing Urie N15s were proving quite incapable of keeping time reliably with even the existing loads.

The Southern's Traffic Manager decided that engines would be required which were capable of maintaining an average speed of 55mph with trains up to 500 tons in weight. To meet this, authority had been given for twenty engines of an entirely new design to be built. These were to be the "Lord Nelsons"; but it was not possible to produce the engines in time especially as the design was entirely novel to the Southern.

Thus there was a problem needing to be quickly solved, and to do this Maunsell had to provide a reliable locomotive in a short space of time. Before the grouping a scheme had been worked out for the reconstruction of ten of the 4 cylinder Drummond 4-6-0s as 2 cylinder engines. Maunsell modified the scheme and decided to replace the Drummond engines entirely by new 4-6-0s with 6ft 7in wheels and the N15 boiler with a new front end. There was also to be a new cylinder design which included large ports, large steam chest and long travel valves, whilst the cylinders were made 20½in diameter by 28in stroke. The boiler pressure was 200lb instead of 180lb as on the N15s. Technically these engines were rebuilds, but in fact they were replacements utilising only the bogies and tenders of the other engines. This had the added advantage in that the Drummond 4-6-0s could remain in service throughout the summer of 1924 to ease the critical locomotive situation.

While these "new" engines were being built a comprehensive series of tests was begun on Urie 4-6-0 No 742, running in ordinary passenger service between Waterloo and Salisbury to try to find the

reason for their shy steaming and erratic performance. Several alterations were made to the whole class as a result, and the same smokebox arrangement as for the new Maunsell 4-6-0s was adopted, including a modified chimney and blast pipe. The valve motion however, was not altered.

There was still a pressing need to get the new engines out as there was no prospect of the "Lord Nelsons" being ready until 1925. Therefore in the autumn of 1924 it was decided to put on order 20 Maunsell N15s and have them built by outside contractors which provided a possibility of having a few engines completed before the 1925 summer service. An order was placed with the North British Loco Co in December and the first four were delivered in May of the following year. Eastleigh completed the first of the new 4-6-0s in February and the class took the numbers 448-457 of the Drummond engines they replaced.

It was decided that these new engines should carry names, and most appropriately in view of the company's association with the West of England, their names recalled the legends of King Arthur and the Round Table. This was a popular move and the engines became firm favourites. The first of the engines, No 453 was named *King Arthur* and the remainder were named after the Knights of the Round Table, with the exception of No 454 *Queen Guinevere*. The Urie N15s were also included in the class and were named after the other associations of the legend. The "King Arthur" class engines were reliable and predictable in performance and entered service just in time to save the Southern's reputation.

In February 1926 a further fourteen locomotives were built at Eastleigh for the Brighton section, and they were paired with 6 wheel tenders in order to fit on the existing turntables.

No 780 *Sir Persant* was provided for the inaugural "Bournemouth Belle" on Sunday 5th July 1931 instead of a "Lord Nelson", and although the down trip was

delayed, the engine put up a good performance on the return trip, arriving one minute early at Waterloo.

The greatest achievement by a "King Arthur" that has been recorded was in September 1934 behind No 777 *Sir Lamiel* (now preserved at Ashford in Kent). No 777 brought a 345 ton "Atlantic Coast Express" up from Salisbury to Waterloo, running the 83.8 miles in 72 minutes 41 seconds. The 54.4 miles from Andover to Surbiton were covered at the amazing average speed of 80.2mph. It has been suggested since that there must have been a strong following wind, for the run was so far above the normal "King Arthur" performance.

The class was in its element on lines where hill climbs existed, and so they held their place on the steeply graded Salisbury to Exeter line against any attempt to introduce "Lord Nelsons" and "Schools" and it was not until the introduction of the larger Bulleid Pacifics that their monopoly was broken. However, despite this the Arthurs could still be relied on for good work when given the chance. They ended their days on the West of England and Bournemouth main lines.

DATA

Driving wheel diameter:	6ft 7in
Bogie wheel diameter:	3ft 7in
Cylinders (2):	20½in x 28in
Boiler pressure:	200lb per sq in
Weight:	138ton 3cwt

Models

Bassett-Lowke produced a Gauge 1 live steam model in 1937 costing £14 4s even in those days. This was a good likeness and was hand painted. Bassett-Lowke (Bing) produced a Gauge O clockwork version for 40s which, although a little dumpy, was a fair representation. Neither of these engines had smoke deflectors.

Currently the only model obtainable new is the Wills OO white metal kit with either a scale or a Hornby chassis.

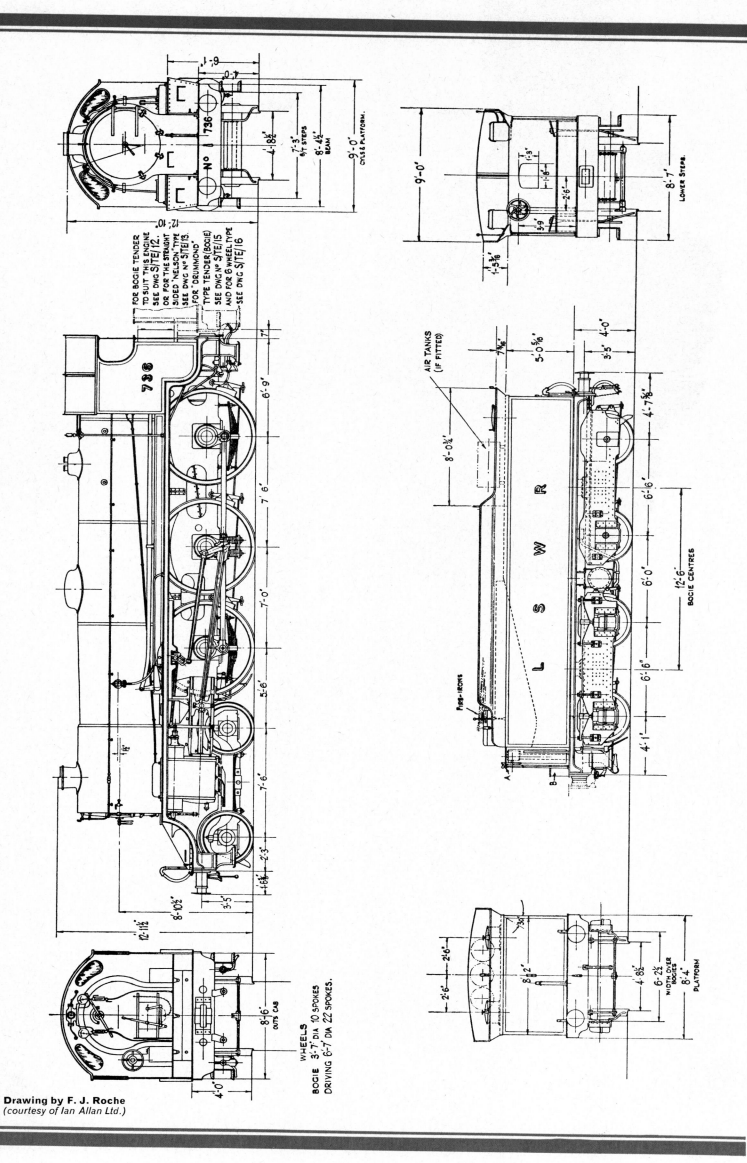

Drawing by F. J. Roche
(courtesy of Ian Allan Ltd.)

GWR 'Castle' Class

Models

The GWR "Castle" class 4-6-0 locomotive was designed by C B Collett in 1923 and was in reality a development of the Churchward design of 1906, known as the "Star" class. The new locomotives somewhat naturally had a similarity with the earlier design, having the same wheelbase and same diameter for the driving wheels and bogie wheels; however, the frame was extended by a foot to accommodate a larger firebox and the cylinder diameter enlarged from 15in to 16in; the obvious external difference is the larger cab with side windows and roof which is carried back over the tender fall plate. There is also a larger boiler, a Standard No 8 in place of a Standard No 1. The locos were a success right from the start, and finally a total of 171 were built, of which 155 were constructed new, the remaining 16 being converted from the "Stars". Twelve different batches were built between the years 1923 and 1950. When the original locos appeared they were given the 3,500 gallon tenders, but subsequent engines had the larger 4,000 gallon type and the earlier ones were soon changed over.

The first locomotive of the new class to emerge from Swindon Works in August 1923 was No 4073 *Caerphilly Castle* which was exhibited at the British Empire Exhibition at Wembley the following year. Another of the class to achieve fame was No 5000 *Launceston Castle* when it was loaned to the LMSR for evaluation purposes prior to the ordering of their "Royal Scot" class. A further loco from the early batch was No 4082 *Windsor Castle* which went to the Darlington Railway Centenary Celebrations and later became the Royal Engine, having been driven by HM King George V when it emerged from Swindon. A plaque recording this event was affixed in the cab.

In 1936 a shorter chimney was fitted to No 5044 and this improved the look of the locos as well as giving better draught; this was later extended to all in the class.

One engine, No 5005 *Manorbier Castle* was the object of some experiments carried out by the GWR on streamlining being given a bullet shaped smokebox front and "fairing" around the cab etc. This phase did not last long, the loco soon reverting to its normal appearance.

During the late forties some of the class were converted to oil burning for a few years. Many (67 in fact) were later rebuilt with a double chimney which improved the draughting.

The class have been responsible for many fast runs that have been recorded over the years, particularly their handling of the "Cheltenham Flyer" express train.

The first of the class was withdrawn from service in December 1958. A few of the locos were renamed during their life, some carrying the names of aircraft of World War II, and others had name changes within the class.

Between 1962/64 fourteen "Castle" class were transferred for service on the London Midland Region of British Railways.

Fortunately five "Castles" are now preserved for posterity: *Caerphilly Castle* in the Science Museum, London; No 7029 *Clun Castle* and No 7027 *Thornbury Castle* at the Standard Gauge Steam Trust, Tyseley; No 4079 *Pendennis Castle* by Hon John Gretton and W H McAlpine and No 5051 *Earl Bathurst* at Didcot by The Great Western Society.

In spite of the great popularity of the prototype with railway enthusiasts, this has not been well represented by the model trade. Models in gauges O and OO were available prior to, and just after the War, from several firms, some of which are no longer in business.

Bassett-Lowke produced an O gauge model in the mid '20s and this was still available, albeit modified, after the War when the locomotive could be hand-painted named and lined to customers' requirements. A standard 4-6-0 by Bing was marketed in the early 1930s. This, when painted and lettered in Great Western colours carried the name *Windsor Castle*. Hornby O gauge had their standard 4-4-2 loco in GWR livery which they numbered 4073 and named *Caerphilly Castle*. In the late 1950s Hornby Dublo Railways introduced their very successful 4mm scale model with its die-cast body and powerful motor. At first this was only available as a three-rail model, but was later also available in two-rail form. It is now marketed by G & R Wrenn Ltd. and is still a popular model.

When the firm of Tri-ang made a brief sojourn into TT gauge, they produced a 3mm scale model of the Castle class, alas no longer manufactured.

There is also a very good 4mm scale model by Wills.

DATA

Diameter of Driving/Coupled wheels:	6ft 8½in
Diameter of bogie wheels:	3ft 2in
Cylinders (4):	16in x 26in
Overall length:	65ft 1¾in
Boiler pressure:	225lbs/sq in
Tractive effort:	31,625lbs

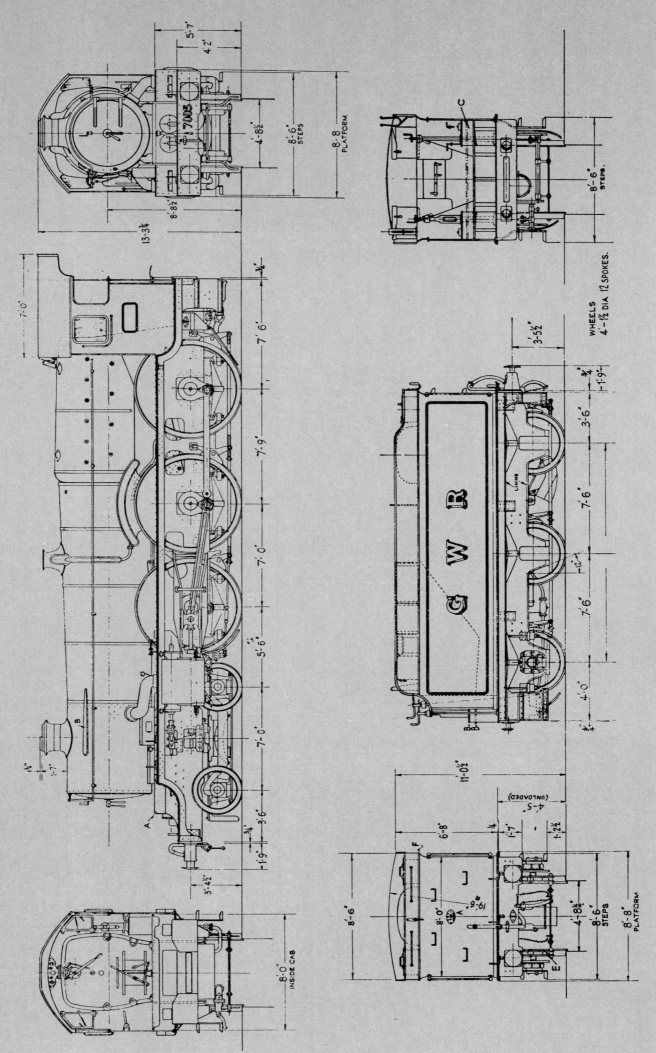

Drawing by F. J. Roche
(courtesy of Ian Allan Ltd.)

LNER J39 CLASS 0-6-0

In 1926 Sir Nigel Gresley designed two classes of 0-6-0 tender locomotives for shorthaul secondary services, both were of similar external design but one had 4ft 8in dia driving wheels, the other 5ft 2in drivers. The classes were designated J38 and J39, respectively and the latter proved so successful that a total of 271 locomotives were built up to 1941.

The first batch of 54 locos were built at Darlington Works and in service they soon proved they were capable of hauling some of the cross-country passenger trains with a good turn of speed. On freight traffic they excelled on moderate length trains of the pick-up goods type, and were generally regarded as good locos by all crews. Their only restriction was the small tenders fitted to those originally built for they only carried 3,500 gallons of water and 5½tons of coal. Later batches as built had varying tenders and a large batch constructed by Beyer Peacock in 1936 were given high and straight sided tenders holding 4,200 gallons of water which is the type shown on our drawing. Other tender variations included 3,940 gallon and 4,125 gallon types.

The locomotives had small 24 element superheaters and these were considered adequate for the non-main line operations for which they were designed. The two inside cylinders had piston valve steam chests above them and the drive was to the middle axle. Ross "pop" safety valves, power reversing gear and mechanical lubricators were all incorporated in the specification.

The J39 class had sturdy looks, and were well proportioned, but the overall height of 13ft with a boiler diameter of 5ft 9in set fairly low on the frames gave them a massive appearance. The crew were given a commodious and well protected cab with two side windows and large spectacle plates.

Westinghouse and vacuum brakes were fitted.

During the war and at times of other emergencies the J39 class were called upon to haul heavy trains, often having to be pressed into service to replace a larger loco which had failed, and on all occasions they acquitted themselves with honour.

Above: Class J39 0-6-0 64747, at Derby in 1951.
H C Casserley

Below: Wills model of J39 in LNER livery built on Triang chassis.
Richard Sharpe Studios

DATA

Diameter of driving wheels:	5ft 2in
2 cylinders:	20in by 26in
Working pressure:	180lbs/sq in
Total weight of loco and tender in working order:	102ton 1cwt
Tractive effort:	25,664lb

Models

In 1928 Bassett-Lowke produced an O gauge model of the class J39 in all metal construction and hand enamelled and finished in full LNER livery; it was available for electric or clockwork propulsion.

Bonds of Euston Road marketed a gauge O model made by Vulcan Models in 1969 which was for 12v DC operation.

In the smaller scales one can still obtain an excellent cast metal kit by Wills Finecast which has been designed to fit a Tri-ang chassis.

L.N.E.R.   J 39
...d goods locomotive introduced in 1926.

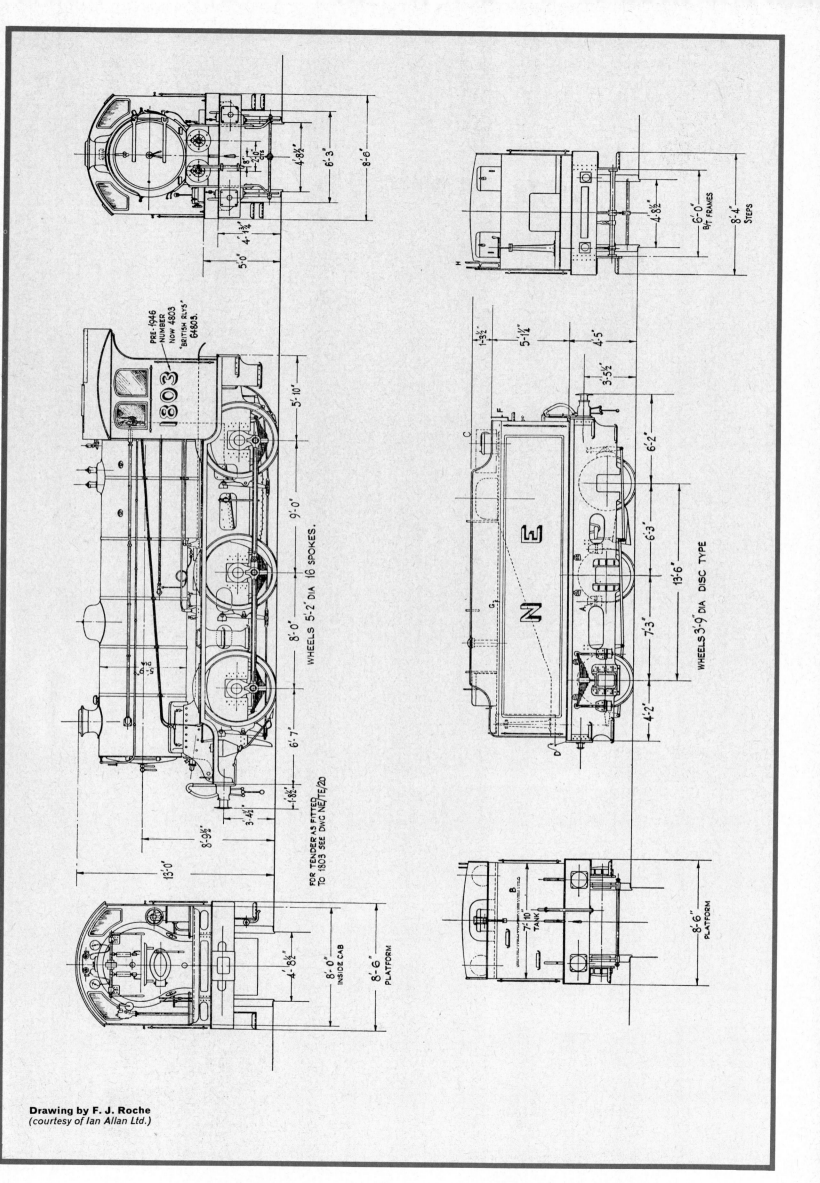

PRE-1946 NUMBER 4803 NOW "BRITISH RLYS" 64805.

WHEELS 5'·2" DIA 16 SPOKES.

FOR TENDER AS FITTED TO 1803 SEE DWG NE/TE/20

WHEELS 3'·9" DIA DISC TYPE

B/T FRAMES

Steps

INSIDE CAB

PLATFORM

TANK

PLATFORM

Drawing by F. J. Roche
(courtesy of Ian Allan Ltd.)

GWR KING CLASS 4-6-0

With the advent of good publicity in the early 1920s public travelling was on the increase and the West Country resorts of Devon were becoming more popular as a holiday centre. Train loadings were increasing and although the "Castle" class locomotives were proving adequate, there was the occasional need for something more powerful. The Great Western who were very publicity conscious were seriously upset when the Southern Railway introduced their "Lord Nelson" class loco in 1926 with the statement that it was "the most powerful passenger locomotive in Great Britain". This stung the General Manager of the GWR, Sir Felix Pole into action and he demanded an even more powerful locomotive to grace the rails of his own company's system. An order was given to C B Collett, the CME that he must produce a locomotive almost immediately. Although Collett had "carte blanche" from the design point of view, time was short and there would be little time for any trials or experiments such as Gresley of the LNER and Fowler of the LMSR, were undertaking. Sir Felix Pole wanted a new big and powerful loco that would work hard and fast and be right at the first go. Collett therefore made extensive use of the proven designs of his predecessor, C J Churchward, and designed a greatly improved version of the "Star" class. Even when the building was commencing, Sir Felix Pole urged more speed for he wanted to show the new locomotive in America in mid-1927 as an example of British loco practice in general and the Great Western's in particular! The result was a 4-6-0 with a compact wheelbase of only 29ft 5in (necessary for the curving Devon main line), the highest boiler pressure of any loco at that time, 250lb; a tractive effort of 40,300lb—well

ahead of its rivals and an axle loading of 22½ton.

In June 1927 the first of the new class emerged from Swindon Works and was named, not as many thought after Cathedrals, but as *King George V*. After a few proving trials the new loco hauled the "Cornish Riviera Express" from Paddington to Plymouth on July 20, taking a record load of ten coaches unassisted up the severe gradients on the South Devon main line. On August 3rd the new loco and tender were shipped to the USA with much publicity, for the GWR were still busy proclaiming the most powerful and graceful new locomotive. No 6000 *King George V* remained in America until October 1927 where it was on show at the Baltimore and Ohio's

centenary celebrations and also hauled a train to Washington and Philadelphia. It put up a most impressive performance against the larger American engines and was presented with a commemorative bell, duly inscribed, which it still carries on the centre of its front buffer beam.

Meanwhile the first five locos of the class had been completed at Swindon and were in service when troubles were experienced with the loco rolling at speeds which finally resulted in a derailment. Fortunately this was not serious, but the cause was found to be instability of the front bogie and immediate modifications were carried out. The result of the findings was advised to William Stanier in America, who was in charge of the American tour, and similar modi-

fications were effected to the loco out there.

When the loco returned to this country in November it again received renewed outbursts of publicity from the GWR, who had never really stopped since the loco first saw the light of day.

By 1930 construction of the 30 locomotives in the class (Nos 6000-6029) was completed and all carried the names of British Monarchs. Modifications to the original design were carried out to the bogies and the covers for the inside valves and feed-pipes. One loco, No 6014 *King Henry VII* was partially streamlined in 1935, but this did not last for long and and the casing was soon removed.

The locos proved popular with the public and the enginemen alike and they produced many record breaking runs, both before, during and after the War.

Following the extensive locomotive exchange trials of 1948 when GWR locos ran on other lines, modifications were made to the superheaters and outside steam pipes and between 1955 and '58 all locos in the class were fitted with improved blast pipes and double chimneys, which again improved their already fine performance.

All the class was withdrawn during 1962 with the exception of No 6000 which has been preserved and at present is at Bulmers Cider Centre at Hereford.

DATA

Dia. of driving wheels:	6ft 6in
Dia of bogie wheels:	3ft
Boiler pressure:	250lb per sq in
Tractive effort:	40,300lb
Cylinders (four):	16¼in by 28in
Weight in working order	
loco:	89ton
tender:	46ton 14cwt
Tender capacity:	4,000 gallon water plus 00 ton coal

Models

Soon after the class was introduced, Bassett-Lowke made an economical model for gauge O, later producing in 1936 a detailed scale model which was available for clockwork, electric at 6-8V DC or 20V AC operation.

In 4mm scale there was a Jamieson sheet metal kit, and Wills Finecast still produce a cast metal kit for this class of loco. Similarly in TT gauge (3mm scale) there is a cast white metal kit produced by G E Mellor.

Above: A 4mm scale model of GWR No 6027 "King Richard I" built from a Wills Finecast kit. *(Courtesy Trent Valley MRS)*

Below: No 6000 "King George V" at Hereford. *R L Ratcliffe*

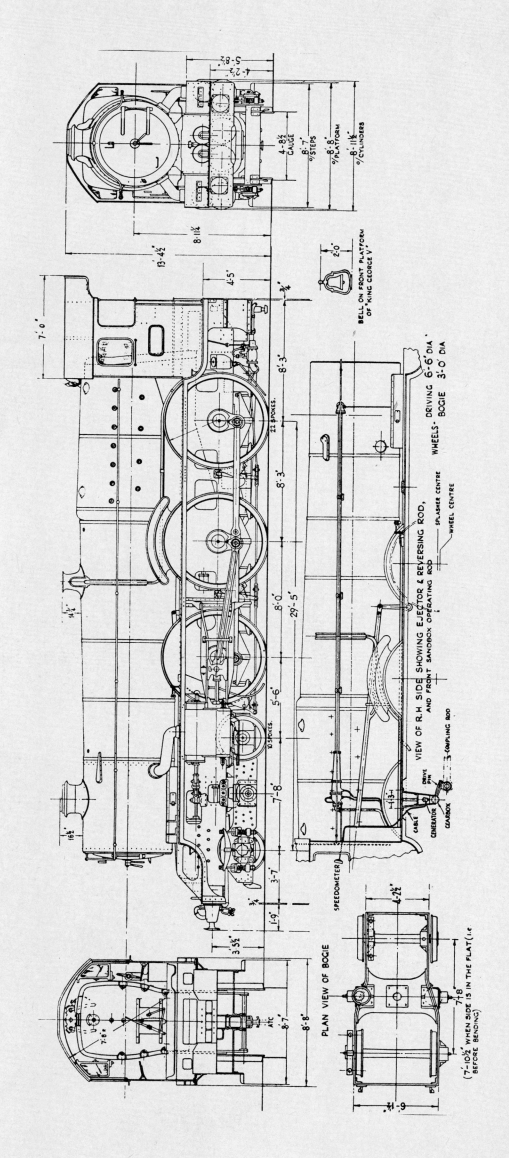

ROYAL SCOT CLASS 4-6-0 LOCOMOTIVE

Up to 1927 the LMSR was having to double-head the majority of its main line express trains, especially on the West Coast route, due to having inherited the old Midland Railway policy of small engines which existed at the Grouping in 1923. To a certain extent the LNWR had followed the Midland idea, for their locos had small boilers and although adequate for the early post-War period, they were not comparable to the modern requirements. Thus the LMSR had an immediate demand for a large boilered express locomotive that could cope with ten coach trains or more, at a reasonable speed. This was forcibly brought home to the LMS by the locomotive exchanges of 1925, so much so that in 1926 the LMSR borrowed a GWR 4-6-0—No 5000 *Launceston Castle*—for a month to work on the West Coast route from Euston-Crewe and then Crewe-Carlisle. The loco performed extremely well easily proving itself capable of hauling the loads required at a high speed and with economy of coal and water. After this the LMSR decided upon a 4-6-0 configuration with a large boiler, a high working pressure and long travel valve gear with three cylinders. A full set of drawings for the Southern Railway's recently introduced "Lord Nelson" class were obtained which were modified to suit LMSR specifications thus there is a similarity between the two classes. Fifty of the new locos (Nos 6100-6149) were ordered direct from the drawing board of the North British Locomotive Co, probably the first time that this has ever happened, for the usual practice is to order one, give it tests and a period of running to assess its performance, before placing further orders. The first loco was delivered in August 1927, and the whole order was completed within twelve months. Twenty more were built at Derby in 1929 (Nos 6150-6169).

Modifications were made to both batches following experience gained with the running and maintenance of the locos, which were originally fitted with a standard type of Midland tender holding 7cwt of coal By 1931/32 developments had been undertaken on the valves, bogies, and axleboxes but these did not affect the external appearance with the exception of the addition of smoke deflectors which stopped steam and smoke from laying along the boiler and obscuring the drivers forward vision. The class were however, renowned as being "rough riders" particularly when they were due for an overhaul.

One more loco was built by the North British (No 6399) which had a high pressure boiler of complex design, but the loco was not a success and finally killed a crew member and injured another when a tube burst. It was later rebuilt by Stanier in 1943 with a tapered boiler and renumbered 6170, having a double chimney and differing heating surfaces etc.

The whole class was rebuilt from 1943 onwards, partly from the experience

Last un-rebuilt "Royal Scot" BR 46163 at Rugby in 1953. *J M Jarvis*

Bottom: Purchased in pieces in a book shop in Carlisle some years ago this O gauge Bassett-Lowke "Royal Scot" of the early 1930s has been fully reconditioned and painted.(Caroline & Andrew collection). *B Monaghan*

Stanier obtained with the rebuilding of the ill-fated No 6399 and also from knowledge gained with his efficient class 5 locomotives.

In 1933 No 6100 *Royal Scot* was sent to America to be exhibited at the Chicago Exhibition where it made a favourable impression for power from such a small loco (by American standards).

All the class were named after British Regiments, although some of the earlier locos received names from old LNWR engines, but these were subsequently changed.

The first loco of the class was withdrawn from service in October 1962.

DATA

Diameter of driving/coupled wheels:	6ft 9in
Diameter of bogie wheels:	3ft 3½in
Overall length:	65ft 2¾in
3 cylinders:	18in by 26in
Weight in working order:	139ton 11cwt

Some Models

Bassett-Lowke were quick off the mark for their 1927 catalogue showed an O gauge model of the loco which was available for clockwork or electric (4-8v DC) operation. The following year Hornby Trains had their O gauge version available, but this, like the *Flying Scotsman*, was a 4-4-2 with the same body painted a different colour, and in no way could it be called a scale model. Bing also produced a gauge "O" model in 1928, though this was not a true replica.

Today there is no ready-to-run model of this famous class of loco, although there are kits by Jamieson (sheet metal) and Wills (cast metal—original version) both in 4mm scale. In TT scale (3mm:1ft) there is a cast metal kit by GEM (G E Mellor) and there was a plastic kit from Kitmaster, but unfortunately these ceased production a few years ago.

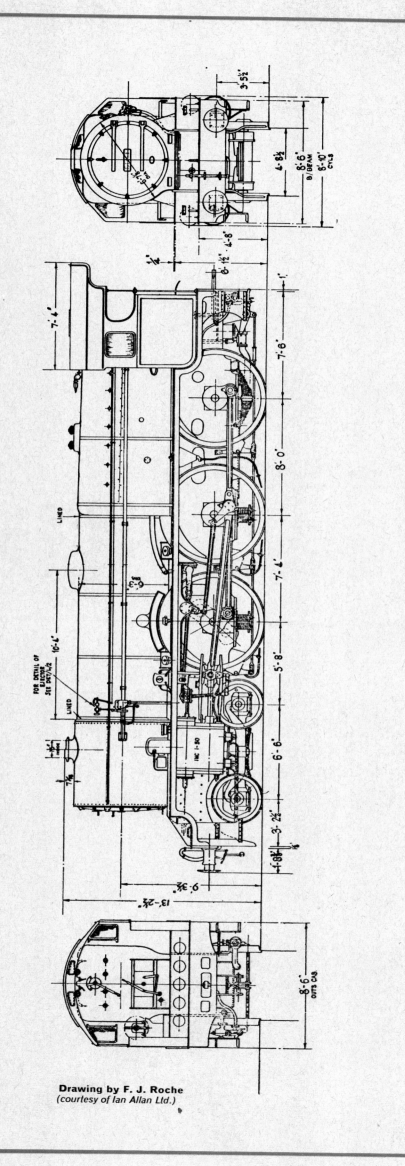
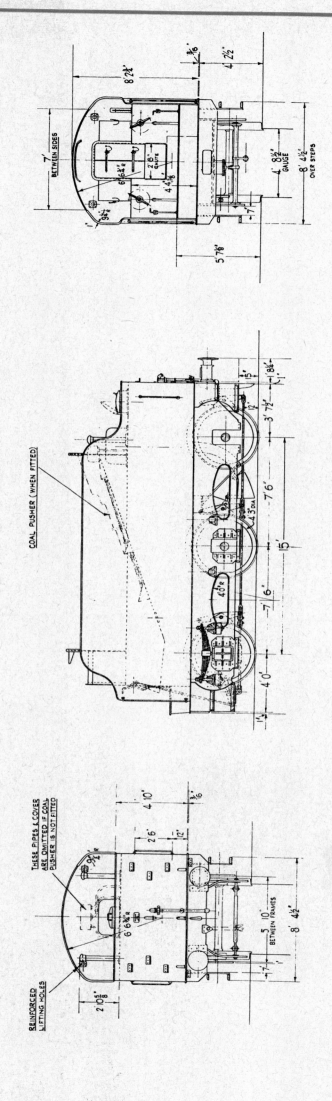

Drawing by F. J. Roche
(courtesy of Ian Allan Ltd.)

GWR 49XX CLASS- THE 'HALLS'

BY C M WHITEHOUSE

The "Hall" Class of the Great Western Railway was one of the most successful mixed traffic engines of its time; these engines worked over most parts of the system and were ideal for use on a very wide range of duties. Their prowess led to the construction of similar types on other railways; for example the Stanier Class 5 of the LMS and the Thompson B1 of the LNER.

The first of the class, totalling 330, was introduced in 1928 after the success of the prototype No 2925 *Saint Martin.* The prototype engine was virtually a Churchward "Saint" class as regards the boiler, cylinders, motion, frames and bogie but with differences of a cylinder centre line co-incident with the driving axle, and 6ft 0in diameter wheels. The outline of the cab was re-designed to be on a par with that used on the "Castles". Collett had not deviated much from the set Churchward pattern.

That 2925 was a great success is shown by the first order for the new "Hall" class which numbered no less than 80 loco-motives. The new engines differed from 2925 (now re-numbered 4900) in that the pitch of the boiler was slightly higher, they possessed outside steam pipes, and the frame work was modified. About half of the first batch were fitted with Church-ward's standard type of 3,500 gallon ten-ders, but with 4958 the larger 4,000 gallon pattern became standard, although a few later engines came out with the earlier type of tender.

A variation on the 49XX class was introduced in 1944 by Hawksworth. These engines, numbering from 6959, differed in outward appearance. The most marked change was the construction method for the underframes: Hawksworth chose to use plate frames throughout (including the bogie) and a new pattern of cylinder and smokebox saddle arrangement, in that the cylinders were bolted on to the outside of the main frames instead of being bolted back to back with the smoke-box saddle. The standard No 1 boiler with a 3 row superheater was also fitted. The engines were paired with the new pattern of straight-sided 4,000 gallon tenders.

At the end of the Second World War there was a vast shortage of coal, and in August 1946 the Minister of Transport ordered that several steam engines should be converted to burn oil. During the latter half of 1946 and early 1947 eleven "Hall" locomotives were so converted, along with other GW engines of dif-ferent classes. They were re-numbered in the 39XX series which they retained until they were converted back to coal again between 1948 and 1950. They burnt a heavy grade fuel oil called "Bunker C" and operated mainly on coal trains in South Wales where two depots were fitted out for their use.

All the class, except one, passed to British Railways in 1948; the exception was 4911 *Bowden Hall* which was a war casualty, receiving a direct hit at Keyham on 29th April 1941, and it was officially condemned at Swindon in June of that year. No 4946 was the first engine to be lettered "British Railways", albeit in the GW style of lettering and shading, and appeared as early as the 16th January 1948. No 6910 was the first of the class to be painted in the experimental livery of lined black, which was eventually adopted for the whole class. No 6990 was selected to take part in the inter-regional locomo-tive exchanges in 1948, and worked between Marylebone and Manchester; it was banned from other lines because of

the generous loading gauge afforded by the GWR as a result of the broad gauge.

An account of the "Hall" Class would be incomplete without an example of the outstanding nature of work they could be called upon to perform. One such oc-casion was recorded in the "Railway Magazine" for January 1955 when a Castle failed at Little Somerford with the "Bristolian". It was replaced by 7904 *Fountains Hall* from a goods train, and the delayed train left 14 minutes later. High speed and hard work by the engine enabled Paddington to be reached in 59 minutes 37 seconds, with some pro-longed hard running; 80-84 mph was sustained for 47 miles between Wantage Road and West Drayton—no mean achievement.

The last member of the class was withdrawn in 1968, but 6998 *Burton Agnes Hall,* officially withdrawn in Janu-ary 1966, is still occasionally at work on special trains. She was purchased by the Great Western Society and restored at their Didcot depot. Although she Is the only member of her class still alive there are plans to restore several more—one of the schemes is to convert a "Hall" back into a "Saint"—so the wheel may turn full circle.

Preserved "Hall" Class Engines

4930 *Hagley Hall* Severn Valley Railway
4983 *Albert Hall* Birmingham Railway Museum
5900 *Hinderton Hall* GW Society, Didcot
6960 *Raveningham Hall* Steamtown, Carn-forth
6998 *Burton Agnes Hall* GW Society, Didcot

DATA

2 cylinders:	18½in by 30in
Diameter of Driving wheels:	6ft 0in
Diameter of Bogie wheels:	3ft 2in
Boiler Pressure:	225lb per sq in
Tractive effort:	27,275lb
Weight of loco and tender in working order:	112ton 10cwt

Note. Tender drawing is as fitted to the early engines. The more usual 4,000 gallon tender was illustrated with the "Castle" Class.

Models

In 4mm scale there is a Wills Finecast white metal kit which will fit either onto a Triang B12 chassis or a special scale one. Hornby Railways produce a prop-rietory model with a plastic injection moulded body in Great Western livery (although it used to be in BR livery); the same firm also produce the same model in bright red, named "Lord West-wood" which is intended to appeal to younger modellers.

In the early 1960s a Jamieson 4mm scale kit appeared, which was an all metal body and chassis which needed soldering and building up, much in the manner of a hand built loco.

In O gauge the only model available is in kit form with nickel-silver parts by Leinster models.

In N gauge Graham Farish produce a "Hall" with a plastic injection moulded body and give a choice of either black or green liveries.

Left Above: Wills Finecast model of G.W.R. "Hall" class.

Left Below: G.W.R. "Hall" Class 4-6-0 No. 6953 'Leighton Hall' at Wolverhampton (Oxley). *Colourviews*

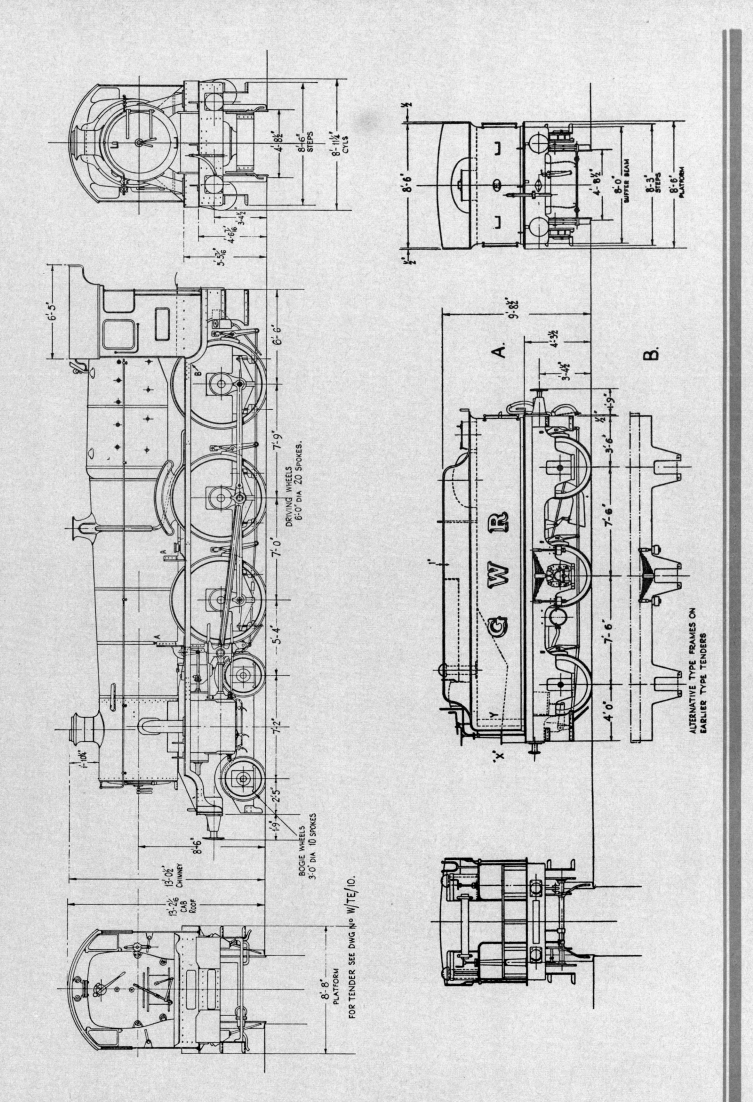

6'-5"

6'-6"

7'-9"

DRIVING WHEELS
6'-0" DIA 20 SPOKES.

7'-0"

5'-4"

7'-2"

BOGIE WHEELS
3'-0" DIA 10 SPOKES

1'-0¼"

2'-5"

1'-9"

8'-6"

13'-0½" CHIMNEY

13'-2⅝" CAB ROOF

8'-8" PLATFORM

FOR TENDER SEE DWG No W/TE/IO.

4'-8½"

8'-6" STEPS

8'-11½" CYLS

4'-6½"

3'-4½"

5'-5⅜"

8'-6"

4'-8½"

8'-0" BUFFER BEAM

8'-3" STEPS

8'-6" PLATFORM

½"

½"

9'-8"

4'-9½"

3'-4½"

A.

4'-9"

5'-6"

7'-6"

7'-6"

4'-0"

B.

'X'

'Y'

GWR

ALTERNATIVE TYPE FRAMES ON
EARLIER TYPE TENDERS

Drawing by F. J. Roche
(courtesy of Ian Allan Ltd.)

57XX TANK

The 0-6-0, or six-coupled pannier tank is synonymous with the Great Western Railway, and for a period of eighty years they have been ubiquitous all over the system; a grand total of 2,393 having been built between 1860-1956. The distinctive design having the side tanks extending up to the boiler top and the length of the boiler is reminiscent of the saddle tank, many of which were rebuilt as pannier tanks. The pannier tank was evolved by the difficulty of fitting a saddle tank onto a Belpaire firebox which was much favoured and thus a happy compromise was made.

The duties of these sturdy little locos were not confined to the humble shunting duties as may be imagined, for they worked local passenger and freight trains with ease and put up some prodigious performances over the years.

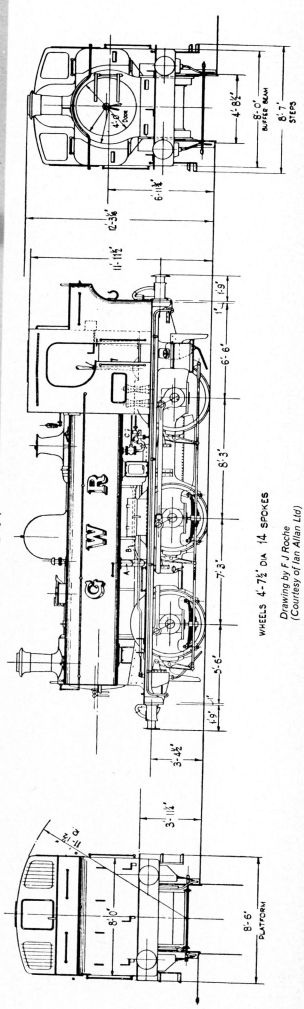

Obviously, over such a long period there were considerable improvements made to the design, particularly the cab where the comfort of the crew was considered and these were made larger in latter years. However, there is a surprising amount of standardisation that has existed in the working parts and dimensions over the years.

Our drawing shows the 57xx class of pannier tank of the later type with the larger cab, giving more protection from the weather for the driver and fireman. This particular class of pannier tank was very similar to the rebuilt 27xx class, which in turn came from the "1813" class. A total of 863 of the 57xx class were built between 1929-50 not only at Swindon Works but on the premises of many of the leading English locomotive builders.

With their small size, low axle loadings the panniers had few restrictions as to the lines which could not accommodate them. The first one was withdrawn from service in March 1956, the last one running long after steam had ceased on British Railways for several of the class were sold to London Transport who used them on their works and stores trains. Some are still working on lines like the Severn Valley Railway or Keighley and Worth Valley Railway. Engines with early and late cabs (7752, 7760 and 9600) are in working order at Tyseley.

Models

Surprisingly, accurate models of pannier tanks have not been commercially produced in the model trade in relation to the widespread use of the prototypes. Bassett-Lowke and the Leeds Model Company both produced gauge O models in the 1930s, the former being available for clockwork or electric propulsion.

Graham Farish produced a pannier in 4mm scale in the 1950s which is now out of production although they have produced another model in N gauge which was released in 1972. In that year Tri-ang (Hornby Railways) also produced a OO gauge model, which was placed on the chassis for their existing LMSR 0-6-0T and thus was not as accurate as it might have been. It has remained in the field of the kit manufacturers of recent years to supply cast white metal kits for pannier tank bodies—GEM with a model of a 57xx class for TT gauge, BEC with a kit for a 94xx class also in TT gauge, while Wills Finecast have produced 4mm scale body kits for a 94xx class and the older 1854 class.

DATA

Cylinders:	17½in by 24in
Boiler pressure:	200lbs/sq in
Diameter of driving wheels:	4ft 7½in
Tank capacity:	1,200 gallons
Bunker capacity:	3¼ton
Tractive effort:	22,515lbs
Weight in working order:	47ton 10cwt

Top: GWR 57XX class 0-6-0 Pannier Tank in TT gauge. Built from a GEM kit.

Left: Great Western Railway 57xx 0-6-0 pannier tank No 7752 in 1947 livery.
C M Whitehouse

Centre left: 57XX Pannier by Triang-Hornby in 4mm scale, produced 1972 – re-painted and lettered.

Top left: Gauge "0" scratch built Pannier.
G Brown

WHEELS 4'-7½' DIA 14 SPOKES

Drawing by F J Roche
(Courtesy of Ian Allan Ltd)

In 1928 the various chiefs of departments of the Southern Railway were having discussions on a new locomotive that was needed to work heavy trains at express speeds on the lines of the Eastern Section, which had a very restricted loading gauge (particularly on the Charing Cross-Hastings line); abounded with quite severe gradients and had some sharp radius curves. The Civil Engineer then made a further restriction that due to shallow track beds the axle loading must not exceed more than 21tons. This could have been done with a six-coupled locomotive, but its length would have been an embarrassment on the tight curves, further there could have been another difficulty with turntables, for the line generally only had turntables capable of taking a loco of 50ft. The existing turntables could, of course, have been rebuilt, but the cost involved was nearly as much as that of a new loco-motive.

The CME of the Southern, R E L Maunsell overcame all these problems and in March 1930 the first of the new locos—class V—left Eastleigh Works. It created quite a furore, for it was of 4-4-0 wheel arrangement, (said by many people to be a moribund design), was compara-tively short, and incorporated many standard parts from the Lord Nelson and King Arthur class locos. The wheels, outside cylinders, valve gear and motion were interchangeable with the Lord Nelson class, while the boiler was a shortened version of the King Arthur class, having a round topped firebox which enabled the cab sides to be in-clined towards the centre, thus coming within the loading gauge.

The locos were a triumph for their designer and became the most powerful 4-4-0 locomotives to have been built in Europe. They surpassed all expectations and not only coped well with the trains of the Eastern Section, but also worked on the Central and Western Sections, on the latter hauling the Waterloo-Bourne-mouth express trains and putting up some very good timings, equal to those of their larger brothers.

A total of 40 locomotives were built between 1930-35, all named after Schools between 1930-35, all named after schools in the southern counties of England,

Few modifications were made, the gravity sanding gear on the first ten was replaced with steam fed type, and smoke deflectors were fitted in 1932. Later, Bulleid experimented with double chim-neys and Lemaitre blast pipes which were retained on some of the locos. The original tenders were six wheeled types holding 4,000 gallons of water and 5tons of coal, but some of these were replaced by tenders from withdrawn "Nelson" class locos in the 1950s. No 932 had a different tender from inception, having higher sides than the rest of the class.

DATA

Diameter of driving/coupled wheels:	6ft 7in
Diameter of bogie wheels:	3ft 1in
Boiler pressure:	220lbs/per sq
Tractive effort:	25,230lbs

Models

Soon after the appearance of the proto-type, Bassett Lowke produced an O gauge model available with three types of propulsion—clockwork, electric at 8volts DC or electric at 20v AC.

A model that would have become very popular had not the War intervened was the Hornby tinplate O gauge version introduced in 1939—No 900 *Eton* was available for clockwork or electric propul-sion.

In the late 1960s Kitmaster produced a plastic 4mm scale kit of the locomotive, which was later purchased by Airfix and also marketed under their name. This is still currently available.

A more advanced kit is available in the Jamieson range, which consists of the various parts cut from nickel-silver, while Wills Finecast kits have recently (April '73) produced a fine 4mm scale kit of white metal castings for the body and tender. A special chassis can also be supplied.

SR 'SCHOOLS' CLASS 4-4-0

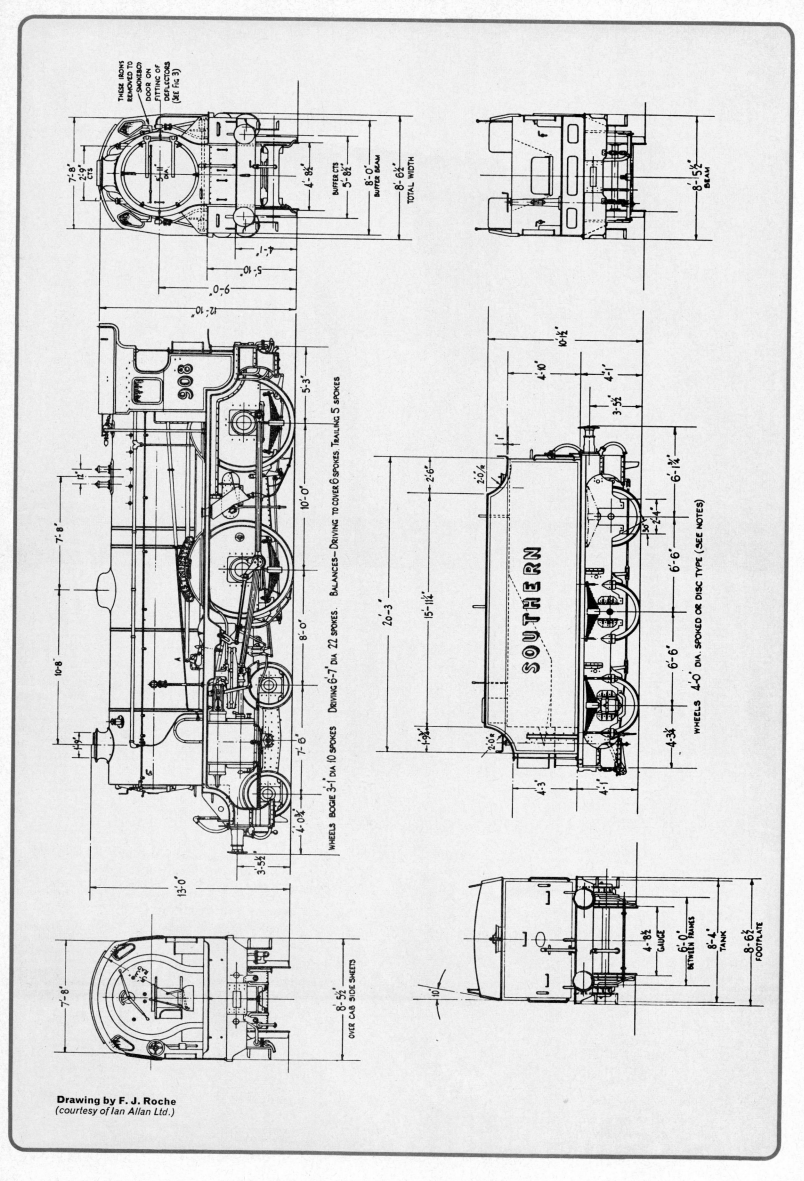

THESE IRONS
REMOVED TO
SMOKEBOX
DOOR ON
FITTING OF
DEFLECTORS
(See Fig 3)

7'-8"
2'-9" CTS
5'-11" DIA

4'-8½"
BUFFER CTS
5'-8½"
BUFFER BEAM
8'-0"
8'-6½"
TOTAL WIDTH

8'-5½"
BEAM

4'-1"
5'-10"
9'-0"
12'-10"

908

5'-3"
10'-0"
8'-0"
7'-6"
4'-0¾"

12"
7'-8"
10'-8"
4½"
3'-5½"
13'-0"

WHEELS BOGIE 3'-1 DIA 10 SPOKES   DRIVING 6'-7 DIA 22 SPOKES.   BALANCES — DRIVING TO COVER 6 SPOKES. TRAILING 5 SPOKES

10'-½"
4'-10"
4'-1"
3'-5½"
1"
2'-6"
2'-0½"
20'-3"
15'-11½"
1'-9½"
2'-0 R

SOUTHERN

6'-1¼"
2'-4"
6'-6"
6'-6"
4'-3¾"
4'-3"
4'-1"

WHEELS 4'-0 DIA. SPOKED OR DISC TYPE (SEE NOTES)

7'-8"
8'-5½"
OVER CAB SIDE SHEETS

4'-8½"
GAUGE
6'-0"
BETWEEN FRAMES
8'-4"
TANK
8'-6½"
FOOTPLATE

10°

Drawing by F. J. Roche
(courtesy of Ian Allan Ltd.)

453

GWR 14XX CLASS

Above : The preserved GWR 14XX 0-4-2T No 1420 at Worcester in 1966.

Above right: A K's kit and box.

Below: A fine hand built 14XX Class as GWR No 4837 by Guy Williams and now at Pendon Museum. *Peter Williams*

Tank engines with an 0-4-2 wheel arrangement were first introduced to the Great Western Railway by George Armstrong of Wolverhampton in the 1860s. The first designs incorporated saddle tanks, but these were altered to side tanks in 1870 and resulted in the well-known 517 class. These engines were allocated to branch and local trains, and under Churchward many were used for auto trains.

The 14XX class were built as a replacement for the 517 class, which were being withdrawn by 1932. At one time or another virtually all the branch lines of the GWR have seen one or more of these engines which proved just as useful as the old 517s.

The engines were originally numbered in the 48XX series, and the first emerged from Swindon in 1932. The design was not new and was derived from nineteenth century ideas, although various points were updated. The most noticeable improvement was the provision of an enclosed cab which was formed flush with the tank sides and bunker; this extra width allowed the provision of very large cab windows. One novelty not previously seen on GW engines was the casing behind the chimney which housed the control cock for the regulator lubricator. The axle load of the engines was kept under 14 tons in order to allow them to run on "uncoloured" routes and to give them the very widest availability.

There were seventy-five engines in the 48XX series, all fitted with Automatic Train Control and auto gear when built. There were a further twenty engines which were numbered in the 58XX series; these were identical except that they were not fitted with either ATC or auto gear. Ten were later fitted for "push and pull" working between 1936 and 1938. The 48XX series were all re-numbered in the 14XX series in 1946 as their original numbers were required for the 28XX 2-8-0 tender engines which had been converted to burn oil.

The appearance of the class remained unchanged except for the addition of large whistle shields (a few engines sported smaller type shields initially) and, from 1944 onwards, the fitting of a top feed which did little to improve their handsome appearance. Also, steps were fitted to the fireman's side of the bunker.

The class was widely dispersed over the Great Western system and became a familiar sight on the many branch lines. However, the closure of several of these meant there was not enough work for all of the class and so six of the 58XXs were put into store at Swindon. The amalgamation and British Railways' policy of closing down unremunerative branch lines resulted in the withdrawal of the 58XX series except 5809, 5815 and 5818 as these were auto fitted. Similarly later, many of the 14XX series became redundant and they too were gradually withdrawn although several remained into the mid-sixties until the latter days of GW steam.

In Great Western times the engines were painted in unlined green. The official livery in BR days was unlined black, but Nos 1465, 1470 and 5818 were lined out. From 1956 onwards they were painted green, and some were even turned out with full lining and polished safety-valve covers.

The Class has been a favourite candidate for preservation with no less than four examples being preserved, of which three are in working order. The exception is 1442 which is on a plinth at Tiverton. The Great Western Society has 1460 at their Didcot depot; this engine, together with an auto coach, were their first acquisitions. Nos 1420 and 1450 can be seen at work on the Dart Valley Railway between Buckfastleigh and Totnes (Riverside), sometimes hauling loads that Collett never dreamed of. Unfortunately they have been painted in lined out green which is not the correct GWR livery.

The Great Western were criticised for producing an outdated design, but the 14XX class have certainly proved their worth as small and economical engines which are capable of a fair turn of speed when necessary: 64 mph has been recorded and it was not unknown for one to overtake an express on parallel lines such as between Reading and Maidenhead.

DATA

Driving wheel diameter:	5ft 2in
Trailing wheel diameter:	3ft 8in
Cylinders (2):	16in diameter x 24in stroke
Boiler pressure:	165lb
Weight (total):	41ton 6cwt

Models

Currently in production are two white metal kits: K's produce one for OO (16.5mm) gauge, and GEM produce one for TT (12mm) gauge. There never have been any ready to run commercial models of 14XXs.

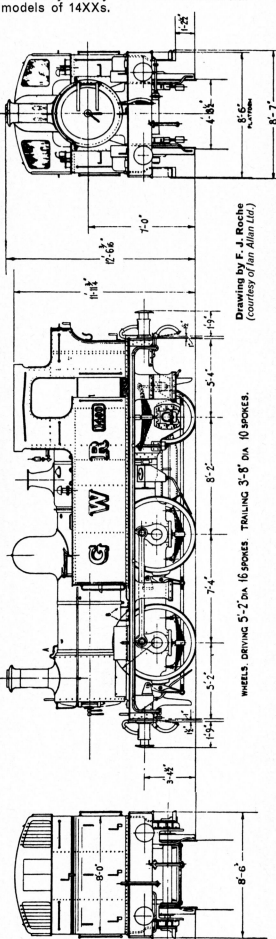

Drawing by F. J. Roche
(courtesy of Ian Allan Ltd.)

WHEELS. DRIVING 5'-2" DIA 16 SPOKES. TRAILING 3'-8" DIA 10 SPOKES.

The SNCF 231 E Pacific

Above: SNCF 231 E 36 at Calais in 1963.   *J E Bell*

Below: A Rivarossi 4 mm model of a Nord 231 E Pacific.   *E S Russell*

In the days of the French pre-nationalised railways each company had its own fleet of Pacifics, some of which dated back to before 1914. Many of these locomotives were rejuvenated during the 1930s with improved steam passages, valves, and high degree superheat. The classic example was a rather unremarkable series of Pacifics built for the Paris-Orleans company in 1909, transformed under the direction of Andre Chapelon into the later SNCF class 231 E with an increase in power output from 2,100 to 3,500hp. The 231 Es were concentrated on the Nord Region and their final days were spent working the Amiens-Calais section until April 10th 1967 when 231 E 22 made its last journey working the Fleche d'Or. Of all French engines, the Chapelon compound Pacifics were the best loved and the best known, their fame crossing the waters of the English Channel.

That Chapelon revolutionised the performance of these and the PLM Pacifics is an understatement. At the time of rebuilding the latter were provided with new low pressure cylinders with large steam passages and the PLM double blast pipe. The old P-O Midi engine—later the 231 Es—had the de Glehn arrangement of independently controlled valve gear and were rather better starters than their PLM sisters.

There were four series of 231 Es. The first (231 E1-20) built by Fives Lille, the second (231 E21-28) built by Ateliers du Nord the third 231 E29-38 built by Forges et Acieries de la Marine et d'Homecourt and the final series 231 E39-48 by Fives Lille. The first series were the rebuilds of 1909-14 locomotives in 1934. The others were constructed in 1936-37. The Nord machines (21-48) differed from those of the P.O. in a few details, dome covers, dynamo etc.

Models

French Pacifics have, in later years, proved to be popular models in HO scale and both Rivarossi and Jouef have produced excellent replicas of the 231 E.

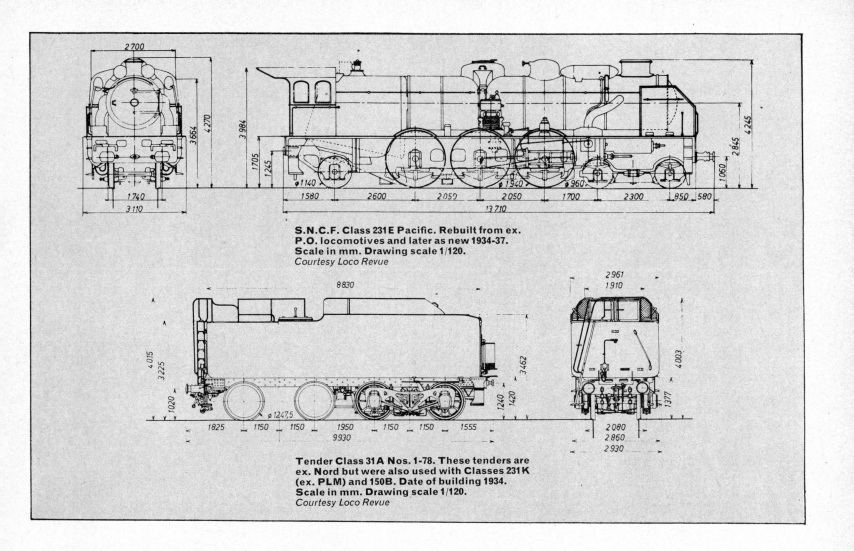

**S.N.C.F. Class 231E Pacific. Rebuilt from ex.
P.O. locomotives and later as new 1934-37.
Scale in mm. Drawing scale 1/120.**
Courtesy Loco Revue

**Tender Class 31A Nos. 1-78. These tenders are
ex. Nord but were also used with Classes 231K
(ex. PLM) and 150B. Date of building 1934.
Scale in mm. Drawing scale 1/120.**
Courtesy Loco Revue

STANIER 2-6-4Ts of the LMSR

The LMSR has always had a large number of 2-6-4T locomotives, yet did not acquire all that number from its constituent companies at the time of the Grouping. Sir Henry Fowler built the first design for the LMSR in 1927 (Nos 2300 etc) and these were quite successful having two cylinders 19in by 26in and 5ft 9in coupled wheels. When Sir William Stanier was appointed as CME he found there was a need for a new and powerful locomotive for the London, Tilbury and Southend line as that Company's locos were becoming time expired, plus the fact that a loco with more speedy acceleration was needed to cope with the growing commuter traffic.

His first design, introduced in 1934, was a three cylinder loco of massive proportions and impressive looks, in keeping with what later became known as the Stanier tradition or characteristic, having strong affinities to Swindon designs, where Stanier was previously employed. The new locos had a domeless taper boiler, driving wheels of 5ft 9in diameter but the three cylinders were 16in by 26in. These engines were numbered 2500-2536 and although they worked the Southend line they could be found on other parts of the LMSR system. In practice it was found that the new locos did not show a marked improvement on the earlier Fowler design. Our drawing shows a locomotive of this early Stanier design, one of which is preserved at Bressingham, Diss, Norfolk.

It perhaps was not surprising that two years later in 1936 Stanier produced another class of loco of similar appearance and dimensions, but having only two cylinders this time measuring 19½in

by 26in. Large numbers of these were built at Derby Works and by the North British Loco Co from 1936 onwards. These locos proved powerful, efficient and economical in service and various locos in the class could be found in practically every part of the LMSR system.

In 1945, C E Fairburn succeeded Stanier as CME and he too, introduced a 2-6-4T loco, which although copying Stanier's design in many respects was slightly smaller, the coupled wheelbase being shortened by 1ft 2in which enabled the locos to work on some of the branch lines with sharp radius curves. The external appearance was changed by the cut-away footplating at the front end, ahead of the cylinders, probably to reduce the overall weight. These locos were widely used, and they became the basis for the design of the British Railways class 4, 2-6-4Ts (Nos 80000 upwards) although there were modifications made such as a shorter cab etc.

It would appear that the 2-6-4T locomotive in its various forms proved popular with the management and operating staffs of the LMSR.

Models

Bassett-Lowke produced an O gauge model of the original Stanier design in 1938 available for clockwork, or 6V and 20V electric operation. A super detailed model appeared about the same time, which was practically handbuilt and to special order. Also in O gauge there is a Dawson (now marketed by CCW) body kit.

In 4mm scale there is a cast white metal kit on the market by Wills Finecast; a Jamieson sheet metal kit (now difficult to obtain); and the popular Hornby Dublo model of the BR locomotive which has a die-cast body and an exceptionally good chassis and motor.

In TT scale (3mm:1ft), there is a BEC kit of the BR type.

DATA
(For Stanier's original design as drawing)

Dia of driving wheels:	5ft 9in
Cylinders (three):	16in by 16in
Tractive effort:	24,600lb
Water capacity:	2,000 gallons
Coal capacity:	3½ton
Weight in working order:	92ton 5 cwt
Boiler pressure:	200lb per sq in

Above: A 7mm scale Stanier 2-6-4T No 2436, a model of one of the 2-cylinder variety of these popular locomotives. Model built by **D W Jackson.** *B Monaghan*

Right: **LMS No 2508 photographed soon after delivery.**

Drawing by F. J. Roche
(courtesy of Ian Allan Ltd.)

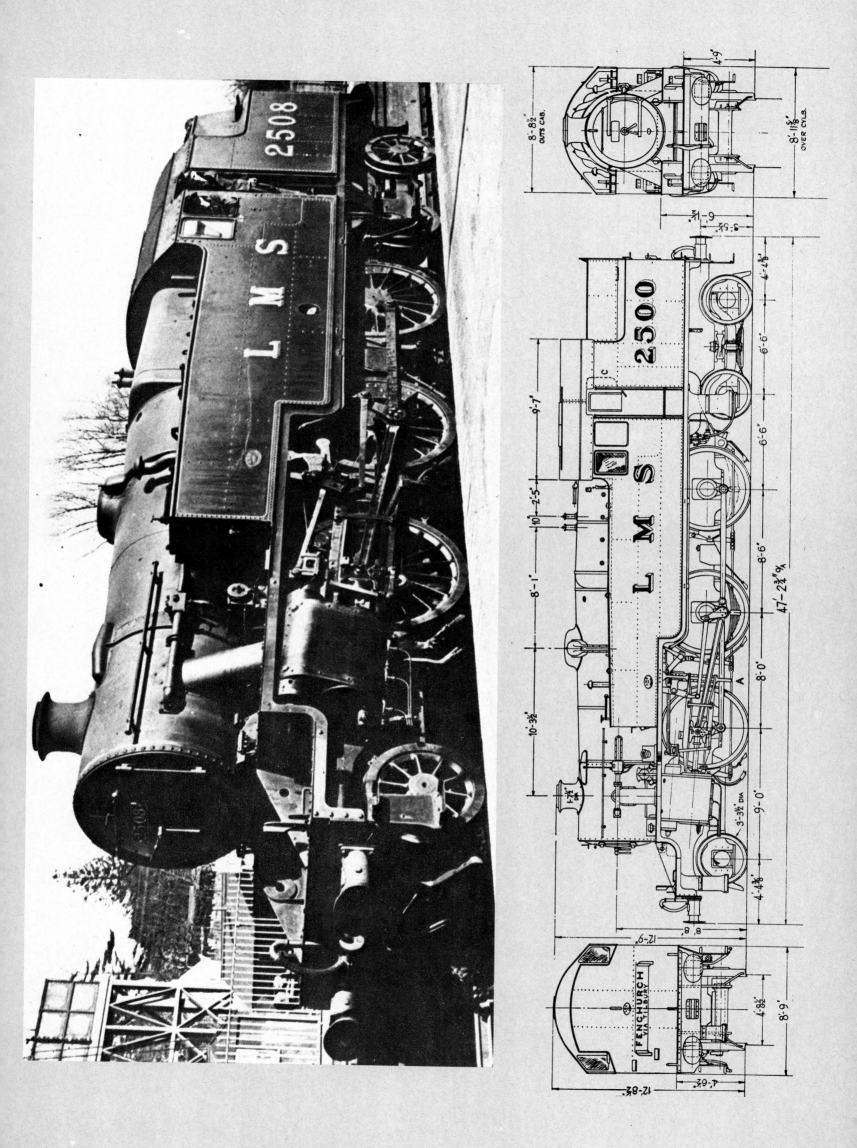

STANIER PACIFIC

Within 17 months of W A Stanier (later Sir William Stanier) taking over from Sir Henry Fowler as CME of the LMSR, he had designed the first LMSR Pacific loco and it had emerged from Crewe Works. Three were built and attracted much publicity; they were Nos 6200 *Princess Royal,* 6201 *Princess Elizabeth* and a third which was a revolutionary turbine locomotive. They were immediately put into service on the West Coast route on trains to and from Scotland, but mechanical troubles arose which necessitated modifications and it was not until 1935 that further locos (Nos 6203-6212) were built. These were also named after members of the Royal Family and the class became known as the "Princess Royal" class. The design was striking for a long tapered boiler was fitted and the locos gave the impression of strength and speed; the class must rank as being one of the most handsome locos at the time. All these locos ran right until their end without having had smoke deflectors fitted.

In 1937 with much attendant publicity the LMSR launched their new "Coronation Scot" train between Euston and Glasgow for which Stanier designed five streamlined locos. The design of the earlier Pacific locomotives was considerably revised having an improved boiler with greatly increased heating surfaces and the whole loco was given a streamlined casing, this being the popular trend at the time. The engines looked very smart for their livery was distinctive, a deep blue with a silver band running from a chevron on the bulbous front end right along the sides to the tender, and incidentally carried on along the carriages. The locos were a great success; a 3in increase in the size of the drivers and the increased heating surfaces over their predecessors plus other internal modifications paid dividends. The following year a further five were built, also streamlined but with a livery of LMS

maroon with gold bands, followed by another five which were not streamlined. The years 1939-1948 saw further batches, fourteen of which were streamlined and ten which were not. The livery was either LMS maroon or, due to wartime restrictions, plain black. One batch (Nos 6230-4) had double chimneys which were later fitted to all of the class. While the locomotives proved highly successful in service, it was found that maintenance was made difficult and took longer for the streamlined variety, thus this casing was removed in 1946/47 and was not replaced. These de-streamlined locos were easily recognisable at first for they had a sloping top to the smokebox and a break in the footplate ahead of the cylinders instead of the graceful curve of the others. All were later rebuilt with normal smokeboxes and footplates and fitted with smoke deflectors.

Many record breaking runs have been recorded for this class, the most famous of which was the 114mph reached near Crewe on a press trip in 1937.

The turbomotive mentioned earlier was finally rebuilt to orthodox form following many mechanical troubles, only to be destroyed in the Harrow accident in 1952.

This class was known as the "Princess Coronation" class and our drawing shows one of the later examples of the prototypes which never carried streamlining.

DATA

Diameter of driving wheels:	6ft 9in
Diameter of bogie wheels:	3ft
Diameter of pony wheels:	3ft 9in
Cylinders:	16½in by 28in
Boiler pressure:	250lbs/sq in
Tractive effort:	40,000lbs
Weight in working order (loco & tender):	161ton 12cwt

Models

In 1937 Hornby produced their finest model for their O gauge system. This was

a detailed model of No 6201 *Princess Elizabeth.* It was a 20v AC electric locomotive which in a presentation box cost only £5 5s 0d. The following year the Hornby Dublo system introduced an LMSR Pacific which is still being produced by Wrenn Ltd today with variations. This was 6231 *Duchess of Atholl* with a diecast 4mm scale body and a 12v DC mechanism which cost 45s in those days!

Bassett-Lowke also produced the Princess Royal class in gauges O (electric and clockwork) and in gauge 1 (electric or live steam), as well as streamlined and non-streamlined Duchess/Coronations.

When the firm of Rovex (later to become Tri-ang) first entered the model railway market in 1950, their original loco was a rather poor model of an LMSR Pacific in OO gauge. The model has been improved many times and is still in the Hornby Railways catalogue.

Naturally with such a popular prototype many models in various scales have been especially made for customers by the model-making concerns.

The streamlined "Coronation" is represented in the catalogues by a OO gauge version from Hornby Railways (ex-Triang) and as a 4mm scale body kit in sheet metal from Jamiesons.

Top Left: Hornby 'OO' early 3 rail model.

Top Right: 46235 'City of Birmingham' at **Saltley.**

Below: Trix-Twin 'OO' Gauge electric model. *(Caroline and Andrew Collection).* *B Monaghan*

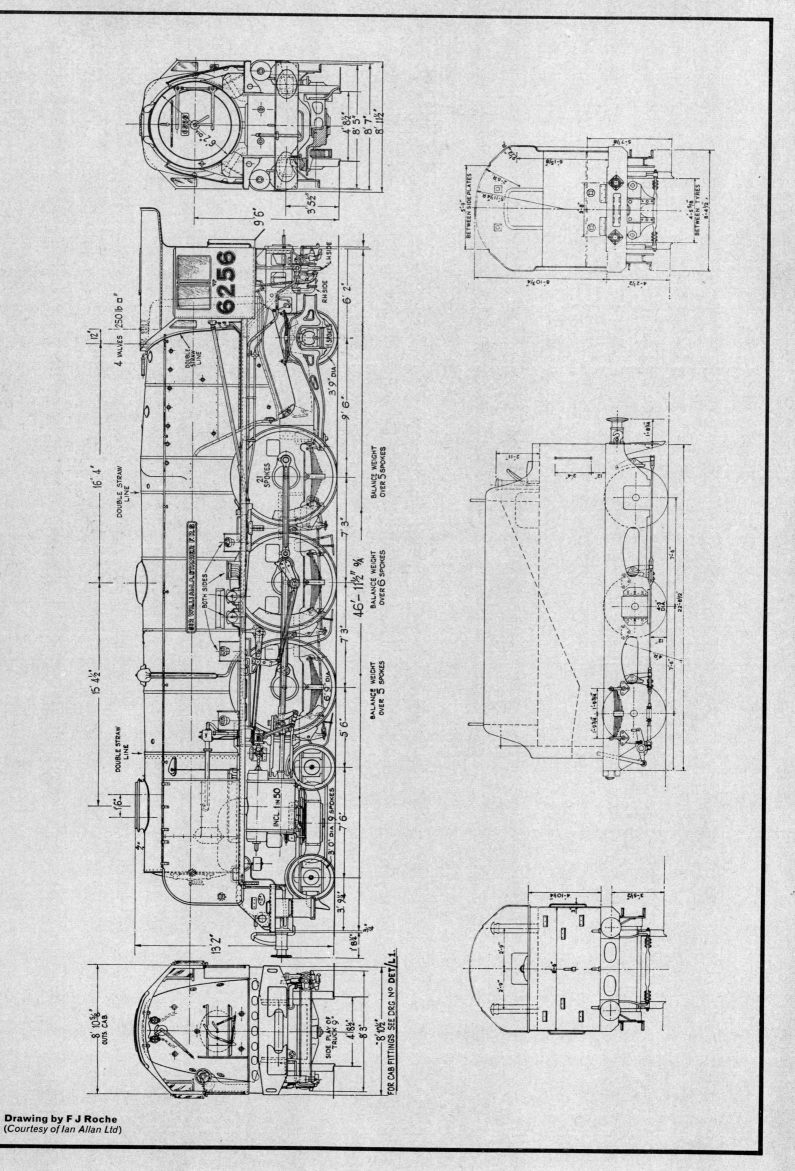

Drawing by F J Roche
(Courtesy of Ian Allan Ltd)

461

The Stanier Class 8F 2-8-0

The story of the Stanier designed class 8F 2-8-0 locomotives has a parallel with the Robinson 2-8-0s which were designed for the Great Central Railway, for both types were adopted by the War Department for use in the two World Wars.

The need for a heavy long distance freight loco was being felt by the LMSR in the mid-thirties when freight traffic was reaching a new peak, thus in June 1935 the first of the new class emerged from Crewe Works. The first batch, (Nos 8000-8011) had domeless tapered boilers, with Walschaerts valve gear, the cylinders and motion being identical with the Stanier class 5 locomotives. These locomotives were given the power classification 7F. Further batches built from 1936 onwards were classified as 8F and had improved tapered boilers, with domes and top feed, larger grates and bigger fireboxes. Eventually the original locos were converted likewise.

All the class had left hand drive with steam sanding gear, permitting a trickle of sand to the front of the leading coupled wheels and to the front and rear of the third pair of wheels; there was also a de-sander which consisted of a jet of water to wash the sand off the rails after it had served its purpose, so that the track circuiting would not be affected by the residue left on the rails.

The tender was the standard 6-wheel type with a capacity of 4,000 gallons of water and 9tons of coal, being of the high sided pattern.

The locomotives proved highly successful in service, even working passenger trains on occasions. A total of 126 had been built up to the end of 1939, when the Ministry of Supply adopted the design for use in occupied countries, thus 240 were ordered with some modifications such as Westinghouse brakes

Top: 2-8-0 BR No 48467 at Kettering.

Bottom: A 4mm scale LMS 2-8-0 No 8153 model by Beeson (*Collection Count Antonio Giansanti Coluzzi*)

instead of the vacuum type and other slight alterations. These were mainly built by the North British Locomotive Co and saw service in the Middle East—Egypt, Turkey, Iran and even Italy. Many of these were converted to oil burning, and some returned to this country after the hostilities, but some were kept by the operating companies in the countries concerned, where they continued to give good service.

During the War the movement of freight, troops and vital supplies were causing problems with the available motive power and with an eye on the opening of the Second Front and our re-entry into France and Germany, the Railway Executive Committee (a Wartime body in charge of the Railways of Britain), selected this class of loco, and many more were built not only in the LMSR works at Crewe and Horwich but in the erecting shops of the other railway companies at Ashford, Brighton, Dar-

lington, Doncaster, Eastleigh and Swindon. These locos were then loaned to the LNER, SR and GWR as well as to the LMSR. Again many were sent overseas after a spell of service in Britain in 1946/47, serving in Europe and further afield, many being lost as the result of enemy action.

The class was the largest built to a Stanier design, a total of 852 being produced, and 666 were in service in the British Isles after the War.

The locos were very free running and appear to have been popular with their crews and they were a familiar sight on main lines throughout the country.

The first loco was withdrawn in October 1960 and several have been preserved.

DATA

2 cylinders:		18½in by 28in
Dia of driving wheels:		4ft 8½in
Dia of pony truck:		3ft 3¼in
Boiler pressure:		225lbs per sq in
Tractive effort:		32,438lbs
Maximum axle load:		16ton
Weight in working order:		
loco	70ton	10cwt
tender	50ton	2cwt
total	124ton	12cwt

Models

Because of the difficulty of getting an eight coupled locomotive model round sharp curves, they have never been as popular as prototypes having a shorter wheelbase. Nevertheless Hornby-Dublo produced an excellent scale model of the class 8F in, 1958 which had a die-cast metal body and a Ringfield Motor. This model was immediately acclaimed by all enthusiasts and proved to be universally popular. It is still available today in the models now being produced by Wrenn.

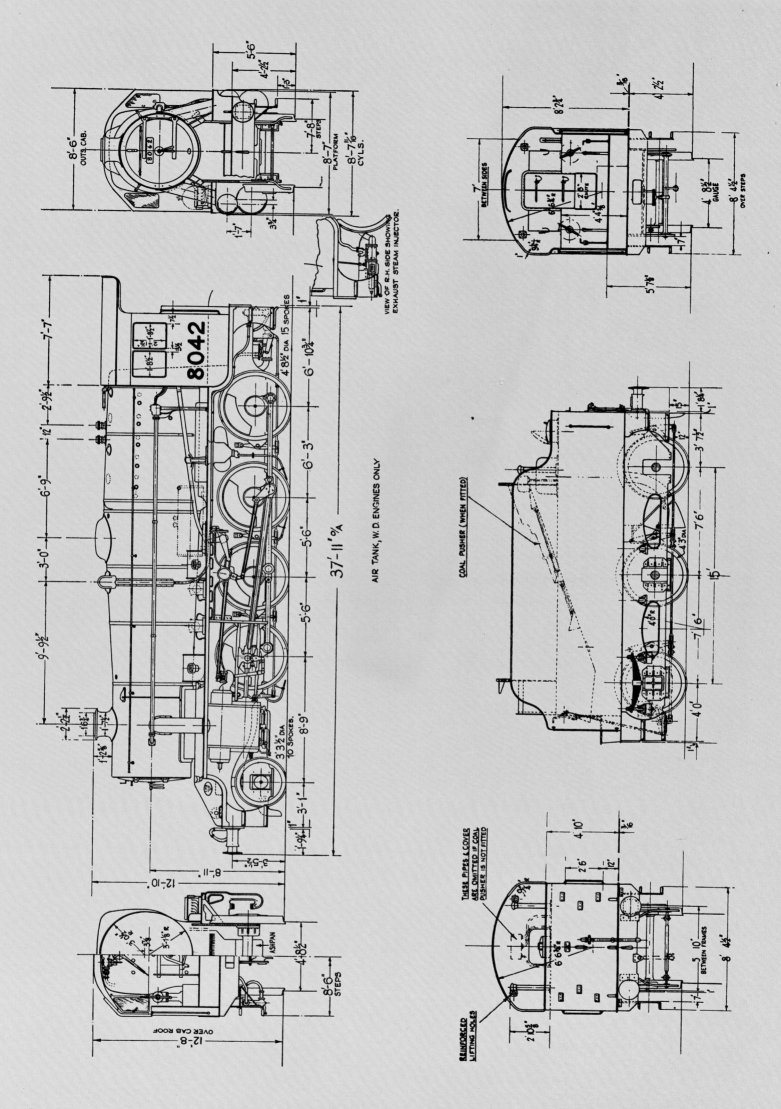

VIEW OF R.H. SIDE SHOWING
EXHAUST STEAM INJECTOR.

AIR TANK, W.D. ENGINES ONLY

8042

COAL PUSHER (WHEN FITTED)

THESE PIPES & COVER
ARE OMITTED IF COAL
PUSHER IS NOT FITTED

REINFORCED
LIFTING HOLES

Drawing by F. J. Roche
(courtesy of Ian Allan Ltd.)

Southern Railway 0·6·0 Q Class

Mr R E L Maunsell designed the Q class of 0-6-0 tender freight locomotives just before he retired; the first of the 20 in the class actually being completed at the Eastleigh Works of the Southern Railway after Mr O V Bulleid had taken over as Chief Mechanical Engineer. At the Grouping of the Railways in 1923, the Southern had inherited a large number of old 0-6-0 locomotives from their constituent companies which had been kept in service due to their light axle loadings. However, as track standards improved the Civil Engineers were able to allow a higher axle loading and with the older locos becoming time expired, there was a need for a replacement which could be more powerful, and in keeping with the modern trend. Although primarily a freight locomotive, it is obvious that Maunsell foresaw that they would be used on passenger duties, for he fitted train heating connections at either end, a sound idea, for later in their life this class of loco worked secondary passenger trains very successfully.

The boiler was of the Belpaire type and had a pressure of 200lb per sq inch—much higher than the locos they were replacing, likewise the tractive effort was raised to 26,160lb, making them quite a powerful and useful addition to the motive power fleet. Long travel piston valves of 10in diameter operated Stephenson link motion through rocking levers which ensured ease of maintenance. Steam reversing gear was fitted as standard, operated through a miniature lever in the cab. Steam sanding gear was placed in front of the leading coupled wheels and behind the centre wheels, while a de-

sander or rail washer was fitted behind the last pair of wheels.

The tender was of standard design as fitted to the class N 2-6-0 locomotives. The axle loadings of 18ton were within the permitted limits imposed by the civil engineers.

In service the locos proved to be rather poor steamers, but this was later improved when Bulleid had fitted Lemaitre multiple blast pipe to his own Q1 class of locomotives. After the war experiments were made and the Q class were fitted

Above: A 16.5mm gauge 4mm scale model built from a Wills' kit. *David Rudkin*

Above: B.R. (Southern Region) 'Q' Class 0-6-0 No 30546 at Eastleigh.

with blast pipes and chimney assemblies the same as used on the BR class 4 2-6-4Ts. This considerably improved the performance of the class and did not spoil the aesthetic looks, but it did not assist the economy of maintenance, and they were later put back to single blast pipes, although still retaining the larger diameter chimney. Two of the locos (Nos 545 and 549) retained their smaller chimneys to the end of their days.

DATA

Two inside cyclinders:	19in by 26in
Dia of driving wheels:	5ft 1in
Weight of loco in working order:	49ton 10cwt
Weight of tender in working order:	40ton 10cwt
Boiler pressure:	200lb per sq in
Tractive effort:	26,260lb

Models

With a locomotive with such simple lines and having the ubiquitous wheel arrangement, it was not long before the model manufacturers added "near likeness" models to their range, using their existing chassis and parts. One such was Bassett-Lowke for gauge "O" in their 1938/39 catalogue. Live steam enthusiasts were catered for by a design of "LBSC" in the "Model Engineer" which had close affinities to the Q class and the GWR 2251 class for a 2½in or 3½in gauge model.

In 4mm scale there is a Wills Finecast white metal kit which is accurate and is designed to fit a standard Triang (now Hornby Railways) chassis.

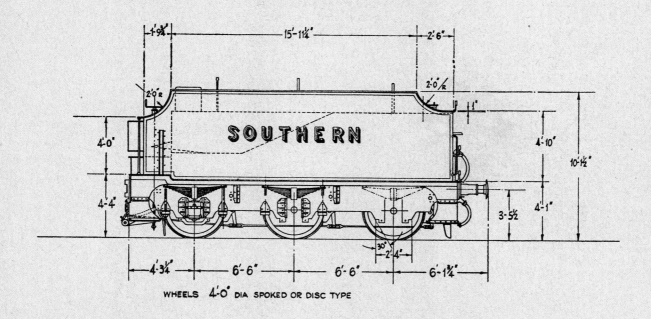

SOUTHERN

WHEELS 4'-0" DIA SPOKED OR DISC TYPE

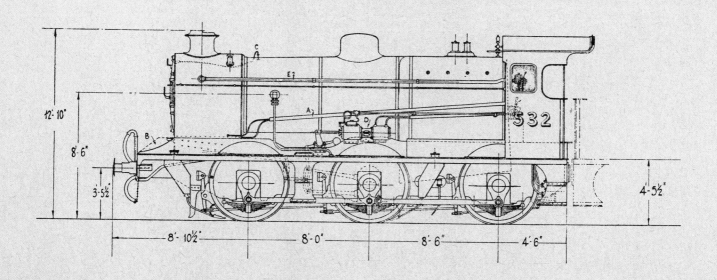

532

Drawing by F. J. Roche
(courtesy of Ian Allan Ltd.)

SR MERCHANT NAVY CLASS
AS ORIGINALLY BUILT

O V Bulleid was appointed Chief Mechanical Engineer of the Southern Railway in 1937 and the first of his new class of locomotives was introduced in February 1941. They created quite a furore for they represented a complete break with tradition, not only in looks but in their mechanics. It was the first Pacific (4-6-2 wheel arrangement) for a tender locomotive on any Southern Railway line, but if its streamlined (or "Air-smoothed" as Bulleid preferred to call it) external appearance shocked the critics, the mechanical aspects utterly confounded them.

The loco had patent disc wheels known as B-F-B (Bulleid Firth-Brown) which was similar to the Box-Pok wheels which were stronger than the conventional spoked variety, yet were 10 per cent lighter. There were three cylinders, but the valve gear was chain driven, the chain drive being in a totally enclosed oil-bath. Electric lighting was fitted throughout the loco, which had an extra deep cab and gave the crew more comfort and weather protection than any loco designed prior to this date. Even the numbering system was new, following the Continental practice, the first loco was 21C1, meaning two bogie axles, one pony or radial truck and three coupled drivers (C), followed by the number of the actual loco.

The difficulty in designing a loco to meet the increased traffic with sufficient power to work heavy trains yet still keep to an axle load of only 21tons was not an easy task, and for this reason Bulleid decided that he must break with the conventional and accepted practices in locomotive design. The normal procedure was for many of the parts to be heavy castings, but by the use of electric welding Bulleid redesigned many of the parts to be fabricated from steel sheet cut to the required shapes and arc welded. The weight saving was considerable as against castings, also when used in place of the normal double thickness of metal where rivets were normally employed.

The usually heavy steel footplates and the running boards and splashers over the wheels were dispensed with and the lightweight air smoothed casing covered all the boiler and many other parts of the loco, and this casing was carried on stays attached to the main frames. The firebox was of steel as against the normal copper.

The tender followed the shape of the cab and coach sides, so that a unified line was given to the loco, especially when used with the Bulleid designed coaches. The tenders were likewise fabricated from steel sheet and again electric welding played its part. The tenders originally carried 6 tons of coal and 5,100 gallons of water, but several changes were made to the tenders over the years.

A total of thirty locomotives were built in three batches of ten in 1941-42, 1944-45 and 1948-49, the last batch coming under the jurisdiction of British Rail. All the locomotives were named after famous shipping lines associated with the Southern Railway and the large nameplates carried a coloured replica of the shipping company's flag in its correct colours. It is interesting to note that these nameplates were made in pairs—both right and left handed so that the flag was always flying in the right position for the direction of travel.

The first locomotive of the Merchant Navy class had their teething troubles, the main one being the boiler and firebox lagging catching fire under the air-smoothed casing, this was aggravated by the odd oil leaks from the chain drive valve gear. Troubles were also experienced with water getting into the oil bath, and there were some difficulties with the steam operated reversing gear. Another major problem was the smoke and exhaust laying along the boiler so that the drivers vision was obscured, and a long series of experiments were conducted to overcome this problem, which resulted in modifications to the frontal appearance of the later locomotives and the earlier ones were then likewise altered. However, the boiler, again of unconventional design, proved to be a perfect generator of steam and the class quickly got the name for being good

steamers with plenty of power. The boiler pressure was later decreased from the original 280lbs per sq in to 250lbs per sq in in an effort to reduce some of the slipping for which the locos were noted when starting from rest.

Many fine performances have been attributed to these locos, which were included in the Locomotive Exchanges of 1948, acquitting themselves well against their rivals on other lines.

In 1945 Bulleid introduced a slightly lighter and fractionally smaller air-smoothed Pacific of which 100 were built up to 1951 and were named after towns and places in the West Country, also some bore names commemorating the defeat of the Luftwaffe known as the "Battle of Britain" class. Many of these were also rebuilt.

Following experiments with one of the class, the whole thirty locos were rebuilt between 1954-56 and the airsmoothed casing removed and many other alterations made including the scrapping of the chain driven valve gear.

Our drawing shows one of the class in the original condition.

DATA

3 cylinders:	18in by 24in
Dia. of driving wheels:	6ft 2in
Boiler pressure:	280phs sq/in (later reduced to 250lbs)
Dia of bogie wheels:	3ft 1in
Dia of pony truck wheels:	3ft 7in
Weight of loco and tender in working order:	144ton (this varied between batches)
Tractive effort:	37,500lb

Models

One of the first models of the Merchant Navy class in its original form was produced by Graham Farish in 4mm scale. This had a die-cast body and a 12v DC motor of unusual design. The firm of Tri-ang have produced a West Country in original condition in both OO and TT scales with a plastic injection moulded body, while Kitmaster produced a 4mm scale plastic kit of a Battle of Britain loco, which is now marketed by Airfix.

Left: Nigel Dyckhoff's TT Gauge (3 mm scale) Merchant Navy No. 35026 "Lamport and Holt Line" painted in BR experimental livery.
N F W Dyckhoff

Centre: West Country 34008 "Padstow" leaving Southampton Central. *Colour views.*

Right: A Tri-ang 00 gauge model of the West Country Class of loco. in original condition. This one is named "Sir Winston Churchill", and is one of the class bearing names commemorating the Battle of Britain.
S W Stevens-Stratten

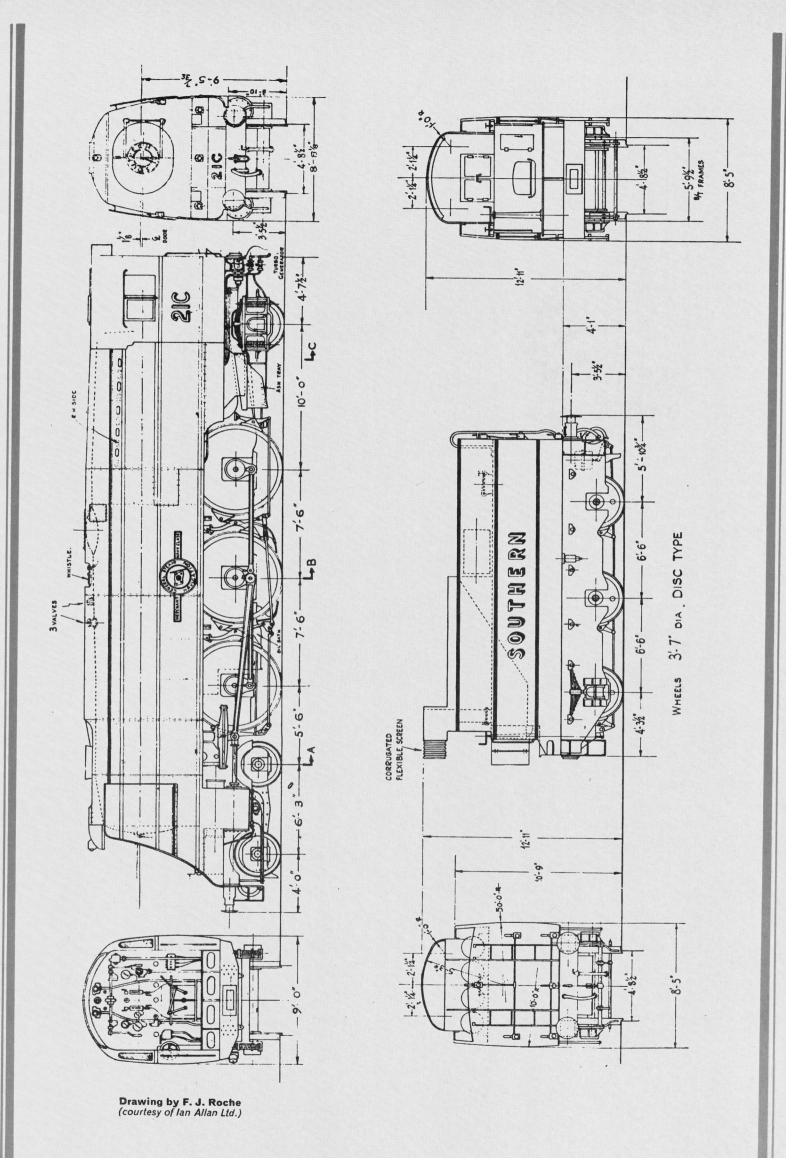

Drawing by F. J. Roche
(courtesy of Ian Allan Ltd.)

WHEELS 3'-7" DIA. DISC TYPE

At the end of the Second World War the French Railways were in dire straights with lack of locomotives and rolling stock and many of their lines severely damaged. This was due to bombing, first by the Germans, then by the Allies; deliberate sabotage by the French under German occupation; the devastation caused by the retreating German armies, and finally by the theft of many good French locos which were sent to other parts of the Third Reich. The total number of locomotives lost is not accurately known but it was in excess of 12,000.

In November 1944, with thoughts of a peace looming on the horizon, a French Mission visited America to discuss the manufacture of replacement locomotives, of a mixed traffic design which were not to be to the Allied Austerity standard. The French technicians wanted a 2-8-2 wheel arrangement, which is so suited to mixed traffic work, especially as before the War they had their own 141P class which, although a four cylinder compound, had proved successful. At that time ideas for a compound four cylinder loco were ruled out, for the design had to be relatively simple, yet produce a robust and powerful loco. Obviously some American influences would have to be accepted if production was to be put in hand quickly, and the result was a blend of French and American standards and practices. Design work settled, production commenced in March 1945 and the first loco was ready for steam trials in July, the first four being delivered to Marseilles in the November of that year. Production of the 700 ordered was quick and was completed by the Spring of 1946 having been shared between three firms —Baldwins (who did the original designs), Alco and Lima. The 700 locos were made available to France under the "Lend-Lease" arrangements then in force to assist the Allies.

The SNCF wanting more of these locomotives immediately ordered a fur-

S.N.C.F.
141 R Class 2·8·2

ther 640, 500 to be split between the three original builders and 140 to be built in Canada.

Some variations existed in the design, some locos having bar frames, while others had Monobloc cast steel frames; variations also existed with Box-Pok and spoke wheels and with the bearings— some having roller bearings others the plain type, while the pony truck varied between the Cole type and the Delta type. The biggest difference was in the fuel used, for 720 were coal burners and 603 oil burners. This makes a total of 1,323 which is correct, for 17 of the locos lie at the bottom of the Atlantic having been lost in transit.

In service the locos proved robust and reliable, easily maintained, good steamers with immense power and popular with the crews for they had a large and well protected cab, as well as a mechanical stoker in the coal fired versions. They were used on all Regions of the SNCF and on both main line passenger and fast heavy freight trains. On the old PLM region, the line along the Mediterranean coast, they virtually monopolised the motive power from Marseille to Ventimiglia often taking heavy passenger trains of 800 tons and over. The majority of the locos put up some very high mileages, approximately $2\frac{1}{2}$ times that of the average French locos, while

the maintenance costs were about $\frac{1}{3}$ less than average. The fuel consumption may have been heavier than some French locos, but the 141R class were robust and well built and served the SNCF right to the end of the Steam loco era.

The locos were delivered in an all black (gloss) paint, which remained on the Nord and Est Regions. The PLM Region gave the locos green livery with full lining as they came into the shops for repairs and overhaul, while the Ouest and SudOuest Regions repainted them in plain green, but the latter had a yellow band.

DATA

Diameter of driving wheels:	5ft 5in
Diameter of bogie wheels:	3ft $\frac{1}{2}$in
Diameter of pony wheels:	3ft 4in
Cylinders, (two):	$23\frac{1}{2}$in by 28in
Boiler pressure:	220lbs/sq in
Weight in working order: +72ton tender (coal fired type)	115ton 10cwt
Maximum speed:	65mph

Models

A few gauge O models have been manufactured for special orders, but the main models are in HO scale (3.5mm: 1ft). In 1961 Tenshode produced a coal burning version, followed by Gerard TAB with an oil burner. The best selling mass production model is the Jouef version, introduced in the Summer of 1969, which is a very fine model of a coal burning type with Box-Pok wheels in black livery and retailing at an attractive price. Jouef have since added two variations, an oil-burning version with spoked wheels available in green or black livery, and very recently the coal burning model is available in green or black livery with spoked wheels. The Italian firm of Lima have also produced HO scale models of the 141R class in green or black with alternate tenders according to the fuel supply, as here Fulgarex

7mm Scale SNCF 141R by Fulgarex, 1971.
Count Giansanti Coluzzi

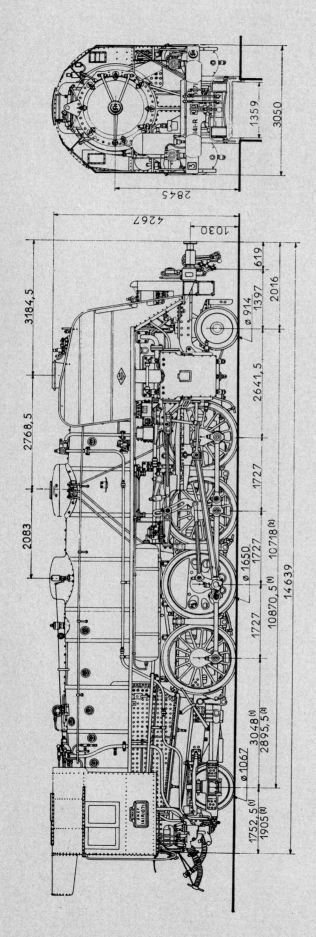

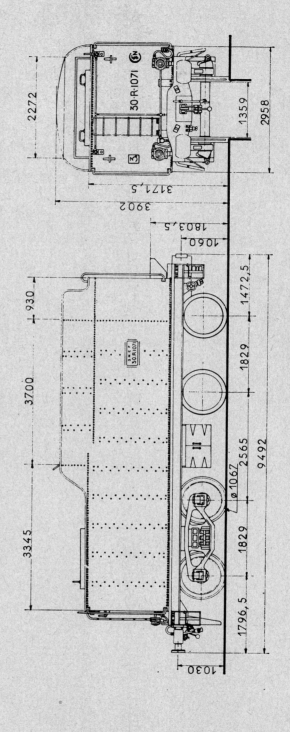

Drawing courtesy Editions Loco-Revue

SNCF 241P 4-8-2 locos

The 241P class of 4-8-2 locomotives were constructed to a Societé Nationale des Chemins de Fer design, under the supervision of Andre Chepelon by the firm of Creusot et Cie between 1948-52. They were among the last designs of steam locomotives and had many novel features. By Continental standards they were very handsome locomotives having a long and powerful look about them, the cabs retaining the traditional PLM shape at the front end. They were superheated compound 4-cylinder locos both high and low pressure cylinders having piston valves. Kylechap blast pipes were fitted and they were equipped with a mechanical stoker so that they could use a low grade of coal.

When the class was introduced they replaced 40 locomotives of the 141P class and were put to work on the old Paris-Lyon-Mediterannean line working between these towns on the main-line express trains. However, with electrifica-tion making very rapid advances it was not long before they were ousted to other lines, including some that went to the Nord system, while others sent to the L'Est, and Ouest regions. Several ended their days on the line from Le Mans to Brest.

The class had similarities with a previous C class, but they had some failings including weak frames and a tendency for overheating of the axleboxes. However, these troubles were overcome with modifications of which many were carried out.

In service the 241P class were popular with their crews and the operating staff as well, for they were powerful, reliable and virtually silent in comparison with the blast of other locos. It was perfectly normal practice to make the gentlest of starts even with the heaviest of trains.

The class was the last of the great French 4-cylinder compounds in regular service, and when they were finally withdrawn in 1970 they were possibly the most powerful steam locomotive remaining in the World. One is now preserved in the SNCF Museum.

DATA

Diameter of drivers:	6ft 7in
Boiler pressure:	290lb per sq in (later reduced to 285)
Cylinders:	Two—$17\frac{3}{4}$in by $25\frac{1}{2}$in Two—$26\frac{3}{4}$in by $27\frac{1}{2}$in
Maximum speed:	120km/h
Weight in working order:	$131\frac{1}{2}$ton
Maximum axle loading:	20ton

Models

Fulgarex have made models of the 241P class in gauges 1 and O, while TAB and Gerard have made hand built models in 3.5mm scale. One of the most popular of the Jouef range of loco models has been their plastic bodied class 241P, which with tender drive is at the present time economically priced for a well detailed model and is far better than comparable priced British made models.

Top: Kitmaster 4mm SNCF 241P.
E S Russell
Below: JOUEF 3.5mm (HO) SNCF 241P.
E S Russell

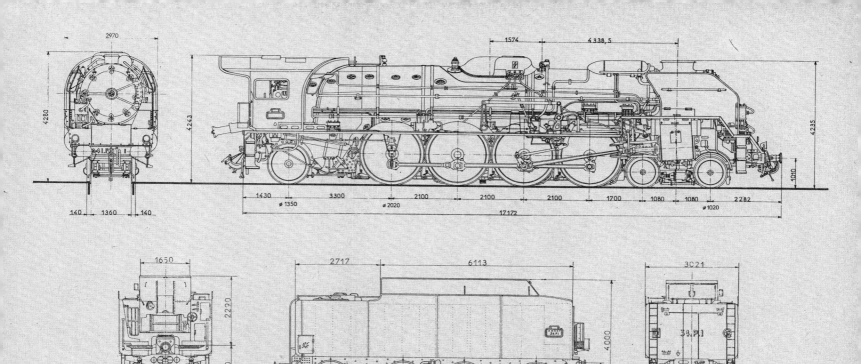

Drawing Courtesy of Loco-Revue

SNCF 241 P.

BR Warship class diesel hydraulic locomotive

The first "Warship" class diesel hydraulic locomotives were introduced on the Western Region of British Rail in 1958 and were an early venture into the realms of regular main line diesel traction in this country.

The initial five locomotives of the class (Nos D600-604) were very different to the 38 locomotives which followed. They were of the A1A-A1A type (having a non-powered axle between the driving ones), built by the North British Loco Co using two MAN 12 cylinder turbocharged diesel engines which developed 1,000hp each and drove the Voight hydraulic transmission. However, it was found that the weight of the locomotives (117½ton in working order) was too heavy for the power available, for the tractive effort was only 50,000lb.

The main body of the class, as shown in our drawing, were introduced later in 1958, having been built at Swindon Works (Nos 800-832 and 866-870). These locomotives were much lighter, only 78½ton in working order also slightly smaller as their length was only 60ft. The locos were built in close collaboration with Krauss-Maffei and were based on the Deutsche Bundesbahn V221 class (originally classified V200), using the same engines—two Maybach diesels manufactured by Bristol-Siddeley under licence. These engines develop a total of 2,300hp which gives a tractive effort of 52,000lb. The transmission is via a single Mekydro torque converter with a 4-speed automatic gearbox to the axles—each one being driven. Speed of the engines is selected by the driver via an 8-step controller and the gear change is by oil pressure.

The advantages of hydraulic transmission over its electrical counterpart has been claimed as a saving in weight also simplicity, but unfortunately the protective and control systems associated with the transmission were very complex and most of the failures of these locos can be attributed to this.

The locomotives have a top speed of 90mph, although on an initial test one locomotive reached 104mph and was able to start a 15 coach train on a 1 in 74 gradient without assistance.

The fuel tanks hold 80 gallons of oil and the water tanks are for 1,000 gallons. The cooling water is pre-heated to enable easier starts to be made, especially in cold weather. A feature of the class is that the bogies have no axleboxes, bolsters or central pivots; instead laminated and coil springs transmit the body weight to the bogie frames and a flexible linkage takes the place of the central pivot.

After initial teething troubles the Warship class have distinguished themselves on the Western Region's Paddington-West of England main line, also on the Waterloo-Exeter workings of the Southern and Western Regions. Many excellent timings have been made by these loco-

Top: D822 "Hercules" at the head of a West of England express at Paddington.

Below: Warship class models. The rear locomotive is an HO scale model by Hamo while in front are two N gauge versions from Minitrex. *S W Stevens-Stratten*

Opposite: Drawing by courtesy of "Model Railway Constructor".

motives, including an Ian Allan Special from Plymouth to Waterloo in 233 minutes for the 230 miles (from Exeter it was 150 minutes for 171 miles) reaching a maximum of 96mph at Andover and passing through Woking at 90mph.

The whole of the class carry names of famous Warships of the Royal Navy. When first introduced they were painted green and later some were repainted in maroon. Later still they were painted in BR rail blue. The first of the class was withdrawn in 1972, and the rest quickly followed. No D821 has, however, been preserved.

Models

The first model was from Trix Products in 1964 and was fractionally small but otherwise acceptable for 4mm, OO scale. Unfortunately it is not available now. In 1967, Märklin produced an HO scale model of the loco to a scale of 3.5mm: 1ft, thus it is of little use to the vast majority of English modellers, although it has a fantastic performance. It was available in two versions—the Märklin for 14v AC stud contact, or the Hamo version for 12v DC two rail. In 1970, the German firm of Minitrix produced an N gauge model which is to exact scale and well detailed. It is available in green or blue livery.

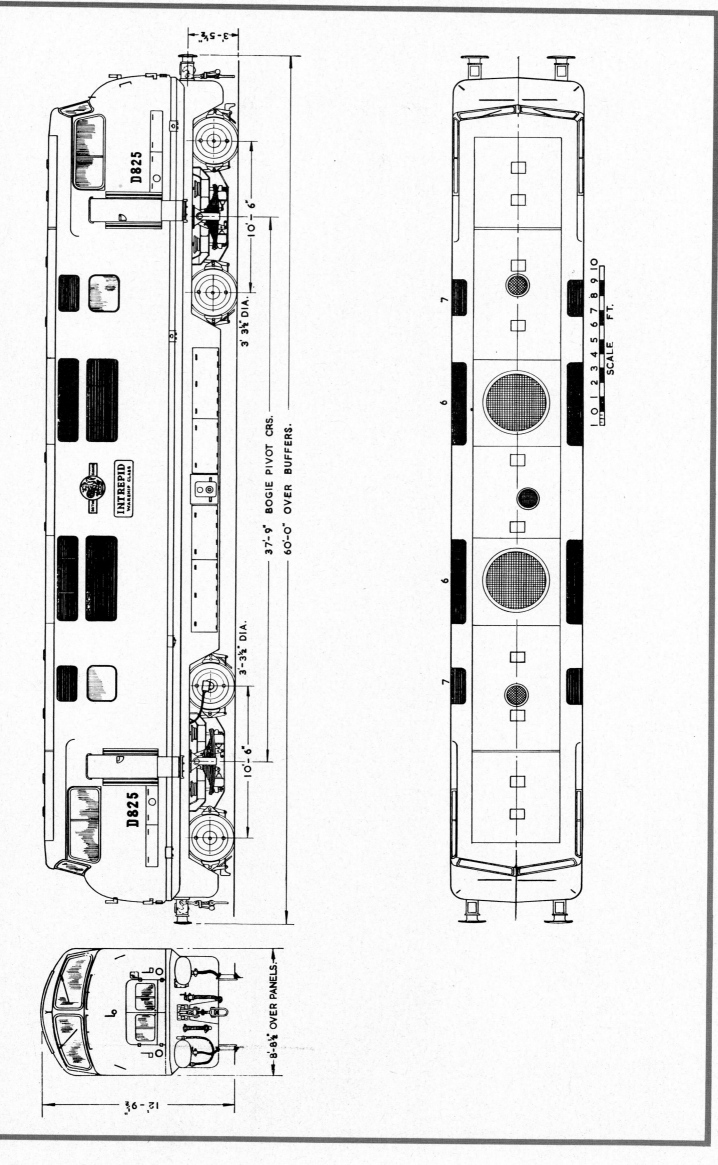

D825

INTREPID
WARSHIP CLASS

D825

3'-5⅜"

10'-6"

3' 3½" DIA.

37'-9" BOGIE PIVOT CRS.

60'-0" OVER BUFFERS.

3'-3½" DIA.

10'-6"

8'-8½" OVER PANELS.

12'-9⅜"

7

6

6

7

0 1 2 3 4 5 6 7 8 9 10

SCALE   FT.

BR 'Western' class 52 Diesel locomotive

Soon after the beginning of the era of diesel traction on British Rail the Western Region realised that the then present power range would be insufficient for their requirements for the future and their basic thoughts turned to a design incorporating a larger power unit. The basic mechanics were to be kept similar to the 2,300hp Warship class which has already been described in this book, and fortunately the Bristol Siddeley Maybach engines used in the earlier locos could easily be up-rated by the addition of extra intercooling to 1,350hp for the same engine speed of 1,500rpm. The Voight hydraulic transmission also has modifications from the initial type used in the Warships Nos D600-604. (The D800 type of Warship have diesel mechanical transmission).

Delivery of the new locos began in 1962 with No D1000 upwards and a total of 74 were ordered—35 to be built at Swindon and 39 to be built at Crewe.

These larger and heavier Western class locos (108ton in working order) had increased axle loading, so a six-wheel bogie unit was designed although it bears a close resemblance to the two-axle Warship type. All three axles are driven.

The design of the body and cab, a prominent feature of the class, was evolved with the assistance of the BTC design panel and many people consider these locos to be the most handsome of the diesel types running on BR. They certainly seem to give an impression of power and strength with their angular but functional appearance.

The maximum speed permitted with these locos is 90mph and the maximum tractive effort is 72,000lb with a continuous tractive effort rated at 14,200lb for 14½mph.

The batteries, fuel (856 gallons) and water (986 gallons) is carried under the floor, between the two bogies. The weight of the body is transmitted to the bogies by brackets supported by large rubber blocks on the buckles of two large laminated springs, through coil springs on the bogie frame; thence through laminated springs to the top of the axle roller bearing casings and so to the axle.

Train heating is supplied by a boiler situated centrally in the locomotive.

The locos were originally operated on the Paddington-Shrewsbury services, but later began running to Bristol and Cardiff, the Devon and Cornwall areas, and from the Midlands to South Western holiday resorts with through trains.

Numbered D1000-1073, the first three were painted in experimental liveries, D1000 (Western Enterprise) was painted a golden yellow called dessert sand; D1001 (Western Pathfinder) was green and D1002 (Western Explorer) an attractive shade of maroon, which was later adopted for all the class, before they were painted in the standard BR rail blue with yellow ends.

Models

Trix made a 3.8mm scale model of the Western class loco which proved very popular and was available in green, maroon or blue livery. It was also available with twin motors if required, but most people found that the one motor as fitted gave sufficient power. The body shape has been used by David Curwen to make several large passenger carrying models in 7½in or 10¼in gauge using a Ford engine.

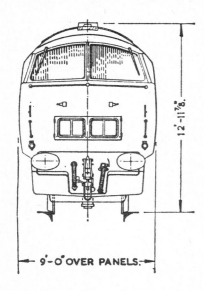

12'-11⅞.

9'-0" OVER PANELS.

All drawings 4mm:1ft scale full size for OO and EM gauges

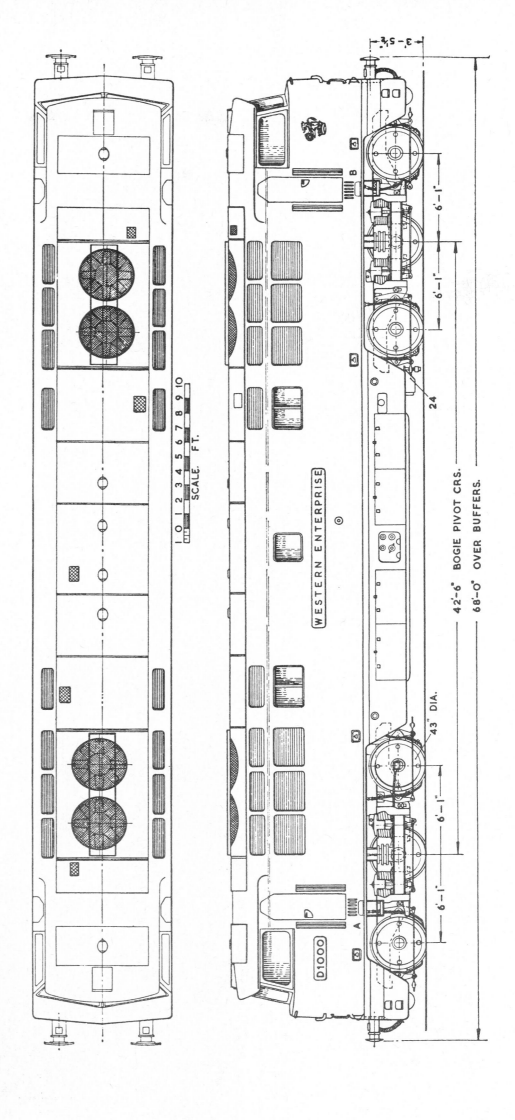

0 1 2 3 4 5 6 7 8 9 10

SCALE.   FT.

WESTERN ENTERPRISE

D1000

3'-5¼"

6'-1"

6'-1"

24

43" DIA.

6'-1"

6'-1"

42'-6" BOGIE PIVOT CRS.

68'-0" OVER BUFFERS.

BR Deltic
diesel-electric locomotives

In 1955 there were only five main line diesel-electric locos on British Railways, and with the thoughts of modernisation a variety of designs were being put forward. In October of that year a brand new and very powerful diesel-electric Co-Co loco was unveiled at the Preston Works of the makers—English Electric Co. This prototype had been built and financed by private enterprise and arrangements were made with British Rail for the loco to run on main line duties for evaluation tests.

The actual diesel engine design was not new for this was born in 1947 when the D Napier & Sons "Deltic" diesel engine was produced for the Admiralty, but it was the first time that such an engine had been utilised for land traction. The engine had 18 cylinders—opposed-piston two-stroke type—with the cylinders arranged in three banks of six with a common crankshaft at each corner of the triangular formation. The construction of the engine made extensive use of light alloys, and with the compact design, the weight was less than for a normal engine of this size or power output. Two such engine units were used in the Deltic locomotive, driving generators which fed the six axle mounted traction motors.

Trials with the loco began in November 1955 on the London Midland Region main line between London (Euston) and Liverpool. It was not long before the huge blue locomotive with its yellow chevrons on the front and rear, and the yellow twin lines on the sides, framing the word "Deltic", became a familiar sight. After a few modifications the loco was tested with special dynamometer equipment on the line from Skipton to Carlisle taking it over Ais Gill summit, where it acquitted itself with honours. It then returned to the Euston-Liverpool run regularly hauling the "Merseyside Express" and the "Shamrock" until late 1959, when it was transferred to the Eastern Region for work on the main line between Kings Cross and Doncaster (also to Newcastle). Again, the prototype was an undoubted success, any teething troubles being of a minor nature and quickly cured, usually by the engineers of the English Electric Company who were travelling with the locomotive.

In April 1958, British Rail ordered 22 of the locomotives for regular work on the Eastern Region main line and delivery started in 1961—six years after the prototype had appeared. In April 1963 the blue painted prototype Deltic locomotive was given to the Science Museum, South Kensington after it had completed something in excess of 400,000 miles.

The production batch of 22 locomotives differed from the prototype in several ways, nearly all externally. They were 1ft 9in longer, and 7ton lighter, but the bogie wheelbase was reduced 14in and the sides given a slight tumblehome so that the locomotive would not be restricted to the major main lines and clearance problems suffered with the prototype would be eliminated, also it would be able to negotiate some sharper radius curves. The driver's visibility was also improved by altering the shape of the bulbous nose of the loco and placing the driver's windows at a slightly different angle. Internally little change took place, for the original "Deltic" design was a very compact machine and there was little room to spare within the body which was built to the maximum permitted by the loading gauge.

The original livery for the production

DATA

	Prototype	Production
Length over buffers:	67ft 9in	69ft 6in
Wheelbase of bogies:	14ft 4in	13ft 6in
Wheel diameter:	3ft 7in	3ft 7in
Weight in working order:	106ton	99ton
Maximum axle loading:	18ton	16½ton
Tractive effort—max:	52,500lb	50,000lb
continuous:	23,500lb	32,000lb
	at 43½mph	at 32½mph
Maximum speed:	105mph	100mph
Total bhp:	3,300	3,300

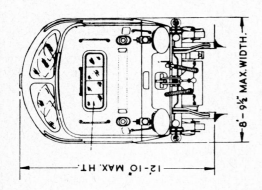

8'-9½" MAX. WIDTH.

12'-10" MAX. HT.

locos was BR loco green (Brunswick green) for the body with an apple green skirt and grey roof with black louvres. The yellow square was first painted on the front and then at a later date the whole of the "nose" including front of cab was painted yellow. The latest livery is of course BR rail blue with the yellow front.

All 22 of the locos (Nos D9000-D9021) were given names, mostly those of regiments of the British Army.

Models

The first model of the prototype Deltic was a 4mm scale plastic kit (non-motorised) produced by Rosebud under the Kitmaster trademark in 1960 which was a well detailed and accurate model, in the original livery.

The Hornby-Dublo models produced a 4mm scale "Deltic" of the production run in January 1961, which is still a popular model and much sought after by the modern image modeller.

Bassett-Lowke also made an O gauge model of the Deltic around 1962, but this also is now off the market.

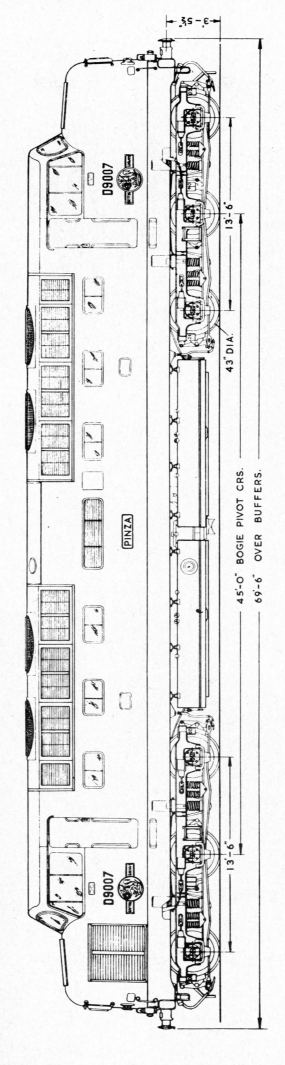

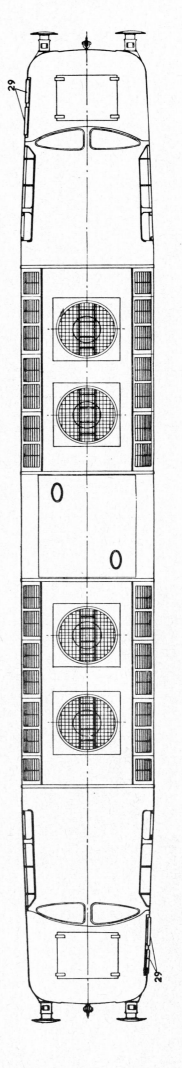

Left: "Deltic" diesel No 9019 hauling the down
Flying Scotsman in 1972.   *D Cross*

MODEL RAILWAY PUBLICATIONS

Facing page: A scene at Bradcaster locomotive depot on Norman Eagles' O gauge clockwork Sherwood Railway. *Richard Sharpe Studios*

Overleaf: Front end of gauge 1 steam model of the celebrated Maffei Pacific of the Bavarian State Railways, built by Wilag, Switzerland.
Richard Sharpe Studios

Locomotives and the 'Model Engineer'

It was over 75 years ago, in January 1898, that a modest magazine known as the "Model Engineer and Amateur Electrician" began to appear on bookstall counters. Now if 75 years is a good age for a person, it is a remarkable one for a magazine; so one must take the greatest pleasure in the fact that it still appears and not only on the bookstalls of Britain but with a world-wide circulation and reputation.

The original title is interesting. In those high and far-off times houses with electricity laid on were not too common and therefore there was considerable scope for amateurs to obtain the convenience of electrical power by fitting up their own plant. By 1923 the "Amateur" had been dropped and the title in full was "Model Engineer and Electrician—A journal of small power engineering". In 1926 it became "The Model Engineer and Light Machinery Review" and, although it is most difficult to detect any justification from the contents, in 1930, "Electrician" came back, this time "Practical" rather than "Amateur" or common-or-garden. In 1937, the plain and honoured title "The Model Engineer" came and stayed for good.

Regardless of these changes of name, it has always carried information, instruction and advice for those who make mechanical things, particularly models, for pleasure. The present satisfactory position is a result of wise guidance by successive editors, beginning with the original founder, owner and proprietor, Percival Marshall. Wise guidance has

always led to a high standard of contents and for this we must thank some remarkable contributors, whose writings down the years have been the principal influence in the development of the Model Engineering hobby.

Miniature locomotives have always been a major item in the magazine and, amongst the many distinguished people who have provided material, one legendary but rather shy and misty figure bestrides the scene, L Lawrence, alias "Curly" or "LBSC", whose famous series of eighteen hundred plus articles appeared nearly every week from 1924 to 1959. There was a brief come-back in 1966 which lasted until his death in 1967.

He was a shy person and seldom or rarely appeared in public. This was with good reason because he had a personal problem that nowadays we would take as a matter of course, but which 50 years ago was a matter to be spoken of in hushed tones. It was this, that the feminine elements which are present in most men's make-up gradually became more and more marked in his.

However, there was no such dubiety about the quality of his written works: these were of genius quality in three particular ways.

First, that he wrote for the beginner, the man who thought a vice was something nasty in the woodshed and a tap something to draw water from, but who longed to build a real steam locomotive fired by coal which he could himself drive. Second, that he covered the whole subject from equipping the workshop to

Above: "Caribou", Martin Evans' Canadian shunter masquerading as a "Rio Grande". Surely everybody knows that Americans painted their steam locomotives "any colour they wished as long as it was black"?
J B Hollingsworth

laying the track, not forgetting driving, firing, and even buying and selling. His rule 1, never part with money until you have seen it in steam, applies to all gauges and particularly 4ft 8½in. Not for nothing were the articles for many years entitled "Shops, Shed and Road—a column of live steam", such was the coverage of his subject.

The third delightful thing was that until the last years they were a "column of live steam" in more senses than one, intimate, to the point, controversial, gritty, wise, crystal clear and often very, very funny. There were all the mythical characters he brought in to make his points, the over-particular Inspector Meticulous, the irrepressible Bert Smiff "cor lumme mate, yer Chevy Chase don't 'alf need a squeeze and squash"— a comment on the importance of adequate lubrication. His real friends, too, we met, such as "Bro. Wholesale", who in 1938 built a 2½in gauge giant track with spirals and flyovers down at Bursledon in Hampshire. On one occasion, LBSC, driving his 4-12-2 "Caterpillar", derailed spectacularly at the highest point, a railroad wreck in the full Hollywood tradition, after which, as he put it, "our hero was found lifting the locomotive to see if a sixpence which fell out of his pocket was underneath".

He was just on the wrong side of 40 when he started his career as a writer, having started on the LB&SCR before the turn of the century, worked his way up to driver, after which he spent some time in mechanical engineering. The war, which came during his sixties, was a bit close at hand sometimes, for he lived in bomb alley alongside his beloved Brighton main line—you could see his track from the trains near Purley Oaks Station. But he carried on and it was not until the war was over that, affected by the strain a little of the fun crept out of, and a few howlers crept into, his work. Nevertheless, his last complete design, a 5in gauge GWR pannier tank, was a winner and many examples of "Pansy"—he always gave an appropriate catchy name—can be found doing the rounds at club tracks in Britain.

In all he provided the "words and music" for 54 steam locomotives in the "Model Engineer" as well as 33 published elsewhere, not counting the two which were unfinished in 1959 and 1967 respectively. His term "words-and-music" implied full how-to-do-it instructions with clear simple drawings and sketches which anyone could follow. The great majority were coal-fired with proper locomotive boilers, the correct number of cylinders as per prototype, and full valve gear. Indeed, the invitation to conduct the weekly articles came about as a result of letters in the correspondence columns of the magazine during 1923—the famous "battle of the boilers" —when he advocated the advantages of following, more closely than was then the fashion, the functional principles of full size practice.

The correspondence battle culminated in a David-and-Goliath trial of strength at the Model Engineer Exhibition of 1924. Henry Greenly, the champion of the anti-LBSC faction had specially built by Bassett-Lowke a spirit-fired 2-8-2 called "Challenger". LBSC produced his little coal burning 4-4-2 "Ayesha," which clearly demonstrated both the practicability and, indeed, superiority of his principles of design, at least in this size of miniature. Henry Greenly, of course, was unchallenged master on the larger sizes, as his superb contemporary work on the Romney, Hythe & Dymchurch Railway showed.

The locomotives which LBSC and his successors designed and described divide into two kinds; simple projects for beginners and more complex and interesting ones for experienced workers. In the former case no assumption of previous experience in metal work was made and in the latter the instructions were aimed one notch higher and assumed that, at least, the builder had already tackled one of the simpler locomotives.

His first locomotive the 1 gauge "Ford Pacific" was an oddball, falling into neither category, but his second, the 2½in gauge "Simple Sally" (1926) was the original tyro's loco. She was a North Eastern 4-4-0 "1619" class with the ultra-simple arrangement of outside cylinders and inside valves with slip-eccentric valve gear. Her successors, such as the LMS 4-4-0 "Annie Boddie" (1934) a locomotive which "any body" could build, and the 0-4-0T· industrial shunter "Juliet" (1946), have introduced many people to a whole new world of pleasurable endeavour.

Amongst his advanced designs, it is hard to single out a "best", but one might mentioned his BR 4-6-2 "Britannia" (1951); he was entrusted with a set of

drawings while the prototype was still under construction and on the secret list, so that, the very day that big sister was revealed to the national press, the Model Engineer carried the first instalment of what was to prove one of the most successful and popular live steam miniatures. One might also mention another design contemporary with the prototype; his "King" class "Kingette" (1928) where he had the more difficult job of squeezing 4 cylinders and inside valve-gear between 2½in gauge frames.

Typically, each serial took about a year to complete; in the advanced designs, certain elementary processes were taken for granted and not described in detail, which compensated for the greater complexity. For most people the actual building would take a good deal longer, two years being a realistic time to spend on building a live steam locomotive.

In addition to all this, there were many general items and accessories, the construction of which was described in full, such as passenger cars, workshop jigs and fixtures, unusual valve gears, overhauls, boiler fittings, donkey pumps, lubricators, and many other blobs and gadgets. Delightful toys for the children just before Christmas were another feature. His toy steam fire-engine (1954) was a particularly delightful example.

He also described and had illustrated locomotives, both his own and others, examples of those which were described in the construction articles and others of interest which were not. We heard about his poverty-stricken childhood in South London, his early days on the "Brighton" railway, even the 0-1-1-1-1-0 (I quote) called Mick he took for walks in the evening between making drawings, writing articles and answering letters; for he personally answered queries, usually by return, of any reader who cared to write enclosing "return carriage".

His epitaph must be the exhaust noise of the many locomotives built to his instructions which continue to perform so excellently on live steam tracks from Edinburgh to Auckland and Norwich to Los Angeles.

In this connection, perhaps the best tribute to his work is paid by a principal Midlands supplier of drawings castings and parts for miniature steam locomotives, in whose catalogues, nearly 15 years after the last complete design appeared, are listed sets for 25 of LBSC's locomotives against 18 for those of all other designers put together. In the Model Engineer's own catalogue of locomotive drawings, LBSC scores 39 against 15 for other designers.

LBSC had the charming habit of referring to the editor of the Model Engineer as our "worthy Knight-of-the-Blue

Pencil" and one is happy to record that his successor as the M.E. locomotive expert was the present editor. The same pattern of beginner's and advanced projects is visible in Martin Evans' authoritative work and gentle style. So far he has given us 15 designs ranging from a little O gauge "Royal Scot" up to what is by far the largest locomotive design ever published in the "Model Engineer", the 7¼in gauge LMS Black Five 4-6-0 "Highlander". It is interesting to note that before the war 2½in gauge was the norm, with the occasional 3½in. Afterwards 3½in became the standard and since then the median size has risen further to 5in with an occasional 7¼in. For example, Martin Evans is in 1973 describing a 5in gauge GWR "Manor" class 4-6-0, while 35 years ago LBSC was giving us a very similar "Grange" in 2½in gauge. Incidentally the difference in style between the two writers is epitomised by the names given to the two designs. The former is correctly called "Torquay Manor" after the first of the class, while LBSC, who lived at 121 Grange Road, Purley, rather impishly called his "Purley Grange", and numbered her 121.

The insatiable appetite of miniature locomotive builders can nowadays only be satisfied by having a second regular contributor and Don Young brings his ability as a designer and his charm and clarity as a writer together to great effect. As an Isle of Wight resident he naturally began with the Island's standard locomotive, the Adams 0-4-4T. So far his

masterpiece has been the Great Central Atlantic "Jersey Lily" in 5in gauge, as lovely as the famous beauty whose name she bears.

To get a word in edgeways amongst these giants might have seemed an impossibility but some have managed it and, as one might expect, with several remarkable designs.

Edgar Westbury, famous for his work in the M.E. on miniature petrol engines, designed a 3½in gauge version of an early LMS diesel shunter, "1831", described in very complete detail before the war. Charles Simpson, later editor of the "Locomotive", with his 7¼in gauge dock shunter "Midge" (1933) contrasted with Alan Sherwood with a live-steam OO gauge GWR 2-8-0T "Rhondda" (1960). No less a famous name than J N Maskelyne, did one design, as one might expect a superb one and as one equally might expect a Great Western one, his outside-frame 5in Armstrong Goods in 1939-40.

Ken Swann with his "Bridget" (1969) added to the exclusive rank of 7¼in gaugers and showed that even an industrial shunter could be a work of art. There was also an excellent series in 1956 on a Sentinel-type geared locomotive, W J Constable's "Sirena".

In addition to all this wisdom put before us by the gentlemen referred to, we also heard something from their victims. Many were the instructive and sometimes amusing articles on "How I built my locomotive" or "How we built our railway". It would be invidious to

single out particular ones for mention, but making an exception in salute to his memory, the late Michael Lloyd's articles on the building of the Hilton Valley Railway (1959) showed him as outstanding a writer as he was an engineer. Most of those who won the Locomotive Championship Cup and, at the other end of the scale, numerous first-timers have told of their heavily contrasting experiences. Suffice it to say that size went from one of the largest miniatures ever, Henry Greenly's "River Esk" (1925) in 15in gauge, for the Ravenglass and Eskdale line, to what must surely be the smallest working steam locomotive ever built, Alan Sherwood's little "Koala" (1957), running on N gauge. Skill ranged from an erecting shop foreman at Crewe Works, describing his cup-winning LMS "Duchess" Pacific to a writer called "Rathlin" who described building a GNR Stirling 4-2-2 (1937) beginning not only without mechanical knowledge and experience but living on an island off the Irish Coast where mechanical contrivances of any kind were a novelty.

Locomotives other than steam have appeared, too; battery electrics emulating straight electrics, petrol emulating diesel, even one with a hot-air engine. C Baker described a clockwork passenger hauler!

Model Railways were rightly the property of the associated "Model Railway News", but one very special one found frequent mention amongst our M.E. box of delights. Victor Harrison described his superb outdoor gauge 1 railway with steam (coal and spirit), clockwork and battery-electric power, laid in his garden at Bishops Stortford. A general description came in 1939, but many particular items appeared between 1920 and 1953.

Turning for a moment from model locomotives to full-size ones, excellent coverage was for many years given in the "M.E.". Between the wars Charles Lake wrote his "Loco-prototypes-News-and-Notes" every week; in those days new designs of steam locomotive appeared in the world as frequently as that. Diesels and electrics have neither the individuality nor, since their mechanisms are much more complex, do they lend themselves in the same way that steam does to reduction in size without severe functional simplification; perhaps this is why prototype information is no longer demanded.

For historical information, two classic series have appeared, both later printed as books; F C Hambleton's "Locomotives Worth Modelling" (1942-1946) and J N Maskelyne "Locomotives I have Known" (1950-1959).

Another famous author who has contributed in the past was O S Nock. His series of 25 articles (1940-1943), unhappily never reprinted in book form, was perhaps the best thing he ever wrote. It dealt with semaphore signals and locking frames, his own professional subject. Each separate pre- and post-1923 company was covered with drawings and photographs, involving difficult original research and giving information

Opposite page top: "Boxhill": A beautifully finished example of Martin Evans' "S" gauge LBSC "Terrier". *J B Hollingsworth*

Opposite page below: "Pansy": LBSC's last design, a fine example out on the road at Kinver. *J B Hollingsworth*

Above: George Barlow drives his "Kingette" at New Romney. Typical of LBSC's designs, "Kingette" has little or no non-functional detail, but nevertheless has four working cylinders and full valve gear. *W R Jones*

not even now available elsewhere.

Naturally, since railways are the basic theme of this account, we have given prominence to how they have been catered for in the "M.E."; however, there were and are a profusion of other fascinating items too varied to list. Petrol engines, steam engines of many varieties, clocks, traction engines, a cine projector and, of course, workshop tools and processes. Ship and boat models were once a great feature, but are now dealt with in a specialist publication. The emphasis always was on things that worked, particularly in some fascinating way. For example, in 1952 the late Dr J Bradbury Winter described from the point of view of a master craftsman, the construction of a Congreve clock, which keeps time by the constant run of a steel ball rolling each way down a zig-zag path cut in a brass plate, rocked to reverse the gradient between each "stroke". Dr Winter's work, in this case on a beautiful model locomotive now in Brighton Museum, was also held up as a shining example back in Issue No 1 of 1898.

So, in conclusion, let us take a look at a typical issue. It is dated 3rd August 1973 and numbered 3469, reflecting the fact that weekly publication became twice monthly some years ago. The advertisements which adorned the cover for so many years gave way in 1939 to a picture; more recently this has been a coloured one and, in the case of issue 3469, showing a beautiful Marenghi Fair Organ. 35 editorial pages, beginning with the editor's commentary "Smoke Rings" (though whether tobacco- or coal- smoke is not clear), in which an echo appears of the battle fought out earlier in the year in in the correspondence columns on oil-firing versus coal-firing for locomotives. Instalments of the six current construction series occupy 21 pages; L C Mason's

why the "Model Engineer" is more than a magazine; why it has become an institution, developing the hobby it serves by encouraging all the inter-dependent ingredients, instruction, supply, self-criticism, competition, reward, example, in a truly excellent manner. Long may it continue to do so.

Left: "Britannia": One of LBSC's most successful designs.   *J B Hollingsworth*

Opposite page Below left: "Doris": LBSC's popular copy of Britain's most numerous locomotive, the LMS "Black Five".
J B Hollingsworth

This page, top to bottom: "Stormy Petrel": Vital organs according to LBSC's "words-and-music", but Inspector Meticulous would be shocked by a "Castle" class cab, "County" splashers, a "Hall" chimney and name and number from an "Achilles" class single.   *J B Hollingsworth*

"Cornwall": The product of a model engineer who has graduated well beyond the need for "how to do it" instructions.   *J B Hollingsworth*

"Firefly": An extremely popular Martin Evans design.   *J B Hollingsworth*

An LBSC design – "Helian Lassie" built for 3½in gauge.   *J B Hollingsworth*

"Mastiff" petrol engine, E Jackson-Stevens' Model Tramway, Don Young's 3½in gauge Festiniog Locomotive, "Mountaineer", W J Hughes' traction engine, Tubal Caine's steam driven fan; the editor puts his head in the lion's mouth with drawings for the chimney and boiler mountings of "Torquay Manor" aforementioned. However, he is certainly safe, the chimney is so good that he will not be eaten even by the most rabid GWR fan.

A further 8 pages were devoted to the doings of Model Engineering Clubs, Bristol opening their new track, Whitchurch celebrating their 25th anniversary and Romford playing host on their track to the Southern Federation. Two pages are devoted to tool matters, and one to a short article on pumps and last, but most certainly not least, we have the famous correspondence columns in which burning questions of the day are hotly debated. Some real fireworks about safety on Live Steam tracks occur very rightly in this issue.

In all, just under one half of the issue is devoted to steam locomotives. This applies also to the advertisers, whom we must not forget, for they have not only helped the magazine with revenue, but also the service they have given over the years has contributed as much to the hobby as the experts, the debates in the correspondence columns and indeed the magazine itself, not to speak of the exhibitions and competitions which the "M.E." regularly sponsors.

When one considers how all these elements have been fitted together, fostered over the years, it can be seen

MODEL RAILWAYS 6ᵈ

Catalogues of delight

SCALE MODEL RAILWAYS
SEASON 1936-37

MILBRO

MILLS

PRICE 6ᵈ

Price 6D.

6200 LMS

BASSETT-LOWKE LTᴰ
NORTHAMPTON
LONDON AND MANCHESTER

1/6

J·L·S

W.H. JUBB LTᴰ
SHEFFIELD

The joy of owning a model railway has almost always been preceded by the equally pleasurable browse round the toy shop and the eager thumbing through makers catalogues. All over the world these booklets setting out the manufacturer's wares are part and parcel of the model railway hobby and give many happy hours of armchair modelling. Today some of the older catalogues, like the models they sold, are in themselves collectors' pieces. Who today, for instance, can easily come by one of the pre-war Hornby Books of Trains printed in full colour for three old pence, or a Bassett-Lowke booklet at sixpence giving details of locomotives from the cheap German built toy at seven and sixpence (35p) to a complete 7¼in guage passenger hauling "George the Fifth" 4-4-0 at £250.00. The war brought a break as the toymakers temporarily went out of business, but today though the old firms are generally defunct new and even better models are on the market and lovingly pictured in colour in their makers advertising. True, the old household names of Bing, Bassett-Lowke, Mills and Bowman have gone to Collector's Corner, but Triang, Peco, Wrenn and Wills all make the mouth water as do Gem and Marklin, Faller and Lilliput amongst a host of others. These illustrations show something of the colour in model railway catalogues and there will be a great deal of nostalgia generated from some of the covers.

The new
FALLER
catalogue
'73|74

FU

231 E 22

2

Jouef
MARQUE DÉPOSÉE

PECO

MODEL
RAILWAY
PRODUCTS

ILLUSTRATED CA
Metal Locomotive Kits

finecast
WILLS

GUREX

鉄道模型 趣味

Hobby of Model Railroading

MAY '72 No. 287 5

■細密モデルC5333
■地下鉄10輌2編成製作記
■市販国鉄蒸機誌上展

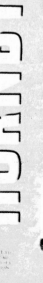

N OO

WILLS
finecast

HORNBY DUBLO *ELECTRIC TRAINS*

PURCHASE TAX SURCHARGE
26th JULY 1961

Some of the prices in this catalogue are now
subject to a small Purchase Tax surcharge.

6ᵈ

PART 21

30p

Canada $1
New Zealand 75c
South Africa 75c
U.S.A. $1
Australia 75c
RECOMMENDED BUT-
NOT OBLIGATORY

HISTORY OF MODEL & MINIATURE RAILWAYS

707

Model Railway Magazines

Many textbooks have been written about modelling railways, but, although some make handy reference books, with the great strides taken in techniques and materials, they are inclined to become out-of-date very rapidly. For the model railway enthusiast in the U.K., there are three magazines published each month which are devoted to this subject and as many modellers are only too willing to talk about their hobby, there is no shortage of material. Additionally there are three monthly magazines devoted to the real railways from which we make our models.

The first magazine to be published which included model railway subjects was the "Model Engineer" which first appeared in 1898. Although this covered many other modelling subjects, it included much on steam locomotives, in what we now call the larger scales, but which at that time were far more common among the few that could actively become involved.

In 1909, after writing for the "Model Engineer", Henry Greenly in partnership with W J Bassett-Lowke published a magazine called "Model Railways and Locomotives" (the cost being 3d a month!). This new magazine was practically exclusively devoted to model

railways but naturally the larger scale models, which nowadays we call miniature railways. Among the articles published was one on the first known O gauge coal-fired live steam locomotive and later an experimental live steam loco half this size. This magazine ceased publication in 1919.

In 1925, Percival Marshall decided to publish a companion magazine to "Model Engineer" and launched the "Model Railway News" on the market—the first of many model railway magazines to be published throughout Europe if not the world.

March 1934 saw the entry of the second British magazine devoted to the hobby and this was "Model Railway Constructor". Both magazines struggled in the depression years and just when the situation became financially more stable, the War intervened, bringing considerable difficulties. Happily both magazines continued and in 1949 were joined by a third magazine, "Railway Modeller", published by Ian Allan. This was sold after the first year to S C Pritchard of Pritchard Patent Products, of PECO model railway fame.

At various times other magazines have included model or miniature railway subjects and at one time "Model Maker"

—not now published as a separate entity—carried a few articles, as does the present "Airfix Magazine".

"Model World"—a short-lived magazine also had a few general articles on the subject, and of course the original "Meccano Magazine" each month had several articles devoted to their own products—Hornby Trains, both for gauge O and OO.

Magazines published in other countries can be obtained in Great Britain to special order, and the most popular, doubtless because they are in English, are the two American periodicals "Model Railroader" and "Model Railroad Craftsman". Other magazines which deal with model railways, some including the prototype systems, are the two French periodicals "Loco Revue" and "Rail Miniature Flash"; the German "Eisenbahn (Modellbahn) Magazin" and "Modelleisenbahner" also "Miniaturbahnen". In Switzerland there is "Eisenbahn-Amateur".

Several of the Continental model railway manufacturers also publish their own magazines, such as Fleischmann and Märklin, but both are in the language of origin.

Now for a closer look at the history of the three English monthly magazines.

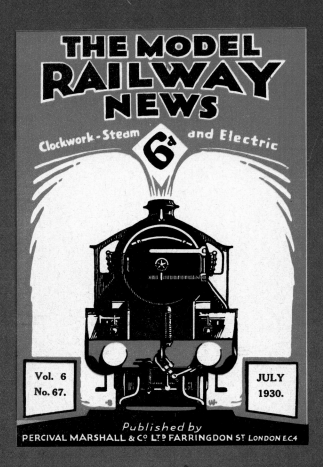

THE MODEL
RAILWAY
NEWS

Clockwork - Steam 6ᵈ and Electric

Vol. 6
No. 67.

JULY
1930.

Published by
PERCIVAL MARSHALL & Cᵒ LTᴰ FARRINGDON ST LONDON E.C.4

RAILWAY
MODELLER

APRIL 1954

For The Average Enthusiast

PUBLISHED 1'6 MONTHLY

RAILWAY
MODELLER

For the average enthusiast   April '74 20p

Nuremberg Report

Model
Railway

IAN ALL

April 1

CONSTRUCTOR

GWR 0 gauge layout   •   BR clan class loco in 4ᵐ
LSWR coaches • NG rolling stock • Nuremberg Toyfair rep

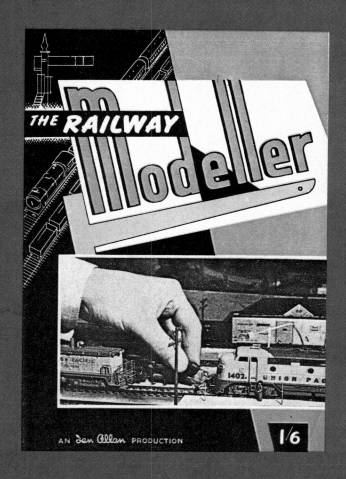

THE RAILWAY modeller

AN Ian Allan PRODUCTION

1/6

THE MODEL RAILWAY CONSTRUCTOR

Vol. 6.   FEBRUARY 1939.   No. 60

G.W.R. Local Train entering Chard, (G.W.R.)
(Photo: W. B. Jacobs)

SOME STANDARD MEASUREMENTS
TAKING STEREOSCOPIC VIEWS
A Unique Electric Loco — A Road Bridge
BUILDING FROM DRAWINGS — "MONOTONY"

Free With This Issue—LARGE FOLDING DIAGRAM, "O" GAUGE FULL-SIZE

PRICE SIXPENCE

Model Railways

APRIL 1974

20p   U.S.A. & CANADA $1

MAP   HOBBY MAGAZINE

INCORPORATING
MODEL RAILWAY NEWS

MEET THE
QUEEN OF
HADES

WAGON BUILDING EXERCISE (4mm)
FOR BEGINNERS

18-31 DECEMBER 1970   First and Third Friday   Volume 136   Number 3407   3/- 15p.

Model Engineer

MAP   (USA & Canada—75 Cents)   HOBBY MAGAZINE

CHRISTMAS NUMBER

Model Railways

This is the title adopted since 1971 for the old "Model Railway News". It was in January 1925 that Percival Marshall, the proprietor and editor launched "Model Railway News" on the market. As the first periodical dealing exclusively with the subject the magazine was quite successful, it dealt with peoples' layouts, gave lessons in metal work, hints and tips and general articles on modelling all aspects of the model railway field. It also gave news of the activities of the model railway clubs which were being rapidly formed in all parts of the country.

After eleven years as Editor, Percival Marshall handed over to J N Maskelyne from January 1936, and it is probably true to say that for the next eleven years the magazine prospered, setting a very high standard, for J N Maskelyne was a brilliant engineer, a competent draughtsman and a very popular editor. He was a meticulous worker and his standards of accuracy were such that his writings or drawings were beyond question. Many fine series of articles and drawings (the latter still referred to by many who hand-build their models), appeared during this time, not only from the editor, but from the pens of other eminent model railway enthusiasts and engineers. Such names as the Rev. Edward Beal, Michael Longridge, Henry Greenly, G P Keen, Leyland Barratt, Bassett-Lowke and many others, who can claim to have had a considerable influence on the hobby.

In 1957, the pressure of editorship, advancing years and health problems led to the partial retirement of J N Maskelyne and he was succeeded by his able assistant Roy E Dock who maintained the standard of his predecessor for eight years until June 1965. In that month Paul Towers took over as Editor whilst Roy Dock stepped up to Managing Editor of Percival Marshall including "Model Railway News" and "Model Engineer".

In November the Percival Marshall organisation was acquired by Model Aeronautical Press (later to change its name to Model and Allied Publications) with a consequent re-organisation and change of style. Paul Towers remained editor eventually taking on the job of Ad Manager; he put forward new and somewhat novel ideas in the magazine including a monthly section on narrow gauge and industrial modelling while still retaining the popular features. In June 1967 he vacated the editorial seat, handing over to Jack Shortland who was a professional modelmaker; he had been on the staff of Percival Marshall for a number of years but had left the firm and had been persuaded to join MAP by Paul Towers; unfortunately ill health caused another change within a year when John Brewer, previously assistant editor, took the helm.

In September 1971, the magazine was completely re-designed in size content and title, now becoming "Model Railways" with Roy Dock back in the chair as Editor. It now has coloured covers, with occasional colour inside and tends to delve more deeply into technical matters than the other magazines, but still covers the entire sphere of model railways and contains many good drawings for the hand-builder of locomotives and rolling stock.

Model Railway Constructor

The first issue of "Model Railway Constructor" was published in March 1934, and it has appeared every month without a break since that date.

From the beginning it was the idea of the editor and proprietor, Ernest F Carter to cater particularly for the constructor with articles on building models for all aspects of model railways, not forgetting the adaption of proprietary models. The first issue was a mere 20 pages of only 8in by 5in, costing 6d. By today's standards it seems incredible that so many plans and drawings coud be crammed into such a small page size.

After two years or so, Carter found that life was too hectic as both proprietor: editor: publishing, distribution and advertising manager! He therefore sold the publishing rights, but remained editor and proprietor and with improved distribution, the circulation began to increase. The first advertiser was Walkers and Holtzaffpel and their successors, W & H (Models) Ltd, still advertise today. After a time, the magazine began losing money and became too much of a strain for Carter, so in 1939 he sold his interests to the late F W Chubb, a professional railwayman and a model railway enthusiast. Chubb was adamant that the model magazine should not be dictated to, or run by the trade—an argument still upheld by the present publishers and editor—but again, just before the War it became uneconomic and the new proprietor was going to give it another three months, when he met R J Raymond at a model railway meeting, and after a discussion appointed him as Editor. At that time articles were written by only two or three people under a variety of nom-de-plumes.

Shortly after taking the editorial chair, Raymond found himself faced with all the difficulties of wartime production —shortages of paper, dislocation caused by bombing, contributors now in the Services etc. These of course were added to the problems already existing. The London offices were bombed and the whole of the editorial department moved to Raymond's private house on the Surrey/Hants border; meanwhile the proprietor had evacuated to a cottage alongside a canal in Berkshire, where his wife coped with the difficulties of the accounts and the subscribers copies— not helped by the fact that the cottage had neither electricity or running water! One foggy night in the blackout, the lorry about to deliver the subscribers' copies turned the wrong way and shot the lot into the canal! Funny to look back at now, but not so at the time! Advertising revenue was virtually nil—none had any items to sell with no materials available and the magazine was reduced to 16 pages—but it kept appearing each month despite the difficulties.

After the War, the magazine began to prosper and with the easing of restrictions more pages were added to each issue. It continued to grow and expand and had built up a healthy circulation when in June 1956, R J Raymond had to resign as editor and joint proprietor (a role he had held since 1946) due to ill health. The "Model Railway Constructor" was taken over by Railway World Ltd with K G Mansell as editor and continued until December 1959 when that firm were purchased by Ian Allan Ltd, the present publishers.

Within six months, G M Kichenside was appointed editor and continued until the end of 1963 when he handed over to Alan Williams who continued for two and a half years until the present editor, S W Stevens-Stratten was appointed.

der modelleisenbahner

FACHZEITSCHRIFT
FUR DEN MODELLEISENBAHNBAU
UND ALLE FREUNDE
DER EISENBAHN   Jahrgang 20

MÄRZ
3/71

EB VERLAG FUR VERKEHRSWESEN
Einzelheftpreis 2.– M · Sonderpreis für die DDR 1.– M   32 542

Overleaf: On the Forest Railway in Cornwall.
J Southern

Looking back over the 40 years there have been many changes in model railways, but the magazine has kept apace with all the new developments. The current issues reflect the healthy state of the hobby for each month the "Model Railway Constructor" contains articles describing layouts, prototype installations of modelling interest, scale plans of rolling stock and ancilliary items and unbiased reviews of commercially produced equipment. Each issue now has coloured covers as well as colour on two of its inside pages.

Railway Modeller

The first issue of "Railway Modeller" appeared in October 1949. It was originally edited by G H Lake, who continued in the post for the first four issues, the present editor, C J Freezer succeeded as from the sixth. Born as it was during the period of the post-war shortages, the early issues reflected the spirit of gallant improvisation common at that time, it comprised only 36 pages inclusive of cover and was just 8in by 5in large. It continued in this way under the original ownership for some twelve issues, appearing at roughly bi-monthly intervals. S C Pritchard, who had a few years previously started on the manufacture of model railway products, and had connections in the printing industry, purchased the magazine in 1951 and formed a new company, Peco Publications and Publicity Ltd to publish "Railway Modeller" and other books.

The first issue under the new proprietorship appeared in November of that year, continuing under the editorship of C J Freezer. The November and December issues remained in the old small format, but with the January 1952 issue a fresh beginning was made, the magazine enlarged to 10in by 8in and new ideas were incorporated. The trend to increase in size continued until it has reached the present A4 format, with an average of 72 pages per issue. At the time of the take-over the sales were a lot less than they are now.

Editorially it caters for the average enthusiast, providing him with a mine of information on all aspects of the hobby. Looking back over the past 20 years one realises just how much the hobby has changed. In the 1940s railway modellers —although the term was hardly ever used—were perhaps a little shy of admitting their hobby for fear of being accused of playing with trains. Today all that is different. It is accepted universally as a wonderfully relaxing adult hobby, promoting as it does so many skills. Possibly in the early days the ardent enthusiast was a little more industrious, since there were no kits and few ready-to-run models available. The change, which has been reflected in the pages of "Railway Modeller", shows that it is the availability of such a range of products that enables so many more people to enjoy the hobby, since the first essential is no longer the ability to make a neat soldered joint.

"Railway Modeller" has always made a practice of using a large number of quality photographic illustrations since it believes that much can be learned from the achievements of others. In the January 1952 issue the first "Railway of the Month" appeared, a 4mm scale model of the Culm Valley Branch by Maurice Deane. This was one of the first published examples of a layout based on an actual prototype, but unlike many present models it was, in those days, possible to visit the small steam worked branches to make drawings and take one's own photographs. This established a precedent, since then the lead article in every issue of "Railway Modeller" has featured a well illustrated layout as the "Railway of the Month".

The introduction of the Railway Modeller Cup, the first fully open major award for model railway construction was made the following year. Originally devised to encourage good articles, the Cup being awarded to what was judged by the readers the best of the year. Ever since, apart from the one exception in 1953, when it was won by Norman Eagles for an article on timetable operation, it has gone to a "Railway of the Month", and has now been officially confined to this category. Time has proved that no matter how attractive may be the locomotive, coaches, wagon and building projects, the other enthusiast's railway does more to encourage good modelling than any other single subject. The Railway Modeller Cup is won outright each year and several outstanding contributors have now more than one on their shelves.

History of the
MODEL RAILWAY PRESS in the UNITED STATES

A model railway press specific to the hobby did not exist in the United States prior to 1934. Nevertheless, starting in the mid-twenties, articles about model railways began to appear in magazines. "The Modelmaker", a monthly dealing with the construction and operation of working scale models commenced publication in Bay Shore, Long Island, New York in 1924. In the beginning it frequently carried descriptive and constructional articles on locomotives and cars and later had articles on model railways in every issue.

"Railroad Stories", now called "Railroad Magazine", a monthly essentially about the prototype railroads, included model railway information up through the thirties but primarily of a news rather than a technical nature. "Popular Science Monthly", a general magazine, began carrying model railway articles on a regular basis as early as 1929 and continued into the fifties. Although much of the information published in "Popular Science" was devoted to modification of the toy trains of that period to make them usable for model railways, some articles were quite sophisticated. An example was the series starting in the December, 1930 issue on building an automatic block-signal system with ATS (Automatic Train Stop).

During this early period, Americans had to depend, to a large extent, both on supplies and publications from England. In addition to the British magazines, four books by Henry Greenly received wide

circulation. As a result certain British railroad terms became part of the hobby language instead of the equivalent American term. Examples are "fishplate" instead of "angle bar" for joining rails and "rodding" instead of "pipe lines" for setting points and signals at manual interlockings.

American books on model railways began appearing in the early thirties, some of the earliest being issued by their authors rather than established publishers. One of the most important of these early works was the "Signal and Control Manual for Miniature and Model Railroads" by William K Walthers in 1932. Walthers is best known for the establishment of one of the earliest (and still one of the largest) model-railroad supply houses and manufacturers but he also was one of the major early contributors of model railroad articles to periodicals as well as the author of several books. Although they never could be expected to become best sellers, he issued books which preserved the history of the hobby such as his "A Booklet on Couplers", a history of couplers, prototype and model, from 1836 to 1942.

March, 1933, with the first issue of the "Model Craftsman" (published in New York City) heralded a new day for model railways. This was not immediately apparent as the Craftsman began as a general hobby magazine, indeed there was only one model railway article in that first issue. However it quickly became

the focus for the articles which theretofore had been scattered among the general magazines. The close personal contact between the publisher and the New York Society of Model Engineers, one of the most important model railroad clubs in the country, did no harm and by 1935 about half its pages were devoted to model railways. Later it became 100% model railroading and changed its name to the "Railroad Model Craftsman".

An important side advantage of a periodical with a specific interest in the hobby was that such a publisher also has an interest in books on the subject. Within a year of its first issue, the "Model Craftsman" published the 255-page "Model Railroad Manual", a still-valuable reference.

The day heralded by the Craftsman dawned in January, 1934 with Vol 1, No 1 of the "Model Railroader", the first of the all model railroad magazines in the US. Initially started on a non-profit basis, the magazine soon became commercial. Published in Milwaukee, Wisconsin, the "Model Railroader" had close contact with the Model Railroad Club of Milwaukee, one of the oldest and largest clubs in the country. In its first year this new magazine grew from 12 pages to 22 per issue and was well on its way to becoming the most prominent periodical in the field in the US.

Above : Bound first volumes of 'Model Railroader', 'Model Craftsman' and 'H.O. Monthly' with first issue cover showing.
Paul Mallery

At the end of 1934, A C Kalmbach & Co, publisher of the "Model Railroader", entered the book field with "Simplified Trackwork for Model Railroad Builders" by W K Walthers. By January 1935, Kalmbach had purchased The Model-maker Corp and adopted that name as publisher of the "Model Railroader". The Modelmaker magazine was continued until 1940, at which time the name of the publisher was again changed, this time to the present Kalmbach Publishing Co. Kalmbach is unusual in the model railroad publishers field in that it long maintained its own printing plant.

An interesting book, "The Model Railroad Right of Way" by O W Wilson, issued in 1934 by the original Model-maker, was continued at least to 1941 by Kalmbach. That book covered British as well as US practice.

Many regard "The Model Railroader Cyclopedia", first edition 1936, to be the most important of the early books. It contained primarily plans but covered all aspects of railways. This book was periodically enlarged up to its sixth and last edition in 1949. In 1960 a large work was published including only steam locomotives under the name "Model Railroader Cyclopedia. Vol 1".

In 1937 Kalmbach published the "Hand-book for Model Railroaders" by W K Walthers, probably the first of the long series of general books on building model railroads to US practice. Also about 1937 the booklet "Choice of Scale and Gauge" by Linn H Westcott appeared, important primarily as the first book by this most important of US model railway authors who is at present the editor of the "Model Railroader" magazine.

Kalmbach continued to expand their line of model railway books. By 1941 they had added "Model Railroad Track and Layout" by A C Kalmbach, "Model Cars and Locomotives" by Edward Beal and Frank Taylor, "Building a Passenger Train" by M D Thornburgh, "Model Railroad Conversion Manual" by Louis Hertz, the latter book being on the conversion of toy equipment to model railroad purposes. In 1941 they issued another in the long series of general books, "Model Railroads" by Edwin P Alexander. Kalmbach was by then, firmly established as the most prominent of model railway book publishers and retains that position today.

Several attempts were made prior to World War II to start other model railway magazines but there were not enough good articles to support more periodicals. One of the longer-lived, 1937 to at least 1940, was the "Model Railroader's Digest" published by Louis H Hertz, New York. This magazine was heavy on information about toy trains.

About 1937 manufacturers began publishing materials to assist beginners. In some cases this information was included as a section of a catalogue, early examples were by Mantua (HO) and by Scale-Craft (O & OO). By 1941 Scale-Craft had 34 pages of such information in its catalogue. Mantua, now called Ty-co, issued books separate from their catalogue, a booklet "Two Rail", first edition by Eric LaNal (pen name for Allan Lake Rice), second edition by this author,

was designed to explain wiring for two rail to beginners. Eric LaNal also wrote an 8,000 word treatise on HO modelling practice for inclusion in "The Mantua HO Handbook" published in 1941.

Lionel, the most prominent US manufacturer of toy trains, for many years published a magazine called the "Model Builder", which, although based on the use of Lionel toy trains and track, had considerable information on building structures, scenery, and layouts in general. In 1940 that company issued a 191-page "Handbook for Model Builders" which, except for layout design, was not tied to Lionel track and equipment.

The entry of the US into World War II created a gap in model railway publishing bridged only by the "Model Railroad" and the "Railroad Model Craftsman" magazines plus some coverage in "Popular Science" and "Railroad Stories". During the war the "Model Railroader", still in its original 7in by 10in format, was reduced to about 50 pages per issue. After the war this rose to about 90 pages and in 1948 its format was changed to that most common in the hobby, $8\frac{1}{2}$in by 11in and had about 76 pages per issue. It has that format today but has grown to about 90 pages.

The great upsurge of interest in model railroading after the war swept HO scale into a dominant position. This change, however, was not totally reflected in the

two existing magazines, in particular they continued to publish plans only in other scales. A V Anderson of Philadelphia recognized that there was an opportunity for a magazine specifically for HO and in May, 1948 the first issue of the "HO Monthly" appeared. In 1950 the name was changed to "Model Trains" but it continued to be HO exclusively. Probably its greatest impact was that following its introduction the other magazines began publishing plans to HO scale. Due to early losses, its printers took over the publication of "Model Trains". It continued to grow in size and stature, reaching 60 pages of $8\frac{1}{2}$in by 11in format by 1953. "Model Trains" was then purchased by Kalmbach Publications, the first issue under the new publisher converting the magazine into an all-gauge beginners periodical which was continued until March, 1962.

A change in the hobby following the war reflected in the publications was the increasing separation of toy trains and model railways. An exception was S scale, $\frac{3}{16}$in = 1ft. The introduction by American Flyer of two-rail semi-scale toy equipment essentially ended S gauge as a significant modelling gauge.

About 1951 two short-lived semi-toy, semi-model railway magazines appeared, "Electric Trains", published by Fox-Shulman of Philadelphia and "Toy Trains", published by the "Railroad Model Craftsman". Following the end of

those periodicals, toy trains ceased to have significant impact on model railway publications except for articles about toy-train collecting in the "Railroad Model Craftsman".

Fox-Shulman also published a 224-page book the "1948 Model Railroad Annual" which was more comprehensive than most general books and contained information and some photographs of many of the clubs then active.

About 1948 publications by model railway hobby organizations began to appear on a regular basis. Most important of these was and remains the Bulletin of the NMRA (National Model Railroad Association) which, at that time, changed from an occasionally-issued news sheet to a monthly. Although primarily concerned with news about the hobby including such things as proposed standards, by 1962 it was carrying technical articles. By 1974 it had grown in size to 64 8½in by 11in pages and serves as a forum for subjects too advanced to be suitable for the commercial press.

members from the east coast to Colorado. Only one year younger and still active is the "Clearboard" of The Model Railroad Club, Union, New Jersey. In 1965 the Standards Manual of the latter club was published as a small 62-page book by Winston Publishers, New York City. This book was sold nationwide as well as at the annual public shows at the club.

With the end of World War II, some of the earlier books, particularly those published by Kalmbach and the Railroad Model Craftsman, again became available. New books, too began appearing, one of the most important, first edition in 1950 and periodically updated is "How to Wire Your Model Railroad" by Linn H Westcott and published by Kalmbach. The latter publisher has consistently added to its line of books not only with special books written for the model railroader such as the "N Scale Primer" by Russ Larson introduced in 1974 but also by reprints of important early works on the prototype railways, an example

exhausted. The second edition of the Electrical Handbook was enlarged to two volumes and published by the Railroad Model Craftsman and the second edition of the Bridge Handbook also was enlarged but published by the Builders' Compendium. Although the word "handbook" has been used before and since for model railway books written as "how-to" books, the handbooks in the series by this author are true handbooks in the engineering sense. That is they are meant to be reference works covering all the established methods and typical model and prototype practice in a given subject.

About 1955 ready-to-run locomotives and cars to HO began to have major impact. This led manufacturers to publish books specifically aimed at assisting beginners to use their commercial products. Although, as described earlier, beginner information had been published by manufacturers as early as the thirties, these latter books were different in that they were written around the use of

One of the most important reference works for model railroading is the NMRA Manual, actually a loose-leaf file of Data Sheets, Recommended Practices, and similar material dealing with all phases of the hobby. Such sheets are issued from time to time and distributed with the Bulletin. By 1974 this Manual had become about 2in thick.

The NMRA is divided into area organizations known as Regions and Divisions, some of which have regular publications which carry plans and prototype information specific to their local areas.

Some of the large clubs maintain regular publications. Perhaps the oldest which is still consistently issued is the "Bell" of the Bell Telephone Laboratories Model Railroad Club. Its first issue was in 1948 and today it serves about 300

being the "Car Builders Cyclopedia of American Practice" originally published by Simmons-Boardman in 1941.

Simmons-Boardman, the leading publisher for the prototype railways including the magazine "Railway Age" entered the model railway field with quality-printed hard-cover books about 1954. They issued general books by Louis H Hertz and what proved to be the start of an expanding series of handbooks in the hobby, "The Electrical Handbook for Model Railroaders" and "The Bridge and Trestle Handbook for Model Railroaders", both by this author. Simmons-Boardman chose not to market its hobby books through hobby channels, depending instead on its normal non-hobby distribution. They withdrew from the hobby field when the first printings were

specific commercial products, for example track layouts using sectional track as manufactured by the publisher of the book. Atlas Tool was and remains the most active in this field both in HO and in N with several layout plan books written by John Armstrong and Thaddeus Stepek, also "Wiring Your Layout" by this author. This latter book describes wiring layouts using the prefabricated Atlas control system. That books published by manufacturers are not an insignificant part of the model railway publishing field is demonstrated in that about 200,000 copies of the above wiring book were sold in the first edition alone.

A collection of books published by Atlas Tool.
Paul Mallery

Around 1960 a new form of model railway publication appeared, the Builders' Compendium". It is a looseleaf book, each page covering a specific product or products by a particular manufacturer. It is available with an up-date service to keep all information current. The chief value of this publication is to model railroaders who do not have access to a well-stocked hobby store.

In 1969 the "Builders' Compendium" entered the bound-book field with the "Trackwork Handbook for Model Railroads" and later with the second edition of the previously-mentioned Bridge Handbook, both by this author. They also have books of prototype information, one a reprint of old Pennsylvania Maintenance-of-Way information.

Special-interest periodicals were published from time to time, some dealing with a specific gauge such as S, but typically they were not successful. An exception is "Traction Models", published by Vane Jones, Indianapolis, which started in 1966. Although nominally covering all forms of electric traction including electrified main-line railroads, it is primarily devoted to tramways and interurban railways of the type common in the US from about 1900 to 1940. In 1974 it made its entry into the book field with the "Model Traction Handbook" by this author. Another periodical specific to tramways, "Street Railways", was being issued in 1974.

With the exception of the previously-mentioned "Electric Trains", every periodical in the field of model railways had been published by a house organized for the purpose. Some, notably Kalmbach Publishing, later expanded into other fields, but they remained mainly model-railway based. However in 1971, Challenge Publications, Canoga Park, California, a large-scale publisher of hobby periodicals in other fields, commenced the "Railroad Modeler". This magazine is heavy on photographs and is set at the beginner and elementary level, roughly the position vacated by the ending of publication of "Model Trains" in 1962.

The situation at the time of writing is that model railroading in the US is served by five major periodicals with wide national distribution, the NMRA Bulletin, the "Model Railroader", the "Railroad Model Craftsman", the "Railroad Modeler", and "Model Traction". Although competitive with all others to some degree, each magazine has its own distinctive features, areas of coverage, and in some cases difference in level.

In addition to magazines and books prepared especially for model railways, there have been and remain many other related publications which have information useful to model railroading, for example "Trains" magazine by Kalmbach Publishing and the many books about various prototype railroads and traction lines. But, as we have here been concerned only with the press specifically publishing for model railways, such related publications, valuable as they are, have, with minor exceptions, been omitted.

Above: Issues of 'Model Railroader' from Volumes 1 and 41. *Paul Mallery*

Top Right: 'Traction Models' published by Vane Jones of Indianapolis. *Paul Mallery*

Right: A selection of handbooks in a series written by the author. *Paul Mallery*

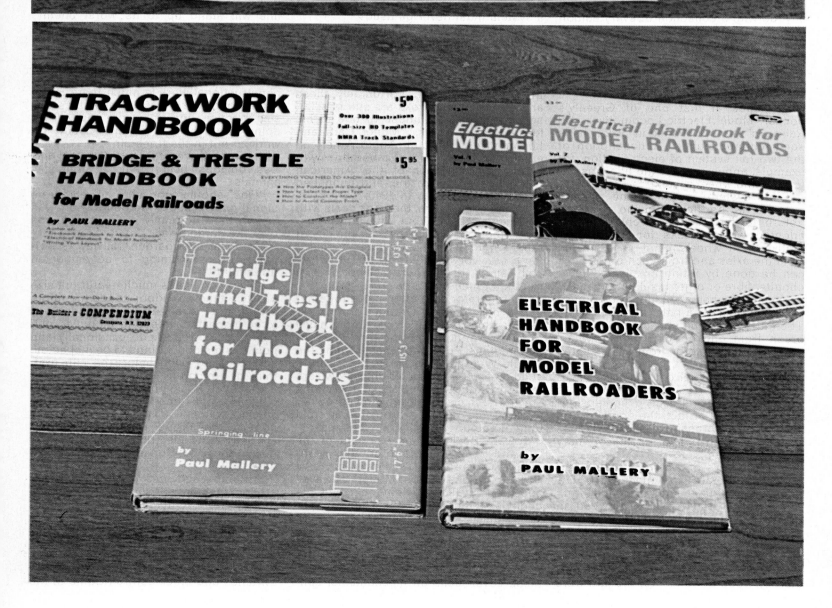

Practical and nostalgic

Some classic model railway books

If the railway modeller read everything published about his hobby, he would probably never have a minute to spare for any actual modelling. The literature is vast; yet though the practical man may scorn the "armchair modeller", both alike need to read at least some of the books on the subject, not only to learn "how to do it" but to take advantage of other people's ideas. It is therefore worth having a look at a few of the more vintage "classic" books, especially one or two that might be less familiar to today's enthusiast.

Such a look reveals some surprises, as well as entertainment. New methods and materials replace old; tinplate and scratch-building have given way to plastics and kits. Yet some "new" ideas are not so new after all; two-rail, the cult of the scenic, even model colour photography, have respectable ancestry. Certain books are now fascinating glimpses of the state of the art at a past moment in time, while others seem to set novel trends that are now commonplace. Yet others fit into no categories, but have their own period charm.

Among "classics", of course, pride of place must go to W J Bassett-Lowke's "Model Railway Handbook", a "bible" to generations of enthusiasts. The many editions span several decades, and anyone with a collection of every edition of this famous work has a treasure indeed! Perhaps less well remembered nowadays are the books of Bassett-Lowke's associate Henry Greenly, though these did much to popularise the hobby during the 1920s.

A glance at just one of Greenly's books, "Model Electric Locomotives and Railways" (first published in 1922), yields some curious points. A description of the two-rail system of electrification, for example, appears under the title "insulated-rail and wheel system", as follows:

"This system, in which one running rail acts as the 'flow' and the other the 'return' for the electric current, has been adopted with success for small locomotives. All wheels must be insulated from the axles and from each other. This can be done by fitting small bushes of ebonite, fibre or other insulating material between the wheels and the axles. These can be turned on a lathe and forced on. The current may be collected by a small brush from one or more of the wheel tyres on each side or from an insulated slip-ring on the axle".

In view of the later complaint that two-rail wiring was "too complicated", it is amusing to read Greenly's conclusion:

"As a matter of fact, the complication at points and crossings is actually less than that which obtains in the ordinary third-rail system".

In these days of readily available rectifiers to obtain the necessary DC supply from the mains for model train operation, it is interesting to read in Greenly of procedures then employed for this purpose. To obtain DC from AC mains, you could make up a chemical rectifier from four glass jars, in which stood aluminium and iron plates separated by wood or vulcanite; the jars were

filled with a saturated solution of ammonium phosphate, and then you could put your current through. Be careful, though, or with three or four hours of overloading, the whole thing would start to boil!

A spine-tingling story is Greenly's account of the use of high-voltage house supply through a resistance. He describes a model railway obtaining its current direct from the mains with only a resistance, made from an ordinary commercial electric firebar, intervening between the controller and the mains, an arrangement which our more safety-conscious age can only regard with horror.

"This installation may be considered as working on the 'fixed amperage' system. Whatever happens, a short circuit of the running and third rail, or any similar fault, which, if the railway were supplied from an accumulator, would cause a large and destructive current to flow, does not matter in the least, except for the waste of current, as no greater current than five amperes can pass through the system".

He concludes that "the system worked quite well, without sparking at the locomotive commutator, and is eminently safe". Nowadays, of course, it cannot be too strongly emphasised that such a system must never be used!

No less a "classic" author is Edward Beal, whose books such as "The Craft of Modelling Railways" and "Scale Railway Modelling Today" inspired many to greater heights in the hobby during the 1930s and after. Fortunately these and others of his books are still familiar, so here is just a glimpse of one of his lesser-known works, "Model Cars and Locomotives", a joint Anglo-American enterprise by Beal in collaboration with Frank Taylor, editor of the American "Modelmaker" magazine, and published in the United States in 1940.

As the title implies, the book deals with American practice, but with an enthusiasm that almost converts the most rabid Anglophile—even if it means learning a new vocabulary (how about a "red ball freight" or a "short fast hot shot"!) Here's a touch of the flavour:

"Refrigerator cars often move together in red ball freights. Oranges from California and Florida, fruit from many orchards, lettuce from the truck gardening regions, dressed meat from the Middle West packing houses start off in solid reefer trains. The bright yellow cars make fine models . . . Special attractions are the fast disappearing private owner reefers—and what an attraction a solid train of colourful beer cars would make!"

Edward Beal was an exponent of the OO and HO gauges, and another advocate of these small scales was E W Twining, whose "Indoor Model Railways" appeared in 1937. Twining claimed his book as "a technical rather than a popular treatise", and it embraces a wealth of intricate detail and scale drawings. He aimed to give "the amateur model maker and railway owner some suggestions which may be useful to them"; these cover ideas on mechanisms, con-

trol, two-rail working, and architectural features, and incidentally make up a review of the material then available to the modeller.

Not the least interesting of Twining's comments are his views on layout and scenery, especially in relation to the typical layout of this period. Many have suggested, he says, that "to make the most complete system it is necessary to pack into a given space as many things as can be thought of". He urges concentration on the railway: "make the railway picturesque and reproduce nature rather than works and factories". Perhaps this is a reflection of Twining's many-sided nature; as well as being a professional modelmaker, he was also the author of books on "Heraldry", "Art in Advertising" and "The Art and Craft of Stained Glass".

From indoor model railways to the great outdoors, and a book that brought a breath of fresh air into the subject. R E Tustin's "Garden Railways", published in 1949, was probably the first book entirely devoted to this specialised area of modelling, and no doubt it tempted many to seek new horizons. Based on his own experiences of an O gauge garden layout that had already been in operation for more than ten years, he shows how to ensure that the line will stand up to its worst enemy, the weather, and extols the virtues of the wide open spaces:

"Why not turn to the garden? You will undoubtedly have fifty times the space that you would have indoors, the actual constructional work is much more interesting, and more closely resembles full size practice, and I am sure you will be doing yourselves a lot more good by working out in the fresh air."

Naturally there are snags, one of the less obvious being that of domestic animals:

"One should not site an elaborate signal gantry just at the point where it is known that the family cat always jumps over the garden wall . . . "

Moreover the garden railway is evidently not something to be embarked upon lightly:

"A garden line is much nearer full size practice than an indoor concern, and its owner must arrange for permanent way to be inspected, weeds to be pulled out, ballast to be repacked occasionally and points and signal fittings to be inspected, adjusted and oiled before he can even think of running trains".

Clearly this is not a project for the sluggard, and those who prefer just to sit and watch it all happen might find more to their liking in an unusual book entitled "Auto-Electric Model Railways". Its author is A Duncan Stubbs and its date 1939.

Intriguing schemes for automatic operation include an automatic timetable that will work your whole railway for you; just switch on and it goes! There are other fascinations, like automatic level crossing gates, and automatic couplings worked by an electro magnet in each wagon, as well as delayed action switches and block control. Some of the

MINIATURE LOCOMOTIVE CONSTRUCTION

JOHN H. AHERN

MODEL RAILWAYS
1838-1939 · Hamilton Ellis

GEORGE ALLEN AND UNWIN

THE MODEL RAILWAY HANDBOOK
W.J. BASSETT-LOWKE M.I.LOCO.E

FIFTEENTH EDITION
SEVEN SHILLINGS & SIXPENCE

MODEL RAILWAY ENGINES
J. E. MINNS

PLEASURES AND TREASURES

methods may appear a trifle Heath Robinsonish in the light of present-day practice; for example, there is a method of operating points by means of a falling weight. This involves a bobbin, which can be released electrically; around this is wound a length of twine, at the end of which is a 1lb weight. Release the bobbin, the weight falls and switches the points. After a time, of course, you have to rewind the twine so that it can start all over again!

But operation is not all; the railway must also have realistic surroundings. Nowadays the scenic setting is an accepted integral part of the whole layout plan rather than an afterthought, but it was not always so. A stimulus towards the present viewpoint was undoubtedly given by a "Modelcraft Planbook" entitled "Scenic Railway Modelling", published in 1944 and probably the first book dealing exclusively with this facet of the hobby. Its author and illustrator was P R Wickham, a commercial artist and already a noted modeller, and it includes plans for the obvious railway features such as bridges, tunnels and stations, as well as for outside items such as factories, shops, houses, and even road vehicles.

The context in which the book appeared is hinted in the review in "Model Railway Constructor": "materials used generally are very simple and wartime conditions need deter no one from turning out some most attractive models". For at this time of shortages of materials, many enthusiasts were obliged to turn to alternatives and so give attention to scenic features that did not involve scarce metals.

One alternative material was cardboard, of which Wickham was an early protagonist. Examples of his work can be seen in another of his books "Commercial Model Making", which devotes one of its three sections to railway modelling and includes the author's ideas on cardboard construction for locomotives and rolling stock.

From the same era of shortages originates another minor classic, E Rankine Gray's "Cardboard Rolling Stock and How to Build it", which is still well-known to the modeller. Though intended first and foremost as an instruction manual for the "ERG" card parts, it is in fact a complete guide to the subject for the scratch builder as well. "There was a time", says Gray, "when no model railway enthusiast would have considered using cardboard for the construction of rolling stock, but few can now doubt that this material has come to stay".

This bleak wartime period also produced a little book which must be a strong contender for the prize for originality. Certainly "Railways" is not the most strikingly original title, and the modeller might be forgiven for thinking that it is not of direct appeal to him, for this is a children's primer of the "I am Fred the engine driver" kind.

But sight of the subtitle brings second thoughts: "Photographed in colour from model railways". For this refreshingly novel work contains 24 colour photographs of model railways, including such celebrated layouts as J H Ahern's Madder Valley, Ronald Shephard's South British, Kenview, Bekonscot, and Victor B Harrison's line. Published in 1944, it must be one of the earliest books (as distinct from catalogues) to feature colour photographs of model railways, a notable achievement under wartime circumstances. And if the present-day

eye may be critical of the quality of a few of the pictures, it remains a delight to revisit colourful Madderport and the South British, as well as to see vintage tinplate such as an operating mail van.

The views of the Madder Valley recall Ahern's quest for scenic perfection, exemplified not only in his models but in his classic books "Miniature Building Construction" (first published as long ago as 1947) and "Miniature Landscape Modelling" (1951). Happily these are now again in print, together with the third member of the trilogy, "Miniature Locomotive Construction", which first appeared in 1948.

Such titles are indicative of specialisation in an expanding hobby, for to compile one book covering every aspect of the subject is an ambitious undertaking. A valiant attempt at the task was made by Ernest F Carter, one of the most prolific of writers on model railways; his "Model Railway Encyclopedia", first published in 1950, is a weighty tome of over 450 pages. He justified the work as follows:

"The need for a really comprehensive constructional and operational manual dealing exclusively with the smaller gauges is greater today than at any period in the history of the model railway hobby. Modern developments have rendered obsolete many of the theories and methods to which the model railway enthusiast has so long rigidly adhered".

The truth of such a statement is clear from an examination of the first edition of the encyclopedia, which paints a picture that now appears entirely remote from today's scene, such has been the rate of change over the past quarter-century. Much of the book, for example, is specially applicable to the then popular O gauge, while OO gauge track still comprised brass rail soldered to brass or tinplate sleepers. Stud contact electrification (for which Carter tells us he was responsible in 1938) was then enjoying a vogue in the face of the upcoming two-rail. These were also the days when the modeller expected to make things from scratch, a pointer to the state of the market at the time; there is, for example, a detailed chapter on building an OO mechanism.

Conditions and methods change, but so also do attitudes, and the last few years have seen the growth of the "vintage mania" and the rise of the collector of obsolete models. Several books mirror this aspect of the hobby, and have no doubt aided in stimulating it. Pioneer of the historical, Hamilton Ellis in his delightful "Model Railways 1838-1939", published in 1962, traces the subject back to surprisingly early beginnings, recalls many old models, and recounts the careers of the principal makers, all in his own characteristic style.

Something on similar lines but of a more elaborate nature is Gustavo Reder's "Mit Uhrwerk, Dampf und Strom", published in Germany in 1970, a glorious book for the historically-minded enthusiast to revel in, with a superb array of illustrations to make any collector envious. Here is a panorama of the commercial model railways of yesteryear: fearful electrical contrivances, elevated railways on stilts, mountain railways, "Katastrophen-Zügen" complete with casualties, double deck coaches with canopies and railings, pseudo-Gothick stations with flags flying, tunnels with castles on top. If ever a book captured the spirit of the model railway heritage, this is it. Appropriately enough, Hamilton Ellis translated it into an English edition in 1972 under the title "Clockwork, Steam and Electric".

On the even more antiquarian side ("veteran" rather than "vintage"?) J E Minns' "Model Railway Engines" (a "Pleasures and Treasures" book of 1969) surveys the subject primarily from the point of view of the early large-scale items that are now in the antique dealers' salerooms rather than in the everyday secondhand shop.

More for the ordinary collector are two books in the short-lived "Troy Model Club Series": "Older Locomotives 1900-42" by P G Gomm and "Recent Locomotives 1947-70" by P E Randall, both dating from 1970. Illustrated throughout in colour, these two slim volumes point out some of the delights the avid collector might still find, even if many of the models are now elusive and expensive; but one thing they do demonstrate is that a model does not have to be so old to be a collector's piece nowadays. Indeed, these two little books are themselves already something of a collector's pieces!

Maybe there is scope for philosophy in such a thought. And if you feel that the hobby has been somewhat light on the metaphysical side, then turn to "Paddington to Seagood" by the poet and critic Gilbert Thomas, published in 1947. Not only does the author relate an absorbing story of his life with model trains (and incidentally the book is embellished with photographs by W J Bassett-Lowke) but he draws up a "balance sheet" in which he expresses a philosophy that probably many have experienced but which few have been able to put into words:

"Whenever, at my desk, I feel my brain running hot, or whenever I am stuck for an idea or a phrase, I wander into the railway room. I may or may not operate a few trains. Often I find it restful just to potter about, doing a little oiling, pushing back a key or two that may have worked loose on the permanent way, or effecting some other minor repair or adjustment. At other times I merely stand and stare; and how good is the staring!"

Indeed, what model railway enthusiast could better Gilbert Thomas's conclusion:

"The hobby has proved so potent an aid to health, balance, and good temper, and consequently to increased output of work, that I am now fully persuaded that, even from the strictly economic point of view, it has been a sound investment."

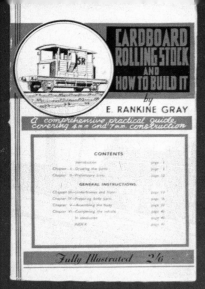

CARDBOARD ROLLING STOCK AND HOW TO BUILD IT
by E. RANKINE GRAY
A comprehensive practical guide covering 4 m.m and 7 m.m construction

CONTENTS

Fully Illustrated 2/6

BUILD MODEL LOCOMOTIVES

SOUTHERN 47

MODEL CARS LOCOMOTIVES
by EDWARD BEAL and FRANK TAYLOR

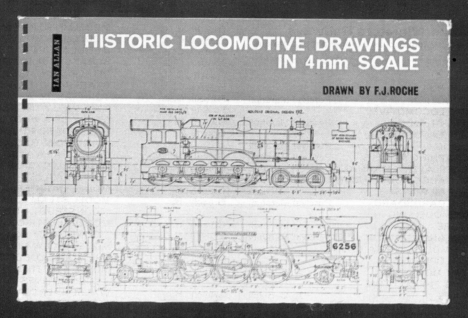

IAN ALLAN

HISTORIC LOCOMOTIVE DRAWINGS IN 4mm SCALE

DRAWN BY F.J.ROCHE

6256

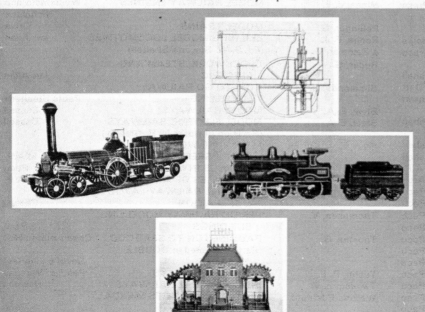

Gustav Reder

Clockwork, Steam and Electric

The History of Model Railways up to 1939

Photographs by Richard Sharpe Studios

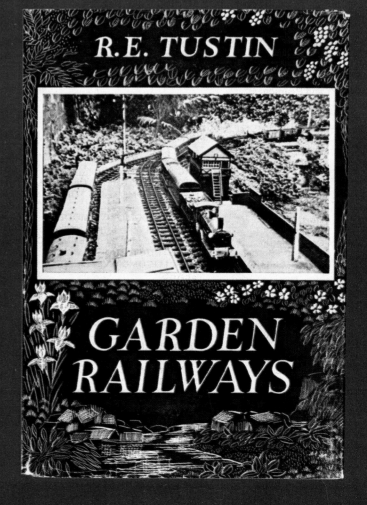

R. E. TUSTIN

GARDEN RAILWAYS

Bibliography for Model and Miniature Railways

This list is not necessarily complete but should act as a guide to those seeking information on the subject.

Ahern, J. H.	MINIATURE BUILDING CONSTRUCTION	Percival Marshall
Ahern, J. H.	MINIATURE LOCOMOTIVE CONSTRUCTION	Percival Marshall
Ahern, J. H.	MINIATURE LANDSCAPE MODELLING	Percival Marshall
Ahern, J. H.	PHOTOGRAPHING MODELS	Percival Marshall
Ahern, J. H.	PECO PLATELAYER'S MANUAL	Peco
Andress, Dr. M.	NARROW GAUGE MODEL RAILWAYS	Allmark
Andress, Dr M.	N GAUGE RAILWAYS	Allmark
Baker, C.	MODELS IN CARDBOARD	Percival Marshall
*Beal, Rev Edward	RAILWAY MODELLING IN MINIATURE	Percival Marshall
Beal, Rev Edward	WEST MIDLAND	Percival Marshall
Beal, Rev Edward	CRAFT OF MODELLING RAILWAYS	Nelson
Beal, Rev Edward	NEW DEVELOPMENTS IN RAILWAY MODELLING	A. C. Black
Beal, Rev Edward	MODELLING THE OLD TIME RAILWAYS	A. C. Black
Beal, Rev Edward	SCALE RAILWAY MODELLING TODAY	A. C. Black
Beal, Rev Edward	RAILWAY MODELLING IN PLAN & PERSPECTIVE	Modelcraft
Boreham, D. A.	NARROW GAUGE RAILWAY MODELLING	Percival Marshall
Boston, Rev E.	RAILS ROUND THE RECTORY	The Book House Loughborough
Boyd-Carpenter, V. and Pearson, G.	OUR MODEL RAILWAYS	Author
Bryand, M. (Ed.)	IAN ALLAN BOOK OF MODEL RAILWAYS	Ian Allan
Butterell, R. Clayton, H. Jacot, M.	MINIATURE RAILWAYS	Oakwood Press
*Carter, E. F.	MODEL RAILWAY ENCYCLOPEDIA	Harold Starke
Denny, Rev. P. B.	BUCKINGHAM GREAT CENTRAL	Peco
Dewhirst, N.	STEAM LOCOMOTIVES FOR O GAUGE	Percival Marshall
Dow, George	WORLD LOCOMOTIVE MODELS	Adams and Dart
Ellis, C. H.	MODEL RAILWAYS 1838-1939	George Allen & Unwin
Evans, Martin	MANUAL OF MODEL STEAM LOCOMOTIVE CONSTRUCTION	Percival Marshall
Evans, Martin	MODEL LOCOMOTIVE VALVE GEARS	Percival Marshall
Evans, Martin	TICH	Percival Marshall
Evans, Martin	MODEL LOCOMOTIVE CONSTRUCTION	M.A.P.
*Freezer, C. J.	RAILWAY MODELLING	Arco
Freezer, C. J.	60 PLANS FOR SMALL RAILWAYS	Peco
Freezer, C. J.	PLANS FOR LARGER LAYOUTS	Peco
Freezer, C. J.	TRACK PLANS	Peco
Freezer, C. J.	A HOME FOR YOUR RAILWAY	Peco
Freezer, C. J.	STARTING IN SCALE OO	Peco
Freezer, C. J.	WIRING THE LAYOUT	Peco
Freezer, C. J.	BUILDING THE BASEBOARD	Peco
Freezer, C. J.	PLANNING THE LAYOUT	Peco
Freezer, C. J.	CAB CONTROL	Peco
Freezer, C. J.	LOW RELIEF MODELLING	Peco
Freezer, C. J.	STATION LAYOUT DESIGN	Peco
Freezer, C. J.	POINT AND SIGNAL CONTROL	Peco
Freezer, C. J.	SIGNALLING THE LAYOUT	Peco
Freezer, C. J.	LANDSCAPE MODELLING	Peco
Freezer, C. J.	OO GAUGE IN THE GARDEN	Peco
Freezer, C. J.	MODELLING BRANCH LINES	Peco
Freezer, C. J.	MODELLING MODERN RAILWAYS	Peco
Freezer, C. J.	METRICATION AND THE MODELLER	Peco
Freezer, C. J.	SCRATCHBUILDING SIMPLIFIED	Peco
Freezer, C. J.	INTRODUCING N GAUGE	Peco
Freezer, C. J.	STARTING WITH A TRAIN SET	Peco
Freezer, C. J.	TURNTABLES AND TRAVERSERS	Peco
Freezer, C. J.	TWO RAIL WITH DEAD FROGS	Peco
Gray, E. R.	STUDY OF A MODEL RAILWAY	ERG
Gray, E. R.	CARDBOARD ROLLING STOCK AND HOW TO BUILD IT	ERG
Greenly, H.	MODEL RAILWAYS	Cassell
Greenly, H.	MODEL ELECTRIC LOCOMOTIVES & RAILWAYS	Cassell
Greenly, H.	MODEL ENGINEERING	Cassell
Greenly, H.	MODEL STEAM LOCOMOTIVE CONSTRUCTION	Cassell
Greenly, H.	MODEL ELECTRIC RAILWAY CONSTRUCTION	Cassell
Greenly, H.	MODEL RAILWAY CONSTRUCTION	Cassell
Greenly, H.	THE MODEL LOCOMOTIVE	Percival Marshall
Greenly, H.	MODEL ELECTRIC LOCOMOTIVES	Percival Marshall
Greenly, H.	WALSCHAERTS VALVE GEAR	Percival Marshall
Greenly, H.	SIGNALS AND SIGNALLING	Percival Marshall
Greenly, H.	PLANNING AND LAYOUT (See also Steel E. A.)	Percival Marshall
Gomm, P. G.	OLDER LOCOMOTIVES	Nelson
Gomm, P. G.	RECENT LOCOMOTIVES	Nelson
Gorham, F. R. (Ed.)	HORNBY BOOK OF TRAINS	Oxford Publishing
Hobbs, E. W.	MODEL RAILWAY MAKING	Cassell
Hobbs, E. W.	MODEL ELECTRIC RAILWAY MAKING	Cassell
Hobbs, E. W.	THE MODEL MAKERS WORKSHOP	Cassell
†LBSC (Lawrence, L.)	SHOP SHED AND ROAD	Percival Marshall
Longridge, M.	MODELLING 4mm SCALE ROLLING STOCK	Rayler
Martin, J.	WORLD OF MODEL RAILWAYS	Percival Marshall
Minns, J. E.	MODEL RAILWAY ENGINES	Weidenfeld and Nicholson
Pollinger, G.	MODEL TRAINS	Orbis
Roche, F. J. & Templar, G. C.	BUILDING MODEL LOCOMOTIVES (Ed. S. W. Stevens-Stratten)	Ian Allan
Reder, G.	CLOCKWORK, STEAM AND ELECTRIC	Ian Allan
Simmonds, N.	HOW TO GO RAILWAY MODELLING	Patric Stephens
Steal, E. A.	MODEL RAILWAYS	Cassell
Steel, E. A.	MODEL ELECTRIC RAILWAYS (Revision of works by H. Greenly)	Cassell
Steel, E. A. & E. H.	MINIATURE WORLD OF HENRY GREENLY	M.A.P.
Stokes Illiffe, G.	BUILDINGS IN MINIATURE	Peco
Strickland, W. A.	CHRONICLES OF A GARDEN RAILWAY	M.A.P.
Taylor, N. G.	OO MODEL RAILWAY LAYOUT & OPERATION	Cassell
Thompson, V.	PERIOD RAILWAY MODELLING, BUILDINGS	Peco
Thomas, G.	PADDINGTON TO SEAGOOD (Partly reprinted in DOUBLE HEADED	Chapman and Hall David & Charles)
Tustin, R. E.	GARDEN RAILWAYS	Percival Marshall
Twining, E. W.	INDOOR MODEL RAILWAYS	Newnes
Watkins Pitchford	PECO PLATELAYER'S MANUAL (2nd Edition)	Peco
Wickham, P. R.	MODELLED ARCHITECTURE	Percival Marshall

*Indicates author has written a number of small handbooks, only major works shown.

†Indicates not in compiler's library, title and provenance not certain.

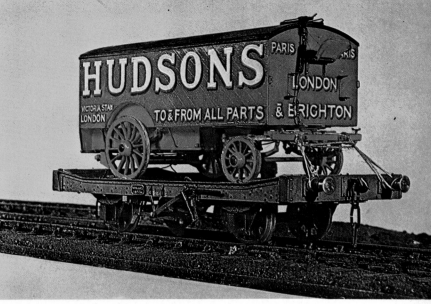

Magazines

GREAT BRITAIN	Model Railways & Locomotives	ceased publication
	Model Railway News	ceased publication
	Model Railway Constructor	Ian Allan
	Railway Modeller	Peco
	Model Railways	M.A.P.
USA	Model Railroader	Kalmbach
	Railroad Model Craftsman	New Jersey
FRANCE	Loco Revue	Auray (Morbihan)
	Rail Miniature Flash	Paris
GERMANY	Moderne Eisenbahn	Dusseldorf
	Miniaturbahnen	Nurnberg
	Der Modelleisenbahner	Berlin
HOLLAND	Hobby Bulletin	Nijverheidswerf
	Redactie Miniatuurbanen	Baarn
JAPAN	Hobby of Model Railroading	Kigei Publishing Co. Ltd.
ITALY	Italmodel	Milano
AUSTRIA	Eisenbahn	Vienna
SWITZERLAND	Eisenbahn-Amateur	Meggen

Prototype

There are a large number of prototype books, many of which contain information useful to the railway modeller. Publications by David & Charles, Ian Allan, Allan & Unwin, Peco, Oakwood, and especially, Oxford Publishing Co. are to be recommended. Oxford Publishing's list now contains a number of books containing scale drawings, mostly to accepted modelling scales.

Pictorial albums by Ian Allan, D. Bradford Barton, and Oxford Publishing Co. are of value for specific prototypes.

Drawings

J. E. Skinley publishes a large range of drawings to accepted modelling scales. The accuracy of certain drawings is suspect. Ian Allan also publish the Roche collection of drawings plus selections of coach and wagon drawings.

Oxford Publishing, in conjunction with British Rail, are microfilming official drawings. The sources vary from weight diagrams to general arrangement drawings; all have been carefully selected for their value to railway modellers.

Society Journals

Most specialist societies publish a journal, monthly or quarterly. In addition the Gauge 1 Association, EM Gauge Society, Gauge O Guild and Protofour Society have prepared useful handbooks relating to their specific interest. The Historical Model Railway Society Journal invariably contains a number of accurate drawings. The Journal of the Stephenson Locomotive Society contains small scale side elevations of locomotives, not to any specific scale. The Railway Observer, the journal of the Railway Correspondence & Travel Society is very accurate on matters of locomotive allocation and current practice. Their series of locomotive histories are both exhaustive and accurate and are highly recommended for information on numbering, naming, building and withdrawal dates, and major changes in detail.

Sources

Many books listed are out of print. Many larger clubs have libraries, frequently with good collections of modelling journals. The Model Railway Club (London) and Manchester Model Railway Society deserve special mention in this respect.

Most recent books can be obtained through the local Public Library through the library interlending scheme. A number of specialist second-hand booksellers can provide copies of out of print books. However, a diligent search in second-hand bookshops and curio shops can often unearth old railway books at very reasonable prices.

Bibliography for Passenger Carrying Miniature Railways of 7¼" Gauge upwards.

This list is not necessarily complete but should act as an adequate guide to those seeking information on this subject.

Butterell, Robin	MINIATURE RAILWAYS	Ian Allan
Clayton, Howard Jacot, Michel	} MINIATURE RAILWAYS Vol 1.	
Butterell, Robin	1-15in GAUGE	Oakwood Press 1971
Clayton, Howard	THE DUFFIELD BANK AND EATON RAILWAYS	Oakwood Press 1968

Davies, W. J.	THE RAVENGLAS AND ESKDALE RAILWAY	David & Charles 1968
Greenly, Henry	MODEL STEAM LOCOMOTIVES First published 1922, since revised on a number of occasions and most recently by E. A. Steel	
Heywood, Sir Arthur	MINIMUM GAUGE RAILWAYS 3rd edition 1898	(published privately)
Shaw, Frederick	LITTLE RAILWAYS OF THE WORLD Published in the USA in 1958	
Steel, E. A. and E. H.	THE MINIATURE WORLD OF HENRY GREENLY	Model and Allied Publications 1973
Strauss, Dr. Walter	LILIPUTBAHNEN	published in Germany 1938
Wilson, B. G.	MINIATURE RAILWAYS	Ian Allan
Woodcock, George	MINIATURE STEAM LOCOMOTIVES	David & Charles 1964

There are a number of guides issued by various miniature railways giving details of the line, rolling stock, etc. and these are generally available from the proprietors.

A number of magazines deal with miniature railway matters from time to time.

MODELS, RAILWAYS AND LOCOMOTIVES published between 1909/1919, edited by Henry Greenly, had many articles on miniature locomotives and railways. Also many issues of THE LOCOMOTIVE, now no longer published, carried articles on locomotives and miniature railways.

Bassett-Lowke published a number of editions of THE MODEL RAILWAY HANDBOOK in the 1920s and 1930s which contained information on a number of their larger scale model locomotives.

The best current sources of information are THE MODEL ENGINEER which is published fortnightly and THE NARROW GAUGE published three times a year by the Narrow Gauge Railway Society. Members of the Society also receive NARROW GAUGE NEWS at approximately two month intervals giving up-to-the-minute information on most miniature lines.

References may also be found from time to time in the monthly magazines, RAILWAY MAGAZINE and RAILWAY WORLD.

Acknowledgement

The Publishers and Editors gratefully acknowledge the help which they have received in the compilation of this work. Without this assistance the task would have been an impossible one, and to all those who have played a part in advising, supplying information and pictures, and in the provision of constructive criticism, thanks is recorded. It is impossible to list all those who have helped, but in particular we wish to acknowledge outstanding assistance from the following:—

Ian Allan Ltd for the use of the Roche Drawings, and the advice of S. W. Stevens-Stratten, Editor of their Magazine "Model Railway Constructor". Peco Publications Ltd for the advice of C. J. Freezer, Editor of their magazine "Railway Modeller".
R. Butterell Esq., and J. B. Hollingsworth Esq., for advice on Miniature Railway matters.
Paul Towers Esq., for advice on Model Railway matters.
Rev. E. Boston for extracts from his book "Rails Round the Rectory". (The Bookhouse, Loughborough)
Gerald Pollinger Esq., for the tables on page 87 from his book "Model Trains" (Orbis).
R. Guy Williams Esq., J. H. Russell Esq., S. C. Pritchard Esq., E. Cornwell Esq., for consultation and help.
J. van Riemsdijk Esq., Count Antonio Giansanti Coluzzi, Sen. Gustavo Reder, Jim Whittaker Esq., and R. McCrindell Esq., for matters relating to tinplate trains.
Loco-Revue for advice on French matters, and drawings.
Pendon, Bristol, Derby, and the London Science Museums for facilities. Model Railway and Model Engineering Societies and Clubs for assistance. E. Jackson Stevens Esq., for advice on Tramway matters.
The Railway Correspondence & Travel Society for material from their series "Locomotives of the Great Western Railway".
Verlag Eisenbahn, Switzerland who now own Bing.

INDEX

THE PUBLISHERS AND EDITORS WOULD LIKE TO EXPRESS THEIR GRATEFUL THANKS TO THE FOLLOWING CONTRIBUTORS TO THIS BOOK:
Allenden, Dennis – 405
Ball, R. – 320
Butterell, Robin, – 148, 158, 172, 175, 184, 187, 197, 201, 207, 233
Clayton, H. – 45, 153
Cook, Mike – 314
Cross, M. S. – 217, 393
Denny, Rev. Peter – 290
Elkin, P. W. – 259
England, Roye – 327, 371
Falaize, Jean – 398
Freezer, C. J. – 23, 83, 89

Girod-Eymery, Henry – 398
Glasby, Ellis – 335
Hine, Stuart – 127
Holoran, E. C. – 360
Hollingsworth, J. B. – 179, 223, 481
Joyce, Jim – 19, 63, 67, 71, 77, 502
Lewis, Mike – 389
Macmillan, Nigel S. C. – 376
Mallery, Paul – 497
Murray, Anthony – 303
Neale, D. H. – 345
Northwood, Ken – 331
Pochin, Ross – 295
Pomroy, John D. – 365
Randall, P. E. – 95
Ray, Jack – 356
Riemsdijk, J. T. van, – 239
Rolt, L. T. C. – 168
Rogers, J. B. – 162
Russell, J. H. – 123, 308
Sharman, Mike – 283
Steel, Ernest A. – 143
Stevens-Stratten, S. W. – 43, 101, 412, 416, 418, 420, 424, 426, 430, 435, 436, 440, 442, 444, 446, 451, 458, 460, 462, 464, 467, 468, 470, 476, 494
Symes-Schutzmann, R. A. – 131
Tidmarsh, J. D. – 211
Towers, Paul – 349, 382
van Riemsdijk, J. T. – 27, 34
Wheldon, J. – 135
Whitehouse, C. M. – 422, 428, 438, 448, 454
Whittaker, Jim – 269, 275
Williams, Geoff – 299